REPRINTS OF ECONOMIC CLASSICS

LIFE OF ADAM SMITH

LIFE

of

ADAM SMITH

By JOHN RAE

[1895]

With an Introduction
"Guide to John Rae's *Life of Adam Smith*"
By Jacob Viner

AUGUSTUS M. KELLEY • PUBLISHERS

First edition 1895
(London: Macmillan and Co., 1895)

Reprinted with Jacob
Viner's introduction
1965 and 1977 by

AUGUSTUS M. KELLEY · PUBLISHERS
Fairfield, New Jersey 07006

Library of Congress Cataloged.
The original printing of this title as follows:

Rae, John, 1845-1915
    Life of Adam Smith.   With an introduction: "Guide to John
Rae's Life of Adam Smith" by Jacob Viner.   New York, A. M.
Kelley, bookseller, 1965.

   145,xv, 449 p.   24cm.   (Reprints of economic classics)
   Bibliographical footnotes.

   1. Smith, Adam, 1723-1790.   I.   Viner, Jacob, 1892-
   HN103.S6.42   1965   330.122094(B)   63-23522

PRINTED IN THE UNITED STATES OF AMERICA

TABLE OF CONTENTS

INTRODUCTION

GUIDE

TO

JOHN RAE'S
LIFE OF ADAM SMITH

BY

JACOB VINER

1965

I. INTRODUCTION

The primary purpose of this "Guide" is to facilitate for the present-day reader the use of John Rae's *Life of Adam Smith*. As a comprehensive biography, it had no substantial predecessor. Seventy years after its publication, it still has no substantial successor. Its original edition, and until the present reissue its only edition, is not only out of print but in booksellers' terminology is "scarce." It has historical importance not only for its merits, which are many, but even for its defects. It has long been the main reliance and for many the sole reliance for the facts of Adam Smith's life; its errors and omissions have thus to a large extent become "institutionalized," standard, for most persons with any interest in Smith.

There were for Rae, and there would continue to be for any new and ambitious biographer of Smith, great difficulties in writing a comprehensive and accurate biography covering his activities, his experiences, and his personal relations with his relatives, his friends and neighbors, his correspondents. In the circle in which he lived, a high value was set both on the privacy of one's own affairs and on the protection of the privacy of those with whom one had had intimate personal relations. It was then quite common, therefore, for men in their old age to carry out, or to leave instructions for carrying out after their death, a massive destruction of their private papers. Adam Smith did this, and it is on record that so also did others whose papers would or might have been valuable sources of biographical information with respect to Smith, notably George Dempster, David Hume and Adam Ferguson.

Even when papers were left in quantity, heirs often did not appreciate their value and either let them perish or deliberately destroyed them. The papers of Dugald Stewart, known to have contained material invaluable for a biography of Smith, were destroyed by his son and heir in 1837, as he himself writes, after "finding myself getting on in life, and despairing of finding a sale for it [his "literary property"] at its real value." Some papers of Thomas Reid, Adam Smith's successor at Glasgow, were as late as 1898 in the possession of a descendant. A philosopher who then examined them reported finding "valuable unpublished material—more indeed than I could avail myself of within narrow limits," but his own interests were philosophical, not biographical nor economic; I can find no record of any economist ever having examined them. Some boxes of papers of John Millar, reportedly Smith's "favorite pupil," were deliberately destroyed by his descendants in 1941 or 1942! These instances can be added to.

Correspondence, of course, is normally a major biographical source, and it is so for Smith. But Adam Smith, in this as in other respects, did nothing himself which was designed to help his future biographers. He avowedly abominated letter-writing, and on all the known evidence he kept it to a minimum. Of the letters he wrote in his youth, scarcely any have survived. Of his later correspondence, Rae has done most to collect and publish it, and after him W. R. Scott, but no complete list is available of the letters written by Smith, published or unpublished, that are known to have survived. As little better than a guess, I would not put the number much higher than 200, of which perhaps 150 have appeared in print, mostly thanks to Rae and to W. R. Scott. Disappointingly small in quantity as the surviving correspondence is, it is only by its aid that one can trace with what seems a fair degree of comprehensiveness Smith's activities and his personal contacts. His letters, however, were sparing in self-revelation and in large part confined themselves to a particular matter of business, personal or public, or to the recommendation of others to the good offices or hospitality of his friends. Hitherto unknown Smith letters still turn up occasionally, but no major discovery has occurred in recent decades. Until, however, a comprehensive search is made for Smithian correspondence, and it is then assembled and annotated, we cannot assume that substantially more information from his correspondence will not be available to a future biographer of Smith than was available to Rae and Scott.

In the Scottish intellectual circles of Smith's time, among whom propriety was sovereign, it was not proper for friendly writers or respectable periodicals to publish personal biographical material about living persons who were not royalty or prominent politicians or military heroes. Even references in serious books to living authors were customarily made as impersonal as possible, so that sometimes only an inner circle could identify the persons to whom reference was being made, and it was considered bad manners publicly to attempt to penetrate the anonymity of published works. When a writer of some prominence died, notice of some kind would be taken by the English "literary" periodicals, and there was a plethora of them. But many of them were little more than gossip-sheets, staffed by hack-writers without time or zeal for research, and seeking mostly the anecdotal and the eccentric. A large fraction of the anecdotes in which Smith figures first appeared immediately after his death in the minor sheets, which plagiarized each other with abandon and with gratuitous embellishment. The intimate friends who survived Smith and were in a position to contribute from direct knowledge to the drawing of his character and the telling of the story of his life were rarely biographically-minded. Smith was a bachelor and left no immediate relatives.[1] There was only one memoir of Smith of substance and range which was written by a personal acquaintance soon enough after Smith's death for its author to be able to rely

---

[1] David Douglas (later Lord Reston), Smith's sole heir, usually referred to as Smith's "nephew" or "cousin," was the son of a nephew of Smith's mother, i.e., the son of a cousin of Smith. He was nevertheless Smith's nearest surviving relative.

on his own memory and on the recollections of surviving members of Smith's circle and soon enough for him to have access to some private papers of Smith which were later to disappear. This was Dugald Stewart's "Account of the Life and Writings of Adam Smith, LL.D.," read to the Royal Society of Edinburgh on January 21 and March 18, 1793.[2]

Stewart's memoir provides the solid core of material in all subsequent accounts of Smith's life up to the appearance of Rae's book in 1895, although some new information of value was contributed in the interval by others, chiefly Lord Brougham, J. R. McCulloch, and Thorold Rogers. Rae himself relied heavily on Stewart's memoir, much more heavily than he explicitly acknowledged. Stewart, alas, used only a fraction of the material available to him, some of it apparently irretrievably lost to later generations, and he devoted a regretfully large proportion of the space made available to him to a description of and commentary on Smith's published writings which later scholars would gladly have exchanged for a few bits of the additional information about Smith which Stewart had on hand, and of which he gives us tantalizingly scanty samples or hints.[3]

---

[2] It was first published in the *Transactions* of the Society, III (1794), part 1, pp. 55-137, but was often reprinted during the next century. Scholars have often overlooked that two later issues of the Account contained additional notes by Stewart: one with thirty pages of added matter in *The Works of Adam Smith, LL.D.*, Dugald Stewart, ed., London, 1811, V, 403-552, and a later one with further additions in Dugald Stewart, *Works*, Sir William Hamilton, ed., Edinburgh, 1858, X, 5-98.

[3] Cf. J. R. McCulloch's comment on Stewart's memoir of Adam Smith: "It is much to be regretted that the information given in this memoir with regard to the distinguishing peculiarities in the character and conduct of Smith is extremely meager and imperfect. Stewart sunk the man in the philosopher; and at this distance of time it is all but impossible to supply his deficiencies." ("Sketch of the Life and Writings of Adam Smith," prefixed to McCulloch's edition of *The Wealth of Nations*, Edinburgh, 1863, p. i. McCulloch published this sketch many times.) Dugald Stewart wrote biographical memoirs as a duty and not as a pleasure. "I hate biography," he exclaimed in a letter of 1797. See John Veitch, "Memoir of Dugald Stewart," in Dugald Stewart, *Works*, X, lxxv, note.

With the aid of skilled and knowledgeable editorial annotation, a considerable amount of biographical information can often be gleaned from an author's published writings which had no autobiographical intentions. It is, for this and for more important reasons, one of the obligations which scholars owe as a group to departed masters of systematically collecting and editing, in conformity with the best prevailing standards of the editorial craft, their writings and papers. This obligation has so far been only very partially fulfilled as far as the admirers of Smith, who have been legion, are concerned. An English scholar, Edwin Cannan, published editions, in 1896 of Smith's Glasgow "Lectures on Justice, Police, Revenue and Arms," hitherto unpublished, and in 1904 of *The Wealth of Nations,* which for the level of their editorial workmanship set new standards for at least English-speaking economists. W. R. Scott has printed, with over-enthusiastic commentary, the texts he discovered of some portions of Smith's economic lectures at Glasgow. Professor John M. Lothian, in 1963, published, with respectable but undistinguished editing, the manuscript report which he had discovered of Smith's Glasgow lectures on "Rhetoric and Belles Lettres."[4] This is nearly the sum total of modern annotated editing in English of Smith's writings, although I would say a word on behalf of McCulloch's various editions of *The Wealth of Nations,* which, until Cannan made his contribution, represented the best editing Smith had received.

There is no complete edition "in print" of Smith's *The Theory of Moral Sentiments.* There is only one first-class edition of *The Theory of Moral Sentiments,* which is in German.[5] There are no separate annotated editions of

---

[4] *Lectures on Rhetoric and Belles Lettres delivered in the University of Glasgow by Adam Smith. Reported by a student in 1762-63.* London & Edinburgh, 1963.

[5] Adam Smith, *Theorie der Ethischen Gefühle,* Dr. Walther Eckstein, ed., Leipzig, 1926, 2 vols., which collates all six editions published in Smith's lifetime.

Smith's minor essays. There has been no reprint for over a century of Smith's first appearances in print (anonymously): two contributions to the short-lived *The Edinburgh Review* of 1755, a review of Samuel Johnson's Dictionary and a "Letter to the Authors of the Edinburgh Review." Given this general situation, it is good news, therefore, that the University of Glasgow, in association with the Clarendon Press, has undertaken to prepare and publish an edition of the complete works of Adam Smith and, as part of the project, a new Life.

Since Rae's *Life of Adam Smith* appeared in 1895, the outstanding contribution of new information about Smith has been by W. R. Scott, especially in his *Adam Smith as Student and Professor,* London, 1937, but also in a series of lesser but valuable papers and essays. When a new Life comes to be written, it seems probable that it will have to depend very heavily on the information which Rae and Scott had discovered or collected. In lesser degree, James Bonar and C. R. Fay have made contributions, and new information has come also and is continuing to come in small packages as a by-product of the work of scholars who have no special interest in Smith but come across material of Smithian interest, including an occasional hitherto unknown letter of Smith, or to Smith, or commenting on Smith, in the papers of other men, and take some notice of it.

It is even possible that for such a new edition there are still to be found unpublished manuscripts of some importance. It is only several years ago that Professor Lothian discovered the Glasgow lectures of Smith on Rhetoric, which he has since edited and published. He found at the same time a manuscript set of notes of Smith's Glasgow lectures on economics, covering the same ground as those edited by Cannan, but apparently taken down by a different hand, and in substantially greater detail. This manuscript is now in the possession of the University of

Glasgow, and I understand is being examined with a view to publication. I know nothing about the nature and contents of this manuscript except the meager information given by Professor Lothian in an article in an Edinburgh newspaper: "about 170,000 [words] of a new version of [Smith's] views on the philosophy of history, law and economics, had suddenly become available," "dated, in great part lecture by lecture, through the academic session of 1762-63."[6]

On my rough count, this means substantially over 50 per cent more matter than is contained in the version of the lectures edited by Edwin Cannan. It may well be also not only a fuller but a more accurate transcript of these lectures. Cannan always emphasized the high quality of the transcript that he published, but later there became available a limited amount of information about two other reports of these lectures which indicated that, as far as they went, they filled some gaps and corrected some errors of substance in the version published by Cannan. In 1938 a Continental scholar, Georg Sacke, reported that he had found a large amount of material borrowed from Smith embodied in the lectures in Moscow University of a former student of Adam Smith, S. Desnickii, which the latter had published in Russian in 1768. Dr. Sacke retranslated into English as a sample a section corresponding with the introductory pages of Cannan's version, and this suffices to show both that it is derived from the same original lecture and that it is a superior report to the one published by Cannan.[7] Studying at Glasgow at the same time was another young Russian, A. Tretiokov, who also borrowed heavily from Adam Smith in his later lectures at Moscow University. In their published works, and perhaps in sur-

[6] John M. Lothian, "Long-Lost MSS. of Adam Smith," *The Scotsman*, Nov. 1, 1961, p. 8.

[7] Georg Sacke, "Die Möskauer Nachschrift der Vorlesungen von Adam Smith," *Zeitschrift für Nationalökonomie*, IX (1938), 351-356.

viving manuscripts of theirs, there may be additional information about the scope and content of Smith's lectures at Glasgow.[8] At about the same time W. R. Scott found, and soon thereafter published, a sizable fragment of another transcript of Smith's lectures which both gives an improved version of some passages, and bridges some gaps in the Cannan and apparently also in the Lothian versions.[9]

It seemed for a time that another sizable Smith manuscript, "Meditations on Seneca's Epistles," hitherto unpublished, was in existence. A listing of this in a bookseller's catalogue, with an attribution of it to Smith, was taken seriously by Henry Higgs, and after him by W. R. Scott. J. A. La Nauze, however, has located the manuscript in an Australian library, and from internal evidence, including its handwriting, attributes it persuasively to Robert Wallace, despite the fact that its dating and the paper on which it was written are consistent with an attribution to Adam Smith.[10]

Rae had no significant contribution to make to the interpretation or appraisal of Smith's thought. The importance of Rae's book is confined to the contribution it made to our knowledge of Smith's background, his personality, activities, associations, and correspondence. In the tradition of Smithian biography then and since, Rae operated on loose standards with respect to precision and accuracy in transmitting information; his handling of bibliographical

---

[8] On Desnitskii and Tretiokov, see: Michael P. Alekseev, "Adam Smith and his Russian Admirers of the Eighteenth Century," in W. R. Scott, *Adam Smith as Student and Professor*, Glasgow, 1937, pp. 424-427; (A. I. Pashkov, ed. of original edition), John M. Letiche, ed. and tr. from the Russian, *A History of Russian Economic Thought, Ninth Through Eighteenth Centuries*, Berkeley, 1964, pp. 507-531.

[9] W. R. Scott, *Adam Smith as Student and Professor*, Glasgow, 1937, Part III, "An Early Draft of Part of *The Wealth of Nations* (c. 1763)," pp. 317-356.

[10] J. A. La Nauze, "A Manuscript Attributed to Adam Smith," *Economic Journal*, LV (1945), 288-291.

material was invariably casual and undisciplined.[11] Plagued as all Smithian biographers are bound to be by frustrating gaps in information, and eager to provide a sustained and unbroken story, he reported with undue readiness to believe what gossip and anecdotes he could gather and tended in subsequent reference to these to promote them to the status of positive knowledge. Where historical data were not available to make an episode intelligible or credible, he resorted somewhat freely to surmise, resting sometimes on no or the flimsiest factual foundations. But Rae was a trained writer on the level of superior journalism. He wrote smoothly and lucidly, and he made his *Life* an interesting and highly readable book. In this respect, he rose above the tradition in which he was operating, while in his lack of precision and rigor in presentation of his historical or bibliographical data and in his readiness to make surmise a substitute for genuine information and to promote gossip to the status of positive fact he was operating in a traditional rut for writers on Smith which his successors upon occasion dug even deeper.

A limited search has furnished only the most meager biographical information about our biographer himself. John Rae was born in 1845 in Wick, a small sea-coast town in Caithnessshire on the north-easternmost coast of Scotland, with the herring fishery as its main industry.[12] His father had for many years been Provost of Wick. He

---

[11] Commenting in the middle of the nineteenth century on the opposition which the authorities at the British Museum encountered from within the literary world when they proposed to reform the Catalogue of its library by listing titles precisely as they appeared on title pages and arranging them in alphabetical order of names of authors or of beginning words of titles, the *Edinburgh Review* said that "there is among men of letters a widespread incompetency to describe books correctly, and a great want of aspiration after a healthier state." (*Edinburgh Review*, XCII (1850), 389). In this respect the nineteenth-century Smithian biographers were perhaps guilty only of not being in advance of their times, but this excuse is not available for twentieth-century writers.

[12] For further reference to Wick, see *infra*, pp. 93-94.

himself was a graduate of Edinburgh University. He remained a bachelor all his life. By major occupation a journalist, living in London, he was for many years assistant editor of *Contemporary Review.* He published, in addition to his *Life of Adam Smith,* two other books, *Contemporary Socialism,* 1884, which reached a fourth edition in 1908, and *Eight Hours for Work,* 1894. He died in 1915, and was buried in Wick.[13]

My main objective in preparing this "Guide" to Rae's *Life* is to provide such help as I can to the reader of the *Life* to identify errors, omissions, ambiguities, uncertainties, in the information Rae presents. Where I can, I supply either supplementary or more precise information, or references to where it can be found. I make no attempt to cover the additional information supplied by W. R. Scott with respect to Smith's official activities as a member of the University of Glasgow faculty, but I refer freely to him on other matters, often, I regret to have to say, to correct or to question his data.[14]

The most satisfactory way, perhaps, of presenting my comments on Rae's text would have been to have added them as immediate annotations to the relevant passages, but the photographic method of reproduction of his text makes this impracticable. I have chosen, instead, to present my material in the form of a series of brief essays or of notes on topics of biographical interest in relation to Smith, linked as closely as possible to Rae's treatment of them. I begin with a series of notes on Smith's relations

---

[13] I derive all this information from the English *Who Was Who* covering persons who died in the year 1915, and Palgrave's *Dictionary of Political Economy,* Henry Higgs, ed., London, 1926, III, 738-739. I have not been able to find an obituary of Rae in *The Economic Journal* or The *Times* of London. University of Edinburgh or Caithness-shire publications which might contain a memoir of him were not available to me.

[14] My references to W. R. Scott, *Adam Smith as Student and Professor,* Glasgow, 1937, will henceforth be abbreviated as "Scott, *ASSP.*" My references to Rae's *Life* will be made mainly in my main text, in the form "(Rae, p.—.)."

with particular persons. I follow this by a series of notes on topics related in some manner to the Scottish milieu in which Smith lived, intended to serve as supplements to the material presented by Rae illustrative of Smith's response to, or failure to respond to, the immediate Scottish background of his time. The chief lesson I derive from this material is that while Smith was a keen observer of his surroundings and used skillfully what he saw to illustrate his general arguments, his loyalties were primarily to the Britain of which Scotland was for him an integral part, not a colony or a subordinate partner, next to what he referred to as "the great society of mankind." I know of no instance where it could justly be made a reproach against Smith that on a broad issue he took an unduly parochial Scottish position, and the specific topics I have chosen for treatment are, I believe, fairly representative of his general disposition to use freely what he observed at first hand in his immediate Scottish neighborhood to illustrate and to support his general doctrines, but to direct these doctrines primarily to the service of a greater community.

I add, as of biographical interest, a survey and appraisal of what has been written by James Bonar and others of Smith's personal library. I close with a brief chronology of events significant in Adam Smith's personal life, based mainly on Rae's account in the *Life* and on the rich material gathered by W. R. Scott.

The sources I have used in preparing this "Guide" are predominantly confined to what is immediately available to me, chiefly in the Princeton University Library, but also in my modest private collection of printed material of Smithian interest and in my accumulation of notes from my reading over the years in other libraries. These notes, unfortunately, having been made for other purposes or for no specific purpose that I can now recall, are often insufficiently precise or full to warrant incorporation without serious hazard of error in my text. I have endeavored, however, to refer readers to material not now available to me for careful examination, wherever I have some reason to suppose that there is a substantial probability that it might contain new information which some readers with easy access to the material might be interested enough to explore or which might help some future biographer of Smith in filling the many gaps and resolving the many puzzles that still persist in our knowledge of Smith the person, as distinguished from Smith the author. For description, interpretation, and appraisal of Smith's writings, and for an account of Smith's sources and his influence, it has not seemed to me that Rae's *Life* was an appropriate starting-point, or this the appropriate occasion, even if I had ambitions in that direction. At a few points, however, I do encroach slightly on this area, chiefly where I believe I have discovered a neglected but promising field for research by Smithian scholars. Throughout this "Guide" I generally offer my comments not as definitive solutions of problems, but as possible contributions to such solution or as warnings to the readers of Rae's *Life* either that they remain unsolved or that they have been solved by other writers since Rae wrote. Since the emphasis is on "problems" wrongly solved or left unsolved by Rae, there would be an unfair distribution of emphasis on flaws in Rae's book, and an unjust disparagement of its positive achievements, if this Guide were presented as an attempt at a balanced appraisal of the value of Rae's book as a whole. Such is not its intent. For what we know of Smith as a person and of the record of his personal life, our major indebtedness is to Rae's *Life,* and after that to Dugald Stewart and to W. R. Scott.

II. THE RELATIONS OF SMITH WITH SELECTED PERSONS

1. *James Anderson.* Rae says that Anderson "won Smith's friendship by a controversial pamphlet challenging some of his doctrines." (Rae, p. 318.) Anderson did make a claim which comes close to this, that his criticism in one of his works[1] of some of Smith's economic analysis, and especially of Smith's views on the export bounties on corn, was "the commencement of a friendly intercourse that subsisted between us during the whole after period of his life,"[2] and he made similar statements in others of his numerous writings. Anderson and Smith could easily have met in Edinburgh, where they were both residents and both members of the Royal Society of Edinburgh. (Rae, p. 421.) Anderson was a persistent critic, sometimes a penetrating one, of Adam Smith's views with respect to agricultural policy; he supported Bentham in the latter's criticism of Smith's support of a legal maximum on interest rates;[3] and he was, with John Knox, one of the promoters of a scheme, which Adam Smith forecast was bound to fail, for helping the Scottish herring fisheries through a joint-stock company which would finance improved fishing-ports and fish-curing stations.[4] The only evidence I know of Smith's feeling towards Anderson is in a letter of 1780 to a Danish correspondent in which Smith refers to Anderson as "A very diligent, laborious honest man," and claims

---

[1] *Observations on the Means of Exciting a Spirit of National Industry,* [Edinburgh, 1777], Dublin, 1779, Postscript to Letter Thirteenth; II, 107-202.

[2] *Selections from the Correspondence of George Washington and James Anderson,* Charleston, S. C., 1800, p. 75.

[3] In a review of Bentham, *Defense of Usury, Monthly Review,* LXXVIII (1788), 361-370.

[4] See *infra,* p. 91 ff.

adequately to have met Anderson's criticisms of his objections in the first edition of *The Wealth of Nations* to the corn-bounty in the "very long chapter" of his *Observations on the Means of Exciting a Spirit of National Industry* by revising in the second edition one sentence in which he now acknowledged that he had been guilty of a "careless expression."[5] The letter contains more autobiographical material than perhaps any other surviving letter of Smith's. Anderson's chapter, which Smith thought he had adequately disposed of by revising a single sentence of *The Wealth of Nations*, was indeed a "very long chapter," some 75 pages long in the Dublin edition.[6]

2. *Jeremy Bentham.* Smith and Bentham never met. In his *Defense of Usury*, 1788, Bentham criticizes Smith for his approval in *The Wealth of Nations* of a legal maximum on the rate of interest. A friend of Bentham's, George Wilson, reported to Bentham in a letter of Dec. 4, 1789, that Smith had in conversation with William Adam, another friend of Bentham, spoken respectfully of Bentham and of his argument in *The Defense of Usury*, and that Smith "seemed to admit that you were right." With only this to go on, Rae states that "Bentham won—what is rarer—his [i.e., Smith's] conversion from the doctrines impugned." (Rae, pp. 318, 422-424.) Professor W. Stark has recently published the draft of a letter of Bentham to

---

[5] A copy of the letter is in Scott, *ASSP*, pp. 281-284.

[6] The claim made by Rae, (pp. 318, 365, 421.), and by others before and after him, that Anderson was "the first and true author of what is known as Ricardo's theory of rent" seems to me a gross exaggeration, since I cannot find in Anderson's writings any recognition of the law of diminishing returns or of the intensive margin of cultivation. But Anderson was a voluminous writer on economic matters, with portions of the text of *The Wealth of Nations* a repeated target. Lists of his writings are given in *The Gentleman's Magazine*, 1808, II, 1051, and in the article devoted to him in the *Supplement* to the Fourth Edition of the *Encyclopaedia Britannica*, but neither list is complete. See also J. H. Hollander, "Adam Smith and James Anderson," *Annals of the American Academy*, VII (1896), 461-464.

Smith written either late in 1789 or early in 1790, in which Bentham reports that he has heard of an apparent acceptance by Smith of Bentham's position, and asks for permission to make public Smith's conversion to Bentham's position. Smith died on July 17, 1790. Bentham received no reply to his letter, but there reached him at the same time as news of Smith's death "a present" from Smith in the form, according to Stark, of a presentation copy of *The Wealth of Nations*.[7] From the information available all that can be safely inferred is that Smith bore Bentham no ill-will for his criticism and possibly did not deny that it had some force.

3. Hugh Blair. Rae (pp. 32-33.) reports some gossip that in his published lectures on rhetoric Blair borrowed with inadequate acknowledgement from the manuscript which Smith had lent him of Smith's prior lectures in Edinburgh.[8] The recent discovery and publication by Professor John M. Lothian of a report of Smith's Lectures on Rhetoric at Glasgow may now make possible a direct comparison by qualified scholars of Smith's and Blair's doctrines in this area.

Blair had a general reputation in Edinburgh as being pompous and conceited, and Smith once commented that

---

[7] See W. Stark, *Jeremy Bentham's Economic Writings,* London, 1952, I, 26-27, 189-190. It seems more likely that it was either a copy of *The Theory of Moral Sentiments* only, or copies of both *The Theory of Moral Sentiments* and *The Wealth of Nations,* which Smith sent to Bentham in 1790. A fifth edition of *The Wealth of Nations* was published in 1789. A sixth edition of *The Theory of Moral Sentiments* was published in 1790, shortly before Smith's death. Bonar reports that University College, London, has Bentham's presentation copy of the sixth edition of *The Theory of Moral Sentiments.* (*A Catalogue of the Library of Adam Smith,* 2d ed., London, 1932, Introduction, p. xxxiii, and pp. 201-203.) John Bowring, Bentham's editor, states that Bentham "received a copy of Smith's *works* which had been sent to him as a token of esteem." (*The Works of Jeremy Bentham,* John Bowring ed., Edinburgh, 1838 ff., III, 52, italics mine.)

[8] See also W. R. Scott, *ASSP,* pp. 52, 119.

"Blair was too puffed up."[9] Scott has published a letter written by Blair to Smith in 1776, upon publication of *The Wealth of Nations,* in which Blair somewhat patronizingly advises Smith on how he could have improved the structure of the book. If, for example, Smith in a future edition were to add a "syllabus," "ten or fifteen additional pages would comprise it all, and they would be the most valuable pages of the whole." Blair also advised the addition of an index.[10]

Smith did not reconstruct the book. But an index was added in the third edition, published in 1784, whether as a response to Blair's advice we do not know. Cannan has speculated as to whether Smith himself prepared the index, but decided that he did not. "We should not expect a man of Adam Smith's character [meaning status? or "indolence?"] to make his own index."[11] Evidence has since come to light that Cannan's surmise was correct, and that the index was prepared by a professional index-maker engaged by Smith's publishers.[12] But Smith saw at least part of the index before it was published, and may therefore have edited it.

4. *Duke of Buccleuch.* It was as tutor of the young Duke of Buccleuch, stepson and ward of Charles Townshend, that Smith gained the opportunity to reside in France for two years and thereafter financial independence on the

---

[9] Rae, p. 421; see also R. M. Schmitz, *Hugh Blair,* New York, 1948.

[10] W. R. Scott, "A Manuscript Criticism of 'The Wealth of Nations' in 1776 by Hugh Blair," *Economic History,* III (1938), 47-53.

[11] In his introduction to his edition of *The Wealth of Nations,* p. xvi. Cannan in this edition reproduces the original index.

[12] Catalogue No. 379, Spring 1954, Item no. 531, of Myers & Co., the London booksellers, offers for sale, from the papers of Thomas Cadell, a partner of William Strahan in the publication of *The Wealth of Nations,* a series of receipts, one of which was for payment to John Noorthouck, "for compiling an Index to Dr. Smith's Origin of the Wealth of Nations." Noorthouck is given an entry in the *Dictionary of National Biography* as professional index-maker as well as an author in his own right.

basis of an annual pension for life of £300 a year, much more than he could have earned from a university professorship. For the rest of Smith's life, Smith and Buccleuch remained mutually devoted and in intimate relations. Smith was often a guest at Dalkeith, the Duke's estate, not far from Edinburgh, and shortly before Smith's death the Duke wrote him a warm letter urging him to come to Dalkeith in the interest of his health.[13] The Duke was by all accounts a much admired person and although never a candidate for important office a person of much influence in Scottish affairs, both locally and as a representative Scottish peer in the House of Lords. There is some evidence that Buccleuch frequently consulted Smith on matters related to public and private business, and that Smith was occasionally appealed to to use his influence with Buccleuch with reference to appointments and to matters which came before the House of Lords. On May 1, 1775, for example, Edmund Burke wrote to Smith asking him to use his influence with Buccleuch in favor of a private bill before the House of Lords whereby Richard Champion, a Bristol potter and constituent of Burke, would be granted an extension of a patent for hard-paste porcelain which Wedgwood and other potters opposed. The decision was in favor of Champion, in effect a victory of the Rockingham Whigs over the Bedford Whigs.[14]

In *The Wealth of Nations*, Smith gives a detailed account of the difficulties and eventual failure, in the early 1770's, of the "Ayr Bank," operating with unlimited liability of the proprietors.[15] The Buccleuch family was one of the principal proprietors, and Cannan attributes to this circumstance the "extremely accurate" account in *The*

---

[13] W. R. Scott, *ASSP*, p. 311.

[14] See G. H. Guttridge, "The American Correspondence of a Bristol Merchant," *University of California Publications in History*, XXII (1934), 57, and C. R. Fay, *The World of Adam Smith*, Cambridge, Eng., 1960, p. 12.

[15] See *The Wealth of Nations*, I, 296-300.

Wealth of Nations of the Ayr Bank's difficulties. Rae (pp.
253-254.) prints a letter written by Smith in 1772, in which
he says that close friends of his were deeply concerned
in the affairs of the Bank and in the financial disturbance
which had ensued throughout Scotland "and my attention
has been a good deal occupied about the most proper
method of extricating them." The financial crisis resulting
from the suspension of payments by the Ayr Bank apparently meant for the Buccleuch family not only that they
suffered heavy losses as investors in the Bank itself, but
that some debtors to the family faced bankruptcy, and
that under Scottish bankruptcy law it was possible for
particular creditors to negotiate agreements with debtors
under which these creditors would have preferred claims
over other creditors. To deal with this situation, the Duke
of Buccleuch helped to steer through parliament in 1772
a special act, The Bankruptcy Laws of Scotland Act:
xiii Geo. iii, c. 73, (1772), which brought Scottish bankruptcy law closer to English law, and deprived debtors of
any role in deciding the order in which creditors' claims
against them should be met. Smith may possibly have
helped in drafting this Act, or a subsequent Act, xiv Geo.
iii, c. 21, (1774), which also was intended to deal with
the conditions created by the Ayr Bank failure. The Ayr
Bank difficulties had a wide impact in Scotland, and
Smith's personal friends in the Carron Company, which
was also in trouble, may also have sought his counsel.[16]

5. *Earl of Buchan.* Rae's references to the Earl of Buchan
(Rae, *passim,* see index.) call for no special comment beyond a warning as to the weight to be attached to Buchan's
reminiscences about Smith which Rae reports. Buchan was
regarded in his own time as highly eccentric. Rae's claim

---

[16] See R. H. Campbell, *Carron Company,* Edinburgh, 1961, p. 133,
for Smith's personal relations with John Roebuck, one of the partners
of the firm.

that Buchan "knew [Smith] well for the last thirty years of his life" (Rae, p. 4.) is to be treated with reserve.[17]

6. *Edmund Burke.* The material presented by Rae bearing on the personal relationships between Smith and Burke, resting largely on anecdotes and correspondence, points strongly to the unbroken friendship, mutual respect, and general harmony in philosophic, political and economic outlooks, of the two men. (See Rae's index under "Burke.") Recent commentators on the relations between the two men give the same impression,[18] as do also the few additional letters between the two men which have come to light since Rae's *Life* was published.[19] In their general lines, these accounts of the tone and character of the personal and intellectual relations between the two men seem to me to be substantially correct. In the following comments, however, I will endeavor to show how even a limited reexamination of the anecdotal material and comparison of their writings on common topics can throw additional light both on the nature of the intellectual agreement

[17] For glimpses at the Earl of Buchan's personality, see Samuel Miller, *Memoir of the Rev. Charles Nisbet, D.D.*, New York, 1840, pp. 191-192 (an autobiographical letter of 1790); Luther P. Eisenhart, "Walter Minto and the Earl of Buchan," *Proceedings of the American Philosophical Society*, XCIV (1950), 282-294; R. P. Gillies, *Memoirs of a Literary Veteran*, London, 1851, I, 338. Thomas Thomson, writing to his father while on a sightseeing tour in 1797, reports: "Spent two nights at Dryburgh Abbey [Buchan's residence] with Lord Buchan, by much the most singular natural curiosity we met with." (C. Innes, *Memoir of Thomas Thomson, Advocate*, Edinburgh, 1854, p. 35.)

[18] W. C. Dunn, "Adam Smith and Edmund Burke: Complementary Contemporaries," *Southern Economic Journal*, VII (1941), 330-346; C. R. Fay, *The World of Adam Smith*, Cambridge, Eng., 1960, ch. 1, "Edmund Burke and Adam Smith." See also J. S. Nicholson, *A Project of Empire*, London, 1909, pp. 18-21, "Adam Smith and Burke."

[19] See especially the letters of Smith to Burke on the change in the latter's political status when Rockingham died in 1782, letters which Rae knew about but believed to be lost, (Rae, p. 738.), but which were later published in Dixon Wecter, "Adam Smith and Burke," *Notes and Queries*, CLXXIV (1938), 311 and in C. R. Fay, *op. cit.*, p. 15.

between them and on limitations to the area of their agreement arising out of differences in both temperament and methodological principles. Once, moreover, Burke had embarked on a political career, political strategy was always an important element in his speeches and writings, whereas in the case of Smith his writings, with only minor qualifications, were dominated by the spirit of the "professor" or the "philosopher," with little express consideration of the limitations, whether imposed from without or self-imposed, under which the "politician" would more or less necessarily operate.

There is a tradition that Smith consulted Burke when he was writing *The Wealth of Nations*.[20] The origin of this tradition seems to be a statement in 1800 by the editor of one of Burke's works that "He was . . . consulted, and the greatest deference was paid to his opinions by Dr. Adam Smith, in the progress of the celebrated work on the Wealth of Nations."[21]

One difficulty with this story is that on the basis of what is known of the activities of the two men the earliest occasion on which they might have met is in London late in 1775, or only a few months before the publication of *The Wealth of Nations*. There is to support it, however, a claim by Burke himself, made in 1796, which seems to refer to a

---

[20] See, e.g., Thomas Moore, *Memoirs, Journal, and Correspondence,* London, 1853-1856, III, 162, reporting a conversation with Wordsworth; Thomas Macknight, *History of the Life and Times of Burke,* London, 1858, I, 57. It is rather surprising that Rae makes no reference to it. C. R. Fay, *The World of Adam Smith,* p. 4, rejects the tradition as "moonshine," perhaps because of the number of persons for whom it has been claimed that they helped Smith in the writing of *The Wealth of Nations* and the paucity of evidence that it was in his pattern of work to solicit or to accept assistance of this kind.

[21] Burke, *Thoughts and Details on Scarcity, originally presented to . . . William Pitt, . . . November, 1795,* London, 1800, editor's preface, p. vi. The editor was probably Dr. French Lawrence, who had worked with Burke before the latter's death on the preparation of his manuscripts for publication. See Donal Barrington, "Edmund Burke as an Economist," *Economica,* N.S. XXI (1954), 257.

period before 1776 and can plausibly be interpreted to be applicable to Adam Smith:

Does his Grace [the Duke of Bedford] think that they, who advised the Crown to make my retreat easy, considered me only as an economist? That, well understood, however, is a good deal. If I had not deemed it of some value, I should not have made political economy an object of my humble studies, from my very early youth to near the end of my service in Parliament, even before (at least to any knowledge of mine) it had employed the thoughts of speculative men in other parts of Europe. At that time it was still in its infancy in England, where, in the last century, it had its origin. Great and learned men thought my studies were not wholly thrown away, and deigned to communicate with me now and then on some particulars of their immortal works. Something of these studies may appear incidentally in some of the earliest things I published. The House has been witness to their effect and has profited of them more or less for above eight and twenty years.[22]

"Learned men" who "deigned to communicate with me now and then on some particulars of their immortal works" could well have included Adam Smith, since it was economics Burke was referring to and it is hard to think of economic works of the time other than *The Wealth of Nations* which Burke would have characterized as "immortal." The "communication" could, of course, have been by correspondence, and there do survive letters of Burke to Smith prior to the publication of *The Wealth of Nations*. If the "communication" between them with relation to *The Wealth of Nations* occurred, however, after rather than before the publication of the first edition, the problem of dating would be largely resolved. There is evidence, although not as definitive as one might wish, that Smith

---

[22] "A Letter to a Noble Lord," [1796], *The Works of . . . Edmund Burke,* Bohn ed., London, 1854-1857, V, 124.

and Burke did discuss one passage in the first edition of *The Wealth of Nations,* that this occurred in 1777, and that Smith as a result of this discussion modified the text of his second or 1778 edition.

In 1773 Burke marshalled through the House of Commons a bill revising but preserving the substance of the British legislation providing for bounties on the export of grain. (13 Geo. iii, c. 43.) In the first edition of *The Wealth of Nations* Smith found fault with some provisions of this Act as even being inferior to the preceding legislation. In a later edition, probably the second one of 1778, Smith softened his criticism by adding the following sentences:

> So far, therefore, this law seems to be inferior to the ancient system. With all its imperfections, however, we may perhaps say of it what was said of the laws of Solon, that, though not the best in itself, it is the best which the interests, prejudices, and temper of the times would admit of. It may perhaps in due time prepare the way for a better.[23]

Francis Horner, writing in 1804, reports Smith's application to the 1773 Act of the saying about the laws of Solon, and adds:

> He probably bore in mind, when he used these expressions, the answer which Mr. Burke had made to him, on being reproached for not effecting a thorough repeal, that it was the privilege of philosophers to conceive their diagrams in geometrical accuracy; but the

---

[23] *The Wealth of Nations,* Cannan ed., II, 45. Cannan's edition is based on the fifth edition, 1789. Cannan notes that "These two [three?] sentences are not in ed. 1," but unlike his usual practice he does not state when they were first added. The second edition is not available for examination, but these sentences are in the third edition, 1784, and I have not found them in the separately published *Additions and Corrections to the First and Second Editions,* 1784. This would imply that they were first added in the second edition of 1778, but Cannan warns us that Smith did not include in *Additions and Corrections* all the "minor alterations" which he made in the third edition (*The Wealth of Nations,* Cannan ed., Editor's Introduction, p. xvi.)

engineer must often impair the symmetry, as well as simplicity of his machine, in order to overcome the irregularities of friction and resistance.[24]

If, as seems probable, the first meeting of Burke and Smith was in 1777 and the "laws of Solon" passage was first inserted in *The Wealth of Nations* in the second, or 1778, edition, everything would hang together: Burke's reported remark to Smith, Smith's concession re the 1773 Act, and an occasion for and at least one item in the content of a consultation between Smith and Burke relating to *The Wealth of Nations*. Francis Horner gives no source for the comment he attributes to Burke, and we are in the dark as to the channel by which it became known to others. But the tenor of Burke's comment, as reported by Horner, fits closely other general statements by Burke bearing on the differences in the patterns of thought appropriate to the practical politician and those followed, whether appropriately or not, by the theorist. One of these, attributed to Burke as having been addressed to Smith, is closely similar to the one reported by Francis Horner:

> You, Dr. Smith, from your professor's chair, may send forth theories upon freedom of commerce as if you were lecturing upon pure mathematics; but legislators must proceed by slow degrees, impeded as they are in their course by the friction of interest and the friction of preference.[25]

This report raises a similar problem of dating. The reference to "your professor's chair" implies a date prior to 1764, for Smith ceased to be a professor in that year. But Smith and Burke had not yet met then, and Smith had lectured on but had not yet published anything relating

---

[24] *The Economic Writings of Francis Horner in the Edinburgh Review*, Frank W. Fetter, ed., London, 1957, p. 98.

[25] Quoted in *The Papers of Thomas Jefferson*, Julian P. Boyd, ed., Princeton, VIII (1953), 59. With an exceptional departure from the normal procedure of this model of editorial rigor and craftsmanship, no indication of source or date is given.

to freedom of commerce. Burke, however, may have used "professor" and "philosopher" as interchangeable terms for those who relied on a priori argument as adequate to solve practical problems. The nearest to acknowledgement by Burke that the statesman could make *any* use of abstract thinking, of "abstractions and universals," in the formulation and execution of policy that I have been able to find is the following passage:

> I do not put abstract ideas wholly out of any question, because I well know that under that name I should dismiss principles, and that without the guide and light of sound, well-understood principles, all reasonings in politics, as in everything else, would be only a confused jungle of particular facts and details, without the means of drawing out any sort of theoretical or practical conclusion.[26]

Smith would perhaps not have found anything to object to here. But Burke elsewhere gave fairly clear expression to the view that "a theory, however plausible it may be," should not carry much weight for a statesman as against respect for vested interests, tradition, his own personal values and prejudices, and so forth.[27] I doubt whether Smith would in principle allow so much personal discretion to the "statesman," although how in fact the two men would act in a comparable practical situation is a matter for conjecture, given the frailties of all men.

That Burke out of office and of active politics was capable of treating economic theory of a most highly abstract and "narrow" kind as adequate guide to policy, to the exclusion of all other considerations, he showed at least once, very late in life. In a memoir of advice to Pitt in 1795 on how to deal with the then prevalent acute eco-

---

[26] "Speech on a Bill . . . respecting religious opinions," [1792] *Works*, VI, 113-114. The whole paragraph from which this is extracted is relevant, but it is too long for full quotation here.

[27] See "Speech Dec. 1, 1783, on Mr. Fox's East-India Bill," *Works*, II, 179-180.

nomic distress, not published until after his death, he warned that no measure of relief should be resorted to which involved "breaking the laws of commerce, which are the laws of nature, and consequently the laws of God," and argued that "labor is . . . a commodity and, as such, an article of trade," and must in consequence "be subject to all the laws and principles of trade, and not to regulations foreign to them, and that may be totally inconsistent with those principles and those laws."[28]

Since neither Burke nor Smith has left a comprehensive statement of his views with respect to these matters, we do not have adequate material upon which to base a firm judgment as to what their degree of harmony was when they were thinking of what was appropriate methodological procedure for men with a responsible practical role, on the one hand, and for "philosophers," on the other. My own impression is that the harmony was substantial, but not complete, and that it was sufficiently incomplete to lead upon occasion to wider divergence of ultimate position than in the case of the export bounties on grain already commented on. But there is difficulty in finding instances to test this. Burke and Smith did upon several concrete issues take contrary positions. But Burke on these issues may have engaged in a level of practice not in full conformity with his own principles as he might expound them before a disinterested audience, while Smith in *The Wealth of Nations* could discuss a problem from a narrowly-technical fiscal or taxation point of view without making it clear, or perhaps without being clear himself, that if he were in a position of authority where it was his responsibility to make, or to participate in making, a relevant policy-decision, he should and would take much more into account than the fiscal aspect.

Except for the "laws of Solon" passage, I know of only one passage in *The Wealth of Nations* which even appears

---

[28] "Thoughts and Details on Scarcity," [Nov. 1795], *Works*, V, 100, 89.

to be concerned with the question of appropriate methodological standards for men operating in different capacities and, more specifically, with the standards appropriate to the man of practice on the one hand and the theorist on the other hand. Smith is discussing whether it is "good policy" to retaliate against another country's discriminating trade restrictions:

> There may be good policy in retaliations of this kind, when there is a probability that they will procure the repeal of the high duties or prohibitions complained of. The recovery of a great foreign market will generally more than compensate the transitory inconveniency of paying dearer during a short time for some sorts of goods. To judge whether such retaliations are likely to produce such an effect, does not, perhaps, belong so much to the science of a legislator, whose deliberations ought to be governed by general principles which are always the same, as to the skill of that insidious and crafty animal, vulgarly called a statesman or politician, whose councils are directed by the momentary fluctuations of affairs.[29]

Economists, especially some of the members of the German historical school, have interpreted this passage as expressing Smith's contempt, as a theorist, for the practical politician and, as a believer in laissez faire, for officialdom and for political activity in general, but the apparent respect shown for the "legislator" should then have puzzled them. I am not confident that this passage is susceptible of a crystal-clear interpretation, but I am sure that it will inevitably be misinterpreted if we fail to recognize that Smith is here using terminology in a specific eighteenth-century semantic pattern which is in some of its aspects foreign to us to-day, but which would have been familiar to his educated contemporaries. What that semantic pattern was Smith makes fairly clear by the words "vulgarly called" in this passage, and by some passages in a section first added in the final (the sixth) edition of the *Theory* of *Moral Sentiments,* where he is characterizing the "states-man," the "legislator," the "politician," and also the "sage" or "philosopher."

Smith here shows awareness that two verbal patterns of usage with respect to these terms were prevalent, one of them substantially belonging to "vulgar" or common dis-course, and the other employed by learned men as inherited from ancient Greek verbal usage[30] as represented in its traditional translations not only into English but also, and perhaps especially, into French. To make his own usage at particular moments somewhat clearer, Smith resorts at times to qualifying adjectives or other expressions, as, for example, "vulgarly called" in the passage cited above from *The Wealth of Nations,* or as the "great statesman," the "great legislator" in the *Theory of Moral Sentiments* where he also refers to "the greatest and noblest of all characters, that of the reformer and legislator of a great state." I cite in illustration one passage from the *Theory of Moral Sentiments:*

> We talk of the prudence of the great general, of the great statesman, of the great legislator . . . This supe-rior prudence, when carried to the highest degree of perfection . . . is the most perfect wisdom combined with the most perfect virtue. It constitutes very nearly the character of Academical or Peripatetic sage as the superior prudence [i.e., the prudence of a high, but lower, order of men] does that of the Epicurean.[31]

This was written when the French Revolution was already in process. We do not appear to have any record of

---

[29] *The Wealth of Nations,* I, 432-433.

[30] See Leo Strauss, "On Classical Political Philosophy," *Social Re-search,* XII (1945), 105-106.

[31] There is no standard edition of the *Theory of Moral Sentiments* in English and no widely-available complete edition of any kind to refer to. I cite here from Part VI. Sect. 1, "Of the Character of the Indi-vidual," in the *Theory of Moral Sentiments* as it appears in Adam Smith, *Essays Philosophical and Literary,* Ward Lock ed., London, n.d., p. 191, or in Bohn Standard Library ed., *Theory of Moral Senti-ments,* London, 1887, p. 316.

Smith's reaction to that Revolution, but there may be in
Part VI. Sect. II, Ch. ii, of the *Theory of Moral Sentiments*
oblique allusions to it which are not fully "Burkean," and
which may even reflect his response to Burke's completely
hostile attitude toward the Revolution. But I refer to this
here only as a suggestion for further research.

In the 1790 edition of the *Theory of Moral Sentiments,*
Smith condemns the "man of system" and the "spirit of
system."[32] But here and elsewhere Smith commends "system" and "systematic" thought. In his works and his correspondence he refers to *The Wealth of Nations* and to the
Theory of Moral Sentiments as "my system" without any
indication that he is confessing sin. He is not being inconsistent but on the contrary is following a usage of his time,
especially in France,[33] under which "system" and "systematic" were neutral or eulogistic terms for more-or-less
abstract and rigorous theory, and "man of system," "spirit
of system," and "system-monger" were derogatory terms
signifying over-attachment to and exaggeration of the
applicability to concrete issues without qualification of
abstract and therefore at its best partial and incomprehen-
sive theorizing. Boswell, writing to a friend in 1764, said:

> Mr. Smith, whose Moral Sentiments you admire so
> much, wrote to me some time ago, 'Your great fault
> is acting upon system.' What a curious reproof to a
> young man from a grave philosopher! It is, however,

---

[32] Part VI. Sect. II, Ch. ii. "Of the Order in which Societies are by
Nature recommended to our Beneficence," in *Essays Philosophical and
Literary,* Ward Lock ed., pp. 206-208; Bohn ed., *Theory of Moral
Sentiments,* pp. 341-343.

[33] See: Condillac, *Traité des Systèmes,* in *Oeuvres Complètes de
Condillac,* Paris, 1803, vol. III; *Oeuvres Complètes de Freret,* Paris,
1796, editor's introductory essay, I, 63-69. For modern accounts of
eighteenth-century French usage see: Pierre Proteau, *Étude sur
Morellet,* Laval, 1910, pp. 64-73; D. Mornet, *La Pensée Française au
XVIIIe Siècle,* Paris, 1929, pp. 86-87. Burke, however, seems to have
used "system" and "systematic" only in a pejorative sense.

a just one, and but too well founded with respect
to me.[34]

I feel sure that Smith would have insisted that there is
nothing curious but only wisdom in even a "systematic"
philosopher advising against "acting upon system."
Acceptance of even the best of "systems" as providing of
itself adequate guidance for action involved the "abuse of
system," not its proper utilization.[35]

It should be understood that this discussion of the extent of harmony between Smith's and Burke's approaches
to problems has not been based on a thorough reading,
with this question in mind, of their writings. Its main purpose is to warn against too ready an acceptance of the
view that there was something approaching perfect harmony between them and to encourage further research
on this question.

7. Adam Ferguson. The information that we have on the
character of the relations between Smith and Ferguson
indicates that while in general they were friendly and even
warm, in at least two and perhaps in three periods whose
duration we do not know there was friction between them.
I will confine myself here to comment on the real or alleged
instances of friction between the two men, all of which
turn, or may turn, on the issue of plagiarism.

---

[34] Cited in Clyde E. Dankert, "Adam Smith and James Boswell,"
Queen's Quarterly, LXVIII (1961), 331.

[35] The references given in Note 33, p. 32, *supra,* deal with this issue
of the distinction between the proper usage of "system" and its abuse
by overdependence on it in actual policy. For its abuse even in the
realm of thought, as distinguished from practice, a modern comment
is of interest.

> In a lecture, and sometimes in a book, we prefer even a false
> system, artificially and too ingeniously imposed upon the facts,
> to the subtleties and complications of truth, because it seems to
> offer us a clue to the labyrinth, a satisfying explanation in which
> our minds can rest, and an easily remembered formula. The mis-
> taking of the appearance of system for profundity is one of the
> most persistent delusions of the human mind. (Paul Shorey,
> *Platonism Ancient and Modern,* Berkeley, 1938, p. 126.)

Dugald Stewart, in his Memoir of Smith, relates that in 1755 Smith made claims against some unnamed person that he had in effect borrowed without acknowledgement from some unpublished lectures that Smith had delivered on economic topics. James Bonar, in the first edition (1894) of his *Catalogue of Adam Smith's Library,* surmises without explanation that Adam Ferguson was the person aimed at. Rae disposes effectively of this surmise by pointing out that at the time Smith had delivered the lectures involved Ferguson was in France as an army chaplain and that Ferguson gave up that post and returned to Scotland only in 1754. (Rae, pp. 61-65.) Until years after 1755, there is no record of Ferguson having published anything or delivered any lectures on economic topics. Bonar nevertheless repeated in 1932 in the second edition of his *Catalogue* that the 1755 manifesto by Smith "may possibly have been provoked by Adam Ferguson." He added to his original note only a blind reference to Rae: "Cf. Rae, (*Life of Adam Smith,* 61 seq.)," and a page reference to a passage on plagiarism which first appeared in the sixth edition, (1790) of Smith's *Theory of Moral Sentiments.* The passage is as follows:

> Unmerited applause a wise man rejects with contempt on all occasions . . . A weak man, however, is often much delighted with viewing himself in this false and delusive light . . . He pretends to have done what he never did, to have written what another wrote, to have invented what another discovered; and is led into all the miserable vices of plagiarism and common lying.[36]

This harsh passage may have been directed against Ferguson,[37] but there is no known ground for associating it with a plagiarism, real or supposed, by Ferguson as early as 1755.

---

[36] Ward Lock ed., p. 109; Bohn ed., p. 177.
[37] See *infra,* p. 37.

Alexander Carlyle does report Smith as complaining that Ferguson had plagiarized him, but in 1767 in his *History of Civil Society*, not in or before 1755:

> [Ferguson's] book on Civil Society ought only to be considered as a college exercise, and yet there is in it a turn of thought and a species of eloquence peculiar to Ferguson. Smith had been weak enough to accuse him of having borrowed some of his inventions without owning them. This Ferguson denied, but owned he had derived many notions from a French author, and that Smith had been there before him.[38]

If we assume that Carlyle's report has some basis, which of Smith's writings or lectures might Smith have thought that Ferguson had drawn upon unfairly, and who could the "French author" have been from whom, according to Ferguson, both Smith and himself had borrowed? Scott suggests that the borrowed matter was in the field of "Jurisprudence," and that the "French author . . . was no doubt Montesquieu."[39] Hazel Van Dyke Roberts, on the other hand, in her zeal for capturing for her hero, Boisguilbert, all laurels remaining unappropriated, reviews the issue and decides that Boisguilbert was the "French author" Ferguson had had in mind, chiefly on the basis of alleged parallelisms of thought.[40]

There is one issue on which Smith and Ferguson cover common ground, as also John Millar, Robert Wallace, and, later, after the publication of *The Wealth of Nations,* a host of writers including notably Karl Marx, and that is the proposition that division of labor tends to degrade labor, the *"Entfremdung"* or "alienation" issue. Here Adam Smith has clear claims to priority as far as British writers are concerned, although according to Marx, who was not

---

[38] *The Autobiography of Dr. Alexander Carlyle,* new ed., London, 1910, p. 299; see Rae, p. 65.

[39] W. R. Scott, *ASSP,* pp. 118-119.

[40] Hazel Van Dyke Roberts, *Boisguilbert,* New York, 1935, pp. 321-335.

acquainted with Smith's contributions to the *Edinburgh Review* in 1755, it was Smith who was taught by Ferguson, rather than the other way around.[41] But all of these, except perhaps Marx, were started on this line of thought by a "French author," or at least an author writing in French, Jean Jacques Rousseau, and none of them made a secret of his indebtedness, although it has since been very nearly universally overlooked, and seemingly universally left unexplored. I offer this as another possible clue to the priority puzzle as between Smith and Ferguson, but I will not pursue this further here.

That there is something, however, in the surmise of Scott, and perhaps others before him, that Montesquieu was the unnamed French author, is supported by the fact that Ferguson in his *History of Civil Society* acknowledges great indebtedness to him and by the following statement of John Millar, which makes in one brief passage a linkage between Montesquieu, Smith, the "History of Civil Society," and his own work in that field.

> [I] had the benefit of hearing his [Smith's] lectures on the History of Civil Society and of enjoying his unreserved conversation on the same subject. The great Montesquieu pointed out the road. He was the Lord Bacon in this branch of Philosophy. Dr. Smith is the Newton..[42]

"History of Civil Society," of course, was the title of the book by Ferguson, about which the question of undue borrowing arose. Was Millar by any chance suggesting that

---

[41] Karl Marx: *Misère de la Philosophie* [1847], Alfred Costes, ed., Paris, 1950, pp. 154-155; *Capital*, Moore and Aveling tr., London, 1889, p. 347.

[42] Cited by Scott, *ASSP*, p. 56, from John Millar, *Historical View of English Government*, 1803, II, 429-430, note. An approximation of this passage is included in one of the extracts from Millar's *Historical View* given in William C. Lehmann, *John Millar of Glasgow*, Cambridge, Eng., 1960, p. 363, note, with "History of Civil Society" for some reason put by the editor in italics.

Ferguson had borrowed even the title of his book from Smith's unpublished lectures?

Adam Ferguson, writing to a friend shortly after Smith's death about his last days, said: "We knew he was dying for some months, and though matters, as you know, were a little awkward when he was in health, upon that appearance I turned my face that way and went to him without further consideration, and continued my attentions to the last." (Rae, p. 433.) The sixth edition of Smith's *Theory of Moral Sentiments,* with its severe passage on plagiarism, was published in 1790. Was Smith when he died still nursing a grievance against Ferguson on the plagiarism issue? In the present state of our knowledge, the only appropriate answer to this question seems to be that we do not know.

8. *Robert Foulis.* Foulis was a distinguished Glasgow printer and publisher, and also for a time operated an Academy of Design which both trained artists and sold their products. The University of Glasgow, whose official printer he was, provided him with facilities on its grounds for his operations, and he also lived in social and intellectual intimacy with the professors of the University, including Smith. With one exception discussed later, this is about all we know with respect to transactions between Smith and Foulis, but Rae, with the aid of a series of surmises, manages to build up an account of repeated transactions.

Rae (p. 76.) believes, on flimsy grounds, that Smith was in personal contact with Foulis before coming to Glasgow, late in 1751, as professor at the University.[43] On the basis of this belief, he says: "I think it is not unreasonable to see traces of Smith's suggestion in the number of early economic books which Foulis reissued after the year 1750, works of writers like Child, Gee, Mun, Law and Petty."

---

[43] See *infra,* pp. 47-48, re Hamilton of Bangour.

This has become standard in Smithian literature,[44] but no real evidence has been supplied by anyone to support it. As far as we know, Smith after leaving Glasgow in 1740 to go to Oxford was never there again until January, 1751, when he was formally appointed to a professorship in the University, but with leave of absence until the autumn session. During this interval in 1751, he came occasionally to Glasgow to attend faculty meetings, but he continued his activities in Edinburgh, and was still writing letters from there as late as September and November (Rae, pp. 44-45.), and there is no record of his taking up residence in Glasgow before the opening in October of the new session of the University.[45]

A catalogue, presumably substantially complete, of Foulis's publications from 1741 to 1776, including reissues, is given in *Notices and Documents Illustrative of the Literary History of Glasgow*, Glasgow, 1831.[46] The catalogue lists 516 items. Of these, only 9 items, including all those mentioned by Rae and including second issues of two of these by Foulis, can be identified as reprints of "early economic tracts." Of these 9 items, 2 were published in 1750, 4 in 1751, mostly early in that year, 1 (Mun, *England's Treasure by Foreign Trade*) in 1755, and 2 (second issues of Gee, *Trade and Navigation* and of John Law,

---

[44] David Murray, *Early Burgh Organization, Glasgow*, Glasgow, 1929, pp. 449-450, says that the post-1750 economic items issued by Foulis "may have been suggested by Smith." Henry Higgs, *Bibliography of Economics 1751-1775*, Cambridge, Eng., 1935, Introduction, p. 4 (with Murray as a reference), says: "Some were no doubt suggested by him [i.e., Smith]." C. R. Fay, *Adam Smith and the Scotland of his Time*, Cambridge, Eng., 1956, p. 122, says: "It was his [i.e., Smith's] teaching that prompted Robert Foulis to publish a series of mercantilist literature . . ."

[45] See *infra*, pp. 47-48.

[46] The book was edited by "W.J.D.," i.e., William James Duncan, (1811-1885), banker and antiquarian? It is often catalogued as by Richard Duncan, who "presented" (that is, financed?) it to The Maitland Club. It consists mainly of material relating to the Foulis brothers. The catalogue, found by W.J.D. in the Foulis papers, is on pages 47-78.

Money and Trade, both of which Foulis first published in 1750) in 1760. On the chance that there might have been omissions in the Foulis Catalogue, I have checked for the years 1749 to 1755 inclusive the Kress Library *Catalogue* (1940) and its *Supplement* (1955) for all entries of economic interest attributed to Glasgow, whether Foulis is expressly indicated as publisher or not. Of Foulis's seven first issues of economic tracts the Kress *Catalogue* lists six (the missing item is Berkeley, *The Querist,* 1751), and it lists no items which would imply incompleteness of the Foulis Catalogue.

If I may assume that books published by Foulis before the end of 1751 would have been decided upon by him before Smith took up residence in Glasgow, late in that year, there remain only three early economic tracts whose publication by Foulis it is at all plausible to attribute to suggestions by Smith, Mun's *England's Treasure,* 1755, and second Foulis printings, in 1760, of John Law's *Money and Trade* and of Gee's *Trade and Navigation,* and this merely because we know that Smith referred to all three in his Glasgow Lectures.[47]

The Catalogue of books published by Foulis, if Francis Hutcheson items are excluded, contains only one item of substantial economic interest which was not an "early" item, and no economic item of which Foulis was the original publisher. Foulis published in a year not specified in the Catalogue an item listed as "Tucker on Naturalization," probably *A Letter to a Friend concerning Naturalization,* first published in London in 1753. I am not aware that Smith ever took any interest in the naturalization issue as such. Tucker is not mentioned or, as far as I can ascertain, alluded to, in any of Smith's published writings or correspondence, and Smith is similarly without mention in Tucker's publications or correspondence, although later in the 1750's Tucker was engaged, directly and indirectly, in

---

[47] See in Cannan ed., *Lectures on Justice,* index under these names.

important correspondence on economic issues with such intimates of Smith as Hume, Lord Kames, and James Oswald.[48] By 1751 also, Tucker had been in correspondence on issues of economic policy with Charles Townshend.[49] But we do not know of any contact before 1759 between Smith and Townshend.[50]

It is implausible, therefore, that Smith had anything to do with the initiation by Foulis of the republication of early economic tracts, and we have no positive supporting evidence that Foulis was encouraged by Smith to continue this activity after 1751.[51]

There is also the question whether Foulis—or anyone else—was engaged in the production of busts of Adam Smith during Smith's Glasgow period. Rae states that "stucco" (i.e., plaster-of-Paris?) busts of Adam Smith appeared in all the bookstores of Glasgow while Smith was teaching at Glasgow. (Rae, pp. 59, 438.) As W. R. Scott maintains, Rae's probable source is the following passage in Strang, *Glasgow Clubs*, (2nd ed., 1857, p. 83.): "Dunlop and Wilson were the most fashionable bibliopoles [for booksellers] in the town. Their windows were ornamented with stucco busts of Adam Smith, David Hume and other literati." The earliest trace of Dunlop and Wilson's operations in Glasgow Scott could find was a 1773 advertisement by the firm.[52] I would add that the credibility of Strang as a witness seems doubtful when he is found reporting so nearly incredible a thing as that busts of Hume were regarded as respectable ornaments for a bookseller's win-

[48] See *infra.*, pp. 53-54.

[49] Historical Manuscripts Commission, *Eleventh Report,* Appendix, Part IV, "The Manuscripts of the Marquess Townshend," London, 1887, pp. 371-379.

[50] See *infra.*, p. 83.

[51] Cf. Scott, *ASSP,* p. 348, to somewhat the same purpose, but Scott uses for the dates of publication of some items the date of a later particular Foulis advertisement thereof, instead of the actual dates of first publication by Foulis, which are in most cases some years earlier.

[52] Scott, *ASSP,* p. 105.

dow in eighteenth-century Scotland. Rae, with his *"all* the bookstores in Glasgow," gratuitously adds a little to Strang's statement. He suggests further that these busts must have been produced in Foulis's Academy of Design, and that James Tassie, who was at one time a student at the Academy and who many years later made the renowned medallions of Smith, may have been the artist who made the bust of Smith. (Rae, p. 438.) Scott and others have searched vigorously for a specimen of a bust of Smith made during his lifetime, but have found no trace of one. Copies survive of a catalogue of the full range of products offered for sale by the Academy of Design, but it lists no busts of living persons and the only Scottish scholar, living or dead, represented in the catalogue is Francis Hutcheson, who had died in 1746, or before the Academy was founded.[53] On the other hand, Foulis's Catalogue announced that "Any person may have a statue or bust done in Paris-plaster, after a picture drawing, or print."[54] This leaves open the possibility, therefore, that the Academy did produce, on special order, a bust of Smith, and even that Tassie had a hand in it. But there is to date nothing but surmise to support it.[55]

---

[53] The catalogue is reprinted in *Notes Illustrative of the Literary History of Glasgow,* pp. 93-115. Francis Hutcheson is listed under "Basrelievo's," "5 inches by 4. Plaister 2s. 6d., Wax 7s. 6d." *Ibid.* p. 114. In Glasgow Bibliographical Society, *Catalogue of the Foulis Exhibition,* Glasgow, 1913, an original copy of the catalogue is listed as item 241:

> 'A Catalogue of Pictures, Drawings, Prints, Statues and Busts in Plaister of Paris, done at the Academy in the University of Glasgow. Published for the Use of Subscribers.' Folio. Foulis, n.d.

Although the catalogue is undated, its probable date is about 1758, for a letter of John Dalrymple (who was a good friend of both Foulis and Smith) to Foulis of Dec. 1, 1757, advises Foulis, who was under financial pressure, to "Be so good as make out a catalogue of your pictures, and as far as you can of your busts, books of drawings, and prints" as part of a program to obtain subscribers for Foulis's products. *Notes Illustrative,* p. 27; see also Rae, p. 75.

[54] *Notes Illustrative,* p. 115.

[55] For another issue in which both Foulis and Smith are involved, see *infra.,* pp. 47-49.

9. *Benjamin Franklin.* Did Franklin and Smith ever meet? If the two men ever met, it must have been in London or in Scotland. There were two occasions on which they were both in Scotland at the same time, and three occasions on which they were in London at the same time. Rae reports or surmises meetings on three of these five occasions. (Rae, pp. 150-151, 264-266.)[56]

Franklin was in Scotland for six weeks in the early autumn (Rae wrongly says in the spring) of 1759 when Smith was teaching in Glasgow. Franklin then visited both Edinburgh and Glasgow, and could have met Smith in either place. Rae accepts Alexander Carlyle's account of meeting Franklin in Edinburgh at a supper given by Principal William Robertson at which Smith, Hume, and others were also present, but Carlyle places the supper in September. (Rae, pp. 150-151.)[57] But Hume in a letter to John Millar of Dec. 18, 1759, writes that he had not been in Edinburgh in that year until November, and this is confirmed by other letters of Hume in that year.[58] Carlyle began writing his Autobiography in 1800, when he was in his seventy-ninth year and continued to work at it until within a few weeks of his death in 1805, so that he recorded his memory of the supper some forty years or more after the event.[59] No supporting evidence has been adduced from other sources.

---

[56] The question is dealt with in: Thomas D. Eliot, "The Relations between Adam Smith and Benjamin Franklin before 1776," *Political Science Quarterly*, XXXIX (1924), 67-96; Lewis J. Carey, *Franklin's Economic Views*, New York, 1928, Ch. vi, "Franklin's Influence on Adam Smith"; J. Bennet Nolan, *Benjamin Franklin in Scotland and Ireland 1759 and 1771*, Philadelphia, 1938. None of them, however, provides any evidence of a meeting between the two men which adds much positively to what Rae says.

[57] *The Autobiography of Alexander Carlyle*, London, 1910, pp. 413-414.

[58] See: *The Letters of David Hume*, J. Y. T. Greig, ed., Oxford, 1932, I, 316; *New Letters of David Hume*, Raymond Klibansky and Ernest C. Mossner, eds., Oxford, 1954, pp. 44-58.

[59] Carlyle, *Autobiography*, pp. 597-598.

Rae prints a letter from Smith to his publisher, Strahan, dated April 4, 1760, which contains the following passage:

"Remember me to the Franklins. I hope I shall have the grace to write to the youngest by next post to thank him, in the name both of the College and of myself, for his very agreeable present." (Rae, p. 150.)

Benjamin Franklin had been accompanied on his Scottish visit by his son William, and Rae comments "it seems from this letter highly probable that Franklin had gone through to Glasgow [from Edinburgh], and possibly stayed with Smith at the College. Why otherwise should the younger, or, as Smith says, youngest, Franklin have thought of making a presentation to Glasgow College, or Smith of thanking him not merely in the name of the College, but in his own?" (Rae, p. 151.) It is possible to imagine other reasons, but the odds seem to me favorable that Smith did meet Franklin in 1759 in Edinburgh, or in Glasgow, or in both. On the basis of published information, this seems as much as can be said.

In 1761, while Franklin was in London toward the end of a stay of some five years, Smith was in London for a few weeks, apparently mainly or solely on University of Glasgow business. There is no report of any meeting between the two men at that time.

In 1766-1767, Smith and Franklin were simultaneously in London from November 1766 to May 1767. Here again there is no report of their meeting.

In the autumn of 1771, while Smith was living in Kirkcaldy, Franklin paid a second visit to Scotland and during his stay in Edinburgh, late in October, was David Hume's house guest.[60] We have almost no information about Smith's activities, or inactivities, in that year, but we do know that sometime in that year Hume had with apparent difficulty obtained a promise by Smith to visit him around

---

[60] Ernest C. Mossner, "Dr. Johnson *In Partibus Infidelium?*" *Modern Language Notes,* LXIII (1948), 516.

Christmas, but that Smith had not kept his promise. (Rae, p. 252.) In any case, there is not on record any information indicating that Smith met Franklin on this occasion.

Adam Smith and Franklin were both living in London in the period May, 1773 to March, 1775. The only basis for the widely-accepted belief that the two men met during this period is the story, which has gained weight with each repetition, that, as Rae reports it, Franklin once said that "the celebrated Adam Smith, when writing his *Wealth of Nations,* was in the habit of bringing chapter after chapter, as he composed it, to himself, Dr. Price, and others of the literati; then patiently hear their observations and profit by their discussions and criticisms, sometimes submitting to write whole chapters anew, and even to reverse some of his propositions." (Rae, pp. 264-265.) In the index to his book, Rae does refer to the story as "alleged assistance to Smith in composing *Wealth of Nations*" (Rae, p. 443, under entry for "Franklin."), but in his text he gives, on what seem to me flimsy grounds, considerable credence to it (Rae, pp. 265-266.).

Rae gives as his source for the story "Watson's *Annals of Philadelphia,* I, 533.[61] Watson's source for the story was undoubtedly Deborah Logan, the widow of Dr. George Logan, the person to whom Franklin was supposed to have told it. The first record of the story is in a letter by Mrs. Logan written in 1829.[62] Watson tells the story for the first time in the 1830 edition of his *Annals.* In later editions, he acknowledges having received help from Mrs. Logan's manuscripts. In the 1856 edition, for instance, he refers to

---

[61] John F. Watson, *Annals of Philadelphia,* either the Philadelphia 1856 edition, which I have consulted, or the 1844 edition which, according to other references, has the same story on the same page. Or Rae may have taken the story at second (or third) hand from James Parton, *Life and Times of Benjamin Franklin,* New York, 1864, I, 537. Rae quotes from Parton the opinion that Franklin could have afforded Smith great help in his treatment of the American Colonies. (Rae, pp. 265-266.)

[62] See *The Historical Magazine,* Second Series, IV (1868), 280.

"the MS collections of Mrs. Logan, kindly lent to me for general use."[63]

Dr. Logan died in 1821, and Mrs. Logan soon thereafter began to write a Memoir of her husband. She completed it before her death in 1839, but it remained unpublished until 1899, when the edited and revised manuscript prepared by a great-granddaughter, Miss Frances A. Logan, was published, a year after the death of Miss Logan.[64] The story is repeated there in substantially identical form and substance as in Watson's *Annals* and in Mrs. Logan's letter of 1829.[65]

The Logans were married in 1781. Franklin could have told the story to Dr. Logan at almost any time prior to 1790, when Franklin died. Franklin and Smith could have met in London to work together on *The Wealth of Nations* at any time between the spring of 1773 and the spring of 1775, when Franklin left England. There are no physical difficulties in connection with the story. Franklin, Dr. Logan, and Mrs. Logan were all reporters of above-average intelligence and integrity. If the story should nevertheless be rejected, the grounds for doing so must rely therefore, in part at least, on the possibility of someone's misunderstanding or lapse of memory; such possibility is always present, as has often been demonstrated. Between the occasion when the reported aid of Franklin to Smith in his writing of *The Wealth of Nations* could have occurred, 1773 to 1775, and the first recorded report of this in writing, 1829, there was a lapse of up to 55 years, with three persons involved, an average lapse per person, therefore, of some 18 years, and a maximum possible lapse, for Mrs. Logan, the key person, of 48 years, (1781, when

---

[63] I, 27; see also I, 77-78.

[64] *Memoir of Dr. George Logan of Stanton by his Widow Deborah Norris Logan,* edited by great-granddaughter Frances A. Logan. Introduction by Charles J. Stillé, Philadelphia, 1899. Mr. Stillé writes that Miss Logan "spent many years in revising and copying the manuscript and preparing it for publication." Introduction, p. 10.

[65] *Ibid.,* pp. 46-47.

she married Logan, to 1829), long periods for the most reliable of reporters and the most retentive of memories.

Franklin left behind him a mass of memorabilia, but to date there is no published evidence that he confided this remarkable story to anyone but Dr. Logan. Smithian memorabilia are admittedly scanty, and Smith himself might be reasonably regarded as having no motive for spreading widely an acknowledgement of having received the kind of aid in writing *The Wealth of Nations* that the story reports. But there is no evidence that Smith ever got help of this sort in the preparation of *any* of his manuscripts.

There remains the reference in the story to Price and other London "literati" participating in the discussions. There is no evidence to make credible that Smith would turn to Price for advice and counsel. To Smith, Price was mainly a political and religious speculator, with unacceptable doctrines, and a practitioner of "political arithmetic." In 1776 Smith put on record that "I have no great faith in political arithmetic,"[66] and he repeated this later in correspondence. Price admired Smith and cherished his acquaintanceship with him. There is evidence that Smith and Price were together at least on one occasion in London, but it was at a dinner party in 1776, or after Franklin had left England, and when it was too late for further work on *The Wealth of Nations*. (Rae, p. 280.) There is no record of Price having told anyone of having helped Smith on *The Wealth of Nations*. In a letter Price wrote shortly after Smith's death, he tells in general terms of his relations with Smith. If he had had any part in the writing of *The Wealth of Nations*, mention of it in this

---

[66] *The Wealth of Nations,* II, 36. More explicitly, in a letter written in 1785, Smith stated: "Price's speculations cannot fail to sink into the neglect that they have always deserved. I have always considered him as a factious citizen, a most superficial philosopher, and by no means an able calculator." (Rae, p. 400.)

letter would have been completely appropriate, but there is no such mention in it.[67] As for the other "literati" who reportedly helped Smith write his *The Wealth of Nations,* apparently none of them thought it worth while to leave a record of it, or to tell others of it who would pass the gossip on to later generations.

The story as it stands, even if written down to allow for exaggeration, is to my mind on the bare outward edge of credibility, although it faces no physical obstacles. The Franklin Papers, now in process of publication, may give substance to the story. But until this happens, or other fresh supporting evidence turns up, the appropriate reaction to the story seems to me to be: *Si populus vult decipi, decipiatur.*

10. *William Hamilton of Bangour (1704-1754).* Foulis published anonymously in 1748 and 1749 an edition of *Poems on Several Occasions* of William Hamilton of Bangour, the "Jacobite poet-laureate."[68] Rae says, on the authority of "the accurate and learned David Laing," that "The task of collecting and editing the poems was entrusted to Adam Smith." (Rae, p. 39.) Others state only

---

[67] See *Proceedings of the Massachusetts Historical Society,* 2nd Series, XVII (1903), 377. On the other hand, it may not have been in character for Price to make such claims. John Howard made written acknowledgement in correspondence with Price of the latter's help in connection with *The State of the Prisons,* 1777, but Price never claimed any credit for Howard's book. (See Carl B. Cone, *Torchbearer of Freedom. The Influence of Richard Price on Eighteenth Century Thought,* Lexington, Ky., 1952, pp. 60-61.)

[68] I write "1748 and 1749", because: in the Foulis catalogue the book is dated 1749, it is often assigned to 1748, and sometimes there is reference to two issues, in 1748 *and* 1749. The 1758 edition, also published by Foulis, is listed in the Foulis catalogue as the "2nd edition," and is so referred to in most references to it. The 1749 issue was probably regarded by Foulis and by others as merely a reissue of the 1748 one, and not a "new edition." I will here refer to the 1758 edition as the second edition and will make no distinction between a 1748 and a 1749 issue. No early editions have been available to me for examination.

that Smith wrote the preface for the 1748 edition.[69] Rae uses Smith's supposed association with the 1748 edition both to support his argument that Smith's associations with Foulis began before his appointment to a professorship at the University of Glasgow,[70] and to mark the beginning of Smith's literary career.

Because of his Jacobite activities, Hamilton had to flee to France in 1747, where he lived in exile until some time in 1750. The publication of the 1748 edition was arranged in his absence by a group of his Scottish friends, acting on their own initiative. Smith was then living and lecturing in Edinburgh, and I know of no real evidence that he already had a connection with either Foulis or Hamilton, or, except for his earlier Glasgow education, with Glasgow. William Hamilton was pardoned in 1750 and returned to Scotland in that year, where he remained, apparently in or near Glasgow, for some two years. In 1752 he returned to France, this time because he was suffering from tuberculosis, and he died in Lyons in 1754.

In 1758, Hamilton's friends arranged once more for a Foulis edition of his poems. This was planned to be dedicated to William Craufurd, a Glasgow businessman, a patron of Hamilton and also a friend of Smith, who had died in 1755. A letter of Dec. 1, 1757, survives, in which John Dalrymple, another friend of Smith and also of Hamilton, and, according to Rae, apparently a nephew of Craufurd, writes to Foulis asking him to try to persuade Smith to write the dedication to Craufurd.[71] In the two

---

[69] The preface to the 1748 edition is reprinted in *The Poems and Songs of William Hamilton of Bangour*, Edinburgh, 1850, where it is attributed to Smith. Philip Gaskell, *A Bibliography of the Foulis Press*, London, 1964, which reached me only after this work was in press, refers to "Adam Smith's Preface" to the 1748 edition, (p. 125) but provides no supporting evidence. This preface contains nothing of interest, at least for present purposes.

[70] See *supra*, p. 37.

[71] See Rae, pp. 40-42 and, for the complete letter, *Notices and Illustrations of the Literary History of Glasgow*, pp. 23-28.

years 1751 to 1752 Smith, it appears, had become a friend
of both Hamilton and Craufurd. There is no clear evidence
that Smith did actually write the dedication to Craufurd
which appears in the 1758 edition, but it seems probable
enough that he did. It does not seem to me that Rae also
attributes to Smith the collecting and editing of the
poems for the 1758 edition, but others have so interpreted
him. The letter from Dalrymple to Foulis of Dec. 1, 1757,
says nothing about collecting and editing, and I don't know
why, after so brief an acquaintance with Hamilton, Smith
should have had any special qualifications for the task.
If the new edition was published *early* in 1758, this would
be presumptive evidence that the collecting and editing
had been done before Smith was asked (December 1, 1757)
to write the dedication to Craufurd, but a search through
the files for 1758 of the *Monthly Review,* the *Critical
Review,* and the *Gentleman's Magazine* has not turned up
a notice of Hamilton's *Poems.*[72]

11. *David Hume.* In 1846 John Hill Burton printed, apparently for the first time, the following passage from a
letter of March 4, 1740, from Hume to Francis Hutcheson:

> My bookseller has sent to Mr. Smith a copy of my
> book, which I hope he has receiv'd, as well as your
> letter. I have not yet heard what he has done with the
> Abstract. Perhaps you have. I have got it printed in
> London . . .

Burton comments as follows:

> The 'Smith' here mentioned as receiving a copy

---

[72] N. S. Bushnell, *William Hamilton of Bangour, Poet and Jacobite,*
Aberdeen, 1957, was not available to me. Clyde E. Dankert, *Thoughts
from Adam Smith,* Hanover, N. H., 1963, p. 36, writes:
"There is some slight question as to whether Smith performed this
task (of "collecting and editing the poems of his friend William
Hamilton") but we shall be giving him the benefit of the doubt, going
along with John Rae, the economist's chief biographer, and N. S. Bushnell, author of a comparatively recent study of Hamilton." But if
Dankert here has the 1758 edition in mind, I do not interpret Rae as
claiming for Smith the collecting and editing of the poems for this
edition.

of the Treatise, we may fairly conclude, notwithstanding the universality of the name, to be Adam
Smith, who was then a student in the University of
Glasgow, and not quite seventeen years. It may be
inferred from Hume's letter, that Hutcheson had
mentioned Smith as a person on whom it would serve
some good purpose to bestow a copy of the Treatise;
and we have here, evidently, the first introduction to
each other's notice, of two friends . . .[73]

Rae, with no more evidence on hand than Burton provides, promotes Adam Smith to being the author rather
than the mere recipient of the 'Abstract.' To explain why
Hutcheson would need to communicate by letter with one
of his students, Rae surmises that Smith may have gone
home to Kirkcaldy to make preparations for Oxford,
though he did not actually set out for Oxford till June.
(Rae, pp. 15-16.)

W. R. Scott, writing in 1900, accepts the story as told
by Burton and Rae. He adds a mite to its credibility by
reporting, on the basis of Carlyle's *Autobiography,* "that
it was customary for Hutcheson and Leechman [another
Glasgow professor] to require promising members of their
classes to prepare abstracts either of new or standard
works, and that these summaries often attracted considerable notice in the University."[74] Lest Smith's youthfulness

---

[73] John Hill Burton, *Life and Correspondence of David Hume,* Edinburgh, 1846, I, 116-117.

[74] W. R. Scott, *Francis Hutcheson,* Cambridge, England, 1900, pp.
120-121. Scott refers to p. 101 of Carlyle's *Autobiography,* but does
not specify the edition. The relevant material I can find in the editions
available to me (e.g., London, 1910, pp. 95, 110-111) indicates that
Leechman prescribed one "discourse" a session to each student, but
says nothing about such a practice on the part of any other professors. It reports two somewhat exceptional instances, only one on
Hutcheson's initiative, where papers written by Carlyle were seen by
Hutcheson. I can find no other evidence that it was routine then at
Glasgow University to assign papers, or reports on books, to students,
and the evidence I have found indicates rather that if students did
prepare papers, it was usually on their own initiative and to be read
at students' clubs.

at the time operate to damage the credibility of the story, Scott proceeds: "This is not to be taken as tending to discredit the early connection of Adam Smith with Hume, rather, it is a remarkable instance of Hutcheson's success as a teacher, and the enthusiasm with which he inspired his pupils for Philosophy."[75]

Many years later Scott was not only still treating the story seriously, but on the strength of it alone made Adam Smith's preparation of the "Abstract" *the* critical point in Smith's career:

> In the lives of many men there is one important decision which once it is made determines their whole career. Such a decision had to be made by Adam Smith while he was still a very young man, though it is quite possible that he never fully realized the consequences. This happened in the following way.

There follows a résumé of the 1749 story as told by Rae. If I read Scott correctly, the "decision" Smith then made was that "philosophy" was not for him.[76]

The only evidence at the command of Burton, Rae, and Scott to connect Smith with Hume as early as 1740 was the letter of March 4, 1740, from Hume to Hutcheson which linked Hume and Hutcheson to a "Mr. Smith" and the indisputable fact that Adam Smith was then a student of Hutcheson's. If "Mr. Smith" should turn out to be another Smith than Adam, the whole story would immediately founder.

It may perhaps be pleaded on behalf of Burton, Rae, and Scott that for modern students of eighteenth century Scottish intellectual life there is an irresistible association

---

[75] Scott, *ibid.*, p. 121.

[76] W. R. Scott, "Adam Smith," *Proceedings of the British Academy,* XI (1923), 437-438. Scott did not abandon the story until learning that J. M. Keynes in 1936 or 1937 had "evidence to prove that the Christian name of the person mentioned was not Adam." W. R. Scott, *ASSP,* pp. 34-35.

of ideas between "Mr. Smith" and Adam Smith. Although
at later stages of his career Smith had full claim to the
titles professor, doctor and commissioner, it was both his
preference and common practice for him to be addressed
and referred to as "Mr. Smith."[77] To this designation, he
had few rivals among men of stature to be confused with.
In the "Smith" entries in the *Epitome* of the *Dictionary
of National Biography* for the period, roughly, of 1730 to
1790, there are only five Smiths who are identifiable from
the *Epitome* alone as Scots, and except for our Adam none
of these is of real prominence. Even of these five, one was
a Catholic bishop *in partibus infidelium* and another was
an M.D., so that for neither would "Mr." have been a
proper appellation. I am skeptical, moreover, that in eighteenth century Scottish oral or written communication it
would have been customary to refer to a sixteen-year-old
student as "Mr."[78]

The story in any case was definitely ruined when the
joint research of J. M. Keynes and Piero Sraffa achieved
the identification of "Mr. Smith," located printed copies of
the "Abstract," and demonstrated that it was an abstract
of Hume's *Treatise of Human Nature*, written by Hume
himself, and intended by him to stimulate the sale of
his *Treatise*. "Mr. Smith" was John Smith, Hutcheson's
Dublin bookseller and publisher, and Hume was seeking,
with Hutcheson's help, to induce John Smith to undertake
a second and revised edition of his *Treatise* in Dublin,
where Hume would be free from the English copyright law

---

[77] See Dugald Stewart's "Account of the Life and Writings of Adam
Smith," in his *The Collected Works,* Edinburgh, 1858, X, 98; also
Rae, p. 234.

[78] According to Edmund S. Morgan, *The Puritan Family,* Boston,
1944, p. 37, "the title 'Mister' or 'Master' was reserved in the seventeenth century for persons of wealth and social distinction." For
eighteenth-century Scotland, it at least seems to be true that "Mr."
was not freely extended as a title to youngsters or persons without
social status.

which in England and Scotland gave his London publisher control over the issue of new editions of his book.[79]

In their introduction, Keynes and Sraffa tell in some detail the history of the legend and summarize its status at the time of their writing in the following words: "To-day it is a commonplace amongst the biographers of Hume and Adam Smith that Adam Smith at seventeen [it should be "in his seventeenth year"] wrote a review of Hume's Treatise." I would put a word in, however, for a German biographer of Smith, Emanuel Leser, who in 1881, with only Burton's story to work on, failed to pierce "Mr. Smith's" identity or to perceive the character of the "Abstract," but nevertheless showed a reasonable degree of skepticism that men of the stature of Hutcheson and Hume would take so seriously the effort of a student in his seventeenth year.[80]

In the years roughly from 1748 to 1758, there occurred a complex network of correspondence involving pioneering discussion of the existence and mode of operation of "natural" processes whereby international economic equilibrium would be maintained, or if disturbed would re-establish itself, without need of extensive or systematic governmental intervention. Major or marginal participants in this discussion were Charles Townshend and Josiah Tucker, Lord Kames and James Oswald, David Hume and Montesquieu. Essays which Hume published in 1752 partly as an outgrowth of this correspondence were to be landmarks in the history of economic thought. In his Glasgow lectures, as reported in the manuscript edited by Cannan, Smith drew substantially on these essays of Hume,

---

[79] See *An Abstract of a Treatise of Human Nature 1740. A Pamphlet hitherto unknown by David Hume. Reprinted with an Introduction by J. M. Keynes and P. Sraffa.* Cambridge, Eng., 1938.

[80] See Emanuel Leser, *Untersuchungen zur Geschichte der National-ökonomie,* I Heft, I, "Aus der Lebengeschichte des Adam Smith," Jena, 1881, pp. 5-8.

but otherwise there is no trace of his participation in the discussion, and in *The Wealth of Nations* there is little sign that Smith had profited from Hume's contribution.[81]

Rae reports an episode which if it occurred as he relates it would imply that Smith had before 1752 at least a small part, which there is no other evidence to support, in this discussion. Rae's account is as follows:

> Early in its first session [of the Literary Society, of Glasgow]—on the 23rd of January 1753—Professor Adam Smith is stated to have read an account of some of Mr. David Hume's Essays on Commerce. These essays had then just appeared, and they had probably been seen by Smith before their publication, for in September 1752 Hume writes Smith asking him for any corrections he had to suggest on the old edition of the Political Essays with which the Commercial Essays were incorporated. We have seen Hume submitting one of these Commercial Essays in 1750 to Oswald and Mure, and when we find him in 1752 asking for suggestions from Smith on the essays already printed, we may safely infer that he had also asked and received suggestions on the new essays which had never before been published. (Rae, pp. 95-96.)

For Adam Smith's paper, Rae's only source is an extract of the Records of the Literary Society for the year 1752 given in *Notices and Illustrations,* p. 132, which reads "Jany. 23. Mr. Smith read an Account of some of Mr. David Hume's Essays on Commerce." There is nothing in

---

[81] For comment on the historical significance of the correspondence, and for material relating to it, see: J. M. Low, "An Eighteenth Century Controversy in the Theory of Economic Progress," *Manchester School,* XX (1952), 311-330; David Hume, *Writings on Economics,* Eugene Rotwein, ed., pp. 187-206; Jacob Viner, *Studies in the Theory of International Trade,* New York, 1937, pp. 84-87. For the possible relations of Townshend to the discussion, see *infra,* pp. 83-84.

Notices and Illustrations to justify or explain the substitution for 1752 of 1753 in Rae's account. I will tentatively take it for granted that this substitution was merely a slip on Rae's part or a typographical error. Disregarding it makes Rae's supposition that Smith had a copy of Hume's essays prior to their publication more rather than less credible.

The only concrete ground that is apparent for Rae's inference that Smith had a copy of Hume's essays prior to their publication is that Smith as early as January 23, 1752, was already able to read a paper on a book published in the same year. Hume published the book under the title *Political Discourses*, which continued to be the title under which all subsequent separate editions were published in Hume's lifetime. All these essays were newly published in 1752,[82] under the collective title of *Political Discourses*, although Rae never refers to them by this title. Most of them were on economic topics. The publication of *Political Discourses* was announced in *Scots Magazine* for January, 1752 (p. 56), and in *Gentleman's Magazine* for February, 1752 (p. 94). The book was reviewed in the *Monthly Review* in two parts, the first of which appeared in January, 1752. It was common eighteenth-century practice, moreover, for publishers to put on title pages of books which were actually issued as late as November of a given year the date of the following year,[83] and from a letter of Hume to Robert Wallace of September 22, 1751, we learn that the *Political Discourses* was then near publication, but not so near that brief additions, or deletions, could not

---

[82] In the 1758 edition, an essay "On the Jealousy of Trade" was added.

[83] See: John Nichols, *Literary Anecdotes of the Eighteenth Century*, London, 1812, III, 249, note; R. M. Schmitz, *Hugh Blair*, New York, 1948, p. 49, note; Robert Kerr, *Memoirs of the Life, Writings, and Correspondence of William Smellie*, Edinburgh, 1811, I, 29.

still be made.[84] There need not, therefore, have been any physical obstacle to Smith reading a paper on Jan. 23rd, 1752, commenting on a book published as of the year 1752, without having had an advance copy or a pre-publication manuscript. *The Monthly Review,* if it appeared on schedule, had been about as prompt in *printing* a review of the book.

Rae appeals, in support of his inference that Smith had seen the essays before their publication, to a letter written by Hume to Smith in September 1752, "asking him for any corrections he had to suggest on the old edition of the Political Essays." (Rae, p. 95.)[85] The letter does demonstrate that in 1752 Hume welcomed suggestions from Smith prior to the republication of his *old* essays. It still leaves it open, however, as to whether he had earlier proceeded in the same manner with respect to the new essays which he published as *Political Discourses* in 1752. Cannan, relying presumably on Rae's account, wrongly interprets Hume's invitation to Smith to provide suggestions for a new edition as applying to a new edition of the *Political Discourses,* instead of to the "Essays moral & political"

---

[84] *New Letters of David Hume,* Raymond Klibansky and Ernest C. Mossner, eds., Oxford, 1954, pp. 28-29. One of the essays in *Political Discourses,* "Of the Populousness of Ancient Nations" was written in response to an essay by Robert Wallace as yet unpublished which he had allowed Hume to read. (See James Bonar, *Theories of Population from Raleigh to Arthur Young,* London, 1931, pp. 174-177.) Hume had sent his own essay on population to Wallace for comment before publishing it, and his letter shows that he had also let Wallace read some of the other essays prior to their publication as *Political Discourses.* Since James Oswald also had read some of these essays before their publication, it is not hard to believe that Smith had seen them before they were published.

[85] Rae is probably relying here on John Hill Burton's *Life* of Hume. The letter, dated Sept. 24, 1752, is available, with relevant editorial notes, in J. Y. T. Greig, *The Letters of David Hume,* I, 167-168. Hume refers in it to "Essays moral & political," first published in 1741/1742, republished in 1748, and now awaiting its republication in 1753 as vol. I. of *Essays and Treatises on Several Subjects,* with vol. II. devoted to philosophical essays of lesser interest to Smith.

of 1741/1742 and 1748, expressly referred to in Hume's letter.[86]

I return to the question raised by Rae's substitution of 1753 for 1752 as the year in which Smith read his Jan. 23rd paper. I thought for a time that this might possibly be a silent correction by Rae of confusion on the part of previous writers with respect to "new style" versus "old style." But if previous writers were using "old style" the year would have been 1751, and if they were using "new style" it would have been 1752. By Jan. 23, 1752 "new style," moreover, there was no longer any ambiguity as to dating, for by an act of 1751, "new style" was made legally effective beginning with the January 1 which followed immediately upon Dec. 31, 1751. In Scotland, furthermore, it had been common practice since 1600 to treat Jan. 1 as the beginning day of the year, and since the 1740's at least, although without statutory basis, as the day on which the year number changed.[87]

Rae says that *Notices and Illustrations* "gives us no information about the papers read in this society [i.e., the Literary Society] after the first six months, except those by Foulis, but no doubt Smith read other papers in the remaining ten years of his connection with the society" (Rae, p. 96.). *Notices and Illustrations* does state, however,

[86] Cannan ed., *The Wealth of Nations,* "Editor's Introduction," p. xlvii, Note 1. Cannan uses this as a basis for a conclusion of some importance on the intellectual relations of the two men.

[87] See W. W. Greg, "Old Style-New Style," in *Joseph Quincy Adams Memorial Studies,* Washington, 1948, pp. 563-569; R. W. Chapman, ed., *The Letters of Samuel Johnson,* Oxford, 1952, I, 42. Referring to a Johnson letter carrying the date March 17, 1752, Chapman writes: "I am assuming, as we are bound to assume, that Johnson was using old style; but dates in these fateful years of change are treacherous things." They are, indeed! Chapman here overlooks that "old style" was abolished as from Dec. 31, 1751 on. His comments, however, are otherwise very helpful. For the references to Greg and Chapman, I am indebted to friends who are knowledgeable on these matters, but if I have nevertheless gone wrong, the fault is mine.

(p. 16) that "Adam Smith read those essays on Taste, Composition, and the History of Philosophy, which he had previously delivered while a lecturer on rhetoric in Edinburgh," which may or may not be correct. John Millar, writing to Smith's "nephew," David Douglas, shortly after Smith's death, says: "Of the discourses which he intended upon the imitative arts, he read two to our Society at Glasgow."[88] These were presumably the two parts of the three-part essay on "The Imitative Arts" which were published posthumously, with a fragment of Part III added.

12. *Samuel Johnson*. There is a substantial body of anecdotes and recollections, much of it of dubious reliability, which points towards some incompatibility of temperament of Smith and Johnson and also a critical attitude of the two men towards each other's works, personality, and intellect. Rae reports some of this material, (See his index, under "Johnson.") and the available material, including that presented by Rae, has been surveyed in two recent articles.[89] It is my impression, however, that these writers minimize on the whole the extent to which what is known of the relations of the two men with each other points to a basic coldness and to the existence of a number of points of potential friction between them. I will not resurvey the material which they have gathered, but will confine myself mostly to material which has not hitherto been referred to in discussions of the relations between Smith and Johnson.

I do not know whether James Boswell exercised much influence on Johnson's opinions or attitudes towards other men, but whatever its extent that influence must have been such in direction as on the whole to nudge Johnson towards dislike of or coldness to Smith. Boswell attended

---

[88] W. R. Scott, *ASSP*, p. 312.

[89] Clyde E. Dankert, "Two Eighteenth-Century Celebrities," *The Dalhousie Review*, XLII (1962), 364-375; John H. Middendorf, "Dr. Johnson and Adam Smith," *Philological Quarterly*, XL (1961), 281-296.

Smith's lectures at the University of Glasgow for one year. They never, as far as we know, became intimate, and we have no record of any reference to Boswell by Smith, but they must have met fairly frequently, in the social life of the Edinburgh intellectuals, at "The Club," "Johnson's Club," in London of which they were both members, in the meeting-places of Scotsmen in London, if not elsewhere. Boswell never expressed any admiration for Smith's personal characteristics, and they had in general inharmonious political, religious, literary views, as far as I can tell. Boswell reported to Johnson such evidence or gossip of the expression by Smith of views critical of Johnson as came his way, and was apparently happy to find opportunities for provoking Johnson into outbursts at Smith's expense which would merit listening to and recording. Like many others, he was angered by Smith's public expression of admiration for David Hume despite the latter's failure to renounce his religious skepticism in the months when he knew that death was impending. On one occasion he proposed to Johnson that the latter should "knock Hume's and Smith's heads together, and make vain and ostentatious infidelity exceedingly ridiculous."[90] He was in close relations with W. J. Mickle, the poet, at a time when the latter was nursing a sense of grievance against Smith.[91] Smith's alignments on the opposite side to his own of the "Douglas Cause" was for Boswell an additional provocation.

Scottish public opinion split violently on the "Douglas Cause," with the "Stewart" side commanding the "popular" support. Boswell espoused the "Stewart" side, while

[90] James Boswell, *Life of Johnson,* (July 9, 1777), Modern Library ed., III, 153. Boswell, in 1776, submitted to the *London Chronicle* an apoplectic rejoinder to a letter in praise of Hume which it had printed. Boswell in effect denied that public avowal of religious skepticism and good character and behavior could coexist in the same person. Boswell's letter is reprinted, as "Remarks on the Character of Mr. Hume," in *Scots Magazine,* XXXVIII (Nov. 1776), 578-579.

[91] See *infra,* p. 70 ff.

Smith was an ardent supporter of the opposing or "Hamilton" side. Lady Jane Douglas (1698-1753), daughter of James, second Marquis of Douglas (1646-1700), and sister of Archibald, third Marquis of Douglas (1694-1761), married Colonel John Stewart in 1746, secretly lest her brother cut off her allowance in consequence. The third Marquis of Douglas had no direct heirs, and if Lady Jane Douglas had a son he would be the lawful heir to the Douglas estates. John Stewart, before the death of the third Marquis, persuaded him that Lady Jane Douglas had been delivered of male twins in July, 1748 (at 51 years of age!), that one of them had died, and that the surviving one, Archibald Douglas Stewart, was thus the lawful heir male of the third Marquis, and before his death the Marquis settled the Douglas estates on Archibald Douglas Stewart. Suit was brought on behalf of the young Duke of Hamilton, in the absence of issue of Lady Jane Douglas the lawful heir of the Douglas estates, on the ground that the claim that the twins born in 1748 were issue of Lady Jane was an imposture. By a majority of one, the Scottish Court of Sessions decided in favor of the claims of the Duke of Hamilton, but on appeal to the House of Lords the decision was reversed in 1769.[92]

Boswell was involved in the case both emotionally and as one of the counsel on the side of Archibald Douglas Stewart. He not only worked on the legal briefs, but published a pamphlet, *The Essence of the Douglas Cause* (which he could not persuade Johnson to read) and, more relevant for present purposes, he is reported to have inserted in the *London Chronicle,* under cover of anonymity, a series of fabrications in support of the Stewart claims,

---

[92] For a history of this case, see Lillian de la Torre, *The Heir of Douglas,* New York, 1952.

one of which was presented as if coming from Smith's pen.[93]

Andrew Stuart, a close friend of Adam Smith, and Baron Mure, another friend and a patron of Smith, were guardians of the Duke of Hamilton, and Andrew Stuart, who was a lawyer, also acted professionally as the principal prosecutor of the young Duke's claims. The Duke of Hamilton was closely related, through his mother, the Duchess of Argyle, to the Duke of Buccleuch. Smith was therefore involved as a friend with the group pressing the Duke of Hamilton's claims. In 1765, when he was in Toulouse as tutor of the Duke of Buccleuch, Smith had been commissioned by Andrew Stuart to take evidence bearing on the authenticity of the testimony gathered in France on the Stewart side to support the claim that Lady Jane Douglas had in fact been delivered of twin sons in Paris in 1748.[94] When the House of Lords in 1769 rejected the claims of the Duke of Hamilton, Smith in a letter to Lord Hailes, a distinguished Scottish jurist, protested vehemently against the reversal by the House of Lords of the decision of the highest Scottish Court, and protested especially against the role played in that reversal by Lord Mansfield and Lord Camden, whom he held to have been primarily responsible and to have catered to the mob. (Rae, pp. 248-250; see also, for relevant material, Rae, pp. 258-259.) Rae comments that Smith's "impeachment of the impartiality of the two great English judges—Lord Camden and Lord Mansfield—cannot seem defensible." (Rae, p. 250.) But Rae, on the same page, prints a letter in which David Hume

---

[93] Lillian de la Torre, *op. cit.,* pp. 213-214. The numbers of the *London Chronicle* containing this series have not been available. There is no reference to the "Douglas Cause" in the only treatment of the relations between Boswell and Smith known to me: Clyde E. Dankert, "Adam Smith and James Boswell," *Queen's Quarterly,* LXVIII (1961), 323-332.

[94] See W. R. Scott, *ASSP,* pp. 259-261.

arraigns as bluntly as did Smith the judicial integrity of the two Law Lords in their conduct in the Douglas case. That Smith's reaction need not have been wholly a matter of personal entanglements with the Hamilton side and of prejudice any reader of the indictment of Lord Mansfield's conduct in the case by Andrew Stuart will, I think, easily be persuaded.[95]

There was published in 1782 an anonymous tract, *Deformities of Dr. Samuel Johnson, Selected from his Works,* Edinburgh, "Printed for the author and sold by W. Creech and T. Longman and J. Stockdale, London." Later in the same year a second edition, somewhat enlarged and again anonymous, was published, "Printed for the Author; and sold by J. Stockdale, London; and W. Creech Edinburgh." The book is commonly attributed to John Callander of Craigforth. If this attribution were correct, Adam Smith would be involved at least by intimate association with a participant in the scurrilous campaign against the character and the literary attainments of Johnson which a sizable group of Scottish writers engaged in.

John Callander was at different stages of his life a wealthy landowner, a practicing advocate in Edinburgh, an agricultural "improver," an antiquarian whose considerable renown as such was, however, destined to be tarnished later by the discovery that he had been guilty of extensive plagiarism, a writer of literary criticism. His personal relations with Adam Smith were of long duration and apparently were close. He attended the lectures on "jurisprudence" which Smith gave in Edinburgh before going to Glasgow as professor; he was a member of Smith's circle

---

[95] Andrew Stuart, *Letters to the Right Honourable Lord Mansfield,* London, 1773. I would think that this book would make fascinating reading for a lawyer interested in the principles of evidence, or for a student of Scottish eighteenth century rhetoric in practice.

of friends in Edinburgh; he once accompanied Smith on a
visit to Kirkcaldy. According to Rae, he was a fellow-
member with Smith of the Literary Club in Glasgow. (Rae,
p. 95; this seems to be Rae's only mention of Callander.)[96]

Deformities of Dr. Samuel Johnson is a bitter attack on
both the personal characteristics and the writings of Johnson. It manifests a strong animus against him, arising apparently mainly from resentment against Johnson's disparagement of Scotland in general and of particular Scottish writers. Adam Smith appears in the tract in several
different connections, but always so as to compare Johnson
with him to Johnson's disadvantage, as inferior to Smith
in personal character, in political judgment, in literary
performance.

After citing from Johnson's *Taxation No Tyranny,* "No
part of the world has yet had reason to rejoice that Colum-
bus found at last reception and employment," *Deformities*
comments:

> This wild opinion is fairly disproved by Dr. Smith, a
> philosopher not much afraid of novelty; for he has
> advanced a greater variety of original, interesting, and
> profound ideas, than almost any other author since
> the first existence of books.[97]

In a reference to an acknowledgement by Johnson that
when writing his *Dictionary* he found himself frequently

---

[96] There are entries for John Callander in the *Dictionary of National
Biography* and in R. Chambers, *Biographical Dictionary of Eminent
Scotsmen.* There is some information about him in John Ramsay of
Octhertyre, *Scotland and the Scotsmen in the Eighteenth Century,*
A. Allardyce, ed., Edinburgh, 1888, II, 238-241. W. R. Scott, *ASSP,*
refers to him, and to "Callander Papers" in the University of Edin-
burgh Library, with reference to Adam Smith (pp. 20, 50, 54, 55, 63).
In none of these, however, is there any mention of the *Deformities of
Dr. Samuel Johnson.*

[97] *Deformities of Dr. Samuel Johnson,* 2nd ed., p. 33.

[98] *Ibid.,* p. 67.

entangled "in the mazes of . . . intricacy," the author asks
whether Johnson's treatment of the particle "But" was
not an example.[98] When Smith reviewed the *Dictionary* in
the *Edinburgh Review* for 1755, he had used Johnson's
treatment of "But" as one of the two examples he chose
to demonstrate how Johnson's method could be improved
upon.[99]

The most striking example of lavish praise of Smith at
the expense of Johnson in *Deformities* is the following
from the final paragraph in the tract:

> Dr. Johnson says, that one of the lowest of all human
> beings is a Commissioner of Excise.[100] This can hardly
> be the case, unless himself or his reverend friend Mr.
> Shaw[101] shall arrive at that dignity. But in the mean-
> time, there is a Commissioner of Excise, or Customs
> (no matter which)[102] who in the scale of human beings

[99] Smith's review is most readily available in *The Works of Adam Smith*, London, 1811, V, 559-562.

[100] I do not know where Johnson says this. His definition of "Excise" in his *Dictionary* is well-known: "a hateful tax levied upon commodities and adjudged not by the common judges of property but by wretches hired by those to whom the excise is paid." The Commissioners of Excise in 1755 sought to have Johnson prosecuted for criminal libel, but William Murray, (later Lord Mansfield) the Attorney-General, while he thought the definition legally a "libel," recommended that Johnson be given a chance to alter his definition before any action was taken. (John Owens, *Plain Papers relating to the Excise Branch*, Linlithgow, 1879, pp. 2-3.)

[101] William Shaw (1749-1831), was a member for a time of Johnson's literary circle, but Johnson apparently ridiculed one of his works, and in 1785, after Johnson's death, Shaw wrote *Memoirs of . . . Dr. Johnson*, which seems to me predominantly hostile to Johnson. *Deformities* is here obviously insulting Shaw, who was not popular in Scotland, because of his long-sustained flirtation with Anglicanism, his denial of the authenticity of Macpherson's *Ossian*, and perhaps also what seemed to some Scotsmen his undue subserviency for a loyal Scot to Samuel Johnson. But I do not pretend to be able to follow all the literary by-play engaged in in this tract.

[102] Adam Smith was at the time, of course, a "Commissioner of Customs." But he was also a "Commissioner of the Salt Duties" and thus also a holder of an office which in England, although not in Scotland, was under the jurisdiction of the Excise Department.

is not much lower than Lexiphanes[103] himself. This couple stand in the most striking contrast, and to draw the character of the first is to write an oblique but most severe censure on the character of the second. Dr. Smith's language is a luscious and pure specimen of strength, elegance, precision, and simplicity. His *Enquiry* into the nature and causes of the wealth of nations deserves to be studied by every member of the community, as one of the most accurate, profound, and persuasive books that ever was written. In *that* performance he displays an intimate and extensive knowledge of mankind, in every department of life, from the cabinet to the cottage; a supreme contempt of national prejudice, and a fearless attachment to liberty, to justice, and to truth. His work is admired as a mass of excellence, a condensation of reasonings, the most various, important, original, and just.[104]

I know of no direct evidence that Smith was aware even of the existence of this tract. But the circumstantial evidence is such as to make it hard to believe that if John Callander were really its author in one way or another it would not have been brought to Smith's attention. It would then have been written by a personal friend. It was published in Edinburgh by William Creech, a prominent local bookseller, who had had a part, although a very minor one, in the publication of the first edition of *The Wealth of Nations*,[105] who was acquainted with all the

---

[103] This is no doubt an allusion to the chief character in [Archibald Campbell], *Lexiphanes,* (2nd ed., London, 1767). A burlesque of Johnson's literary style, *Lexiphanes* was in imitation of Lucian. The original "Lexiphanes" was a character in one of Lucian's satires whom Lucian ridiculed for his atrocious literary style. Campbell applies the name "to our English Lexiphanes *the Rambler.*" He mentions Johnson's adverse comments on things Scottish, pp. 24, 36, 118-119, note, and as a rejoinder points to the many uncomplimentary things Scottish authors had written about Johnson.

[104] *Deformities of Dr. Samuel Johnson,* 2nd ed., p. 89.

[105] The Kress Library of Harvard University has a copy of a variant first edition of *The Wealth of Nations* which carries the following information on its title-page: "London, Printed for W. Strahan and T. Cadell, and for W. Creech at Edinburgh, 1776."

literati of Edinburgh, and of whom it was said in an obituary of him in an Edinburgh newspaper: "With Lord Kames, Dr. Robertson, Dr. Blair, Dr. George Campbell, Dr. Adam Smith . . . he was in the habits of constant intimacy."[106] It was noticed in the reviews.[107] Even if the author did not see to it that Smith should receive a copy, it must have been talked about in town, and someone must have drawn his attention to the fact that he figured rather prominently in it. In any case, if Smith did read it, he must have become aware that in some minds if not in his own the relations between himself and Samuel Johnson were regarded as somewhat hostile.

There is another tract, which has many resemblances to *Deformities of Dr. Samuel Johnson* and is related to it closely, *A Critical Review of the Works of Dr. Samuel Johnson,* 1783. The tract is extremely scarce, and I have seen only a film of the second edition, whose title-page reads: "London. Printed for the Author, and sold by T. Cadell and J. Stockdale, at Edinburgh, by J. Dickson and W. Creech, 1783." The coincidences between *Deformities* and *A Critical Review* are too many to be wholly fortuitous. They were printed in successive years, each in two editions, and in both cases apparently the book originated in Edinburgh and then later in the year received a London edition. Both were published anonymously. William Creech of Edinburgh and J. Stockdale of London were involved in the publication of both tracts. Both tracts have Samuel Johnson as their subject and treat him with scorn and anger. Both refer favorably to Adam Smith. Both are attributed to Scottish authors, with nearly identical surnames, John Callander in the case of *Deformities of Dr.*

---

[106] See the "Life of Mr. Creech," prefixed to a posthumous second edition of William Creech, *Edinburgh Fugitive Pieces,* Edinburgh, 1815, p. xxxix.

[107] *The Critical Review,* LIX (August, 1782), 140-142; *The Monthly Review,* LXVIII (February, 1783), 185-186, (adversely in each case). I have not found a Scottish review. Smith, however, once declared himself not to be an admirer or even reader of the reviews.

Samuel Johnson, James T. Callender in the case of *A Critical Review.* The latter tract makes repeated references to *Deformities of Dr. Samuel Johnson* as if it had the same authorship, and its back outer cover carries an advertisement of the second edition of *Deformities.*[108]

There are in *A Critical Review* only two references, and these minor ones, to Adam Smith. After criticizing Johnson for excessive use, without explanation, of words borrowed from other languages, it comments: "Let us see how the best writers of the present age have acted in this respect," and then brings in evidence from a number of writers, all of them Scotsmen, and one of them Adam Smith. Of him, it says: "In an Enquiry into the nature and causes of the wealth of nations, I am *almost,* certain that the writer has not left a single foreign phrase unexplained, except the word *entrepôt,* which he adopts as an English noun."[109] Elsewhere it cites Smith's remark in *The Wealth of Nations* that at Oxford the professors had almost given up teaching.[110]

---

[108] James Thomson Callender (1758-1803), a native of Scotland, was a journalist in London, until he emigrated to the United States in 1794 after prosecution for libel on account of a political pamphlet he wrote. In the United States he was first patronized by Jefferson but later became embroiled with him. He died by drowning in a Virginia river, reportedly by suicide. There are articles on him in the *Dictionary of National Biography* and in the *Dictionary of American Biography,* but only the most meager information is given on his career prior to and during the 1780's. In the articles on James Anderson in Robert Chambers, *A Biographical Dictionary of Eminent Scotsmen* and in the *Dictionary of National Biography,* it is said that when the government was pressing Anderson, editor of *The Bee,* to disclose the authorship of a series of political articles which it regarded as libellous, Callender named Lord Gardenstone, against whom he had a personal grievance, to the authorities as the author, and that this forced Anderson, against his usual practice, to disclose that the true author was Callender himself. Chambers' *Biographical Dictionary* characterized Callender as a "worthless person." I have not found anywhere any references to possible relations of Callender with Samuel Johnson, Adam Smith, or John Callander.

[109] *A Critical Review,* p. 28; italics in original.

[110] *Ibid.,* p. 38.

I am indebted to Herman W. Liebert for bringing *A Critical Review* to my attention and for warning me that J. T. Callender, its author, was probably also the author of *Deformities of Dr. Samuel Johnson*. Dr. Liebert also has informed me that there is in the possession of an American collector of Johnsoniana a letter from J. T. Callender to J. Stockdale, the publisher, dated October 4, 1783, in which Callender asks for the delivery to him of the unsold copies of *Deformities of Dr. Samuel Johnson*. Attempts on my part to gain access to this letter have proved unsuccessful. Even without recourse to this letter, however, sufficient evidence is provided by the text of *A Critical Review* that it and *Deformities of Dr. Samuel Johnson* had common authorship. That the author was James T. Callender, not John Callander, the letter, as reported, provides the most convincing although not the sole evidence. *A Critical Review contains* this passage:

> In a work lately published by Mr. Callander of Craigforth, that gentleman (Introduction, p. 7) observes: "That had the laborious Johnson been better acquainted with the oriental tongues, or had he ever understood the first rudiments of the northern languages from which the English and Scots derive their origin, his bulky volumes had not presented to us the melancholy truth, that unwearied industry, *devoid of settled principles,* avails only to add one error to another."[111]

This seems adequate evidence by itself to acquit John Callander of any responsibility for authorship of either *Deformities of Samuel Johnson* or *A Critical Review*. I have not been able to identify the publication from which this quotation was taken. If, however, it is a fair sample of how John Callander dealt with Johnson in that publication, he may have rivalled J. T. Callender in scurrility, and thus the question may still be relevant as to whether

---

[111] Introduction, p. iv. The italics are in *A Critical Review*.

Adam Smith's intimate personal association with John Callander implicates him in any way with the campaign of exaggerated attack on Johnson as author and as person which some hyperpatriotic Scots engaged in.

In *Deformities of Samuel Johnson,* it will be remembered, one of the objections made against Johnson was that he had applied abusive terms to excise officers, and Adam Smith was there cited to demonstrate that an excise officer could be an admirable character. It is ironical that within less than ten years James T. Callender was writing, apparently in the pay of victims of their manipulations, to expose the corrupt practices of Scottish excise officers. It seems that it was on account of such writings that he was prosecuted for seditious publication and found it expedient to flee to America.[111a]

When he arrived in the United States, J. T. Callender continued to write in criticism of excise officers, perhaps still in the pay of their victims, and also published new editions of *The Political Progress of Britain.* In a new work, *A Short History of the Nature and Consequences of Excise Laws,* which he published in Philadelphia in 1795, he seems to have been attempting both to explain and to qualify his earlier praise of Adam Smith despite Smith's being an excise officer and an admirer of excise taxation:

> Dr. Adam Smith treated the laws, and parliament itself, with the utmost freedom. Speaking of one statute, he says, that happily the morals of the great body of the people were never so thoroughly corrupted, as the morals of those who made that law. He has ex-

---

[111a] The relevant publications of his in this connection seem to be *An Impartial Account of the Conduct of the Excise towards the Breweries in Scotland, Particularly in Edinburgh,* Edinburgh, 1791, and *The Political Progress of Britain,* Edinburgh, 1792 (neither of which were available for examination), and a closely-related series of anonymous contributions to *The Bee,* of which "On the Conduct of the Excise," a review of *An Impartial Account, The Bee,* IV (1791), 183-186, and a letter, *ibid.,* pp. 257-258, are probably representative, although I cannot demonstrate that they were products of his pen.

plained many of the faults of excise, but he was not in a profligate opposition, for he was a Scots commissioner of salt excise, and as holding that office, authorized or countenanced those enormities which his writings condemned.[111b]

13. *William Julius Mickle.* Mickle, a Scottish poet, the translator into English verse of Camoens' epic, *The Lusiad*, was a bitter critic of Smith. Rae (pp. 316-318.) bases his account on a life of Mickle attached by the Rev. John Sim as a preface to his edition of *The Poetical Works of William Julius Mickle*, London, 1806. This has not been available to me.[112]

Rae rebuts Sim's statement that Mickle began his attack on Smith's criticism of the (British) East India Company in *The Wealth of Nations* in the first complete edition of his *The Lusiad*, on the ground that the former was not published until 1776 whereas the latter was published in 1775. The first edition of *The Lusiad* carried the date 1776 on its title page. Rae may have had evidence that it was actually published late in 1775; in a letter to a friend dated Jan. 22, 1776, Mickle already is able to report on the reception of his poem.[113]

Other sources make it clear, however, that the criticism of *The Wealth of Nations* first appeared in the second edi-

---

[111b] *A Short History,* pp. 115-116. To this passage he attaches a note, whose relevance is not apparent to me, but which is clearly not friendly in intent: "This gentleman left behind him a thousand pages on *Sympathy.*"

[112] I have used the following sources: Mickle, *The Lusiad; or, The Discovery of India,* 2nd ed., Oxford, 1778, 3rd ed., London, 1798; *The Poetical Works of William Mickle,* C. Cooke, ed., London, n.d. (1799?), prefixed by a "Life" which is based largely on the item following: "An Account of the Life and Writings of William Julius Mickle," *The European Magazine,* XVI (1789), 155-157, 317-321. Sister M. E. Taylor, *William Julius Mickle* (1734-1788). *A Critical Study,* Washington, 1937, has no independent biographical information.

[113] Cooke, p. xii. On the other hand, the problem is complicated by the fact that Mickle had for several years previous been circulating portions of *The Lusiad* in printed form as he completed them.

tion of *The Lusiad,* published in June, 1778. *The Gentle-man's Magazine* reviewed the first edition of *The Lusiad* in the August number of 1776, or after the date of publication (March 9, 1776), of *The Wealth of Nations.* It noted that Mickle's account and Smith's account of the Portuguese East India trade differed radically. When in 1778 the *Gentleman's Magazine* reviewed the second edition of *The Lusiad,* with its added material critical of *The Wealth of Nations,* it claimed that its 1776 review had drawn Mickle's attention to Smith's contrary views. For itself, it strongly supported Mickle, and took special objection to the position it attributed to Smith, that "to raise a royal [i.e., fiscal or public] revenue in distant countries is the great use of colonization."[114]

Between the appearance of the first edition of *The Lusiad* and the attack on Smith in the second edition, more had happened, however, to embitter Mickle against Smith than merely the differences with respect to colonial policy between the two. Mickle had, with his consent, dedicated to the Duke of Buccleuch the first edition of *The Lusiad,* and had sent him a special copy. When a friend called on the Duke for the good offices which Mickle expected in return, he was allegedly rebuffed by the Duke with the statement that he had not read *The Lusiad,* having been informed that it had not the merit it had been presented to him as having. Mickle is supposed to have believed that this informant was Smith. (See Rae, pp. 316-317.)[115] Mickle also disapproved strongly, on religious grounds, of

---

[114] *The Gentleman's Magazine,* XLVIII (September 1778), 427-428. On Smith's views with respect to fiscal relations with colonies, see *infra.,* pp. 85-86.

[115] See Cooke, p. xiv, for a report of a letter by Mickle to a friend, August 22, 1776, telling of the cold reception of Mickle's intermediary by the Duke. According to the account in *The European Magazine,* XVI (1789), 157, the rebuff from the Duke of Buccleuch resulted from "the malicious insinuations of a certain person about the patron," an allusion, according to later commentators, to Adam Smith. Mickle nevertheless retained the dedication to the Duke of Buccleuch in the second edition of the *Lusiad.*

Smith's association with and open admiration of David Hume.

Other considerations, no doubt, entered into Mickle's mind. He had long been anxious for financial security, and had looked hopefully towards a post with the East India Company. As far back as 1771 he had written to Joseph Warton, a fellow-poet (who, incidentally, has been said to have been an intimate friend of Smith) telling of possible intermediaries on his behalf with the Company and stating "I am so far from disliking to venture abroad, that, should I fail of poetical success, to the East Indies I certainly will go."[116]

Rae says that Mickle "very probably came to entertain better views of Smith, for he seems to have been not only quick to suspect injuries, but ready after a space to perceive his error." (Rae, p. 317.) I have found nothing which indicates that Mickle's attitude towards Smith changed. In 1779, Mickle published anonymously a pamphlet, which I have not seen, but which from its title was clearly in part a continuation of his criticism of Smith: *A Candid Examination of the Reasons for Depriving the East-India Company of its charter . . . together with Strictures on Some of the Self-Contradictions, and Historical Errors, of Dr. Smith, in his Reasons for the Abolition of the Said Company*, London, 1779.

Mickle's criticism of Adam Smith's economics was not limited to Smith's specific applications of his general laissez faire and free competition doctrines to the East India Company issue, but included a frontal attack on these doctrines themselves. I give one sample of the character of his criticism of Smith's general views. After remarking, with clear allusion to Smith, that "The fable of Procrustes, and his iron bed, was perhaps designed by the ancients to signify a system builder and his system," he gives, as an example

---

[116] See Rev. John Wooll, *Biographical Memoirs of the late Rev'd Joseph Warton*, London, 1806, pp. 379-380.

of excess simplification, Smith's proposition that "Every individual is continually exerting himself to find the most advantageous employment for whatever capital he can command."[117] Mickle replies:

> But this position, absolutely necessary to our author's system, we flatly deny. There is not only a torpor on the general mind of such districts as are ignorant of commerce, which requires to be routed into action by those of superior intelligence; but there is also a stubborn attachment in such minds to their ancient usages, which half a century can hardly remove. Our author might have seen both their stupor and obstinacy strongly exemplified in the vast difficulty of introducing modern agriculture into a certain country [i.e., Scotland?].[118]

It was not Smith's custom publicly to acknowledge, still less, formally to reply to, or to make explicit concessions to, adverse criticism of himself or his writings, and he seems never publicly to have referred to Mickle. Although in the third edition (1784) of *The Wealth of Nations* he introduced new material on the East India Company and its history which was on the whole even more critical than his original attack on the Company, he did on one point make a concession which brought him closer to Mickle's position:

> When a company of merchants undertake, at their own risk and expense, to establish a new trade with some remote and barbarous nation, it may not be unreasonable to incorporate them into a joint stock company, and to grant them, in case of their success, a monopoly of the trade for a certain number of years. It is the easiest and most natural way in which the

---

[117] *The Wealth of Nations,* 1st ed., II, 32; Cannan ed., I, 419.

[118] *The Lusiad,* 3rd ed., London, 1798, Introduction, p. ccxliv, note. Mickle's criticism of Smith is on pages ccxxiii-ccxlix of the Introduction in this edition, (pp. clxi-clxxvi in the 2nd ed., 1778). Mickle attacks Smith's general position, but the section of *The Wealth of Nations* he examines most closely is, in the Cannan edition, II, 129-140.

state can recompense them for hazarding a dangerous and expensive experiment, of which the public is afterwards to reap the benefit. A temporary monopoly of this kind may be indicated upon the same principles upon which a like monopoly of a new machine is granted to its inventor, and that of a new book to its author.[119]

But Smith was not adopting here a new principle for him. In his Glasgow *Lectures* of 1763 he had already made this concession: "... exclusive privileges ... are generally the creatures of the civil law. Such are monopolies and all privileges of corporations, which, *though they might once be conducive to the interest of the country*, are now prejudicial to it."[120]

There is no reason to suppose, therefore, that Smith introduced his concession in the 1784 edition of *The Wealth of Nations* as a response to Mickle's argument in the *Lusiad*.

14. *Henry Moyes.* James Currie (1756-1805), a native of Scotland, educated at the Universities of Edinburgh and Glasgow, practiced medicine in Liverpool, where he became a leading citizen. He maintained his Scottish intellectual contacts, however, sent his son to study in Edinburgh, carried on an active correspondence with Dugald Stewart, and wrote a biography of Robert Burns.[121] On the basis of Currie's unpublished papers, Professor Sydney Checkland reports that in a letter to Thomas Creevey of February 24, 1793, Currie writes:

When Dr. Adam Smith was writing his profound work on the 'Wealth of Nations' at Kirkcaldy in Scotland,

---

[119] Cannan ed., II, 245. For this passage first appearing in the 1784 ed., I am relying on Cannan's note, *ibid.*, II, 223, n. 1.

[120] *Lectures on Justice, Police, Revenue and Arms,* E. Cannan, ed., pp. 129-130. Italics are mine.

[121] See W. W. Currie, *Memoir of the Life of James Currie,* London, 1831. There are in this volume a few scraps of information supplied to Dugald Stewart by James Currie relating to Smith while in France as tutor to the Duke of Buccleuch which do not seem to have been reported elsewhere.

he used to wander in the evenings on the foreshore. In these excursions a blind boy of the village of humble situation, but of great ingenuity, became his constant companion.

Professor Checkland reports further, apparently on the basis of this letter, that the boy was Shadrach Moyes and that Smith, after tutoring him himself, sent him to David Hume, who obtained for him a bursary at Edinburgh and so set him on the path of becoming a successful lecturer on chemistry and the philosophy of natural history. The occasion for mention of him by Currie in his 1793 letter to Creevey was that Moyes had turned up in Liverpool and had asked for introductions in London.[122]

The only other accounts I have seen of a blind boy born in Kirkcaldy who became a successful lecturer on natural science do not seem to be wholly reconcilable with James Currie's account.[123]

In the first place, there is the question of the boy's name. According to all other accounts, Moyes, at least in his later years, called himself and was universally referred to as "Henry," and there is no mention of "Shadrach" in the other accounts. It is conceivable, of course, that Moyes had two given names and used one at one time and the other at other times. But James Currie refers to him as "Shadrach" in 1793, where the other accounts agree in referring to him only as "Henry." Moreover, the giving of a middle name to a child seems to have been very uncommon in both England and Scotland except for the nobility until the nineteenth century. There were such cases, but if

---

[122] Sydney Checkland, "Economic Attitudes in Liverpool, 1793-1807," *Economic History Review,* 2nd Series, V (1952), 72.

[123] John A. Harrison, "Blind Henry Moyes, 'an Excellent Lecturer in Philosophy,'" *Annals of Science,* XIII (1957), 109-125; John Kay, *A Series of Original Portraits and Caricature Etchings,* new ed., Edinburgh, 1877 (1st ed. 1837), "Dr. Henry Moyes," I, 177-179. Harrison cites as an important source for Moyes's early life, C. W. Hatfield, *Historical Notices of Doncaster,* Doncaster, 1866, vol. I. This was not available to me.

eighteenth-century scholars make a try at naming a few examples offhand, I know from experiments I have tried that they will not be very successful.[124]

John A. Harrison, in his article on Henry Moyes, writes of his early years as follows:

> So successful was the boy at his lessons that his prowess spread outside the school [Kirkcaldy Grammar School] to the town of Kirkcaldy itself, where his name came to the notice of Adam Smith. Smith, himself an old pupil of the school, was then engaged in writing at his mother's home in the town his great work *Inquiry into the Nature and Causes of the Wealth of Nations.*[125]

Harrison's account and Currie's account are here in agreement, but a difficulty remains. Adam Smith was living in Kirkcaldy, working on *The Wealth of Nations*, only in the period from 1768 to 1774. His only other periods of residence in Kirkcaldy were from 1723 to 1737, from 1746 to 1748, and from 1776 to 1778. Henry Moyes, according to the Baptismal Register of his birthplace, was born on Christmas Day, 1749, and was baptized on July 23, 1751.[126] This would make the earliest possible encounter of Smith with Henry Moyes occur in 1768, when Moyes would already have been over eighteen years of age, old enough in eighteenth-century Scotland to have graduated from college. Perhaps Moyes's blindness caused him to remain in grammar school for some years beyond the normal school-leaving age, but this would conflict somewhat with his reputed intellectual prowess while at school. On the other hand, if Moyes stayed in grammar school for some

---

[124] It was a Shadrach Moyes, a Treasury Agent in Edinburgh, to whom Adam Smith paid the required fee in 1777 when appointed a Commissioner of Customs for Scotland. (See Rae, p. 322.) It is possible that Currie knew, or knew of, this Shadrach Moyes and confused Henry Moyes with him when writing his 1793 letter.

[125] Harrison, *op. cit.,* p. 110.

[126] *Ibid.*

years beyond the normal period, it would help to explain why the records of Edinburgh University and of Glasgow University, both of which he was reported to have attended, do not provide confirmation of this. If he studied at either of these universities at an age higher than the normal age, he would neither have "matriculated" nor received a degree, but would have been received as a "special" student. On the other hand, I have found no explanation of how or where he obtained the title of "Dr." which he freely used in his advertising of his lectures. Degrees, however, were purchasable at some Scottish universities in the eighteenth century; at least the M.D. degree was.[127]

15. *Pierre Quesnay.* Rae states without indicating his source that Smith so admired Quesnay as an economist "that he meant to have dedicated the *Wealth of Nations* to Quesnay had the venerable French economist been alive at the time of its publication." (Rae, p. 216.) The source is undoubtedly Dugald Stewart, and Stewart's source is Adam Smith himself: "If he had not been prevented by Quesnay's death, Mr. Smith had once an intention (as he told me himself) to have inscribed to him his Wealth of Nations."[128]

In a 1923 lecture, W. R. Scott stated that "du Pont spoke of him [Smith] as a fellow disciple of Quesnay to whom Smith had intended to dedicate *The Wealth of Nations,* a pious aspiration which was frustrated by the death of Quesnay in 1774."[129] Scott gives no source reference. Stewart's memoir was in print by 1795. Dupont died in 1817, and had kept on writing until near his death; he may, therefore, have been relying on Stewart as his authority for the statement.

---

[127] See *infra,* pp. 101-103.

[128] Dugald Stewart, "Account of the Life and Writings of Adam Smith," *Works,* X, 48.

[129] "Adam Smith," *Proceedings of the British Academy,* XI (1923), 451.

16. *Robert Raikes*. Rae states that "The Sunday School Movement, . . . started by Thomas Raikes two or three years before [1787], won Smith's strongest commendation." Rae bases this on a letter of July 27, 1787 from Raikes to William Fox (for which Rae gives no source) which contains this statement: "Dr. Adam Smith, who has very ably written on the wealth of nations, says, 'no plan has promised to effect a change of manners with equal ease and simplicity since the days of the Apostles.' " Rae comments that Raikes "writes as if the remark had been made in conversation with himself." (Rae, p. 407.)

Robert Raikes was a Gloucester printer and newspaper publisher and a pioneer propagandist for Sunday Schools. Thomas Raikes, whose name by some slip Rae substitutes for that of Robert Raikes, was a nephew of Robert, a London merchant, dandy and diarist of some prominence, whose commerce was not typically with Sunday Schools. Rae probably found the letter he refers to in some biography of Robert Raikes.[130] I cannot see that the letter itself tells us whether Smith made the statement attributed to him in some publication of his, in correspondence, in conversation with Robert Raikes, or in conversation with some third person. I know of no other record of a reference to Sunday Schools by Smith.

17. *Thomas Reid*. In November 1763, when Smith was about to give up his professorship at the University of Glasgow in the middle of an academic session to become tutor to the Duke of Buccleuch, he recommended, and the University agreed, that Thomas Young be appointed as substitute lecturer for the balance of the academic year. In the normal Scottish pattern, manoeuvering began with respect to the appointment of a successor to Smith's professorship. Non-academic persons with influence had a part to play in the selection. Some of the professors at Glasgow

---

[130] It is in Alfred Gregory, *Robert Raikes,* New York, n.d., p. 107; see also p. 85.

were pressing for Thomas Young's appointment, while pressure came from outside the University on behalf of Thomas Reid, then a professor at Aberdeen. Rae (p. 171.) gives a vague account of what went on, relying for the most part on a letter of Feb. 2, 1764, from James Stuart Mackenzie, Lord Privy Seal for Scotland and brother of Lord Bute, the great dispenser of patronage in Scotland, to Baron Mure, for which letter he gives no source.

There were, in fact, at least two relevant letters from Mackenzie to Mure, dated Feb. 2, 1764, and March 7, 1764. In the first of these, Mackenzie states that Smith has told him "that his recommendation of Mr. Young was merely to teach his class this winter, and nothing more;" in the second Mackenzie comments, with respect to Baron Mure's opinion, presumably expressed in a previous letter, that the faculty would like William Wight, the professor of Church History, as the successor to Smith: "I learn, elsewhere, that Wight is very well where he is, but knows no more of Smith's branch [moral philosophy? economics? jurisprudence?] than he does of the secrets of state."[131]

W. R. Scott supplies a bit of additional information: a letter of Feb. 2, 1764, from John Millar, a professor at Glasgow, to Smith, then in London en route to France, reporting that there was pressure to elect Thomas Reid as Smith's successor, and asking Smith to use his influence on behalf of Young. Scott comments that "The expressions of Reid, whether in his writings or in his letters, are much less cordial [to Smith] than might have been expected," and, on the basis of John Millar's letter to Smith, he remarks: "It now appears that Adam Smith and his friends had been exerting their influence to secure the election of Thomas Young, . . . Evidently Reid remembered that Adam Smith had not only failed to support him, but had actively promoted the interests of another, and certainly a much

---

[131] Maitland Club, *Selections from the Family Papers Preserved at Caldwell*, Glasgow, 1854, Part II, vol. I, pp. 232, 241.

less distinguished candidate."[132] Since we do not know what Smith replied to Millar, nor what Reid knew of Smith's part, if any, in the proceedings, Scott was going beyond the available evidence in assuming that Smith had done something to obstruct Reid's election, and that Reid was aware of it and resented it.

There may, however, have been coldness towards Smith on Reid's part. Reid differed from Smith in his political and philosophical views and on some points at least with respect to economic policy and theory. There seems to be no record of their ever meeting, except perhaps at formal gatherings at the University of Glasgow, nor of their ever having corresponded with each other. The references to Smith by Reid that I have found in his published writings or in his correspondence are most courteous and respectful, but they are sometimes critical. Reid opened his inaugural lecture at Glasgow with this reference to Smith:

> I had not the happiness of his personal acquaintance, for want of opportunity; though I wished for it, and now wish for it more than ever. . . . I am much a stranger to his system, unless so far as he hath published it to the world.[133]

Non-committal, perhaps, but not hostile. I know of no reference, direct or indirect, by Smith to Reid, or to his ideas, whether in his published works or in his correspondence. But Rae reports (p. 440.) that "Among other relics of Smith that are still extant are four medallions by Tassie, which very probably hung in his library. They are medallions of his personal friends." Of these four medallions, three were of Joseph Black the chemist, James Hutton the geologist and Andrew Lumisden the antiquarian, all three members of Smith's most intimate circle in Edinburgh in his last years and Black and Hutton his closest friends. The fourth was of Thomas Reid.

---

[132] Scott, *ASSP,* pp. 97, 257.
[133] A. Campbell Fraser, *Thomas Reid,* Edinburgh, [1888], p. 77.

18. *William Thom.* Rae does not mention William Thom, who was a somewhat eccentric Glasgow minister who was critical of the University of Glasgow and of its professors, and wrote a series of tracts of a satirical or burlesque character directed at the faculty. W. R. Scott comments on two of these in which Adam Smith was a target, as the supposed drafter on behalf of the University of an address presented to the King in 1762 on the birth of the Prince of Wales. *A Letter containing a Defence of the College of G-W against an insidious attempt to depreciate the Ability and Taste of its Professors,* 1762, is a mock apology for the literary flaws in the address. Its sequel, *Donaldsoniad: J-n D-n Detected,* 1763, claims that Adam Smith had undertaken to take responsibility for the Address and that the Faculty had rewarded him for this by granting an LL.D. to him. Scott shows that none of this was according to the facts.[134]

Thom comments on Adam Smith in at least one other tract. Thom had a project for the establishment of a Commercial Academy in Glasgow, and wrote at least two pamphlets in support of it: *The Defects of an University Education, and its Unsuitableness to a Commercial People,* n.p., 1762; *Remarks upon a Pamphlet concerning the Necessity of Erecting an Academy at Glasgow,* Glasgow, 1762.[135] In *The Defects,* Thom argues that a specialized institution with a different curriculum is needed for the training of young men for business, and that the University does not adequately perform this function. Its curriculum is unsuitable, its professors fail to give the needed individual attention to students and to have sufficient personal contacts with them, and the procedure whereby it requires each regular student to attend on the same day lectures on Latin, Greek, mathematics and philosophy has no other

---

[134] W. R. Scott, *ASSP,* pp. 75-76.

[135] A third pamphlet, also attributed to Thom, *The Scheme, for Erecting an Academy at Glasgow, Set Forth in its own Proper Colours,* Glasgow, 1762, was not available to me.

apparent logic than that of leaving the professors with
spare time which they can devote to more remunerative
private classes for special students who pay higher fees.

Thom concedes that the University lectures on moral
philosophy are delivered by a very able master "and in a
very ingenious manner," but he claims that this master,
that is, Adam Smith, uses them for the exposition of singular ideas rather than communication of knowledge, and
that they are not of much use. Especially useless is the
search for the "origin" of morality, with each professor
destroying the system of his predecessor. Morality should
be taught instead. For his own Academy he proposes a
curriculum consisting of "practical mathematics, history in
general, history of our own country and of those in the
neighborhood, or with which we carry on commerce, natural history, geography, the history of commerce, and practical morality." Of the fare the University offers, the only
thing he would have the students of his academy partake
of is, surprisingly enough after what he has said, the opportunity of Smith's "Ethic class":

> to which many of our citizens will send their sons,
> after their course in our own Academy is finished.
> When they have first learned useful and necessary
> things, those of them who are in easy circumstances,
> and have genius, will be entertained with the ingenious
> and amusing theory of so eminent a master.[136]

In *Remarks upon a Pamphlet*, Thom repeats his criticism of spending much time on schemes of moral philosophy
instead of emphasizing the importance of practicing morality, and argues that the change from system to system with
each change of professor is dangerous, but does not seem
to have Smith particularly in mind.[137]

As perhaps the first prospectus in the English-speaking
world for a school of business, *The Defects of an University*

---

[136] *The Defects of an University Education,* pp. 5-13, 17-52.
[137] *Remarks,* pp. 16-17, 20.

Education is an interesting, as well as in its way an unintentionally amusing, document. What is curious is that Thom should find a place in the educational program of the students of his proposed business Academy for Smith's lectures on the theory of moral sentiments but should make no reference to his lectures on economics.

19. *Charles Townshend.* The first mention of Townshend in Rae is in his report of a letter of Hume to Smith, April 12, 1759, in which Hume, among other matters, reports Townshend's admiration of the just-published *Theory of Moral Sentiments* and his intention to put his ward and step-son, the Duke of Buccleuch, then a student at Eton, in Smith's charge when he was through with Eton. (Rae, p. 147.) In Sept. 1759, when Townshend was, for the first and only time, in Scotland, Smith writes to Townshend, offering condolences on the death of Townshend's brother. Smith here notes that this is his first letter to Townshend; he refers to a previous meeting shortly before, at which time the Duke of Buccleuch's educational future was presumably discussed. (Rae, p. 148.) Later references by Rae to Townshend deal only with Smith's tutorship of the young Duke. (Rae, pp. 164, 222-224.) Rae gives no indication of any contact between Townshend and Smith prior to 1759.

Charles Townshend was already somewhat of an economist on his own account before we know of any association on his part with Adam Smith. He corresponded with Josiah Tucker in 1751 and 1752, and in that correspondence showed strong free-trade tendencies, pushing Tucker in that direction rather than being pushed by him.[138] In his *National Thoughts Recommended to the Serious Attention of the Public*,[139] as in his correspondence with Tucker, he

---

[138] Historical Manuscripts Commission, *Eleventh Report,* Appendix, Part IV, "The Manuscripts of the Marquess of Townshend," London, 1887, pp. 371-379.

[139] Undated, but published not long before March, 1752, when he sent a copy to Tucker.

strongly opposed the export bounty on corn, and on this, as on other matters, he converted Tucker to his views.

In 1754, Townshend offered Cambridge University the funds to provide prizes for essays, to promote the study at the University of the "theory of trade," and suggested a list of possible questions for the essays. The first question he suggested was "The Influence of Trade on Morals." The University, somewhat hesitantly since it clearly had misgivings whether economics was a respectable field of study for dons or students, accepted the offer, but without consulting Townshend tampered with his list of questions, and in particular deleted his first question. Townshend became aware of this, apparently through reading an advertisement of the essay-writing competition. He protested, and it was explained to him that the authorities at the University had decided that since "great corruption [had been] for some time visible among the trading part of our nation" it was not an expedient time to invite essays on "the influence of trade on morals." Townshend replied indignantly:

> There is not any moral duty which is not of a commercial nature. Freedom of trade is nothing more than a freedom to be moral agents, and since a free moral inquiry into this most interesting theory, on the observance of which the happiness of this life and of the next do entirely depend, cannot be allowed at your University I have done, and have nothing more to add . . .

Townshend refused to read the winning essay, and so ended, disastrously, Cambridge University's first entry into the field of economics.[140] At about the same time, Adam Smith was reading his 1755 manifesto in Glasgow in favor of free trade and laissez faire. It was appropriate that the two men should soon thereafter come into close association.

---

[140] H. M. C., *Eleventh Report,* Appendix, Part IV, pp. 384-391.

On his return from France late in 1766, Adam Smith remained in London from some time in October, 1766, to some time in May, 1767. Rae is somewhat at a loss in trying to account for Smith's activities during these six months or so. (Rae, pp. 232-238.) In October, 1766, Townshend had moved up in the Chatham Ministry to the Chancellorship of the Exchequer, and "pledged himself to find a revenue in America." It now seems clear that Smith's main activity during his stay in London at this time was work with Townshend on his disastrous taxation project.[141] W. R. Scott takes it for granted that Smith was opposed to Townshend's proposals: "If his [Smith's] views on taxation and representation were the same as those he expressed in 1776 and 1778, and from his whole type of thought there is no reason to doubt it, he may have expressed his disagreement forcibly and returned to Scotland."[142]

Smith did believe in "representation" in the law-making authority, including representation on a territorial basis, but his criteria of "representation" were not democratic ones and he never expressed dissatisfaction with the Scottish situation, where only a tiny minority had a vote, and on as fortuitous and irrational a basis as can be imagined. In his discussion of colonial relations, the fiscal aspect always received major emphasis. This was also true of Townshend from at least 1753 on. A recent biography of Townshend which scarcely touches on his intellectual history and concentrates on his flaws of character and personality and on his political manoeuvres fails to mention Smith's name and identifies as Townshend's chief adviser in drafting his ill-fated proposals for taxing the colonies a Samuel Touchet, a member of Parliament, and merchant

---

[141] See W. R. Scott, "Adam Smith at Downing Street, 1766-7," *Economic History Review*, VI (1935), 79-89.

[142] *Ibid.*, pp. 88-89.

adventurer, who in 1766 became financial adviser to Townshend at the Exchequer.[143]

C. R. Fay once commented, with reference to the consequences on Britain's relations with its American Colonies of the Townshend taxes of 1767, "I submit, though the temple fall on me as I say it, that in the last analysis it was professional advice which lost us [i.e., Britain] the first empire."[144] It was, I presume, Adam Smith, and not Samuel Touchet, that Fay had in mind. In any case, whatever attraction there was for Smith in the concept of an ideal "Empire," one condition that had to be met to make empire acceptable to him was that no province should be retained within the Empire if it could not "be made to contribute towards the support of the whole empire." With respect to the East Indies, which "are represented as more fertile, more extensive, and, in proportion to their extent, much richer and more populous than Great Britain," he seemed to think that it could be possible "to draw a great revenue from them."[145] As between on the one hand, increased taxation or increased debt in Britain, and on the other hand, a shrunken empire, Smith would have to all appearances chosen the shrunken empire.

20. *Alexander Webster.* Rae prints two letters by Smith, dated Dec. 22, 1785, and Jan. 3, 1786, to an addressee

[143] Sir Lewis Namier and John Brooke, *Charles Townshend,* London, 1964, pp. 107, 173-174, 179; Namier and Brooke, *The History of Parliament,* III, 533-536. In this latter item, which is a condensed biography of Touchet, it is stated that "among Charles Townshend's papers there is a draft in Touchet's handwriting of Townshend's American duties exactly as introduced in the House on 13 May 1767" and that Townshend credited Touchet with "the choice of taxes" (p. 535). The only other biographical material relating to Touchet that I have been able to find is in *A Letter to a Merchant at Bristol, concerning a Petition of S— T—, Esq., to the King, for an Exclusive Grant to the Trade of the River Senegal.* By a Merchant of London, London, 1762. This gives an unfavorable account of some of Touchet's business operations and his relations with the Government.

[144] C. R. Fay, *Adam Smith and the Scotland of His Day,* Cambridge, Eng., 1956, p. 116.

[145] *The Wealth of Nations,* II, 433, 431.

unknown to him, which refer to Webster as a political arithmetician. The letters turn on the question whether population was increasing or decreasing. William Eden had in 1780 engaged in controversy with Richard Price on this question, and on the strength of the fact that Price figures in Smith's letters, Rae surmises that William Eden was the addressee. (Rae, pp. 398-401.) W. R. Scott, however, prints a letter of Smith dated Nov. 10, 1785, which is unquestionably linked with the two letters referred to above as letters in a series to the same person, and this letter is addressed to George Chalmers.[146]

In the letter printed by Scott, Smith refers to Webster as "of all the men I have ever known the most skilful in Political Arithmetic." The three letters turn on the quality of Webster's work in his census or "enumeration" of the population of Scotland in 1755. Smith liked Webster personally, and was predisposed to thinking him innocent of the absurdities to which he thought other political arithmeticians were prone. James Bonar, however, has commented on Webster's 1755 census: "We see that the 'enumeration' is full of conjectures, 'computations,' and assumptions," precisely the defects charged against political arithmetic by its eighteen-century detractors.[147] Rae's account of Webster's career as statistician needs to be checked against the accounts of Bonar and others.[148]

---

[146] W. R. Scott, *ASSP*, 294-295. The letter Scott prints had already been published, but without identification of the addressee, in Historical Manuscripts Commission, *Report on the Laing Manuscripts preserved in the University of Edinburgh*, vol. II, London, 1925, p. 522.

[147] See Jacob Viner, "The Economist in History," *The American Economic Review*, LIII (1963), 15-16.

[148] See James Bonar, *Theories of Population from Raleigh to Arthur Young*, London, 1931, pp. 178-183. Since in Smith's correspondence Richard Price figures as a political arithmetician in whose calculations Smith had no confidence, it is of interest that Price began with a low opinion of Alexander Webster's proficiency as a demographer, but later withdrew his criticism of his statistical soundness and referred to him as "ingenious." (*Observations on Reversionary Payments*, 6th ed., W. Morgan, ed., London, 1803, I, 108-115.)

III. SMITH AND THE SCOTLAND
OF HIS TIME

1. *The Highland Economy*

From the 1770's on, there was an extensive literature expressing concern about the economic plight of the Highlanders (including the Islanders as such). The Highland economy had some features special to it, as for example, its poverty in natural resources, its rugged terrain and harsh climate, the survival of ancient feudal patterns of land tenure and of landlords' rights and obligations, and the relative absence of regional government with staff, financial resources, and authority to meet the distinctive needs of the area. But there were important aspects of the eighteenth-century Highland economy which would make it a good subject for a case study in the history of the theory of economic development as economists now expound it, and the contemporary literature dealing with the Highlands was rich in information and insights.

Smith in *The Wealth of Nations* gave some attention to the special economic problems of the Highlands, but what attention to them he did there give was not focused on the plight of the Highlanders but was merely incidental to his search for illustrative material in connection with his general treatment of the problems of taxation, of bounties, of the economics of landlordism. Several of the most prominent contemporary investigators of economic conditions in the Highlands were acquaintances and neighbors of Smith, most notably James Anderson, George Dempster, Sir John Sinclair.[1] Smith seems never to have visited the Highlands

---

[1] The only important investigators in Smith's time of conditions in the Highlands for whom I am unable to establish a personal link of some kind with Smith are John Knox, a Scot, who was a bookseller in London, and David Loch, an Edinburgh merchant.

except for one trip of a few days' duration in 1759 to call on the Duke of Argyle on his estate in Inverary. There seems to be no record of Smith ever having been officially consulted on problems specially affecting the Highlands.[2]

Much of the Highlands area was, or was believed to be, unsuitable for tillage or for cattle-raising and was uninhabited. The land suitable for tillage was largely in scattered patches, and the grazing land was mostly rough and poor, and with little growth serviceable for winter feed. The usable land was mainly worked by tenants and subtenants, each with several tiny patches of land of varying degrees of fertility and proximity to his cabin. Rents were payable partly in money and in products, partly in feudaltype services often due at times inconvenient to the tenants, or to the landlords, or to both, and with no effective procedures for commuting them into money-payments. The fisheries, a source of income supplementary to farming for those living close to the sea, operated under handi-

---

[2] W. R. Scott says that Adam Smith was one of the witnesses before the House of Commons Committee on the British Fisheries of 1785 (*Scottish Economic Literature to 1800,* Glasgow, 1911, p. 67). The only reference to Smith in the Reports of the Committee that I can find is a statement that it had been referred to Smith's comments in *The Wealth of Nations* (third ed., 1784) on the bounties to Scottish herring-boats and a brief quotation from these comments. (*Third Report,* reprinted in *Reports from Committees of the House of Commons, 1785-1801,* 1803, X, 48-49.)

Another House of Commons Committee dealing with somewhat related matters, The Committee on Smuggling and other Illicit Practices used in Defrauding the Revenue, met from Dec. 1783 to March, 1784. George Dempster, a member of the Committee, writing on behalf of William Eden, the Chairman, on Dec. 18, 1783, asked Smith either to present in person or submit in a memoir to the Committee his "ideas for the most effectual means to prevent smuggling." (W. R. Scott, *ASSP,* pp. 287-288.) The Committee Report, published in Vol. XI of *Reports from Committees of the House of Commons, 1785-1801,* 1803, does not contain, or refer to, a presentation by Smith. The Report of the Committee was followed in 1786 by the enactment of a bill (26 Geo. iii, c. 40) systematically revising the regulations governing ship manifests, inspection, packaging, etc., intended to prevent smuggling and illegitimate claims of customs drawbacks, but it contained no special provisions for Scotland.

caps of climate, geography, and dispersed settlement, plus the burdensome regulations connected with the administration of the taxes on salt, an essential for curing the fish both for sale and for direct consumption in the absence of ice and of known technology for its use in the preservation of fish. In these circumstances, population, though sparse in relation to area, was excessive in relation to natural resources and to employment opportunities, and the level of living was meager and for many subject to the hazards of recurrent famines because of crop failures and the failure of fish to appear in the neighboring waters at the expected seasons.

Possibilities of emigration, mostly to America, were of course available as a means of escape. But emigration was itself costly to the emigrants in money-terms, and meant a prospectively permanent separation from their ancestral homes and their kindred. It meant also, even with some prospect of successful establishment abroad, a sacrifice of the measure of economic security, meager though it might be, which customary land-tenure rights and traditional claims, in times of distress, on the bounty of the lairds, provided for many of the Highlanders. From the point of view of the landlords—this was prior to the days of extensive resort to sheep-grazing—and of upper-class Scottish opinion in general, emigration signified "depopulation," an economically and sentimentally inacceptable mode of adjustment to poverty. The possibility of the development of industry as a substitute for the traditional occupations was limited by the scarcity of natural resources providing raw materials for processing or fabrication, by the absence of roads and of towns, and by the poverty of the area in capital, in educational facilities, in harbors, in postal services, and, according to some commentators, in initiative and ambition on the part of the mass of the population. The inflow of guidance, financial assistance, enterprise, from outside the area, was minimal in extent, and the home supply of talent had already begun its flight to greener pastures in the Lowlands, in England, and overseas.[3]

In 1786 there was founded the British Society for Extending the Fisheries, with a charter from Parliament giving it the privilege of operating as a joint-stock limited-liability company. It was primarily a philanthropic enterprise, although it offered subscribers the prospect of modest dividends and of ultimate repayment of principal, a combination of philanthropic objectives and a business-corporation set-up which was by no means unusual in the eighteenth century. Its sponsors had accepted the advice of John Knox, James Anderson, and others, that an effective means of helping the Highland economy attain prosperity was to remedy certain defects in the mode of operation of the fisheries whose roots lay in the maldistribution of its coastal population. With the fishing population scattered along the coast, and using only small boats, they could be only part-time fishermen, operating with inadequate equipment which they in large part had to make and maintain themselves, with limited and difficult access to markets, and without much cooperation or division of labor. The Society hoped that by taking the initiative in establishing new small towns as fishing-stations and marketing and industrial centers it would promote the use of larger and better-equipped boats able to venture into the outer waters where the fish were more regularly present, specialization in occupations, and the use of improved harbor facilities (to be provided in part at least by government aid), and that above all it would help to bring the scattered fishermen into more concentrated settlements where division of labor could be extended, and educational and other services could be economically provided.

Adam Smith in 1787, in conversation with William

---

[3] I base this account mostly on contemporary materials. The most informative modern accounts are in Malcolm Gray, *The Highland Economy 1750-1850*, Edinburgh, 1957, and Henry Hamilton, *An Economic History of Scotland in the Eighteenth Century*, Oxford, 1963.

Wilberforce, an English philanthropist who was taking an active interest in the British Society, expressed scepticism about the financial future of the Society and of the prospect that any benefit would result from its activities. (Rae, p. 407.)

Wilberforce's account of his conversation with Smith is as follows:

> Dr. Smith, with certain characteristic coolness, observed to me that he looked for no other consequence from the scheme than the entire loss of every shilling that should be expended in it, granting, however, with uncommon candour, that the public would be no great sufferer, because he believed the individuals meant to put their hands only in their own pockets.[4]

Rae says of the project that "It was indeed the grand philanthropic scheme of the day" and this seems to be true for Scotland at least. I have found no adverse comment on the project by a Scotsman except for Smith's, and only one English one, by Jeremy Bentham. In 1783 James Anderson sent to Bentham for comment the manuscript of a book which he proposed to publish, probably the tract which he printed for private circulation later that year, *The True Interest of Great Britain Considered, or a Proposal for Establishing Northern British Fisheries*. I have not seen this tract, but it probably contained an exposition of the town-building ideas which he in later works strongly advocated.[5]

Bentham, in a letter whose severe tone he later regretted, advised Anderson against publication. The scheme, he wrote, was not new, for Sir James Steuart and John

---

[4] R. I. and Samuel Wilberforce, eds., *The Correspondence of William Wilberforce*, London, 1840, I, 40-41.

[5] See, for example, his *An Account of the Present State of the Hebrides and Western Coasts of Scotland*, Edinburgh, 1785, "Large and Small Towns compared with regard to their Effects on Society," pp. xxxiv-lvii. See also, *ibid.*, Appendix No. X, "Hints for the Civil Police of a Town," pp. 416-443, for a quite utopian picture of how one of the proposed new towns could be laid out and governed.

Campbell had previously espoused it. Any subsidization or financial encouragement of such a scheme would be in violation of economic principle, since the direction of the investment of capital should be left to the initiative of its owners. The appropriate remedy for the poverty of the Highlanders was emigration, especially to America.[6]

According to Rae, the subsequent history of the British Society confirms Smith's pessimistic forecast. The first attempts to set up new fishing villages all failed immediately; the one even partially successful venture of the Society was a real-estate project in Wick, which was fairly successful financially although with "as near nil" effect on the development of the Highland fisheries as Smith had predicted. When Rae wrote, the Society was still in existence but was in process of liquidation, with the prospect that after a record of meager dividend payments it would return to its shareholders about £15,000 of its original capital of £35,000. (Rae, pp. 407-410.) It should be noted that, through his connection with Wick, Rae was in a favored position to be well-informed.[7]

No history of the British Society seems ever to have been written. From the early accounts of the objectives of the Society, it appears that the prospects of substantial dividends were a minor element in attracting subscribers. The Act incorporating the Society (26 Geo. iii, c. 106) stated its object to be to remedy the conditions "in which the dispersed situation of the inhabitants hath hitherto proved a great impediment to their active exertions." The

---

[6] Jeremy Bentham, *Works,* X, 117-129. See also W. Stark, *Jeremy Bentham's Economic Writings,* London 1952, I, 15-16. Steuart had proposed in 1767 a town-building project on behalf of the Highland economy. In his scheme, gratuitous financing from government funds would have a major role, and there would be established some form of profit-sharing, in addition to wages or other earnings, for the workmen engaged in the auxiliary enterprises serving the fisheries. (Sir James Steuart, *An Inquiry into the Principles of Political Economy* [1767], *The Works,* London, 1805, II, 194-195). I have not located John Campbell's discussion.

[7] See *supra,* p. 13.

Society was intended more to provide a central organization for effort by persons of means to help the development
of the Highlands than to finance such development from
its own capital resources. The maximum limit for its own
capitalization was set at £150,000, with a maximum subscription for any shareholder of £500, and the Society was
not authorized to borrow. There is some evidence that the
Society did make a significant contribution, although only
after several decades, by its investment in Wick, towards
converting a small village to a substantial and flourishing
little town which for a while was the greatest herring-
fishing center in the world.[8] But there can be no doubt that
the original sponsors of the British Society were grossly
over-optimistic with respect to what it could accomplish,
no matter how sound in principle its analysis of the needs
of the Highland economy may have been, with the resources
it was planning to accumulate. John Knox, for instance,
in the year following the foundation of the British Society,
assured its members that "The public have caught the
generous flame, and, from present appearances, there is
every reason to believe, that the year MDCCLXXXVI will
form an aera in the British annals."[9]

[8] See Henry Hamilton, *An Economic History of Scotland*, p. 123,
James Fergusson, *Letters of George Dempster to Sir Adam Fergusson
1756-1813,* London, 1934, pp. 200-201, and *The New Statistical Account
of Scotland,* Edinburgh, 1845. XV, 151-154.

[9] John Knox, *Tour through the Highlands of Scotland and the
Hebrides Isles,* London, 1787, Dedication (to the British Society),
p. vi. See also George Dempster, *A Discourse, containing a Summary
of the Proceedings of the Directors of the Society for Extending the
Fisheries and Improving the Sea Coasts of Great Britain,* 1789, as
reported in *Scots Magazine,* Appendix, 1789, pp. 640-643, and James
Fergusson, *Letters of George Dempster,* pp. 198-201. Dempster, a
member of Parliament, guided through Parliament the 1786 Act which
granted the British Society its charter, and devoted much effort to the
affairs of the Society. He was a fellow-member with Smith of the
Poker Club (Rae, pp. 136-137.) and the Select Society in Edinburgh.
In addition to the biographical material supplied in James Fergusson,
op. cit., there are brief biographies of Dempster in Robert Chambers,
Biographical Dictionary of Eminent Scotsmen and in Sir Lewis Namier
and John Brooke, *The History of Parliament. The House of Commons
1754-1790,* London, 1964, II, 313-317.

Smith in the third edition of *The Wealth of Nations* (1784) added to his discussion of bounties in general a detailed discussion of the bounties on herring "busses," (that is, fishing vessels of some size and with decks, so that they could operate in the open seas). Rae refers to this addition as apparently "prompted by current agitations of the stream of political opinion." (Rae, p. 363.)

In a passage in the previous editions of *The Wealth of Nations* Smith had qualified his general condemnation of bounties by conceding that "it is reasonable" to tax other branches of industry to support the production of commodities necessary for national defense if such production could not otherwise be maintained at home. He weakened this concession in the third edition.[10]

Smith does not deny that the fisheries bounties may contribute to the national defence by augmenting the number of seamen and the amount of shipping. But the existing bounties were granted as annual tonnage (i.e., weight of ship) bounties, not as bounties proportioned to the quantity of fish caught. Only "busses" of fifteen tons and over tonnage were eligible for the bounties. According to Smith: "A boat [i.e., small boat] fishery . . . seems to be the mode of fishing best adapted to the peculiar situation of Scotland; the fishers carrying the herrings on shore, as fast as they are taken, to be either cured or consumed fresh." This is because it is in the "lochs," (in West Scotland usage this term includes arms of the sea projecting

---

[10] See *The Wealth of Nations,* Cannan ed., II, 19, editor's note. Cannan here says that the enlarged discussion of the herring bounties is "in place of" this passage. The passage, however, remains in the third and later editions, although placed in a different location, shortened somewhat, and "it might not be unreasonable" substituted for "it is reasonable." See *ibid.,* II, 24, last paragraph.

far inland, or, as Smith calls them, "sea-lochs," as well as fresh-water lakes), that the herrings congregate.[11]

Smith claimed, moreover, that the fact that the bounties were granted on a tonnage basis regardless of how many or how few fish were caught made them both excessive and ineffective in stimulating an increase in the amount of fish caught. The bounty "is proportional to the burden of the ship, not to her diligence or success in the fishery; and it has, I am afraid, been too common for vessels to fit out for the sole purpose of catching, not the fish, but the bounty."[12]

There was wide agreement at the time that the tonnage bounty was being exploited in the manner Smith describes,[13] and the Act of 1786 dealing with the fisheries (26 Geo. iii, c. 81) revised the bounty legislation so as to make the bounties paid to buss operators depend partly

---

[11] *Ibid.*, II, 20-21. Contemporary accounts differ. The shoals of fish appeared highly irregularly in any specific loch, and the small boats could not move freely from loch to loch, partly because of the distance and the hazard of the intervening open seas, partly because they had shore privileges only in their own home lochs. In open sea fishing with decked boats which could stay out at sea indefinitely, the fish could be sought out and netted wherever they happened to be, and the fishing therefore could be sustained for long periods. But conditions varied in different parts of the northern coasts, and therefore also, presumably, the relative profitability of small-boat and buss fishing. Smith, however, obviously believed that it was generally true that small-boat fishing was low-cost fishing as long as enough fish could be caught in the inshore waters to satisfy the market demand, and that when that ceased to be true additional fish could be caught in the open seas from larger boats but only at higher costs. "The real price of this commodity, [i.e. fish] therefore, rises in the progress of improvement [with which Smith associates a greater demand for fish]. It has accordingly done so, I believe, more or less in every country." *Ibid.*, I, 234-235. This is the nearest, I think, that Smith ever comes to a formulation of a law of production under conditions of increasing cost. (Cf., however, *ibid.*, I, 94.)

[12] *Ibid.*, II, 21.

[13] See, e.g., David Loch, *Essay on the Trade, Commerce, and Manufacture of Scotland*, Edinburgh, 1775, pp. 61-64; James Anderson, *Observations on the Means of Exciting a Spirit of National Industry* [1777], Dublin ed., 1779, II, 342-358.

on the quantity of fish caught and to provide a separate bounty per barrel of fish caught by the small boats not eligible to share in the tonnage bounties. It may be asked why seemingly so absurd a method of granting bounties had ever been adopted and permitted to survive so long. (It was not finally terminated, I believe, until 1830.) The explanation is that a major objective of the bounties was to increase the national supply of "seamen" able to navigate the high seas, to handle complicated equipment, and ready at all times to perform the duties of skilled sailors on merchant ships and warships.[14] Inshore fishermen, who were primarily occupied in agriculture, were for the purposes of the bounty legislation not "seamen." Smith does not consider this element in the case for the tonnage bounties.

In his computation of the amount of bounties granted per barrel of herring exported, Smith includes both the tonnage bounties and the amount of exemption from salt-duties enjoyed by the buss operators, despite his concession that "the loss of duties upon herrings exported cannot, perhaps, properly be considered as bounty."[15] Smith elsewhere distinguishes several times between a bounty properly so called and a "drawback" or remission of a tax or duty, and warns against confusing the latter with the former,[16] but in the case of export herring he does not adhere fully to his own distinction, if it be accepted that special exemption from a tax is the economic equivalent of a "drawback" of the amount of tax paid.

The salt duties were some twelve times the pre-tax value of the domestic salt of the kind used in curing fish for

[14] See David Loch, *Essay on the Trade, Commerce, and Manufacture of Scotland,* p. 63.

[15] *The Wealth of Nations,* II, 435-437.

[16] *Ibid.,* I, 416, I, 417, II, 1-2, II, 24. The Committee on the Fisheries in 1785, in computing the amount of bounty per barrel of exported herring, expressly excluded from the computation of the amount of bounty "the allowance of using salt duty-free." *Third Report, loc. cit.,* p. 49.

export and the duties were still higher on foreign salt. The total amount of the revenue from all the salt duties actually collected in the Highlands (including the Islands) was nevertheless negligible. For the six northern counties (Argyle, Inverness, Ross, Sutherland, Caithness, and Orkney and Shetland), covering more than half the area of Scotland, the aggregate gross yield of the salt taxes in the ten years 1775 to 1784 was £1,273.[17] The exemption from salt duty of salt used in curing export fish and the poverty of the area were in large part the explanation of this low yield of the salt tax. But the abuse of the exemption by users of salt for legally non-exempt purposes and the use of smuggled salt no doubt also played a part. Despite this low yield of the tax, the burden of the salt duties was the most emphasized non-natural obstacle to the prosperity of the fisheries in the literature concerning itself with the Highland economy.

The explanation of this apparent paradox is that to gain exemption from the salt-tax by fulfilling all the procedural requirements for such exemption was often as burdensome as to surrender one's legal right to exemption and thus escape the administrative straitjacket, or as to use smuggled salt and become subject to the terrible penalties imposed if one was caught, or as to give up catching and curing fish.[18] The Committee of 1785 on the British Fisheries described the situation as follows:

> From the concurring testimony of all the witnesses, it appears to your Committee, that the present system of the Salt Laws is peculiarly embarrassing and vexatious to those who are concerned in the fisheries

---

[17] See John Girvin, *The Impolicy of Prohibiting the Exportation of Rock Salt from England to Scotland,* London, 1799, Appendix 6.

[18] The burdens of meeting the requirements for exemption were many and could be incredibly grievous. See especially, James Fergusson, *Letters of George Dempster,* pp. 148-152. See also: Malcolm Gray, *The Highland Economy,* pp. 112-113, and Edward Hughes, *Studies in Administration and Finance 1558-1825, with Special Reference to the History of Salt Taxation in England,* Manchester, 1934, pp. 447-450.

of this kingdom. And it also appears to your Committee, that the beneficent and wise intentions of the Legislature in allowing the use of salt duty-free in the curing of fish for exportation are, in a great measure, frustrated by the various regulations and restrictions which from time to time have been judged necessary for the purpose of preventing a fraudulent abuse of the indulgence.[19]

Adam Smith was very much interested in the technical problems of taxation and its administration. Excise taxes on non-necessaries of wide consumption were his favorite form of taxation from the point of view of equitable distribution and productivity, but in the belief that the poor threw off on others taxes on essentials he accepted as suitable for taxation commodities which were essentials for all classes. He was revenue-minded, and his famous four canons of taxation said nothing with reference to the possible burdensomeness for legal *non*-taxpayers of the administrative measures employed to protect the revenue from tax-evaders. In Scotland, unlike England, the administration of the salt taxes was assigned to the Customs instead of to the Excise so that Smith, from 1780 on, was a Commissioner of the Salt Duties as well as a Commissioner of Customs. From 1780 on, therefore, Smith must have been especially well-informed with respect to the mode of operation of the salt taxes in Scotland, and must have been aware of the widespread complaints against their impact on the fisheries. There is no hint in *The Wealth of Nations,* however, that there was anything wrong, or in need of justification, with respect to the British salt taxes, from the point of view of equity, of administrative burdensomeness, or of productivity of revenue.

In England from early times a tax had been imposed on sea-borne coal from which coal transported from the mines to its point of use by road (or river) was free, apparently because of the insuperable administrative problems that

---

[19] *First Report, loc. cit.,* p. xii.

would be associated with the attempt to collect a tax on coal transported by land. With the Act of Union, the tax on sea-borne coal was extended to Scotland. It was a heavy tax, and it involved burdensome administrative regulations as well. For the Highlanders (including the Islanders) coal was dear in any case because of their distance from the mines, and was available only by sea-transport. The coal tax was therefore more of a burden for them than for the inhabitants of the Lowlands. Smith mentions the tax on sea-borne coal as the one important exception from the beneficial general rule in Britain that coastwise traffic (like road and river traffic) was free of tax, and elsewhere points out that it is a heavy tax, "upon most sorts of coal . . . more than sixty percent. of the original price at the coal-pit," with the result that "where they are naturally cheap, they are consumed duty free; where they are naturally dear, they are loaded with a heavy duty;"[20] but he left it to others to apply this to the plight of the Highlanders.

In *The Wealth of Nations* Smith mentions another special handicap of the Highland economy, the charge by owners of land adjoining the sea of rent for the privilege of gathering kelp. The Highlanders (including their womenfolk) gathered this species of seaweed, which grew along some of their coasts between the low- and high-water marks, and burned it on the adjoining shores in large iron pots (incidentally, with heavily-taxed sea-borne coal) to abstract its soda content. From the sale of the soda ash, they derived a welcome cash supplement to their income from their agricultural and fishing activity.[21] But to use

---

[20] *The Wealth of Nations,* II, 384; II, 358. For contemporary comment on the adverse impact of the coal-tax on the Highlands, see John Knox, *Tour through the Highlands of Scotland,* 1787, pp. (cli)-(cliii), and James Anderson, *Observations on the Effect of Coal Duty upon the Remote and Thinly Peopled Coast of Britain,* Edinburgh, 1792. (This last item has not been available to me.)

[21] See in Archibald and Nan L. Clout, *The Chemical Revolution,* London, 1952, the references listed in the index under "Kelp" and "Kelping."

the shore for this purpose, they had to pay a rent to the owners of the adjoining land. Smith uses this as an illustration of the landlord who "sometimes demands rent for what is altogether incapable of human improvement." "The landlord . . . , whose estate is bounded by a kelp shore of this kind, demands a rent for it as much as for his corn fields." He goes on to say that in the Shetlands the landlords charge rent to their tenants "in proportion, not to what the farmer can make by the land, but to what he can make both by the land and by the water. It is partly paid in sea-fish; and one of the very few instances in which rent makes a part of the price of that commodity, is to be found in that country."[22]

The absence in *The Wealth of Nations* of a discussion of the general economic state of the Highlands seems as puzzling to me in the light of the wide prevalence in his time and in his community of such discussion as has been to many readers of that otherwise all-embracing work the absence of any general comment on the problem of poor relief. This is a kind of biographical problem which the discovery of a single hitherto unknown letter or manuscript of Smith could conceivably solve.

2. *Scottish Medical Degrees*

The medical professors at the University of Edinburgh, under the leadership of William Cullen, a friend of Smith's, were disturbed by the lax manner in which medical degrees were granted by rival Scottish universities, and presented a memorial to the Duke of Buccleuch asking him to sponsor legislation in Parliament to regulate the licensing of physicians to practice. The Duke asked Dr. Cullen to submit

---

[22] *The Wealth of Nations,* I, 146. In one of his earliest ventures into economics, Karl Marx quotes Smith's passage on kelp approvingly, but uses it to expose what he regards as the absurdity of Smith's statement elsewhere in *The Wealth of Nations* (II, 248) that the interest of the landlord is always identical with that of society. (Karl Marx, *Early Writings,* T. B. Bottomore, tr. and ed., New York, 1961, pp. 103-104.)

the memorial to Adam Smith, and Smith replied to Cullen in a long letter expressing his skepticism about the efficiency and integrity of universities, or of professional guilds, as administrators of licensing to practise medicine. He declared his preference for leaving to their customers the decision as to the competence of the physicians. (Rae, pp. 271-280.) There is no record of Cullen's having replied directly to Smith, and Smith's letter apparently led to the abandonment of any effort by Cullen to get legislative action. But in a discourse in Latin given shortly after at the University of Edinburgh Cullen did in effect reply to Smith.[23] This issue as to the need for educational prerequisites for the practice of medicine and for agencies to enforce them of course antedated Smith. As we shall see, it continued to be a live issue in Scotland.

In *The Wealth of Nations* there is a passage which echoes Smith's letter to Dr. Cullen:

> The privileges of graduates in arts, in law, *physic* and divinity, when they can be obtained only by residing a certain number of years in certain universities, necessarily force a certain number of students to such universities, independent of the merit or reputation of the teachers. The privileges of graduates are a sort of statutes of apprenticeship, which have contributed to the improvement of education, just as the other statutes of apprenticeship have to that of arts and manufactures.[24]

Read literally, this would seem to be in direct conflict with the spirit of Smith's letter to Dr. Cullen. But Smith,

---

[23] Rae bases his account on Dr. John Thomson, *An Account of the Life, Lectures, and Writings of William Cullen* (1st ed., Edinburgh, 1832; enlarged ed., Edinburgh, 1859) which is not available to me. J. R. McCulloch, ed., *The Wealth of Nations by Adam Smith*, new ed., Edinburgh, 1863, pp. 582-588, reproduces some of Thomson's material, and gives in translation some extracts from Cullen's Latin discourse. See also Raymond Pearl, "Adam Smith on Medical Education and Related Matters," *Journal of the American Medical Association*, LXXXV (1925), 1663-1665 (based on McCulloch's account).

[24] *The Wealth of Nations*, Cannan ed., II, 252. (Italics mine.)

I think, is here expecting his readers to remember that a full volume back he had denied that apprenticeship rules applying to arts and manufactures render any useful service and to recognize therefore the ironic tone in which this passage is written.[25]

Smith, however, would apparently have supported a requirement for a "liberal," as distinguished from a professional, education as a prerequisite applicable to "every person before he was permitted to exercise any liberal profession, or before he could be received as a candidate for any honorable office of trust or profit,"[26] and presumably he would include as a "liberal profession" the practice of medicine.

In the 1850's the issue was further complicated for Scotland by the refusal of the English professional authorities to recognize without further examination degrees obtained outside of England, and by a shortage of doctors in the rural areas of Scotland for which the allegedly excessive requirements by that time of the Scottish medical colleges were held responsible. In 1857, in a review of two pamphlets dealing with these questions, the *Edinburgh Medical Journal* summarized the views of Cullen and Smith, and sided with Smith against any governmental interference. To Cullen's argument that mankind can judge of its carpenters, but not of its doctors, it replied: "We believe that the same common sense regulates, or at least may regulate, the choice of your family doctor, as it does the choice of your architect, engineer, or teacher."[27]

3. *Pins (and Needles) and Nails*

All readers of *The Wealth of Nations* know that Smith used both pin-making and nail-making to illustrate the gain in "dexterity" of the workman resulting from division

---

[25] See *Ibid.,* I, 123-125.
[26] *Ibid.,* II, 281.
[27] "Medical Reform," *Edinburgh Medical Journal,* Dec. 1857, pp. 543-551.

of labor. Smith, however, distinguishes between the manner in which and degree to which division of labor increases dexterity in the two industries because of the differences in their respective technologies. In the nailery, each worker confines himself to nail-making, i.e., there is division of occupation by product, but each worker carries on all the operations necessary to make a nail from the heating of the iron to the finished nail ready for use. In the pin-factory, there is *sub*division of labor, so that it takes eighteen different laborers to carry out all the operations which are involved in the making of a single pin.[28]

> ... in the way in which this business [i.e., pin-making] is now carried on, not only the whole work is a peculiar trade, but it is divided into a number of branches, of which the greater part are likewise peculiar trades. One man draws out the wire, another straights it. . . . a third cuts it, a fourth points it, a fifth grinds it at the top for receiving the head; [etc.]
>
> * * *
>
> The making of a nail . . . is by no means one of the simplest operations. The same person blows the bellows, stirs or mends the fire as there is occasion, heats the iron, and forges every part of the nail . . . The different operations into which the making of a pin . . . is subdivided, are all of them much more simple, and the dexterity of the person, of whose life it has been the sole business to perform them, is usually much greater.[29]

Rae, I think, misses the distinction Smith draws between the two industries (Rae, p. 8.):

> Kirkcaldy . . . had a nailery or two, which Smith is said to have been fond of visiting as a boy, and to have acquired in them his first rough idea of the value of

---

[28] See Adam Smith, *Lectures on Justice,* pp. 163-164, 255, for pin-making; *The Wealth of Nations,* I, 6-7 for pin-making, I, 9-10 for nail-making and pin-making.

[29] *The Wealth of Nations,* I, 6, 10.

division of labor. However that may be, Smith does draw some of his illustrations of the division of labor from that particular business, which would necessarily be very familiar to his mind, and it may have been in Kirkcaldy that he found the nailers paid their wages in nails, and using these nails afterwards as a currency in making their purchases from the shopkeepers.[30]

It was the *limited* extent to which division of labor was carried in a nailery that made it practicable to pay the nailers in nails instead of in money. The pin-maker could not have been paid his wages in pins which he had himself made.

T. S. Ashton makes the following comment on Smith's use of pin-making to illustrate the effects of division of labor:

> An economic historian once asked why Adam Smith had drawn his illustration of the effects of the division of labor from his 'silly pin manufactory' when a few miles away from his home stood the great Carron iron works. The answer is obvious: Adam Smith was anxious to isolate the results of the application of his celebrated principle from those of the use of machinery and power. The pin trade employed only simple appliances, it was almost ideal for his purpose. Most English industrial establishments came somewhere between the extremes represented by the pin works and Carron.[31]

A more careful reading of *The Wealth of Nations* would have explained to the "economic historian" why Smith chose the "silly pin manufactory," (which Smith referred

---

[30] W. R. Scott, *ASSP*, pp. 26-27, 333-334, also misses the contrast between the two industries which Smith draws, and directs his attention only to the similarity between them.

[31] T. S. Ashton, *An Economic History of England: The 18th Century*, London, 1955, p. 103.

to as "a very trifling manufacture") and also the nailery,
rather than the Carron iron works, to illustrate the division
of labor principle.

> . . . in those trifling manufactures which are destined
> to supply the small wants of but a small number of
> people, the whole number of workmen must neces-
> sarily be small; and those employed in every different
> branch of the work can often be collected into the
> same workhouse, and placed at once under the view
> of the spectator. In those great manufactures, on the
> contrary, which are destined to supply the great wants
> of the great body of the people, every different branch
> of the work employs so great a number of workmen,
> that it is impossible to collect them all into the same
> workhouse. We can seldom see more, at one time, than
> those employed in one single branch. Though in such
> manufactures, therefore, the work may really be di-
> vided into a much greater number of parts, than in
> those of a more trifling nature, the division is not near
> so obvious, and has accordingly been much less
> observed.[32]

Smith was familiar with nail-making. He knew something of the more advanced technique of pin-making in his
time. The near-by Carron iron works must have been
familiar to him. Its major owners were personal friends of
his. In the 1760's the Carron Company was involved with
the nail-making industry of the Kirkcaldy region as sup-
plier of iron rods (as a substitute for iron scrap) as the
raw material of the naileries and as wholesale distributor

---

[32] *The Wealth of Nations,* I, 6. There follow immediately Smith's
description of the manner in which the pin-making business "is now
carried on," his statement of his having seen "a small manufactory of
this kind where ten men only were employed, and where some of
them consequently performed two or three distinct operations" with
less use of machinery, and a reference to other "trifling" industries
where "the labor can neither be so much subdivided, nor reduced to
so great a simplicity of operation [e.g., the nail-making industry?]."

of the nails made from its own iron rods.[33] I am ignorant in these matters, but I am under the impression that modern commentators have failed to appreciate at its true worth the perceptiveness of Smith in detecting and interpreting the differences in degree and kind of the application of division of labor in different industries. There is no difficulty in finding references to division of labor through all the ages from ancient Greece on, but I doubt whether anyone anticipated Smith in tracing its relationship to scale of industry, to scale of plant, and to the essential seasonal and raw-material characteristics of the various industries.

It has been claimed by Anton Tautscher that a German writer, Ernst Ludwig Carl, writing in 1722-1723, and not Adam Smith, was the true founder of political economy. He bases this claim largely on Carl's treatment of division of labor.[34] In some respects, according to Tautscher, Carl was superior to Smith in his treatment of division of labor, especially in his insistence that individual initiative did not suffice to bring about the appropriate extent, limits, and direction of division of labor, and that, to attain this, comprehensive, direct and detailed operation and regulation of industry by the prince was requisite. Except by vague implication, indeed, Carl in fact assigns no role at all to individual responses to patterns of relative costs and demands as the major force governing the extent and direction of division of labor. Tautscher, naturally enough

---

[33] See R. H. Campbell, *Carron Company,* Edinburgh, 1961, pp. 14, 64, 78-82.

[34] Anton Tautscher, *Ernst Ludwig Carl (1682-1743) der Begründer der Volkswirtschaftslehre,* Jena, 1939; Tautscher, "Der Begründer der Volkswirtschaftslehre—ein Deutscher," *Schmollers Jahrbuch,* LXIV (1940), 79-106; Tautscher, "Die Arbeitsteilung als Grundproblem der Nationalökonomie bei Ernst Ludwig Carl (1722)," *Zeitschrift für Nationalökonomie,* X (1941), 1-24; Tautscher, "Ernst Ludwig Carl und Adam Smith," *Weltwirtschaftliches Archiv,* LIV (1941), 13-57.

writing where and when he did, presents this, in effect, as a virtue, not a defect, of Carl.[35]

Tautscher finds so much similarity in ideas and even in language in the treatment of division of labor by Carl and by Smith that he accepts it as at the least highly probable that Smith was influenced by Carl, either directly, or through some intermediate source. There are some mildly impressive parallelisms, as, for instance, when Smith speaks of pin-making as a business in which "not only the whole work is a peculiar trade, but it is divided into a number of branches" and Carl refers to "Cette séparation de métier de tailleur en plusieurs branches." What is for present purposes even more interesting is that Carl uses pin-making and nail-making as his major illustrations of division of labor, for the first time, according to Tautscher, in the literature of economics.[36]

There are differences, however, between Carl's and Smith's treatments of pin-making and nail-making which Tautscher overlooks. Carl uses nails, pins, needles interchangeably to illustrate division of labor. The special feature of pin-making which attracted the attention of Smith, the extreme subdivision of labor within a single plant, in contrast to the absence of division of labor within a nailery, and in contrast also to its dispersion among many estab-

---

[35] Carl published his work in France, under cover of semi-anonymity: *Traité de la Richesse des Princes,* Paris, 1722-1723, three volumes, by "C. C. d. P. d. B. Allemand," that is, Carl Conseiller du Prince de Brandenburg, German. (See *The Kress Library of Business and Economics Catalogue,* 1940, p. 178, item No. 3459.) E. R. A. Seligman knew of this work, but only from eighteenth-century references to it. The earliest and the only extensive comment on it in English that I know of is by Leopold Katscher, of Budapest, "A Bibliographical Discovery in Political Economy," *Journal of Political Economy,* IX (1901), 423-436, which seems to have been unknown to Tautscher. It seems to be based, however, solely on second-hand accounts of the book, contains nothing of relevance for present purposes, and does not identify the author.

[36] The most relevant passages in Carl are in the *Traité,* I, 17-20; II, 113-119, 134-135, 240-250, 371-372.

lishments in the iron industry, received no comment from Carl, perhaps because pin-making had not yet reached this stage when he wrote.

4. *"Slavery" in the Scottish Mines*

By Scottish statutes dating back to 1606 and by judicial decisions under Scottish law, workers in and about coal-mines and salt pits were bound to the mines for life; they could not leave for employment in another occupation or in another mine without the consent of the owner and another employer was subject to penalty if he hired them without the consent of the owner of the mine to which they were bound. The bondage was not in legal theory hereditary, but it was substantially so in practice. Anyone, man or woman, who worked for a year in a particular mine or accepted a year's wages in advance thereby bound himself to that mine for life. (I do not know what happened if the mine became exhausted.) Children could be contracted into bondage for life by their parents; by court decisions, children who worked with their parents in the mines thereby bound themselves for life; it was common practice for parents to "arl" their children, that is, contract them into bondage for a premium at the time of their baptism; at the age of fourteen or older children could bind themselves for life, subject to the approval of kirk-sessions in the country or of magistrates in the towns.

Until 1747, the bondage was absolute; only the mine-owner could end it and on his own terms. By an Act of that year (20 Geo. ii, c. 19), applying to all Britain unless an express exception was stipulated in the Act, all workers in all occupations hired for one year or longer could be freed by justices upon complaint of abuse or maltreatment. In general, however, all the local judicial and administrative machinery of government was available to the mine-owners by right for the enforcement of the bondage and for the punishment of insurgent colliers. The right of habeas corpus was expressly withheld from bonded miners.[37]

The coalminers and salters of Scotland were not freed until 1799, by a British Act (39 Geo. iii, c. 56) although a previous Act of 1775 (15 Geo. iii, c. 28) had made some partial and ineffective steps in that direction. The evidence seems to me overwhelming that humanitarian considerations had almost nothing to do with the passage of these Acts, and that the major factor leading to their framing and enactment was that the bondage system had become unprofitable and nearly unworkable for the mineowners but that to the individual mineowner it seemed too great a risk to free his miners in the hope that he could rehire them or hire others on a free contract basis at reasonable rates of pay as long as coalminers, colliers' settlements, and the coal-mining craft as a whole bore the social stigma of servility. The Acts seem to have passed without any debate in Parliament or discussion in the press. I have found ref-

---

[37] There does not appear to be a comprehensive study either of the history or of the economics of serfdom in the Scottish mines. The above account is based mainly on the following sources: "Slavery in Modern Scotland," *Edinburgh Review,* CLXXXIX (1899), 119-148; Thomas Johnston, *The History of the Working Classes in Scotland,* Glasgow, n.d. (c. 1928), pp. 64-65, 69, 78-84 (based largely on the previous item); T. S. Ashton and Joseph Sykes, *The Coal Industry of the Eighteenth Century,* Manchester, 1929, pp. 70-83; R. Page Arnot, *A History of the Scottish Miners,* London, 1955, pp. 1-13; The Stair Society, *An Introduction to Scottish Legal History,* Edinburgh, 1958, pp. 59, 136-140; R. H. Campbell, *Carron Company,* Edinburgh, 1961, pp. 48, 50, 64-71; Henry Hamilton, *An Economic History of Scotland in the Eighteenth Century,* Oxford, 1963, pp. 367-372. Items that are, or may be, relevant, but were not available to me, are: *Memorial for the Colliers of Scotland,* July 23, 1762; [Archibald Cochrane], *Description of the Estate and Abbey of Culross,* Edinburgh, 1793; *Considerations on the Present Scarcity and High Prices of Coals in Scotland,* Edinburgh, 1793; Robert Ball, *General View of the Coal Trade in Scotland,* 1808; James Barrowman, "Slavery in the Coal Mines of Scotland," *Transactions of the Federated Institute of Mining Engineers,* XIV (1897-1898).

erences to only two persons who prior to the passage of the 1775 Act had publicly expressed unfriendly views with respect to the system of bondage in the mines. One of these was John Millar, who in 1771, as part of a general hostile discussion of slavery, commented critically on the remnant of it in the Scottish mines but criticized it more for its unprofitability, as he saw it, to the proprietors than its injurious effects on the miners, for whom, he said, "their servitude is not very grievous" and is offset by higher than normal wages.[38] The other was John Stevenson, whose name recurs in accounts of the bondage in the Scottish mines of the eighteenth century as an opponent of the institution, but about whom I have not succeeded in obtaining much additional information.[39]

If I were to try to explain the failure of the Scottish eighteenth-century "Enlightenment" to show more awareness and uneasiness about what seems to later commentators a skeleton in its own local closet, I would put most weight on the proposition that each age has its own very special blindspots and on my interpretation of eighteenth-century Scottish intellectualism as being only vestigially

---

[38] *Observations Concerning the Distinction of Ranks in Society,* [London, 1771], Dublin ed., 1771, pp. 236-238; also in later editions: see, e.g., 3rd ed. corrected and enlarged, London, 1781, 340-341, 353-356. Millar may, however, have taken a more vigorous stand elsewhere, for Ronald Meek reports that "he took an active part in the struggle to abolish slavery, both at home and abroad," ("The Scottish Contribution to Marxist Sociology," John Saville, ed., *Democracy and the Labour Movement,* London, 1954, p. 97.)

[39] A tract by him which relates to the Scottish colliers I know only by title: *Letters in Answer to Dr. Price's Two Pamphlets on Civil Liberty . . . Also Copies of Four Letters, concerning the Slavery of the Colliers, Coal-bearers, and Salters in Scotland, Addressed to the Members of the House of Commons in the year 1774,* London, 1778. He is sometimes referred to as "of London," and he has been identified as a "Dissenter" (Anthony Lincoln, *Some Political & Social Ideas of English Dissent 1763-1800,* Cambridge, Eng., 1938, p. 149), which may mean that he was not a Scotsman.

"reformist" where social and political structure and property rights were involved. There were also other special features which helped the institution of serfdom in the mines to survive without major controversy. The bondage system was of indigenous origin; it was a peculiarly Scottish system, but it would require British legislation to end it. It was a vested interest of the top layer of Scottish society. Both coal and salt were vital to the Scottish economy and there was a common belief that with free labor it would be extremely difficult to maintain an adequate labor supply, a belief which the Scottish lawyers promoted to the principle of "necessary servitude." The legal fiction also that the servitude was voluntarily entered into by those subject to it pacified some otherwise possibly uneasy consciences.

Bishop Joseph Butler, in the midst of a romantic eulogy of British liberty, found it necessary to refer to the bondage in the Scottish mines, and took refuge in its "voluntary" character.

> We are certainly a freer nation than any other we have an account of, and as free, it seems, as the very nature of government will permit. Every man is equally under the protection of the laws; may have equal justice against the most rich and powerful; and securely enjoy all the common blessings of life, with which the industry of his ancestors, or his own, has furnished him. In some other countries the upper part of the world is free, but in Great Britain, the whole body of the people is free. For we have at length, to the distinguished honor of those who began, and have more particularly labored in it, emancipated our northern provinces of their *legal* remains of slavery; for *voluntary* slavery cannot be abolished at least not directly by law. I take leave to speak of this long-desired work as done; since it wants only his concur-

rence, who, as we have found by many years' experience, considers the good of his people as his own."[40]

John Erskine (1695-1768), professor of Scots Law at the University of Edinburgh (and incidentally a colliery-owner himself) held that "there appears nothing contrary either to reason or to the peculiar doctrines of Christianity in a contract by which one binds himself to perpetual service under a master, who on his part is obliged to maintain the other in all the necessaries of life."[41]

The preamble to the Act of 1775 explained as motives for its enactment that the stigma attached to bondage was an obstacle to recruiting sufficient workers and the act would therefore benefit the public "without doing any injury to the present masters, and would remove the reproach of allowing such a state of servitude to exist in a free country."[42] But who was making such a reproach at the time, and why would it trouble those in power? The date may be significant. The American Revolution was about to begin, and "freedom" was the issue. In 1770 Benjamin Franklin had published a piece "Conversation on Slavery" in an English newspaper, the London *Public Advertiser,* as a rejoinder to the "many reflections being thrown against the Americans, . . . on account of their keeping slaves in

---

[40] "Sermon . . . preached before the House of Lords, . . . June 11, 1747," *The Works of Joseph Butler,* W. E. Gladstone, ed., 1896, II, 364-365 (the italics are in the original text). Gladstone explains in a note that the last two sentences in the above quotation are an allusion to 20 Geo. ii, c. 19 (referred to *supra,* p. 109), which was then awaiting George II's signature. What Butler says here indicates that relief of the colliers' plight was a major objective of the Act, and that it was a response to a humanitarian movement. I have not noticed any mention of the Act in the accounts of the colliers' bondage that I have read. In any case, Bishop Butler was overoptimistic in his expectations as to the significance of the Act for the colliers.

[41] Cited from an early edition of John Erskine, *Institute of the Law of Scotland,* in "Slavery in Modern Scotland," *Edinburgh Review,* CLXXXIX (1899), 143. I have not been able to find the passage in the later edition available to me.

[42] *The Statutes at Large of England and of Great Britain,* London, 1811, XIV, 19.

their country." Addressing himself to a hypothetical Scotsman, Franklin wrote:

> But, Sir, as to your observation, that if we had a
> real love of liberty, we should not suffer such a thing
> as slavery among us, I am a little surprised to hear
> this from you, a North Briton, in whose own country,
> Scotland, slavery still subsists, established by law.
>
>   *   *   *
>
> I mean the slavery in your mines. All the wretches
> that dig coal for you, in those dark caverns under
> ground, unblessed by sunshine, are absolute slaves by
> law, and their children after them, from the time they
> first carry a basket to the end of their days. They are
> bought and sold with the colliery, and have no more
> liberty to leave it than our negroes have to leave their
> master's plantation . . . Their skin is white, . . . they
> are honest good people, and at the same time are your
> own countrymen.[43]

Franklin's argument was, no doubt, not a significant
factor in preparing the way for the passage of the Act of
1775, but it may, however, help to explain the wording
of its preamble.

Adam Smith could not have avoided knowing a good
deal at first hand about colliers' and salters' servitude.
Kirkcaldy, where he was born, was a coal-mining as well
as a salt-pit town. (Rae, p. 8.) There were coal-mines and
colliers' settlements in the vicinity of Edinburgh,[44] and also
not far from Glasgow. There were coal-mine owners or
lessees among Smith's personal friends. As Commissioner
of the Salt Duties from 1780 on, he needed to be well-
informed about the salteries. There is, however, no mention

---

[43] Reprinted in Verner W. Crane, ed., *Benjamin Franklin's Letters
to the Press, 1758-1775,* Chapel Hill, 1950, pp. 186-192.

[44] Hugh Miller, (1802-1856), in his *My Schools and Schoolmasters,*
Edinburgh, [1st ed., 1852] n.d., pp. 315-318, writes of a colliers'
settlement near where he was born, within four miles of Edinburgh,
whose population when he was young still bore physical and psycho-
logical scars of their own and their parents' degraded status.

of Scottish miners' bondage in *The Wealth of Nations.*
There are even passages which indicate that he was capable
of forgetting its existence. Smith, for instance, writes: "A
collier working by the piece is supposed, at Newcastle, to
earn commonly about double and in many parts of Scotland about three times the wages of common labor. His
high wages arise altogether from the hardship, disagree-
ableness, and dirtiness of his work." In his lectures at
Glasgow, however, he had attributed the high wages of
Scottish colliers in part to their dislike of their bondage;
the Scottish miners run away to Newcastle, where "though
they have less wages, . . . they have liberty."[45] Elsewhere
in *The Wealth of Nations,* discussing agrarian serfdom, he
writes: "It is only in the western and southwestern provinces of Europe, that it has gradually been abolished
altogether."[46]

In his lectures, Smith used the high wages of the Scotch
colliers as support of his general thesis that, as John U. Nef
puts it, "slave is dearer [to the employer] than free labor."
Nef is doubtful that the Scottish collier did in fact earn
higher wages than the English ones when computed on a
comparable basis,[47] but John Millar presented some wage-
data which seem to confirm Smith's observation.[48] For
Smith's thesis, moreover, it is total production cost per
ton which is significant, and comparative wages per day,
or per week, or even per ton, do not suffice to decide the
comparative total cost per ton according to whether it is

---

[45] *The Wealth of Nations,* I, 106; *Lectures,* Cannan ed., pp. 99-100.
[46] *The Wealth of Nations,* I, 364. J. R. McCulloch, in the editions
of *The Wealth of Nations* which he brought out, noted that "The
species of slavery, alluded to in the text, was not altogether extinct
in Scotland when *The Wealth of Nations* was published," and pointed
out that the coalminers and salters were then "in the exact condition
of the *adscripti glebae* of the middle ages." See, e.g., the Edinburgh
1828 edition, II, 186, note, and the Edinburgh 1863 edition, p. 172,
note.
[47] *The Rise of the British Coal Industry,* London, 1932, II, 190-191.
[48] *The Origin of the Distinction of Ranks,* 1781 ed., pp. 354-355, note.

slave labor or free labor that is used. Comparative labor discipline, regularity of work, care in handling tools and equipment and in treating the coal-seams, and many other such factors, should enter into the calculation. R. H. Campbell's account of the experience of the Carron Company seems here to offer strong support for Smith's proposition. The Carron Company found it profitable to import colliers from England on a free contract basis at premium wages over the Newcastle rates and with specially favorable working facilities provided for the English colliers, because the English colliers apparently were more efficient, better disciplined and more loyal workers.[49]

The fact that Smith never came out strongly against colliers' serfdom on humanitarian or on ethical grounds does not, of course, demonstrate that he was not strongly opposed to it. Smith did not have great faith in the efficacy of moral principles when they clashed with economic interest. "The late resolution of the Quakers in Pennsylvania to set at liberty all their negro slaves, may satisfy us that their number cannot be very great. Had they made any considerable part of their property, such a resolution could never have been agreed to."[50] Smith may have thought that a more effective way of ending slavery than preaching moral principle or humanity to slave-owners was to persuade them that free labor would be more profitable to them than slave labor. It is curious, nevertheless, that he did not find the Act of 1775 worthy of comment in *The Wealth of Nations* or appeal to it as evidence supporting one of his favorite theses.

---

[49] R. H. Campbell, *Carron Company,* pp. 48, 50.
[50] *The Wealth of Nations,* I, 365.

IV. ADAM SMITH'S LIBRARY

1. *Its Size and Contents according to Bonar's Catalogue*

Since information concerning the contents of Smith's library has become available in any quantity, scholars interested in the sources from which Smith may have derived theories or concepts have made use of such information more for the negative purpose of excluding specific authors or groups of authors as influences on Smith than for the positive purpose of tracing such influence. It is the main concern of this section to bring out the limitations of the kind of information we have as to the contents of Smith's library when this information is used for the purpose of excluding any particular book or author as a possible or probable influence on Smith.

There are four major sources of information with respect to the books owned by Smith: a list compiled by James Bonar in 1894; a revision of this list published by Bonar in 1932; a "Catalogue of 1781" prepared for Smith himself and carrying annotations in his hand, which was first published in 1951; and reports by librarians, collectors, booksellers, and others of the location of books carrying Adam Smith's bookplate or label, with the bookplate as the essential criterion as to whether a book was once in Smith's library. These are overlapping sources, and the complete listing of books known to have been owned at some time by Smith would require a fuller collocation of the information derivable from them than has yet been performed. Even if it were performed, moreover, there would still be abundant reason to suppose that we did not possess an even approximately complete list of the books that had at some time or other been in Smith's library, although I think we can approximate the size of his library at the time of his death. To explain the nature of our main sources of information with respect to the extent and contents of Smith's library, their known and potential shortcomings, and their relationships to each other, calls for a sketch of the history of Smith's library after his death. For our knowledge of this history James Bonar is the chief source.[1]

David Douglas, later Lord Reston, Adam Smith's sole heir, inherited all his books. As far as is known, he kept Smith's library intact until his own death in 1819. He bequeathed his estate, in equal portions, to his two daughters, a Mrs. Bannerman and Mrs. W. B. Cunningham, and it is taken for granted by Bonar and others that they shared equally in the books. Mrs. Bannerman kept her portion of Smith's library intact until her death in 1884. In that year, her son gave some and in 1894 the remainder of the Smith books to New College, Edinburgh, so that a presumptive half of Smith's library, with no known or suspected leakage from it since Smith's death, should still be intact on the shelves of New College today. Bonar states that until 1878 the Cunningham family also kept intact its half of the Smith library. In that year, Mrs. Cunningham, the daughter of Lord Reston, sold some of the Smith books to Edinburgh booksellers and gave the remainder to her son, R. O. Cunningham, a professor at Queen's College, Belfast. He in turn gave some of the books to Queen's College, but is believed to have retained the rest until his death in 1918.

In 1894, Bonar compiled his first catalogue of Smith's library, based on what he characterized as "full reports"

---

[1] See especially James Bonar, *A Catalogue of the Library of Adam Smith*, 2nd ed. Prepared for the Royal Economic Society, London, 1932, (henceforth referred to as Bonar, *Catalogue II*), Introduction, pp. xvi-xix. See also Rae, pp. 439-440. Rae here says that "a small number" of Smith's books were sold in 1878. His sole source of information is Bonar's account, but I can find in the latter nothing to support a positive statement that the number was "small." The size of the sales in 1878 has important bearing for the appraisal of the degree of completeness of our present information about the contents of Smith's library.

made to him of their then holdings by the Bannerman family, the Cunningham family, Queen's College, Belfast, and New College, Edinburgh, as well as on what information he could gather about books carrying Adam Smith's bookplate or label held elsewhere than in these four locations. If Bonar's account of the history of Smith's library was accurate, the one gap of any consequence in our knowledge of the contents of that library at the time of Smith's death would therefore be as to the extent and contents of the Cunningham sales of 1878, and any stray copies of books carrying the Smith label that turned up and could not be otherwise accounted for would be attributable to the portion of the Cunningham holdings sold in 1878.[2]

After 1878 there is again no record of any leakages from the major depositaries until 1918, this time again by the Cunningham family, who in that year sold the remainder of their holdings to Dulau & Co. Ltd., London booksellers. There is obscurity as to what happened between 1918 and July, 1920. A University of Tokyo professor who was in London in 1920 saw an advertisement of the Smith books in a Dulau & Co. catalogue, bought all that the firm still held, amounting to 148 "books or entries" or 308 volumes, and donated them to the University of Tokyo, where they still are. Whether or not Dulau & Co. between 1918 and July, 1920, had already sold any Smith books has not been explored.[3]

All of the books sold to Dulau & Co. in 1918 by the Cunninghams had presumably been reported by them to

[2] James Bonar, *Catalogue of the Library of Adam Smith*, 1st ed., London, 1894. (Henceforth referred to as Bonar, *Catalogue I*.) Most of the information in this edition is reproduced in the second edition, so that my references to Bonar's *Catalogue* will be mainly to the latter edition.

[3] The only information available as to the Dulau & Co. transactions is in Tadao Yanaihara, ed., *A Full and Detailed Catalogue of Books which belonged to Adam Smith now in the Possession of the . . . University of Tokyo*, Tokyo, 1951, pp. v-vi. (Henceforth referred to as Yanaihara, *A Full Catalogue*) There may be relevant information in catalogues issued or advertisements by Dulau & Co.

Bonar for the first edition of his *Catalogue* in 1894. When Bonar was preparing his second edition, he was provided a list of the University of Tokyo holdings by Professor Eijiro Kawaii of Tokyo, found in it some twenty items which he could not identify in the list of Cunningham holdings as of 1894 in the first edition of the *Catalogue,* and added them to his list in the second edition. On the basis of the additional and more accurate information supplied by Professor Yanaihara in his *Full Catalogue* and of a fresh scrutiny of the data in the Bonar and the Yanaihara catalogues I believe I can reduce the number of relevant entries in the Tokyo Catalogue which are not traceable as Cunningham holdings in 1894 as then reported to Bonar to not more than 12 out of a total of 135 "entries," comprising 23 volumes out of a total of some 300 volumes. This is not a large number, but it is puzzling nevertheless, and may indicate that the Cunningham reporting in 1894 was not "full." I will nevertheless tentatively assume that it may be disregarded.[4]

I venture here on an estimate of the size of Smith's library at the time of his death and of the extent of the Cunningham leakage in 1878 through sale of Smith books on the market, basing my estimate on the information derivable from Bonar, *Catalogue II* and on a series of assumptions which Bonar and others have made and which I will tentatively accept: (1) that the Bannerman and Cunningham holdings were originally approximately equal in number of volumes; (2) that there were no significant leakages to the market at any time from the Lord Reston and the Bannerman holdings; (3) that the only significant sales from the Cunningham holdings were in 1878 and

---

[4] For information with respect to the relations of Bonar's listing of the books held in Tokyo and the list given by Yanaihara, see Bonar, *Catalogue II,* Introduction, p. xviii and p. 214, and Yanaihara, *Full Catalogue,* Introduction, p. vi. As to what entries are to be treated as relevant, I reject all Yanaihara's entries which he does not expressly list as carrying the Adam Smith label.

in 1918; and (4) that Bonar's informants in 1894 did in fact submit "full reports" of their holdings at that time, aside from any possible minor errors of listing and identification. On this basis, the list in Bonar, *Catalogue II* represents a total of approximately 2240 relevant volumes, of which 1400 are identifiable as Bannerman holdings, and the remaining 840 represent Cunningham holdings as they were in 1894, plus previous Cunningham donations to Queen's College, Belfast. The approximate number of volumes in Smith's library at his death was consequently 2800, and the Cunningham leakage of 1878 amounted to approximately 560 volumes. At the most, less than 100 volumes not listed in Bonar can now be located in their present resting-places and identified by the Adam Smith labels they carry, leaving over 400 volumes in Smith's library at his death which cannot now be identified unless they are represented in the Catalogue of 1781 which was discovered in 1920.

2. *Smith's own Catalogue of 1781*

With the books purchased by the University of Tokyo in 1920 was included a manuscript catalogue of Smith's library as of 1781, with annotations in Smith's hand. Bonar was told of the existence of this catalogue in time to mention it in the second edition of his *Catalogue,* 1932, but was not given a copy nor any account of its contents.[5] By 1937, W. R. Scott had received from Tokyo a photographic copy of the Catalogue of 1781 and had made a brief and somewhat misleading comment on it, tending unduly to minimize its importance.[6] Later, in an undated mimeographed memorandum which he distributed not long before his death in 1940, Scott described the Catalogue and presented a selected list of works recorded in it which he could not

---

[5] See Bonar, *Catalogue II,* p. 214.
[6] W. R. Scott, *ASSP,* p. 172.

identify in Bonar, *Catalogue II*. He commented further on
the Catalogue of 1781 as follows:

> I went through it systematically incorporating any
> entry I could not find in Dr. Bonar's *Catalogue,* on the
> blank pages of an interleaved copy of that Catalogue.
> It seemed to me that the right thing was for Dr.
> Bonar to complete his work of almost fifty years by
> making a supplement to his *Catalogue,* and accord-
> ingly I sent him the material above mentioned. That
> may take some time, since in the Catalogue of 1781
> scarcely any data are given about the particular edi-
> tion of the works recorded.[7]

Bonar was then 87 or 88 years of age, but he outlived
W. R. Scott, who died in 1940. Bonar died in January, 1941,
aged 89. G. Findlay Shirras, in an obituary of Bonar,
reported that Bonar had bequeathed to him "an inter-
leaved edition of Bonar's Catalogue of Adam Smith's
library, with Professor Scott's scholarly notes (which
Bonar greatly valued)."[8] Shirras himself died in 1955.

The book edited by Professor Yanaihara and published
in Tokyo in 1951 included, as Appendix II, a complete
reproduction of the Catalogue of 1781, thus making it
available for the first time to scholars generally. According
to Yanaihara, "The Catalogue of 1781 contains about 1100
books or entries (2300 volumes)."[9] Bonar estimated
(counted?) the number of "entries" in his first list at
about 1000, and the number of "volumes" at about 2000.[10]
I cannot find that Bonar presented similar estimates for
his second list, but Henry Higgs, in his review of Bonar,

---

[7] From a copy of the mimeographed memorandum in my possession.

[8] G. Findlay Shirras, "James Bonar 1852-1941," *Proceedings of the
British Academy,* XXVII (1941), 374, note. I hope that this volume
will be appropriately protected from the fate which so often has befallen
material of Smithian interest.

[9] Yanaihara, *Full Catalogue,* Introduction, p. viii.

[10] Bonar, *Catalogue I,* Introduction, p. viii.

Catalogue II, stated that "It includes 1100 books or pamphlets and 2200 volumes."[11]

It would be a mistake, however, if even with respect to the count of "volumes," where ambiguity is less than for "books" or "entries" or "items" and where the correspondence in counts between the various lists is especially close, this correspondence in total numbers is taken to mean a similar correspondence in detailed contents of the lists. Yanaihara marked each volume-entry in the Catalogue of 1781 that he could identify as also being represented in Bonar, *Catalogue II,* but he presented no count of them. On the basis of my own counting, of the 1120 total "entries" and 2300 total "volumes" in the Catalogue of 1781, there were some 490 "entries" and 940 "volumes" which Yanaihara could not identify as in the Bonar list. While I think it is possible by further comparison of the two lists substantially to lower the count of non-corresponding items, I am convinced that there is considerable irreducible listing in the Catalogue of 1781 of items which are not represented in Bonar, *Catalogue II.*

Comparison between the 1781 and the Bonar lists in their present form is difficult and time-consuming because of the divergent and for this purpose at least frustrating ways in which the two lists were constructed. The titles in the Catalogue of 1781 are given in abbreviated fashion, with fairly full indication of authorship when known to Smith but as a rule without date or place of publication or other indication of the edition. The Catalogue of 1781, moreover, is a shelf-list, with location in Smith's library as the only governing principle for the order of listing. Bonar's list is in large degree arranged alphabetically by authors' names. This does not apply, however, to pamphlets of diverse authorship bound together in volumes, listed separately under "Pamphlets," and to books of authorship unknown to Bonar which are usually listed

---

[11] *The Economic Journal,* XLII (1932), 625.

under some major word in the title or under the subject
of the book. It of course does not apply to volumes of
periodicals, to official documents, or to other items of un-
specifiable or joint authorship. It would require a complete
reconstruction of both lists, on a consistent alphabetical
basis, to obtain a reliable estimate of the number of items
in the 1781 Catalogue which are missing from Bonar,
Catalogue II.

No one, as far as I know, has made any attempt to compare the two lists with the obverse purpose of determining
which, and how many, items listed by Bonar are absent
from the Catalogue of 1781. Such absences are easier to
explain, and generally of less significance for present purposes, than the absences from Bonar's list of items listed
in the Catalogue of 1781. The two lists correspond to in-
ventories at two different dates, 1781 and 1790. Smith
continued to acquire books, by purchase[12] and by gift,
after 1781. Perhaps more important, we must not take
for granted that the Catalogue of 1781 as we now know it
was a complete record of Smith's book holdings in 1781.
The Catalogue, as a shelf-list, identifies four numbered
"Divisions" and under these "Rows;" "top," "upper" and
"lower" "Shelves;" and "Bookcases." Outside the "Divisions," it locates other "Bookcases," and refers to a "Locked
Press" and a "closet." All this suggests to me that the
Catalogue of 1781 as we now know it was for a single floor,
perhaps for a single large room, a "Library Room" proper.
We know that Smith's house, "Panmure House," had more
than one story, and it of course had more than one room
in which shelves and books could have been located. One
item in the 1781 Catalogue has what may be a highly
relevant notation: "Carried up stairs."[13]

---

[12] Cf. Smith to Cadell, Dec. 7, 1782: "I bought at London a good
many partly new books or editions that were new to me." (Rae, p. 362.)
[13] Yanaihara, *A Full Catalogue*, p. 82.

3. *Discrepancies between the Two Catalogues*

It seems probable that the bulk of any discrepancy between the size and contents of the Catalogue of 1781 and Bonar's *Catalogue II* can in the main be explained by incompleteness of the 1781 Catalogue, by acquisitions of additional books by Smith between 1781 and his death in 1790, and by the Cunningham "leakage" of 1878. We should consider also, however, the possibility of additional leakages, between 1790 and 1894, perhaps not confined to the Cunningham holdings, as well as the possibility already referred to that there was not full reporting to Bonar by the main holders in 1894 of their actual holdings at that time.

Bonar has identified one volume as having passed out of the Cunningham holdings prior to the 1878 leakage. This volume is in Reading University Library, carries the Adam Smith label, and has an annotation in the hand of J. R. McCulloch, the economist, that it was given to him by the Rev. Mr. Cunningham, the son-in-law of Lord Reston, in 1854.[14] There may, of course, have been other such instances of Cunningham gifts, but it seems reasonable, in the absence of further information, to treat it as exceptional.

Bonar states in his *Catalogue II* that a two-volume set of Berkeley's *Works* carrying the Smith label reported to him in 1894 as being in the Cunningham holdings and so recorded in *Catalogue I* was purchased by Glasgow University from a London bookseller in 1903. This indicates a leakage from these holdings after 1894 but before 1918. More puzzling, this item had been underscored by some reader, something rarely if ever reported for an item carrying the Smith book label, and this reader made a marginal notation "July 2, 1827. J.H.B.C." Unless J.H.B.C. was a member of the Cunningham family, how did these volumes

---

[14] Bonar, *Catalogue II,* p. 199.

get into his hands, and then back again into the Cunningham collection?[15]

Another puzzle has come to my attention too late fully to explore. In 1940 a scholar published a list of the books carrying the Adam Smith label in the Hutzler Collection at the Johns Hopkins University, of which 14 entries were identified as recorded in Bonar, *Catalogue II* and 24 entries were not so recorded.[16] This list was known to me but I took it for granted that the items in it not recorded in Bonar, *Catalogue II,* stemmed from the Cunningham 1878 leakage. One entry did attract my attention: a 1788 tract, with which was bound a 1793 tract, that is, one published after Smith's death. I surmised that the cover which carried the Smith label belonged originally to the 1788 item, and that in 1793 or later the original binder's boards had been used to cover both the 1788 and 1793 items. I gave the matter no further thought until I was almost ready to send this material to press, when a new book drew my interest to the 1793 item.[17] I thereupon sought additional information from Dean Evans at the Johns Hopkins University. Each additional bit of information I received gave rise to new questions on my part, and I now must leave my inquiry in mid-air. I can report now that the items listed by Claude Jones as not in Bonar, *Catalogue II* correspond closely but not identically to a list of 25 volumes offered in one lot to the Johns Hopkins University by the

---

[15] Bonar, *Catalogue II,* pp. 24-25. The puzzle is added to by Bonar's attempt at an explanation. He previously had informed us that Professor R. O. Cunningham died in 1918 (*Ibid.,* Introduction, p. xvii.), and on p. 25 he states that these volumes were in Cunningham's possession in 1894. He proceeds: "It seems probable that on his death some of the books . . . came on the market. This Berkeley was purchased . . . July 9, 1903." Bonar must have forgotten both that it was in 1918 that R. O. Cunningham died, rather than before 1903, and that he had already told us that R. O. Cunningham's books were sold in 1918 after his death.

[16] Claude Jones, "Adam Smith's Library: Some Additions," *Economic History,* IV (1940), 326-328.

[17] See *infra,* p. 133 ff.

Museum Book Store, London, in 1912, none of which volumes is listed by Bonar. This of itself would suggest that they came from the Cunningham 1878 leakage. The volume containing both a 1788 and a 1793 tract raises doubts, however. It carries on its left-hand inside cover the Adam Smith label and also a signature which, from a photograph, I read as Wm. J. Powell, Esq., and also a place-name, Abergavenny. The title page of the 1788 item carries what I take to be the same signature. The title page of the 1793 item carries in a distinctly different hand the signature Wm. Powell, Grays Inn, 179 , the remainder of the date being cut off, apparently by a binder's slicing of the tract to make it match in width the 1788 tract (and the 1788 covers?). I cannot identify either of the Powells, but Abergavenny is an ancient town at the Welsh border of Monmouthshire, and I have found in an old tour book the statement that Powells were numerous and prominent in its area, the name Powell being an early Anglicization of the common Welsh surname Ap Howell. The question arises, how explain the presence in the 1790's outside of Lord Reston's holdings of a book carrying the Adam Smith label? If this were a single instance, it would be a matter of little consequence, since it could have been a gift by Smith, or by Lord Reston. But personal inspection of the other items bought by the Johns Hopkins University in 1912 from the Museum Book Store might indicate that all or many of them came from a hitherto unsuspected leakage of possibly sizable proportions from the Adam Smith library while it was in the possession of Lord Reston, or even of Adam Smith himself. Inquiry into this, however, will have to be deferred to a future occasion.[18]

We now know, with thanks due chiefly to Bonar, a great

---

[18] I must here express my thanks for the trouble Dean G. Heberton Evans, Jr. of the Johns Hopkins University has taken in finding answers to my burdensome inquiries, and for the help his astute suggestions have been to me in constructing hypotheses which would contribute to an explanation of the place of the Johns Hopkins collection in the history of Adam Smith's library.

deal about the extent and contents of Smith's library. It should also be clear by now, however, that there must have been in his library at one time or another many books, possibly some hundreds of them, as to which we have no record. Because of this, it must be regarded as hazardous to conclude from our present knowledge relating to his library that any specific book or category of books was not at some time included in it.

4. *The Use by Scholars of Information concerning the Contents of Smith's Library*

Immediately after the publication of Bonar, *Catalogue I* there began the process of using it to minimize the possibility that at some specified period Smith was already acquainted with the writings of the Physiocrats in general, and of Turgot's *Réflexions sur la Formation et Distribution des Richesses* in particular, and thus influenced by them. I will cite two examples, first of an author making such use of Bonar's *Catalogue* and second of an author making similar use of the Catalogue of 1781.

Edwin Cannan, although he was generally an outstandingly careful and accurate scholar did, I think, systematically put more weight than was warranted on absences from Bonar, *Catalogue I* of physiocratic items as negative evidence of what Smith at different periods had owned or read. Consider the following passages:

> Turgot's book . . . was only published six years before *The Wealth of Nations,* and then only in the periodical *Éphémérides du Citoyen.* As this was not in the Advocates' Library at Edinburgh in 1776, and is not among the collections of Adam Smith's books which Dr. James Bonar has catalogued, we are not justified in assuming that Adam Smith had so much as seen the work.[19]

---

[19] E. Cannan, ed., *Lectures of Adam Smith,* Editor's Introduction, p. xxiii. Cannan is probably concerned here only with the period prior to 1776.

[Dr. Bonar's] Catalogue tells us what books Smith had in his possession at his death, fourteen years after *The Wealth of Nations* was published . . .[20]

not a particle of evidence has ever been produced to show that he had used or even seen the book in question [i.e., Turgot's *Réflexions*].[21]

In his exposition of Physiocratic doctrine, Smith does not appear to follow any book closely. His library contained Du Pont's *Physiocratie, ou constitution naturelle du gouvernement le plus avantageux au genre humain,* 1768 (see Bonar, *Catalogue,* p. 92) and he refers lower down to La Rivière, *L'ordre naturel et essentiel des sociétés politiques,* 1767, but he probably relied largely on his recollection of conversations in Paris, see Rae, *Life of Adam Smith,* pp. 215-22.[22]

In at least four respects, these passages inflate the weight of the absence of positive evidence as to the extent of Smith's reading into a kind of presumption that what we do not positively know him to have read he had not in fact read. They imply that Bonar, *Catalogue I* contained a complete list of the contents of Smith's library, although Bonar had himself warned his readers against so interpreting his list. They imply that books were generally inaccessible to Smith in Edinburgh for reading unless they were in his own library or in the Advocates' Library, which is not credible. They do not report fully the physiocratic literature which Bonar does list in his *Catalogue I* as having been in Smith's library. They suggest that Cannan had some real evidence to support the opinion that Smith learnt from talk rather than from reading, although I would argue that all the real evidence we have points fairly strongly to the opposite conclusion. It is only conversation with Frenchmen, moreover, which is here in issue, and we know that

---

[20] *The Wealth of Nations,* Cannan ed. [1904] Editor's Preface, p. vii.
[21] *Ibid.,* Editor's Introduction, p. xlvii.
[22] *Ibid.,* II, 163, note.

Smith spoke French very badly and that in the eighteenth century even educated Frenchmen could mostly not speak, or even read, English at all.

Cannan in 1898 came across and published a letter from Adam Smith dated March 25, 1766, addressed from a London address to his London bookseller, Thomas Cadell, asking that four boxes be sent for him to Edinburgh, and that they be insured for £200. As Cannan points out, the date is puzzling, for the available evidence points strongly to Smith having been in France (and Geneva) continuously from early in 1764 to late in 1766. Cannan suggests as a solution of this problem that the notoriously absent-minded Smith wrote 1766 for 1767.[23] The latter date would raise no difficulty, for we know that Smith had returned from France late in 1766 and remained in London until May, 1767. W. R. Scott adds some surmises about this letter, stated as fact. "When [Smith] returned [from France] he had brought with him at least four boxes of books which were to be insured for £200 for the journey from London to Kirkcaldy." Scott cites this letter solely to minimize Smith's acquaintance with physiocratic literature prior to his visit to France.[24]

Since from 1767 on Smith was to concentrate on the writing of *The Wealth of Nations,* and since he was never again to write anything non-economic in nature for which French works could be important sources of facts or ideas, resort to plausible surmise would permit the assumption that if it was *French* books which the four boxes contained, they would be largely books on economics. Quite a number of books could then have been covered by £200 of insurance, perhaps even a substantial collection of the prior publications of all the leading physiocrats. Since, as we shall see in a moment, Scott found reason for believing that

---

[23] E. Cannan, "Two Letters of Adam Smith's," *The Economic Journal,* VIII (1898), 402-403.

[24] W. R. Scott, *ASSP,* p. 126.

the books Smith brought back from France were mainly not on economics, this should not have troubled him. If Cannan also had thought that the four boxes contained mostly or solely books from France, it should have troubled him later, in 1904, when he surmised that Smith knew physiocratic doctrine more from conversation in France than from reading.

I return to Turgot's *Réflexions*. The Catalogue of 1781 lists a number of physiocratic works, although Scott, who accepts the Catalogue as a list of *all* Smith's books, minimizes, on the flimsiest of grounds, both the number and the significance of the economic books there listed.

> The manuscript Catalogue does not add many to the list of economic books. What it does suggest—and that very definitely—is that the volumes Adam Smith brought back from France were acquired very largely through personal relations and recommendations. To that extent there is something of an accidental character in this portion of his library.[25]

Does the Catalogue include Turgot's *Réflexions?* This was first published in three instalments, in the numbers of November 1769, December 1769, and January 1770 of the *Éphémérides du Citoyen.*[26] A version of the *Réflexions,* corrected by Turgot, was also printed separately in 1770, although in only 100 to 150 copies. Turgot in that year sent a copy of this separately-printed version, to which he referred as a "brochure," to Josiah Tucker.[27] I can find no

---

[25] W. R. Scott, *ASSP,* pp. 124-125. The "economics" books which are in the Catalogue of 1781 and which have not been identified as also in Bonar's *Catalogue* seem to me fairly substantial in number and impressive in importance.

[26] See Gustav Schelle, "Pourquoi les "Réflexions" de Turgot . . . ne sont-elles pas exactement connues," *Journal des Économistes,* XLIII (1888), 5.

[27] See *Ibid.,* and also *Oeuvres de Turgot,* Gustav Schelle ed., *Paris,* 1919, III, 421. Cf. Cannan, *supra,* p. 128, for the belief that *Réflexions* was printed only in the *Éphémérides.*

trace of this separate issue of the *Réflexions* in the Catalogue of 1781. But the Catalogue has four entries for the
Éphémérides, three entries for a consecutive run of three
full years (36 "tomes") for 1767 to 1769 and another
entry for a half-a-year's run (6 "tomes") for an unspecified
year.[28] The periodical ran from 1767 to 1772. If Smith's
reported holdings were a wholly consecutive run, they
would cover January 1767 to June 1770, and he would have
owned the complete text of the *Réflexions*. If his holdings
were not wholly consecutive, he would have owned at least
two-thirds of the *Réflexions*. This was evidence not available to Cannan, although it was available to Scott. But
even in the case of Cannan, granting that I have the advantage of hindsight, I cannot help feeling that he took
more seriously than was even then justified the evidence
provided by Bonar's *Catalogue* as to what books Smith
had *not* read or even seen.

5. *Adam Smith the Translator of Turgot's* Réflexions?

There are of course other procedures than investigation
of what books a man once owned for inquiring into whether
he had been influenced by specific books, the most obvious,
in the absence of explicit testimony by the man himself,
being to look into the writings of this man to see whether
they contain parallelisms of language or of thought with
the books in question. Cannan found no such parallelisms
in the *Réflexions* and *The Wealth of Nations* which were
clear enough or significant enough to provide any support
for the thesis that Smith had read the *Réflexions* before

---

[28] Yanahaira, *Full Catalogue*, p. 98. Scott says that the Catalogue
lists only three years of the *Éphémérides,* but he must have overlooked
the separate entry for six "tomes" of unspecified date. *ASSP*, p. 125.

publication of *The Wealth of Nations* and he rejected with contempt Thorold Rogers' claim that he had discovered some significant parallelisms.[29]

Shortly before this manuscript was to be sent to the publisher for printing, there reached me a new book, by I. C. Lundberg, dealing solely with the relationships of Adam Smith to Turgot's *Réflexions*.[30] The major thesis of this study is that there are grounds for believing that Adam Smith was (or probably was, or perhaps was, or could have been, these being competing theses of the author) the author of a translation of *Réflexions* into English published in 1793. A secondary thesis is that it can be shown by internal evidence in the form of correspondence between verbal usage in the *Réflexions* and in *The Wealth of Nations* that Smith read the *Réflexions* before the publication of *The Wealth of Nations* in 1776. I will comment first on the latter thesis.

Miss Lundberg claims that Smith makes use of verbal expressions in *The Wealth of Nations* which he could have derived only from a French source, or French sources, and that the correspondence between Smith's usage and that of Turgot in *Réflexions* is so extensive and so close that the *Réflexions* must have been this source. She puts most of her emphasis on Smith's frequent use of the terms "*a* capital" and "capital*s*" (in the plural) on the ground

---

[29] Cannan, ed., Smith, *Lectures,* Editor's Introduction, p. xxiv, note. The most extensive presentation of possible parallelisms between *The Wealth of Nations* and the physiocratic writings I know of is by Emanuel Leser, *Der Begriff des Reichtums bei Adam Smith,* Heidelberg, 1874, pp. 79-92. The *Réflexions* plays only a minor role here, however, and Leser's quotations are largely from editions not readily available to me. I have made no attempt, therefore, to check Leser's conclusions, especially since Cannan did not deny and no one now would deny that there is convincing evidence of physiocratic influence in some portions of *The Wealth of Nations;* in my opinion, for what it is worth, much of this influence was in fact overinfluence and was regrettable.

[30] I. C. Lundberg, *Turgot's Unknown Translator: The Réflexions and Adam Smith,* The Hague, 1964.

that nowhere but in France could Smith have found a precedent for such usage. I understand her also to claim that nowhere but in Turgot's *Réflexions* could Smith have found even in France so systematic or extensive or otherwise significant an adherence to this usage.

> Nothing in the whole of an *Inquiry* is more significant than the term Smith uses hundreds of times, 'a capital.' No other term is more revealing of his French sources, and none, as we shall see, so completely identifies *Réflexions* as its source.[31] . . . For Smith not only uses 'capitals' profusely, but he uses 'a capital' profusely. That he could have had any but a French source for this terminology is out of the question.[32]

It is true that Smith in *The Wealth of Nations* repeatedly uses expressions like "a capital," "an equal capital," "two capitals," "their capitals," and so forth, and I suppose it is also true that English-speaking persons before and after Smith would in similar contexts normally write "capital," "capital equal in amount," and so forth, if they used the word "capital" at all. I also concede the probability that Smith was here influenced by French usage and especially by Turgot's usage in the *Réflexions*. Miss Lundberg's demonstration of the verbal correspondences between *The Wealth of Nations* and the *Réflexions* I accept, therefore, as a significant addition to the case against Cannan's skepticism with respect to Smith's even having seen the *Réflexions* before writing *The Wealth of Nations*, and it uses a type of evidence, verbal similarity as distinguished from similarity of ideas and concepts, which Cannan does not seem to have explored. Miss Lundberg also contributes one new bit of external evidence; she shows that between 1766 and 1776 there was a wider range of ways and forms in which the text of the *Réflexions* could

---

[31] *Ibid.,* p. 60. A turning of the pages of *The Wealth of Nations* suggests that the "hundreds of times" reflects sheer enthusiasm on the part of the author. "Tens of times," however, could easily be confirmed.

[32] *Ibid.,* p. 65.

have reached Smith than had been realized by Cannan and other writers.

I am not persuaded, however, that Smith's usage of the words "capital" and "capitals" was as exclusively French as Miss Lundberg claims, or that even if Smith's source was French it need have been as preeminently *Réflexions* as she claims. There is an extensive literature on the history of the use of the word "capital" (and its linguistic equivalents in other languages than English). But this literature did not examine the distinctions that may have been made in practice between: (1) "capital" as a generic term not taking a plural form; (2) "a capital" used in the singular to designate the holdings of a particular person, firm, or country, or the portion of the aggregate holdings of a particular person, firm, or country which had a specific form or had been given a specific employment (as, for example, "a fixed capital," "a circulating capital," "a capital used in agriculture" or "in commerce," "a foreign capital"); and (3) "capitals," as the plural form of (2); all of these usages are to be found in *The Wealth of Nations*. It has not been possible for me at this time to explore the history of usage along this line, but a hasty inspection of material immediately at hand turned up some evidence that Miss Lundberg's generalizations in this area were too sweeping (especially with respect to the use of the plural form, "capitals").

Cannan, writing in 1929, reports W. R. Scott as finding, with reference to the investments of particular individuals in joint-stock enterprises, that "After 1614 payments [by the companies of dividends to such individuals] expressed in terms of one or more 'capitals' are frequent."[33] Menasseh Ben Israel, in 1655, wrote: "But as for the Jews, they aspire at nothing, but to prefer themselves in their way of

---

[33] Edwin Cannan, *A Review of Economic Theory*, London 1929, p. 137.

merchandize, and so employing their capitals ...."[34] My German dictionary gives *Kapitalien* as the plural of *Kapital,* and the Kress Library *Catalogue* lists: Philip Zorer, *Rechtmessiges ... vorschlag ... wie es nemlich ... in schuldsachen wegen der Kapitalien und deren vertagten interesse bezahlung ...* , Nürnberg, 1638.[35] M. Postlethwayt, writing in 1757, stated that money used to buy government securities was "a dead capital for the sake of a domestic interest money only."[36]

Despite Miss Lundberg's rejection of Cantillon as a possible source of Smith's "a capital," "capitals" usage, on the ground that Cantillon's terms were *"un fond, des fonds, ce fond,"* I find that Cantillon used the plural term, *"capitaux,"* freely.[37]

In some way not clear to me, Miss Lundberg found in the "uncanny similarity" between the usages of the term "capital" by Turgot, by Adam Smith, and by the translator into English of *Réflexions* whose translation was published in 1793,[38] justification for receptivity to the surmise that Adam Smith and the translator in question were one and the same person, and for speculation as to Smith's and Turgot's reasons for keeping this collaboration between them secret.

This investigation, after the first intimation of what Smith's French usage of "capital" might presage, has been pursued in the clear awareness that at the bottom of it lies a secret compact which two men entered upon,

---

[34] *To His Highnesse the Lord Protector of the Commonwealth ... The Humble Addresses of Menasseh Ben Israel,* [London, 1655], reprint in Lucien Wolf, *Menasseh Ben Israels Mission to Oliver Cromwell,* London, 1901, p. 9.

[35] The Kress Library of Business and Economics, *Catalogue Supplement ... Through 1776,* Boston, 1956, p. 17, item S. 266.

[36] M. Postlethwayt, *Great-Britain's True System,* London, 1757, p. 30.

[37] See *Turgot's Unknown Translator,* p. 60, and Richard Cantillon, *Essai sur le Commerce,* [1755], Boston, 1892, pp. 273, 291, 294, 420, 421 (twice), 422 (twice).

[38] See the rear cover of *Turgot's Unknown Translator.*

and which neither one violated or permitted anyone after him to violate. One cannot even presume to say how long this secret has existed. Is it as old as *Réflexions?* Or was it 'sealed' just before Turgot died? What circumstances surrounded the participants, to make concealment essential?

These are fascinating questions, and for none is there at present any answer.[39]

These questions do fascinate me, but only because I cannot find a single sentence in the study, or anything in the translation itself, which offers any warrant for their being asked. As for the translation, not only does the date of its first publication present a formidable obstacle to any hypothesis that Smith was its author, but its only express references to Smith are such as to make it as incredible as can be that Smith could ever have written them.

The translation has two references to Smith. The title-page has on it, in English translation, the following quotation from Condorcet, *Vie de Monsieur Turgot*, 1786. "This Essay [i.e., *Réflexions*] may be considered as the germ of the Treatise on *The Wealth of Nations*, written by the celebrated Smith." In the translator's foreword or introduction, he calls the *Réflexions* "a work, on the foundation of which was formed, one of the most approved and justly celebrated treatises in the English language, Dr. Adam Smith's Essays on *The Wealth of Nations*."[40] I cannot imagine Smith quoting the first passage or composing the second, except on the hypothesis that his purpose was to prevent anyone from thinking that he was in any way involved in the translation.

Once it is conceded that Smith probably had read the *Réflexions* before completing *The Wealth of Nations*, there is nothing mysterious in the close resemblance in the use

---

[39] *Ibid.*, p. 76.
[40] *Reflections on the Formation and Distribution of Wealth*, by M. Turgot. Translated from the French. London, 1793, title-page and p. ii of foreword.

of "capital" terminology between the *Réflexions, The Wealth of Nations,* and a later translation of the *Réflexions* by someone who could have had a copy of *The Wealth of Nations* before him. Nor was anonymity a rare phenomenon in the eighteenth century, especially in so hack-ridden an activity as the translation of French works into English.

The only bit of evidence that I know of that does point to a personal linkage of any kind of Adam Smith to the 1793 translation of *Réflexions,* Miss Lundberg has missed. There is in the library of the Johns Hopkins University a copy of the 1793 translation of the *Réflexions* which is bound together with another work published in 1788 in covers which carry the Adam Smith book label.[41] There is no other well-authenticated record of the discovery of this label on any post-1790 volume. If this evidence does not provide any support to the thesis that Smith himself was the translator, it does at least seem to implicate his ghost.

---

[41] See Claude Jones, "Adam Smith's Library—Some Additions," *Economic History,* IV (1940), 327, and *supra,* pp. 126-127.

V. AN ADAM SMITH CHRONOLOGY

I. *Life*

1723–1737 Born Kirkcaldy (exact date unknown; date of baptism, June 5, 1723, given by Rae, p. 1, as date of birth). (Father, also named Adam Smith, married Margaret Douglas, 1720; died *ca.* Jan. 25, 1723). Attended Burgh School, Kirkcaldy, *ca.* 1730–1737.

1737–1740 Student at University of Glasgow.

1740–1746 Student at Oxford University; Snell Fellowship, Balliol College (£40 per annum) not surrendered until Feb. 1749; nominated to Warner Exhibition (£20 per annum) Nov. 1742. Never in Oxford again after 1746.

1746–1748 Lived in Kirkcaldy with mother.

1748–1751 Lived in Edinburgh; gave several courses of public lectures in belles lettres and "jurisprudence." Half-brother, Hugh Smith, died 1750; Adam Smith his heir. Elected professor of logic, University of Glasgow, Jan. 9, 1751.

1751–1763 Lived in Glasgow, Oct. (?) 1751—Dec. 1763. Elected professor of moral philosophy, April 29, 1752. Rode to York, for reasons of health, and visited Lord Shelburne at Wyecombe, 1759 or 1760. In Inverary for several days to call on Duke of Argyle in 1760. First visit to London, on University business, sometime between Aug. 27 and Oct. 15, 1761. Made Burgess of City of Glasgow, May 3, 1762, LL.D., University of Glasgow, Oct. 1762. Obtained contingent leave of absence, preliminary to resigning, Nov. 8, 1763.

1764–1766 Left Glasgow for London, Jan. 1764, en route to France as tutor of Duke of Buccleuch. Left London for France, late Jan. or early Feb. 1764. Formally resigned professorship at Glasgow, Feb. 14, 1764. In Paris, 10 days, in Toulouse, 18 months; travel in south of France, 2 months; in Geneva, (Oct.–Dec. 1765), 2 months; in Paris again (Dec. 1765–Oct. 1766), 10 months.

1766–1767 In London, working with Charles Townshend, about six months, Oct. 1766–spring 1767. Elected Fellow Royal Society (London), May 21, 1767 (admitted, May 27, 1773).

1767–1773 In Kirkcaldy, living with mother, working on *The Wealth of Nations,* May 1767–April 1773. Received Freedom of City, Edinburgh, June 1770.

1773–1776 In London, April 1773–*ca.* May 1776, working on *The Wealth of Nations* (published March 9, 1776).

1776 In Kirkcaldy, *ca.* May to December, with brief stop in Edinburgh to stay with David Hume (who died Aug. 27, 1776).

1777 In London, Jan.–*ca.* Nov.

1777–1778 In Edinburgh and Kirkcaldy, Nov. 1777–Jan. 1778. Appointed a Commissioner of Customs for Scotland (£500 a year) and a Commissioner of the Salt Duties for Scotland (£100 a year) Jan. 1778.

1778–1790 In Edinburgh, living in his own house, Panmure House, with his mother, his cousin, Jane (Jean, Janet) Douglas, and the son of a nephew of his mother, David Douglas, later Lord Reston, whom he was to make his sole heir. In London for several months in 1782, when he attended dinners of "the Club" ("Samuel Johnson's Club"). Participated in founding of Royal Society of Edinburgh, 1783. Accompanied Edward Burke to Glasgow, to attend his installation as Rector of the University, April, 1784. Mother (Margaret Douglas Smith) died, May 23, 1784. In London, to consult the physician, John Hunter, April–May, 1786. In London, *ca.* March–Aug. 1787, on leave; consulted by William Pitt on tax matters. Rector of Glasgow University,

1787–1789. His cousin, Jane Douglas, died, 1788. Adam Smith died, July 17, 1790.

II. *Publications*
(first appearances in print only; correspondence published posthumously not included)

1. "A Dictionary of the English Language, by Samuel Johnson," *The Edinburgh Review,* No. 1, Appendix, Jan. 1755 (anonymous).

2. "A Letter to the Authors of the Edinburgh Review," *ibid.,* No. 2, July, 1755 (anonymous).

3. *The Theory of Moral Sentiments,* London, 1759.

4. "Considerations concerning the First Formation of Languages, and the Different Genius of Original and Compounded Languages," *The Philological Miscellany,* I (1761), 440–479.

5. *An Inquiry into the Nature and Causes of the Wealth of Nations,* London, (March 9) 1776.

6. A letter to William Strahan concerning the death of David Hume, Nov. 9, 1776, *Scots Magazine,* XXXIX (Jan. 1777), 5–7.

7. *Essays on Philosophical Subjects,* Joseph Black and James Hutton, eds., Edinburgh, 1795.

8. *Lectures on Justice, Police, Revenue and Arms delivered in the University of Glasgow reported by a Student in 1763,* Edwin Cannan, ed., Oxford, 1896.

9. (Memoir to Lord North on the American Revolution), G. H. Guttridge, ed., "Adam Smith on the American Revolution: an Unpublished Memorial," *American Historical Review,* xxxviii (1933), 714–720.

10. "An Early Draft of Part of the Wealth of Nations," W. R. Scott, ed., in W. R. Scott, *Adam Smith as Student and Professor,* Glasgow, 1937, pp. 322–356.

11. *Lectures on Rhetoric and Belles Lettres delivered in the University of Glasgow . . . 1762–63,* John M. Lothian, ed., London and Edinburgh, 1963.

INDEX OF NAMES OF PERSONS

(No entries are made for John Rae and Adam Smith)

143

Life of Adam Smith

BY

JOHN RAE

London

MACMILLAN & CO.

AND NEW YORK

1895

PREFACE

THE fullest account we possess of the life of Adam Smith
is still the memoir which Dugald Stewart read to the
Royal Society of Edinburgh on two evenings of the
winter of 1793, and which he subsequently published
as a separate work, with many additional illustrative notes,
in 1810. Later biographers have made few, if any, fresh
contributions to the subject. But in the century that has
elapsed since Stewart wrote, many particulars about Smith
and a number of his letters have incidentally and by very
scattered channels found their way into print. It will be
allowed to be generally desirable, in view of the continued
if not even increasing importance of Smith, to obtain as
complete a view of his career and work as it is still in our
power to recover; and it appeared not unlikely that some
useful contribution to this end might result if all those particulars and letters to which I have alluded were collected
together, and if they were supplemented by such unpublished letters and information as it still remained possible to
procure. In this last part of my task I have been greatly
assisted by the Senatus of the University of Glasgow,
who have most kindly supplied me with an extract of
every passage in the College records bearing on Smith;
by the Council of the Royal Society of Edinburgh, who
have granted me every facility for using the *Hume Corre-*

spondence, which is in their custody; and by the Senatus of the University of Edinburgh for a similar courtesy with regard to the *Carlyle Correspondence* and the David Laing MSS. in their library. I am also deeply indebted, for the use of unpublished letters or for the supply of special information, to the Duke of Buccleuch, the Marquis of Lansdowne, Professor R. O. Cunningham of Queen's College, Belfast, Mr. Alfred Morrison of Fonthill, Mr. F. Barker of Brook Green, and Mr. W. Skinner, W.S., late Town Clerk of Edinburgh.

CONTENTS

CHAPTER I

EARLY DAYS AT KIRKCALDY

CHAPTER II

STUDENT AT GLASGOW COLLEGE

CHAPTER III

AT OXFORD

CHAPTER IV

LECTURER AT EDINBURGH

CHAPTER V

PROFESSOR AT GLASGOW

CHAPTER VI

THE COLLEGE ADMINISTRATOR

CHAPTER VII

AMONG GLASGOW FOLK

CHAPTER VIII

EDINBURGH ACTIVITIES

CHAPTER IX

THE "THEORY OF MORAL SENTIMENTS"

CHAPTER X

FIRST VISIT TO LONDON

CHAPTER XI

LAST YEAR IN GLASGOW

CHAPTER XII

TOULOUSE

CHAPTER XIII

GENEVA

CHAPTER XIV

PARIS

CHAPTER XV

LONDON

CHAPTER XVI

KIRKCALDY

CHAPTER XVII

LONDON

CHAPTER XXII

VARIOUS CORRESPONDENCE IN 1778

CHAPTER XXIII

FREE TRADE FOR IRELAND

CHAPTER XXIV

THE "WEALTH OF NATIONS" ABROAD AND AT HOME

CHAPTER XXV

SMITH INTERVIEWED

CHAPTER XXVI

THE AMERICAN QUESTION AND OTHER POLITICS

CHAPTER XXXI

REVISION OF THE "THEORY"

CHAPTER XXXII

LAST DAYS

CHAPTER I

ADAM SMITH was born at Kirkcaldy, in the county of Fife, Scotland, on the 5th of June 1723. He was the son of Adam Smith, Writer to the Signet, Judge Advocate for Scotland and Comptroller of the Customs in the Kirkcaldy district, by Margaret, daughter of John Douglas of Strathendry, a considerable landed proprietor in the same county.

Of his father little is known. He was a native of Aberdeen, and his people must have been in a position to make interest in influential quarters, for we find him immediately after his admission to the Society of Writers to the Signet in 1707, appointed to the newly-established office of Judge Advocate for Scotland, and in the following year to the post of Private Secretary to the Scotch Minister, the Earl of Loudon. When he lost this post in consequence of Lord Loudon's retirement from office in 1713, he was provided for with the Comptrollership of Customs at Kirkcaldy, which he continued to hold, along with the Judge Advocateship, till his premature death in 1723. The Earl of Loudon having been a zealous Whig and Presbyterian, it is perhaps legitimate to infer that his secretary must have been the same, and from the public appointments he held we may further gather that he was a man of parts. The office of Judge Advocate for Scotland, which was founded at the Union, and which he was the first to fill, was a position of considerable responsibility, and was occupied after him by men, some of them of great distinction. Alexander Fraser Tytler, the historian, for example, was Judge Advocate till he went to the bench as Lord Woodhouselee. The Judge Advocate was clerk and legal adviser to the Courts Martial, but as military trials were not frequent in Scotland, the duties of this office took up but a minor share of the elder Smith's time. His chief business, at least for the last ten years of his life, was his work in the Custom-house, for though he was bred a Writer to the Signet—that is, a solicitor privileged to practise before the Supreme Court—he never seems to have actually practised that profession. A local collectorship or controllership of the Customs was in itself a more important administrative office at that period, when duties were levied on twelve hundred articles, than it is now, when duties are levied on twelve only, and it was much sought after for the younger, or even the elder, sons of the gentry. The very place held by Smith's father at Kirkcaldy was held for many years after his day by a Scotch baronet, Sir Michael Balfour. The salary was not high. Adam Smith began in 1713 with £30 a year, and had only £40 when he died in 1723, but then the perquisites of those offices in the Customs were usually twice or thrice the salary, as we know from the *Wealth of Nations* itself (Book V. chap. ii.). Smith had a cousin, a third Adam Smith, who was in 1754 Collector of Customs at Alloa with a salary of £60 a year, and who writes his cousin, in connection with a negotiation the latter was conducting on behalf of a friend for the purchase of the office, that the place was worth £200 a year, and that he would not sell it for less than ten years' purchase.[1]

Smith's father died in the spring of 1723, a few months before his famous son was born. Some doubt has been cast upon this fact by an announcement quoted by Presi-

[1] Original letter in possession of Professor Cunningham, Belfast.

dent M'Cosh, in his *Scottish Philosophy*, from the Scots
Magazine of 1740, of the promotion of Adam Smith,
Comptroller of the Customs, Kirkcaldy, to be Inspector-
General of the Outports.   But conclusive evidence exists
of the date of the death of Smith's father in a receipt for
his funeral expenses, which is in the possession of Professor
Cunningham, and which, as a curious illustration of the
habits of the time, I subjoin in a note below.[1]   The promotion of 1740 is the promotion not of Smith's father but
of his cousin, whom I have just had occasion to mention,
and who appears from Chamberlayne's *Notitia Angliæ*
to have been Comptroller of the Customs at Kirkcaldy

---

[1] A COUNT OF MONEY DEBURSED ABOUT MR. SMITH'S FUNERALL

	£	s	d
To eight bottles of ale	£0	12	0
To butter and eggs to the seed cake	1	4	0
To four bottles of ale	0	6	0
To three pounds fresh butter for bread . . .	0	14	0
To one pound small candles	0	4	6
To two pounds bisquet	1	4	0
To sixteen bottles of ale	1	4	0
To money sent to Edinr. for bisquet, stockings, and necessars	25	4	0
To three expresses to Edinburgh	2	14	0
To a pair of murning shous to Hugh	1	10	0
To horse hyre with the wine from Kinghorn . . .	0	15	0
To the poor	3	6	0
To six bottles and eight pints of ale to the beadels, etc. .	1	10	4
To pipes and tobacco	0	4	0
To four pints of ale to the workmen	0	12	8
To the postage of three letters	0	6	0
To making the grave	3	0	0
To caring the mourning letters thro' the town and country .	1	10	0
To the mort cloth	3	12	0
To Robert Martin for his services	1	4	0
To Deacon Lessels for the coffin and ironwork . .	28	4	0
To Deacon Sloan for lifting the stone	1	11	0

Summa is £80 16 6

On the back is the docquet, "Account of funeral charges, Mr. Adam
Smith, 1723," and the formal receipt as follows : "Kirkaldie, Apl. 24,
1723.   Received from Mr. James of Dunekier eighty pund sexteen
shilling six penes Scots in full of the within account depussd by
me.　　　　　　　　　　　　　　　　　　　MARGRATE DOUGLASS."

"Mr. James of Dunekier" is Mr. James Oswald of Dunnikier, the
father of Smith's friend, the statesman of the same name, and he had
apparently as a friend of the family undertaken the duty of looking
after the funeral arrangements.

from about 1734 till somewhere before 1741. In the *Notitia Angliæ* for 1741 the name of Adam Smith ceases to appear as Comptroller in Kirkcaldy, and appears for the first time as Inspector-General of the Outports, exactly in accordance with the intimation quoted by Dr. M'Cosh. It is curious that Smith, who was to do so much to sweep away the whole system of the Customs, should have been so closely connected with that branch of administration. His father, his only known relation on his father's side, and himself, were all officials in the Scotch Customs.

On the mother's side his kindred were much connected with the army. His uncle, Robert Douglas of Strathendry, and three of his uncle's sons were military officers, and so was his cousin, Captain Skene, the laird of the neighbouring estate of Pitlour. Colonel Patrick Ross, a distinguished officer of the times, was also a relation, but on which side I do not know. His mother herself was from first to last the heart of Smith's life. He being an only child, and she an only parent, they had been all in all to one another during his infancy and boyhood, and after he was full of years and honours her presence was the same shelter to him as it was when a boy. His friends often spoke of the beautiful affection and worship with which he cherished her. One who knew him well for the last thirty years of his life, and was very probably at one time a boarder in his house, the clever and bustling Earl of Buchan, elder brother of Lord Chancellor Erskine, says the principal avenue to Smith's heart always was by his mother. He was a delicate child, and afflicted even in childhood with those fits of absence and that habit of speaking to himself which he carried all through life. Of his infancy only one incident has come down to us. In his fourth year, while on a visit to his grandfather's house at Strathendry on the banks of the Leven, the child was stolen by a passing band of gipsies, and for a time could not be found. But presently a gentleman arrived who had met a gipsy woman a few miles down the road carrying a child that was crying piteously. Scouts were immediately despatched in the direction indicated, and they came upon the woman in Leslie wood. As soon as she saw them she threw her burden down and escaped, and the child was brought back to his mother. He would have made, I fear, a poor gipsy. As he grew up in boyhood his health became stronger, and he was in due time sent to the Burgh School of Kirkcaldy.

The Burgh School of Kirkcaldy was one of the best secondary schools of Scotland at that period, and its principal master, Mr. David Millar, had the name of being one of the best schoolmasters of his day. When Smith first went to school we cannot say, but it seems probable that he began Latin in 1733, for *Eutropius* is the class-book of a beginner in Latin, and the *Eutropius* which Smith used as a class-book still exists, and contains his signature with the date of that year.[1] As he left school in 1737, he thus had at least four years' training in the classics before he proceeded to the University. Millar, his classical master, had adventured in literature. He wrote a play, and his pupils used to act it. Acting plays was in those days a common exercise in the higher schools of Scotland. The presbyteries often frowned, and tried their best to stop the practice, but the town councils, which had the management of these schools, resented the dictation of the presbyteries, and gave the drama not only the support of their personal presence at the performances, but sometimes built a special stage and auditorium for the purpose. Sir James Steuart, the economist, played the king in *Henry the Fourth* when he was a boy at the school of North Berwick in 1735. The pupils of Dalkeith School, where the historian Robertson was educated, played *Julius Cæsar* in 1734. In the same year the boys of Perth Grammar School played *Cato* in the teeth of an explicit presbyterial anathema, and again

[1] In possession of Professor Cunningham.

in the same year—in the month of August—the boys of
the Burgh School of Kirkcaldy, which Smith was at the
time attending, enacted the piece their master had written.
It bore the rather unromantic and uninviting title of
" A Royal Council for Advice, or the Regular Education
of Boys the Foundation of all other Improvements."
The *dramatis personæ* were first the master and twelve
ordinary members of the council, who sat gravely round
a table like senators, and next a crowd of suitors, standing
at a little distance off, who sent representatives to the
table one by one to state their grievances—first a tradesman, then a farmer, then a country gentleman, then a
schoolmaster, a nobleman, and so on. Each of them
received advice from the council in turn, and then, last of
all, a gentleman came forward, who complimented the
council on the successful completion of their day's labours.[1]
Smith would no doubt have been present at this performance, but whether he played an active part either as
councillor or as spokesman for any class of petitioners,
or merely stood in the crowd of suitors, a silent super,
cannot now be guessed.

Among those young actors at this little provincial
school were several besides Smith himself who were to
play important and even distinguished parts afterwards on
the great stage of the world. James Oswald—the Right
Hon. James Oswald, Treasurer of the Navy—who is sometimes said to have been one of Smith's schoolfellows, could
not have been so, as he was eight years Smith's senior, but
his younger brother John, subsequently Bishop of Raphoe,
doubtless was ; and so was Robert Adam, the celebrated
architect, who built the London Adelphi, Portland Place,
and—probably his finest work—Edinburgh University.
Though James Oswald was not at school with Smith, he
was one of his intimate home friends from the first.
The Dunnikier family lived in the town, and stood on such a
footing of intimacy with the Smiths that, as we have seen,

[1] Grant's *Burgh Schools of Scotland*, p. 414.

it was " Mr. James of Dunnikier "—the father of the
James Oswald now in question—who undertook on behalf
of Mrs. Smith the arrangements for her husband's funeral ;
and the friendship of James Oswald, as will presently
appear, was, after the affection of his mother, the best
thing Smith carried into life with him from Kirkcaldy.
The Adam family also lived in the town, though the
father was a leading Scotch architect—King's Mason for
Scotland, in fact—and was proprietor of a fair estate not far
away ; and the four brothers Adam were the familiars of
Smith's early years.   They continued to be among his
familiars to the last.   Another of his school companions
who played a creditable part in his time was John Drysdale,
the minister's son, who became one of the ministers of
Edinburgh, doctor of divinity, chaplain to the king,
leader of an ecclesiastical party—of the Moderates in
succession to Robertson—twice Moderator of the General
Assembly, though in his case, as in so many others, the path
of professional success has led but to oblivion.   Still he
deserves mention here, because, as his son-in-law, Professor
Dalzel tells us, he and Smith were much together again
in their later Edinburgh days, and there was none of all
Smith's numerous friends whom he liked better or spoke
of with greater tenderness than Drysdale.[1]   Drysdale's
wife was a sister of the brothers Adam, and Robert Adam
stayed with Drysdale on his visits to Edinburgh.

A small town like Kirkcaldy — it had then only
1500 inhabitants—is a not unfavourable observatory for
beginning one's knowledge of the world.   It has more
sorts and conditions of men to exhibit than a rural district
can furnish, and it exhibits each more completely in all
their ways, pursuits, troubles, characters, than can possibly
be done in a city.   Smith, who, spite of his absence of
mind, was always an excellent observer, would grow up
in the knowledge of all about everybody in that little
place, from the " Lady Dunnikier," the great lady of the

---

[1] Drysdale's *Sermons*, Preface by Dalzel.

town, to its poor colliers and salters who were still
bondsmen.   Kirkcaldy, too, had its shippers trading with
the Baltic, its customs officers, with many a good smuggling
story, and it had a nailery or two, which Smith is said to
have been fond of visiting as a boy, and to have acquired
in them his first rough idea of the value of division of
labour.[1]   However that may be, Smith does draw some
of his illustrations of the division of labour from that
particular business, which would necessarily be very
familiar to his. mind, and it may have been in Kirkcaldy
that he found the nailers paid their wages in nails, and using
these nails afterwards as a currency in making their purchases from the shopkeepers.[2]

At school Smith was marked for his studious disposition, his love of reading, and his power of memory; and by
the age of fourteen he had advanced sufficiently in classics
and mathematics to be sent to Glasgow College, with a
view to obtaining a Snell exhibition to Oxford.

[1] Campbell, *Journey from Edinburgh through North Britain*, 1802,
ii. p. 49.
[2] *Wealth of Nations*, Book I. chap. iv.

CHAPTER II

SMITH entered Glasgow College in 1737, no doubt in
October, when the session began, and he remained there
till the spring of 1740.   The arts curriculum at that time
extended over five sessions, so that Smith did not complete
the course required for a degree.   In the three sessions
he attended he would go through the classes of Latin,
Greek, Mathematics, and Moral Philosophy, and have
thus listened to the lectures of the three eminent teachers
who were then drawing students to this little western
College from the most distant quarters, and keeping its
courts alive with a remarkable intellectual activity.   Dr. A.
Carlyle, who came to Glasgow College for his divinity
classes after he had finished his arts course at Edinburgh,
says he found a spirit of inquiry and a zeal for learning
abroad among the students of Glasgow which he remembered nothing like among the students of Edinburgh.
This intellectual awakening was the result mainly of the
teaching of three professors—Alexander Dunlop, Professor
of Greek, a man of fine scholarship and taste, and an
unusually engaging method of instruction ; Robert Simson,
the professor of Mathematics, an original if eccentric
genius, who enjoyed a European reputation as the restorer
of the geometry of the ancients ; and above all, Francis
Hutcheson, a thinker of great original power, and an unrivalled academic lecturer.

Smith would doubtless improve his Greek to some extent under Dunlop, though from all we know of the work of that class, he could not be carried very far there. Dunlop spent most of his first year teaching the elements of Greek grammar with Verney's Grammar as his text-book, and reading a little of one or two easy authors as the session advanced. Most of the students entered his class so absolutely ignorant of Greek that he was obliged to read a Latin classic with them for the first three months till they learnt enough of the Greek grammar to read a Greek one. In the second session they were able to accompany him through some of the principal Greek classics, but the time was obviously too short for great things. Smith, however, appears at this time to have shown a marked predilection for mathematics. Dugald Stewart's father, Professor Matthew Stewart of Edinburgh, was a class-fellow of Smith's at Glasgow; and Dugald Stewart has heard his father reminding Smith of a "geometrical problem of considerable difficulty by which he was occupied at the time when their acquaintance commenced, and which had been proposed to him as an exercise by the celebrated Dr. Simson." The only other fellow-student of his at Glasgow of whom we have any knowledge is Dr. Maclaine, the translator of Mosheim, and author of several theological works; and Dr. Maclaine informed Dugald Stewart, in private conversation, of Smith's fondness for mathematics in those early days. For his mathematical professor, Robert Simson himself, Smith always retained the profoundest veneration, and one of the last things he ever wrote—a passage he inserted in the new edition of his *Theory of Moral Sentiments*, published immediately before his death in 1790—contains a high tribute to the gifts and character of that famous man. In this passage Smith seeks to illustrate a favourite proposition of his, that men of science are much less sensitive to public criticism and much more indifferent to unpopularity or neglect than either poets or painters, because the

excellence of their work admits of easy and satisfactory
demonstration, whereas the excellence of the poet's work
or the painter's depends on a judgment of taste which is
more uncertain; and he points to Robert Simson as a
signal example of the truth of that proposition. "Mathematicians," he says, "who may have the most perfect
assurance of the truth and of the importance of their discoveries, are frequently very indifferent about the reception which they may meet with from the public. The
two greatest mathematicians that I ever have had the
honour to be known to, and I believe the two greatest
that have lived in my time, Dr. Robert Simson of Glasgow
and Dr. Matthew Stewart of Edinburgh, never seemed to
feel even the slightest uneasiness from the neglect with
which the ignorance of the public received some of their
most valuable works." [1]   And it ought to be remembered
that when Smith wrote thus of Simson he had been long
intimate with D'Alembert.

But while Smith improved his Greek under Dunlop,
and acquired a distinct ardour for mathematics under
the inspiring instructions of Simson, the most powerful
and enduring influence he came under at Glasgow was undoubtedly that of Hutcheson—"the never-to-be-forgotten
Hutcheson," as he styled him half a century later in recalling
his obligations to his old College on the occasion of his
election to the Rectorship. No other man, indeed, whether
teacher or writer, did so much to awaken Smith's mind or
give a bent to his ideas. He is sometimes considered a
disciple of Hume and sometimes considered a disciple
of Quesnay; if he was any man's disciple, he was
Hutcheson's. Hutcheson was exactly the stamp of man
fitted to stir and mould the thought of the young. He
was, in the first place, one of the most impressive lecturers
that ever spoke from an academic chair. Dugald Stewart,
who knew many of his pupils, states that every one of
them told of the extraordinary impression his lectures used

[1] *Theory of Moral Sentiments*, i. 313.

to make on their hearers. He was the first professor in Glasgow to give up lecturing in Latin and speak to his audience in their own tongue, and he spoke without notes and with the greatest freedom and animation. Nor was it only his eloquence, but his ideas themselves were rousing. Whatever he touched upon, he treated, as we may still perceive from his writings, with a certain freshness and decided originality which must have provoked the dullest to some reflection, and in a bracing spirit of intellectual liberty which it was strength and life for the young mind to breathe. He was not long in Glasgow, accordingly, till he was bitterly attacked by the older generation outside the walls of the College as a " new light " fraught with dangers to all accepted beliefs, and at the same time worshipped like an idol by the younger generation inside the walls, who were thankful for the light he brought them, and had no quarrel with it for being new. His immediate predecessor in that chair, Professor Gershom Carmichael, the reputed father of the Scottish Philosophy, was still a Puritan of the Puritans, wrapt in a gloomy Calvinism, and desponding after signs that would never come. But Hutcheson belonged to a new era, which had turned to the light of nature for guidance, and had discovered by it the good and benevolent Deity of the eighteenth century, who lived only for human welfare, and whose will was not to be known from mysterious signs and providences, but from a broad consideration of the greater good of mankind—" the greatest happiness of the greatest number." Hutcheson was the original author of that famous phrase.

All this was anathema to the exponents of the prevailing theology with which, indeed, it seemed only too surely to dispense ; and in Smith's first year at Glasgow the local Presbytery set the whole University in a ferment by prosecuting Hutcheson for teaching to his students, in contravention of his subscription to the Westminster Confession, the following two false and dangerous doctrines : 1st, that the standard of moral goodness was the promotion of the happiness of others ;, and 2nd, that we could have a knowledge of good and evil without and prior to a know- ledge of God.   This trial of course excited the pro- foundest feeling among the students, and they actually made a formal appearance before the Presbytery, and defended their hero zealously both by word and writing. Smith, being only a bajan—a first year's student—would play no leading part in these proceedings, but he could not have lived in the thick of them unmoved, and he certainly—either then or afterwards, when he entered Hutcheson's class and listened to his lectures on natural theology, or perhaps attended his private class on the Sundays for special theological study—adopted the religious optimism of Hutcheson for his own creed, and continued under its influence to the last of his days.

In politics also Hutcheson's lectures exercised im- portant practical influence on the general opinion of his students.   The principles of religious and political liberty were then so imperfectly comprehended and so little accepted that their advocacy was still something of a new light, and we are informed by one of Hutcheson's leading colleagues, Principal Leechman, that none of his lectures made a deeper or wider impression than his exposition of those principles, and that very few of his pupils left his hands without being imbued with some of the same love of liberty which animated their master.   Smith was no exception, and that deep strong love of all reasonable liberty which characterised him must have been, if not first kindled, at any rate quickened by his contact with Hutcheson.

Interesting traces of more specific influence remain. Dugald Stewart seems to have heard Smith himself admit that it was Hutcheson in his lectures that suggested to him the particular theory of the right of property which he used to teach in his own unpublished lectures on jurisprudence, and which founded the right of property on the general sympathy of mankind with the reasonable expectation of the occupant to enjoy unmolested the object which he had acquired or discovered.[1] But it is most probable that his whole theory of moral sentiments was suggested by the lectures of Hutcheson, perhaps the germs of it even when he was passing through the class. For Hutcheson in the course of his lectures expressly raises and discusses the question, Can we reduce our moral sentiments to sympathy? He answered the question himself in the negative, on the ground that we often approve of the actions of people with whom we have no sympathy, our enemies for example, and his pupil's contribution to the discussion was an ingenious attempt to surmount that objection by the theory of sympathy with an impartial spectator.

Hutcheson's name occurs in no history of political economy, but he lectured systematically on that subject— as Smith himself subsequently did—as a branch of his course on natural jurisprudence, a discussion of contracts requiring him to examine the principles of value, interest, currency, etc., and these lectures, though fragmentary, are remarkable for showing a grasp of economic questions before his time, and presenting, with a clear view of their importance, some of Smith's most characteristic positions. He is free from the then prevailing mercantilist fallacies about money. His remarks on value contain what reads like a first draft of Smith's famous passage on value in use and value in exchange. Like Smith, he holds labour to be the great source of wealth and the true measure of value, and declares every man to have the natural right to use his faculties according to his own pleasure for his own ends in any work or recreation that inflicts no injury on the persons or property of others, except when the public interests may otherwise require. This is just Smith's system of natural liberty in matters industrial, with a general limitation in the public interest such as Smith also approves. In the practical enforcement

[1] Stewart's *Works*, vii. 263.

of this limitation he would impose some particular restraints which Smith might not, but, on the other hand, he would abolish other particular restraints which Smith, and even Quesnay, would still retain, *e.g.* the fixing of interest by law. His doctrine was essentially the doctrine of industrial liberty with which Smith's name is identified, and in view of the claims set up on behalf of the French Physiocrats that Smith learnt that doctrine in their school, it is right to remember that he was brought into contact with it in Hutcheson's class-room at Glasgow some twenty years before any of the Physiocrats had written a line on the subject, and that the very first ideas on economic subjects which were presented to his mind contained in germ—and in very active and sufficient germ—the very doctrines about liberty, labour, and value on which his whole system was afterwards built.

Though Smith was a mere lad of sixteen at that time, his mind had already, under Hutcheson's stimulating instructions, begun to work effectively on the ideas lodged in it and to follow out their suggestions in his own thought. Hutcheson seems to have recognised his quality, and brought him, young though he was, under the personal notice of David Hume. There is a letter written by Hume to Hutcheson on the 4th of March 1740 which is not indeed without its difficulties, but if, as Mr. Burton thinks, the Mr. Smith mentioned in it be the economist, it would appear as if Smith had, while attending Hutcheson's class,—whether as a class exercise or otherwise,— written an abstract of Hume's *Treatise of Human Nature*, then recently published, that Smith's abstract was to be sent to some periodical for publication, and that Hume was so pleased with it that he presented its young author with a copy of his own work. " My bookseller," Hume writes, " has sent to Mr. Smith a copy of my book, which I hope he has received as well as your letter. I have not yet heard what he has done with the abstract. Perhaps you have. I have got it printed in London, but not in the *Works of*

the Learned, there having been an article with regard to
my book somewhat abusive before I sent up the abstract."
If the Mr. Smith of this letter is Adam Smith, then he
must have been away from Glasgow at that time, for
Hutcheson was communicating with him by letter, but
that may possibly be explained by the circumstance that
he had been appointed to one of the Snell exhibitions at
Balliol College, Oxford, and might have gone home to
Kirkcaldy to make preparations for residence at the
English University, though he did not actually set out for
it till June.

These Snell exhibitions, which were practically in the
gift of the Glasgow professors, were naturally the prize of
the best student of Glasgow College at the time they fell
vacant, and they have been held in the course of the two
centuries of their existence by many distinguished men,
including Sir William Hamilton and Lockhart, Archbishop Tait and Lord President Inglis. They were
originally founded by an old Glasgow student, a strong
Episcopalian, for the purpose of educating Scotchmen for
the service of the Episcopal Church in Scotland. By
the terms of his will the holders were even to be bound
under penalty of £500 " to enter holy orders and return
to serve the Church in Scotland," and it has sometimes
been concluded from that circumstance that Smith must
have accepted the Snell exhibition with a view to the Episcopal ministry. But the original purpose of the founder
was frustrated by the Revolution settlement, which made
" the Church in Scotland " Presbyterian, and left scarce any
Episcopal remnant to serve, and the original condition has
never been practically enforced. The last attempt to impose
it was made during Smith's own tenure of the exhibition,
and failed. In the year 1744 the Vice-Chancellor and
the heads of Colleges at Oxford raised a process in the
Court of Chancery for compelling the Snell exhibitioners
" to submit and conform to the doctrines and discipline of
the Church of England, and to enter into holy orders

when capable thereof by the canons of the Church of England"; but the Court of Chancery refused to interfere, and the exhibitioners were left entirely free to choose their sect, their profession, and their country, as seemed best to themselves. It may be added that in Smith's time the Snell foundation yielded five exhibitions of £40 a year each, tenable for eleven years.

Of Smith's friends among his fellow-students at Glasgow, no names have been preserved for us except those already mentioned, Professor Matthew Stewart, and Dr. Maclaine, the embassy chaplain at the Hague. He continued on a footing of great intimacy with Stewart, whom, as we have seen, he considered to be, after Robert Simson, the greatest mathematician of his time, and he seems to have enjoyed occasional opportunities of renewing his acquaintance with Dr. Maclaine, though the opportunities could not have been frequent, as Maclaine spent his whole active life abroad as English chaplain at the Hague. But the remark made by Smith to Dr. William Thompson, a historical writer of the last century, seems to imply his having had some intercourse with his early friend. Thompson, Dr. Watson the historian of Philip II., and Dr. Maclaine, seem all to have been writing the history of the Peace of Utrecht, and Smith, who knew all three, said Watson was much afraid of Maclaine, and Maclaine was just as much afraid of Watson, but he could have told them of one they had much more cause to fear, and that was Thompson himself.

CHAPTER III

SMITH left Scotland for Oxford in June 1740, riding the whole way on horseback, and, as he told Samuel Rogers many years afterwards, being much struck from the moment he crossed the Border with the richness of the country he was entering, and the great superiority of its agriculture over that of his own country. Scotch agriculture was not born in 1740, even in the Lothians; the face of the country everywhere was very bare and waste, and, as he was rather pointedly reminded on the day of his arrival at Oxford, even its cattle were still lean and poor, compared with the fat oxen of England. Among the stories told of his absence of mind is one he is said by a writer in the *Monthly Review* to have been fond of relating himself whenever a particular joint appeared on his own table. The first day he dined in the hall at Balliol he fell into a reverie at table and for a time forgot his meal, whereupon the servitor roused him to attention, telling him he had better fall to, because he had never seen such a piece of beef in Scotland as the joint then before him. His nationality, as will presently appear, occasioned him worse trouble at Oxford than this good-natured gibe.

He matriculated at the University on the 7th of July. Professor Thorold Rogers, who has collected the few particulars that can now be learned of Smith's residence at Oxford from official records, gives us the matriculation entry : " Adamus Smith e Coll. Ball., Gen. Fil. Jul. 7mo 1740," [1] and mentions that it is written in a round school-boy hand—a style of hand, we may add, which Smith retained to the last. He has himself said that literary composition never grew easier to him with experience ; neither apparently did handwriting. His letters are all written in the same big round characters, connected together manifestly by a slow, difficult, deliberate process.

He remained at Oxford till the 15th of August 1746 ; after that day his name appears no longer in the Buttery Books of the College ; but up till that day he resided at Oxford continuously from the time of his matriculation. He did not leave between terms, and was thus six years on end away from home. A journey to Scotland was in those days a serious and expensive undertaking ; it would have taken more than half Smith's exhibition of £40 to pay for the posting alone of a trip to Kirkcaldy and back. When Professor Rouet of Glasgow was sent up to London a few years later to push on the tedious twenty years' lawsuit between Glasgow College and Balliol about the Snell exhibitions, the single journey cost him £11 : 15s., exclusive of personal expenses, for which he was allowed 6s. 8d. a day.[2] Now Smith out of his £40 a year had to pay about £30 for his food ; Mr. Rogers mentions that his first quarter's maintenance came to £7 : 5s., about the usual cost of living, he adds, at Oxford at that period. Then the tutors, though they seem to have ceased to do any tutoring, still took their fees of 20s. a quarter all the same, and Smith's remaining £5 would be little enough to meet other items of necessary expenditure. It appears from Salmon's *Present State of the Universities*, published in 1744, during Smith's residence at Oxford, that an Oxford education then cost £32 a year as a minimum, but that there was scarce a commoner in the University who spent less than £60.

[1] Rogers's edition of the *Wealth of Nations*, I. vii.
[2] Laing MSS., Edinburgh University.

Smith's name does not appear in Bliss's list of Oxford graduates, and although in Mr. Foster's recent *Alumni Oxonienses* other particulars are given about him, no mention is made of his graduation ; but Professor Rogers has discovered evidence in the Buttery Books of Balliol which seems conclusively to prove that Smith actually took the degree of B.A., whatever may be the explanation of the apparent omission of his name from the official graduation records. In those Buttery Books he is always styled Dominus from and after the week ending 13th April 1744. Now Dominus was the usual designation of a B.A., and in April 1744 Smith would have kept the sixteen terms that were then, we may say, the only qualification practically necessary for that degree. He had possibly omitted some step requisite for the formal completion of the graduation.

Smith's residence at Oxford fell in a time when learning lay there under a long and almost total eclipse. This dark time seems to have lasted most of that century. Crousaz visited Oxford about the beginning of the century and found the dons as ignorant of the new philosophy as the savages of the South Sea. Bishop Butler came there as a student twenty years afterwards, and could get nothing to satisfy his young thirst for knowledge except " frivolous lectures " and " unintelligible disputations." A generation later he could not even have got that ; for Smith tells us in the *Wealth of Nations* that the lecturers had then given up all pretence of lecturing, and a foreign traveller, who describes a public disputation he attended at Oxford in 1788, says the Præses Respondent and three Opponents all sat consuming the statutory time in profound silence, absorbed in the novel of the hour. Gibbon, who resided there not long after Smith, tells that his tutor neither gave nor sought to give him more than one lesson, and that the conversation of the common-room, to which as a gentleman commoner he was privileged to listen, never touched any point of literature or scholarship, but "stagnated

in a round of College business, Tory politics, personal
anecdotes, and private scandal." Bentham, a few years
after Gibbon, has the same tale to tell ; it was absolutely
impossible to learn anything at Oxford, and the years he
spent there were the most barren and unprofitable of his
life. Smith's own account of the English universities in
the *Wealth of Nations*, though only published in 1776,
was substantially true of Oxford during his residence there
thirty years before. Every word of it is endorsed by
Gibbon as the word of " a moral and political sage who
had himself resided at Oxford." Now, according to that
account, nobody was then taught, or could so much as find
" the proper means of being taught, the sciences which it is
the business of those incorporated bodies to teach." The
lecturers had ceased lecturing ; "the tutors contented themselves with teaching a few unconnected shreds and parcels"
of the old unimproved traditionary course, " and even
these they commonly taught very negligently and superficially"; being paid independently of their personal industry,
and being responsible only to one another, " every man
consented that his neighbour might neglect his duty provided he himself were allowed to neglect his own " ; and the
general consequence was a culpable dislike to improvement
and indifference to all new ideas, which made a rich and
well-endowed university the " sanctuary in which exploded
systems and obsolete prejudices find shelter and protection
after they have been hunted out of every corner of the
world." Coming up from a small university in the
North, which was cultivating letters with such remarkable
spirit on its little oatmeal wisely dispensed, Smith concluded that the stagnation of learning which prevailed in
the wealthy universities of England was due at bottom to
nothing but their wealth, because it was distributed on a
bad system.

Severely, however, as Smith has censured the order of
things he found prevailing at Oxford, it is worthy of notice
that he never, like Gibbon and Bentham, thought of the

six years he spent there as being wasted. Boswell and others have pronounced him ungrateful for the censures he deemed meet to pass upon that order of things, but that charge is of course unreasonable, because the censures were undeniably true and undeniably useful, and I refer to it here merely to point out that as a matter of fact Smith not only felt, but has publicly expressed, gratitude for his residence at the University of Oxford. He does so in his letter to the Principal of Glasgow College in 1787 accepting the Rectorship, when in enumerating the claims which Glasgow College had upon his grateful regard, he expressly mentions the fact that it had sent him as a student to Oxford. In truth, his time was not wasted at Oxford. He did not allow it to be wasted. He read deeply and widely in many subjects and in many languages ; he read and thought for six years, and for that best kind of education the negligence of tutors and lecturers, such as they then were, was probably better than their assiduity.

For this business of quiet reading Smith seems to have been happily situated in Balliol. Balliol was not then a reading college as it is now. A claim is set up in behalf of some of the other Oxford colleges that they kept the lamp of learning lit even in the darkest days of last century, but Balliol is not one of them. It was chiefly known in that age for the violence of its Jacobite opinions. Only a few months after Smith left it a party of Balliol students celebrated the birthday of Cardinal York in the College, and rushing out into the streets, mauled every Hanoverian they met, and created such a serious riot that they were sentenced to two years' imprisonment for it by the Court of King's Bench ; but for this grave offence the master of the College, Dr. Theophilus Leigh, and the other authorities, had thought the culprits entitled to indulgence on account of the anniversary they were celebrating, and had decided that the case would be sufficiently met by a Latin imposition. If Balliol, however, was not more enlightened than any of the other colleges of the day, it had one great advantage, it possessed one of the best college libraries at Oxford. The Bodleian was not then open to any member of the University under the rank of a bachelor of arts of two years' standing, and Smith was only a bachelor of arts of two years' standing for a few months before he finally quitted Oxford. He could therefore have made little use of the Bodleian and its then unrivalled treasures, but in his own college library at Balliol he was allowed free range, and availed himself of his privilege with only too great assiduity, to the injury of his health.

His studies took a new turn at Oxford ; he laid aside the mathematics for which he showed a liking at Glasgow, and gave his strength to the ancient Latin and Greek classics, possibly for no better reason than that he could get nobody at Oxford to take the trouble of teaching him the former, and that the Balliol library furnished him with the means of cultivating the latter by himself. He did so, moreover, to some purpose, for all through life he showed a knowledge of Greek and Latin literature not only uncommonly extensive but uncommonly exact. Dalzel, the professor of Greek at Edinburgh, was one of Smith's most intimate friends during those latter years of his life when he was generally found with one of the classical authors before him, in conformity with his theory that the best amusement of age was to renew acquaintance with the writers who were the delight of one's youth ; and Dalzel used always to speak to Dugald Stewart with the greatest admiration of the readiness and accuracy with which Smith remembered the works of the Greek authors, and even of the mastery he exhibited over the niceties of Greek grammar.[1] This knowledge must of course have been acquired at Oxford. Smith had read the Italian poets greatly too, and could quote them easily ; and he paid special care to the French classics on account of their style, spending much time indeed, we are told, in

[1] Stewart's *Life of Adam Smith*, p. 8.

trying to improve his own style by translating their writings into English.

There was only one fruit in the garden of which he might not freely eat, and that was the productions of modern rationalism. A story has come down which, though not mentioned by Dugald Stewart, is stated by M'Culloch to rest on the best authority, and by Dr. Strang of Glasgow to have been often told by Smith himself, to the effect that he was one day detected reading Hume's *Treatise of Human Nature*—probably the very copy presented him by the author at the apparent suggestion of Hutcheson—and was punished by a severe reprimand and the confiscation of the evil book. It is at least entirely consistent with all we know of the spirit of darkness then ruling in Oxford that it should be considered an offence of peculiar aggravation for a student to read a great work of modern thought which had been actually placed in his hands by his professor at Glasgow, and the only wonder is that Smith escaped so lightly, for but a few years before three students were expelled from Oxford for coquetting with Deism, and a fourth, of whom better hopes seem to have been formed, had his degree deferred for two years, and was required in the interval to translate into Latin as a reformatory exercise the whole of Leslie's *Short and Easy Method with the Deists*.[1]

Except for the great resource of study, Smith's life at Oxford seems not to have been a very happy one. For one thing, he was in poor health and spirits a considerable part of the time, as appears from the brief extracts from his letters published by Lord Brougham. When Brougham was writing his account of Smith he got the use of a number of letters written by the latter to his mother from Oxford between 1740 and 1746, which probably exist somewhere still, but which, he found, contained nothing of any general interest. " They are almost all," he says, "upon mere family and personal matters, most

[1] Tyerman's *Wesley*, i. 66.

of them indeed upon his linen and other such necessaries, but all show his strong affection for his mother." The very brief extracts Brougham makes from them, however, inform us that Smith was then suffering from what he calls "an inveterate scurvy and shaking in the head," for which he was using the new remedy of tar-water which Bishop Berkeley had made the fashionable panacea for all manner of diseases. At the end of July 1744 Smith says to his mother : "I am quite inexcusable for not writing to you oftener. I think of you every day, but always defer writing till the post is just going, and then sometimes business or company, but oftener laziness, hinders me. Tar-water is a remedy very much in vogue here at present for almost all diseases. It has perfectly cured me of an inveterate scurvy and shaking in the head. I wish you'd try it. I fancy it might be of service to you." In another and apparently subsequent letter, however, he states that he had had the scurvy and shaking as long as he remembered anything, and that the tar-water had not removed them. On the 29th of November 1743 he makes the curious confession : "I am just recovered from a violent fit of laziness, which has confined me to my elbow-chair these three months."[1] Brougham thinks these statements show symptoms of hypochondria ; but they probably indicate no more than the ordinary lassitude and exhaustion ensuing from overwork. Hume, when about the same age, had by four or five years' hard reading thrown himself into a like condition, and makes the same complaints of "laziness of temper" and scurvy. The shaking in the head continued to attend Smith all his days.

But low health was only one of the miseries of his estate at Oxford. There is reason to believe that Balliol College was in his day a stepmother to her Scotch sons, and that their existence there was made very uncomfortable not merely at the hands of the mob of young gentlemen among whom they were obliged to live, but even

[1] Brougham, *Men of Letters*, ii. 216.

more by the unfair and discriminating harshness of the College authorities themselves. Out of the hundred students then residing at Balliol, eight at least were Scotch, four on the Snell foundation and four on the Warner, and the Scotch eight seem to have been always treated as an alien and intrusive faction. The Snell exhibitioners were continually complaining to the Glasgow Senatus on the subject, and the Glasgow Senatus thought them perfectly justified in complaining. In a letter of 22nd May 1776, in which they go over the whole long story of grievances, the Glasgow Senatus tell the Master and Fellows of Balliol plainly that the Scotch students had never been "welcomely received" at Balliol, and had never been happy there. If an English undergraduate committed a fault, the authorities never thought of blaming any one but himself, but when one of the eight Scotch undergraduates did so, his sin was remembered against all the other seven, and reflections were cast on the whole body; "a circumstance," add the Senatus, "which has been much felt during their residence at Balliol." Their common resentment against the injustice of this kind of tribal accountability that was imposed on them naturally provoked a common resistance; it developed "a spirit of association," say the Senatus, which "has at all periods been a cause of much trouble both to Balliol and to Glasgow Colleges." [1] In 1744, when Smith himself was one of them, the Snell exhibitioners wrote an account of their grievances to the Glasgow Senatus, and stated "what they wanted to be done towards making their residence more easy and advantageous"; [2] and in 1753, when some of Smith's contemporaries would still be on the foundation, Dr. Leigh, the master of Balliol, tells the Glasgow Senatus that he had ascertained in an interview with one

[1] Letter from Senatus of Glasgow College to Balliol College, in Laing MSS., Edinburgh University.

[2] Letter of A. G. Ross of Gray's Inn to Professor R. Simson, Glasgow, in Edinburgh University Library.

of the Snell exhibitioners that what they wanted was to be transferred to some other college, because they had " a total dislike to Balliol." [1]

This idea of a transference, I may be allowed to add, continued to be mooted, and in 1776 it was actually proposed by the heads of Balliol to the Senatus of Glasgow to transfer the Snell foundationers altogether to Hertford College; but the Glasgow authorities thought this would be merely a transference of the troubles, and not a remedy for them, that the exhibitioners would get no better welcome at Hertford than at Balliol if they came as " fixed property" instead of coming as volunteers, and that they could never lose their national peculiarities of dialect and their habits of combination if they came in a body. Accordingly, in the letter of 22nd May 1776, which I have already quoted,[2] they recommended the arrangement of leaving each exhibitioner to choose his own college,—an arrangement, it may be remembered, which had just then been strongly advocated as a general principle by Smith in his newly-published *Wealth of the Nations*, on the broader ground that it would encourage a wholesome competition between the colleges, and so improve the character of the instruction given in them all.

Now if the daily relations between the Scotch exhibitioners at Balliol and the authorities and general members of the College were of the unhappy description partially revealed in this correspondence, that may possibly afford some explanation of what must otherwise seem the entirely unaccountable circumstance that Smith, so far as we are able to judge, made almost no permanent friends at Oxford. Few men were ever by nature more entirely formed for friendship than Smith. At every other stage of his history we invariably find him surrounded by troops of friends, and deriving from their company his chief solace and delight. But here he is six or seven years at Oxford, at

[1] Laing MSS., Edinburgh University.
[2] Edinburgh University Library.

the season of manhood when the deepest and most lasting friendships of a man's life are usually made, and yet we never see him in all his subsequent career holding an hour's intercourse by word or letter with any single Oxford contemporary except Bishop Douglas of Salisbury, and Bishop Douglas had been a Snell exhibitioner himself. With Douglas, moreover, he had many other ties. Douglas was a Fifeshire man, and may possibly have been a kinsman more or less remote; he was a friend of Hume and Robertson, and all Smith's Edinburgh friends; and he was, like Smith again, a member of the famous Literary Club of London, and is celebrated in that character by Goldsmith in the poem " Retaliation," as " the scourge of impostors, the terror of quacks." I have gone over the names of those who might be Smith's contemporaries at Balliol as they appear in Mr. Foster's list of *Alumni Oxonienses*, and they were a singularly undistinguished body of people. Smith and Douglas themselves are indeed the only two of them who seem to have made any mark in the world at all.

An allusion has been made to the Scottish dialect of the Snell exhibitioners; it may be mentioned that Smith seems to have lost the broad Scotch at Oxford without, like Jeffrey, contracting the narrow English; at any rate Englishmen, who visited Smith after visiting Robertson or Blair, were struck with the pure and correct English he spoke in private conversation, and he appears to have done so without giving any impression of constraint.

Smith returned to Scotland in August 1746, but his name remained on the Oxford books for some months after his departure, showing apparently that he had not on leaving come to a final determination against going back. His friends at home are said to have been most anxious that he should continue at Oxford; that would naturally seem to open to him the best opportunities either in the ecclesiastical career for which. they are believed to have destined him, or in the university career for which nature herself designed him. But both careers were practically barred against him by his objection to taking holy orders, the great majority of the Oxford Fellowships being at that time only granted upon condition of ordination, and Smith concluded that the best prospect for him was after all the road back to Scotland. And he never appears to have set foot in Oxford again. When he became Professor at Glasgow he was the medium of intercourse between the Glasgow Senate and the Balliol authorities, but beyond the occasional interchange of letters which this business required, his relations with the Southern University appear to have continued completely suspended. Nor did Oxford, on her part, ever show any interest in him. Even after he had become perhaps her greatest living alumnus, she did not offer him the ordinary honour of a doctor's degree.

CHAPTER IV

In returning to Scotland Smith's ideas were probably fixed from the first on a Scotch university chair as an eventual acquisition, but he thought in the meantime to obtain employment of the sort he afterwards gave up his chair to take with the Duke of Buccleugh, a travelling tutorship with a young man of rank and wealth, then a much-desired and, according to the standard of the times, a highly-re-munerated occupation. While casting about for a place of that kind he stayed at home with his mother in Kirk-caldy, and he had to remain there without any regular employment for two full years, from the autumn of 1746 till the autumn of 1748. The appointment never came ; because from his absent manner and bad address, we are told, he seemed to the ordinary parental mind a most unsuitable person to be entrusted with the care of spirited and perhaps thoughtless young gentlemen. But the visits he paid to Edinburgh in pursuit of this work bore fruit by giving him quite as good a start in life, and a much shorter cut to the professorial position for which he was best fitted. During the winter of 1748-49 he made a most successful beginning as a public lecturer by delivering a course on the then comparatively untried subject of English litera-ture, and gave at the same time a first contribution to English literature himself by collecting and editing the poems of William Hamilton of Bangour. For both these undertakings he was indebted to the advice and good offices of Lord Kames, or, as he then was, Mr. Henry Home, one of the leaders of the Edinburgh bar, with whom he was made acquainted, we may safely assume, by his friend and neighbour, James Oswald of Dunnikier, whom we know to have been among Kames's most intimate friends and correspondents. Kames, though now fifty-two, had not yet written any of the works which raised him afterwards to eminence, but he had long enjoyed in the literary society of the North something of that position which Voltaire laughs at him for trying to take towards the world in general ; he was a law on all questions of taste, from an epic poem to a garden plot. He had little Latin and no Greek, for he never was at college, and the classical quotations in his *Sketches* were translated for him by A. F. Tytler. But he had thrown himself with all the greater zeal on that account into English literature when English literature became the rage in Scotland after the Union, and he was soon crossing steel with Bishop Butler in metaphysics, and the accepted guide of the new Scotch poets in literary criticism. Hamilton of Bangour confesses that he himself

> From Hume learned verse to criticise,

the Hume meant being his early friend, Henry Home of Kames, and not his later friend, David Hume the historian.[1] Home's place in the literature of Scotland corresponds with his place in its agriculture ; he was the first of the improvers ; and Smith, who always held him in the deepest veneration, was not wrong when, on being complimented on the group of great writers who were then reflecting glory on Scotland, he said, " Yes, but we must every one of us acknowledge Kames for our master." [2]

---

[1] Home and Hume, it may be mentioned, are only different ways of spelling the same name, which, though differently spelt, was not differently pronounced. [2] Tytler's *Life of Kames*, i. 218.

When Home found Smith already as well versed in the English classics as himself, he suggested the delivery of this course of lectures on English literature and criticism. The subject was fresh, it was fashionable, and though Stevenson, the Professor of Logic, had already lectured on it, and lectured on it in English too to his class, nobody had yet given lectures on it open to the general public, whose interest it had at the moment so much engaged. The success of such a course seemed assured, and the event fully justified that prognostication. The class was attended among others by Kames himself; by students for the bar, like Alexander Wedderburn, afterwards Lord Chancellor of England, and William Johnstone, who long played an influential part in Parliament as Sir William Pulteney; by young ministers of the city like Dr. Blair, who subsequently gave a similar course himself; and by many others, both young and old. It brought Smith in, we are informed, a clear £100 sterling, and if we assume that the fee was a guinea, which was a customary fee at the period, the audience would be something better than a hundred. It was probably held in the College, for Blair's subsequent course was delivered there even before the establishment of any formal connection with the University by the creation of the professorship.

The lectures Smith then delivered on English literature were burnt at his own request shortly before his death. Blair, who not only heard them at the time, but got the use of them—or, at least, of part of them—afterwards for the preparation of his own lectures on rhetoric, speaks as if there was some hope at one time that Smith would publish them, but if he ever entertained such an intention, he was too entirely preoccupied with work of greater importance and interest to himself to obtain leisure to put them into shape for publication. It has been suggested that they are practically reproduced in the lectures of Blair. Blair acknowledges having taken a few hints for his treatment of simplicity in style from the manuscript of Smith's lectures. His words are : "On this head, of the general characters of style, particularly the plain and the simple, and the characters of those English authors who are classed under them, in this and the following lecture, several ideas have been taken from a manuscript treatise on rhetoric, part of which was shown to me many years ago by the learned and ingenious author, Dr. Adam Smith ; and which it is hoped will be given by him to the public."[1] Now many of Smith's friends considered this acknowledgment far from adequate, and Hill, the biographer of Blair, says Smith himself joined in their complaint. It is very unlikely that Smith ever joined in any such complaint, for Henry Mackenzie told Samuel Rogers an anecdote which conveys an entirely contrary impression. Mackenzie was speaking of Smith's wealth of conversation, and telling how he often used to say to him, "Sir, you have said enough to make a book," and he then mentioned that Blair frequently introduced into his sermons some of Smith's thoughts on jurisprudence, which he had gathered from his conversation, and that he himself had told the circumstance to Smith. "He is very welcome," was the economist's answer ; "there is enough left."[2] And if Smith made Blair welcome to his thoughts on jurisprudence, a subject on which he intended to publish a work of his own, we may be certain he made him not less heartily welcome to his thoughts on literature and style, on which he probably entertained no similar intention. Besides, if we judge from the two chapters regarding which he owns his obligation to Smith, Blair does not seem to have borrowed anything but what was the commonest of property already. He took only what his superficial mind had the power of taking, and the pith of Smith's thinking must have been left behind. To borrow even a hat to any purpose, the two heads must be something of a size.

---

[1] Blair's _Lectures on Rhetoric and Belles-Lettres_, i. 381.

[2] Clayden's _Early Life of Samuel Rogers_, p. 168.

We cannot suppose, therefore, that we have any proper representation or reflection of Smith's literary lectures in the lectures of Blair, but it would be quite possible still, if it were desired, to collect a not inadequate view of his literary opinions from incidental remarks contained in his writings or preserved by friends from recollections of his conversation. Wordsworth, in the preface to the *Lyrical Ballads*, calls him "the worst critic, David Hume excepted, that Scotland, a soil to which this sort of weed seems natural, has produced," and his judgments will certainly not be confirmed by the taste of the present time. He preferred the classical to the romantic school. He thought with Voltaire that Shakespeare had written good scenes but not a good play, and that though he had more dramatic genius than Dryden, Dryden was the greater poet. He thought little of Milton's minor poems, and less of the old ballads collected by Percy, but he had great admiration for Pope, believed Gray, if he had only written a little more, would have been the greatest poet in the English language, and thought Racine's *Phædrus* the finest tragedy extant in any language in the world. His own great test of literary beauty was the principle he lays down in his Essay on the Imitative Arts, that the beauty is always in the proportion of the difficulty perceived to be overcome.

Smith seems at this early period of his life to have had dreams of some day figuring as a poet himself, and his extensive familiarity with the poets always struck Dugald Stewart as very remarkable in a man so conspicuous for the weight of his more solid attainments. "In the English language," says Stewart, "the variety of poetical passages which he was not only accustomed to refer to occasionally, but which he was able to repeat with correctness, appeared surprising even to those whose attention had never been attracted to more important acquisitions." The tradition of Smith's early ambition to be a poet is only preserved in an allusion in Caleb Colton's

" Hypocrisy," but it receives a certain support from a remark of Smith's own in conversation with a young friend in his later years.   Colton's allusion runs as follows :—

> Unused am I the Muse's path to tread,
> And curs'd with Adam's unpoetic head,
> Who, though that pen he wielded in his hand
> Ordain'd the *Wealth of Nations* to command ;
> Yet when on Helicon he dar'd to draw,
> His draft return'd and unaccepted saw.
> If thus like him we lay a rune in vain,
> Like him we'll strive some humbler prize to gain.

Smith's own confession is contained in a report of some conversations given in the *Bee* for 1791.   He was speaking about blank verse, to which he always had a dislike, as we know from an interesting incident mentioned by Boswell.   Boswell, who attended Smith's lectures on English literature at Glasgow College in 1759, told Johnson four years after that Smith had pronounced a strong opinion in these lectures against blank verse and in favour of rhyme—always, no doubt, on the same principle that the greater the difficulty the greater the beauty.   This delighted the heart of Johnson, and he said, " Sir, I was once in company with Smith, and we did not take to each other, but had I known that he loved rhyme as much as you tell me he does, I should have hugged him."   Twenty years later Smith was again expressing to the anonymous interviewer of the *Bee* his unabated contempt for all blank verse except Milton's, and he said that though he could never find a single rhyme in his life, he could make blank verse as fast as he could speak.   " Blank verse," he said ; " they do well to call it blank, for blank it is.   I myself even, who never could find a single rhyme in my life, could make blank verse as fast as I could speak."   The critic would thus appear here again to have been the poet who has failed, though in this case he had the sense to discover the failure without tempting the judgment of the public.

Indeed he had already begun to discover his true
vocation, for besides his lectures on English literature,
which he delivered for three successive winters, he delivered at least one winter a course on economics; and
in this course, written in the year 1749, and delivered
in the year 1750-51, Smith advocated the doctrines
of commercial liberty on which he was nurtured by
Hutcheson, and which he was afterwards to do so much
to advance. He states this fact himself in a paper read
before a learned society in Glasgow in 1755, which
afterwards fell into the hands of Dugald Stewart, and
from which Stewart extracts a passage or two, which
I shall quote in a subsequent chapter. They certainly
contain a plain enough statement of the doctrine of
natural liberty; and Smith says that a great part of
the opinions contained in the paper were "treated of at
length in some lectures which I have still by me, and
which were written in the hand of a clerk who left my
service six years ago"—that is, in 1749—and adds that
"they had all of them been the subjects of lectures which
I read at Edinburgh the winter before I left it, and I can
adduce innumerable witnesses both from that place and
from this who will ascertain them sufficiently to be mine."[1]
These ideas of natural liberty in industrial affairs were
actively at work, not only in Smith's own mind, but in
the minds of others in his immediate circle in Scotland in
those years 1749 and 1750. David Hume and James
Oswald were then corresponding on the subject, and though
it is doubtful whether Smith had seen much or anything
of Hume personally at that time (for Hume had been
abroad with General St. Clair part of it, and did not live
in Edinburgh after his return), it was in those and the two
previous years that Smith was first brought into real
intellectual contact with his friend and townsman, James
Oswald.

Oswald, it may be mentioned, though still a young

[1] Stewart's *Works*, ed. Hamilton, vol. x. p. 68.

man—only eight years older than Smith—had already made his mark in Parliament where he sat for their native burgh, and had been made a Commissioner of the Navy in 1745. He had made his mark largely by his mastery of economic subjects, for which Hume said, after paying him a visit at Dunnikier for a week in 1744, that he had a "great genius," and "would go far in that way if he persevered." He became afterwards commissioner of trade and plantations, Lord of the Treasury, and Vice-Treasurer of Ireland, and would have certainly gone further but for his premature death in 1768 at the age of fifty-two. Lord Shelburne once strongly advised Lord Bute to make him Chancellor of the Exchequer. Smith thought as highly of Oswald as Hume. He used to "dilate," says Oswald's grandson, who heard him, "with a generous and enthusiastic pleasure on the qualifications and merits of Mr. Oswald, candidly avowing at the same time how much information he had received on many points from the enlarged views and profound knowledge of that accomplished statesman." [1] Dugald Stewart saw a paper written by Smith which described Oswald not only as a man of extensive knowledge of economic subjects, but a man with a special taste and capacity for the discussion of their more general and philosophical aspects. That paper, we cannot help surmising, is the same document of 1755 I have just mentioned in which Smith was proving his early attachment to the doctrines of economic liberty, and would naturally treat of circumstances connected with the growth of his opinions. However that may be, it is certain that Smith and Oswald must have been in communication upon economic questions about that period, and Oswald's views at that period are contained in the correspondence to which reference has been made.

Early in 1750 David Hume sent Oswald the manuscript of his well-known essay on the Balance of Trade, afterwards published in his *Political Essays* in 1752, asking

---

[1] *Correspondence of James Oswald*, Preface.

for his views and criticisms ; and Oswald replied on the 10th of October in a long letter, published in the *Caldwell Papers*,[1] which shows him to have been already entirely above the prevailing mercantilist prejudices, and to have very clear conceptions of economic operations. He declares jealousies between nations of being drained of their produce and money to be quite irrational ; that could never happen as long as the people and industry remained. The prohibition against exporting commodities and money, he held, had always produced effects directly contrary to what was intended by it. It had diminished cultivation at home instead of increasing it, and really forced the more money out of the country the more produce it prevented from going. Oswald's letter seems to have been sent on by Hume, together with his own essay, to Baron Mure, who was also interested in such discussions. The new light was thus breaking in on groups of inquirers in Scotland as well as elsewhere, and Smith was from his earliest days within its play.

Amid the more serious labours of these literary and economic lectures, it would be an agreeable relaxation to collect and edit the scattered poems, published and unpublished, of Hamilton of Bangour, the author of what Wordsworth calls the " exquisite ballad " of " The Braes o' Yarrow," beginning—

> Busk ye, busk ye, my bonny, bonny bride,
> Busk ye, busk ye, my winsome marrow,
> Busk ye, busk ye, my bonny, bonny bride,
> And think no more on the Braes o' Yarrow.

This ballad had appeared in Allan Ramsay's *Tea-Table Miscellany* so long ago as 1724, and it was followed by Hamilton's most ambitious effort, the poem " Contemplation," in 1739, but the general public of Scotland only seem to have awakened to their merits after the poet espoused the Jacobite cause in 1745, and celebrated the

[1] *Caldwell Papers*, i. 93.

victory of Prestonpans by his "Ode to the Battle of Gladsmuir"—the name the Jacobites preferred to give the battle. This ode, which had been set to music by M'Gibbon, became a great favourite in Jacobite households, and created so much popular interest in the author's other works that imperfect versions of some of his unpublished poems, and even of those which were already in print, began to appear. The author was himself an outlaw, and could not intervene. The ode which had lifted him into popularity had at the same time driven him into exile, and he was then living with a little group of young Scotch refugees at Rouen, and completely shattered in bodily health by his three months' hiding among the Grampians. Under those circumstances his friends thought it advisable to forestall the pirated and imperfect collections of his poems which were in contemplation by publishing as complete and correct an edition of them as could possibly be done in the absence of the author. And this edition was issued from the famous Foulis press in Glasgow in 1748. In doing so they acted, as they avow in the preface, "not only without the author's consent, but without his knowledge," but it is absurd to call an edition published under those circumstances, as the new *Dictionary of National Biography* calls it, a "surreptitious edition." It was published by the poet's closest personal friends as a protection for the poet's reputation, and perhaps as a plea for his pardon.

The task of collecting and editing the poems was entrusted to Adam Smith. We are informed of this fact by the accurate and learned David Laing, and though Laing has not imparted his authority for the information, it receives a certain circumstantial corroboration from other quarters. We find Smith in the enjoyment of a very rapid intimacy with Hamilton during the two brief years the poet resided in Scotland between receiving the royal pardon in 1750 and flying again in 1752 from a more relentless enemy than kings—the fatal malady of consumption, from which he died two years later at Lyons. Sir John Dalrymple, the historian, speaks in a letter to Robert Foulis, the printer, of "the many happy and flattering hours which he (Smith) had spent with Mr. Hamilton." We find again that when Hamilton's friends propose to print a second edition of the poems, they come to Smith for assistance. This edition was published in 1758, and is dedicated to the memory of William Craufurd, merchant, Glasgow, a friend of the poet mentioned in the preface to the first edition as having supplied many of the previously unpublished pieces which it contained. Craufurd appears to have been an uncle of Sir John Dalrymple, and Sir John asks Foulis to get Smith to write this dedication. "Sir," says he, in December 1757, "I have changed my mind about the dedication of Mr. Hamilton's poems. I would have it stand 'the friend of William Hamilton,' but I assent to your opinion to have something more to express Mr. Craufurd's character. I know none so able to do this as my friend Mr. Smith. I beg it, therefore, earnestly that he will write the inscription, and with all the elegance and all the feelingness which he above the rest of mankind is able to express. This is a thing that touches me very nearly, and therefore I beg a particular answer as to what he says to it. The many happy and the many flattering hours which he has spent with Mr. Hamilton and Mr. Craufurd makes me think that he will account his usual indolence a crime upon this occasion. I beg you will make my excuse for not wryting him this night, but then I consider wryting to you upon this head to be wryting to him." [1] It is unlikely that Smith would resist an appeal like this, and the dedication bears some internal marks of his authorship. It describes Mr. Craufurd as "the friend of Mr. Hamilton, who to that exact frugality, that downright probity and pliancy

[1] Duncan's *Notes and Documents illustrative of the Literary History of Glasgow*, p. 25.

of manners so suitable to his profession, joined a love of learning and of all the ingenious arts, an openness of hand and a generosity of heart that was far both from vanity and from weakness, and a magnanimity that would support, under the prospect of approaching and inevitable death, a most torturing pain of body with an unalterable cheerfulness of temper, and without once interrupting even to his last hour the most manly and the most vigorous activity of business." This William Craufurd is confounded by Lord Woodhouselee, and through him by others, with Robert Crauford, the author of " The Bush aboon Traquair," " Tweedside," and other poems, who was also an intimate friend of Hamilton of Bangour, but died in 1732.

Another link in the circumstantial evidence corroborating David Laing's statement is the fact that Smith was certainly at the moment in communication with Hamilton's personal friends, at whose instance the volume of poems was published. Kames, who was then interesting himself so actively in Smith's advancement, was the closest surviving friend Hamilton possessed. They had been constant companions in youth, leading spirits of that new school of dandies called " the beaux "—young men at once of fashion and of letters—who adorned Scotch society between the Rebellions, and continued to adorn many an after-dinner table in Edinburgh down till the present century. Hamilton owns that it was Kames who first taught him " verse to criticise," and wrote to him the poem " To H. H. at the Assembly"; while Kames for his part used in his old age, as his neighbour Ramsay of Ochtertyre informs us, to have no greater enjoyment than recounting the scenes and doings he and Hamilton had transacted together in those early days, of which the poet himself writes, when they " kept friendship's holy vigil " in the subterranean taverns of old Edinburgh " full many a fathom deep."

CHAPTER V

THE Edinburgh lectures soon bore fruit. On the death of Mr. Loudon, Professor of Logic in Glasgow College, in 1750, Smith was appointed to the vacant chair, and so began that period of thirteen years of active academic work which he always looked back upon, he tells us, "as by far the most useful and therefore by far the happiest and most honourable period" of his life. The appointment lay with the Senatus—or, more strictly, with a section of the Senatus known as the Faculty Professors—some of whom, of course, had been his own teachers ten years before, and knew him well ; and the minutes state that the choice was unanimous. He was elected on the 9th of January 1751, and was admitted to the office on the 16th, after reading a dissertation *De origine idearum*, signing the Westminster Confession of Faith before the Presbytery of Glasgow, and taking the usual oath *De fideli* to the University authorities ; but he did not begin work till the opening of the next session in October. His engagements in Edinburgh did not permit of his undertaking his duties in Glasgow earlier, and his classes were accordingly conducted, with the sanction of the Senatus, by Dr. Hercules Lindsay, the Professor of Jurisprudence, as his substitute, from the beginning of January till the end of June. During this interval Smith went through to Glasgow repeatedly to attend meetings of the Senatus, but

he does not appear to have given any lectures to the
students.   If he was relieved of his duties in the summer,
however, he worked double tides during the winter, for
besides the work of his own class, he undertook to carry
on at the same time the work of Professor Craigie of the
Moral Philosophy chair, who was laid aside by ill health,
and indeed died a few weeks after the commencement of
the session.   This double burden was no doubt alleviated
by the circumstance that he was able in both the class-
rooms to make very considerable use of the courses of
lectures he had already delivered in Edinburgh.   By the
traditional distribution of academic subjects in the Scotch
universities, the province of the chair of Logic included
rhetoric and belles-lettres, and the province of the chair
of Moral Philosophy included jurisprudence and politics,
and as Smith had lectured in Edinburgh both on rhetoric
and belles-lettres and on jurisprudence and politics, he
naturally took those branches for the subjects of his
lectures this first session at Glasgow.   Professor John
Millar, the author of the *Historical View of the English
Government* and other works of great merit, was a member
of Smith's logic class that year, having been induced, by
the high reputation the new professor brought with him
from Edinburgh, to take out the class a second time,
although he had already completed his university curriculum ; and Millar states that most of the session was
occupied with "the delivery of a system of rhetoric and
belles-lettres."   In respect to the other class, jurisprudence
and politics were specially suggested to him as the subjects
for the year when he was asked to take Professor Craigie's
place.   The proposal came through Professor Cullen, who
was probably Craigie's medical attendant, and Cullen
suggested those particular subjects as being the most likely
to suit Smith's convenience and save him labour, inasmuch
as he had lectured on them already.   Smith replied that
these were the subjects which it would be most agreeable
to him to take up.

EDINBURGH, 3rd Sept. 1751.

DEAR SIR—I received yours this moment. I am very glad that Mr. Craigie has at last resolved to go to Lisbon. I make no doubt but he will soon receive all the benefit he expects or can wish from the warmer climate. I shall, with great pleasure, do what I can to relieve him of the burden of his class. You mention natural jurisprudence and politics as the parts of his lectures which it would be most agreeable for me to take upon me to teach. I shall very willingly undertake both. I shall be glad to know when he sets out for Lisbon, because if it is not before the first of October I would endeavour to see him before he goes, that I might receive his advice about the plan I ought to follow. I would pay great deference to it in everything, and would follow it implicitly in this, as I shall consider myself as standing in his place and representing him. If he goes before that time I wish he would leave some directions for me, either with you or with Mr. Leechman, were it only by word of mouth.—I am, dear doctor, most faithfully yours, ADAM SMITH.[1]

Smith would begin work at Glasgow on the 10th of October, and before the middle of November he and Cullen were already deeply immersed in quite a number of little schemes for the equipment of the College. There was first of all the affair of the vacancy in the Moral Philosophy chair, which was anticipated to occur immediately through the death of Mr. Craigie—referred to in the following letter as " the event we are afraid of." This vacancy Cullen and Smith were desirous of seeing filled up by the translation of Smith from the Logic to the Moral Philosophy chair, and the Principal (Dr. Neil Campbell) seems to have concurred in that proposal, and to have mentioned Smith's name with approbation to the Duke of Argyle, who, though without any power over the appointment to any except the Crown chairs, took much interest in, and was believed to exercise much influence over, the appointment to all. This was the Duke Archibald— better known by his earlier title of the Earl of Islay—who

[1] Thomson's *Life of Cullen*, i. 605.

was often called the King of Scotland, because he practically ruled the affairs of Scotland in the first half of last century, very much as Dundas did in the second. Smith seems to have gone through to Edinburgh to push his views with the Duke, and to have waited on him and been introduced to him at his levee.

Then there was the affair of Hume's candidature for the Logic chair, contingent on Smith's appointment to the other. There was the affair of the Principal's possible retirement, with, no doubt, some plan in reserve for the reversion, probably in favour of Professor Leechman, mentioned in the previous letter, who did in the event succeed to it. Then there was Cullen's " own affair," which Smith was promoting in Edinburgh through Lord Kames (then Mr. Home), and which probably concerned a method of purifying salt Cullen had then invented, and wanted to secure a premium for. At any rate, Lord Kames did speak to the Duke of Argyle on this subject in Cullen's behalf a few months later.

While immersed in this multiplicity of affairs Smith wrote Cullen the following letter :—[1]

Edin., *Tuesday, November* 1751.

Dear Sir—I did not write to you on Saturday as I promised, because I was every moment expecting Mr. Home to town. He is not, however, yet come.

I should prefer David Hume to any man for the College, but I am afraid the public would not be of my opinion, and the interest of the society will oblige us to have some regard to the opinion of the public. If the event, however, we are afraid of should happen we can see how the public receives it. From the particular knowledge I have of Mr. Elliot's sentiments, I am pretty certain Mr. Lindsay must have proposed it to him, not he to Mr. Lindsay. I am ever obliged to you for your concern for my interest in that affair.

When I saw you at Edinburgh you talked to me of the Principal's proposing to retire. I gave little attention to it at that time, but upon further consideration should be glad to listen to

---

[1] Thomson's *Life of Cullen*, i. 606.

any proposal of that kind. The reasons of my changing my opinion I shall tell you at meeting. I need not recommend secrecy to you upon this head. Be so good as to thank the Principal in my name for his kindness in mentioning me to the Duke. I waited on him at his levee at Edinburgh, when I was introduced to him by Mr. Lind, but it seems he had forgot.

I can tell you nothing particular about your own affair more than what I wrote you last till I see Mr. Home, whom I expect every moment.—I am, most dear sir, ever yours,

A. SMITH.

The event they were afraid of happened on the 27th of November, and Smith was, without any opposition, appointed Craigie's successor on the 29th of April 1752. It would appear from this letter as if Cullen had heard from his colleague, Professor Lindsay, of a possible rival to Smith for that chair in the person of Mr. Elliot—no doubt Mr. Gilbert Elliot, a man of brilliant parts and accomplishments, who afterwards attained high political eminence as Sir Gilbert Elliot, but who was at this time a young advocate at the Edinburgh bar, with no liking for law and a great liking for letters and philosophy. Smith, however, who was a personal friend of Elliot's, knew that the latter had no such designs, and eventually his own candidature was unopposed. But in anticipation of this result, the keenest contest was carried on all winter over the election to the Logic chair, which he was to leave. David Hume came forward as a candidate, and there is an erroneous, though curiously well-supported tradition that Edmund Burke was a candidate also. One of Burke's biographers, Bisset, states that Burke actually applied for the post, but applied too late.[1] Another of his biographers, Prior, says that Burke being in Scotland at the time, took some steps for the place, but finding his chances hopeless, withdrew;[2] while Professor Jardine, a subsequent occupier of the chair himself, asserts that Burke was thought of by

[1] Bisset's *Burke*, i. 32.
[2] Prior's *Burke*, p. 38.

some of the electors, but never really came forward.[1] But Smith, who was not only the previous occupant of the office, but, as Professor of Moral Philosophy, was one of the electors of his successor, stated explicitly to Dugald Stewart (as Stewart wrote to Prior[2]) " that the story was extremely current, but he knew of no evidence on which it rested, and he suspected it took its rise entirely from an opinion which he had himself expressed at Glasgow upon the publication of Burke's book on the *Sublime and Beautiful*, that the author of that book would be a great acquisition to the College if he would accept of a chair." Had anything been known in Glasgow of Burke's candidature for a chair there five years before, it would unquestionably be recollected on the occasion of the publication of so notable a work, but Burke's very name was so unfamiliar to the circle interested in the election that when Hume first met him in London in 1759, he mentions him in a letter to Smith as " a Mr. Burke, an Irish gentleman who has written a very pretty book on the *Sublime and Beautiful*." [3]

The interest of the contest is sufficiently great from the candidature of one philosopher of the first rank, and to Smith himself—already that philosopher's very close friend—it must have been engrossing. It will be observed that in his letter to Cullen he expresses himself with great caution on the subject. He is quite alive to the fact that the appointment of a notorious sceptic like Hume might be so unpopular with the Scottish public as to injure the interests of the University. But when Hume came forward Cullen threw himself heart and soul into his cause, as we know from Hume's own acknowledgments ; and if Cullen and Smith are found acting in concert at the initiation of the candidature, it is not likely that Smith lagged behind Cullen in the prosecution of the canvass, though nothing remains to give us any decisive informa-

---

[1] *Outlines of the Philosophy of Education*, p. 23.
[2] Prior's *Life of Burke*, Bohn's ed. p. 38.
[3] Burton's *Life of Hume*, ii. 55.

tion on the point. Their exertions failed, however, in consequence, Hume himself always believed, of the interference of the Duke of Argyle, and the chair was given to a young licentiate of the Church named Clow, who was at the time entirely unknown, and indeed never afterwards established any manner of public reputation.

Smith's preference for the Moral Philosophy chair came mainly no doubt from preference for the subjects he would be called upon to teach in it, but the emoluments also seem to have been somewhat better, for Smith was expressly required, as a condition of acceptance of the office, to content himself until the 10th of October of that year (the opening day of the new session) " with the salary and emoluments of his present profession of Logic," even though he might be actually admitted to the other professorship before that date. It must not be supposed, however, that the emoluments of his new office were by any means very lordly. They accrued partly from a moderate endowment and partly from the fees paid by the students who attended the lectures—a principle of academic payment which Smith always considered the best, because it made the lecturer's income largely dependent on his diligence and success in his work. The endowment was probably no more than that of the Mathematical chair, and the endowment of the Mathematical chair was £72 a year.[1] The fees probably never exceeded £100, or even came up to that figure, for Dr. Thomas Reid, Smith's successor in the Moral Philosophy chair, writes an Aberdeen friend, after two years' experience of Glasgow, that he had more students than Smith ever had, and had already touched £70 of fees, but expected, when all the students arrived, to make £100 that session.[2] The income from fees in the Scotch chairs in last century seems to have been subject to considerable variations from session to session. A bad harvest would sometimes tell

---

[1] *Caldwell Papers*, i. 170.
[2] Hamilton's *Reid*, p. 40.

seriously on the attendance, and a great crisis like that of
1772, when the effects of a succession of bad harvests were
aggravated by ruinous mercantile speculations, deprived
Adam Ferguson in the Edinburgh Moral Philosophy
chair of half his usual income from fees.   It may also be
mentioned as a curious circumstance that in those days a
professor used to lose regularly many pounds a year by
light money.   When Lord Brougham, as a young student
of chemistry in Edinburgh, paid his fee to Black, the
great chemist weighed the guineas carefully on a weighing
machine he had on the table before him, and observed in
explanation, "I   am   obliged   to   weigh   when   strange
students come, there being a very large number who bring
light guineas, so that I should be defrauded of many
pounds every year if I did not act in self-defence against
this class of students." [1]

Smith kept an occasional boarder in his house, and
would of course make a trifle by that, but his regular
income from his class work would not exceed £170 a
year.   £170 a year, however, was a very respectable
income at a period when, as was the case in 1750, only
twenty-nine ministers in all broad Scotland had as much
as £100 a year, and the highest stipend in the Church
was only £138.[2]

Besides his salary Smith had a house in the College—
one of those new manses in the Professors' Court which
Glasgow people at the time considered very grand ; and
though the circumstance is trifling, it is a little curious
that he changed his house three times in the course of his
thirteen years' professorship.   It was the custom when a
house fell vacant for the professors to get their choice of
it in the order of their academical seniority.   There seems
to have been no compulsion about the step, so that it is
not beneath noticing that Smith should in so short a term
have elected to make the three removes which proverbial

---

[1] *Brougham's Life and Times*, i. 78.
[2] Chamberlayne's *Angliæ Notitia* for 1750.

wisdom deprecates. When his friend Cullen was translated to Edinburgh in 1756, Smith, who was next in
seniority, having been made professor in Glasgow a few
months after the eminent physician, removed to Cullen's
house; then he quitted this house in 1757 for the house
of Dr. Dick, Professor of Natural Philosophy, who died
in that year; and he left Dick's house in turn for Dr.
Leechman's, on the promotion of that divine to the
Principalship in 1762. These houses are now demolished
with the rest of the old College of Glasgow, so that we
cannot mark the gradation of comfort that may have
determined these successive changes; and besides they
may have been determined by no positive preference of
the economist himself, but by the desires of his mother
and his aunt, Miss Jane Douglas, who both lived with
him in Glasgow, and whose smallest wishes it was the
highest ambition of his affectionate nature to gratify.

In Smith's day there were only some 300 students
at Glasgow College in all, and the Moral Philosophy
chair alone had never more than 80 or 90 in the public
class and 20 in the private. The public class did
not mean a free class, as it does on the Continent; it
really was the dearer of the two, the fee in the private
class being only a guinea, while the fee of the public class
was a guinea and a half. The public class was the
ordinary class taken for graduation and other purposes,
and obligatory by academic authority; the private was a
special class, undertaken, with the permission of the Senatus,
for those who wished to push the subject further; and to
harmonise this account of them with what has been previously said of the income Smith drew from fees, it is
necessary to explain that many of the students who
attended these classes paid no fees, according to a custom
which still prevails in Scotch universities, and by which
one was considered a *civis* of a class he had attended for two
years, and might thereafter attend it whenever he chose
without charge. Many in this way attended the Moral

Philosophy class four or five years, and among them, as Dr. Reid informs us, quite a number of preachers and advanced students of divinity and law, before whom, the worthy doctor confesses, he used to stand in awe to speak without the most careful preparation.

The College session was then longer than it is now, extending from the 10th of October to the 10th of June, and the classes began at once earlier in the morning and continued later at night. Smith commenced his labours before daybreak by his public class from 7.30 to 8.30 A.M. ; he then held at 11 A.M. an hour's examination on the lecture he delivered in the morning, though to this examination only a third of the students of the morning class were in the habit of coming ; and he met with his private class twice a week on a different subject at 12. Besides these engagements Smith seems to have occasionally read for an hour like a tutor with special pupils ; at least one is led to infer so much from the remarks of a former pupil, who, under the *nom de plume* of Ascanius, writes his reminiscences of his old master to the editor of the *Bee* in June 1791. This writer says that he went to Glasgow College after he had gone through the classes at St. Andrews, Edinburgh, and even Oxford, in order that he might, "after the manner of the ancients, walk in the porticoes of Glasgow with Smith and with Millar, and be imbued with the principles of jurisprudence and law and philosophy" ; and then he adds: "I passed most of my time at Glasgow with those two first-rate men, and Smith read private lectures to me on jurisprudence, and accompanied them with his commentaries in conversation, exercises which I hope will give a colour and a substance to my sentiments and to my reason that will be eternal."

There is no difficulty in identifying this enthusiastic disciple with the eccentric and bustling Earl of Buchan, the elder brother of Lord Chancellor Erskine, and of the witty and greatly beloved Harry Erskine of the Scotch bar, and the subject of the Duchess of Gordon's well-known *mot :* " The wit of your lordship's family has come by the mother, and been all settled on the younger branches." We know that this Earl of Buchan was a contributor to the *Bee* under various fictitious signatures, because he has himself republished some of his contributions, and we know that he attended Smith's class at Glasgow, because he says so in a letter to Pinkerton, the historian, mentioning having seen in Smith's library at that time a book of which Pinkerton could not find a single copy remaining anywhere—the memoirs of Lockhart of Lee, Cromwell's ambassador to France, which had been suppressed (as the Earl had been told by his maternal uncle, Sir James Steuart, the economist) at the instance of Lockhart, the famous advocate, afterwards Lord Covington, because the family had turned Jacobite, and disliked the association with the Commonwealth.[1] The Earl gives the year of his attendance at Glasgow as 1760, but he must have continued there more than one session, for he attended Millar's lectures as well as Smith's, and Millar was not there till the session 1761-62 ; and it is on the whole most likely that this is the very young nobleman whom Dr. Alexander Carlyle met in company with Smith at a large supper party in April 1763, and concerning whom he mentions that he himself whispered after a little to Smith that he wondered how he could set this young man so high who appeared to be so foolish, and Smith answered, " We know that perfectly, but he is the only lord in our College."

It will be observed that Lord Buchan says Smith *read* private lectures to him. Smith's public lectures he was not accustomed to read in any of his classes, but he seems

---

[1] Smith's copy of this book seems to have gone out of existence like the others, for his cousin and heir, David Douglas, wrote Lord Buchan in January 1792 that he had searched for it in Smith's library without any success, and that though a catalogue of the library had since then been made out, Lockhart's Memoirs was not contained in it. Douglas's letter is in the Edinburgh University Library.

to have found it more convenient in teaching a single pupil to read them, and interpose oral comments and illustrations as he went along. Others of Smith's old students besides Lord Buchan express their obligations to the conversations they were privileged to have with him. Dugald Stewart, Brougham informs us, used to decline to see his students, because he found them too disputatious, and he disliked disputing with them about the correctness of the doctrines he taught. But Smith, by all accounts, was extremely accessible, and was even in the habit of seeking out the abler men among them, inviting them to his house, discussing with them the subjects of his lectures or any other subject, and entering sympathetically into their views and plans of life. John Millar, having occasion to mention Smith's name in his *Historical View of the English Government*, takes the opportunity to say : " I am happy to acknowledge the obligations I feel myself under to this illustrious philosopher by having at an early period of life had the benefit of his lectures on the history of civil society, and enjoying his unreserved conversation on the same subject." [1]

Millar, it may be added, was one of Smith's favourite pupils, and after obtaining the chair of Jurisprudence in his old College, one of his chief associates, and Smith held so high an opinion of Millar's unique powers as a stimulating teacher that he sent his cousin, David Douglas, to Glasgow College for no other purpose but to have the advantage of the lectures and conversation of Millar. Jeffrey used to say that the most bracing exercises a student in Glasgow underwent in those days were the supper disputations at Professor Millar's house, and that, able and learned as his works are, " they revealed nothing of that magical vivacity which made his conversation and his lectures still more full of delight than of instruction." Though he always refused to accept Smith's doctrine of free trade, Millar was the most effective

[1] Book II. chap. x.

and influential apostle of Liberalism in Scotland in that age, and Jeffrey's father could never forgive himself for having put his son to Glasgow, where, though he was strictly forbidden to enter Millar's class-room, "the mere vicinity of Millar's influence" had sent him back a Liberal.[1]

Now it is this interesting and famous lecturer from whom we obtain the fullest account of Smith's qualities as a lecturer and of the substance of his lectures.

"In the professorship of logic," he says, "to which Mr. Smith was appointed on his first introduction into this University, he soon saw the necessity of departing widely from the plan that had been followed by his predecessors, and of directing the attention of his pupils to studies of a more interesting and useful nature than the logic and metaphysics of the schools. Accordingly, after exhibiting a general view of the powers of the mind, and explaining as much of the ancient logic as was requisite to gratify curiosity with respect to an artificial method of reasoning which had once occupied the universal attention of the learned, he dedicated all the rest of his time to the delivering of a system of rhetoric and belles-lettres."

In moral philosophy "his course of lectures," says Millar, "was divided into four parts. The first contained natural theology, in which he considered the proofs of the being and attributes of God, and those principles of the human mind upon which religion is founded. The second comprehended ethics, strictly so called, and consisted chiefly of the doctrines which he afterwards published in his *Theory of Moral Sentiments*. In the third part he treated at more length of that branch of morality which relates to *justice*, and which, being susceptible of precise and accurate rules, is for that reason capable of a full and particular explanation.

"Upon this subject he followed the plan that seems

[1] Cockburn's *Life of Jeffrey*, p. 12.

to be suggested by Montesquieu, endeavouring to trace the gradual progress of jurisprudence, both public and private, from the rudest to the most refined ages, and to point out the effects of those arts which contribute to subsistence and to the accumulation of property, in producing correspondent improvements or alterations in law and government. This important branch of his labours he also intended to give to the public ; but this intention, which is mentioned in the conclusion of the *Theory of Moral Sentiments*, he did not live to fulfil.

" In the last of his lectures he examined those political regulations which are founded, not upon the principle of *justice* but that of *expediency*, and which are calculated to increase the riches, the power, and the prosperity of a state. Under this view he considered the political institutions relating to commerce, to finances, to ecclesiastical and military establishments. What he delivered on those subjects contained the substance of the work he afterwards published under the title of *An Inquiry into the Nature and Causes of the Wealth of Nations*." [1]

Under the third part were no doubt included those lectures on the history of civil society to which Millar expresses such deep obligation, and of which another pupil of Smith's, Professor Richardson of the Humanity chair in Glasgow—a minor poet of considerable acceptance in his day—also speaks with lively gratitude, particularly of those " on the nature of those political institutions that succeeded the downfall of the Roman Empire, and which included an historical account of the rise and progress of the most conspicuous among the modern European governments." [2]

Richardson tells us, too, that Smith gave courses of lectures on taste, on the history of philosophy, and on belles-lettres, apparently continuing to utilise his old lectures on this last subject occasionally even after his

[1] Stewart's *Works*, x. 12.
[2] Richardson's *Life of Arthur*.   See *Arthur's Discourses*, p. 510.

translation from the chair to which they properly apper-
tained, and that he was very fond of digressing into
literary criticism from his lectures on any subject.
" Those who received instruction from Dr. Smith," says
Richardson, " will recollect with much satisfaction many
of those incidental and digressive illustrations and discussions, not only in morality but in criticism, which were
delivered by him with animated and extemporaneous
eloquence as they were suggested in the course of question
and answer. They occurred likewise, with much display
of learning and knowledge, in his occasional explanations
of those philosophical works, which were also a very
useful and important subject of examination in the class
of moral philosophy." [1]

His characteristics as a lecturer are thus described by
Millar :—

" There was no situation in which the abilities of
Mr. Smith appeared to greater advantage than as a
professor. In delivering his lectures he trusted almost
entirely to extemporary elocution. His manner, though
not graceful, was plain and unaffected, and as he seemed to
be always interested in the subject, he never failed to
interest his hearers. Each discourse consisted commonly
of several distinct propositions, which he successively
endeavoured to prove and illustrate. These propositions
when announced in general terms had, from their extent,
not unfrequently something of the air of a paradox. In his
attempts to explain them, he often appeared at first not to
be sufficiently possessed of the subject, and spoke with
some hesitation. As he advanced, however, his manner
became warm and animated, and his expression easy and
fluent. On points susceptible of controversy you could
easily discern that he secretly conceived an opposition to
his opinions, and that he was led upon this account to
support them with greater energy and vehemence. By the
fulness and variety of his illustrations the subject gradually

---

[1] Richardson's *Life of Arthur*. See *Arthur's Discourses*, p. 508.

swelled in his hands and acquired a dimension which, without a tedious repetition of the same views, was calculated to seize the attention of his audience, and to afford them pleasure as well as instruction in following the same subject through all the diversity of shades and aspects in which it was presented, and afterwards in tracing it backwards to that original proposition or general truth from which this beautiful train of speculation had proceeded." [1]

One little peculiarity in his manner of lecturing was mentioned to the late Archdeacon Sinclair by Archibald Alison the elder, apparently as Alison heard it from Smith's own lips. He used to acknowledge that in lecturing he was more dependent than most professors on the sympathy of his hearers, and he would sometimes select one of his students, who had more mobile and expressive features than the rest, as an unsuspecting gauge of the extent to which he carried with him the intelligence and interest of the class. "During one whole session," he said, "a certain student with a plain but expressive countenance was of great use to me in judging of my success. He sat conspicuously in front of a pillar : I had him constantly under my eye. If he leant forward to listen all was right, and I knew that I had the ear of my class ; but if he leant back in an attitude of listlessness I felt at once that all was wrong, and that I must change either the subject or the style of my address." [2]

The great majority of his students were young men preparing for the Presbyterian ministry, a large contingent of them—quite a third of the whole—being Irish dissenters who were unfairly excluded from the university of their own country, but appear to have been no very worthy accession to the University of Glasgow. We know of no word of complaint against them from Smith, but they were a sore trial both to Hutcheson and to Reid. Reid says he always felt in lecturing to those " stupid Irish teagues " as

[1] Stewart's *Works*, x. 12.
[2] Sinclair's *Old Times and Distant Places*, p. 9.

St. Anthony must have felt when he preached to the fishes,[1] and Hutcheson writes a friend in the north of Ireland that his Irish students were far above taking any interest in their work, and that although he had "five or six young gentlemen from Edinburgh, men of fortune and fine genius, studying law, these Irishmen thought them poor bookworms."[2] Smith had probably even more of this stamp of law students than Hutcheson. Henry Erskine attended his class on jurisprudence as well as his elder brother. Boswell was there in 1759, and was made very proud by the certificate he received from his professor at the close of the session, stating that he, Mr. James Boswell, was "happily possessed of a facility of manners."[3] After the publication of the *Theory of Moral Sentiments*, students came even from a greater distance. Lord Shelburne, who was an enthusiastic admirer of that work, sent his younger brother, the Honourable Thomas Fitzmaurice, for a year or two to study under Smith, before sending him to Oxford in 1761 to read law with Sir William Blackstone. Mr. Fitzmaurice, who married the Countess of Orkney, and is the progenitor of the present Orkney family, rose to a considerable political position, and would have risen higher but for falling into ill health in the prime of life and remaining a complete invalid till his death in 1793, but he never forgot the years he spent as a student in Smith's class and a boarder in Smith's house. Dr. Currie, the well-known author of the *Life of Burns*, was his medical attendant in his latter years, and Dr. Currie says his conversation always turned back to his early life, and particularly to the pleasant period he had spent under Smith's roof in Glasgow. Currie has not, however, recorded any reminiscences of those conversations.[4] Two Russian students came in 1762, and Smith had twice to

---

[1] Hamilton's *Reid*, p. 43.
[2] M'Cosh, *Scottish Philosophy*, p. 66.
[3] Boswell's *Correspondence with Erskine*, p. 26.
[4] Currie's *Memoirs of James Currie, M.D.*, ii. 317.

give them an advance of £20 apiece from the College funds, because their remittances had got stopped by the war. Tronchin, the eminent physician of Geneva, the friend of Voltaire, the enemy of Rousseau, sent his son to Glasgow in 1761 purposely "to study under Mr. Smith," as we learn from a letter of introduction to Baron Mure which the young man received before starting from Colonel Edmonston of Newton, who was at the time resident in Geneva. It was of Tronchin Voltaire said, "He is a great physician, he knows the mind," and he must have formed a high idea of the *Theory of Moral Sentiments* to send his son so far to attend the lectures of its author. It was this young man who, on his way back from Glasgow, played a certain undesigned part in originating the famous quarrel between Rousseau and Hume, of which we shall have more to hear anon. He was living with Professor Rouet of Glasgow, at Miss Elliot's lodging-house in London, when Hume brought Rousseau there in January 1866, and the moment Rousseau saw the son of his old enemy established in the house to which he was conducted, he flew to the conclusion that young Tronchin was there as a spy, and that the good and benevolent Hume was weaving some infernal web about him.

Smith's popularity as a lecturer grew year by year. It was felt that another and perhaps greater Hutcheson had risen in the College. Reid, when he came to Glasgow to succeed him in 1764, wrote his friend Dr. Skene in Aberdeen that there was a great spirit of inquiry abroad among the young people in Glasgow—the best testimony that could be rendered of the effect of Smith's teaching. It had taught the young people to think. His opinions became the subjects of general discussion, the branches he lectured on became fashionable in the town, the sons of the wealthier citizens used to go to College to take his class though they had no intention of completing a university course, stucco busts of him appeared in the booksellers' windows, and the very peculiarities of his voice and pronunciation received the homage of imitation. One point alone caused a little—in certain quarters not a little—shaking of heads, we are told by John Ramsay of Ochtertyre. The distinguished professor was a friend of "Hume the atheist"; he was himself ominously reticent on religious subjects ; he did not conduct a Sunday class on Christian evidences like Hutcheson; he would often too be seen openly smiling during divine service in his place in the College chapel (as in his absent way he might no doubt be prone to do); and it is even stated by Ramsay that he petitioned the Senatus on his first appointment in Glasgow to be relieved of the duty of opening his class with prayer, and the petition was rejected ; that his opening prayers were always thought to "savour strongly of natural religion"; that his lectures on natural theology were too flattering to human pride, and induced "presumptuous striplings to draw an unwarranted conclusion, viz. that the great truths of theology, together with the duties which man owes to God and his neighbours, may be discovered by the light of nature without any special revelation,"[1] as if it were a fault to show religious truth to be natural, for fear young men should believe it too easily. No record of the alleged petition about the opening prayers and its refusal remains in the College minutes, and the story is probably nothing but a morsel of idle gossip unworthy of attention, except as an indication of the atmosphere of jealous and censorious theological vigilance in which Smith and his brother professors were then obliged to do their work.

In his lectures on jurisprudence and politics he had taught the doctrine of free trade from the first, and not the least remarkable result of his thirteen years' work in Glasgow was that before he left he had practically converted that city to his views. Dugald Stewart was explicitly informed by Mr. James Ritchie, one of the most eminent Clyde merchants of that time, that Smith had,

[1] Ramsay, *Scotland and Scotsmen*, i. 462, 463.

during his professorship in Glasgow, made many of the leading men of the place convinced proselytes of free trade principles.[1] Sir James Steuart of Coltness, the well-known economist, used, after his return from his long political exile in 1763, to take a great practical interest in trying to enlighten his Glasgow neighbours on the economical problems that were rising about them, and having embraced the dying cause in economics as well as in politics, he sought hard to enlist them in favour of protection, but he frankly confesses that he grew sick of repeating arguments for protection to these " Glasgow theorists," as he calls them, because he found that Smith had already succeeded in persuading them completely in favour of a free importation of corn.[2] Sir James Steuart was a most persuasive talker ; Smith himself said he understood Sir James's system better from his talk than from his books,[3] and those Glasgow merchants must have obtained from Smith's expositions a very clear and complete hold indeed of the doctrines of commercial freedom, when Steuart failed to shake it, and was fain to leave such theorists to their theories. Long before the publication of the *Wealth of Nations*, therefore, the new light was shining clearly from Smith's chair in Glasgow College, and winning its first converts in the practical world. One can accordingly well understand the emotion with which J. B. Say sat in this chair when he visited Glasgow in 1815, and after a short prayer said with great fervour, " Lord, let now thy servant depart in peace."

Dugald Stewart further states, on the authority of gentlemen who were students in the moral philosophy class at Glasgow in 1752 or 1753, that Smith delivered so early as that lectures containing the fundamental principles of the *Wealth of Nations* ; and in 1755—

[1] Steuart's *Works*, vi. 379.
[2] *Ibid.* vi. 378.
[3] Dr. Cleland's account of Glasgow in *New Statistical Account of Scotland*, vi. 139.

the year Cantillon's *Essai* first saw the light, and the year before Quesnay published his first economic writing —Smith was not only expounding his system of natural liberty to his students, but publicly asserting his claim to the authorship of that system in a Glasgow Economic Society—perhaps the first economic club established anywhere. The paper in which Smith vindicates this claim came somehow into the possession of Dugald Stewart, and so escaped the fire to which Smith committed all his other papers before his death, but it is believed to have been destroyed by Stewart's son, very possibly after his father's directions. For Stewart thought it would be improper to publish the complete manuscript, because it would revive personal differences which had better remain in oblivion, and consequently our knowledge of its contents is confined to the few sentences which he has thought right to quote as a valuable evidence of the progress of Smith's political ideas at that very early period. It will be observed that, as far as we can collect from so small a fragment of his discourse, he presents the doctrine of natural liberty in a more extreme form than it came to wear after twenty years more of thought in the *Wealth of Nations*. Stewart says that many of the most important opinions in the *Wealth of Nations* are detailed in this document, but he cites only the following :—

" Man is generally considered by statesmen and projectors as the materials of a sort of political mechanics. Projectors disturb nature in the course of her operations on human affairs, and it requires no more than to leave her alone and give her fair play in the pursuit of her ends that she may establish her own designs. . . . Little else is required to carry a state to the highest degree of affluence from the lowest barbarism but peace, easy taxes, and a tolerable administration of justice ; all the rest being brought about by the natural course of things. All governments which thwart this natural course, which force things into another channel, or which endeavour to arrest the progress of society at a particular point, are unnatural, and, to support themselves, are obliged to be oppressive and tyrannical. . . . A great part of the opinions enumerated in this paper is treated of at length in some lectures which I have still by me, and which were written in the hand of a clerk who left my service six years ago. They have all of them been the constant subjects of my lectures since I first taught Mr. Craigie's class the first winter I spent in Glasgow down to this day without any considerable variations. They had all of them been the subjects of lectures which I read at Edinburgh the winter before I left it, and I can adduce innumerable witnesses both from that place and from this who will ascertain them sufficiently to be mine." [1]

The distinction drawn in the last sentence between *that* place, Edinburgh, and *this* place, shows that the paper was read to a society in Glasgow. Smith was a member of two societies there, of which I shall presently have something more to say, the Literary Society and a society which we may call the Economic, because it met for the discussion of economic subjects, though we do not know its precise name, if it had any. Now this paper of Smith's was not read to the Literary Society—at least, it is not included in the published list of papers read by it— and we may therefore conclude that it was read to the Economic Society.

Nothing is now known of the precise circumstances in which the paper originated, except what Stewart tells us, that Smith " was anxious to establish his exclusive right " to " certain leading principles both political and literary," " in order to prevent the possibility of some rival claims which he thought he had reason to apprehend, and to which his situation as a professor, added to his unreserved communications in private companies, rendered him peculiarly liable " ; and that he expressed himself " with a good deal of that honest and indignant warmth which is perhaps unavoidable

---

[1] Stewart's *Works*, ed. Hamilton, x. 68.

by a man who is conscious of the purity of his intentions when he suspects that advantages have been taken of the frankness of his temper." It would appear that some one, who had got hold of Smith's ideas through attending his class or frequenting his company, either had published them, or was believed to be going to publish them as his own.

The writer of the obituary notice of Smith in the *Monthly Review* for 1790 alleges that in this Glasgow period Smith lived in such constant apprehension of being robbed of his ideas that, if he saw any of his students take notes of his lectures, he would instantly stop him and say, " I hate scribblers." But this is directly contradicted by the account of Professor John Millar, who, as we have seen, was a student in Smith's classes himself, and who expressly states both that the permission to take notes was freely given by Smith to his students, and that the privilege was the occasion of frequent abuse. " From the permission given to students of taking notes," says Millar, " many observations and opinions contained in these lectures (the lectures on rhetoric and belles-lettres) have either been detailed in separate dissertations or engrossed in general collections which have since been given to the public." In those days manuscript copies of a popular professor's lectures, transcribed from his students' note-books, were often kept for sale in the booksellers' shops. Blair's lectures on rhetoric, for example, were for years in general circulation in this intermediate state, and it was the publication of his criticism on Addison, taken from one of the unauthorised transcripts, in Kippis's *Biographia Britannica*, that at length instigated Blair to give his lectures to the press himself. A professor was thus always liable to have his unpublished thought appropriated by another author without any acknowledgment at all, or published in such an imperfect form that he would hardly care to acknowledge it himself. If Smith, therefore, exhibited a jealousy over his rights to his own thought,

as has been suggested, Millar's observation shows him to
have had at any rate frequent cause; but neither at that
time of his life nor any other was he animated by an
undue or unreasonable jealousy of this sort such as he has
sometimes been accused of; and if in 1755 he took
occasion to resent with "honest and indignant warmth"
a violation of his rights, there must have been some special
provocation.

Mr. James Bonar suggests that this manifesto of 1755
was directed against Adam Ferguson, but that is not
probable. Ferguson's name, it is true, will readily occur
in such a connection, because Dr. Carlyle tells us that
when he published his *History of Civil Society* in 1767
Smith accused him of having borrowed some of his ideas
without owning them, and that Ferguson replied that he
had borrowed nothing from Smith, but much from some
French source unnamed where Smith had been before him.
But, however this may have been in 1767, it is unlikely
that Ferguson was the occasion of offence in 1755. Up
till that year he was generally living abroad with the
regiment of which he was chaplain, and it is not probable
that he had begun his *History* before his return to Scotland,
or that he had time between his return and the composition of Smith's manifesto to do or project anything to
occasion such a remonstrance. Then he is found on the
friendliest footing with Smith in the years immediately
following the manifesto, and Stewart's allusion to the circumstances implies a graver breach than could be healed so
summarily. Besides, had Ferguson been the cause of
offence, Stewart would have probably avoided the subject
altogether in a paper to the Royal Society, of which
Ferguson was still an active member.

CHAPTER VI

THE COLLEGE ADMINISTRATOR

A COMMON misconception regarding Smith is that he was as helpless as a child in matters of business. One of his Edinburgh neighbours remarked of him to Robert Chambers that it was strange a man who wrote so well on exchange and barter was obliged to get a friend to buy his horse corn for him. This idea of his helplessness in the petty transactions of life arose from observing his occasional fits of absence and his habitual simplicity of character, but his simplicity, nobody denies, was accompanied by exceptional acuteness and practical sagacity, and his fits of absence seem to have been neither so frequent nor so prolonged as they are commonly represented. Samuel Rogers spent most of a week with him in Edinburgh the year before his death, and did not remark his absence of mind all the time. Anyhow, during his thirteen years' residence at Glasgow College, Smith seems to have had more to do with the business of the College, petty or important, than any other professor, and his brethren in the Senate of that University cannot have seen in him any marked failing or incapacity for ordinary business. They threw on his shoulders an ample share of the committee and general routine work of the place, and set him to audit accounts, or inspect the drains in the College court, or see the holly hedge in the College garden uprooted, or to examine the encroachments on the College lands on the Molendinar Burn, without any fear of his forgetting his business on the way.   They entrusted him for years with the post of College Quæstor or Treasurer, in which inattention or the want of sound business habits might inflict injury even on their pecuniary interests. They made him one of the two curators of the College chambers, the forty lodgings provided for students inside the College gates.   And when there was any matter of business that was a little troublesome or delicate to negotiate, they seem generally to have chosen Smith for their chief spokesman or representative.   It was then very common for Scotch students to bring with them from home at the beginning of the session as much oatmeal as would keep them till the end of it, and by an ancient privilege of the University they were entitled to bring this meal with them into the city without requiring to pay custom on it ; but in 1757 those students were obliged by the tacksman of the meal-market to pay custom on their meal, though it was meant for their own use alone. Smith was appointed along with Professor Muirhead to go and represent to the Provost that the exaction was a violation of the privileges of the University, and to demand repayment within eight days, under pain of legal proceedings.   And at the next meeting of Senate " Mr. Smith reported that he had spoken to the Provost of Glasgow about the ladles exacted by the town from students for meal brought into the town for their own use, and that the Provost promised to cause what had been exacted to be returned, and that accordingly the money was offered by the town's ladler [1] to the students."

Smith was often entrusted with College business to transact in Edinburgh—to arrange with Andrew Stuart, W.S., about promoting a bill in Parliament, or to wait on the Barons of Exchequer and get the College accounts passed ; and he was generally the medium of communication

---

[1] The words ladles and ladler seem to have descended from a time when the exactions were made in kind by ladling the quantity out of the sack.

between the Senatus and the authorities of Balliol College during their long and troublesome contentions about the Snell property and the Snell exhibitioners.

He was Quæstor from 1758 till he left in 1764, and in that capacity had the management of the library funds and some other funds, his duties being subsequently divided between the factor and the librarian. The professors, we are told by Professor Dickson, used to take this office in turn for a term of two or three years, but Smith held the office longer than the customary term, and on the 19th of May 1763 the Senate agreed that "as Dr. Smith has long executed the office of Quæstor, he is allowed to take the assistance of an amanuensis." He was Dean of Faculty from 1760 to 1762, and as such not only exercised a general supervision over the studies of the College and the granting of degrees, but was one of the three visitors charged with seeing that the whole business of the College was administered according to the statutes of 1727. While still filling these two offices, he was in 1762 appointed to the additional and important business office of Vice-Rector, by his personal friend Sir Thomas Miller, the Lord-Advocate of Scotland (afterwards Lord President of the Court of Session), who was Rector of the University that year. As Sir Thomas Miller was generally absent in consequence of his public engagements in London or his professional engagements in Edinburgh, Smith as Vice-Rector had to preside over all University meetings—meetings of the Senatus, of the Comitia, of the Rector's Court—at a time when this duty was rendered delicate by the contentions which prevailed among the professors. The Rector's Court, it may be added—which consisted of the Rector and professors—was a judiciary as well as administrative body, which at one time possessed the power of life and death, and according to the Parliamentary Report of 1829, actually inflicted imprisonment in the College steeple on several delinquents within the preceding fifty years. It may be mentioned that some time elapsed after Sir Thomas Miller's election to the Rectorship before he was able to appoint a Vice-Rector, because he could not appoint a Vice-Rector till he was himself admitted, and he could not attend personally to be admitted on account of engagements elsewhere.   During this interval Smith was elected præses of the University meetings by the choice of his colleagues, and as the position was at the time one of considerable difficulty, they would not be likely to select for it a man of decided business incapacity.

Some idea of the difficulty of the place, on account of the dissensions prevailing in the College during Smith's residence there, may be got from a remark of his successor, Dr. Reid.   In the course of the first year after his arrival in Glasgow, Reid writes one of his Aberdeen friends complaining bitterly of being obliged to attend five or six College meetings every week, and meetings, moreover, of a very disagreeable character, in consequence of "an evil spirit of party that seems to put us in a ferment, and, I am afraid, will produce bad consequences." [1]   A writer in the *Gentleman's Magazine*, in noticing Smith's death in 1790, says that these divisions turned on questions of academic policy, and that Smith always took the side which was popular with people of condition in the city.   The writer offers no further particulars, but as far as we can now ascertain anything about the questions which then kept the Glasgow Senate in such perpetual perturbation, they were not questions of general policy or public interest such as his words might suggest, and on the petty issues they raised it makes no odds to know whether Smith sided with the kites or with the crows.   The troubles were generated, without any public differences, out of the constitution of the University itself, which seemed to be framed, as if on purpose, to create the greatest possible amount of friction in its working.   By its constitution, as that is described in the Parliamentary Report of 1830, Glasgow University was at that time under one name really two distinct cor-

[1] Hamilton's *Reid*, p. 43.

porations, with two distinct governing bodies : (1) the University governed by the Senate, which was composed of the Rector, the Dean of Faculty, the Principal, the thirteen College or Faculty professors, and the five regius professors ; and (2) the College governed by the Faculty, as it was called, which consisted of the thirteen College professors alone, who claimed to be the sole owners and administrators of the older endowments of the College, and to have the right of electing the occupants of their own thirteen chairs by co-optation. Within the Faculty again there was still another division of the professors into gown professors and other professors. The gown professors, who seem to have been the representatives of the five regents of earlier times, were the professors of those classes the students of which wore academical gowns, while the students of the other classes did not; the gown classes being Humanity, Greek, Logic, Natural Philosophy, and Moral Philosophy. These several bodies held separate meetings and kept separate minutes, which remain to this day. The meetings of the Senate were called University meetings or Rector's meetings, because they were presided over by the Rector; and the meetings of the Faculty were called Faculty meetings or Principal's meetings, because they were presided over by the Principal. Even the five gown professors with the Principal held separate meetings which the other professors had no right to attend—meetings with the students every Saturday in the Common Hall for the administration of ordinary academic discipline for petty offences committed by the students of the five gown classes. Smith belonged to all three bodies ; he was University professor, Faculty or College professor, and gown professor too. It is obvious how easily this complicated and unnatural system of government might breed incessant and irritating discussions without any grave division of opinion on matters of serious educational policy. Practical difficulties could scarce help arising as to the respective functions of the

University and the College, or the respective claims of the
regius professors and the Faculty professors, or the respective powers of the Rector and the Principal ; and Smith
himself was one of a small committee which presented a
very lengthy report on this last subject to the Senate of
the University on the 13th of August 1762. The report
was adopted, but two of the professors dissented on the
ground that it was too favourable to the powers of the
Principal.

But, wrangle as they might over petty points of constitutional right or property administration, the heads of
Glasgow College were guided in their general policy at
this period by the wisest and most enlightened spirit of
academic enlargement. Only a few years before Smith's
arrival they had recognised the new claims of science by
establishing a chemical laboratory, in which during Smith's
residence the celebrated Dr. Black was working out his
discovery of latent heat. They gave a workshop in the
College to James Watt in 1756, and made him mathematical instrument maker to the University, when the
trade corporations of Glasgow refused to allow him to
open a workshop in the city ; and it was in that very
workshop and at this very period that a Newcomen's
engine he repaired set his thoughts revolving till the
memorable morning in 1764 when the idea of the separate
condenser leapt to his mind as he was strolling past the
washhouse on Glasgow Green. They had at the same
time in another corner of the College opened a printing
office for the better advancement of that art, and were
encouraging the University printer, the famous Robert
Foulis, to print those Homers and Horaces by which he
more than rivalled the Elzevirs and Etiennes of the
past. To help Foulis the better, they had with their own
money assisted the establishment of the type - foundry
of Wilson at Camlachie, where Foulis procured the types
for his *Iliad ;* they appointed Wilson type-founder to the
University, and in 1762 they erected for him a founding-

house, as they called it, in their own grounds. They had just before endowed a new chair of astronomy, of which they had made their versatile type-founder the first professor, and built for him an astronomical observatory, from which he brought reputation to the College and himself by his observation of the solar spots. They further gave Foulis in 1753 several more rooms in the College, including the large room afterwards used as the Faculty Hall, to carry out his ill-fated scheme of an Academy of Design ; so that the arts of painting, sculpture, and engraving were taught in the College as well as the classics and mathematics, and Tassie and David Allan were then receiving their training under the same roof with the students for the so-called learned professions. The Earl of Buchan, while walking, as he said, " after the manner of the ancients in the porticoes of Glasgow with Smith and with Millar," unbent from the high tasks of philosophy by learning to etch in the studio of Foulis. This was the first school of design in Great Britain. There was as yet no Royal Academy, no National Gallery, no South Kensington Museum, no technical colleges, and the dream of the ardent printer, which was so actively seconded by the heads of the University, was to found an institution which should combine the functions of all those several institutions, and pay its own way by honest work into the bargain. In all these different ways the College of Glasgow was doing its best, as far as its slender means allowed, to widen the scope of university education in accordance with the requirements of modern times, and there was still another direction in which they anticipated a movement of our own day. They had already done something for that popularisation of academic instruction which we call university extension. Professor John Anderson, an active and reforming spirit who deserves to be held in honour in spite of his troublesome pugnacity, used then to deliver within the College walls, with the complete concurrence and encouragement of his colleagues, a series of evening

lectures on natural philosophy to classes of working-
men in their working clothes, and the lectures are
generally acknowledged to have done great service to the
arts and manufactures of the West of Scotland, by improving the technical education of the higher grades of
artisans.

Now in all these new developments Smith took a
warm interest ; some of them he actively promoted.
There is nothing in the University minutes to connect
Smith in any more special way than the other professors
with the University's timely hospitality to James Watt ;
but as that act was a direct protest on behalf of industrial
liberty against the tyrannical spirit of the trade guilds so
strongly condemned in the *Wealth of Nations*, it is at
least interesting to remember that Smith had a part in it.
Watt, it may be recollected, was then a lad of twenty,
who had come back from London to Glasgow to set up
as mathematical instrument maker, but though there was
no other mathematical instrument maker in the city, the
corporation of hammermen refused to permit his settlement because he was not the son or son-in-law of a
burgess, and had not served his apprenticeship to the
craft within the burgh.   But in those days of privilege
the universities also had their privileges.   The professors
of Glasgow enjoyed an absolute and independent authority
over the area within college bounds, and they defeated the
oppression of Watt by making him mathematical instrument maker to the University, and giving him a room in
the College buildings for his workshop and another at the
College gates for the sale of his instruments.   In these
proceedings Smith joined, and joined, we may be sure,
with the warmest approval.   For we know the strong
light in which he regarded the oppressions of the corporation laws.   " The property which every man has in his
labour," he says, " as it is the original foundation of all
other property, so it is the most sacred and inviolable.
The patrimony of the poor man lies in the strength and

dexterity of his hands, and to hinder him from employing this strength and dexterity in what manner he thinks proper without injury to his neighbour is a plain violation of this most sacred property. It is a manifest encroachment upon the just liberty both of the workman and of those who might be disposed to employ him."[1] Watt's workshop was a favourite resort of Smith's during his residence at Glasgow College, for Watt's conversation, young though he was, was fresh and original, and had great attractions for the stronger spirits about him. Watt on his side retained always the deepest respect for Smith, and when he was amusing the leisure of his old age in 1809 with his new invention of the sculpture machine, and presenting his works to his friends as "the productions of a young artist just entering his eighty-third year," one of the first works he executed with the machine was a small head of Adam Smith in ivory.[2]

In the Foulis press and the Academy of Design Smith took a particular interest. He was himself a book-fancier, fond of fine editions and bindings, and he once said to Smellie the printer, whom he observed admiring some of the books in his library, "I am a beau in nothing but my books." And he was a man, as Dugald Stewart informs us, with a carefully-cultivated taste for the fine arts, who was considered by his contemporaries an excellent judge of a picture or a sculpture, though in Stewart's opinion he appeared interested in works of art less as instruments of direct enjoyment than as materials for speculative discussions about the principles of human nature involved in their production. Smith seems to have been one of Foulis's chief practical advisers in the work of the Academy of Design, in settling such details, for example, as the pictures which ought to be selected to be copied by the pupils, or the subjects which ought to be chosen for original work from Plutarch or other classical

[1] *Wealth of Nations*, Book I. chap. ix.
[2] Muirhead's *Life of Watt*, p. 470.

sources, and which would be most likely to suit modern taste.

Sir John Dalrymple, who appears to have been one of Foulis's associates in the enterprise, and to have taken an active concern in the sale of the productions of the Academy in its Edinburgh agency shop, writes Foulis on the 1st of December 1757 regarding the kind of work that ought to be sent for sale there. " In the History pictures that you send in, I beg you will take the advice of Mr. Smith and Dr. Black. Your present scheme should be to execute not what you think the best, but what will sell the best. In the first you may be the better judge, since you are the master of a great Academa, but in the last I think their advice will be of use to you."[1] The letter concludes : " Whether it is an idea or not, I am going to give you a piece of trouble. Be so good as make out a catalogue of your pictures, and as far as you can of your busts, books of drawings, and prints. Secondly, your boys, and how employed. Thirdly, the people who have studied under you with a view to the mechanical art. And lastly, give some account of the prospects which you think you have of being of use either to the mechanical or to the fine arts of your country. Frame this into a memorial and send it to me. I shall have it tryed here by some who wish well to you, and as I go to London in the spring, I shall, together with Mr. Wedderburn and Mr. Elliot, consider what are the most prudent measures to take for your sake, or whether to take any. Mr. Smith is too busy or too indolent, but I flatter myself Dr. Black will be happy to make out this memorial for you. Let me know if I have any chance of seeing you this winter. I have none of being at Glasgow, and therefore wish you and Mr. Smith would come here, or you by yourself would come here in the Christmas vacance."

The memorial alluded to in this letter was no doubt a memorial to Government in behalf of a project then

[1] Duncan's *Notes and Documents*, p. 25.

promoted by the Earl of Selkirk and other friends of Foulis, of settling a salary on him for directing an institution so useful to the nation as the Academy of Design. Whether Smith overcame his alleged indolence and drew up the memorial I cannot say, but this whole letter shows that Smith and Black were the two friends in Glasgow whom Foulis was in the habit of principally consulting, and the last sentence seems to indicate that Smith's hand in the business was hardly less intimate than Dalrymple's own. It may be noticed too how completely Sir John Dalrymple's ideas of Smith, as implied in this letter, differ from those which are current now, and how he sends a tradesman to the philosopher for advice on practical points in his trade. As to pure questions of art, whether this work or that is finest, he thinks Foulis himself may possibly be the best judge, but when it comes to a question as to which will sell the best—and that was the question for the success of the project—then he is urged to take the practical mind of Smith to his counsels. Though Smith's leanings were not to practical life, his judgment, as any page of the *Wealth of Nations* shows, was of the most eminently practical kind. He had little of the impulse to meddle in affairs or the itch to manage them that belongs to more bustling people, but had unquestionably a practical mind and capacity.

If Smith was consulted by Foulis in this way about the management of the Academy of Design, we may safely infer that he had also more to do with the Foulis press than merely visiting the office to see the famous *Iliad* while it was on the case. Smith's connection with Foulis began before he went to Glasgow, by the publication of Hamilton of Bangour's poems by the University press, and I think it not unreasonable to see traces of Smith's suggestion in the number of early economic books which Foulis reissued after the year 1750, works of writers like Child, Gee, Mun, Law, and Petty.

In the University type-foundry Smith took an active interest, because he was a warm friend and associate of the accomplished type-founder.   Wilson had been bred a physician, but gave up his practice to become type-founder, and devoted himself besides, as I have just mentioned, to astronomy, to which Smith also at this period of his life gave some attention.   Smith indeed was possibly then writing his fragment on the history of astronomy, which, though not published till after his death, was, we are informed by Dugald Stewart, the earliest of all his compositions, being the first part of an extensive work on the history of all the sciences which he had at this time projected.   Wilson, having gone to large expense both of time and money to cast the Greek type for the University Homer, and having never found another customer for the fount except the University printer, went up to London in 1759 to push around, if possible, for orders, and was furnished by Smith with a letter of recommendation to Hume, who was then residing there.   Hume writes to Smith on the 29th of July : " Your friend Mr. Wilson called on me two or three days ago when I was abroad, and he left your letter.   I did not see him till to-day.   He seems a very modest, sensible, ingenious man.   Before I saw him I spoke to Mr. A. Millar about him, and found him much disposed to serve him.   I proposed particularly to Mr. Millar that it was worthy of so eminent a bookseller as he to make a complete elegant set of the classics, which might set up his name equal to the Alduses, Stevenses, or Elzevirs, and that Mr. Wilson was the properest person in the world to assist him in such a project.   He confessed to me that he had sometimes thought of it, but that his great difficulty was to find a man of letters that could correct the press.   I mentioned the matter to Wilson, who said he had a man of letters in his eye—one Lyon, a nonjuring clergyman of Glasgow.   I would desire your opinion of him." [1]

[1] Burton, *Life of Hume*, ii. 59.

When Wilson came to reside in the College in 1762, after his appointment to the chair of Astronomy, he found it inconvenient to go to and fro between the College and Camlachie to attend to the type-foundry, and petitioned the Senate to build him a founding-house in the College grounds, basing his claim on their custom of giving accommodation to the arts subservient to learning, on his own services to the University in the matter of the Greek types before mentioned, and on his having undertaken, in spite of the discouraging results of that speculation, to cast a large and elegant Hebrew type for the University press. He estimated that the building would cost no more than the very modest sum of £40 sterling, and he offered to pay a fair rent. This memorial came up for consideration on the 5th of April, and it was Smith who proposed the motion which was ultimately carried, to the effect that the University should build a new foundry for Mr. Wilson on the site most convenient within the College grounds, at an expense not exceeding the sum of £40 sterling, on condition (1) that Mr. Wilson pay a reasonable rent, and (2) that if the house should become useless to the College before the Senate were sufficiently recouped for their expenditure, Mr. Wilson or his heirs should be obliged to make adequate compensation. The foundry was erected in the little College garden next the Physic Garden ; it cost £19 more than the estimate, and was let for £3 : 15s. a year, from which it would appear that $6\frac{1}{2}$ per cent on the actual expenditure (irrespective of any allowance for the site) was considered a fair rent by the University authorities in those days.

The Senate of this little college, which was thus actively encouraging every liberal art, which had in a few years added to the lecture-room of Hutcheson and Smith the laboratory of Black, the workshop of Watt, the press of Foulis, the academy of painting, sculpture, and engraving, and the foundry and observatory of Wilson, entertained in 1761 the idea of doing something for the promotion of athletics among the students, and had under consideration a proposal for the establishment of a new academy of dancing, fencing, and riding in the University.   One of the active promoters of this scheme appears again to have been Adam Smith, for it is he who is chosen by the Senate on the 22nd December 1761 to go in their name and explain their design to the Rector, Lord Erroll, and request his assistance.   This idea seems, however, to have borne no fruit.   Dancing was an exercise they required to be observed with considerable moderation, for they passed a rule in 1752 that no student should be present at balls or assemblies or the like more than thrice in one session, but they treated it with no austere proscription.

One art alone did they seek to proscribe, the art dramatic, and in 1762 the Senate was profoundly disturbed by a project then on foot for the erection of the first permanent theatre in Glasgow.   The affair originated with five respectable and wealthy merchants, who were prepared to build the house at their own expense, the leading spirit of the five being Robert Bogle of Shettleston, who had himself, we are told by Dr. Carlyle, played " Sempronius " in a students' performance of *Cato* within the walls of Glasgow College in 1745.   Carlyle played the title *rôle*, and another divinity student, already mentioned as a college friend of Smith's, Dr. Maclaine of the Hague, played a minor part.   But an amateur representation of an unexceptionable play under the eye of the professors was one thing, the erection of a public playhouse, catering like other public playhouses for the too licentious taste of the period, was another, and the project of Mr. Bogle and his friends in 1762 excited equal alarm in the populace of the city, in the Town Council, and in the University.   The Council refused to sanction a site for the theatre within the city bounds, so that the promoters were obliged to build it a mile outside ; but the anger of

the multitude pursued them thither, and on the very eve
of its opening in 1764 by a performance in which Mrs.
Bellamy was to play the leading part, it was set on fire
by a mob, at the instigation of a wild preacher, who said
he had on the previous night been present in a vision at
an entertainment in hell, and the toast of the evening,
proposed in most flattering terms from the chair, was the
health of Mr. Millar, the maltster who had sold the site
for this new temple of the devil.

During the two years between the projection of this
building and its destruction it caused the Senate of the
College no common anxiety, and Smith went along with
them in all they did. On the 25th of November 1762
he was appointed, with the Principal and two other professors, as a committee, to confer with the magistrates
concerning the most proper methods of preventing the
establishment of a playhouse in Glasgow, and at the same
time to procure all the information in their power concerning the privileges of the University of Oxford with
respect to their ability to prevent anything of that kind
being established within their bounds, and concerning the
manner in which those privileges, if they existed, were
made effectual. On the recommendation of this committee the University agreed to memorialise the Lord
Advocate on the subject, and to ask the magistrates of
the city to join them in sending the memorial. The
Lord Advocate having apparently suggested doubts as to
the extent of their ancient powers or privileges in the
direction contemplated, Smith was appointed, along with
the Principal and one or two other professors, as a special
committee of inquiry into the ancient privileges and constitution of the University, and the Principal was instructed meanwhile to express to his lordship the earnest
desire of the University to prevent the establishment of a
playhouse. While this inquiry was proceeding, the magistrates of the city, on their part, had determined, with the
concurrence of a large body of the inhabitants, to raise an

action at law against the players if they should attempt to act plays in the new theatre, and at a meeting over which Smith presided, and in whose action he concurred, the University agreed to join the magistrates in this prosecution. The agitation against the playhouse was still proceeding when Smith resigned his chair in 1764, but shortly afterwards, finding itself without any legal support, it gradually died away.

The part Smith took in this agitation may seem to require a word of explanation, for he not only entertained no objection to theatrical representations, but was so deeply impressed with their beneficial character that in the *Wealth of Nations* he specially recommends them for positive encouragement by the State, and expressly dissociates himself from those " fanatical promoters of popular frenzies " who make dramatic representations " more than all other diversions the objects of their peculiar abhorrence." The State encouragement he wants is nothing in the nature of the endowment of a national theatre, which is sometimes demanded nowadays. All the encouragement he asks for is liberty—" entire liberty to all those who from their own interest would attempt, without scandal or indecency, to amuse and divert the people by painting, poetry, music, dancing, by all sorts of dramatic representations and exhibitions." But in pressing for this liberty, he expresses the strongest conviction that "the frequency and gaiety of public diversions" is absolutely essential for the good of the commonwealth, in order to " correct whatever is unsocial or disagreeably rigorous in the morals of all the little sects into which the country is divided," and to " dissipate that melancholy and gloomy humour which is almost always the source of popular superstition and enthusiasm." [1] Yet here we seem to find him in alliance with the little sects himself, and trying to crush that liberty of dramatic representations which he declares to be so vital to the health of the community.

[1] *Wealth of Nations*, Book V. chap. i. art. iii.

The reason is not, moreover, that he had changed his opinions in the interval between the attempts to suppress the Glasgow playhouse in 1762 and the publication of his general plea for playhouses in the *Wealth of Nations* in 1776. He had not changed his opinions. He travelled with a pupil to France, still warm from this agitation in Glasgow, and, as we learn from Stewart, was a great frequenter and admirer of the theatre in that country,[1] and a few years before the agitation began he was as deeply interested as any other of John Home's friends in the representations of the tragedy of *Douglas*, and as much a partisan of Home's cause. He does not appear indeed, as is sometimes stated, to have been present either at the public performance of Home's tragedy in Edinburgh in 1756, or at the previous private performance, which is alleged to have taken place at Mrs. Ward the actress's rooms, and in which the author himself, and Hume, Carlyle, Ferguson, and Blair are all said to have acted parts. But that he was in complete sympathy with them on the subject is manifest from an undated letter of Hume to Smith, which must have been written in that year. In this letter, knowing Smith's sentiments, he writes : " I can now give you the satisfaction of hearing that the play, though not near so well acted in Covent Garden as in this place, is likely to be very successful. Its great intrinsic merit breaks through all obstacles. When it shall be printed (which shall be soon) I am persuaded it will be esteemed the best, and by French critics the only tragedy of our language." After finishing his letter he adds : " I have just now received a copy of *Douglas* from London. It will instantly be put on the press. I hope to be able to send you a copy in the same parcel with the dedication." [2] These sentences certainly imply that Smith's ideas of theatrical representations were in harmony with those of Hume and his other Edinburgh friends, but

[1] Stewart's *Works*, x. 49.
[2] Burton's *Life of Hume*, ii. 16.

shortly afterwards he is seeking to revive obsolete academic privileges to prevent the erection of a theatre.

The explanation must be looked for in the line of the conditional clause with which he limits his claim for entire liberty to dramatic entertainments—they must be " without scandal or indecency." There is never any question that if free trade and public morals clash, it is free trade that must give way, and his opposition to the project of the Glasgow playhouse must have originated in his persuasion that it was not attended, as things then went, with sufficient practical safeguards against scandal and indecency. In considering that point due weight must be given not only to the general improprieties permissible on the English stage at that time, but to the fact that locally great offence had quite recently been given in Scotland by the profane or immoral character of some of the pieces presented on the Scottish boards,[1] and that Glasgow itself had had experience of a disorderly theatre already—the old wooden shed where hardy playgoers braved opinion and listened to indifferent performances under the protection of troops, and where, it will be remembered, Boswell, then a student at the College, made the acquaintance of Francis Gentleman, the actor. That house was not a licensed house, but the new house was not to be a licensed house either, and it is quite possible for one who thought a theatre generally, with due safeguards, a public benefit, to think that a particular theatre without those safeguards might constitute a public danger, especially in a university town.

On two delicate questions of professorial duty Smith made a decided stand in behalf of the stricter interpretation. In 1757 Professor John Anderson, the founder of the Andersonian University, who was then Professor of Oriental Languages in Glasgow, became a candidate for the chair which he afterwards filled for so many years with great credit and success—the chair of Natural Philosophy ; and, as the appointment lay with the professors, Professor

[1] See Doran's *Annals of the Stage*, ii. 377.

Anderson was one of the electors, and was quite within his legal right in voting for himself. But Smith, impressed with the importance of keeping such appointments free from any leaven of personal interest, tabled a formal protest on three successive occasions against the intervention of that distinguished but headstrong professor in the business of that particular election. He protested first against Anderson voting on a preliminary resolution respecting the election; he protested the second time against him taking part in the election itself; and he protested a third time after the election, desiring it to be recorded expressly "that he did not vote in the election of Mr. Anderson as Professor of Natural Philosophy, not from objection to Mr. Anderson, in whose election he would willingly have concurred, but because he regarded the method of proceeding as irregular and possibly establishing a bad precedent." As patrons of University chairs, the professors were trustees for the community, and ought each to be bound by a tacit self-denying ordinance, at least to the extent of refraining from actively using this public position to serve his private interest. Smith himself, it will be remembered, was one of his own electors to the Moral Philosophy chair, but then that election was uncontested, and Smith was not present at the meeting which appointed him.

The other personal question arose also out of circumstances which have their counterpart in Smith's own history. Professor William Rouet, Professor of Ecclesiastical and Civil History, made an engagement in 1759 to travel abroad as tutor with Lord Hope, the eldest son of Lord Hopetoun; but when Lord Hopetoun wrote requesting leave of absence for Professor Rouet, the Senate by a majority refused to grant the request. Smith was one of that majority, and took an active part in the subsequent transactions arising out of their decision. Rouet persists in going abroad in the teeth of the refusal, and the University by a majority deprive him of office for

his negligence of duty. The Crown, however, at first
refuse to appoint a successor, on the ground of informality
in the act of deprivation, and Lord Bute tells the Rector,
Lord Erroll, that " the king's orders " are that the business
must be done over again *de novo*, or " else it may be of
the worst consequences to the University." The University take the opinion of eminent counsel, Ferguson of
Pitfour and Burnet of Mountbodie (Monboddo), and are
prepared to face the consequences threatened, but are
eventually saved the trouble by the resignation of Rouet
in 1761. Now in these transactions Smith seems to bear
a leading part. He was one of the small committee
appointed to draw up answers to the protest tabled by
the minority of the Senatus ; it was to him Lord Erroll
communicated the intimation of Lord Bute, though he
was not then either Vice-Rector or Dean of Faculty ; and
it was he and Professor Millar who were sent through
to Edinburgh to consult the two advocates.

Smith was probably on the best terms with Rouet
himself, who was an intimate friend of David Hume and
a cousin of their common friend Baron Mure, and it was
not an uncommon practice for the Scotch universities at
that period to sanction the absence of a professor on a
tutorial engagement. Adam Ferguson left England as
tutor to Lord Chesterfield while he was Professor of
Moral Philosophy at Edinburgh, and Dalzel resided at
Oxford as tutor to Lord Maitland after he was Professor
of Greek in the same University. The Senate of Glasgow had itself already permitted Professor John Anderson
to remain another winter in France with a son of the
Primate of Ireland, when he was chosen Professor of
Oriental Languages in 1756, and Smith had concurred in
giving the permission. But Anderson's absence was
absence to fulfil an already-existing engagement, like the
absence granted to Smith himself in the first year of his
own appointment, while Rouet's was absence to fulfil a
new one ; and Smith, as his own subsequent conduct

shows, held pluralities and absenteeism of that sort to be a wrong and mischievous subordination of the interest of the University to the purely private interest or convenience of the professors. They had too many temptations to accommodate one another by such arrangements at the expense of the efficiency of the College; and his action both in Rouet's case and his own is entirely in the spirit of his criticism of the English universities in the *Wealth of Nations*.

CHAPTER VII

AMONG GLASGOW FOLK

SMITH was not only teacher in Glasgow, he was also learner, and the conditions of time and place were most favourable, in many important ways, for his instruction. Had he remained at Oxford, he would probably never have been an economist; had he not spent so many of his best years in Glasgow, he would never have been such an eminent one. It was amid the thickening problems of the rising trade of the Clyde, and the daily discussions they occasioned among the enterprising and intelligent merchants of the town, that he grew into a great economist.

It need scarce be said that the Glasgow of the middle of last century was a very different city from the Glasgow of to-day. It was in size and appearance a mere provincial town of 23,000 inhabitants. Broom still grew on the Broomielaw; a few cobles were the only craft on the river; and the rude wharf was the resort of idlers, watching the fishermen on the opposite side cast for salmon, and draw up netfuls on the green bank. The Clyde was not deepened till 1768. Before that the whole tonnage dues at Glasgow were only eight pounds a year, and for weeks together not a single vessel with a mast would be seen on the water. St. Enoch Square was a private garden; Argyle Street an ill-kept country road; and the town herd still went his rounds every morning with his horn, calling the cattle from the Trongate and the Saltmarket to their pasture on the common meadows in the now densely-populated district of the Cowcaddens.

Glasgow in these its younger days struck every traveller chiefly for its beauty. Mrs. Montagu thought it the most beautiful city in Great Britain, and Defoe, a few years before, said it was " the cleanest and beautifullest and best built city in Britain, London excepted." As Mrs. Bellamy approached it on the occasion I have mentioned in order to open the new theatre in 1764, she says "the magnificence of the buildings and the beauty of the river . . . elated her heart" ; and Smith himself, we know, once suffered for praising its charms. It was at a London table, and Johnson was present, who, liking neither Smith nor his Scotch city, cut him short by asking, " Pray, sir, have you seen Brentford ? " Boswell, who took a pride in Glasgow himself, calling it " a beautiful city," afterwards expostulated with the doctor for this rough interruption : " Now, sir," said he, " was not that rude ? " The full rudeness is only apparent when we remember that Brentford was in that day a byword for dreariness and dirt—Thomson in the *Castle of Indolence* calls it " a town of mud." When Johnson visited Glasgow, however, he joined the troop of its admirers himself, and Boswell took the opportunity to put him then in mind of his question to Smith, and whisper to him, " Don't you feel some remorse ? "

But Glasgow had already begun its transition from the small provincial to the great commercial capital, and was therefore at a stage of development of special value to the philosophical observer. Though still only a quiet but picturesque old place, nestling about the Cathedral and the College and two fine but sleepy streets, in which carriers built their haystacks out before their door, it was carrying on a trade which was even then cosmopolitan. The ships of Glasgow were in all the waters of the world, and its merchants had won the lead in at least one important branch of commerce, the West India tobacco trade, and were founding fresh industries every year with the greatest possible enterprise. The prosperity of Glasgow is a fruit of the Union which first opened the colonial markets to Scotch merchandise, and enabled the merchants of the Clyde to profit by the advantages of their natural situation for trading with the American plantations. Before the middle of the century the Clyde had become the chief European emporium for American tobacco, which foreign countries were not then allowed to import directly, and three-fourths of the tobacco was immediately on arrival transhipped by the Glasgow merchants for the seaports of the Mediterranean, the Baltic, and the North Sea.

As they widened their connections abroad, they naturally developed their industries at home. They founded the Smithfield ironworks, and imported iron from Russia and Sweden to make hoes and spades for the negroes of Maryland. They founded the Glasgow tannery in 1742, which Pennant thought an amazing sight, and where they employed 300 men making saddles and shoes for the plantations. They opened the Pollokshaws linen print-field in 1742, copper and tin works in 1747, the Delffield pottery in 1748. They began to manufacture carpets and crape in 1759, silk in 1759, and leather gloves in 1763. They opened the first Glasgow bank—the Ship— in 1750, and the second—the Arms—in 1752. They first began to improve the navigation of the Clyde by the Act of 1759 ; they built a dry dock at their harbour of Port Glasgow in 1762 ; while in 1768 they deepened the Clyde up to the city, and began (for this also was mainly their work) the canal to the Forth for their trade with the Baltic. It was obvious, therefore, that this was a period of unique commercial enterprise and expansion. We can easily believe Gibson, the historian of Glasgow, when he states that after 1750 " not a beggar was to be seen in the streets," and " the very children were busy " ; and we can as easily understand Smith when, contrasting Glasgow and Edinburgh among other places, he says the residence of a

few spirited merchants is a much better thing for the
common people of a place than the residence of a court.

Now it was those spirited merchants who had then so
much to do with the making of Glasgow that had also
something to do with the making of Adam Smith. Plain
business men of to-day sometimes smile at the " Virginian
Dons " and " tobacco lords " of last century as they picture
them gathering to the Glasgow Plainstanes at the hour of
'Change in the glory of scarlet cloaks, cocked hats, and gold-
headed canes, and the plain citizens of that time all making
way for their honours as they passed. But there was much
enlightenment and sagacity concealed under that finery.
Mrs. Montagu, who visited Glasgow in 1767, wrote Sir
A. Mitchell, the Ambassador, that she was more delighted
with it than with any other commercial town she had seen,
because gain did not usurp people's whole attention, but
" the sciences, the arts, and the love of agriculture had
their share." [1] Their fortunes were small compared with
the present standard. Sir John Dalrymple, speaking of
three of the foremost merchants of Glasgow (one of them,
John Glassford, the richest man in the city), computes that
they had a quarter of a million between the three, and Dr.
Reid, explaining the anxiety caused in Glasgow by the
American troubles in 1765, says Glasgow owners possessed
property in the American plantations amounting to
£400,000. But these figures meant large handling and
large dealings in those times, and perhaps more energy,
mind, and character than the bigger figures of the present
day ; and we are told that commercial men in Glasgow still
look back to John Glassford and Andrew Cochrane as
perhaps the greatest merchants the Clyde has seen.

Andrew Cochrane was Smith's particular friend among
them, and Dr. Carlyle tells that " Dr. Smith acknowledged his obligations to this gentleman's information
when he was collecting materials for his *Wealth of
Nations ;* and the junior merchants who have flourished

[1] Add. MSS., 6856.

since his time and extended their commerce far beyond what was then dreamt of, confess with respectful remembrance that it was Andrew Cochrane who first opened and enlarged their views."[1]   Dr. Carlyle informs us, moreover, that Cochrane founded a weekly club in the " forties " —a political economy club—of which " the express design was to inquire into the nature and principles of trade in all its branches, and to communicate knowledge and ideas on that subject to each other," and that Smith became a member of this club after coming to reside in Glasgow. This was probably the first political economy club in the world, for Carlyle was in Glasgow in 1743, and it is of that period he speaks when he says, " I was not acquainted with Provost Cochrane at this time, but I observed that the members of this society had the highest admiration of his knowledge and talents."

Cochrane was indeed one of the remarkable men of that time.   Smollett describes him in *Humphrey Clinker* as " one of the first sages of the Scottish kingdom," and " a patriot of a truly Roman spirit."   He was Provost of Glasgow during the Rebellion, and while the Government and the Horse Guards slumbered and dawdled, and let Prince Charlie march from the Highlands to Edinburgh, and from Edinburgh up into the heart of England, Cochrane had already raised two regiments in Glasgow to resist the invader, which, however, this same dawdling Government, from mistaken suspicions of Scottish loyalty, refused to permit him to arm.   The Prince, on his return from England, actually occupied Glasgow, and taxed it severely, but Cochrane's sagacious management piloted the city through the crisis, so that it neither yielded to the popular Prince's arts nor provoked him to hostilities ; and, looking back at these difficulties when he laid down the Provostship a few years later, he said, " I thank my God that my magistracy has ended without reproach."   His correspondence, published by the Maitland Club, contains some

----

[1] Carlyle's *Autobiography*, p. 73.

terse descriptions of the "prodigious slavery" he underwent, "going through the great folks" in London day
after day for two months trying to recover from the
Government some compensation for the Prince's exactions.
And it may be added that it was his banking firm—
Cochrane, Murdoch and Co., generally known, however, as
the Glasgow Arms Bank, because they printed the Glasgow
arms on their notes—that fell on the happy expedient of
paying in sixpences when the Bank of Scotland made the
infamous attempt to "break" it in 1759 by first collecting
its notes for some time, and then suddenly presenting the
whole number collected for immediate payment. The
agent of the Bank of Scotland presented £2893 of notes
on the 14th of December, and after thirty-four successive
days' attendance he wrote his employers that he had only
received £1232, because "the partners vied with each other
in gaining time by miscounting and other low arts, and
when the partners became wearied or ashamed of the task,
their porter, a menial servant, would act the part of
teller." [1]

Of the Political Economy Club, founded by this able
man, we know nothing except what Dr. Carlyle tells us,
and the only other member of it besides Smith and
Cochrane whose name Carlyle mentions is Dr. Wight,
Professor of Ecclesiastical and Civil History. But it met
once a week all the thirteen years Smith resided in Glasgow,
and must have discussed many commercial problems during
that time. We know, indeed, some of the principal
practical questions which were then agitating the minds of
Glasgow merchants, and may be sure those, at least, would
be among the questions discussed at the club. Some of
them concerned the removal of trade restrictions, but the
restrictions which those Glasgow merchants were anxious to
remove were restrictions on the import of raw materials
for their manufactures, such as iron and linen yarn, and
manufacturers, of course, are not necessarily free-traders

[1] Fleming's *Scottish Banking*, p. 53.

because they want free import of raw materials. That was advocated as strongly from the old mercantilist standpoint as it is now from the free-trade one; it was merely sanctioning a little addition to our imports in order to produce a much greater addition to our exports.

In 1750 we find Provost Cochrane in correspondence with Smith's friend, James Oswald, M.P., concerting parliamentary action for the entire removal of the import duty on American iron. The Glasgow ironworks—the nailery, as it was called—with which Mr. Cochrane was connected used at that time 400 tons of iron in the year, and the iron had to be all imported at a high price from Russia and Sweden, because the native ores of Scotland were not then discovered, and American iron, by an iniquitous piece of preferential legislation in favour of the English manufacturer, was allowed to come duty free into English but not into Scotch seaports. Cochrane wants Oswald to get the law amended so as to "allow bar iron from our colonies to be imported to Scotland duty free." "It would," he says, "save our country very great sums, and no way hurt the landed interest. It would lower the price of iron, and consequently of all our manufactures, which would increase the consumpt and sale; it would serve for ballast to our ships from North America, and when tobacco is scarce, fill up part of the tonnage ; would increase our exports, and no way interfere with our neighbours in the South." [1] That language might be held indifferently by the mercantilist and the free-trader.

In advocating the abolition of the duty on foreign linen yarns, which they succeeded in obtaining in 1756, the Glasgow merchants seem certainly to have had no thought of free trade, or probably anything else but their own obvious interest as manufacturers, for they never dreamt of abolishing either the export bounty on home-made linen cloth or of repealing the law of 1748, which gave their

[1] Oswald's *Correspondence*, p. 229.

own Glasgow linen factory a considerable lift, and which forbade the import of foreign linen, and fined husbands for letting their wives wear it. Still the discussion of these subjects would open up various points of view, and it may be remembered that this duty on foreign linen yarns is one which Smith himself, free-trader though he was, was against abolishing, not out of any favour for the flax-growers, but for the protection of the poor women scattered in the cottages of the kingdom who made their livelihood by spinning yarn.

On the question of paper money we find Mr. Cochrane and Mr. Glassford—both of whom were bankers as well as merchants—in communication with Baron Mure and Sir James Steuart, the economist, soon after Smith left Glasgow. Sir James would almost certainly be a member of the club, because he resided in the neighbourhood, but as he was only pardoned a few months before Smith resigned his chair, it is improbable that the two economists ever met together at the club meetings. But the questions the two leading merchants were then discussing with Sir James would, no doubt, have been occasionally subjects of conversation at the club during the time of Smith's attendance. What, we find them asking, are the effects of paper money on prices? on the currency? on the exchanges with other countries? What was the effect of small notes? what of notes not payable on demand? They differed on various points. For example, Glassford would let the banks issue notes for any sums they liked, and had no objection to the small ten-shilling and five-shilling notes which were then common. Cochrane would abolish all notes for less than a pound,[1] and Smith—at least in 1776— would abolish all notes less than five pounds.[2] But all alike had a firm grasp of the true nature and operation of money.

Another society of which Smith was a member, and

[1] *Caldwell Papers*, ii. 3.
[2] *Wealth of Nations*, Book II. chap. ii.

indeed a founder, was the Literary Society of Glasgow. It was a general debating society composed mainly of professors in the University—Cullen, Black, Wilson the astronomer ; Robert Simson, Leechman the divinity professor and principal ; Millar, and indeed nearly the whole Senatus ; with a few merchants or country gentlemen of literary tastes such as William Craufurd, the friend of Hamilton of Bangour; William Mure of Caldwell, M.P. for Renfrewshire ; Sir John Dalrymple, the historian, who was a proprietor in the West country ; John Callander of Craigforth, the antiquary ; Thomas Miller, Town Clerk of Glasgow, and afterwards Lord Justice-Clerk of Scotland; Robert Foulis, the printer ; James Watt, who said he derived much benefit from it ; Robert Bogle of Shettleston, the promoter of the theatre already mentioned ; David Hume, and the Earl of Buchan, elected while residing as a student in 1762.

The Literary Society was founded in 1752, and met every Thursday evening from November to May at half-past six. Its minutes are probably still in existence somewhere, but a few extracts from them have been published by the Maitland Club,[1] and from them we learn that Smith was one of the first contributors to its proceedings. Early in its first session—on the 23rd of January 1753— Professor Adam Smith is stated to have read an account of some of Mr. David Hume's Essays on Commerce. These essays had then just appeared, and they had probably been seen by Smith before their publication, for in September 1752 Hume writes Smith asking him for any corrections he had to suggest on the old edition of the Political Essays with which the Commercial Essays were incorporated. We have seen Hume submitting one of these Commercial Essays in 1750 to Oswald and Mure, and when we find him in 1752 asking for suggestions from Smith on the essays already printed, we may safely infer that he

[1] *Notices and Documents illustrative of the Literary History of Glasgow*, p. 132.

had also asked and received suggestions on the new essays which had never been published.

The Maitland Club volume gives us no information about the papers read in this society after the first six months, except those read by Foulis, but no doubt Smith read other papers in the remaining ten years of his connection with the society. Its debates were often very keen ; the metaphysical and theological combats between Professor Millar—a most brilliant debater—and Dr. Reid, the father of the common-sense philosophy, were famous in their day ; and on one occasion tradition informs us that Smith engaged in a strenuous discussion on some subject for a whole evening against the entire assembly, and, having lost his point by an overwhelming majority, was overheard muttering to himself, " Convicted but not convinced." [1]

After their high controversies in the Literary Society and their keener but less noble contentions in the Senate Hall, the Glasgow professors used to unbend their bows again in the simple convivialities of " Mr. Robin Simson's Club." Mr. Robin Simson was the venerable Professor of Mathematics, equally celebrated and beloved, known through all the world for his rediscovery of the porisms of Euclid, but in Glasgow College—whose bounds he rarely quitted—the delight of all hearts for the warmth, breadth, and uprightness of his character, for the charming simplicity of his manner, and the richness of his weighty and sparkling conversation. It was his impressions of Simson that first gave Smith the idea that mathematicians possessed a specific amiability and happiness of disposition which placed them above the jealousies and vanities and intrigues of the lower world. For fifty years Simson's life was spent almost entirely within the two quadrangles of Glasgow College ; between the rooms he worked and slept in, the tavern at the gate, where he ate his meals, and the College gardens, where he took his daily walk of a fixed number of hundred paces, of which, according

[1] Strang's *Clubs of Glasgow*, 2nd ed. p. 314.

to some well-known anecdotes, he always kept count as
he went, even under the difficulties of interruption.   Mr.
Robin, who was unmarried, never went into general
society, but after his geometrical labours were over
finished the day with a rubber of whist in the tavern at
the College gate.   Here one or another of the professors
used to join him, and the little circle eventually ripened
into a regular club, which met for supper at this tavern
every Friday evening, and went out to Anderston for
dinner on Saturday.   It was then known as the Anderston
Club, as well as by its former designation from the name of
its founder.   Anderston was at that time quite a country
village.   It was very soon afterwards made busy enough
with the cotton factory of James Monteith, but at this time
James Monteith's father was using the spot as a market
garden.   It contained, however, a cosy little "change-
house," capable of providing the simple dinner then in
vogue.   The dinner consisted of only one course.   Mr.
M'George says the first dinner of two courses ever given
in Glasgow was given in 1786 ; and Principal M'Cormick
of St. Andrews, writing Dr. Carlyle about that date,
praises the dinner-parties of St. Andrews to the skies,
but says nobody gave two courses except Mrs. Prebendary Berkeley, and Mrs. Prebendary Berkeley was
the daughter-in-law of a bishop.   The course at the
Anderston dinner, moreover, consisted every week of the
same dish ; it was invariably chicken-broth, which Smollett
classes with haggis, singed sheepshead, fish and sauce, and
minced collops, as one of the five national dishes of
Scotland.   He describes it as "a very simple preparation
enriched with eggs in such a manner as to give the air of
a spoiled fricassee " ; but adds that "notwithstanding its
appearance, it is very delicate and nourishing."   The
chicken-broth was accompanied with a tankard of sound
claret, and then the cloth was removed for whist and a
bowl of punch.   At whist Smith was not considered an
eligible partner, for, says Ramsay of Ochtertyre, if an

idea struck him in the middle of the game he " either renounced or neglected to call,"[1] and he must have in this way given much provocation to the amiability of Simson, who, though as absent-minded as Smith ever was at common seasons, was always keenly on the alert at cards, and could never quite forgive a slip of his partner in the game. After cards the rest of the evening was spent in cheerful talk or song, in which again Simson was ever the leading spirit. He used to sing Greek odes set to modern airs, which the members never tired of hearing again, for he had a fine voice and threw his soul into the rendering. Professor Robison of Edinburgh, who was one of his students, twice heard him—no doubt at this club, for Simson never went anywhere else—sing a Latin hymn to the Divine Geometer, apparently of his own making, and the tears stood in the worthy old gentleman's eyes with the emotion he put into the singing of it. His conversation is said to have been remarkably animated and various, for he knew most other subjects nearly as well as he did mathematics. He was always full of hard problems suggested by his studies of them, and he threw into the discussion much whimsical humour and many well-told anecdotes. The only subject debarred was religion. Professor Traill says any attempt to introduce that peace-breaking subject in the club was checked with gravity and decision. Simson was invariably chairman, and so much of the life of the club came from his presence that when he died in 1768 the club died too.

Three at least of the younger men who shared the simple pleasures of this homely Anderston board—Adam Smith, Joseph Black, and James Watt—were to exert as important effects on the progress of mankind as any men of their generation. Watt specially mentions Smith as one of the principal figures of the club, and says their conversation, " besides the usual subjects with young men,

[1] Ramsay's *Scotland and Scotsmen in Eighteenth Century*, i. 468.

turned principally on literary topics, religion, morality, belles-lettres, etc., and to this conversation my mind owed its first bias towards such subjects in which they were all my superiors, I never having attended a college, and being then but a mechanic." [1] According to this account religion was not proscribed, but Professor Traill's assertion is so explicit that probably Watt's recollection errs. It is, however, another sign of the liberal spirit that then animated these Glasgow professors to find them welcoming on a footing of perfect equality one who, as he says, was then only a mechanic, but whose mental worth they had the sense to recognise. Dr. Carlyle, who was invited by Simson to join the club in 1743, says the two chief spirits in it then were Hercules Lindsay, the Professor of Law, and James Moor, the Professor of Greek, both of whom were still members in Smith's time. Lindsay, who, it will be remembered, acted as Smith's substitute in the logic class, was a man of force and independence, who had suffered much abuse from the Faculty of Advocates in Edinburgh for giving up the old practice of delivering his lectures in Latin, and refusing to return to it. Moor was the general editor of the famous editions of the classics printed by his brother-in-law, Robert Foulis, a man, says Dugald Stewart, of "a gaiety and levity foreign to this climate," much addicted to punning, and noted for his gift of ready repartee. He was always smartly dressed and powdered, and one day as he was passing on the Plainstanes he overheard two young military officers observe one to the other, " He smells strongly of powder." " Don't be alarmed, my young soldier," said Moor, turning round on the speaker, "it is not gunpowder." A great promoter of the merriment of the club was Dr. Thomas Hamilton, Professor of Anatomy, the grandfather of Sir William, the metaphysician, who is thus described in some verses by Dr. John Moore, the author of *Zelucco*—

[1] Smiles's *Lives of Boulton and Watt*, p. 112.

He who leads up the van is stout Thomas the tall,
Who can make us all laugh, though he laughs at us all ;
But *entre nous*, Tom, you and I, if you please,
Must take care not to laugh ourselves out of our fees.

Then we remember what Jeffrey says of "the magical vivacity" of the conversation of Professor John Millar.

CHAPTER VIII

DURING his residence in Glasgow Smith continued to maintain intimate relations with his old friends in Edinburgh. He often ran through by coach to visit them, though before the road was improved it took thirteen hours to make the journey ; he spent among them most part of many of his successive vacations ; and he took an active share, along with them, in promoting some of those projects of literary, scientific, and social improvement with which Scotland was then rife. His patron, Henry Home, had in 1752 been raised to the bench as Lord Kames, and was devoting his new-found leisure to those works of criticism and speculation which soon gave him European fame. David Hume, after his defeat at Glasgow, had settled for a time into the modest post of librarian to the Faculty of Advocates, and was writing his *History of England* in his dim apartments in the Canongate. Adam Ferguson, who threw up his clerical calling in 1754, and wrote Smith from Groningen to give him "clerical titles" no more, for he was "a downright layman," came to Edinburgh, and was made Hume's successor in the Advocates' Library in 1757 and professor in the University in 1759. Robertson did not live in Edinburgh till 1758, but he used to come to town every week with his neighbour John Home before the latter left Scotland in 1757, and they held late sittings with Hume and the other men of letters in the evening. Gilbert

Elliot entered Parliament in 1754, but was always back during the recess with news of men and things in the capital. The two Dalrymples—Sir David of Hailes, and Sir John of Cousland—were toiling at their respective histories, and both were personal friends of Smith's ; while another, of whom Smith was particularly fond—Wilkie, the eccentric author of the *Epigoniad*—was living a few miles out as minister of the parish of Ratho. Wilkie always said that Smith had far more originality and invention than Hume, and that while Hume had only industry and judgment, Smith had industry and genius. His mind was at least the more constructive of the two. A remark of Smith's about Wilkie has also been preserved, and though it is of no importance, it may be repeated. Quoting Lord Elibank, he said that whether it was in learned company or unlearned, wherever Wilkie's name was mentioned it was never dropped soon, for everybody had much to say about him.[1] But that was probably due to his oddities as much as anything else. Wilkie used to plough his own glebe with his own hands in the ordinary ploughman's dress, and it was he who was the occasion of the joke played on Dr. Roebuck, the chemist, by a Scotch friend, who said to him as they were passing Ratho glebe that the parish schools of Scotland had given almost every peasant a knowledge of the classics, and added, " Here, for example, is a man working in the field who is a good illustration of that training ; let us speak with him." Roebuck made some observation about agriculture. "Yes, sir," said the ploughman, " but in Sicily they had a different method," and he quoted Theocritus, to Roebuck's great astonishment.

Among Smith's chief Edinburgh friends at this period was one of his former pupils, William Johnstone—son of Sir James Johnstone of Westerhall, and nephew of Lord Elibank—who was then practising as an advocate at the Scotch bar, but ultimately went into Parliament, married

[1] Southey's *Life of A. Bell*, i. 23.

the greatest heiress of the time, Miss Pulteney, niece of the Earl of Bath, and long filled an honoured and influential place in public life as Sir William Pulteney. He was, as even Wraxall admits, a man of "masculine sense" and "independent as well as upright" character, and he devoted special attention to all economic and financial questions. It was Pulteney who in his speech on the suspension of cash payments by the Bank of England in 1797—in which he proposed the establishment of another bank—quoted from some unknown source the memorable saying which is generally repeated as if it were his own, that Smith "would persuade the present generation and govern the next." He quoted the words as something that had been "well said." Between him and Smith there prevailed a warm and affectionate friendship for more than forty years, and we shall have occasion again to mention his name. But I allude to him at present because a letter still exists which was given him by Smith at this period to introduce him, during a short stay he made in London, to James Oswald, then newly appointed to office at the Board of Trade. This is the only letter that happens to be preserved of all the correspondence carried on by Smith with Oswald, and while both the occasion of it and its substance reveal the footing of personal intimacy on which they stood, its ceremonious opening and ending indicate something of the reverence and gratitude of the client to the patron :—

SIR—This will be delivered to you by Mr. William Johnstone, son of Sir James Johnstone of Westerhall, a young gentleman whom I have known intimately these four years, and of whose discretion, good temper, sincerity, and honour I have had during all that time frequent proofs. You will find in him too, if you come to know him better, some qualities which from real and unaffected modesty he does not at first discover ; a refinement and depth of observation and an accuracy of judgment, joined to a natural delicacy of sentiment, as much improved as study and the narrow sphere of acquaintance this country affords can improve it. He had, first when I knew him, a good deal of vivacity and humour, but he has studied them away. He is an advocate ; and though I am sensible of the folly of prophesying with regard to the future fortune of so young a man, yet I could almost venture to foretell that if he lives he will be eminent in that profession. He has, I think, every quality that ought to forward, and not one that should obstruct his progress, modesty and sincerity excepted, and these, it is to be hoped, experience and a better sense of things may in part cure him of. I do not, I assure you, exaggerate knowingly, but could pawn my honour upon the truth of every article. You will find him, I imagine, a young gentleman of solid, substantial (not flashy) abilities and worth. Private business obliges him to spend some time in London. He would beg to be allowed the privilege of waiting on you sometimes, to receive your advice how he may employ his time there in the manner that will tend most to his real and lasting improvement.

I am sensible how much I presume upon your indulgence in giving you this trouble ; but as it is to serve and comply with a person for whom I have the most entire friendship, I know you will excuse me though guilty of an indiscretion ; at least if you do not, you will not judge others as you would desire to be judged yourself ; for I am very sure a like motive would carry you to be guilty of a greater.

I would have waited on you when you was last in Scotland had the College allowed me three days' vacation ; and it gave me real uneasiness that I should be in the same country with you, and not have the pleasure of seeing you. Believe it, no man can more rejoice at your late success,[1] or at whatever else tends to your honour and prosperity, than does, Sir, your ever obliged and very humble servant,   ADAM SMITH.

GLASGOW, 19*th January* 1752, N.S.[2]

Pulteney abandoned the law in which Smith prophesied eminence for him, but he was happily not cured entirely of his sincerity by his subsequent experience, for it was greatly from that quality that he derived the weight he enjoyed in the House of Commons. His contemporary in Parliament, Sir John Sinclair, says Pulteney's influence

[1] Oswald had just been appointed commissioner for trade and plantations.

[2] *Correspondence of James Oswald*, p. 124.

arose from the fact that he was known to be a man who never gave a vote he did not in his heart believe to be right. Having no taste for display, he lived when he had £20,000 a year about as simply as he did when he had only £200, and on that account he is sometimes accused of avarice, though he was constantly doing acts of signal liberality.

Smith's chief friend in Edinburgh was David Hume. Though their first relations were begun apparently in 1739, they could not have met much personally before Smith's settlement in Glasgow. For when Smith came to Edinburgh in 1748 Hume was abroad as secretary to General St. Clair in the Embassy at Vienna and Turin, and though he left this post in 1749, he remained for the next two years at Ninewells, his father's place in Berwickshire, and only settled in Edinburgh again just as Smith was removing to Glasgow. He would no doubt visit town occasionally, however, and before Smith was a year in Glasgow he had already entered on that correspondence with the elder philosopher which, beginning with the respectful " dear sir," grew shortly into the warmer style of " my dearest friend " as their memorable and Roman friendship ripened. Hume never paid Smith a visit in Glasgow, though he had often promised to do so, but Smith in his runs to Edinburgh spent always more and more of his time with Hume, and latterly at any rate made Hume's house his regular Edinburgh home.

In 1752 Hume had already taken Smith as one of his literary counsellors, and consulted him about the new edition of his *Essays, Moral and Political*, and his historical projects, and I may be permitted here and afterwards to quote parts of Hume's letters which throw any light on Smith's opinions or movements.

On the 24th of September 1752 he writes—

DEAR SIR—I confess I was once of the same opinion with you, and thought that the best period to begin an English History was about Henry the Seventh, but you will please to observe that the change which then happened in public affairs was very insensible, and did not display its influence for many years afterwards. . . . I am just now diverted for the moment by correcting my *Essays, Moral and Political* for a new edition. If anything occur to you to be inserted or retrenched, I shall be obliged if you offer the hint. In case you should not have the last edition by you I shall send you a copy of it. . . . I had almost lost your letter by its being wrong directed. I received it late, which was the reason you got not sooner a copy of *Joannes Magnus*.[1]

On the 17th of December 1754 Hume gives Smith an account of his quarrel with the Faculty of Advocates, and his resolution to stay as librarian after all, for the sake of the use of the books, which he cannot do without, but to give Blacklock, the blind poet, a bond of annuity for the salary. Three weeks later he writes again, and as the letter mentions Smith's views on some historical subjects, it may be quoted :—

EDINBURGH, *9th January* 1755.

DEAR SIR—I beg you to make my compliments to the Society, and to take the fault on yourself if I have not executed my duty, and sent them this time my anniversary paper. Had I got a week's warning I should have been able to have supplied them. I should willingly have sent some sheets of the History of the Commonwealth or Protectorship, but they are all of them out of my hand at present, and I have not been able to recall them.[2]

I think you are extremely in the right that the Parliament's

---

[1] Burton's *Life of Hume*, i. 375.

[2] Mr. Burton thinks the Society mentioned in this paragraph to be "evidently the Philosophical Society" of Edinburgh, but it seems much more likely to have been the Literary Society of Glasgow, of which Hume was also a member. Of the Philosophical Society he was himself Secretary, and would therefore have been in the position of giving warning rather than receiving it ; nor would he have spoken of sending that Society a paper which he would be on the spot to read himself. Whether Smith was Secretary of the Glasgow Literary Society I do not know, but even if he were not it would be nothing strange though the communications of the Society with Hume were carried on through Smith, his chief friend among the members, and his regular correspondent.

bigotry has nothing in common with Hiero's generosity. They were themselves violent persecutors at home to the utmost of their power. Besides, the Huguenots in France were not persecuted; they were really seditious, turbulent people, whom their king was not able to reduce to obedience. The French persecutions did not begin till sixty years after.

Your objection to the Irish massacre is just, but falls not on the execution but the subject. Had I been to describe the massacre of Paris I should not have fallen into that fault, but in the Irish massacre no single eminent man fell, or by a remarkable death. If the elocution of the whole chapter be blamable, it is because my conceptions laboured most to start an idea of my subject, which is there the most important, but that misfortune is not unusual.—I am, etc.[1]

In 1752 Smith was chosen a member of the Philosophical Society of Edinburgh, which, after an interregnum caused by the rebellion, was revived in that year, with David Hume for Secretary, and which was eventually merged in the Royal Society in 1784. But we know of no part he took, if he took any, in its proceedings. Of the Rankenian Society, again—the famous old club in Ranken's Coffee-house, to which Colin Maclaurin and other eminent men belonged, and some of whose members carried on a philosophical controversy with Berkeley, and, if we can believe Ramsay of Ochtertyre, were pressed by the good bishop to accompany him in his Utopian mission to Bermuda—Smith was never even a member, though it survived till 1774. But he took a principal part in founding a third society in 1754, which far eclipsed either of these—at least for a time—in *éclat*, and has left a more celebrated name, the Select Society.

The Select Society was established in imitation of the academies which were then common in the larger towns of France, and was partly a debating society for the discussion of topics of the day, and partly a patriotic society for the promotion of the arts, sciences, and manufactures of Scotland. The idea was first mooted by Allan Ramsay,

---

[1] Burton's *Life of Hume*, i. 417.

the painter, who had travelled in France as long ago
as 1739, with James Oswald, M.P., and was struck
with some of the French institutions. Smith was one
of the first of Ramsay's friends to be consulted about
the suggestion, and threw himself so heartily into it that
when the painter announced his first formal meeting for
the purpose on the 23rd of May 1754, Smith was not
only one of the fifteen persons present, but was entrusted
with the duty of explaining the object of the meeting and
the nature of the proposed institution. Dr. A. Carlyle,
who was present, says this was the only occasion he ever
heard Smith make anything in the nature of a speech,
and he was but little impressed with Smith's powers as a
public speaker. His voice was harsh, and his enunciation
thick, approaching even to stammering.[1] Of course
many excellent speakers often stutter much in making a
simple business explanation which they are composing as
they go along, and Smith always stuttered and hesitated
a deal for the first quarter of an hour, even in his class
lectures, though his elocution grew free and animated,
and often powerful, as he warmed to his task.

The Society was established and met with the most
rapid and remarkable success. The fifteen original mem-
bers soon grew to a hundred and thirty, and men of the
highest rank as well as literary name flocked to join it.
Kames and Monboddo, Robertson and Ferguson and
Hume, Carlyle and John Home, Blair and Wilkie and
Wallace, the statistician; Islay Campbell and Thomas
Miller, the future heads of the Court of Session; the Earls
of Sutherland, Hopetoun, Marchmont, Morton, Rosebery,
Erroll, Aboyne, Cassilis, Selkirk, Glasgow, and Lauderdale; Lords Elibank, Garlies, Gray, Auchinleck, and
Hailes; John Adam, the architect; Dr. Cullen, John Coutts,
the banker and member for the city; Charles Townshend,
the witty statesman; and a throng of all that was distinguished in the country, were enrolled as members, and,

---

[1] Carlyle's *Autobiography*, p. 275.

what is more, frequented its meetings. It met every Friday evening from six to nine, at first in a room in the Advocates' Library, but when that became too small for the numbers that began to attend its meetings, in a room hired from the Mason Lodge above the Laigh Council House; and its debates, in which the younger advocates and ministers—men like Wedderburn and Robertson—took the chief part, became speedily famous over all Scotland as intellectual displays to which neither the General Assembly of the Kirk nor the Imperial Parliament could show anything to rival. Hume wrote in 1755 to Allan Ramsay, who had by that time gone to settle in Rome, that the Select Society "has grown to be a national concern. Young and old, noble and ignoble, witty and dull, laity and clergy, all the world are ambitious of a place amongst us, and on each occasion we are as much solicited by candidates as if we were to choose a member of Parliament." He goes on to say that "our young friend Wedderburn has acquired a great character by the appearance he has made," and that Wilkie, the minister, "has turned up from obscurity and become a very fashionable man, as he is indeed a very singular one. Monboddo's oddities divert, Sir David's (Lord Hailes) zeal entertains, Jack Dalrymple's (Sir John of the *Memoirs*) rhetoric interests. The long drawling speakers have found out their want of talents and rise seldomer. In short, the House of Commons is less the object of general curiosity to London than the Select Society is to Edinburgh. The ' Robin Hood,' the ' Devil,' and all other speaking societies are ignoble in comparison." [1]

At the second regular meeting, which was held on the 19th of June 1754, Mr. Adam Smith was Præses, and gave out the subjects for debate on the following meeting night: (1) Whether a general naturalisation of foreign Protestantism would be advantageous to Britain ; and (2) whether bounties on the exportation of corn be advantageous to trade and

[1] Burton's *Scot Abroad*, ii. 340.

manufactures as well as to agriculture.[1]   Lord Campbell
in mentioning this circumstance makes it appear as if Smith
chose the latter subject of his own motion, in accordance
with a rule of the society whereby the chairman of one
meeting selected the subject for debate at the next meeting ;
and it would have been a not uninteresting circumstance if
it were true, for it would show the line his ideas were
taking at that early period of his career ; but as a matter
of fact the rule in question was not adopted for some time
after the second meeting, and it is distinctly mentioned in
the minutes that on this particular occasion the Præses
" declared before he left the chair the questions that were
agreed upon by the majority of the meeting to be the
subject of next night's debate." [2]   It is quite possible, of
course, that the subjects may have been of Smith's suggestion, but that can now only be matter of conjecture.
Indeed, whether it be due to his influence or whether it
arose merely from a general current of interest moving in
that direction at the time, the subjects discussed by this
society were very largely economic ; so much so that
in a selection of them published by the *Scots Magazine*
in 1757 every one partakes of that character.   " What
are the advantages to the public and the State from grazing ? what from corn lands ? and what ought to be most
encouraged in this country ?   Whether great or small farms
are most advantageous to the country ?   What are the most
proper measures for a gentleman to promote industry on
his own estate ?   What are the advantages and disadvantages
of gentlemen of estate being farmers ?   What is the best and
most proper duration of leases of land in Scotland ?   What
prestations beside the proper tack-duty tenants ought to
be obliged to pay with respect to carriages and other
services, planting and preserving trees, maintaining enclosures and houses, working freestone, limestone, coal, or
minerals, making enclosures, straightening marches, carry-

Minutes of Select Society, Advocates' Library, Edinburgh.
[2] *Ibid.*

ing off superfluous water to other grounds, and forming
drains? and what restrictions they should be put under
with respect to cottars, live stock on the farm, winter
herding, ploughing the ground, selling manure, straw, hay,
or corn, thirlage to mills, smiths or tradesmen employed
on business extrinsic to the farm, subsetting land, granting
assignations of leases, and removals at the expiration of
leases? What proportion of the produce of lands should
be paid as rent to the master? In what circumstances
the rents of lands should be paid in money? in what in
kind? and in what time they should be paid? Whether
corn should be sold by measure or by weight? What is
the best method of getting public highways made and
repaired, whether by a turnpike law, as in many places in
Great Britain, by county or parish work, by a tax, or by
what other method? What is the best and most equal
way of hiring and contracting servants? and what is the
most proper method to abolish the practice of giving of
vails?"[1]   The society had what may be termed a special
agricultural branch, to which I shall presently refer, and
which met once a month and discussed chiefly questions of
husbandry and land management; and the above list of
subjects looks, from its almost exclusively agrarian character, as if it had been rather the business of this branch of
the society merely than of the society as a whole. Still
the same causes that made rural economy predominate in
the monthly work of the branch would give it a large
place in the weekly discussions of the parent association. The members were largely connected with the
landed interest, and agricultural improvement was then on
the order of the day.

In this society accordingly, which Smith attended very
frequently, though he does not appear to have spoken in
the debates, he had with respect to agrarian problems precisely what he had in the economic club of Glasgow with
respect to commercial problems, the best opportunities of

[1] *Scots Magazine*, xix. 163.

hearing them discussed at first hand by those who were practically most conversant with the subjects in all their details.
Of course the society sometimes discussed questions of literature or art, or familiar old historical controversies, such as
whether Brutus did well in killing Cæsar? Indeed, no
subject was expressly tabooed except such as might stir up
the Deistic or Jacobite strife—in the words of the rules,
" such as regard revealed religion, or which may give
occasion to vent any principles of Jacobitism." But the
great majority of the questions debated were of an economic or political character,—questions about outdoor relief,
entail, banking, linen export bounties, whisky duties,
foundling hospitals, whether the institution of slavery
be advantageous to the free? and whether a union with
Ireland would be advantageous to Great Britain? Sometimes more than one subject would be got through in a
night, sometimes the debate on a single subject would be
adjourned from week to week till it was thought to be
thrashed out ; and every member might speak three times
in the course of a debate if he chose, once for fifteen
minutes, and the other twice for ten.

The Select Society was, however, as I have said, more
than a debating club ; it aimed besides at doing something
practical for the promotion of the arts, sciences, manufactures, and agriculture, in the land of its birth, and
accordingly, when it was about ten months in existence,
it established a well-devised and extensive scheme of prizes
for meritorious work in every department of human labour,
to be supported by voluntary subscriptions. In the prospectus the society issued it says that, after the example of
foreign academies, it had resolved to propose two subjects
for competition every year, chosen one from polite letters
and the other from the sciences, and to confer on the
winner some public mark of distinction in respect to his
taste and learning. The reward, however, was not in this
case to be of a pecuniary nature, for the principle of the
society was that rewards of merit were in the finer arts to

be honorary, but in the more useful arts, where the merit
was of a less elevated character, they were to be lucrative.
On the same principle, in the arts the highest place was
allowed to be due to genius, and therefore a reward for a
discovery or invention was set at the very top of the tree,
but still it was of a purely honorary character, a pecuniary
recognition being thought apparently unsuitable to the
dignity of that kind of service. " The art of printing,"
the prospectus goes on to say—with a glance of satisfaction
cast doubtless at the Foulis Press—" the art of printing
in this country needs no encouragement, yet as to pass it
by unnoticed were slighting the merit of those by whose
means alone it has attained that eminence, it was resolved
that the best printed and most correct book which shall
be produced within a limited time be distinguished by an
honorary reward.", On the other hand, the manufacture
of paper was a thing that required encouragement in Scotland, because the Scotch at that time imported their paper
from abroad, " from countries," says the prospectus, " which
use not half the linen that is here consumed " ; and " to
remove this defect, to render people more attentive to their
own interest as well as to the interest of their country, to
show them the consequence of attention to matters which
may seem trivial, it was resolved that for the first, second,
third, fourth, and fifth parcels of linen rags gathered within
a limited time a reward be assigned in proportion to the
quantity and goodness of each parcel." In other cases
manufactures were already well established in the country,
and the thing that still needed to be encouraged by prizes
was improvement in the workmanship. For example,
" manufactures of cotton and linen prints are already
established in different places of this country ; in order to
promote an attention to the elegance of the pattern and to
the goodness of the colouring, as well as to the strength
of the cloth, it was resolved that for the best piece of
printed linen or cotton cloth made within a certain period
a premium should be allotted." The art of drawing,

again, "being closely connected with this art and serviceable to most others, it was resolved that for the best drawings by boys or girls under sixteen years of age certain premiums be assigned." Then there was a considerable annual importation into Scotland of worked ruffles and of bone lace and edging which the Select Society thought might, under proper encouragement, be quite as well produced at home; and it was therefore resolved to give both honorary and lucrative rewards for superior merit in such work, the honorary for "women of fashion" who might compete, and the lucrative for those "whose laudable industry contributes to their own support." Scotch stockings had then a great reputation for the excellence of their workmanship, but Scotch worsted, to make them with, was not so good, and consequently a premium was to be offered for the best woollen yarn. There was a great demand at the time for English blankets, and no reason why the Scotch should not make quite as good blankets themselves out of their own wool, so a premium was proposed for the best imitation of English blankets. Carpet-making was begun in several places in the country, and a prize for the best-wrought and best-patterned carpet would encourage the manufacturers to vie with each other. Whisky-distilling, too, was established at different places, and Scotch strong ale had even acquired a great and just reputation both at home and abroad; but the whisky was " still capable of great improvement in the quality and taste," and the ale trade "might be carried to a much greater height," and these ends might be severally promoted by prizes for the best tun of whisky and the best hogshead of strong ale.

The practical execution of this scheme was committed to nine members of the society, who were to be chosen annually, and were to meet with the society once a month to report progress or receive instructions; but to keep this new task quite distinct from the old, the society resolved, like certain mercantile firms when they adopt a new branch of business, to carry it on under a new firm name, and for this purpose the Select Society of Edinburgh became " The Edinburgh Society for encouraging arts, sciences, manufactures, and agriculture in Scotland"; and the executive committee of nine were termed the "ordinary managers of the Edinburgh Society," who were assisted by other nine "extraordinary managers." The Edinburgh Society was not, however, a separate institution; it was really only a special committee of the Select Society. It met once a month at a separate time from the usual weekly meeting of the parent society, and the business of this monthly meeting came, from the predominant interest of the members, who were so largely composed of the nobility and gentry, to be engrossed almost wholly with agricultural discussions. To render these discussions more effective and profitable, a resolution was passed in 1756 to admit a certain number of practical farmers to the membership.

This extension of the scope of the society's work was not approved by its founder, Allan Ramsay, who thought it beneath the dignity of such an institution to take an interest in the making of ruffles or the brewing of strong ale, and feared besides that it would introduce a new set of very unintellectual members, to the serious prejudice of the society's debates. An essay on taste was very well, and when it came out he would ask Millar, the bookseller, to send it out to him in Rome, but a prize for the biggest bundle of linen rags! " I could have wished," he writes Hume, " that some other way had been fallen upon by which porter might have been made thick and the nation rich without our understanding being at all the poorer for it. Is not truth more than meat, and wisdom than raiment? "[1] But however Ramsay might look down on the project, his coadjutor in the founding of the society, Adam Smith, entertained a very different idea of its importance. A stimulus to the development of her

[1] Burton's _Scot Abroad_, ii. 343.

industries was the very thing Scotland most needed at the moment, and he entered heartily into the new scheme, and took a prominent part in carrying it out. He was not one of the nine managers to whom the practical execution of the idea was at first entrusted, but when a few months afterwards the work was divided among four separate committees or sections of five members each, all chosen by another committee of five, nominated expressly for that purpose, Smith is one of this nominating committee, and is by it appointed likewise a member of one of the four executive committees. The other four members of the nominating committee were Alexander Monro *Primus*, the anatomist ; Gilbert Elliot, M.P. for Selkirkshire ; the Rev. William Wilkie, author of the *Epigoniad;* and the Rev. Robert Wallace, the predecessor and at least in part the stimulator of Malthus in his speculations on the population question. The five members of this committee were directed by the society to put their own names on one or other of the four executive committees, and they placed the name of Smith, together with that of Hume, on the committee for Belles-Lettres and Criticism. As yet he was evidently best known as literary critic, though the questions propounded by him in this society, and the subjects treated by him in the Literary Society of Glasgow, show that his tastes were already leading him into other directions.

Sufficient contributions soon flowed in ; Hume in his letter to Ramsay speaks of £100 being already in hand, and of several large subscriptions besides being promised from various noblemen, whom he names ; and accordingly an advertisement was published in the newspapers on the 10th of April 1755, offering the following prizes:—

I. Honorary premiums, being gold medals with suitable devices and inscriptions :—

 1. For the best discovery in science.
 2. For the best essay on taste.

3. For the best dissertation on vegetation and the principles of agriculture.

II. Honorary premiums, being silver medals with proper devices and inscriptions :—

4. For the best printed and most correct book of at least 10 sheets.
5. For the best printed cotton or linen cloth, not under 28 yards.
6. For the best imitation of English blankets, not under six.
7. For the next best ditto, not under six.
8. For the best hogshead of strong ale.
9. For the best hogshead of porter.

III. Lucrative premiums :—

10. For the most useful invention in arts, £21.
11. For the best carpet as to work, pattern, and colours, of at least 48 yards, £5 : 5s.
12. For the next best ditto, also 48 yards, £4 : 4s.
13. For the best drawings of fruits, flowers, and foliages by boys or girls under sixteen years of age, £5 : 5s.
14. For the second best, £3 : 3s.
15. For the third best, £2 : 2s.
16. For the best imitation of Dresden work in a pair of man's ruffles, £5 : 5s.
17. For the best bone lace, not under 20 yards, £5 : 5s.
18. For the greatest quantity of white linen rags, £1 : 10s.
19. For the second ditto, £1 : 5s.
20. For the third ditto, £1.
21. For the fourth ditto, 15s.
22. For the fifth ditto, 10s.

The articles were asked to be delivered to Mr. Walter Goodall (David Hume's assistant in the work of librarian), at the Advocates' Library, before the first Monday of December.[1] On the 19th of August the following additional prizes were offered :—

23. To the farmer who plants the greatest number (not under 1000) of timber trees, oak, beech, ash, or elm, in hedge-rows before December 1756, £10.

---

[1] *Scots Magazine* for year 1755, p. 126.

24. Second ditto (not under 500), £5.
25. To the farmer who shall raise the greatest number (not under 2000) of young thorn plants before December 1758, £6.
26. Second ditto (not under 1000), £4.

In the following year the society increased the number of its prizes to 92 ; in 1757 to 120, in 1758 to 138, and in 1759 to 142 ; and they were devoted to the encouragement of every variety of likely industry — kid gloves, straw hats, felt hats, soap, cheese, cradles to be made of willow grown in Scotland. One premium was offered to the person who would " cure the greatest number of smoky chimneys to the satisfaction of the society."

The prize for the best essay on taste was won by Professor Gerard of Aberdeen, and the essay was published, and is still well known to students of metaphysics ; and the prize for the best dissertation on vegetation and agriculture fell to Dr. Francis Home. The best invention was a piece of linen made like Marseille work but on a loom, and for this £20 were awarded to Peter Brotherton, weaver in Dirleton, East Lothian. Foulis won in 1757 the prize for the best printed book in Roman characters by his *Horace*, and for the best printed book in Greek characters by his *Iliad* ; and in 1759 Professor Gerard again won a prize by his dissertation on style.

This society, while it lasted, undoubtedly exercised a most beneficial influence in developing and improving the industrial resources of Scotland. The carpet manufacture alone rose £1000 in the year after the establishment of the prizes, and the rise was believed to be due to the stimulus they imparted. But, useful and active and celebrated as it was, the Select Society died within ten years of its origin. The usual explanation is that it owed its death to the effects of a sarcasm of Charles Townshend's. Townshend was brought to hear one of the wonderful debates, which were thought to reflect a new glory on Edinburgh, and was even elected a member of the society, but he observed when he came out that, while he admitted the eloquence of the orators, he was unable to understand a word they said, inasmuch as they spoke in what was to him a foreign tongue. "Why," he asked, "can you not learn to speak the English language, as you have already learnt to write it?"[1]

This was to touch Scotchmen of that period who made any pretensions to education at one of their most sensitive parts. Scotch—the broad dialect of Burns and Fergusson—was still the common medium of intercourse in polite society, and might be heard even from the pulpit or the bench, though English was flowing rapidly into fashion, and the younger and more ambitious sort of people were trying their best to lose the native dialect. We know the pains taken by great writers like Hume and Robertson to clear their English composition of Scotch idioms, and the greater but less successful pains taken by Wedderburn to cure himself of his Scotch pronunciation, to which he reverted after all in his old age. Under these circumstances Townshend's sarcasm occasioned almost a little movement of lingual reform. Thomas Sheridan, who was about this time full of a method he had invented of imparting to foreigners a proper pronunciation of the English language by means of sounds borrowed from their own, and who had just been giving lessons to Wedderburn, and probably practising the new method on him, was brought north in 1761 and delivered a course of sixteen lectures in St. Paul's Chapel, Carrubber's Close, to about 300 gentlemen—"the most eminent," it is reported, "in the country for rank and abilities." Immediately thereafter the Select Society organised a special association for promoting the writing and speaking of the English language in Scotland, and engaged a teacher of correct English pronunciation from London. Smith was not

[1] Lord Campbell's *Lives of the Chancellors*, vi. 32.

one of the directors of this new association, but Robertson, Ferguson, and Blair were, together with a number of
peers, baronets, lords of Session, and leaders of the bar.
But spite of the imposing auspices under which this simple
project of an English elocution master was launched, it
proved a signal failure, for it touched the national
vanity.   It seemed to involve a humiliating confession of
inferiority to a rival nation at the very moment when that
nation was raging with abuse of the Scotch, when Wilkes
was publishing the *North Briton*, and Churchill was
writing his lampoons ; and when it was advertised in the
Edinburgh newspapers, it provoked such a storm of anti-
pathy and ridicule that even the honourable society which
furthered the scheme began to lose favour, its subscriptions and membership declined, and presently the
whole organisation fell to pieces.   That is the account
commonly given of the fall of the Select Society, and the
society certainly reached its culminating point in 1762.
After that subscribers withdrew their names, or refused to
pay their subscriptions, and in 1765 the society had no
funds to offer more than six prizes and ceased to exist,
its own explanation being that it died of the loss of
novelty.   "The arrears of subscriptions seem," it says, "to
confirm an observation that has sometimes been made,
that in Scotland every disinterested plan of public utility
is slighted as soon as it loses the charm of novelty." [1]

Another interesting but even more abortive project
which Smith took a leading part in promoting at this same
period was the publication of a new literary magazine,
entitled the *Edinburgh Review*, of which the first number
appeared in July 1755, and the second and last in January
1756.   This project also originated, like the Select Society,
in a sentiment of Scotch patriotism.   It was felt that
though Scotland was at the time stirring with an important
literary and scientific movement, the productions of the
Scotch press were too much ignored by the English literary

[1] *Scots Magazine*, xxvi. 229.

periodicals, and received inadequate appreciation even in Scotland itself for want of a good critical journal on the spot. "If countries may be said to have their ages with respect to improvement," says the preface to the first number of the new *Review*, "then North Britain may be considered as in a state of early youth, guided and supported by the more mature strength of her kindred country. If in anything her advances have been such as to make a more forward state, it is in science." After remarking that the two obstacles to the literary advancement of Scotland had hitherto been her deficiency in the art of printing and her imperfect command of good English, and that the first of these obstacles had been removed entirely, and the second shown by recent writers to be capable of being surmounted, it proceeds : " The idea therefore was that to show men at this particular stage of the country's progress the gradual advance of science would be a means of inciting them to a more eager pursuit of learning, to distinguish themselves and to do honour to their country." The editor was Alexander Wedderburn, who afterwards became Lord High Chancellor of England and Earl of Rosslyn, but had in 1755 only just passed as an advocate at the Scotch bar ; and the contributors were Robertson, who wrote eight review articles on new historical publications ; Blair, who gave one or two indifferent notices of works in philosophy ; Jardine, one of the ministers of Edinburgh, who discussed Ebenezer Erskine's sermons, a few theological pamphlets, and Mrs. Cleland's Cookery Book ; and Adam Smith, who contributed to the first number a review of Dr. Johnson's *Dictionary*, and to the second a remarkable letter to the editor proposing to widen the scope of the *Review*, and giving a striking survey of the state of contemporary literature in all the countries of Europe. Smith's two contributions are out of sight the ablest and most important articles the *Review* published.

He gives a warm and most appreciative welcome to

Johnson's *Dictionary*, but thinks it would have been improved if the author had in the first place more often censured words not of approved use, and if in the second he had, instead of simply enumerating the several meanings of a word, arranged them into classes and distinguished principal from subsidiary meanings. Then to illustrate what he wants, Smith himself writes two model articles, one on *Wit* and the other on *Humour*, both acute and interesting. He counts humour to be always something accidental and fitful, the disease of a disposition, and he considers it much inferior to wit, though it may often be more amusing. " Wit expresses something that is more designed, concerted, regular, and artificial ; humour something that is more wild, loose, extravagant, and fantastical ; something which comes upon a man by fits which he can neither command nor restrain, and which is not perfectly consistent with true politeness. Humour, it has been said, is often more diverting than wit ; yet a man of wit is as much above a man of humour as a gentleman is above a buffoon ; a buffoon, however, will often divert more than a gentleman."

In his second contribution—a long letter to the editor published in the appendix to the second number—Smith advocates the enlargement of the scope of the *Review* so as to give some account of works of importance published abroad, even though space had to be provided for the purpose by neglecting unimportant publications issued from the Scotch press, and, in fact, he considers this substitution as a necessity for the continued life of the *Review*. For, says he, " you will oblige the public much more by giving them an account of such books as are worthy of their regard than by filling your paper with all the insignificant literary news of the time, of which not an article in a hundred is likely to be thought of a fortnight after the publication of the work that gave occasion to it." He then proceeds to a review of contemporary continental literature, which he says meant at that time the literature of France. Italy had ceased to produce literature, and Germany produced only science. A sentence or two may be quoted from his comparison between French and English literature, because they show that he was not, as he is sometimes accused of being, an unfair depreciator of the great writers of England and a blind admirer of those of France. He will be owned to have had a very just opinion of the specific merits of each.

" Imagination, genius, and invention," he says, " seem to be the talents of the English ; taste, judgment, propriety, and order, of the French. In the old English poets, in Shakespeare, Spenser, and Milton, there often appears, amidst some irregularities and extravagancies, a strength of imagination so vast, so gigantic and supernatural, as astonishes and confounds the reader into that admiration of their genius which makes him despise as mean and insignificant all criticism upon the inequalities of their writings. In the eminent French writers such sallies of genius are more rarely to be met with, but instead of them a just arrangement, an exact propriety and decorum, joined to an equal and studied elegance of sentiment and diction, which, as it never strikes the heart like those violent and momentary flashes of imagination, so it never revolts the judgment by anything that is absurd or unnatural, nor ever wearies the attention by any gross inequality in the style or want of connection in the method, but entertains the mind with a regular succession of agreeable, interesting, and connected objects."

From poetry he passes to philosophy, and finds that the French encyclopedists had left their native Cartesian system for the English system of Bacon and Newton, and were proving more effective expositors of that system than the English themselves. After reviewing the *Encyclopédie* at considerable length, he gives an account of the recent scientific works of Buffon and Reaumur, and, among books in metaphysics, of Rousseau's famous *Discourse on the Origin and Foundation of the Inequality of Mankind*, which was then only a few months out, and in which, Smith says, Rousseau, " by the help of his style, together with a little philosophical chemistry," has made " the principles and ideas of the profligate Mandeville seem to have all the purity and simplicity of the morals of Plato, and to be only the true spirit of a republican carried a little too far." He gives a summary of the book, translates a few specimen passages, and concludes by saying, " I shall only add that the dedication to the Republic of Geneva, of which M. Rousseau has the honour of being a citizen, is an agreeable, animated, and I believe, too, a just panegyric."

Sir James Mackintosh, who republished these two numbers of the first *Edinburgh Review* in 1818 after the second *Edinburgh Review* had made the name famous, considers it noteworthy, as showing the contributors to have taken up a very decided political position for so early a period, that the preface to the first number speaks boldly in praise of George Buchanan's " undaunted spirit of liberty." But Smith's warm expression of admiration for the Republic of Geneva, to which he reckons it an honour to belong, is equally notable. He seems to have been always theoretically a republican, and he certainly had the true spirit of a republican in his love of all rational liberty. His pupil and lifelong friend, the Earl of Buchan, says : " He approached to republicanism in his political principles, and considered a commonwealth as the platform for the monarchy, hereditary succession in the chief magistrate being necessary only to prevent the commonwealth from being shaken by ambition, or absolute dominion introduced by the consequences of contending factions."[1]

Smith's scheme for the improvement of the *Review* was never carried out, for with that number the *Review* itself came to a sudden and premature end. The reason for giving it up is explained by Lord Woodhouselee to have been that the strictures passed by it on some fanatical publications of the day had excited such a clamour

[1] The *Bee* for June 1791.

"that a regard to the public tranquillity and their own determined the reviewers to discontinue their labours."[1] Doubt has been expressed of the probability of this explanation, but Lord Woodhouselee, who was personally acquainted with several of the contributors, is likely to have known of the circumstances, and his statement is borne out besides by certain corroborative facts. It is true the theological articles of the two numbers appear to us to be singularly inoffensive. They were entrusted to the only contributor who was not a young man, Dr. Jardine, the wily leader of the Moderate party in the Church, the Dean of the Thistle mentioned in Lord Dreghorn's verses as governing the affairs of the city as well as the Church through his power over his father-in-law—

> The old Provost, who danced to the whistle
> Of that arch politician, the Dean of the Thistle.

The arch politician contrived to make his theological criticism colourless even to the point of vapidity, but that did not save him or his *Review*; it perhaps only exposed them the more to the attacks of zealots. His notice of the sermons of Ebenezer Erskine, the Secession leader, provoked a sharp pamphlet from Erskine's son, in which the reviewers were accused of teaching unsound theological views, of putting the creature before the Creator by allowing the lawfulness of a lie in certain situations, of throwing ridicule on the Bible and the Westminster *Confession of Faith*, and of having David Hume, an atheist, among their number.

This last thrust was a mere controversial guess, and, strangely enough, it guessed wrong. A new literary review is started in Edinburgh by a few of Hume's younger friends, and Hume himself—the only one of them who had yet made any name in literature, and the most distinguished man of letters then in Scotland—is

[1] Tytler's *Life of Lord Kames*, i. 233.

neither asked to contribute to the periodical, nor even admitted to the secret of its origination. When the first number appeared he went about among his acquaintances expressing the greatest surprise that so promising a literary adventure should be started by Edinburgh men of letters without a whisper of it ever reaching his ears. More than that, his very name and writings were strangely and studiously ignored in its pages. His *History of the Stewarts* was one of the last new books, having been published in the end of 1754, and was unquestionably much the most important work that had recently come from any Scotch pen, yet in a periodical instituted for the very purpose of devoting attention to the productions of Scotch authors, this work of his remained absolutely unnoticed.

Why this complete boycott of Hume by his own household? Henry Mackenzie "thinks he has heard" two reasons given for it : first, that Hume was considered too good-natured for a critic, and certain to have insisted on softening remarks his colleagues believed to be called for ; and second, that they determined to keep him out of the secret entirely, because he could not keep a secret.[1] But this explanation does not hold together. If Hume was so good-natured, he would be less difficult rather than more difficult to manage ; and as for not being able to keep a secret, that, as Mr. Burton observes, is a very singular judgment to pass on one who had been Secretary of Legation already and was soon to be Secretary of Legation again, and Under Secretary of State, without having been once under the shadow of such an accusation. Besides, neither of these reasons will explain the ignoring of his writings.

A more credible explanation must be looked for, and it can only be discovered in the intense *odium theologicum* which the name of Hume excited at the moment, and which made it imperative, if the new *Review* was to get

[1] *Life of John Home*, p. 24.

justice, that it should be severed from all association with his detested name. Scotland happened to be at that very hour in an exceptional ferment about his theological heresies, and one of the strangest of proposals had come before the previous General Assembly of the Kirk, backed by a number of the most respected country clergy. It was no other than to summon the great sceptic to their bar, to visit his *Inquiry concerning the Principles of Morals* with censure, and to pronounce against the author the major ban of excommunication.

The wise heads who rule the Scotch Church courts of course threw out this inconvenient proposal by the favourite ecclesiastical device of passing an abstract resolution expressive of concern at the growing evils of the day, without committing the Church to any embarrassing practical action; and Hume himself was, as Wedderburn told them he likely would be, hardened enough to laugh at the very idea of their anathema. But the originators of the agitation only returned to the battle, and prepared for a victory in the next Assembly in May 1756. Between the two Assemblies Hume wrote his friend Allan Ramsay, the painter, who was in Rome : " You may tell that reverend gentleman the Pope that there are men here who rail at him, and yet would be much greater persecutors had they equal power. The last Assembly sat on me. They did not propose to burn me, because they cannot, but they intended to give me over to Satan, which they think they have the power of doing. My friends, however, prevailed, and my damnation is postponed for a twelvemonth, but next Assembly will surely be upon me." [1]   And so in truth it was. An overture came up calling for action regarding " one person calling himself David Hume, Esq., who hath arrived at such a degree of boldness as publicly to avow himself the author of books containing the most rude and open attacks upon the glorious Gospel of Christ," and a

---

[1] Burton's *Scot Abroad*, ii. 343.

motion was made for the appointment of a committee
"to inquire into the writings of this author, to call him
before them, and prepare the matter for the next General
Assembly." This motion was again defeated, and the
heresy-hunters passed on to turn their attention to Lord
Kames, and to summon the printers and publishers of his
Essays before the Edinburgh Presbytery to give up the
author's name (the book having been published anonymously), "that he and they may be censured according to
the law of the Gospel and the practice of this and all other
well-governed churches."

It is open to us to believe that Hume's friends contemplated no more than a temporary exclusion of him
from their counsels until this storm should pass by ; but
at any rate, as they launched their frail bark in the very
thick of the storm, it would have meant instant swamping
at that juncture to have taken the Jonah who caused all
the commotion and made him one of their crew. For the
same reason, when they found that, for all their precautions,
the clamour overtook them notwithstanding, they simply
put back into port and never risked so unreasoning and
raging an element again.

It may indeed be thought that they declined Hume's
co-operation, because they expressly hoisted the flag of
religion in their preface, and professed one of their
objects to be to resist the current attacks of infidelity.
But there would have been no inconsistency in engaging
the co-operation of an unbeliever on secular subjects, so long
as they retained the rudder in their own hands, and men
who were already Hume's intimate personal friends were
not likely to be troubled with such unnecessary scruples
about their consistency. The true reason both of Hume's
exclusion from their secret and of their own abandonment of
their undertaking is undoubtedly the reason given by Lord
Woodhouselee, that they wanted to live and work in peace.
They did not like, to use a phrase of Hamilton of Bangour,
to have "zeal clanking her iron bands" about their ears.

Hume, on the other hand, rather took pleasure in the din he provoked, and had he been a contributor the rest would have had difficulty—and may have felt so—in restraining him from gratifying that taste when any favourable opportunities offered.

While these things were going on in Edinburgh a book had made its appearance from the London press, which is often stated to have been written for the express purpose of converting Adam Smith to a belief in the miraculous evidences of Christianity. That book is the *Criterion of Miracles Examined*, by Smith's Oxford friend Bishop Douglas, then a country rector in Shropshire. It is written in the form of a letter to an anonymous correspondent, who had, in spite of his "good sense, candour, and learning," and on grounds "many of them peculiar to himself and not borrowed from books," "reasoned himself into an unfavourable opinion of the evidences of Christianity"; and this anonymous correspondent is said in Chalmers's *Biographical Dictionary* to have been "since known to be Adam Smith." From Chalmers's *Dictionary* the same statement has been repeated in the same words in subsequent biographical dictionaries and elsewhere, but neither Chalmers nor his successors reveal who it was to whom this was known, or how he came to know it; and on the other hand, Macdonald, the son-in-law and biographer of Douglas, makes no mention of Smith's name in connection with this work at all, and explicitly states that the book was written for the satisfaction of more than one of the author's friends, who had been influenced by the objections of Hume and others to the reality of the Gospel miracles.[1] This leaves the point somewhat undetermined.

Smith was certainly a Theist, his writings leave no doubt of that, but he most probably discarded the Christian miracles; and if Douglas's book is addressed to his particular position, discarded them on the ground that there is no possible criterion for distinguishing true

[1] Douglas's *Select Works*, p. 23.

miracles from false, and enabling you to accept those of Christianity if you reject those of profane history. The Earl of Buchan, apostrophising Smith, asks, " Oh, venerable and worthy man, why was you not a Christian?" and tries to let his old professor down as gently as possible by suggesting that the reason lay in the warmth of his heart, which always made him express strongly the opinions of his friends, and carried him in this instance into sympathy with those of David Hume. That is obviously a lame conclusion, because Smith's friendship for Hume never made him a Tory, nor even on the point of religion were his opinions identical with those of Hume; but Lord Buchan's words may be quoted as an observation by an acute man of a feature in Smith's character not without biographical interest. " Had he (Smith) been a friend of the worthy ingenious Horrox," says his lordship, " he would have believed that the moon sometimes disappeared in a clear sky without the interposition of a cloud, or of another truly honest and respectable man, that a professor of mathematics at Upsala had a tail of six inches long to his rump."[1]

In 1756 the literary circle in Edinburgh was much excited by the performance of John Home's tragedy of *Douglas*. Smith was not present at that performance; but he is stated by Henry Mackenzie, in his *Life of John Home*, to have been present at some of the previous rehearsals of the play, and at any rate he was deeply interested in it; and Hume, as soon as he hears of the continued success of the play in London, hastens to communicate the welcome news to his friend in Glasgow, with whom he was in correspondence about his own historical plans. Smith seems to have been advising him, instead of following up his *History of the Stewarts* by the history of succeeding periods, to go back and write the history of the period before the Stewarts.

After mentioning John Home, Hume proceeds : " I

[1] The *Bee* for 1791.

can now give you the satisfaction of hearing that the play, though not near so well acted in Covent Garden as in this place, is likely to be very successful. Its great intrinsic merit breaks through all obstacles. When it shall be printed (which shall be soon) I am persuaded it will be esteemed the best, and by French critics the only tragedy of our language! . . .

"Did you ever hear of such madness and folly as our clergy have lately fallen into? For my part, I expect that the next Assembly will very solemnly pronounce the sentence of excommunication against me, but I do not apprehend it to be a matter of any consequence ; what do you think?

"I am somewhat idle at present and somewhat indifferent as to my next undertaking. Shall I go backwards or forwards in my History? I think you used to tell me that you approved more of my going backwards. The other would be the more popular subject, but I am afraid I shall not find materials sufficient to ascertain the truth, at least without settling in London, which I own I have some reluctance to. I am settled here very much to my mind, and would not wish at my years to change the place of my abode.

"I have just now received a copy of *Douglas* from London. It will instantly be put in the press. I hope to be able to send you a copy in the same parcel with the dedication."[1]

Hume was now very anxious to have his friend nearer him, and thought in 1758 an opportunity could be contrived of translating Smith to a chair in the University of Edinburgh. There was at that time some probability of Professor Abercromby resigning the chair of Public Law (then styled the chair of the Law of Nature and Nations), and as Smith, though not a lawyer, was yet a distinguished professor of jurisprudence, his friends in Edinburgh immediately suggested his candidature, especially as they

[1] Burton's *Life of Hume*, ii. 16.

believed such a change would not be unacceptable to himself. The chair of the Law of Nature and Nations was one of the best endowed in the College, having a revenue of £150 a year independently of fees, but it had been founded as a job, and continued ever since to be treated as a sinecure. Not a single lecture had ever been delivered by any of its incumbents, in spite of repeated remonstrances on the part of the Faculty of Advocates, and Hume believed that if the Town Council, as administrators of the College, could be got to press for the delivery of the statutory lectures, the present professor would prefer the alternative of resignation. In that event the vacant office might easily, in Hume's opinion, be obtained by Smith, inasmuch as the patronage was in the hands of the Crown, and Crown patronage in Scotland at the time was virtually exercised through Lord Justice-Clerk Milton (a nephew of Andrew Fletcher of Saltoun, the patriot), who had been, ever since the death of Lord President Forbes, the chief confidential adviser of the Duke of Argyle, the Minister for Scotland, and was personally acquainted with Smith through his daughter Mrs. Wedderburn of Gosford, the friend of Robertson and John Home.

Others of Smith's Edinburgh friends zealously joined Hume in his representations, especially the faithful Johnstone (afterwards Sir W. Pulteney), who actually wrote Smith a letter on the subject along with Hume's. Hume's letter is as follows :—

DEAR SMITH — I sit down to write to you along with Johnstone, and as we have been talking over the matter, it is probable we shall employ the same arguments. As he is the younger lawyer, I leave him to open the case, and suppose that you have read his letter first. We are certain that the settlement of you here and of Ferguson at Glasgow would be perfectly easy by Lord Milton's Interest. The Prospect of prevailing with Abercrombie is also very good. For the same statesman by his influence over the Town Council could oblige him either to attend, which he never would do, or dispose of the office for the money which he gave for it. The only real difficulty is then with you. Pray then consider that this is perhaps the only opportunity we shall ever have of getting you to town. I dare swear that you think the difference of Place is worth paying something for, and yet it will really cost you nothing. You made above a hundred pound a year by your class when in this Place, though you had not the character of Professor. We cannot suppose that it will be less than a hundred and thirty after you are settled. John Stevenson[1]—and it is John Stevenson—makes near a hundred and fifty, as we were informed upon Enquiry. Here is a hundred pounds a year for eight years' Purchase, which is a cheap purchase, even considered in the way of a Bargain. We flatter ourselves that you rate our company at something, and the Prospect of settling Ferguson will be an additional inducement. For though we think of making him take up the Project if you refuse it, yet it is uncertain whether he will consent ; and it is attended in his case with many very obvious objections. I beseech you therefore to weigh all these motives over again. The alteration of these circumstances merit that you should put the matter again in deliberation. I had a letter from Miss Hepburn, where she regrets very much that you are settled at Glasgow, and that we had the chance of seeing you so seldom.—I am, dear Smith, yours sincerely, DAVID HUME.

8th June 1758.

P.S.—Lord Milton can with his finger stop the foul mouths of all the Roarers against heresy.[2]

The postscript shows what we have already indicated, that Smith had not escaped the general hue and cry against heresy which was now for some years abroad in the country.

The Miss Hepburn who regrets so much the remoteness of Smith's residence is doubtless Miss Hepburn of Monkrig, near Haddington, one of those gifted literary ladies who were then not infrequently to be found in the country houses of Scotland. It was to Miss Hepburn and her sisters that John Home is said to have been indebted

[1] Professor of Logic.
[2] Burton's *Life of Hume*, ii. 45.

for the first idea of *Douglas*, and Robertson submitted to
her the manuscript of his *History of Scotland* piece by
piece as he wrote it. When it was finished the historian
sent her a presentation copy with a letter, in which he
said : "Queen Mary has grown up to her present form
under your eye ; you have seen her in many different
shapes, and you have now a right to her. Were I a
galante writer now, what a fine contrast might I make
between you and Queen Mary ? What a pretty string of
antitheses between your virtues and her vices. I am glad,
however, she did not resemble you. If she had, Rizzio
would have only played first fiddle at her consort (*sic*),
with a pension of a thousand merks and two benefits in
a winter ; Darnley would have been a colonel in the
Guards ; Bothwell would, on account of his valour, have
been Warden of the Middle Marches, but would have been
forbid to appear at court because of his profligacy. But
if all that had been done, what would have become of my
History ?"[1]

Smith seems to have declined, for whatever reason, to
take up the suggestion of Hume about this chair of Law,
for we find Hume presently trying hard to secure the
place for Ferguson. The difficulty may have been about
the price, for though Hume speaks of £800, it seems
Abercromby wanted more than £1000, and Ferguson too
had no mind to begin life with such a debt on his
shoulders. But the world is probably no loser by the
difficulty, whatever it was, which kept Smith five years
longer among the merchants and commercial problems of
Glasgow.

Smith was one of the founders, or at least the original
members, of the Edinburgh Poker Club in 1762. Every
one has heard of that famous club, but most persons
probably think of it as if it were merely a social or convivial society ; and Mr. Burton lends some countenance
to that mistake by declaring that he has never been able

---

[1] Fraser's *The Lennox*, p. xliv.

to discover any other object it existed for except the drinking of claret. But the Poker Club was really a committee for political agitation, like the Anti-Corn-Law League or the Home Rule Union ; only, after the more genial manners of those times, the first thing the committee thought requisite for the proper performance of their work was to lay in a stock of sound Burgundy that could be drawn from the wood at eighteenpence or two shillings a quart, to engage a room in a tavern for the exclusive use of the members, and establish a weekly or bi-weekly dinner at a moderate figure, to keep the *poker* of agitation in active exercise. The club got its name from the practical purpose it was instituted to serve ; it was to be an instrument for *stirring* opinion, especially in high quarters, on a public question which was exciting the people of Scotland greatly at the moment, the question of the establishment of a national Scotch militia. Some of the members thought that when that question was settled, the club should go on and take up others. George Dempster of Dunnichen, for example, an old and respected parliamentary hand of that time, wrote Dr. Carlyle in 1762 that when they got their militia, they ought to agitate for parliamentary reform, " so as to let the industrious farmer and manufacturer share at last in a privilege now engrossed by the great lord, the drunken laird, and the drunkener baillie." [1] But they never got the length of considering other reforms, for the militia question was not settled in that generation. It outlived the Poker Club, and it outlived the Younger Poker Club which was enrolled to take up the cause in 1786, and it was not finally settled till 1793.

The Scotch had been roused to the defenceless condition of their country by the alarming appearance of Thurot in Scotch waters in 1759, and had instantly with one voice raised a cry for the establishment of a national militia. The whole country seemed to have set its mind

[1] *Carlyle Correspondence*, Edinburgh University Library.

on this measure with a singular unanimity, and a bill for
its enactment was accordingly introduced into the House
of Commons in 1760 by two of the principal Scotch
members, both former ministers of the Crown—James
Oswald and Gilbert Elliot ; but it was rejected by
a large majority, because within only fifteen years of
the Rebellion the English members were unwilling to
entrust the Scotch people with arms. The rejection of
the bill provoked a deep feeling of national indignation,
the slur it cast on the loyalty of Scotland being resented
even more than the indifference it showed to her perils.
It was under the influence of this wave of national sentiment that the Poker Club was founded in 1762, to procure
for the Scotch at once equality of rights with the English
and adequate defences for their country.

The membership of the club included many of the
foremost men in the land—great noblemen, advocates,
men of letters, together with a number of spirited county
gentlemen on both sides of politics, who cried that they
had a militia of their own before the Union, and must
have a militia of their own again. Dr. Carlyle says most
of the members of the Select Society belonged to it, the
exceptions consisting of a few who disapproved of the
militia scheme, and of others, like the judges, who
scrupled, on account of their official position, to take
any part in a political movement. Carlyle gives a list
of the members in 1774, containing among other names
those of the Duke of Buccleugh, Lords Haddington,
Glasgow, Glencairn, Elibank, and Mountstuart ; Henry
Dundas, Lord Advocate ; Baron Mure, Hume, Adam
Smith, Robertson, Black, Adam Ferguson, John Home,
Dr. Blair, Sir James Steuart the economist, Dempster,
Islay Campbell, afterwards Lord President; and John
Clerk of Eldin. The first secretary of the club was
William Johnstone (Sir William Pulteney), and, as has
been frequently told, David Hume was jocularly appointed
to a sinecure office created for him, the office of assassin,

and lest Hume's good-nature should unfit him for the duties, Andrew Crosbie, advocate (the original of Scott's "Pleydell"), was made his assistant. The club met at first in Tom Nicholson's tavern, the Diversorium, at the Cross, and subsequently removed to more fashionable quarters at the famous Fortune's in the Stamp Office Close, where the Lord High Commissioner to the General Assembly held his levees, and the members dined every Friday at two and sat till six. However the club may have pulled wires in private, their public activity seems to have been very little; so far at least as literary advocacy of their cause went, nothing proceeded from it except a pamphlet by Dr. Carlyle, and a much-overlauded squib by Adam Ferguson, entitled "A History of the Proceedings in the Case of Margaret, commonly called Sister Peg."

Smith was, as I have said, one of the original members of the club, and from Carlyle's list would appear to have continued a member till 1774; but he was not a member of the Younger Poker Club, established in 1786. In the interval he had expressed in the *Wealth of Nations* a strong preference for a standing army over a national militia,[1] after instituting a very careful examination of the whole subject. Whether his views had changed since 1762, or whether he had joined in the agitation for a militia merely as a measure of justice to Scotland or as an expedient of temporary necessity, without committing himself to any abstract admiration for the institution in general, I have no means of deciding; but we can hardly think he ever shared that kind of belief in the principle of a militia which animated men like Ferguson and Carlyle, and which, according to them, animated the other members of the club also at its birth. Ferguson says the club was founded "upon the principle of zeal for a militia and a conviction that there could be no lasting security for the freedom and independence of these

---

[1] *Wealth of Nations*, Book V. chap. i.

islands but in the valour and patriotism of an armed
people " ;[1] and when, during his travels in Switzerland
in 1775, he saw for the first time in his life a real
militia—the object of his dreams—actually moving before
him in the flesh, and going through their drill, his heart
came to his mouth, and he wrote his friend Carlyle: " As
they were the only body of men I ever saw under arms
on the true principle for which arms should be carried, I
felt much secret emotion, and could have shed tears."[2]
He was deeply disappointed a year later with Smith's
apostasy on this question, or at least opposition, for
Ferguson makes no accusation of apostasy. After reading
the *Wealth of Nations*, he wrote Smith on the 18th
of April 1776: " You have provoked, too, so far the
Church, the universities, and the merchants, against all
of whom I am willing to take your part ; but you have
likewise provoked the militia, and there I must be against
you. The gentlemen and peasants of this country do not
need the authority of philosophers to make them supine
and negligent of every resource they might have in themselves in the case of certain extremities, of which the
pressure, God knows, may be at no great distance. But
of this more at Philippi."[3]

But many others besides Smith had in this interval
either found their zeal for a militia grown cool or their
opinion of its value modified, and when Lord Mountstuart
introduced his new Scotch Militia Bill in 1776, it received
little support from Scotch members, and its rejection
excited nothing like the feeling roused by the rejection
of its predecessor in 1760, although it was attended this
time with the galling aggravation that what was refused
to the Scotch was in the same hour granted to the Irish,
then the less disliked and distrusted nation of the two.
Opinions had grown divided. Old Fletcher of Saltoun's

[1] " Memoirs of Black," *Transactions*, R.S.E., v. 113.
[2] *Carlyle Correspondence*, Edinburgh University.
[3] Small, *Sketch of A. Ferguson*, p. 23.

idea of a citizen army with universal compulsory service was still much discussed, but many now objected to the compulsion, and others, among whom was Lord Kames, to the universality of the compulsion, rallying to the idea of Fencibles—*i.e.* regiments to be raised compulsorily by the landed proprietors, each furnishing a number of men proportioned to their valued rent.[1] Smith said a militia formed in this way, like the old Highland militia, was the best of all militias, but he held that the day was past for militias of men with one hand on the sword and the other on the plough, and that nothing could now answer for what he calls "the noblest of all arts," the art of war, but the division of labour, which answered best for the arts of peace, and a standing army of soldiers by exclusive occupation.

Divided counsels and diminished zeal supply, no doubt, the main reason for the decay of the Poker Club, but other causes combined. Dr. Carlyle, who was an active member of the club, says it began to decline when it transferred itself to more elegant quarters at Fortune's, because its dinners became too expensive for the members ; and Lord Campbell attributes its dissolution definitely to the new taxes imposed on French wines to pay the cost of the American War. His statement is very explicit : " To punish the Government they agreed to dissolve the ' Poker,' and to form another society which should exist without consumption of any excisable commodity." [2] But he gives no authority for the statement, and they are at least not likely to have been such fools as to think of punishing the Government by what was after all only an excellent way of punishing themselves. The wine duty was no doubt a real enough grievance ; it was raised five or six times during the club's existence, and many a man who enjoyed his quart of Burgundy when the duty was less than half-a-crown a gallon, was obliged to do without

[1] Kames, *Sketches of Man*, Book II. chap. ix.
[2] Campbell's *Lives of the Lord Chancellors*, vi. 28.

it when the duty rose to seven shillings.   It may be worth
adding, however, that the Poker Club was revived as the
Younger Poker Club in the very year, 1786, when the
duty on Burgundy was reduced again by the new Commercial Treaty with France.

CHAPTER IX

SMITH enjoyed a very high Scotch reputation long before his name was known to the great public by any contribution to literature. But in 1759 he gave his *Theory of Moral Sentiments* to the press, and took his place, by almost immediate and universal recognition, in the first rank of contemporary writers. The book is an essay supporting and illustrating the doctrine that moral approbation and disapprobation are in the last analysis expressions of sympathy with the feelings of an imaginary and impartial spectator, and its substance had already been given from year to year in his ordinary lectures to his students, though after the publication he thought it no longer necessary to dwell at the same length on this branch of his course, giving more time, no doubt, to jurisprudence and political economy. The book was published in London by Andrew Millar in two vols. 8vo. It was from the first well received, its ingenuity, eloquence, and great copiousness of effective illustration being universally acknowledged and admired. Smith sent a copy to Hume in London, and received the following reply, which contains some interesting particulars of the reception of the book there :—

LONDON, *12th April* 1759.

DEAR SIR—I give you thanks for the agreeable present of your *Theory*. Wedderburn and I made presents of our copies to such of our acquaintances as we thought good judges and proper to spread the reputation of the book. I sent one to the Duke of Argyle, to Lord Lyttelton, Horace Walpole, Soame Jenyns, and Burke, an Irish gentleman who wrote lately a very pretty treatise on the Sublime. Millar desired my permission to send one in your name to Dr. Warburton.

I have delayed writing you till I could tell you something of the success of the book, and could prognosticate with some probability whether it should be finally damned to oblivion or should be registered in the temple of immortality. Though it has been published only a few weeks, I think there appear already such strong symptoms that I can almost venture to foretell its fate. It is, in short, this——

But I have been interrupted in my letter by a foolish impertinent visit of one who has lately come from Scotland. He tells me that the University of Glasgow intend to declare Rouet's office vacant upon his going abroad with Lord Hope. I question not but you will have our friend Ferguson in your eye, in case another project for procuring him a place in the University of Edinburgh should fail. Ferguson has very much polished and improved his *Treatise on Refinement*, and with some amendments it will make an admirable book, and discovers an elegant and singular genius. The *Epigoniad*, I hope, will do, but it is somewhat uphill work. As I doubt not but you consult the Reviews sometimes at present, you will see in *The Critical Review* a letter upon that poem ; and I desire you to employ your conjectures in finding out the author. Let me see a sample of your skill in knowing hints by guessing at the person.

I am afraid of Kames's *Law Tracts*. The man might as well think of making a fine sauce by a mixture of wormwood and aloes as an agreeable combination by joining metaphysics and Scottish law. However, the book, I believe, has merit, though few people ever take the pains of inquiring into it. But to return to your book and its success in this town. I must tell you——

A plague to interruptions ! I ordered myself to be denied, and yet here is one that has broke in upon me again. He is a man of letters, and we have had a good deal of literary conversation. You told me that you was curious of literary anecdotes, and therefore I shall inform you of a few that have come to my knowledge. I believe I have mentioned to you already Helvetius's book *De l'Esprit*. It is worth your reading, not for its philosophy, which I do not highly value, but for its agreeable composition. I had a letter from him a few days ago, wherein he tells me that my name was much oftener in the manuscript, but that the censor of books at Paris obliged him to strike it out.

Voltaire has lately published a small work called *Candide, ou l'Optimisme.* I shall give you a detail of it. But what is all this to my book, say you? My dear Mr. Smith, have patience; compose yourself to tranquillity. Show yourself a philosopher in practice as well as profession. Think on the impotence and rashness and futility of the common judgments of men, how little they are regulated by reason on any subject, much more on philosophical subjects, which so far exceed the comprehension of the vulgar—

> Non, si quid turbida Roma
> Elevet, accedas : examenve improbum in illâ
> Castiges trutinâ : nec te quaesiveris extra.

A wise man's kingdom is his own heart ; or, if he ever looks farther, it will only be to the judgment of a select few, who are free from prejudices and capable of examining his work. Nothing, indeed, can be a stronger presumption of falsehood than the approbation of the multitude ; and Phocion, you know, always suspected himself of some blunder when he was attended with the applause of the populace.

Supposing, therefore, that you have duly prepared yourself for the worst by all these reflections, I proceed to tell you the melancholy news that your book has been very unfortunate, for the public seem disposed to applaud it extremely. It was looked for by the foolish people with some impatience ; and the mob of literati are beginning already to be very loud in its praises. Three bishops called yesterday at Millar's shop in order to buy copies, and to ask questions about the author. The Bishop of Peterborough said he had passed the evening in a company where he heard it extolled above all books in the world. The Duke of Argyle is more decisive than he used to be in its favour. I suppose he either considers it as an exotic, or thinks the author will be very serviceable to him in the Glasgow elections. Lord Lyttelton says that Robertson and Smith and Bower [1] are the glories of English literature. Oswald protests he does not know whether he has reaped more instruction or entertainment from it, but you may easily judge what reliance can be placed on his judgment. He has been engaged all his life in public business, and he never sees any faults in his friends. Millar exults and brags that

---

[1] Burton thinks with great probability that this junction of names was meant as a sarcasm on Lord Lyttelton's taste.

two-thirds of the edition are already sold, and that he is now sure of success. You see what a son of the earth that is, to value books only by the profit they bring him. In that view, I believe, it may prove a very good book.

Charles Townshend, who passes for the cleverest fellow in England, is so much taken with the performance that he said to Oswald he would put the Duke of Buccleugh under the author's care, and would make it worth his while to accept of that charge. As soon as I heard this I called on him twice with a view of talking with him about the matter, and of convincing him of the propriety of sending that young gentleman to Glasgow, for I could not hope that he could offer you any terms which would tempt you to renounce your professorship ; but I missed him. Mr. Townshend passes for being a little uncertain in his resolutions, so perhaps you need not build much on his sally.

In recompense for so many mortifying things, which nothing but truth could have extorted from me, and which I could easily have multiplied to a greater number, I doubt not but you are so good a Christian as to return good for evil, and to flatter my vanity by telling me that all the godly in Scotland abuse me for my account of John Knox and the Reformation. I suppose you are glad to see my paper end, and that I am obliged to conclude with —Your humble servant.[1]

On the 28th of July Hume again writes from London on the same subject :—

I am very well acquainted with Bourke,[2] who was much taken with your book. He got your direction from me with a view of writing to you and thanking you for your present, for I made it pass in your name. I wonder he has not done it. He is now in Ireland. I am not acquainted with Jenyns,[3] but he spoke very highly of the book to Oswald, who is his brother in the Board of Trade. Millar showed me a few days ago a letter from Lord Fitzmaurice,[4] where he tells him that he has carried over a few copies to the Hague for presents. Mr. York [5] was very much taken with it, as well as several others who had read it.

---

[1] Burton's *Life of Hume*, ii. 55.
[2] Edmund Burke.
[3] Soame Jenyns.
[4] Afterwards the Earl of Shelburne, the statesman.
[5] Probably Charles Yorke, afterwards Lord Chancellor Morden.

I am told that you are preparing a new edition, and propose to make some additions and alterations in order to obviate objections. I shall use the freedom to propose one ; which, if it appears to be of any weight, you may have in your eye. I wish you had more particularly and fully proved that all kinds of sympathy are agreeable. This is the hinge of your system, and yet you only mention the matter cursorily on p. 20. Now it would appear that there is a disagreeable sympathy as well as an agreeable. And, indeed, as the sympathetic passion is a reflex image of the principal, it must partake of its qualities, and be painful when that is so. Indeed, *when we converse with a man with whom we can entirely sympathise,* that is when there is a warm and intimate friendship, the cordial openness of such a commerce overbears the pain of a disagreeable sympathy, and renders the whole movement agreeable, but in ordinary cases this cannot have place. A man tired and disgusted with everything, always *ennuié,* sickly, complaining, embarrassed, such a one throws an evident damp on company, which I suppose would be accounted for by sympathy, and yet is disagreeable.

It is always thought a difficult problem to account for the pleasure from the tears and grief and sympathy of tragedy, which would not be the case if all sympathy was agreeable. An hospital would be a more entertaining place than a ball. I am afraid that on p. 99 and 111 this proposition has escaped you, or rather is interwoven with your reasoning. In that place you say expressly, " It is painful to go along with grief, and we always enter into it with reluctance." It will probably be requisite for you to modify or explain this sentiment, and reconcile it to your system.[1]

Burke, who was thus reported by Hume to have been so much taken with the book, reviewed it most favourably in the *Annual Register*, and not only recognised Smith's theory as a new and ingenious one, but accepted it as being " in all its essential parts just and founded on truth and nature." " The author," he says, " seeks for the foundation of the just, the fit, the proper, the decent, in our most common and most allowed passions, and making approbation and disapprobation the tests of virtue and vice, and showing that these are founded on sympathy, he raises from this simple truth one of the most beautiful

[1] Burton's *Hume*, ii. 59.

fabrics of moral theory that has perhaps ever appeared. The illustrations are numerous and happy, and show the author to be a man of uncommon observation. His language is easy and spirited, and puts things before you in the fullest light ; it is rather painting than writing." [1] One of the most interesting characteristics of the book, from a biographical point of view, is that mentioned by this reviewer ; it certainly shows the author to have been a man of uncommon observation, not only of his own mental states, but of the life and ways of men about him ; as Mackintosh remarks, the book has a high value for " the variety of explanations of life and manners which embellish " it, apart altogether from the thesis it is written to prove.[2]

Charles Townshend adhered to his purpose about Smith with much more steadiness than Hume felt able to give him credit for. Townshend, it need perhaps hardly be said, was the brilliant but flighty young statesman to whom we owe the beginnings of our difficulties with America. He was the colonial minister who first awoke the question of " colonial rights," by depriving the colonists of the appointment of their own judges, and he was the Chancellor of the Exchequer who imposed the tea duty in 1767 which actually provoked the rebellion. " A man," says Horace Walpole, " endowed with every great talent, who must have been the greatest man of his age if he had only common sincerity, common steadiness, and common sense." " In truth," said Burke, " he was the delight and ornament of this house, and the charm of every private society which he honoured with his presence. Perhaps there never arose in this country nor in any other a man of a more pointed and finished wit, and (when his passions were not concerned) of a more refined and exquisite and penetrating judgment." He had in 1754 married the Countess of Dalkeith, daughter and co-heiress of the famous Duke of

[1] *Annual Register*, 1776, p. 485.
[2] Mackintosh, *Miscellaneous Works*, i. 151.

Argyle and Greenwich, and widow of the eldest son of the Duke of Buccleugh. She had been left with two sons by her first husband, of whom the eldest had succeeded his grandfather as Duke of Buccleugh in 1751, and was now at Eton under the tutorship of Mr. Hallam, father of the historian. On leaving Eton he was to travel abroad with a tutor for some time, and it was for this post of tutor to the Duke abroad that Townshend, after reading the *Theory of Moral Sentiments*, had set his heart on engaging its author.

Townshend bore, as Hume hints, a bad character for changeability. He was popularly nicknamed the Weathercock, and a squib of the day once reported that Mr. Townshend was ill of a pain in his side, but regretted that it was not said on which side. But he stood firmly to his project about Smith ; paid him a visit in Glasgow that very summer, saw much of him, invited him to Dalkeith House, arranged with him about the selection and despatch of a number of books for the young Duke's study, and seems to have arrived at a general understanding with Smith that the latter should accept the tutorship when the time came. Townshend of course delighted the Glasgow professors during this visit, as he delighted everybody, but he seems in turn to have been delighted with them, for William Hunter wrote Cullen a little later in the same year that Townshend had come back from Scotland passing the highest encomiums on everybody. Smith seems to have acted as his chief cicerone in Glasgow, as appears from one of the trivial incidents which were all that the contemporary writers of Smith's obituary notices seemed able to learn of his life. He was showing Townshend the tannery, one of the spectacles of Glasgow at the time—" an amazing sight," Pennant calls it—and walked in his absent way right into the tanpit, from which, however, he was immediately rescued without any harm.

In September 1759, on the death of Mr. Townshend's brother, Smith wrote him the following letter :—[1]

---

[1] *Buccleuch MSS.*, Dalkeith Palace.

SIR—It gives me great concern that the first letter I ever have done myself the honour to write to you should be upon so melancholy an occasion. As your Brother was generally known here, he is universally regretted, and your friends are sorry that, amidst the public rejoicings and prosperity, your family should have occasion to be in mourning. Everybody here remembers you with the greatest admiration and affection, and nothing that concerns you is indifferent to them, and there are more people who sympathise with you than you are aware of. It would be the greatest pedantry to offer any topics of consolation to you who are naturally so firm and so manly. As your Brother dyed in the service of his country, you have the best and the noblest consolation : That since it has pleased God to deprive you of the satisfaction you might have expected from the continuance of his life, it has at least been so ordered that ye manner of his death does you honour.

You left Scotland so much sooner than you proposed, when I had the pleasure of seeing you at Glasgow, that I had not an opportunity of making you a visit at Dalkieth (*sic*), as I intended, before you should return to London.

I sent about a fortnight ago the books which you ordered for the Duke of Buccleugh to Mr. Campbell at Edinburgh.[1] I paid for them, according to your orders, as soon as they were ready. I send you enclosed a list of them, with the prices discharged on the back. You will compare with the books when they arrive. Mr. Campbell will further them to London. I should have wrote to you of this a fortnight ago, but my natural dilatoriness prevented me.—I ever am, with the greatest esteem and regard, your most obliged and most obedient humble servant,

ADAM SMITH.

COLLEGE OF GLASGOW,
17*th September* 1759.

The second edition of the *Theory*, which Hume was anticipating immediately in 1759, did not appear till 1761, and it contained none of the alterations or additions he expected; but the *Dissertation on the Origin of Languages* was for the first time published along with it. The reason for the omission of the other additions is difficult to discover, for the author had not only prepared

[1] Mr. Campbell was the Duke's law-agent.

them, but gone the length of placing them in the printer's hands in 1760, as appears from the following letter. They did not appear either in the third edition in 1767, or the fourth in 1774, or the fifth in 1781 ; nor till the sixth, which was published, with considerable additions and corrections, immediately before the author's death in 1790. The earlier editions were published at 6s., and the 1790 edition at 12s. This was the last edition published in the author's lifetime, and it has been many times republished in the century that has elapsed since.

This is the letter just referred to :—

DEAR STRAHAN—I sent up to Mr. Millar four or five Posts ago the same additions which I had formerly sent to you, with a good many corrections and improvements which occurred to me since. If there are any typographical errors remaining in the last edition which had escaped me, I hope you will correct them. In other respects I could wish it was printed pretty exactly according to the copy which I delivered to you. A man, says the Spanish proverb, had better be a cuckold and know nothing of the matter, than not be a cuckold and believe himself to be one. And in the same manner, say I, an author had sometimes better be in the wrong and believe himself in the right, than be in the right and believe or even suspect himself to be in the wrong. To desire you to read my book over and mark all the corrections you would wish me to make upon a sheet of paper and send it to me, would, I fear, be giving you too much trouble. If, however, you could induce yourself to take this trouble, you would oblige me greatly ; I know how much I shall be benefitted, and I shall at the same time preserve the pretious right of private judgment, for the sake of which our forefathers kicked out the Pope and the Pretender. I believe you to be much more infallible than the Pope, but as I am a Protestant, my conscience makes me scruple to submit to any unscriptural authority.

Apropos to the Pope and the Pretender, have you read Hook's Memoirs ?[1] I have been ill these ten days, otherwise I should have written to you sooner, but I sat up the day before yesterday in my bed and read them thro' with infinite satisfaction, tho' they are by no

---

[1] *The Secret History of Colonel Hooke's Negotiations in Scotland in Favour of the Pretender in* 1707, written by himself. London, 1760.

means well written. The substance of what is in them I knew before, tho' not in such detail. I am afraid they are published at an unlucky time, and may throw a damp upon our militia. Nothing, however, appears to me more excusable than the disaffection of Scotland at that time. The Union was a measure from which infinite good has been derived to this country. The Prospect of that good, however, must then have appeared very remote and very uncertain. The immediate effect of it was to hurt the interest of every single order of men in the country. The dignity of the nobility was undone by it. The greater part of the gentry who had been accustomed to represent their own country in its own Parliament were cut out for ever from all hopes of representing it in a British Parliament. Even the merchants seemed to suffer at first. The trade to the Plantations was, indeed, opened to them. But that was a trade which they knew nothing about ; the trade they were acquainted with, that to France, Holland, and the Baltic, was laid under new embar(r)assments, which almost totally annihilated the two first and most important branches of it. The Clergy, too, who were then far from insignificant, were alarmed about the Church. No wonder if at that time all orders of men conspired in cursing a measure so hurtful to their immediate interest. The views of their Posterity are now very different ; but those views could be seen by but few of our forefathers, by those few in but a confused and imperfect manner.

It will give me the greatest satisfaction to hear from you. I pray you write to me soon. Remember me to the Franklins. I hope I shall have the grace to write to the youngest by next post to thank him, in the name both of the College and of myself, for his very agreeable present. Remember me likewise to Mr. Griffiths. I am greatly obliged to him for the very handsom character he gave of my book in his review.—I ever am, dear Strahan, most faithfully and sincerely yours,   ADAM SMITH.

GLASGOW, *4th April* 1760.[1]

The Franklins mentioned in this letter are Benjamin Franklin and his son, who had spent six weeks in Scotland in the spring of the previous year—" six weeks," said Franklin, " of the densest happiness I have met with in any part of my life." We know from Dr. Carlyle that during this visit Franklin met Smith one evening at supper at

[1] Bonar's *Catalogue of Adam Smith's Library*, p. x.

Robertson's in Edinburgh, but it seems from this letter highly probable that he had gone through to Glasgow, and possibly stayed with Smith at the College.   Why otherwise should the younger, or, as Smith says, youngest, Franklin have thought of making a presentation to Glasgow College, or Smith of thanking him not merely in the name of the College, but in his own ?   Strahan was one of Franklin's most intimate private friends.   They took a pride in one another as old compositors who had risen in the world ; and Smith had no doubt heard of, and perhaps from, the Franklins in some of Strahan's previous letters.

The Mr. Griffiths to whom Smith desires to be remembered was the editor of the *Monthly Review*, in which a favourable notice of his book had appeared in the preceding July.

CHAPTER X

SMITH visited London for the first time in September 1761, when Hume and probably others of his Scotch friends happened to be already there. He had not visited London in the course of his seven years' residence at Oxford, for, as Mr. Rogers reports, the Balliol Buttery Books show him never to have left Oxford at all during that time, and he had not visited London in the course of the first ten years he spent in Glasgow, otherwise the University would be certain to have preserved some record of it. For Glasgow University had much business to transact in London at that period, and would be certain to have commissioned Smith, if he was known to be going there, to transact some of that business for it. It never did so, however, till 1761. But in that year, on the 16th of June, the Senate having learned Smith's purpose of going to London, authorise him to get the accounts of the ordinary revenue of the College and the subdeanery for crops 1755, 1756, 1757, and 1758 cleared with the Treasury (that public office being then always in deep arrears with its work) ; to meet with Mr. Joshua Sharpe and settle his accounts with respect to the lands given to the College by Dr. Williams (the Dr. Williams of Williams's Library) ; to inquire into the state of the division of Snell's estate as to Coleburn farm, and the affair of the Prebends of Lincoln ; and to get all particulars about the

£500 costs in the Snell lawsuit with Balliol, which had to be paid to the University. Those documents were delivered, on the 27th of August, to Smith *in præsentia*, and then on the 15th of October, after his return, he reported what he had done, and produced a certificate, signed by the Secretary to the Treasury, finding that the University had in the four years specified and the years preceding expended above their revenue the sum of £2631 : 6 : 5$\frac{11}{12}$. I mention all these details with the view of showing that during Smith's residence in Glasgow the University had a variety of important and difficult business to transact in London, which they would be always glad to get one of their own number to attend to personally on the spot, and that as Smith was never asked to transact any of this business for them except in 1761, it may almost with certainty be inferred that he never was in London on any other occasion during his connection with that University.

Now this journey to London in 1761 is memorable because it constituted the economic " road to Damascus " for a future Prime Minister of England. It was during this journey, I believe, that Smith had Lord Shelburne for his travelling companion, and converted the young statesman to free trade. In 1795 Shelburne (then become Marquis of Lansdowne) writes Dugald Stewart : " I owe to a journey I made with Mr. Smith from Edinburgh to London the difference between light and darkness through the best part of my life. The novelty of his principles, added to my youth and prejudices, made me unable to comprehend them at the time, but he urged them with so much benevolence, as well as eloquence, that they took a certain hold which, though it did not develop itself so as to arrive at full conviction for some few years after, I can truly say has constituted ever since the happiness of my life, as well as the source of any little consideration I may have enjoyed in it." [1]

Shelburne was the first English statesman, except per-

[1] Stewart's *Life of Smith; Works*, ed. Hamilton, vol. x. p. 95.

haps Burke, who grasped and advocated free trade as a broad political principle; and though his biographer, Lord Edmond Fitzmaurice, attributes his conversion to Morellet, it is plain from the letter to Stewart that Morellet had only watered, it was Smith that sowed.

It is important, therefore, to fix if possible the date of this interesting journey. It occurred, Lord Shelburne says, in his own youth, and the only journeys to London Smith made during the period which with any reasonable stretching may be called Shelburne's youth, were made in 1761, 1763, and 1773. Now we have no positive knowledge of Shelburne being in Scotland any of these years, but in 1761 his brother, the Hon. Thomas Fitzmaurice, who had been studying under Smith in Glasgow, and living in Smith's house, left Glasgow for Oxford ; and Shelburne, who, since his father's death that very year, was taking, as we know from his correspondence with Sir William Blackstone on the subject, a very responsible concern in his younger brother's education and welfare, may very probably have gone to Scotland to attend him back. This circumstance seems to turn the balance in favour of 1761 and against the other two dates.

It is almost certain that the journey was not in 1773, for Shelburne would hardly have thought of himself as so young at that date, six years after he had been Secretary of State, and besides he had probably cast off his prejudices by that time, and was already (as we shall presently find) receiving instruction from Smith on colonial policy in 1767 ; and whether it was 1761 or 1763, it in either case shows at what a long period before the appearance of the *Wealth of Nations* Smith was advocating those broad principles which struck Shelburne at the time for their " novelty," and were only fully comprehended and accepted by him a few years afterwards.

Of Smith's visit to London on this occasion we know almost no particulars, but I think the notorious incident of his altercation with Johnson at the house of Strahan the printer must be referred to this visit. The story was told by Robertson to Boswell and Allan Ramsay, the painter, one evening in 1778, when they were dining together at the painter's house, and Johnson was expected as one of the guests. Before the doctor arrived the conversation happened to turn on him, and Robertson said, "He and I have always been very gracious. The first time I met him was one evening at Strahan's, when he had just had an unlucky altercation with Adam Smith, to whom he had been so rough that Strahan, after Smith was gone, had remonstrated, and told him that I was coming soon, and that he was uneasy to think that he might behave in the same way to me. 'No, no, sir,' said Johnson, 'I warrant you Robertson and I shall do very well.' Accordingly he was gentle and good-humoured and gracious with me the whole evening, and he has been so on every occasion that we have met since. I have often said laughing that I have been in a great measure indebted to Smith for my good reception." [1]

Now this incident must have occurred years before 1778, the date of Ramsay's dinner-party at which it was related, for Robertson speaks of having met Johnson many times between; and it probably occurred before 1763, because in 1763 Boswell mentions in his journal having told Johnson one evening that Smith had in his lectures in Glasgow expressed the strongest preference for rhyme over blank verse, and Johnson alludes in his reply to an unfriendly meeting he had once had with Smith. "Sir," said he, "I was once in company with Smith, and we did not take to each other, but had I known that he loved rhyme so much as you tell me he does I should have hugged him." [2] This answer seems to imply that the meeting was not quite recent—not in 1763—and if it occurred before 1763, it must have been in 1761.

It was, no doubt, this unhappy altercation that gave rise to the legendary anecdote which has obtained an im-

---

[1] Boswell's *Johnson*, ed. Hill, iii. 331.   [2] *Ibid.* i. 427.

mortality it ill deserved, but which cannot be passed over here, because it has been given to the world by three independent authorities of such importance as Sir Walter Scott, Lord Jeffrey, and Bishop Wilberforce. Scott communicates the anecdote to Croker for his edition of Boswell's *Johnson*, as it was told him by Professor John Millar of Glasgow, who had it from Smith himself the night the affair happened. Wilberforce gives it ostensibly as it was heard by his father from Smith's lips; and Jeffrey, in reviewing Wilberforce's book in the *Edinburgh Review*, says he heard the story, in substantially the same form as Wilberforce tells it, nearly fifty years before, "from the mouth of one of a party into which Mr. Smith came immediately after the collision."

The story, as told by Scott, is in this wise:[1] "Mr. Boswell has chosen to omit (in his account of Johnson's visit to Glasgow), for reasons which will be presently obvious, that Johnson and Adam Smith met at Glasgow; but I have been assured by Professor John Millar that they did so, and that Smith, leaving the party in which he had met Johnson, happened to come to another company where Millar was. Knowing that Smith had been in Johnson's society, they were anxious to know what had passed, and the more so as Dr. Smith's temper seemed much ruffled. At first Smith would only answer, 'He's a brute; he's a brute;' but on closer examination it appeared that Johnson no sooner saw Smith than he attacked him for some point of his famous letter on the death of Hume. Smith vindicated the truth of his statement. 'What did Johnson say?' was the universal inquiry. 'Why, he said,' replied Smith, with the deepest impression of resentment, 'he said, You lie.' 'And what did you reply?' 'I said, You are a son of a —— !' On such terms did these two great moralists meet and part, and such was the classical dialogue between two great teachers of philosophy."

Wilberforce's version is identical with Scott's, except

[1] Boswell's *Johnson*, ed. Hill, v. 369.

that it commits the absurdity of making Smith tell not
the story itself, but the story of his first telling it.   " ' Some
of our friends,' said Adam Smith, ' were anxious that we
should meet, and a party was arranged for the purpose in
the course of the evening.   I was soon after entering
another society, and perhaps with a manner a little confused.   " Have you met Dr. Johnson?" my friends exclaimed.   " Yes, I have."   " And what passed between
you?"'" and so on.   All this at any rate is legendary
outgrowth on the very face of it, and nonsensical even for
that.   But even the story itself, as told so circumstantially
by Scott, is demonstrably mythical in most of its circumstances.   Johnson was never in Glasgow except one day,
the 29th of October 1773, and in October 1773 Smith
was in London, and as we know from an incidental
parenthesis in the *Wealth of Nations*,[1] engaged in the
composition of that great work.   Hume, again, did not die
till 1776, so that there were better and more " obvious
reasons" than Scott imagined for Boswell's omitting
mention of a meeting between Johnson and Smith at
Glasgow which never took place, and a collision between
them about a famous letter which was not then written.
Time, place, and subject are all alike wrong, but these
Scott might think but the mortal parts of the story, and
he sometimes varied them in the telling himself.   Moore
heard him tell it at his own table at Abbotsford somewhat
differently from the version he gave to Croker.[2]   But
when so much is plainly the insensible creation of the
imagination, what reliance can be placed on the remainder?
All we know is that apparently at their very first meeting
those two philosophers did, in Strahan's house in London
in September 1761, have a personal altercation of an
outrageous character, at which, if not the very words
reported by Scott, then words quite as strong must manifestly have passed between them ; that their host declared

[1] Book IV. chap. vii.
[2] Russell's *Life of Moore*, p. 338.

Johnson to be entirely in the wrong, and that Smith withdrew from the company, and would very possibly go, as the story relates, to another company, his Scotch friends at the British Coffee-House in Cockspur Street, then the great Scotch resort,—a house which was kept by the sister of his friend Bishop Douglas, which was frequented much by Wedderburn, John Home, and others, and to which Smith's own letters used to be addressed.

One thing remains to be said : if the world has never been able to suffer this little morsel of scandal to be forgotten, the two principals in the feud themselves were able to forget it entirely. Smith was at a later period in the habit of meeting Johnson constantly at the table of common friends in London, and was elected in 1775 a member of Johnson's famous club, which would of course have been impossible—and indeed in so small a society never have been thought of—had the slightest remnant of animosity continued on either side. Johnson, it is true, was still occasionally rude to Smith, as he was occasionally rude to every other member of the club ; and certainly Smith never established with him anything of the cordial personal friendship he enjoyed with Burke, Gibbon, or Reynolds ; but their common membership in the Literary Club is proof of the complete burial of their earlier quarrel.

CHAPTER XI

In 1763 the Rev. William Ward of Broughton, chaplain to the Marquis of Rockingham, was bringing out his *Essay on Grammar*, which Sir William Hamilton thought "perhaps the most philosophical essay on the English language extant," and sent an abstract of it to Smith through a common friend, Mr. George Baird, to whom Smith wrote the following letter on the subject:— [1]

GLASGOW, *7th February* 1763.

DEAR SIR—I have read over the contents of your Friend's work with very great pleasure ; and heartily wish it was in my power to give, or to procure him all the encouragement which his ingenuity and industry deserve. I think myself greatly obliged to him for the very obliging notice he has been pleased to take of me, and should be glad to contribute anything in my power to compleating his design. I approve greatly of his plan for a Rational Grammar, and am convinced that a work of this kind, executed with his abilities and industry, may prove not only the best system of grammar, but the best system of logic in any language, as well as the best history of the natural progress of the human mind in forming the most important abstractions upon which all reasoning depends. From the short abstract which Mr. Ward has been so good as to send me, it is impossible for me to form any very decisive judgment concerning the propriety of every part of his method, particularly of some of his divisions.

---

[1] Nichol's *Literary Illustrations*, iii. 515.

If I was to treat the same subject, I should endeavour to begin with the consideration of verbs ; these being in my apprehension the original parts of speech, first invented to express in one word a compleat event ; I should then have endeavoured to show how the subject was divided to form the attribute, and afterwards how the object was distinguished from both ; and in this manner I should have tried to investigate the origin and use of all the different parts of speech and of all their different modifications, considered as necessary to express the different qualifications and relations of any single event. Mr. Ward, however, may have excellent reasons for following his own method ; and perhaps if I was engaged in the same task I should find it necessary to follow the same ; things frequently appearing in a very different light when taken in a general view, which is the only view I can pretend to have taken of them, and when considered in detail.

Mr. Ward, when he mentions the definitions which different authors have given of nouns substantive, takes no notice of that of the Abbé Girard, the author of the book called *Les Vrais Principes de la Langue Françoise*, which made me think it might be possible that he had not seen it. It is the book which first set me a thinking upon these subjects, and I have received more instruction from it than from any other I have yet seen upon them. If Mr. Ward has not seen it, I have it at his service. The grammatical articles, too, in the French *Encyclopédie* have given me a good deal of entertainment. Very probably Mr. Ward has seen both these works, and as he may have considered the subject more than I have done, may think less of them. Remember me to Mrs. Baird and Mr. Oswald, and believe me to be, with great truth, dear sir, sincerely yours,

ADAM SMITH.

Shortly after the date of this letter, Smith, who was now probably beginning to see the approach of the day when he would lay down his Glasgow professorship in order to superintend the studies of the young Duke of Buccleugh, writes David Hume, pressing for his long-promised visit to the West. The occasion of the letter is to introduce a young gentleman of whom I know nothing, but who was doubtless one of the English students who were attracted to Glasgow by Smith's rising fame. He was possibly the first Earl of Carnarvon, of whose uncle, Nicholas Herbert, Smith told Rogers the story that he had read over once a list of the Eton boys and repeated it four years afterwards to his nephew, then Lord Porchester. Smith said he knew him well. The letter is as follows :—

MY DEAR HUME—This letter will be presented to you by Mr. Henry Herbert, a young gentleman who is very well acquainted with your works, and upon that account extremely desirous of being introduced to the authour. As I am convinced that you will find him extremely agreeable, I shall make no apology for introducing him. He proposes to stay a few days in Edinburgh while the company are there, and would be glad to have the liberty of calling upon you sometimes when it suits your conveniency to receive him. If you indulge him in this, both he and I will think ourselves infinitely obliged to you.

You have been long promising us a visit at Glasgow, and I have made Mr. Herbert promise to endeavour to bring you along with him. Though you have resisted all my sollicitations, I hope you will not resist his. I hope I need not tell you that it will give me the greatest pleasure to see you.—I ever am, my dear friend, most affectionately and sincerely yours,
                                        ADAM SMITH.

GLASGOW, *22nd February* 1763.[1]

To that letter Hume returned the following answer :—

DEAR SMITH—I was obliged to you both for your kind letter and for the opportunity which you afforded me of making acquaintance with Mr. Herbert, who appears to me a very promising young man. I set up a chaise in May next, which will give me the liberty of travelling about, and you may be sure a journey to Glasgow will be one of the first I shall undertake. I intend to require with great strictness an account how you have been employing your Leisure, and I desire you to be ready for that purpose. Wo be to you if the Ballance be against you. Your friends here will also expect that I should bring you with me. It seems to me very long since I saw you.—Most sincerely,
                                        DAVID HUME.

EDINBURGH, *28th March* 1763.[2]

---

1 *Hume Correspondence*, R.S.E. Library.
2 *Ibid.* Printed by Burton.

This long-meditated visit was apparently never accomplished, the chaise notwithstanding. Only a few months more pass and the scene completely changes; the two friends are one after the other transported suddenly to France on new vocations, and their first meeting now was in Paris.

Hume writes Smith from Edinburgh on the 9th of August 1763 intimating his appointment as Secretary to the English Embassy at Paris, and bidding him adieu. " I am a little hurried," he says, " in my preparations, but I could not depart without bidding you adieu, my good friend, and without acquainting you with the reasons of so sudden a movement. I have not great expectations of revisiting this country soon, but I hope it will not be impossible ; but we may meet abroad, which will be a great satisfaction to me." [1]

Smith's reply has not been preserved, but it seems to have contained among other things a condemnation, in Smith's most decisive style, of the recent proceedings of his friend Lord Shelburne in connection with various intrigues and negotiations set agoing by the Court and Lord Bute with the view of increasing the power of the Crown in English politics. That appears from a letter Hume writes Smith from London on 13th September, wanting information about his new chief's eldest son, Lord Beauchamp, regarding whom he had once heard Smith mention something told by " that severe critic Mr. Herbert," and to whom Hume was now to act in the capacity of tutor in conjunction with his official duties as Secretary of Legation. Then after relating the story of Bute's negotiations with Pitt through Shelburne, and stating that Lord Shelburne resigned because he found himself obnoxious on account of his share in that negotiation, he says : " I see you are much incensed with that nobleman, but he always speaks of you with regard. I hear that your pupil, Mr. Fitzmaurice, makes a very good figure at Paris." [2]

[1] Burton's *Life of Hume*, ii. 157.
[2] *Ibid.*, ii. 163.

Smith was always a stout Whig, strongly opposed to any attempt to increase the power of the Crown, and cordially denounced Bute and all his works. He was delighted with the famous No. 45 of the *North Briton*, published in the April of this very year 1763, and after reading it exclaimed to Dr. Carlyle, "Bravo! this fellow (Wilkes) will either be hanged in six months, or he will get Lord Bute impeached."[1] Shelburne after his resignation in September voted against the Court in the Wilkes affair, but up till then, at any rate, his public conduct could not be viewed by a man of Smith's political principles with anything but the most absolute condemnation, and the condemnation would be all the stronger because, from personal intercourse with his lordship, Smith knew that he was really a man of liberal mind and reforming spirit, from whom he had a right to look for better things.

When Hume arrived in France the first letter he wrote to any of his friends at home was to Smith. He had been only a week in the country, and describes his first experiences of the curious transformation he then suddenly underwent : from being the object of attack and reproach and persecution for half a lifetime among the honest citizens of Edinburgh, he had become the idol of extravagant worship among the great and powerful at the Court of France.

"During the last days in particular," he says, "that I have been at Fontainebleau I have *suffered* (the expression is not improper) as much flattery as almost any man has ever done in the same time, but there are few days in my life when I have been in good health that I would not rather pass over again.

"I had almost forgot in this effusion, shall I say, of my misanthropy or my vanity to mention the subject which first put my pen in my hand. The Baron d'Holbach, whom I saw at Paris, told me that there was one under his eye

[1] Carlyle's *Autobiography*, p. 431.

that was translating your *Theory of Moral Sentiments*, and
desired me to inform you of it. Mr. Fitzmaurice, your
old friend,[1] interests himself strongly in this undertaking.
Both of them wish to know if you propose to make any
alteration on the work, and desire you to inform me of
your intentions in that particular."[2]

Hume's hope of their "not impossible" meeting in
Paris was destined to be gratified sooner than he could
have conjectured. A few days before Smith received this
letter from Hume he had received likewise the following
letter from Charles Townshend, intimating that the time
had now come for the Duke of Buccleugh to go abroad,
and renewing to Smith the offer of the post of travelling
tutor to his Grace :—

DEAR SIR—The time now drawing near when the Duke of
Buccleugh intends to go abroad, I take the liberty of renewing
the subject to you : that if you should still have the same disposition to travel with Him I may have the satisfaction of informing
Lady Dalkeith and His Grace of it, and of congratulating them
upon an event which I know that they, as well as myself, have so
much at heart. The Duke is now at Eton: He will remain
there until Christmass. He will then spend some short time in
London, that he may be presented at Court, and not pass in-
stantaneously from school to a foreign country ; but it were to
be wished He should not be long in Town, exposed to the habits
and companions of London, before his mind has been more formed
and better guarded by education and experience.

I do not enter at this moment upon the subject of establishment, because if you have no objection to the situation, I know
we cannot differ about the terms. On the contrary, you will find
me more sollicitous than yourself to make the connection with
Buccleugh as satisfactory and advantageous to you as I am persuaded it will be essentially beneficial to him.

The Duke of Buccleugh has lately made great progress both in
his knowledge of ancient languages and in his general taste for
composition. With these improvements his amusement from
reading and his love of instruction have naturally increased. He

---

[1] See above, p. 58.
[2] Burton's *Life of Hume*, ii. 168.

has sufficient talents : a very manly temper, and an integrity of heart and reverence for truth, which in a person of his rank and fortune are the firmest foundation of weight in life and uniform greatness. If it should be agreeable to you to finish his education, and mould these excellent materials into a settled character, I make no doubt but he will return to his family and country the very man our fondest hopes have fancied him.

I go to Town next Friday, and should be obliged to you for your answer to this letter.—I am, with sincere affection and esteem, dear sir, your most faithful and most obedient humble servant,   C. TOWNSHEND.

Lady Dalkeith presents her compliments to you.

ADDERBURY, 25*th October* 1763.[1]

Smith accepted the offer. The terms were a salary of £300 a year, with travelling expenses while abroad, and a pension of £300 a year for life afterwards. He was thus to have twice his Glasgow income, and to have it assured till death. The pension was no doubt a principal inducement to a Scotch professor in those days to take such a post, for a Scotch professor had then no resource in his old age except the price he happened to receive for his chair from his successor in the event of his resignation ; and we find several of them — Professors Moor and Robert Simson of Glasgow among others— much harassed with pecuniary cares in their last years. Smith's remuneration was liberal, but nothing beyond what was usual in such situations at the time. Dr. John Moore, who gave up his medical practice in Glasgow a few years later to be tutor to the young Duke of Hamilton, got also £300 a year while actively employed in the tutorship and a pension of £100 a year afterwards.[2] Professor Rouet, who, as already mentioned, sacrificed his chair in Glasgow for his tutorial appointment, is said to have received a pension of £500 a year from Lord

[1] Original in possession of Professor Cunningham, Belfast.
[2] *Caldwell Papers*, i. 192.

Hopetoun, in addition to a pension of £50 he received, in consideration of previous services of the same kind, from Sir John Maxwell; and Professor Adam Ferguson, who was appointed tutor to the Earl of Chesterfield on Smith's recommendation, had £400 a year while on duty, and a pension of £200 a year, which he lived to enjoy for forty years after, receiving from first to last nearly £9000 for his two years' work. Smith did almost as well, for with the pension, which he drew for twenty-four years, he got altogether more than £8000 for his three years' service.

This residence abroad for a few years with a competent tutor was then a common substitute for a university education. The Duke of Buccleugh, for example, was never sent to a university after he came back from his travels with Smith, but married almost immediately on his return, and entered directly into the active duties of life. It was generally thought that travel really supplied a more liberal education and a better preparation for life for a young man of the world than residence at a university; and it is not uninteresting to recall here how strongly Smith disagrees with that opinion in the *Wealth of Nations*, while admitting that some excuse could be found for it in the low state of learning into which the English universities had suffered themselves to fall :—

" In England it becomes every day more and more the custom to send young people to travel in foreign countries immediately upon their leaving school, and without sending them to any university. Our young people, it is said, generally return home much improved by their travels. A young man who goes abroad at seventeen or eighteen, and returns home at one-and-twenty, returns three or four years older than he was when he went abroad; and at that age it is very difficult not to improve a good deal in three or four years. In the course of his travels he generally acquires some knowledge of one or two foreign languages; a knowledge, however, which is seldom sufficient to enable him either to speak or write them with propriety.   In other respects he commonly returns home more conceited, more unprincipled, more dissipated, and more incapable of any serious application, either to study or to business, than he could well have become in so short a time had he lived at home.   By travelling so very young, by spending in the most frivolous dissipation the most precious years of his life, at a distance from the inspection and controul of his parents and relations, every useful habit which the earlier parts of his education might have had some tendency to form in him, instead of being riveted and confirmed, is almost necessarily either weakened or effaced.   Nothing but the discredit into which the universities are allowing themselves to fall could ever have brought into repute so very absurd a practice as that of travelling at this early period of life.   By sending his son abroad, a father delivers himself, at least for some time, from so disagreeable an object as a son unemployed, neglected and going to ruin before his eyes." [1]

Smith must have written Townshend accepting the situation almost immediately on receiving the offer of it, and he at the same time applied to the University authorities for leave of absence for part of the session.   He does not as yet resign his chair, nor does he make in his application any formal mention of the nature of the business that required his absence ; he merely asks for their sanction to some highly characteristic arrangements which he desired to make in connection with the conduct of his class by a substitute.   On the 8th of November 1763, according to the Faculty Records, " Dr. Smith represented that some interesting business would probably require his leaving the College some time this winter, and made the following proposals and request to the meeting :—

" 1st, That if he should be obliged to leave the College without finishing his usual course of lectures, he should pay back to all his students the fees which he shall have

[1] *Wealth of Nations*, Book V. chap. i. art. ii.

received from them ; and that if any of them should refuse to accept of such fees, he should in that case pay them to the University.

" 2nd, That whatever part of the usual course of lectures he should leave unfinished should be given gratis to the students, by a person to be appointed by the University, with such salary as they shall think proper, which salary is to be paid by Dr. Smith.

" The Faculty accept of the above proposals, and hereby unanimously grant Dr. Smith leave of absence for three months of this session if his business shall require, and at such time as he shall find it necessary."

The reason he asks in the first instance only for this temporary and provisional arrangement is no doubt to be found in the fact that the precise date for the beginning of the tutorship was not yet determined. As it might very possibly be fixed upon suddenly and involve a somewhat rapid call for his services, the precaution of obtaining beforehand a three months' leave of absence would enable him to remain in constant readiness to answer that call whenever it might come, without in the meanwhile requiring him to give up his duties to his Glasgow class prematurely ; and it would at the same time allow ample time to the University to make more permanent arrangements before the temporary provision expired. The call when it came did come rather suddenly. Up till the middle of December Smith never received any manner of answer from Townshend, and the matter was not settled till after the Christmas holidays. For on the 12th of December 1763 Smith writes Hume, who was now in Paris :—

MY DEAR HUME — The day before I received your last letter I had the honour of a letter from Charles Townshend, renewing in the most obliging manner his former proposal that I should travel with the Duke of Buccleugh, and informing me that his Grace was to leave Eton at Christmas, and would go abroad very soon after that. I accepted the proposal, but at the same time expressed to Mr. Townshend the difficulties I should have in leaving the University before the beginning of April, and begged to know if my attendance upon his Grace would be necessary before that time. I have yet received no answer to that letter, which, I suppose, is owing to this, that his Grace is not yet come from Eton, and that nothing is yet settled with regard to the time of his going abroad. I delayed answering your letter till I should be able to inform you at what time I should have the pleasure of seeing you. . . . . I ever am, my dearest friend, most faithfully yours,   ADAM SMITH.[1]

After the Duke reached London, however, at the Christmas recess, it seems to have been quickly settled to send him out on his travels without more delay, and on the 9th of January 1764 Smith intimated to the Faculty of Glasgow College that he was soon to leave that city under the permission granted him by the Dean of Faculty's meeting of the 8th of November, and that he had returned to the students all the fees he had received that session. He likewise acquainted the meeting that he proposed to pay his salary as paid by the College for one half-year, commencing the 10th of October previous, to the person who should teach his class for the remainder of the session. Mr. Thomas Young, student of divinity, was, on Smith's recommendation, chosen for this purpose. A committee was appointed to receive from Smith the private library of the Moral Philosophy class ; next day at a meeting of Senatus he was paid the balance due to him on his accounts as Quæstor, and was entrusted with a copy of Foulis's large *Homer*, which they asked him to carry to London and deliver, in their name, to Sir James Gray, as a present to his Sicilian majesty, who had shown them some favour ; and the Senate-room of Glasgow knew him no more.

His parting with his students was not quite so simple. They made some difficulty, as he seems to have anticipated, about taking back the fees they had paid him for his class, and he was obliged to resort almost to force before he succeeded in getting them to do so. The curious scene is

[1] Fraser's *Scotts of Buccleuch*, ii. 403.

described by Alexander Fraser Tytler (Lord Woodhouse-lee) in his *Life of Lord Kames:* " After concluding his last lecture, and publicly announcing from the chair that he was now taking a final leave of his auditors, acquainting them at the same time with the arrangements he had made, to the best of his power, for their benefit, he drew from his pocket the several fees of the students, wrapped up in separate paper parcels, and beginning to call up each man by his name, he delivered to the first who was called the money into his hand. The young man peremptorily refused to accept it, declaring that the instruction and pleasure he had already received was much more than he either had repaid or ever could compensate, and a general cry was heard from every one in the room to the same effect. But Mr. Smith was not to be bent from his purpose. After warmly expressing his feelings of gratitude and the strong sense he had of the regard shown to him by his young friends, he told them this was a matter betwixt him and his own mind, and that he could not rest satisfied unless he performed what he deemed right and proper. ' You must not refuse me this satisfaction ; nay, by heavens, gentlemen, you shall not ; ' and seizing by the coat the young man who stood next him, he thrust the money into his pocket and then pushed him from him. The rest saw it was in vain to contest the matter, and were obliged to let him have his own way." [1]

This is a signal proof of the scrupulous delicacy of Smith's honour ; he had firmly determined not to touch a shilling of this money, and if the students had persisted in refusing it he intended, as we have seen, to give it to the funds of the University. Many may think his delicacy even excessive, for it is common enough for a professor's class to be conducted by a substitute in the absence, through ill-health or other causes, of the professor himself, and nobody thinks the students suffer any such injury by the arrangement as to call for even a reduction of the fees.

[1] Tytler's *Kames*, i. 278.

What Smith would have done had his absence been due to ill-health one cannot say, but as his engagement with the students for a session's lectures was broken off by his own spontaneous acceptance of an office of profit, he felt he could not honourably retain the wages when he had failed to implement the engagement,—a thing which a barrister in large practice does without scruple every day.

The same sense of right led Smith to resign his chair. He did not do so till he reached France, but he manifestly contemplated doing it from the first, for he only made arrangements for paying his substitute till the end of the first half of the session, by which time he would expect his successor to have entered on office, as indeed actually happened, for Reid came there in the beginning of June. Moreover, his resignation was evidently an understood thing at the University long before it was really sent in, for a good deal of intriguing had already been going on for the place. The Lord Privy Seal (the Hon. James Stuart Mackenzie, Lord Bute's brother), who was Scotch Minister, writes Baron Mure on the 2nd February 1764, a fortnight before Smith resigned, asking whether it was true the University were to appoint Dr. Wight to succeed Smith, and mentions incidentally having had some conversation with Smith himself (apparently in London) on the subject, particularly with regard to the possible claims of Mr. Young, his substitute, to the appointment.

It was not always necessary—nor, indeed, does it seem to have been the more usual practice—for a Scotch professor to resign his chair on accepting a temporary place like a travelling tutorship. Adam Ferguson fought the point successfully with the Edinburgh Town Council when he left England as tutor to Lord Chesterfield ; and Dalzel, when Professor of Greek in Edinburgh, went to live at Oxford as tutor to Lord Maitland ; but we have already seen, in connection with the case of Professor Rouet, that Smith held strong views against the encouragement of absenteeism and the growth of any feeling that the

University was there for the convenience of the professors, instead of the professors being there for the service of the University.

Under these circumstances it was natural for Smith to resign his chair on his acceptance of the tutorship; and although he only sent the letter of resignation after his arrival in France, it is perhaps more convenient to print it here in its natural connection with Glasgow University affairs than to defer it to its more strictly chronological place in the chapter describing his French travels. The letter is addressed " To the Right Hon. Thomas Miller, Esq., His Majesty's Advocate for Scotland," Lord Rector of Glasgow University at the time; and it runs as follows :

My Lord — I take this first opportunity after my arrival in this place, which was not till yesterday, to resign my office into the hands of your lordship, of the Dean of Faculty, of the Principal of the College, and of all my other most respectable and worthy colleagues. Into your and their hands, therefor, I do hereby resign my office of Professor of Moral Philosophy in the University of Glasgow and in the College thereof, with all the emoluments, privileges, and advantages which belong to it. I reserve, however, my right to the salary for the current half year, which commenced at the 10th of October for one part of my salary and at Martinmas last for another ; and I desire that this salary may be paid to the gentleman who does that part of my duty which I was obliged to leave undone, in the manner agreed on between my very worthy colleagues and me before we parted. I never was more anxious for the good of the College than at this moment ; and I sincerely wish that whoever is my successor may not only do credit to the office by his abilities, but be a comfort to the very excellent men with whom he is likely to spend his life, by the probity of his heart and the goodness of his temper.— I have the honour to be, my lord, your lordship's most obedient and most faithful servant,   ADAM SMITH.

Paris, 14*th February* 1764.[1]

The Senate accepted his resignation on the 1st of March, and expressed their regret at his loss in the following

[1] Glasgow University Records.

terms : "The University cannot help at the same time expressing their sincere regret at the removal of Dr. Smith, whose distinguished probity and amiable qualities procured him the esteem and affection of his colleagues ; whose uncommon genius, great abilities, and extensive learning did so much honour to this society ; his elegant and ingenious *Theory of Moral Sentiments* having recommended him to the esteem of men of taste and literature throughout Europe. His happy talents in illustrating abstracted subjects, and faithful assiduity in communicating useful knowledge, distinguished him as a professor, and at once afforded the greatest pleasure and the most important instruction to the youth under his care."

CHAPTER XII

SMITH joined his pupil in London in the end of January 1764, and they set out together for France in the beginning of February. They remained abroad two years and a half—ten days in Paris, eighteen months in Toulouse, two months travelling in the South of France, two months in Geneva, and ten months in Paris again. Smith kept no journal and wrote as few letters as possible, but we are able from various sources to fill in some of the outlines of their course of travel.

At Dover they were joined by Sir James Macdonald of Sleat, a young baronet who had been at Eton College with the Duke of Buccleugh, and who had been living in France almost right on since the re-establishment of peace. Sir James was heir of the old Lords of the Isles, and son of the lady who, with her factor Kingsburgh, harboured Prince Charlie and Flora Macdonald in Skye ; and he was himself then filling the world of letters in Paris and London alike with astonishment at the extent of his knowledge and the variety of his intellectual gifts. Walpole, indeed, said that when he grew older he would choose to know less, but to Grimm he seemed the same marvel of parts as he seemed to Hume. He accompanied Smith and the Duke to Paris, where they arrived (as we know from Smith's letter to the Rector of Glasgow University) on the 13th of February.

In Paris they did not remain long—not more than ten

days at most, for it took at that period six days to go
from Paris to Toulouse, and they were in Toulouse on the
4th of March. Smith does not appear during this short
stay in Paris to have made the personal acquaintance of
any of the eminent men of letters whom he afterwards
knew so well, for he never mentions any of them in his
subsequent letters to Hume from Toulouse, though he
occasionally mentions Englishmen whose acquaintance he
first made at that time. He probably could not as yet
speak French, for even to the last he could only speak it
very imperfectly. Most of their time in Paris seems,
therefore, to have been spent with Hume and Sir James
Macdonald and Lord Beauchamp, who was Hume's pupil
and Sir James's chief friend. Paris, moreover, was merely
a halting-place for the present; their immediate destination was Toulouse, at that time a favourite resort of the
English. It was the second city of the kingdom, and
wore still much of the style of an ancient capital. It was
the seat of an archbishopric, of a university, of a parliament, of modern academies of science and art which made
some ado with their annual *Jeux Floraux*, and the nobility
of the province still had their town houses there, and lived
in them all winter. The society was more varied and refined
than anywhere else in France out of Paris.

Among the English residents was a cousin of David
Hume, who had entered the Gallican Church, and was
then Vicar-General of the diocese of Toulouse, the Abbé
Seignelay Colbert. Smith brought a letter from Hume to
the Abbé, and the Abbé writes Hume in reply on the 4th
of March, thanking him for having introduced Smith,
who, he says, appeared to be all that was said of him in the
letter. "He has only just arrived," the Abbé proceeds,
"and I have only seen him for an instant. I am very
sorry that they have not found the Archbishop here. He
went some six weeks ago to Montpellier, whence he will
soon go to Paris. He told me he had a great desire to
make your acquaintance. I fear that my long black

cassock will frighten the Duke of Buccleugh, but apart from that I should omit nothing to make his stay in this town as agreeable and useful as possible."[1] He writes again on the 22nd of April, after having a month's experience of his new friends : " Mr. Smith is a sublime man. His heart and his mind are equally admirable. Messrs. Malcolm and Mr. Urquhart of Cromartie are now here. The Duke, his pupil, is a very amiable spirit, and does his exercises well, and is making progress in French. If any English or Scotch people ask your advice where to go for their studies, you could recommend Toulouse. There is a very good academy and much society, and some very distinguished people to be seen here." In a subsequent letter he says, " There are many English people here, and the district suits them well."[2]

This Abbé Colbert, who was Smith's chief guide and friend in the South of France, was the eldest son of Mr. Cuthbert of Castlehill in Inverness-shire, and was therefore head of the old Highland family to which Colbert, the famous minister of Louis XIV., was so anxious to trace his descent. That minister had himself gone the length of petitioning the Scotch Privy Council for a birth-brieve, or certificate, to attest his descent from the Castle-hill family, and the petition was refused through the influence of the Duke of Lauderdale. But his successor, the Marquis de Seignelay, found the Scotch Parliament more accommodating in 1686 than the Scotch Privy Council had been, and obtained the birth-brieve in an Act of that year, which was passed, as it states, in order that " this illustrious and noble family of Colbert may be restored to us their friends and to their native country," and which declared that the family came from the south of Scotland, took their name from St. Cuthbert (pronounced, says the Act, by the Scotch Culbert, though " soaftened " by the French into Colbert), and received their arms for their valour in the battle of Harlaw.

[1] *Hume Correspondence*, R.S.E. Library.   [2] *Ibid.*

The link between the Scotch Cuthberts and the French Colberts, thus attested by Act of Parliament, may or may not be fabulous, but it was a link of gold to many members of the family of Castlehill, who emigrated to France, and were advanced into high positions through the interest of their French connections. One of these was the present Abbé, who had come over in 1750 a boy of fourteen, was now at twenty-eight Vicar-General of Toulouse, and was in 1781 made Bishop of Rodez. As Bishop he distinguished himself by the work he did for the improvement of agriculture and industry in his diocese, and, as member of the States General in 1789, he became the hero of the hour in Paris and was carried shoulder-high through the streets for proposing the union of the clergy with the Third Estate. When the Civil Constitution of the clergy was declared he refused to submit, and returning to this country, spent the remainder of his days here as Secretary to Louis XVIII.

It would appear from the Abbé's first letter that Smith had either brought with him from Paris an introduction to the Archbishop of Toulouse, or that Hume had asked his cousin to give him one. This Archbishop — who was so desirous to make Hume's acquaintance — was the celebrated Loménie de Brienne, afterwards Cardinal and Minister of France, who was thought at this time, Walpole says, to be the ablest man in the Gallican Church, and was pronounced by Hume to be the only man in France capable of restoring the greatness of the kingdom. When he obtained the opportunity he signally falsified Hume's prognostication, and did much to precipitate the Revolution by his incapacity. Smith must no doubt have met him occasionally during his protracted sojourn at Toulouse, though we have no evidence that he did, and the Archbishop was rather notorious for his absence from his see. If he did meet his Grace he would have found him as advanced an economist as himself, for having been a college friend of Turgot and Morellet at the Sorbonne, he became a strong advocate of their new economic principles, and succeeded in getting the principle of free trade in corn adopted by the States of Languedoc. Whether they were personally acquainted or not, the Archbishop does not appear to have cherished any profound regard for Smith, for when he was Minister of France he refused his friend Morellet the trifling sum of a hundred francs, which the Abbé asked to pay for the printing of his translation of the *Wealth of Nations*.

During Smith's first six months at Toulouse he does not seem to have seen the Archbishop, or to have seen much of anybody, as the following letter shows. Indeed he found the place extremely dull, the life he led in Glasgow having been, he says, dissipation itself in comparison. They had not received the letters of recommendation they had expected from the Duc de Choiseul, and for society they were as yet practically confined to the Abbé Colbert and the English residents. For a diversion Smith contemplates an excursion to Bordeaux, and suggests a visit for a month from Sir James Macdonald, for the sake not only of his agreeable society, but of the service " his influence and example " would render the Duke. Personally he had, to mitigate his solitude, taken a measure no less important than effectual —he had begun to write a book—the *Wealth of Nations* —"to pass away the time. You may believe I have very little to do."

They had arrived in Toulouse on the 3rd or 4th of March, but it is the 5th of July before Smith thinks of writing Hume ; at least the following letter reads as if it were the first since they parted :—

My dearest Friend—The Duke of Buccleugh proposes soon to set out for Bordeaux, where he intends to stay a fortnight or more. I should be much obliged to you if you could send us recommendations to the Duke of Richelieu, the Marquis de Lorges, and the Intendant of the Province. Mr. Townshend

assured me that the Duc de Choiseul was to recommend us to
all the people of fashion here and everywhere else in France.
We have heard nothing, however, of these recommendations,
and have had our way to make as well as we could by the help of
the Abbé, who is a stranger here almost as much as we. The
Progress indeed we have made is not very great. The Duke is
acquainted with no Frenchman whatever. I cannot cultivate
the acquaintance of the few with whom I am acquainted, as I
cannot bring them to our house, and am not always at liberty to
go to theirs. The life which I led at Glasgow was a pleasurable
dissipated life in comparison of that which I lead here at Present.
I have begun to write a book in order to pass away the time.
You may believe I have very little to do. If Sir James would
come and spend a month with us in his travels, it would not only
be a great satisfaction to me, but he might by his influence and
example be of great service to the Duke. Mention these matters,
however, to nobody but to him. Remember me in the most
respectful manner to Lord Beauchamp and to Dr. Trail,[1] and
believe me, my dear friend, ever yours,   ADAM SMITH.

TOULOUSE, *5th July* 1764.[2]

The trip to Bordeaux was taken probably in August,
and in the company of Abbé Colbert. At Bordeaux they
fell in with Colonel Barré, the furious orator, whose invec-
tive made even Charles Townshend quail, but who was
now over on a visit to his French kinsfolk, and making the
hearts of these simple people glad with his natural kind-
nesses. He seems to have been much with Smith and
his party during their stay in Bordeaux, and to have
accompanied them back to Toulouse. For he writes
Hume on the 4th of September from the latter town,
and says : " I thank you for your last letter from Paris,
which I received just as Smith and his *élève* and L'Abbé
Colbert were sitting down to dine with me at Bordeaux.
The latter is a very honest fellow and deserves to be a

---

[1] Lord Beauchamp was the eldest son of the English Ambassador,
the Earl of Hertford, and Dr. Trail, or properly Traill, was the
Ambassador's chaplain, who was made Bishop of Down and Connor soon
afterwards, when Lord Hertford became Lord-Lieutenant of Ireland.

[2] *Hume Correspondence*, R.S.E. Library.

bishop ; make him one if you can. . . . Why will you triumph and talk of *platte couture ?*   You have friends on both sides. Smith agrees with me in thinking that you are turned soft by the *délices* of the French Court, and that you don't write in that nervous manner you was remarkable for in the more northern climates. Besides, what is still worse, you take your politics from your Elliots, Rigbys, and Selwyns." [1]

Smith was already acquainted with Barré before he left Scotland, where the colonel, for services rendered to Lord Shelburne, held the lucrative post of Governor of Stirling Castle ; and now he could not go sight-seeing in a French town under two better guides than Barré and Colbert—a Frenchman who had become an English politician, and an Englishman who had become a French ecclesiastic. He seems to have been struck with the contrast between the condition of the working class in Bordeaux and their condition in Toulouse, as he had already been struck with the same contrast between Glasgow and Edinburgh. In Bordeaux they were in general industrious, sober, and thriving ; in Toulouse and the rest of the parliament towns they were idle and poor; and the reason was that Bordeaux was a commercial town, the *entrepôt* of the wine trade of a rich wine district, while Toulouse and the rest were merely residential towns, employing little capital more than was necessary to supply their own consumption. The common people were always better off in a town like Bordeaux, where they lived on capital, than in a town like Toulouse, where they lived on revenue.[2] But while he speaks as if he thought the people of Bordeaux more sober as well as more industrious than the people of Toulouse, he looked upon the inhabitants of the southern provinces of France generally as among the soberest people in Europe, and ascribes their sobriety to the cheapness of their liquor. " People are seldom

---

[1] Burton's *Letters of Eminent Persons to David Hume*, p. 37.
[2] *Wealth of Nations*, Book II. chap. iii.

guilty of excess," he says, "in what is their daily fare." He tells that when a French regiment came from some of the northern provinces of France, where wine was somewhat dear, to be quartered in the southern, where wine was very cheap, the soldiers were at first debauched by the cheapness and novelty of good wine; but after a few months' residence the greater part of them became as sober as the rest of the inhabitants. And he thinks the same effect might occur in this country from a re-duction of the wine, malt, and ale duties.[1]

Besides seeing the places, they visited some of the notabilities, to whom the Earl of Hertford had sent them the letters of introduction for which Smith had asked through Hume. The governor of the province was away from home at the time, however; but Smith hoped to see him on a second visit to Bordeaux he was presently to pay to meet his pupil's younger brother on his way round from Paris to Toulouse. But they found the Duke of Richelieu at home, and the gallant old field-marshal, the hero of a hundred fights and a thousand scandals, seems to have received them with great civility and even distinction. Smith used to have much to say ever afterwards of this famous and ill-famed man.

The excursion to Bordeaux in August was so agreeable that they made another—probably in September—up to the fashionable watering-place Bagnères de Bigorre, and in October, when Smith wrote the following letter to Hume, they were on the eve of the second visit to Bordeaux of which I have spoken, and even contemplating after that a visit to Montpellier, when the States of Languedoc—the local assembly of the province—met there in the end of November.

TOULOUSE, 21st October 1764.

MY DEAR HUME—I take this opportunity of Mr. Cook's going to Paris to return to you, and thro' you to the Ambas-

---

[1] *Wealth of Nations*, Book I. chap. xi.

sador, my very sincere and hearty thanks for the very honourable manner in which he was so good as to mention me to the Duke of Richelieu in the letter of recommendation which you sent us. There was, indeed, one small mistake in it. He called me Robinson instead of Smith. I took upon me to correct this mistake myself before the Duke delivered the letter. We were all treated by the Marechal with the utmost Politeness and attention, particularly the Duke, whom he distinguished in a very proper manner. The Intendant was not at Bordeaux, but we shall soon have an opportunity of delivering his letter, as we propose to return to that place in order to meet my Lord's Brother.

Mr. Cook [1] goes to Caen to wait upon Mr. Scot, and to attend him from that place to Toulouse. He will pass by Paris, and I must beg the favour of you that as soon as you understand he is in town you will be so good as to call upon him and carry him to the Ambassador's, as well as to any other place where he would chuse to go. I must beg the same favour of Sir James. Mr. Cook will let you know when he comes to town. I have great reason to entertain the most favourable opinion of Mr. Scot, and I flatter myself his company will be both useful and agreeable to his Brother. Our expedition to Bordeaux and another we have made since to Bagnères has made a great change upon the Duke. He begins now to familiarise himself to French company, and I flatter myself I shall spend the rest of the time we are to live together not only in Peace and contentment, but in gayetty and amusement.

When Mr. Scot joins us we propose to go to see the meeting of the States of Languedoc at Montpelier. Could you promise us recommendations to the Comte d'Eu, to the Archbishop of Narbonne, and to the Intendant? These expeditions, I find, are of the greatest service to my Lord.—I ever am, my dear friend, most faithfully yours, ADAM SMITH.[2]

A few days after the date of that letter Smith writes Hume again, introducing one of the English residents in Toulouse, Mr. Urquhart of Cromartie, as Abbé Colbert describes him in one of his letters, a descendant therefore probably of Sir Thomas. The letter is of no importance, but it shows at least Smith's hearty liking for a good fellow.

[1] The Duke's servant.
[2] *Hume Correspondence*, R.S.E. Library.

My dear Friend—This letter will be delivered to you by Mr. Urquhart, the only man I ever knew who had a better temper than yourself. You will find him most perfectly amiable. I recommend him in the most earnest manner to your advice and protection. He is not a man of letters, and is just a plain, sensible, agreeable man of no pretensions of any kind, but whom you will love every day better and better.—My dear friend, most faithfully yours, Adam Smith.

Toulouse, 4*th November* 1764.[1]

Smith and his two pupils made their proposed expedition to Montpellier during the sittings of the States, for we find them visited there by Horne Tooke,[2] then still parson of Brentford, who had been on a tour in Italy, and stayed some time in Montpellier on his way back. Tooke, it may be said here, was no admirer of Smith; he thought the *Theory of Moral Sentiments* nonsense, and the *Wealth of Nations* written for a wicked purpose,[3] and this is the only occasion on which they are known to have met.

The little provincial assembly which Smith had come to Montpellier to see was at that period, it ought to be mentioned, attracting much attention from all the thinkers and reformers of France, and was thought by many of the first of them to furnish the solution of the political question of that age. The States of Languedoc were almost the only remains of free institutions then left in France. In all the thirty-two provinces of the country except six the States had been suppressed altogether, and in five of these six they were too small to be important or vigorous; but Languedoc was a great province, containing twenty-three bishoprics and more territory than the kingdom of Belgium, and the States governed its affairs so well that its prosperity was the envy of the rest of France. They dug canals, opened harbours,

[1] *Hume Correspondence*, R.S.E. Library.
[2] Stephen's *Life of Horne Tooke*, i. 75.
[3] Samuel Rogers told this to his friend the Rev. John Mitford. See Add. MSS. 32,566.

drained marshes, made roads, which Arthur Young singles out for praise, and made them without the *corvée* under which the rest of rural France was groaning. They farmed the imperial taxes of the province themselves, to avoid the exactions of the farmers-general. They allowed the *noblesse* none of the exemptions so unfairly enjoyed by them elsewhere. The *taille*, which was a personal tax in other parts of the kingdom, was in Languedoc an equitable land tax, assessed according to a valuation periodically revised. There was not a poorhouse in the whole province, and such was its prosperity and excellent administration that it enjoyed better credit in the market than the Central Government, and the king used sometimes, in order to get more favourable terms, to borrow on the security of the States of Languedoc instead of his own.[1]

Under those circumstances it is not surprising that one of the favourite remedies for the political situation in France was the revival of the provincial assemblies and the suppression of the intendants—"Grattan's Parliament and the abolition of the Castle." Turgot, among others, favoured this solution, though he was an intendant himself. Necker had just put it into execution when the Revolution came and swept everything away. Smith himself has expressed the strongest opinion in favour of the administration of provincial affairs by a local body instead of by an intendant, and he must have witnessed with no ordinary interest the proceedings of this remarkable little assembly at Montpellier, with its 23 prelates on the right, its 23 barons on the left, and the third estate—representatives of 23 chief towns and 23 dioceses—in the centre, and on a dais in front of all, the President, the Archbishop of Narbonne. The Archbishop, to whom, it will be remembered, Smith asked, and no doubt received, a letter of introduction from Lord Hertford, was a countryman of his own, Cardinal Dillon, a prince of

[1] Tocqueville, *State of Society in France*, pp. 265, 271.

prelates, afterwards Minister of France; a strong champion
of the rights of the States against the pretensions of the
Crown, and, if we may judge from the speech with which
Miss Knight heard him open the States of Languedoc in
1776, a very thorough free-trader.

With all these excursions, Smith was now evidently
realising in some reasonable measure the "gayetty and
amusement" he told Hume he anticipated to enjoy during
the rest of his stay in the South of France.   His command
of the language, too, grew easier, though it never became
perfect, and he not only went more into society, but was
able to enjoy it better.   Among those he saw most of in
Toulouse were, he used to tell Stewart, the presidents and
counsellors of the Parliament, who were noted, like their
class in other parliament towns, for their hospitality, and
noted above those of other parliament towns for keeping
up the old tradition of blending their law with a love of
letters.   They were men, moreover, of proved patriotism
and independence; in no other society would Smith be
likely to hear more of the oppressed condition of the
peasantry, and the necessity for thoroughgoing reforms.
In those days the king's edict did not run in a province
till it was registered by the local parliament, and the
Parliament of Toulouse often used this privilege of theirs
to check bad measures.   They had in 1756 remonstrated
with the king against the *corvée*, declaring that the condition of the peasantry of France was "a thousand times
less tolerable than the condition of the slaves in America."
At the very moment of Smith's first arrival in Toulouse
they were all thrown in prison—or at least put under
arrest in their own houses—for refusing to register the
centième denier, and Smith no doubt had that circumstance
in his mind when he animadverted in the *Wealth of Nations*
on the violence practised by the French Government to
coerce its parliaments.   He thought very highly of those
parliaments as institutions, stating that though not very
convenient courts of law, they had never been accused or

even suspected of corruption, and he gives a curious reason for their incorruptibility ; it was because they were not paid by salary, but by fees dependent on their diligence.

During Smith's residence in Toulouse the town was raging (as Abbé Colbert mentions in his letters to Hume) about one of the judgments of this Parliament, and for the most part, strangely enough, taking the Parliament's side. This was its judgment in the famous Calas case, to which Smith alludes in the last edition of his *Theory*. Jean Calas, it may be remembered, had a son who had renounced his Protestantism in order to become eligible for admission to the Toulouse bar, and then worried himself so much about his apostasy that he committed suicide in his father's house ; and the father was unjustly accused before the Parliament of the town of having murdered the youth on account of his apostasy, was found guilty without a particle of proof, and then broken on the wheel and burnt on the 9th of March 1762. But the great voice of Voltaire rose against this judicial atrocity, and after three years' agitation procured a new trial before a special court of fifty masters of requests, of whom Turgot was one, on the 9th of March 1765, with the result that Calas was pronounced absolutely innocent of the crime he suffered for, and his family was awarded a compensation of 36,000 livres. The king received them at court, and all France rejoiced in their rehabilitation except their own townsfolk in Toulouse. On the 10th of April 1765—a month after the verdict—Abbé Colbert writes Hume : " The people here would surprise you with their fanaticism. In spite of all that has happened, they every man believe Calas to be guilty, and it is no use speaking to them on the subject." [1]

Smith makes use of the incident to illustrate the proposition that while unmerited praise gives no satisfaction except to the frivolous, unmerited reproach inflicts the keenest suffering even on men of exceptional endurance,

[1] *Hume Correspondence*, R.S.E. Library.

because the injustice destroys the sweetness of the praise, but enormously embitters the sting of the condemnation. "The unfortunate Calas," he writes—"a man of much more than ordinary constancy (broken upon the wheel and burnt at Tholouse for the supposed murder of his own son, of which he was perfectly innocent)—seemed with his last breath to deprecate not so much the cruelty of the punishment, as the disgrace which the imputation must bring upon his memory. After he had been broke, and when just going to be thrown into the fire, the monk who attended the execution exhorted him to confess the crime for which he had been condemned. 'My father,' said Calas, 'can you bring yourself to believe that I was guilty?'"

CHAPTER XIII

GENEVA

In the end of August Smith and his pupils left Toulouse and made what Stewart calls an extensive tour in the South of France. Of this tour no other record remains, but the Duke's aunt, Lady Mary Coke, incidentally mentions that when they were at Marseilles they visited the porcelain factory, and that the Duke bought two of the largest services ever sold there, for which he paid more than £150 sterling. They seem to have arrived in Geneva some time in October, and stayed about two months in the little republic of which, as we have seen, Smith had long been a fervent admirer. In making so considerable a sojourn at Geneva, he was no doubt influenced as a political philosopher by the desire to see something of the practical working of those republican institutions which he regarded speculatively with so much favour, to observe how the common problems of government worked themselves out on the narrow field of a commonwealth with only 24,000 inhabitants all told, which yet contrived to keep its place among the nations, to sit sometimes as arbiter between them, and to surpass them all in the art of making its people prosperous. He had the luck to observe it at an interesting moment, for it was in the thick of a constitutional crisis. The government of the republic had hitherto been vested in the hands of 200 privileged families, and the rest of the citizens were now pressing their right to a share in it, with the active assistance of Voltaire. This important struggle for the conversion of the aristocratic into the democratic republic continued all through the period of Smith's visit, and the city of Geneva, which in its usual state was described by Voltaire as "a tedious convent with some sensible people in it," was day after day at this time the animated scene of the successive acts of that political drama.

During his stay there Smith made many personal friends, both among the leading citizens of the commonwealth and among the more distinguished of the foreign visitors who generally abounded there. People went to Geneva in those days not to see the lake or the mountains, but to consult Dr. Tronchin and converse with Voltaire. Smith needed no introduction to Tronchin, who, as we have seen, held so high an opinion of his abilities that he had sent his own son all the way to Glasgow to attend his philosophical classes ; and it was no doubt through Tronchin, Voltaire's chief friend in that quarter, that Smith was introduced to Voltaire. Smith told Rogers he had been in Voltaire's company on five or six different occasions, and he no doubt enjoyed, as most English visitors enjoyed, hospitable entertainment at Ferney, the beautiful little temporality of the great literary pontiff, overlooking the lake.

There was no living name before which Smith bowed with profounder veneration than the name of Voltaire, and his recollections of their intercourse on these occasions were always among those he cherished most warmly. Few memorials, however, of their conversation remain, and these are preserved by Samuel Rogers in his diary of his visit to Edinburgh the year before Smith's death. They seem to have spoken, as was very natural, of the Duke of Richelieu, the only famous Frenchman Smith had yet met, and of the political question as to the revival of the provincial assemblies or the continuance of government by royal intendants. On this question Smith said that Voltaire expressed great aversion to the States and favoured the side of the royal prerogative. Of the Duke of Richelieu Voltaire said that he was an old friend of his, but a singular character. A few years before his death his foot slipped one day at Versailles, and the old marshal said that was the first *faux pas* he had ever made at court. Voltaire then seems to have told anecdotes of the Duke's being bastilled and of his borrowing the Embassy plate at Vienna and never returning it, and to have passed the remark he made elsewhere that the English had only one sauce, melted butter. Smith always spoke of Voltaire with a genuine emotion of reverence. When Samuel Rogers happened to describe some clever but superficial author as "a Voltaire," Smith brought his hand down on the table with great energy and said, "Sir, there is only one Voltaire."[1] Professor Faujas Saint Fond, Professor of Geology in the Museum of Natural History in Paris, visited Smith in Edinburgh a few years before Rogers was there, and says that the animation of Smith's countenance was striking when he spoke of Voltaire, whom he had known personally, and whose memory he revered. "Reason," said Smith one day, as he showed M. Saint Fond a fine bust of Voltaire he had in his room, "reason owes him incalculable obligations. The ridicule and the sarcasm which he so plentifully bestowed upon fanatics and heretics of all sects have enabled the understanding of men to bear the light of truth, and prepared them for those inquiries to which every intelligent mind ought to aspire. He has done much more for the benefit of mankind than those grave philosophers whose books are read by a few only. The writings of Voltaire are made for all and read by all." On another occasion he observed to the same visitor, "I cannot pardon the Emperor Joseph II., who pretended to travel as a philosopher, for passing Ferney without doing homage to the historian of the Czar Peter I. From this circumstance I concluded that Joseph was but a man of inferior mind."[2]

[1] Clayden's *Early Life of Samuel Rogers*, p. 110.
[2] Faujas Saint Fond, *Travels in England, Scotland, and the Hebrides*, ii. 241.

One of the warmest of Smith's Swiss friends was
Charles Bonnet, the celebrated naturalist and metaphysician,
who, in writing Hume ten years after the date of this
visit, desires to be remembered "to the sage of Glascow,"
adding, "You perceive I speak of Mr. Smith, whom
we shall always recollect with great pleasure." [1]   On
the day this letter was written by Bonnet to Hume,
another was written to Smith himself by a young Scotch
tutor then in Geneva, Patrick Clason, who seems to have
carried an introduction from Smith to Bonnet, and who
mentions having received many civilities from Bonnet on
account of his being one of Smith's friends.   Clason then
goes on to tell Smith that the Syndic Turretin and M. Le
Sage also begged to be remembered to him.   The Syndic
Turretin was the President of the Republic, and M. Le
Sage was the eminent Professor of Physics, George Louis
Le Sage, who was then greatly interested in Professor
Black's recent discoveries about latent heat and Professor
Matthew Stewart's in astronomy, and was one of a group
who gathered round Bonnet for discussions in speculative
philosophy and morals, at which, it may be reasonably
inferred, Smith would have also occasionally assisted.   Le
Sage seems to have met Smith first, however, and to have
been in the habit of meeting him often afterwards, at the
house of a high and distinguished French lady, the Duchesse
d'Enville, who was living in Geneva under Tronchin's treatment, and whose son, the young and virtuous Duc de la
Rochefoucauld, who was afterwards stoned to death in the
Revolution, was receiving instruction from Le Sage himself.   Le Sage writes the Duchesse d'Enville on 5th
February 1766, "Of all the people I have met at your
house, that is, of all the *élite* of our good company, I have
only continued to see the excellent Lord Stanhope and
occasionally Mr. Smith.   The latter wished me to make
the acquaintance of Lady Conyers and the Duke of

[1] *Hume Correspondence*, R.S.E. Library.

Buckleugh, but I begged him to reserve that kindness for me till his return." [1]

This letter shows that Smith was so much taken with Geneva that he meant to pay it a second visit before he ended his tutorial engagement, but the intention was never fulfilled, in consequence of unfortunate circumstances to be presently mentioned.

The Duchesse d'Enville, at whose house Smith seems to have been so steady a guest, was herself a Rochefoucauld by blood, a grand-daughter of the famous author of the *Maxims*, and was a woman of great ability, who was popularly supposed to be the inspirer of all Turgot's political and social ideas, the chief of the "three Maries" who were alleged to guide his doings. Stewart tells us that Smith used to speak with very particular pleasure and gratitude of the many civilities he received from this interesting woman and her son, and they seem on their part to have cherished the same lively recollection of him. When Adam Ferguson was in Paris in 1774 she asked him much about Smith, and often complained, says Ferguson in a letter to Smith himself, " of your French as she did of mine, but said that before you left Paris she had the happiness to learn your language." [2] After two and a half years' residence in France, Smith seems then to have been just succeeding in making himself intelligible to the more intelligent inhabitants in their own language, and this agrees with what Morellet says, that Smith's French was very bad. The young Duc de la Rochefoucauld, who, like his mother, was a devoted friend of Turgot, became presently a declared disciple of Quesnay, and sat regularly with the rest of the economist sect at the economic dinners of Mirabeau, the " Friend of Man." When Samuel Rogers met him in Paris shortly after the outbreak of the Revolution, he expressed to Rogers the highest admiration for Smith,

[1] Prevost, *Notice de la Vie et des écrits de George Louis Le Sage de Geneva*, p. 226.

[2] Small's *Biographical Sketch of Adam Ferguson*, p. 20.

then recently dead, of whom he had seen much in Paris as well as Geneva, and he had at one time begun to translate the *Theory of Moral Sentiments* into French, abandoning the task only when he found his work anticipated by the Abbé Blavet's translation in 1774. The only surviving memorial of their intercourse is a letter from the Duke, which will be given in its place, and in which he begs Smith to modify the opinion pronounced in the *Theory* on the writer's ancestor, the author of the *Maxims*.

The Earl Stanhope, whom Smith used to meet at the Duchess's, and with whom he established a lasting friendship, was the second Earl, the editor of Professor Robert Simson's mathematical works, and himself a distinguished mathematician. He took no part in public life, but his opinions were of the most advanced Liberal order. He had come to Geneva to place his son, afterwards also so distinguished in science, under the training of Le Sage. The Lady Conyers, to whom the Scotch was so anxious to introduce the Swiss philosopher, was the young lady who a few years afterwards ran away from her husband, the fifth Duke of Leeds, with the poet Byron's father, whom she subsequently married, and by whom she became the mother of the poet's sister Augusta.

CHAPTER XIV

PARIS

SMITH left Geneva in December for Paris, where he arrived, according to Dugald Stewart, about Christmas 1765. The Rev. William Cole, who was in Paris in October of the same year, notes in his journal on the 26th of that month, that the Duke of Buccleugh arrived in Paris that day from Spa along with the Earl and Countess of Fife; but this must be a mistake, for Horace Walpole, who was also in Paris that autumn, writes on the 5th of December that the Duke was then expected to arrive in the following week, and as Walpole was staying in the hotel where the Duke and Smith stayed during their residence in that city—the Hotel du Parc Royal in the Faubourg de St. Germain—he probably wrote from authentic information about the engagement of their rooms. It may be taken, therefore, that they arrived in Paris about the middle of December, just in time to have a week or two with Hume before he finally left Paris for London with Rousseau on the 3rd of January 1766. Hume had been looking for Smith ever since midsummer. As far back as the 5th of September he wrote, " I have been looking for you every day these three months," but that expectation was probably founded on reports from Abbé Colbert, for Smith himself does not seem to have written Hume since the previous October, except the short note introducing Mr. Urquhart. At any rate in this letter of September 1765 Hume, as if in reply to Smith's account of his pupil's improvement in his letter of October 1764, says, "Your satisfaction in your pupil gives me equal satisfaction." It is no doubt possible that Smith may have written letters in the interval which have been lost, but he had clearly written none for the previous three months, and it is most probable, with his general aversion to writing, that he wrote none for the four or five months before that. Hume's own object in breaking the long silence is, in the first place, to inform him that, having lost his place at the Embassy through the translation of his chief to the Lord-Lieutenancy of Ireland, he should be obliged to return to England in October before Smith's arrival in Paris ; and in the next, to consult him on a new perplexity that was distressing him, whether he should not come back to Paris and spend the remainder of his days there. In compensation for the loss of his place, he had obtained a pension of £900 a year, without office or duty of any kind—" opulence and liberty," as he calls it. But opulence and liberty brought their own cares, and he was rent with temptations to belong to different nations. "As a new vexation to temper my good fortune," he writes to Smith, "I am in much perplexity about fixing the place of my future abode for life. Paris is the most agreeable town in Europe, and suits me best, but it is a foreign country. London is the capital of my own country, but it never pleased me much. Letters are there held in no honour ; Scotsmen are hated ; superstition and ignorance gain ground daily. Edinburgh has many objections and many allurements. My present mind this forenoon, the 5th of September, is to return to France. I am much press'd also to accept of offers which would contribute to my agreeable living, but might encroach on my independence by making me enter into engagements with Princes and great lords and ladies. Pray give me your judgment." [1]

Events soon settled the question for him. He was

[1] _Hume MSS._, R.S.E. Partially published in Burton's _Life_.

appointed Under Secretary of State in London by Lord Hertford's brother, General Conway, and left Paris, as I have just said, early in January 1766. Rousseau had been in Paris since the 17th of December waiting to accompany Hume to England, and Smith must no doubt have met Rousseau occasionally with Hume during that last fortnight of 1765, though there is no actual evidence that he did. Before leaving, moreover, Hume would have time to introduce his friend to the famous men of Paris itself, and to initiate him into those literary and fashionable circles in which he had moved like a demigod for the preceding two years. The philosophe was then king in Paris, and Hume was king of the philosophes, and everything that was great in court or salon fell down and did him obeisance. "Here," he tells Robertson, "I feed on ambrosia, drink nothing but nectar, breathe incense only, and walk on flowers. Every one I meet, and especially every woman, would consider themselves as failing in the most indispensable duty if they did not favour me with a lengthy and ingenious discourse on my celebrity." Hume could, therefore, open to his friend every door in Paris that was worth entering, but Smith's own name was also sufficiently known and esteemed, at least among men of letters, in France to secure to him a cordial welcome for his own sake. *The Theory of Moral Sentiments* had been translated, at the suggestion of Baron d'Holbach, by E. Dous, and the translation had appeared in 1764 under the title of *Métaphysique de l'Ame.* It was unfortunately a very bad translation, for which Grimm makes the curious apology that it was impossible to render the ideas of metaphysics in a foreign language as you could render the images of poetry, because every nation had its own abstract ideas.[1] But though the book got probably little impetus from this translation, it had been considerably read in the original by men of letters when it first came out, and many of them had then formed, as Abbé

---

[1] *Correspondance Littéraire*, I. iv. 291.

Morellet says he did, the highest idea of Smith's sagacity and depth, and were prepared to meet the author with much interest.

Smith went more into society in the few months he resided in Paris than at any other period of his life. He was a regular guest in almost all the famous literary salons of that time—Baron d'Holbach's, Helvetius', Madame de Geoffrin's, Comtesse de Boufflers', Mademoiselle l'Espinasse's, and probably Madame Necker's. Our information about his doings is of course meagre, but there is one week in July 1766 in which we happen to have his name mentioned frequently in the course of the correspondence between Hume and his Paris friends regarding the quarrel with Rousseau, and during that week Smith was on the 21st at Mademoiselle l'Espinasse's, on the 25th at Comtesse de Boufflers', and on the 27th at Baron d'Holbach's, where he had some conversation with Turgot. He was a constant visitor at Madame Riccoboni the novelist's. He attended the meetings of the new economist sect in the apartments of Dr. Quesnay, and though the economic dinners of the elder Mirabeau, the " Friend of Men," were not begun for a year after, he no doubt visited the Marquis, as we know he visited other members of the fraternity. He went to Compiègne when the Court removed to Compiègne, made frequent excursions to interesting places within reach, and is always seen with troops of friends about him. Many of these were Englishmen, for after their long exclusion from Paris during the Seven Years war, Englishmen had begun to pour into the city, and the Hotel du Parc Royal, where Smith lived, was generally full of English guests. Among others who were there, as I have just mentioned, was Horace Walpole, who remained on till Easter, and with whom Smith seems to have become well acquainted, for in writing Hume in July he asks to be specially remembered to Mr. Walpole.

So much has been written about the literary salons

of Paris in last century that it is unnecessary to do more here than describe Smith's connection with them. The salon we happen to hear most of his frequenting is the salon of the Comtesse de Boufflers-Rouvel, but that is due to the simple circumstance that the hostess was an assiduous correspondent of David Hume. She was mistress to the Prince de Conti, but ties of that character, if permanent, derogated nothing from a lady's position in Paris at that period. Abbé Morellet, who was a constant guest at her house, even states that this connection of hers with a prince of the blood, though illicit, really enhanced rather than diminished her consideration in society, and her receptions were attended by all the rank, fashion, and learning of the city. The Comtesse was very fond of entertaining English guests, for she spoke our language well, and had been greatly pleased with the civilities she had received during her then recent visit to England in 1763. Smith was not long in Paris till he made her acquaintance, and received a very hearty welcome for the love of Hume. She began to read his book, moreover, and it became eventually such a favourite with her that she had thoughts of translating it.

Hume writes to her from Wootton on the 22nd of March 1766 : "I am glad you have taken my friend Smith under your protection. You will find him a man of true merit, though perhaps his sedentary recluse life may have hurt his air and appearance as a man of the world." The Comtesse writes Hume on the 6th of May : "I think I told you that I have made the acquaintance of Mr. Smith, and that for the love of you I had given him a very hearty welcome. I am now reading his *Theory of Moral Sentiments*. I am not very far advanced with it yet, but I believe it will please me." And again on the 25th of July, in the same year, when Hume's quarrel with Rousseau was raging, she appends to a letter to Hume on that subject a few words about

Smith, who had apparently called upon her just as she had finished it : " I entreated your friend Mr. Smith to call upon me. He has just this moment left me. I have read my letter to him. He, like myself, is apprehensive that you have been deceived in the warmth of so just a resentment. He begs of you to read over again the letter to Mr. Conway. It does not appear that he (Rousseau) refuses the pension, nor that he desires it to be made public." [1] The *Theory of Moral Sentiments*, which she had then begun to read, grew more and more in favour with her, and a few years after this—in 1770— when the two sons of Smith's friend, Sir Gilbert Elliot, visited her, they found her at her studies in her bedroom, and talking of translating the book, if she had time, because it contained such just ideas about sympathy. She added that the book had come into great vogue in France, and that Smith's doctrine of sympathy bade fair to supplant David Hume's immaterialism as the fashionable opinion, especially with the ladies.[2] The vogue would probably be aided by Smith's personal introduction into French literary circles, but evidence of its extent is found in the fact that although one French translation of the work had already appeared, three different persons were then preparing or contemplating another—the Abbé Blavet, who actually published his ; the Duc de la Rochefoucauld, who discontinued his labour when he found himself forestalled by the Abbé ; and the Comtesse de Boufflers who perhaps did little more than entertain the design. The best translation was published some years after by another lady, the widow of Condorcet.

The Baron d'Holbach's weekly or bi-weekly dinners, at one of which it has been mentioned Smith had a conversation with Turgot, were, as L. Blanc has said, the regular states - general of philosophy. The usual guests were the philosophes and encyclopedists and men

[1] Burton's *Letters of Eminent Persons to David Hume*, p. 238.
[2] Lady Minto, *Memoirs of Hugh Elliot*, p. 13.

of letters—Diderot, Marmontel, Raynal, Galiani.   The conversation ran largely towards metaphysics and theology, and, as Morellet, who was often there, states, the boldest theories were propounded, and things spoken which might well call down fire from heaven.   It was there that Hume observed he had neither seen an atheist, nor did he believe one existed, and was informed by his host in reply, " You have been a little unfortunate ; you are here at table with seventeen for the first time."

Morellet mentions that it was at the table of Helvetius, the philosopher, he himself first met Smith.   Helvetius was a retired farmer-general of the taxes, who had grown rich without practising extortion, and instead of remaining a bachelor, as Smith says other farmers-general in France did, because no gentlewoman would marry them, and they were too proud to marry anybody else, he had married a pretty and clever wife, an early friend of Turgot's, who helped to make his Tuesday dinners among the most agreeable entertainments in Paris.   He had recently returned from a long sojourn in England, so enchanted with both country and people that d'Holbach, who could find nothing to praise in either, declared he could really have seen nothing in England all the time except the persecution for heresy which he had shortly before suffered in France, and would have escaped in our freer air ; and he was always very hospitable to English celebrities, so that it may be inferred that Smith enjoyed many opportunities of conversation with this versatile and philosophical financier during his stay in Paris.

Morellet, whose acquaintance Smith made at Helvetius' house, became one of his fastest friends in France, and on leaving Paris Smith gave him for a keepsake his own pocket-book,—a very pretty English-made pocket-book, says the Abbé, which " has served me these twenty years." Morellet, besides being an advanced economist, whose views ran in sympathy with Smith's own, was the most delightful of companions, uniting with strong sense and a deep love

of the right an unfailing play of irony and fun, and ever
ready, as Fanny Burney found him still at eighty-five, to
sing his own songs for the entertainment of his friends.
The Abbé was a metaphysician as well as an economist,
but, according to his account of his conversations with
Smith, they seem to have discussed mainly economic subjects—"the theory of commerce," he says, "banking, public
credit, and various points in the great work which Smith
was then meditating,"[1] *i.e.* the *Wealth of Nations*. This
book had therefore by that time taken shape so far that
the author made his Paris friends aware of his occupation
upon it, and discussed with them definite points in the
scheme of doctrine he was unfolding. Morellet formed a
very just estimate of him. "I regard him still," he says,
"as one of the men who have made the most complete
observations and analyses on all questions he treated of,"
and he gave the best proof of his high opinion by writing
a translation of the *Wealth of Nations* himself. Smith
would no doubt derive some assistance towards making
his observations and analyses more complete from the
different lights in which the matters under consideration
would be naturally placed in the course of discussions with
men like Morellet and his friends; but whatever others
have thought, Morellet at least sets up no claim, either on
his own behalf or on behalf of his very old and intimate
college friend Turgot, or of any other of the French
economists, of having influenced or supplied any of Smith's
ideas. The Scotch inquirer had been long working on
the same lines as his French colleagues, and Morellet
seems to have thought him, when they first met, as he
thought him still, when he wrote those memoirs, as being
more complete in his observations and analyses than the
others.

A frequent resort of Smith in Paris was the salon
of Mademoiselle de l'Espinasse, which differed from the
others by the greater variety of the guests and by the

[1] Morellet's *Mémoires*, i. 237.

presence of ladies. The hostess—according to Hume, one of the most sensible women in Paris—had long been Madame du Deffand's principal assistant in the management of her famous salon, but having been dismissed in 1764 for entertaining Turgot and D'Alembert on her own account without permission, she set up a rival salon of her own on improved principles, with the zealous help of her two eminent friends ; and to her unpretending apartments ambassadors, princesses, marshals of France, and financiers came, and met with men of letters like Grimm, Condillac, and Gibbon. D'Alembert indeed lived in the house, having come there to be nursed through an illness and remaining on afterwards, and as D'Alembert was one of Smith's chief friends in Paris, his house was naturally one of the latter's chief resorts.

Here, moreover, he often met Turgot, as indeed he did everywhere he went, and of all the friends he met in France there was none in whose society he took more pleasure, or for whose mind and character he formed a profounder admiration, than that great thinker and statesman. If his conversation with Morellet ran mainly on political and economic subjects, it would most probably run even more largely on such subjects with Turgot, for they were both at the moment busy writing their most important works on those subjects. Turgot's *Formation and Distribution of Wealth* was written in 1766, though it was only published three years later in the *Éphémérides du Citoyen;* and it cannot, I think, be doubted that the ideas and theories with which his mind was then boiling must have been the subject of discussion again and again in the course of his numerous conversations with Smith. So also if Smith brought out various points in the work he was undertaking for discussion with Morellet, he may reasonably be inferred to have done the same with Morellet's greater friend Turgot, and all this would have been greatly to their mutual advantage. No vestiges of their intercourse, however, remain, though some critics profess to see its results writ very large on the face of their writings.

Professor Thorold Rogers thinks the influences of Turgot's reasoning on Smith's mind to be easily perceptible to any reader of the *Formation and Distribution of Wealth* and of the *Wealth of Nations*. Dupont de Nemours once went so far as to say that whatever was true in Smith was borrowed from Turgot, and whatever was not borrowed from Turgot was not true ; but he afterwards retracted that absurdly-sweeping allegation, and confessed that he had made it before he was able to read English; while Leon Say thinks Turgot owed much of his philosophy to Smith, and Smith owed much of his economics to Turgot.[1]   Questions of literary obligation are often difficult to settle.   Two contemporary thinkers, dealing with the same subject under the same general influences and tendencies of the time, may think nearly alike even without any manner of personal intercommunication, and the idea of natural liberty of trade, in which the main resemblance between the writers in the present case is supposed to occur, was already in the ground, and sprouting up here and there before either of them wrote at all. Smith's position on that subject, moreover, is so much more solid, balanced, and moderate than Turgot's, that it is different in positive character; the extremer form of the doctrine taught by Turgot appears to have been taught also by Smith in earlier years and abandoned.   At least the fragment published by Stewart of Smith's Society paper of 1755—eleven years before Turgot wrote his book or saw Smith—proclaims individualism of the extremer form, and intimates that he had taught the same views in Edinburgh in 1750.   Smith had thus been teaching free trade many years before he met Turgot, and teaching it in Turgot's own form ; he had converted many of the merchants of Glasgow to it and a future Prime

---

[1] Schelle, *Dupont de Nemours et les Physiocrates*, p. 159.

Minister of England; he had probably, moreover, thought out the main truths of the work he was even then busy upon. He was therefore in a position to meet Turgot on equal terms, and give full value for anything he might take, and if obligations must needs be assessed and the balance adjusted, who shall say whether Smith owes most to the conversation of Turgot or Turgot owes most to the conversation of Smith? The state of the exchange cannot be determined from mere priority of publication; no other means of determining it exist, and it is of no great moment to determine it at all.

Turgot and Smith are said—on authority which cannot be altogether disregarded, Condorcet, the biographer of Turgot—to have continued their economic discussions by correspondence after Smith returned to this country; but though every search has been made for this correspondence, as Dugald Stewart informs us, no trace of anything of the kind was ever discovered on either side of the Channel, and Smith's friends never heard him allude to such a thing. "It is scarcely to be supposed," says Stewart, "that Mr. Smith would destroy the letters of such a correspondent as M. Turgot, and still less probable that such an intercourse was carried on between them without the knowledge of Mr. Smith's friends. From some inquiries that have been made at Paris by a gentleman of this society[1] since Smith's death, I have reason to believe that no evidence of the correspondence exists among the papers of M. Turgot, and that the whole story has taken its rise from a report suggested by the knowledge of their former intimacy."[2] Some of Hume's letters to Turgot—one from this year 1766, combating among other things Turgot's principle of the single tax on the net product of the land—still exist among the Turgot family archives, but none from Smith, for Leon Say

---

[1] *i.e.* the Royal Society of Edinburgh, to whom Stewart first read his *Life of Smith*.

[2] Stewart's *Works*, v. 47.

examined those archives a few years ago with this purpose among others expressly in view.

An occasional letter, however, certainly did pass between them, for, as Smith himself mentions in a letter which will appear in a subsequent chapter, it was " by the particular favour of M. Turgot " that he received the copy of the *Mémoires concernant les Impositions*, which he quotes so often in the *Wealth of Nations*. This book was not printed when he was in France, and as it needed much influence to get a copy of it, his was most probably got after Turgot became Controller-General of the Finances in 1774. But in any case it would involve the exchange of letters.

Smith, with all his admiration for Turgot, thought him too simple-hearted for a practical statesman, too prone, as noble natures often are, to underrate the selfishness, stupidity, and prejudice that prevail in the world and resist the course of just and rational reform. He described Turgot to Samuel Rogers as an excellent person, very honest and well-meaning, but so unacquainted with the world and human nature that it was a maxim with him, as he had himself told David Hume, that whatever is right may be done.[1]

Smith would deny the name of statesman altogether to the politician who did not make it his aim to establish the right, or, in other words, had no public ideal ; such a man is only " that crafty and insidious animal vulgarly termed a statesman." But he insists that the truly wise statesman in pressing his ideal must always practise considerable accommodation. If he cannot carry the right he will not disdain to ameliorate the wrong, but, " like Solon, when he cannot establish the best system of laws, he will endeavour to establish the best that the people can bear." [2] Turgot made too little account, he thought, of the resisting power

---

[1] Clayden's *Early Life of Samuel Rogers*, p. 95.
[2] *Theory of Moral Sentiments*, Part VI. sec. ii.

of vested interests and confirmed habits. He was too optimist, and the peculiarity attaches to his theoretical as well as his practical work. Smith himself was prone rather to the contrary error of overrating the resisting power of interests and prejudices. If Turgot was too sanguine when he told the king that popular education would in ten years change the people past all recognition, Smith was too incredulous when he despaired of the ultimate realisation of slave emancipation and free trade; and under a biographical aspect, it is curious to find the man who has spent his life in the practical business of the world taking the more enthusiastic view we expect from the recluse, and the man who has spent his life in his library taking the more critical and measured view we expect from the man of the world.

Another statesman whom Smith knew well in Paris was Necker. His wife had very possibly begun by this time her rather austere salon, where free-thinking was strictly tabooed, and Morellet, her right-hand man in the entertainment of the guests, confesses the restraint was really irksome; and if she had, Morellet would probably have brought Smith there. But anyhow Sir James Mackintosh, who had means of hearing about Smith from competent sources, states explicitly that he was upon intimate terms with Necker during his residence in the French capital, that he formed only a poor opinion of that minister's abilities, and that he used to predict the fall of his political reputation the moment his head was put to any real proof, always saying of him with emphasis, " He is a mere man of detail." [1] Smith was not always lucky in his predictions, but here for once he was right.

While Smith was frequenting these various literary and philosophical salons they were all thrown into a state of unusual commotion by the famous quarrel between Rousseau and Hume. The world has long since ceased to take any interest in that quarrel, having assured itself

[1] Mackintosh, *Miscellaneous Works*, iii. 13.

that it all originated in the suspicions of Rousseau's insane fancy, but during the whole summer of 1766 it filled column after column of the English and continental newspapers, and it occupied much of the attention of Smith and the other friends of Hume in Paris. It will be remembered that when Rousseau was expelled from Switzerland, Hume, who was an extravagant admirer of his, offered to find him a home in England, and on the offer being accepted, brought him over to this country in January 1766. Hume first found quarters for him at Chiswick, but the capricious philosopher would not live at Chiswick because it was too near town. Hume then got him a gentleman's house in the Peak of Derby, but Rousseau would not enter it unless the owner agreed to take board. Hume induced the owner to gratify even this whim, and Rousseau departed and established himself comfortably at Wootton in the Peak of Derby. Hume next procured for him a pension of £100 a year from the king. Rousseau would not touch it unless it were kept secret; the king agreed to keep it secret. Rousseau then would not have it unless it were made public; the king again agreed to meet his whim. But the more Hume did for him the more Rousseau suspected the sincerity of his motives, and used first to assail him with the most ridiculous accusations, and then fall on his neck and implore forgiveness for ever doubting him. But at last, on the 23rd of June, in reply to Hume's note intimating the king's remission of the condition of secrecy, and the consequent removal of every obstacle to the acceptance of the pension, Rousseau gave way entirely to the evil spirit that haunted him, and wrote Hume the notorious letter, declaring that his horrible designs were at last found out.

Hume lost no time in going with his troubles to Smith, and asking him to lay the true state of the case before their Paris friends. To that letter Smith wrote the following reply :—

PARIS, *6th July* 1766.

MY DEAR FRIEND—I am thoroughly convinced that Rousseau is as great a rascal as you and as every man here believe him to be. Yet let me beg of you not to think of publishing anything to the world upon the very great impertinence which he has been guilty of. By refusing the pension which you had the goodness to solicit for him with his own consent, he may have thrown, by the baseness of his proceedings, a little ridicule upon you in the eyes of the court and the ministry. Stand this ridicule ; expose his brutal letter, but without giving it out of your own hand, so that it may never be printed, and, if you can, laugh at yourself, and I will pawn my life that before three weeks are at an end this little affair which at present gives you so much uneasiness shall be understood to do you as much honour as anything that has ever happened to you. By endeavouring to unmask before the public this hypocritical pedant, you run the risk of disturbing the tranquillity of your whole life. By leaving him alone he cannot give you a fortnight's uneasiness. To write against him is, you may depend upon it, the very thing he wishes you to do. He is in danger of falling into obscurity in England, and he hopes to make himself considerable by provoking an illustrious adversary. He will have a great party—the Church, the Whigs, the Jacobites, the whole wise English nation—who will love to mortify a Scotchman, and to applaud a man who has refused a pension from the king. It is not unlikely, too, that they may pay him very well for having refused it, and that even he may have had in view this compensation. Your whole friends here wish you not to write,—the Baron, D'Alembert, Madame Riccoboni, Mademoiselle Rianecourt, M. Turgot, etc. etc. M. Turgot, a friend every way worthy of you, desired me to recommend this advice to you in a particular manner as his most earnest entreaty and opinion. He and I are both afraid that you are surrounded with evil counsellors, and that the advice of your English *literati*, who are themselves accustomed to publishing all their little gossiping stories in newspapers, may have too much influence upon you. Remember me to Mr. Walpole, and believe me, etc.

P.S.—Make my apology to Millar for not having yet answered his last very kind letter. I am preparing the answer to it, which he will certainly receive by next post. Remember me to Mrs. Millar. Do you ever see Mr. Townshend ? [1]

---

[1] Brougham's *Men of Letters*, ii. 226.

The deep love of tranquillity this letter breathes, the dislike of publicity as a snare fatal to future quiet, the contempt for the petty vanity that makes men of letters run into print with their little personal affairs, as if they were of moment to anybody but themselves, are all very characteristic of Smith's philosophic temper of mind ; and there is also—what appears on other occasions as well as this in the intercourse of the two philosophers—a certain note of affectionate anxiety on the part of the younger and graver philosopher towards the elder as towards a man of less weight of natural character and experience, and perhaps less of the wisdom of this world, than himself.

Smith seems to have shown Hume's letter to their common friends in Paris, and while deeply interested, as was only natural, in the quarrel, they with one consent took Hume's side, the only possible view of the transaction. The subject continued to furnish matter of conversation and conference among Hume's French literary friends during the whole time of Smith's residence in Paris. Hume sent Smith another letter a little later on in the month of July, which he asked him specially to show to D'Alembert. This Smith did on the 21st, when he met D'Alembert at dinner at Mademoiselle de l'Espinasse's, in company with Turgot, Marmontel, Roux, Morellet, Saurin, and Duclos ; and on the same evening D'Alembert wrote Hume that he had just had the honour of seeing Mr. Smith, who had shown him the letter he had received, and that they had talked much together about Hume and his affairs. Apparently Smith's objections to Hume publishing anything on the quarrel were now overcome ; at all events, the result of this consultation of Hume's French friends was to advise publication ; and accordingly a week or two later Hume sent on a complete narrative of his relations with Rousseau, together with the whole correspondence from first to last, to D'Alembert, with full permission to make any use of it he thought best, and he wrote Smith at the same time asking him to go and get a sight of it.

" Pray tell me," he adds, " your judgment of my work, if it deserves the name. Tell D'Alembert I make him absolute master to retrench or alter what he thinks proper in order to suit it to the latitude of Paris." [1]

On the 27th of July Turgot writes Hume, mentioning that he had that day met Smith at Baron d'Holbach's, and they had discussed the Rousseau affair together. Smith had told him of the letter from Rousseau to General Conway, which he had been shown on the 25th by the Comtesse de Boufflers, and had repeated to him the same interpretation of that letter which he had already expressed to the Comtesse, viz. that Rousseau had not made the secrecy a ground for refusing the pension, but merely regretted that that condition made it impossible for him adequately to show his gratitude. Smith was thus inclined to give Rousseau the benefit of a better construction when a better construction was possible, but Hume writes Turgot on the 5th of August that Smith was quite wrong in that supposition.

One of those two letters of Smith's on the Rousseau affair mentions the name of Madame Riccoboni among those of Hume's friends with whom he had been in communication on the subject, and Madame Riccoboni about the same date writes Garrick that Smith and Changuion, the English ambassador's private secretary, were her two great confidants on the business of this famous quarrel. Madame Riccoboni had been a popular actress, but giving up the stage for letters, had become the most popular novelist in France. Her *Letters of Fanny Butler* and her *History of Miss Jenny* were dividing the attention of Paris with the novels of our own Richardson ; and Smith, in the 1790 edition of his *Theory*, brackets her with Racine, Voltaire, and Richardson as instructors in " the refinements and delicacies of love and friendship." She was an effusive admirer of Smith, as, indeed, she was of Changuion, and of that *bel Anglais*

---

[1] Burton's *Hume*, ii. 348.

Richard Burke, and of Garrick himself ;—" you are," she writes the player, " the dearling of my heart " ;—and when Smith was returning home from France, she gave him the following letter of introduction to Garrick :—

Je suis bien vaine, my dear Mr. Garrick, de pouvoir vous donner ce que je perds avec un regret très-vif, le plaisir de voir Mr. Smith. Ce charming philosopher vous dira combien il a d'esprit, car je le défie de parler sans en montrer. Je sui vraiment fâchée que la politesse m'oblige à lui donner ma lettre ouverte : cet usage établi retient mon cœur tout prêt à lui rendre justice, mais sa modestie est aussi grande que son mérite, et je craindrois que la plus simple vérité ne parût à ses yeux une grosse flaterie ; je puis vous dire de lui, ce qu'il disoit un jour d'un autre—le métier de cet homme-là est d'être aimable. J'ajouterai,—et de mériter l'estime de tous ceux qui ont le bonheur de le connoitre. Oh ces Ecossois ! ces chiens d'Ecossois ! ils viennent me plaire et m'affliger. Je suis comme ces folles jeunes filles qui écoutent un amant sans penser au regret, toujours voisin du plaisir. Grondez-moi, battez-moi, tuez-moi ! mais j'aime Mr. Smith, je l'aime beaucoup. Je voudrois que le diable emportât tous nos gens de lettres, tous nos philosophes, et qu'il me rapportât Mr. Smith. Les hommes supérieurs se cherchent. Rempli d'estime pour Mr. Garrick, désirant le voir et l'entretenir, Mr. Smith a voulu être introduit par moi. Il me flate infiniment par cette préférence, bien des gens se mêlent de présenter un ami à un autre ami, peu sont comme moi dans le cas d'être sûre de la reconnoissance des tous deux. Adieu, mon très-aimable et très-paresseux ami. Embrassez pour moi vôtre gracieuse compagne. La mienne vous assure l'un et l'autre de sa plus tendre amitié. RICCOBONI.[1]

Not content with this letter of recommendation which she gave to Smith to deliver, Madame Riccoboni at the same time sent Garrick another through the post, and shows the sincerity of the feelings of high esteem she had expressed in the open letter by expressing them again quite as decisively in the closed one :—

6 Octobre.

Aujourd'huy je vous écris uniquement pour vous prévenir sur une visite que vous recevrez à Londres. Mr. Smith, un Ecossois,

---

[1] *Garrick Correspondence*, ii. 550.

homme d'un très grand mérite, aussi distingué par son bon naturel, par la douceur de son caractère que par son esprit et son sçavoir, me demande une lettre pour vous. Vous verrez un philosophe moral et pratique ; gay, riant, à cent lieues de la pédanterie des nôtres. Il vous estime beaucoup et désire vous connoître particulièrement. Donnez son nom à votre porte, je vous en prie, vous perdriez beaucoup à ne pas le voir, et je serois désolée de ne pas recevoir de lui un détail du bon accueil que vous lui aurez fait. . . . Donnez son nom à votre porte, je vous le répète. S'il ne vous voit pas, je vous étrangle.[1]

Smith had apparently begged of her also a letter of introduction to R. Burke, and she wrote him one, but he went away without it ; as she says to Garrick, in a letter of 3rd January 1767 : " Ma bête de philosophe est partie sans songer à la prendre." Nor apparently had Smith as yet delivered her letter to Garrick, for she asks, " Vous ne l'avez pas encore vu Mr. Smith ? c'est la plus distraite créature ! mais c'est une des plus aimables. Je l'aime beaucoup et je l'estime encore d'avantage." [2] A few weeks later, on the 29th of January, she again returns to the subject of Smith, asking Garrick whether he had yet seen him, whether he was in London or had delivered her letter, and adding, " C'est un homme charmant, n'est-il pas ? " [3]

Madame Riccoboni was not the only Frenchwoman who was touched with Smith's personal charms ; we hear of another, a marquise, " a woman too of talents and wit," who actually fell in love with him. It was during an excursion Smith made from Paris to Abbeville, with the Duke of Buccleugh and several other English noblemen and a certain Captain Lloyd, a retired officer, who was afterwards a friend, perhaps a patient, of Dr. Currie, the author of the *Life of Burns*, and told the doctor this and many other anecdotes about the economist. Lloyd was, according to Currie, a most interesting and accomplished man, and his acquaintance with Smith was one of

[1] *Garrick Correspondence*, ii. 549.   [2] *Ibid.* ii. 501.   [3] *Ibid.* ii. 511.

great intimacy. The party seem to have stayed some days at Abbeville—to visit Crecy, no doubt, like patriotic Englishmen, and this French marquise was stopping at the same hotel. She had just come from Paris, where she found all the world talking about Hume, and having heard that Smith was Hume's particular friend and almost as great a philosopher as he, she was bent on making so famous a conquest, but after many persistent efforts was obliged eventually to abandon the attempt. Her philosopher could not endure her, nor could he—and this greatly amused his own party—conceal his embarrassment; but it was not philosophy altogether that steeled his breast. The truth, according to Lloyd, was that the philosopher was deeply in love with another, an English lady, who was also stopping in Abbeville at the time. Of all Currie heard concerning Smith from Captain Lloyd this is the only thing he has chosen to record, and slight though it is, it contributes a touch of nature to that more personal aspect of Smith's life of which we have least knowledge. Stewart makes mention of an attachment which Smith was known to have cherished for several years in the early part of his life to a young lady of great beauty and accomplishment, whom Stewart had himself seen when she was past eighty, but "still retained evident traces of her former beauty," while "the powers of her understanding and the gaiety of her temper seemed to have suffered nothing from the hand of time." Nobody ever knew what prevented their union, or how far Smith's addresses were favourably received, but she never married any more than he. Stewart says that "after this disappointment he laid aside all thoughts of marriage"; but the Abbeville attachment seems to have been a different one from this and a later.

While in Paris Smith was a very steady playgoer. He was always a great admirer of the French dramatists, and now enjoyed very much seeing their plays actually represented on the stage, and discussing them afterwards, we may be sure, with an expert like Madame Riccoboni.

Speaking of his admiration for the great French dramatists, Dugald Stewart states that "this admiration (resulting originally from the general character of his taste, which delighted more to remark that pliancy of genius which accommodates itself to general rules than to wonder at the bolder flights of an undisciplined imagination) was increased to a great degree when he saw the beauties that had struck him in the closet heightened by the utmost perfection of theatrical exhibition."[1] The French theatre, indeed, gave him much material for reflection. In his later years his thoughts and his conversation often recurred to the philosophy of the imitative arts. He meant had he lived to have written a book on the subject; he has actually left us a single essay, one of the most finished pieces of work he ever did; and among his friends he was very fond in those days of speaking and theorising on that topic, and supporting his conclusions by illustrations from his wide reading and his observation of life. These illustrations seem to have been drawn frequently from his experiences of the French theatre.

The Earl of Buchan says that Smith had no ear for music, but there are few things he seems to have nevertheless enjoyed better than the opera, both serious and comic. He thought the "sprightly airs" of the comic opera, though a more "temperate joy" than "the scenes of the common comedy," were still a "most delicious" one.[2] "They do not make us laugh so loud, but they make us smile more frequently." And he held the strongest opinion that music was always on virtue's side, for he says the only musical passions are the good ones, the bad and unsocial passions being, in his view, essentially unmelodious. But he thought scenery was much abused on the French operatic stage. "In the French operas not only thunder and lightning, storms and tempests, are commonly represented in the ridiculous manner above

---

[1] Stewart's *Works*, x. 49, 50.
[2] "Essay on the Imitative Arts," *Works*, v. 281.

mentioned, but all the marvellous, all the supernatural of epic poetry, all the metamorphoses of mythology, all the wonders of witchcraft and magic, everything that is most unfit to be represented upon the stage, are every day exhibited with the most complete approbation and applause of that ingenious nation." [1]

Amid all this gaiety of salons and playhouses Smith found a graver retreat with the philanthropic sect of the economists in the apartments of the king's physician, Dr. Quesnay, in Paris and Versailles.   Dupont de Nemours told J. B. Say that he had often met Smith at their little meetings, and that they looked on him as a judicious and simple man, and apparently nothing more, for, he adds, Smith had not at that time shown the stuff he was made of. [2] If they did not then recognise his paramount capacity as they afterwards did, there were some things about his opinions which Dupont thought they learnt better then than they could from the great work in which he subsequently expounded them.   In a note to one of Turgot's works, of which he was editor, Dupont appeals from an opinion expressed, or understood to be expressed, by Smith in his published writings, to the opinion on the same subject which he used to hear from Smith's own lips in the unreserved intercourse of private life.   " Smith at liberty," he says, " Smith in his own room or in that of a friend, as I have seen him when we were fellow-disciples of M. Quesnay, would not have said that." [3]

Though Smith met with them, and was indeed their very close scientific as well as personal associate, it is of course impossible, strictly speaking, to count him, as Dupont does, among the disciples of Quesnay.   He was no more a disciple of Quesnay than Peter was a disciple of Paul, although, it is true, Paul wrote first.   He neither agreed with all the creed of the French economists, nor

[1] *Works*, v. 294.
[2] Say, *Cours Complet*, *Œuvres*, p. 870.
[3] Turgot's *Œuvres*, v. 136.

did he acquire the articles he agreed with from the teaching of their master. He had been for sixteen years before he met them teaching the two principal truths which they set themselves to proclaim : (1) that the wealth of a country does not consist in its gold and silver, but in its stock of consumable commodities; and (2) that the true way of increasing it is not by conferring privileges or imposing restraints, but by assuring its producers a fair field and no favour. He had taught those truths in 1750, and Quesnay had not written anything bearing on them till 1756. Moreover, much in their system on which they laid most stress he has publicly repudiated. Still he speaks both of their system and of their master with a veneration which no disciple could easily surpass. He pronounces the system to be, " with all its imperfections, perhaps the nearest approximation to the truth that has yet been published upon the subject of political economy," and the author of the system to be " ingenious and profound," "a man of the greatest simplicity and modesty, who was honoured by his disciples with a reverence not inferior to that of any of the ancient philosophers for the founders of their respective systems." [1] He might not, like the Marquis de Mirabeau, call Quesnay a greater than Socrates, or the *Economic Table* a discovery equal to the invention of printing or of money, but he thought him so clearly the head of the economic inquirers of the world that he meant to have dedicated the *Wealth of Nations* to Quesnay had the venerable French economist been alive at the time of its publication. Smith was therefore a very sympathetic associate of this new sect, though not a strict adherent.

It may be well to explain in a word to the general reader that this sect were patriots and practical social and political reformers quite as much as theoretical economists. They believed the condition of the French people to have grown so bad as to be a grave danger to the State, and

[1] *Wealth of Nations*, Book IV. chap. ix.

they preached their system as a revelation of the only way of salvation. They were too earnest for the Paris wits. Voltaire always sneered at them till he came to know Turgot. Grimm calls them "the pietists of philosophy," and Hume, bantering Morellet, wonders how a man like Turgot could herd with such cattle, "the most chimerical and the most arrogant that now exist since the annihilation of the Sorbonne." But they were grappling with living problems, and seeing into the real situation so much further than their contemporaries, that an historian like de Tocqueville thinks the best key to the Revolution is to be found in their writings. The malady of the age, they held, was the ever-increasing distress of the agricultural population. The great nobles, the financiers, the farmers-general, the monopolists, were very rich ; but the agriculturists — the vast body of the people — were sinking into a hopeless impoverishment, for between tithes and heavy war taxes and farmer-generals' extortions, and the high rents which, to Turgot's despair, the smaller peasantry would persist in offering without reflecting in the least on the rise in their burdens, — between all these things, the net product of agriculture — what was left in the hands of the cultivator after all expenses were paid away —was getting less and less every year, and the ruin of the peasantry meant the ruin of the nation. "Poor peasants, poor kingdom," said they ; "poor kingdom, poor king."

And the remedy was plain : the net product of agriculture must somehow be made to rise instead of fall. They supported their contention with a certain erroneous theory that agriculture is the sole source of wealth, but the error made little practical difference to the argument, for agriculture is always a sufficiently important source of wealth to make its improvement a national concern. How then was the net product to be increased ? By better methods of cultivation, by removal of legal and official interferences, and by lightening the public burdens through the abolition of all existing · taxes and of the existing system of collecting them through farmers-general, and the institution instead of a single tax on the net product of the soil, to be collected directly by responsible officials. According to the reminiscences of strangers who happened to fall into their company, the talk of the economists always ran much on the net product and the single tax, for they believed the two great needs of the country were agricultural improvement and financial reform. When Quesnay was offered a farmer-generalship of the taxes for his son, he said, "No ; let the welfare of my children be bound up with the public prosperity," and made his son a farmer of the land instead.

In Quesnay's rooms in the palace of Versailles Smith would sometimes hear words that would sound very strange in the house of the king. Mercier de la Rivière, Quesnay's favourite disciple, while writing his book on the *Natural and Essential Order of Political Societies*, published in 1767, almost lived in Quesnay's apartments, discussing the\work point by point with the master. The Marquis de Mirabeau mentions having seen him there six whole weeks running, "moulding and remoulding his work, and consequently denying father and mother" for the time. One day Madame du Hausset heard a memorable conversation there between these two economists. "This kingdom," observed Mirabeau, "is in a miserable state. There is neither energy in the nation nor money to serve in its place." "No," replied Mercier de la Rivière, counsellor of the Parliament of Paris and late Governor of Martinico, "it cannot be regenerated except by a conquest like that of China, or by a great internal convulsion ; but woe to those who will be there then, for the French people does nothing by halves." The words made the little lady-in-waiting tremble, and she hurried out of the room ; but M. de Marigny, brother of the king's mistress, who was also present, followed her, and bade her have no fear, for these were honest men, if a little chimerical, and they were

even, he thought, on the right road, though they knew
not when to stop and went past the goal.[1]

The doctor's room was a little sanctuary of free speech
pitched by an odd chance in the heart of a despotic court,
but his loyalty was known to be as sterling as his patriotism, and Louis himself would come round and listen to
his economic parables, and call him the king's thinker—
as indeed he was, for he was no believer in states-general
or states-particular, he had no interest in court or party
intrigues, and his thought was always for the power of the
king as well as for the welfare of the people. Marmontel,
who used to come to him feigning an interest in the net
product and the single tax, merely, as he confesses, to secure
the doctor's word with Madame de Pompadour about an
appointment he wanted, writes that " while storms gathered
and dispersed again underneath Quesnay's *entre-sol*, he
wrought at his axioms and his calculations in rural
economy as calmly and with as much indifference to the
movements of the court as if he were a hundred leagues
away. Below they discussed peace and war, the choice of
generals, the dismissal of ministers, while we up in the
entre-sol reasoned about agriculture and calculated the net
product, or sometimes dined gaily with Diderot, D'Alembert, Duclos, Helvetius, Turgot, Buffon ; and Madame de
Pompadour, not being able to get that company of philosophers to descend into her salon, used to come up there
herself to see them at table, and have a talk with them."[2]
None of the famous men mentioned here were members of
the sect except Turgot.

The year 1766 was a year of exceptional activity in
this economist camp. Turgot, as we have seen, was writing
an important work, and Mercier de la Riviere another.
The other members of the group were busy too, for they
had just for the first time secured an organ in the press in
the *Journal de l'Agriculture du Commerce et des Finances*,

---

[1] *Memoirs of Madame du Hausset*, p. 141.
[2] Marmontel's *Memoirs*, English Translation, ii. 37.

of which their youngest convert, Dupont de Nemours, was made editor in June 1765, and in which Quesnay himself wrote an article almost every month till Dupont's dismissal in November 1766. The Government, moreover, which had thrown Mirabeau into prison for his first book and had suppressed his second only a year or two before, now ceased from troubling, and gave even a certain official countenance to the *Journal de l'Agriculture*, for after the war it no longer shut its eyes to the distress that prevailed, and began to give an ear to remedies. They were making converts too, among others the Abbé Baudeau, who used to write them down in his journal, the *Éphémérides du Citoyen*, but now offered to make it their organ when they lost the *Journal de l'Agriculture*. They were thus in the first flush of their active propaganda, which in a year or two more made political economy, Grimm says, the *science de la mode* in France, and won converts to the single tax among the crowned heads of Europe. Quesnay too had taken apartments in town in the house of a disciple to be nearer his friends for pushing the propaganda, so that Smith had especially abundant opportunities of seeing him and them that year.

No memorial of all their intercourse, however, has survived except the slight and rather indefinite reminiscence of Dupont de Nemours, to which allusion has been made. Dupont remembers that Smith used to discuss with them a question, which they no doubt would be often discussing, for they were greatly interested in it,—the question of the effect upon the wages of labour of a tax upon the commodities consumed by the labourers ; and he says that Smith, in the freedom of private intercourse with them, expressed quite a different opinion upon that subject from that which he delivered in the *Wealth of Nations*, with the fear of vested interests before his eyes. Dupont could not have read the *Wealth of Nations* very carefully when he hinted this accusation of timidity before vested interests, for there was scarcely a vested interest existing at the time that has not incurred in its turn most vigorous censure in that work. But as the alleged difference amounts merely to this, that Smith in his book asserts a principle with a certain specific limitation to it which he used to assert in conversation without the limitation, it probably represents no real change of opinion, but only a difference between the more exact expositions of the book and the less exact expositions of conversation. The point was this. Smith held, with Dupont and his friends, that a direct tax on the wages of labour, like the French industrial *taille*, would, if the demand for labour and the price of provisions remained the same, have the effect of raising the wages of labour by the sum required to pay the tax. He held, again, with them that an indirect tax on the commodities consumed by the labourers would act in exactly the same way if the commodities taxed were necessaries of life, because a rise in the price of necessaries would imperil the labourer's ability to bring up his family. But what seemed new to Dupont was that Smith now in his book held that if the commodities taxed were luxuries, the tax would not act in that way. It would act as a sumptuary law. The labourer would merely spend less on such superfluities, and since this forced frugality would probably increase rather than diminish his ability to bring up a family, he would neither require nor obtain any rise of wages. The high tobacco duty in France and England and a recent rise of three shillings on the barrel of beer had no effect whatever on wages.

That is what Dupont says Smith would not have contended in France. He would not have drawn this distinction between the taxation of a necessary and the taxation of a luxury, and he only drew it in his book to avert the clamour of offended interests, though against his real convictions. The imputation of dissimulation, though explicitly enough made, may be disregarded. The alternative of a real change of opinion is quite possible, inasmuch as the position Smith has actually reached on this question in his book is far from final or perfect; it is obvious at a glance that in a community such as he supposes, where the labourers are in the habit of consuming both necessaries and luxuries, a tax on necessaries would have exactly the same effect as he attributes to a tax on luxuries; it would force the labourer to give up some of his luxuries. But there might be no real change of opinion, and yet a good deal of apparent difference between the loose statements of a speaker in a language of which he had only imperfect command and his more complete and precise statements in a written book. Dupont, it may be added, seems to think that Smith in his talks with the French economists expressed much more unfavourable views of the inconveniences, changes, and general evils of the English system of taxation than would be gathered from the *Wealth of Nations*.

Before Smith left France he had occasion, unhappily, to resort to Quesnay the physician as well as to Quesnay the economist. He had been in the habit while in Paris of taking his pupils for excursions to interesting places in the vicinity, as he had done from Toulouse, and in August 1766 they went to Compiègne to see the camp and the military evolutions which were to take place during the residence of the Court there. In Compiègne the Duke of Buccleugh took seriously ill of a fever,—the consequence of a fall from his horse while hunting, says his aunt, Lady Mary Coke,—and, as will be seen from the following letter, he was watched and nursed by his distinguished tutor with a care and devotion almost more than paternal. The letter is written to Charles Townshend, the Duke's step-father :—

COMPIÈGNE, *26th August* 1766.

DEAR SIR—It is, you may believe, with the greatest concern that I find myself obliged to give you an account of a slight fever from which the Duke of Buccleugh is not yet entirely recovered, though it is this day very much abated. He came here to see the camp and to hunt with the King and the Court. On Thursday last he returned from hunting about seven at night very hungry, and ate heartily of a cold supper with a vast quantity of sallad, and drank some cold punch after it. This supper, it seems, disagreed with him. He had no appetite next day, but appeared well and hearty as usual. He found himself uneasy on the field and returned home before the rest of the company. He dined with my Lord George Lennox, and, as he tells me, ate heartily. He found himself very much fatigued after dinner and threw himself upon his servant's bed. He slept there about an hour, and awaked about eight at night in a good deal of disorder. He vomited, but not enough to relieve him. I found his pulse extremely quick. He went to bed immediately and drank some vinegar whey, quite confident that a night's rest and a sweat, his usual remedy, would relieve him. He slept little that night but sweat profusely. The moment I saw him next day (Sunday) I was sure he had a fever, and begged of him to send for a physician. He refused a long time, but at last, upon seeing me uneasy, consented. I sent for Quenay, first ordinary physician to the King. He sent me word he was ill. I then sent for Senac ; he was ill likewise. I went to Quenay myself to beg that, notwithstanding his illness, which was not dangerous, he would come to see the Duke. He told me he was an old infirm man, whose attendance could not be depended on, and advised me as his friend to depend upon De la Saone, first physician to the Queen. I went to De la Saone. He was gone out, and was not expected home that night. I returned to Quenay, who followed me immediately to the Duke. It was by this time seven at night. The Duke was in the same profuse sweat which he had been in all day and all the preceding night. In this situation Quenay declared that it was improper to do any-thing till the sweat should be over. He only ordered him some cooling ptisane drink. Quenay's illness made it impossible for him to return next day (Monday) and De la Saone has waited on the Duke ever since, to my entire satisfaction. On Monday he found the Duke's fever so moderate that he judged it unnecessary to bleed him. . . . To-day, Wednesday, upon finding some little extraordinary heat upon the Duke's skin in the morning, he pro-posed ordering a small quantity of blood to be taken from him at two o'clock, but upon returning at that hour he found him so very cool and easy that he judged it unnecessary. When a French physician judges bleeding unnecessary, you may be sure that the fever is not very violent. The Duke has never had the smallest headache nor any pain in any part of his body ; he has good spirits ; his head and his eye are both clear ; he has no extraordinary redness in his face ; his tongue is not more foul than in a common cold.   There is some little quickness in his pulse, but it is soft, full, and regular.   In short, there is no one bad symptom about him, only he has a fever and keeps his bed. . . . De la Saone imagines the whole illness owing to the indigestion of Thursday night.   Some part of the undigested matter having got into his blood, the violent commotion which this had occasioned had burst, he supposes, some small vessel in his veins. . . . Depend upon hearing from me by every post till his perfect recovery ; if any threatening symptom should appear I shall immediately despatch an express to you ; so keep your mind as easy as possible.   There is not the least probability that any such symptom ever will appear. I never stirr from his room from eight in the morning till ten at night, and watch for the smallest change that happens to him.   I should sit by him all night too if the ridiculous, impertinent jealousy of Cook, who thinks my assiduity an encroachment upon his duty, would not be so much alarmed, as it gave some disturbance even to his master in his present illness.

The King has inquired almost every day at his levée of my Lord George and of Mr. De la Saone concerning the Duke's illness.   The Duke and Dutchess of Fitzjames, the Chevalier de Clermont, the Comte de Guerchy, etc. etc., together with the whole English nation here and at Paris, have expressed the greatest anxiety for his recovery.   Remember me in the most respectful manner to Lady Dalkeith, and believe me to be with the greatest regard, dear sir, your most obliged and most humble servant,   ADAM SMITH.

COMPIÈGNE, *26th August* 1766.
Wednesday, 5 o'clock afternoon.[1]

Could there be a more pleasing exhibition of the thorough kindness of a manly heart than this picture of the great philosopher sitting day after day by the bedside of his pupil, watching eagerly every indication of change, and only consenting to leave the room for a time at night out of consideration for the silly jealousy of the valet, who thought the tutor's presence an invasion of his own rights ?

The Duke recovered and they returned to Paris.   But while still at Compiègne they heard of a sad event that

[1] Fraser's *Scotts of Buccleuch*, ii. 405.

could not fail to shock them greatly, the death of their greatly esteemed young friend and fellow-traveller, Sir James Macdonald. "Were you and I together, dear Smith," writes Hume at this time, "we should shed tears at present for the death of poor Sir James Macdonald. We could not possibly have suffered a greater loss than in that valuable young man."[1]

In this letter Hume had dropped a remark showing that he was still clinging to the idea which he had repeatedly mentioned to Smith of returning and making his home for the remainder of his days somewhere in France—in Paris, or "Toulouse, or Montauban, or some provincial town in the South of France, where "—to quote his words to Sir G. Elliot—"I shall spend contentedly the rest of my life with more money, under a finer sky and in better company than I was born to enjoy." Of this idea Smith strongly disapproved. He thought that Hume would find himself too old to transplant, and that he was being carried away by the great kindness and flatteries he had received in Paris into entertaining a plan which could never promote his happiness, because, in the first place, it would probably prove fatal to work, and in the next, it would certainly deprive him of the support of those old and rooted friendships which could not be replaced by the incense of an hour. For his own part, and with a view to his own future, Smith was of an entirely opposite mind. The contrast between the two friends in natural character stands out very strongly here. Smith had enjoyed his stay in France almost as much as Hume, and had been welcomed everywhere by the best men and women in the country with high respect, but now that the term of his tutorship is approaching its end, he longs passionately for home, feels that he has had his fill of travel, and says if he once gets among his old friends again, he will never wander more. This appears from a letter he wrote Millar, the bookseller, probably after his return from Compiègne,

---

[1] Burton's *Life of Hume*, ii. 348.

of which Millar sent the following extract to Hume : "Though I am very happy here, I long passionately to rejoin my old friends, and if I had once got fairly to your side of the water, I think I should never cross it again. Recommend the same sober way of thinking to Hume. He is light-headed, tell him, when he talks of coming to spend the remainder of his days here or in France. Remember me to him most affectionately." [1]

His return, for which he was then looking with so much desire, came sooner than he anticipated, and came, unfortunately, with a cloud. His younger pupil, the Hon. Hew Campbell Scott, was assassinated in the streets of Paris, on the 18th of October 1766, in his nineteenth year; [2] and immediately thereafter they set out for London, bringing the remains of Mr. Scott along with them, and accompanied by Lord George Lennox, Hume's successor as Secretary of Legation. The London papers announce their arrival at Dover on the 1st of November. The tutorship, which ended with this melancholy event, was always remembered with great satisfaction and gratitude by the surviving pupil. "In October 1766," writes the Duke of Buccleugh to Dugald Stewart, "we returned to London, after having spent near three years together without the slightest disagreement or coolness, and, on my part, with every advantage that could be expected from the society of such a man. We continued to live in friendship till the hour of his death, and I shall always remain with the impression of having lost a friend whom I loved and respected, not only for his great talents, but for every private virtue."

Smith's choice for this post of travelling tutor was thought in many quarters at the time to be a very strange choice. Shrewd old Dr. Carlyle thought it so strange

[1] Hill's *Letters of Hume*, p. 59. Original in R.S.E.
[2] *New Statistical Account of Scotland*, i. 490. (Account of Dalkeith by the late Dr. Norman Macleod, then minister of that parish, and Mr. Peter Steel, Rector of Dalkeith Grammar School.)

that he professes to be quite unable as a man of the world
to understand Charles Townshend making it, except "for
his own glory of having sent an eminent Scotch philosopher to travel with the Duke." [1] He thought Smith had
too much "probity and benevolence" in his own soul to
suspect ill in another or check it, and that a man who
seemed too absent to make his own way about could
hardly be expected to look efficiently after the goings
of another. "He was," says Carlyle, "the most absent
man in company I ever knew," and "he appeared very
unfit for the intercourse of the world as a travelling
tutor." [2]

Still Townshend's choice was thoroughly justified by the
result, and Carlyle admits it, but thinks that was due less
to the efficiency of the tutor than to the natural excellence
of the pupil. And there is no doubt that Smith was
exceptionally fortunate in his pupil. In his after life this
Duke Henry took little part in politics, but he made himself
singularly beloved among his countrymen by a long career
filled with works of beneficence and patriotism, and
brightened by that love of science which has for generations
distinguished the house of Buccleuch. It may be true that
with such a pupil Smith's natural defects would find little
opportunity of causing trouble, but it seems certain, as
I have before said, that these defects were habitually exaggerated by Smith's contemporaries, and Carlyle himself
acknowledges that Smith's travels with the Duke cured
him considerably of his fits of abstraction. This is confirmed by Ramsay of Ochtertyre, who says that Smith grew
smarter during his stay abroad, and lost much of the
awkwardness of manner he previously exhibited.

Stewart is disposed to think, however, that the public
have not the same reason to be satisfied with Smith's
acceptance of this tutorship as either he himself or his
pupil had, and that the world at large has been seriously
the loser for it, because "it interrupted that studious

[1] *Autobiography*, p. 280.					[2] *Ibid.*

leisure for which nature seemed to have designed him, and in which alone he could have hoped to accomplish those literary projects which had flattered the ambition of his youthful genius." Now it is, of course, idle to speculate on the things that might have been. Kant was never forty miles from Königsberg, and had Smith remained in Glasgow all his days there is no reason to doubt he could have produced works of lasting importance. But it is a truism to say that the works would have been other and different from what we have. To a political philosopher foreign travel is an immense advantage, and there never was a country where graver or more interesting problems, both economic and constitutional, offered themselves for study than France in the latter half of last century, nor any political philosopher who enjoyed better opportunities than Smith of discussing such problems with the ablest and best-informed minds on the spot. Smith's residence in France, whatever it was to his pupil, must have been an invaluable education to himself, supplying him day after day with constant materials for fresh comparison and thought. Samuel Rogers was greatly struck with the difference between Smith and the historian Robertson. The conversation of Robertson, who, as we know, had never been out of his own country, was much more limited in its range of interest, but Smith's was the rich conversation of a man who had seen and known a great deal of the world. It does not appear that Smith suffered in France from any such want of literary leisure as Stewart speaks of, for he began writing a book in Toulouse because he had so little else to do, and he had not attempted anything of the kind in Glasgow, so far as we know, for five years; but, at all events, for the wealth of illustration which his new book exhibits, the variety of its points of view, the copiousness of its data drawn from personal observation, the world is greatly indebted to the author's residence abroad. And had Smith lived to finish his work on Government we should probably have had more results of his observation of France, but the *Wealth of Nations* itself contains many.

M'Culloch has expressed astonishment that for all his long stay in France Smith should have never perceived any foreshadowings of the coming Revolution, such as were visible even to a passing traveller like Smollett. But Smith was quite aware of all the gravities and possibilities of the situation, and occasionally gave expression to anticipations of vital change. He formed possibly a less gloomy view of the actual condition of the French people than he would have heard uttered in Quesnay's room at Versailles, because he always mentally compared the state of things he saw in France with the state of things he knew in Scotland, and though it was plain to him that France was not going forward so fast as Scotland, he thought the common opinion that it was going backward to be ill founded.[1] Then France was a much richer country, with a better soil and climate, and "better stocked," he says, "with all those things which it requires a long time to raise up and accumulate, such as great towns and convenient and well-built houses both in town and country."[2] In spite of these advantages, however, the common people in France were decidedly worse off than the common people of Scotland. The wages of labour were lower—the real wages—for the people evidently lived harder. Their dress and countenance showed it at once. " When you go from Scotland to England the difference which you may remark between the dress and countenance of the common people in the one country and in the other sufficiently indicates the difference in their condition. The contrast is still greater when you return from France." In England nobody was too poor to wear leather shoes; in Scotland even the lowest orders of men wore them, though the same orders of women still went about barefooted. But " in France

[1] *Wealth of Nations*, Book I. chap. ix.
[2] *Ibid.*, Book V. chap. ii. art. iii.

they are necessaries neither to men nor to women ; the lowest rank of both sexes appearing there publicly, without any discredit, sometimes in wooden shoes and sometimes barefooted." [1] Another little circumstance struck him as a proof that the classes immediately above the rank of labourer were worse off in France than they were here. The taste for dressing yew-trees into the shape of pyramids and obelisks by " that very clumsy instrument of sculpture " the gardener's shears had gone out of fashion in this country, merely because it got too common, and was discarded by the rich and vain. The multitude of persons able to indulge the taste was sufficiently great to drive the custom out of fashion. In France, on the other hand, he found this custom still in good repute, " notwithstanding," he adds, " that inconstancy of fashion with which we sometimes reproach the natives of that country." The reason was that the number of people in that country able to indulge this taste was too few to deprive the custom of the requisite degree of rarity. " In France the condition of the inferior ranks of people is seldom so happy as it frequently is in England, and you will there seldom find even pyramids and obelisks of yew in the garden of a tallow-chandler. Such ornaments, not having in that country been degraded by their vulgarity, have not yet been excluded from the gardens of princes and great lords." [2]

He discusses one great cause of the poorer condition of the French than of the English people. It was generally acknowledged, he says, that " the people of France was much more oppressed by taxation than the people of Great Britain "; and the oppression he found, by personal investigation, to be all due to bad taxes and bad methods of collecting them. The sum that reached the public treasury represented a much smaller burden per head of population than it did in this country. Smith calculated

[1] *Wealth of Nations*, Book V. chap. ii. art. iv.
[2] " Essay on the Imitative Arts," *Works*, v. 260.

the public revenue of Great Britain to represent an assessment of about 25s. a head of population, and in 1765 and 1766, the years he was in France, according to the best, though, he admits, imperfect, accounts he could get of the matter, the whole sum passed into the French treasury would only represent an assessment of 12s. 6d. per head of the French population.[1]   Taxation ought thus to be really lighter in France than in Great Britain, but it was made into a scourge by vicious modes of assessment and collection.   Smith even suggested for France various moderate financial reforms, repealing some taxes, increasing others, making a third class uniform over the kingdom, and abolishing the farming system ; but though these reforms would be sufficient to restore prosperity to a country with the resources of France, he had no hope of it being possible to carry them against the active opposition of individuals interested in maintaining things as they were.

Smith was thus perfectly alive to the prevailing poverty and distress of the French population, to the oppression they suffered, to the extreme difficulty, the hopelessness even, of any improvement of their situation while the existing distribution of political forces continued, and was able to defeat all efforts at reform.   Now from all this it was not very far to the idea of a political upheaval and a new distribution of political forces, and Smith saw tendencies abroad in that direction also.   He told Professor Saint Fond in 1782 that the " Social Compact " would one day avenge Rousseau for all the persecutions he had suffered from the powers that were.

[1] *Wealth of Nations*, Book V. chap. ii. art. iv.

CHAPTER XV

1766–1767.   *Aet.* 43

ARRIVING in London early in November, Smith seems to
have remained on in the capital for the next six months.
The body of his unfortunate pupil, which he brought over
with him, was ultimately buried in the family vault at
Dalkeith, for Dr. Norman Macleod and Mr. Steel say so ;
but the interment there does not seem to have taken place
immediately after the arrival from France, for the London
journals, which announce the Duke of Buccleugh's landing
at Dover on the 1st of November, mention his presence at
the Guildhall with his stepfather, Mr. Townshend, Chancellor of the Exchequer, on the 10th, Lord Mayor's Day ;
and the Duke, who is stated by Dr. Macleod to have
brought his brother's remains north, could not have been
to Scotland and back in that interval.   Smith was accordingly not required to proceed to Scotland on that sad duty,
and on the 22nd of November Andrew Millar, the publisher, writing to David Hume in Edinburgh, mentions the
fact that Smith was then in London and moving about
among the great.   This letter was written about a question
on which Hume had sought Smith's counsel, and on which
Millar had held some conversation with Smith, the upshot
of which he now communicates to Hume—the question
whether he should continue his *History of England.*
While Smith was still in Paris Hume had written saying :
"Some push me to continue my *History*.   Millar offers

any price. All the Marlborough papers are offered me, and I believe nobody would venture to refuse me, but *cui bono?* Why should I forego dalliance and sauntering and society, and expose myself again to the clamours of a stupid factious public? I am not yet tired of doing nothing, and am become too wise either to want censure or praise. By and by I shall be too old to undergo so much labour."[1]

Smith does not appear to have answered this letter at the time, but his opinion is communicated to Hume in this letter from Millar, who no doubt had a conversation with him on the subject. Millar says: "He is of opinion, with many more of your very good sensible friends, that the history of this country from the Revolution is not to be met with in books yet printed, but from MSS. in this country, to which he is sure you will have ready access, from all accounts he learns from the great here; and therefore you should lay the groundwork here after your perusal of the MSS. you may have access to, and doing it below will be laying the wrong foundation. I think it my duty to inform you the opinion of your most judicious friends, and I think he and Sir John Pringle may be reckoned amongst that number."[2]

Smith was himself publishing with Millar at this time a new edition of his *Theory of Moral Sentiments*—the third, which appeared in 1767, containing, like the second, the addition of the *Dissertation upon the Origin of Languages*. One of his reasons for staying so long in London this winter was no doubt to see the sheets through the press. The book was printed by Strahan, who was also a partner in Millar's publishing business; and there is a letter to him from Smith which, though bearing no date but Friday and no place of writing at all, must have been written, as indeed those two very circumstances indicate, in London, and some time during the winter of 1766-67.

[1] Burton's *Life of Hume*, ii. 392. [2] *Ibid.*

My dear Strahan—I go to the country for a few days this afternoon, so that it will be unnecessary to send me any more sheets till I return. The *Dissertation upon the Origin of Languages* is to be printed at the end of the *Theory*. There are some literal errors in the printed copy of it which I should have been glad to have corrected, but have not the opportunity, as I have no copy by me. They are of no great consequence. In the titles, both of the *Theory* and *Dissertation*, call me simply Adam Smith without any addition either before or behind.—I ever am, etc.,

ADAM SMITH.

Friday.[1]

When the *Wealth of Nations* came out in 1776 the author described himself on the title-page as LL.D. and F.R.S., late Professor of Moral Philosophy in Glasgow University, but he wants here on the *Theory* nothing but plain Adam Smith, his mind being at this period apparently averse to making use of his degree even on public and formal occasions, as it always was to using it in private life. He described himself on his visiting cards as " Mr. Adam Smith," he was known in the inner circle of his personal friends as Mr. Smith, and when Dugald Stewart was found fault with by certain critics for speaking of him so in his memoirs, he replied that he never heard Smith called anything else.

But while Smith was superintending the republication of his first book, he was at the same time using his opportunities in London to read up at the British Museum, then newly established, or elsewhere, for his second and greater, of which he had laid the keel in France. One of the subjects which he was engaged in studying at that time was colonial administration. He seems to have been discussing the subject with Lord Shelburne, who was now Secretary of State, and he gives that statesman the results of his further investigations into at least one branch of the subject in the following letter, written in the first

[1] *New York Evening Post.* Original in possession of Mr. David A. Wells of Norwich, U.S.A.

instance, like so many others of Smith's extant letters, to do a service to a friend. He wished to interest Lord Shelburne in the claims of a Scotch friend, Alexander Dalrymple, for the command of the exploring expedition which it was then in contemplation to send to the South Sea, and which was eventually committed to Captain Wallis. This Alexander Dalrymple was afterwards the well-known Hydrographer to the Admiralty and the East India Company, to whom the progress of geographical knowledge lies under deep obligations. He was one of the numerous younger brothers of Lord Hailes, the Scotch judge and historian, and having returned in 1765 from thirteen years' work in the East India Company's service, had devoted himself since then to the study of discoveries in the South Sea, and arrived at a confident belief in the existence of a great undiscovered continent in that quarter. Lord Shelburne would have given him the command of this expedition had not Captain Wallis been already engaged, and next year he was actually offered, and had he been granted naval rank, which he thought essential for maintaining discipline on board ship, he would have undertaken command of the more memorable expedition to observe the transit of Venus, which made Captain Cook the most famous explorer of his age.

The following is Smith's letter :—

My Lord—I send you enclosed Quiros's memorial, presented to Philip the Second after his return from his voyage, translated from the Spanish in which it is published in Purchass. The voyage itself is long, obscure, and difficult to be understood, except by those who are particularly acquainted with the geography and navigation of those countries, and upon looking over a great number of Dalrymple's papers I imagined this was what you would like best to see. He is besides just finishing a geographical account of all the discoveries that have yet been made in the South Seas from the west coast of America to Tasman's discoveries. If your lordship will give him leave, he would be glad to read this to you himself, and show you on his map the geographical ascertainment of the situation of each island. I have seen it ; it is extremely short; not much longer than this memorial of Quiros. Whether this may be convenient for your lordship I know not; whether this continent exists or not may perhaps be uncertain; but supposing it does exist, I am very certain you never will find a man fitter for discovering it, or more determined to hazard everything in order to discover it. The terms that he would ask are, first, the absolute command of the ship, with the naming of all the officers, in order that he may have people who both have confidence in him and in whom he has confidence; and secondly, that in case he should lose his ship by the common course of accidents before he gets into the South Sea, that the Government will undertake to give him another. These are all the terms he would insist upon. The ship properest for such an expedition, he says, would be an old fifty-gun ship without her guns. He does not, however, insist upon this, as a *sine quâ non*, but will go in any ship from an hundred to a thousand tons. He wishes to have but one ship with a good many boats. Most expeditions of this kind have miscarried from one ship's being obliged to wait for the other, or losing time in looking out for the other.

Within these two days I have looked over everything I can find relating to the Roman Colonys. I have not yet found anything of much consequence. They were governed upon the model of the Republic: had two consuls called *duumviri*; a senate called *decuriones* or *collegium decurionum*, and other magistrates similar to those of the Republic. The colonists lost their right of voting or of being elected to any magistracy in the Roman comitia. In this respect they were inferior to many municipia. They retained, however, all the other privileges of Roman citizens. They seem to have been very independent. Of thirty colonies of whom the Romans demanded troops in the second Carthaginian war, twelve refused to obey. They frequently rebelled and joined the enemies of the Republic; being in some measure little independent republics, they naturally followed the interests which their peculiar situation pointed out to them.—I have the honour to be, with the highest regard, my lord, your lordship's most obedient humble servant, ADAM SMITH.

Tuesday, 12*th February* 1767.[1]

The problem of colonial rights and responsibilities had just come rapidly to the forefront of public questions in

[1] Lansdowne MSS.

England. The abandonment of North America by the French in 1763 had given a new importance to the plantations, and seemed to develop at the same time a stronger disposition to assert colonial rights on the one side of the Atlantic, and to interfere with them on the other. The Stamp Act of 1765 had already begun the struggle against imperial taxation which Charles Townshend's tea duty, imposed a few months after this letter was written, was to precipitate into rebellion. There was therefore very good reason why statesmen like Lord Shelburne should be studying the relations of dependencies to mother countries, and turning their attention to earlier colonial experiments such as those of ancient Rome. It will be observed that Smith came in the *Wealth of Nations* to modify somewhat the view he expresses in this letter of the independence of the Roman colonies, and explains that the reason they were less prosperous than the Greek colonies was because they were not, like the latter, independent, and were " not always at liberty to manage their own affairs in the way that they judged most suitable to their own interest." [1]

Smith's absent-minded habit, while it seems from various accounts to have been lessened by his travels abroad, was not entirely removed by them, for on the 11th of February 1767 Lady Mary Coke writes her sister that Lady George Lennox and Sir Gilbert Elliot had happened to meet while visiting her, and had talked of " Mr. Smith, the gentleman that went abroad with the Duke of Buccleugh," saying many things in his praise, but adding that he was the most absent man they ever knew. Sir Gilbert mentioned that Mr. Damer (probably Mr. John Damer, Lord Milton's son) had paid Smith a visit a few mornings before as he was sitting down to breakfast, and falling into discourse Smith took a piece of bread and butter, and after rolling it round and round put it into the teapot and poured the water upon it. Shortly after he poured out a cup, and on tasting it declared it

[1] *Wealth of Nations*, Book IV. chap. vii.

was the worst tea he had ever met with. " I have not the least doubt of it," said Mr. Damer, " for you have made it of bread and butter instead of tea." [1]

The Duke of Buccleugh was married in London on the 3rd of May 1767 to Lady Betsy, only daughter of the Duke of Montagu, and Smith probably returned to Scotland immediately after that event. For in writing Hume from Kirkcaldy on the 9th of June 1767, he mentions having now been settled down to his work for about a month. Another circumstance confirms this inference. He was elected a Fellow of the Royal Society of London on the 21st of May 1767, but was not admitted till the 27th of May 1773, and that seems to imply that he had left London before the former date, and never returned to it again till shortly before the latter one.

[1] Lady Mary Coke's *Journal,* i. 141.

CHAPTER XVI

KIRKCALDY

1767–1773. *Aet.* 44–50

WHEN Smith left Glasgow his mother and cousin went back again to Kirkcaldy, and he now joined them and remained with them there for the next eleven years. Hume, who thought the country an unsuitable place for a man of letters, used every endeavour to persuade him to remove to Edinburgh, but without success. The gaiety and fulness of city life were evidently much less to him than they were to Hume, and he must have found what sufficed him in the little town of his birth. He had his work, he had his mother, he had his books, he had his daily walks in the sea breeze, and he had Edinburgh always in the offing as a place of occasional resort. He is said to have taken much real pleasure, like Shakespeare at Stratford, in mingling again with the simple old folk who were about him in his youth, and he had a few neighbours whose pursuits corresponded more nearly with his own. James Oswald, indeed, was now struck down with illness—"terrible distress" is Smith's expression—and he died in the second year after Smith's return to Scotland. Oswald spent some months in Kirkcaldy, however, in the fall of 1767, and probably again in 1768. One of Smith's other literary neighbours, whom he saw much of during this eleven years' residence in Fife, was Robert Beatson, author of the *Political Index* and other works, to whom there will be occasion to refer again later on. His chief resource, however, throughout this period was his work, which engaged his mind late and early till it told hard, as we shall presently see, on his health.

After being established in Kirkcaldy for some weeks Smith wrote Hume that he was immersed in study, which was the only business he had, that his sole amusements were long solitary walks by the seaside (which, with a man of his gift or infirmity of abstraction, would only be protractions of the study that preoccupied him), and that he never was happier or more contented in all his life. The immediate object of this letter, as so usual with Smith, was to serve a friend — a motive which never failed to overcome his aversion to writing. A French friend — "the best and most agreeable friend I had in France," says Smith — was then in London, and Smith wishes Hume, who was now Under Secretary of State, to show him some attentions during his residence there. This friend was Count de Sarsfield, a gentleman of Irish extraction, an associate of Turgot and the other men of letters in Paris, and a man who added to almost universal knowledge a special predilection for economics, and indeed wrote a number of essays on economic questions, though he never published any of them. He seems to have really been, as Smith indicates, the perfection of an agreeable companion. John Adams, the second President of the United States, when envoy for that country in Paris, was very intimate with him, and says that Sarsfield was the happiest man he knew, for he led the life of a peripatetic philosopher. "Observation and reflection are all his business, and his dinner and his friend all his pleasure. If a man were born for himself alone, I would take him for a model." [1] He was "the greatest rider of hobby-horses" in all President Adams's acquaintance, and some of his hobbies were for the most serious studies. He published a work in metaphysics, and wrote essays against serfdom and slavery, and on a number of other subjects, which were found in

[1] Adams's *Works*, ix. 589.

MS. among President Adams's papers. Yet he was a problem—and not a very soluble one—to the worthy President, for he laid a weight on the merest trifles of ceremony or etiquette which seemed difficult to reconcile with his devotion to profound and learned studies. He visited Adams at Washington during his presidency, and used constantly to lecture the President on his little omissions. After any entertainment Sarsfield would say, writes Adams, "that I should have placed the Ambassador of France at my right hand and the Minister of Spain at my left, and have arranged the other principal personages; and when I rose from the table I should have said, Messieurs, voudrez vous, etc., or Monsieur or Duc voudrez vous, etc. . . . How is it possible to reconcile these trifling contemplations of a master of the ceremonies with the vast knowledge of arts, sciences, history, government, etc., possessed by this nobleman?"[1] Sarsfield kept a journal about all the people he met with, from which Adams makes some interesting quotations, and which, if extant, might be expected to add to our information regarding Smith. Having said so much of Smith's "best and most agreeable friend in France," I will now give the letter :—

KIRKALDY, *7th June* 1767.

MY DEAREST FRIEND—The Principal design of this Letter is to Recommend to your particular attention the Count de Sarsfield, the best and most agreeable friend I had in France. Introduce him, if you find it proper, to all the friends of yr. absent friend, to Oswald and to Elliot in particular. I cannot express to you how anxious I am that his stay in London should be rendered agreeable to him. You know him, and must know what a plain, worthy, honourable man he is. I enclose a letter for him, which you may either send to him, or rather, if the weighty affairs of State will permit it, deliver it to him yourself. The letter to Dr. Morton[2] you may send by the Penny Post.

---

[1] Adams's *Works*, iii. 276.
[2] Secretary of the Royal Society. The letter was probably in acknowledgment of the intimation of his election as Fellow.

My Business here is study, in which I have been very deeply engaged for about a month past. My amusements are long solitary walks by the seaside. You may judge how I spend my time. I feel myself, however, extremely happy, comfortable, and contented. I never was perhaps more so in all my life.

You will give me great comfort by writing to me now and then, and by letting me know what is passing among my friends at London. Remember me to them all, particularly to Mr. Adams's family and to Mrs. Montagu.[1]

What has become of Rousseau? Has he gone abroad because he cannot contrive to get himself sufficiently persecuted in Great Britain?

What is the meaning of the bargain that your ministry have made with the India Company? They have not, I see, prolonged their charter, which is a good circumstance.[2]

The rest of the sheet is torn.

Hume replies on the 13th that Sarsfield was a very good friend of his own, whom he had always great pleasure in meeting, as he was a man of merit; but that he did not introduce him, as Smith desired, to Sir Gilbert Elliot, because "this gentleman's reserve and indolence would make him neglect the acquaintance"; nor to Oswald, because he found his intimacy with Oswald, which had lasted more than a quarter of a century, was broken for ever. He goes on to describe his quarrel with Oswald's brother the bishop; and concludes: "If I were sure, dear Smith, that you and I should not some day quarrel in some such manner, I should tell you that I am yours affectionately and sincerely."[3] Count de Sarsfield seems to have gone on to Scotland to pay Smith a visit, for on the 14th of July Hume writes Smith, enclosing a packet, which he desires to be delivered to the Count.

Smith did not reply to either of these letters till the 13th of September, when he writes from Dalkeith House,

[1] Mr. Adams is Adam the architect, and Mrs. Montagu is the well-known Mrs. Elizabeth Montagu of Portman Square, whose hospitable house was a rival to any of the most brilliant salons of Paris.

[2] *Hume MSS.*, R.S.E. Library.

[3] Burton's *Life of Hume*, ii. 390.

where he has gone for the home-coming of the Duke and Duchess of Buccleugh. After expressing his mind in the plainest terms about the bishop with whom Hume had the tussle—" He is a brute and a beast," says Smith—he goes on to bespeak Hume's favour for a young cousin of his who happened to be living in the same house with Hume in London, Captain David Skene, afterwards of Pitlour, who was in 1787 made inspector of military roads in Scotland.

> Be so good (he says) as convey the enclosed letter to the Count de Sarsfield. I have been much in the wrong for having delayed so long to write both to him and you.
>
> There is a very amiable, modest, brave, worthy young gentleman who lives in the same house with you. His name is David Skeene. He and I are sisters' sons, but my regard for him is much more founded on his personal qualities than upon the relations in which he stands to me. He acted lately in a very gallant manner in America, of which he never acquainted me himself, and of which I came to the knowledge only within these few days. If you can be of any service to him you could not possibly do a more obliging thing to me.
>
> The Duke and Dutchess of Buccleugh have been here now for almost a fortnight. They begin to open their house on Monday next, and, I flatter myself, will both be very agreeable to the People of this country. I am not sure that I have ever seen a more agreeable woman than the Dutchess. I am sorry that you are not here, because I am sure you would be perfectly in love with her. I shall probably be here some weeks. I could wish, however, that both you and the Count de Sarsfield would direct for me as usual at Kirkaldy. I should be glad to know the true history of Rousseau before and since he left England. You may perfectly depend upon my never quoting you to any living soul upon that subject.—I ever am, dear sir, most faithfully yours,

> ADAM SMITH.[1]

The Duke of Buccleugh had never been at Dalkeith since his infancy—if indeed he had been even then, for Dr. Carlyle's words in describing this celebration are,

[1] *Hume MSS.*, R.S.E. Library.

"where his grace had never been before"—because his stepfather, Charles Townshend, was afraid he might grow up too Scotch in accent and feeling ; and his home-coming now, with his young and beautiful bride, excited the liveliest interest and expectation, not only on the Buccleugh estates, but over the whole lowlands of Scot-land, from the Forth to the Solway. The day originally fixed for the celebration was the Duke's birthday, the 13th of September, the very day Smith wrote Hume ; but the event had to be postponed in consequence of the sudden death of Townshend, from an attack of putrid fever, between the day of the Duke's arrival at Dalkeith and the anniversary of his birth. It came off, however, two or three weeks later. An entertainment was given to about fifty ladies and gentlemen of the neighbourhood ; but Dr. Carlyle, who was present, and wrote indeed an ode for the occasion, says that though the fare was sumptuous, the company was formal and dull, because the guests were all strangers to their host and hostess except Adam Smith, and Adam Smith, says Carlyle, "was but ill qualified to promote the jollity of a birthday." "Had it not been for Alexander Macmillan, W.S., and myself," he proceeds, "the meeting would have been very dull, and might have been dissolved without even drinking the health of the day. . . . Smith remained with them (the Duke and Duchess) for two months, and then returned to Kirkcaldy to his mother and his studies. I have often thought since that if they had brought down a man of more address than he was, how much sooner their first appearance might have been."[1]

The ice, which Smith is thus blamed for not being able to break on this first meeting of his pupil with his Scotch neighbours, was not long in melting naturally away under the warmth of the Duke's own kindness of heart. He almost settled among them, for on Townshend's death he gave up the idea on which that statesman had set

[1] Carlyle's *Autobiography*, p. 489.

his heart, and which was one of his reasons for committing the training of the young Duke to the care of
a political philosopher,—the idea of going into politics
as an active career ; and he lived largely on his Scotch
estates ; becoming a father to his numerous tenantry,
and a powerful and enlightened promoter of all sound
agricultural improvement.   Dr. Carlyle says the family
were always kind to their tenants, but Duke Henry
"surpassed them all, as much in justice and humanity
as he did in superiority of understanding and good
sense."   Without claiming for Smith's teaching what
must in any case have been largely the result of a fine
natural character, it is certain that no young man could
live for three years in daily intimacy with Adam Smith
without being powerfully influenced by that deep love
of justice and humanity which animated Smith beyond
his fellows, and ran as warmly through his conversation
in private life as we see it still runs through his published
writings.   Smith was always vigorous and weighty in
his denunciation of wrong, and so impatient of anything
in the nature of indifference or palliation towards it,
that he could scarce feel at ease in the presence of the
palliator.   "We can breathe more freely now," he once
said when a person of that sort had just left the company ; "that man has no indignation in him."[1]

Smith remained the mentor of his pupil all his life.
At "Dalkeith, which all the virtues love," he was always
a most honoured guest, and Dugald Stewart says he
always spoke with much satisfaction and gratitude of his
relations with the family of Buccleugh.   Several of the
traditional anecdotes of Smith's absence of mind are
localised at Dalkeith House.   Lord Brougham, for
example, has preserved a story of Smith breaking out
at dinner into a strong condemnation of the public
conduct of some leading statesman of the day, then
suddenly stopping short on perceiving that statesman's

[1] Sinclair's *Life of Sir John Sinclair*, i. 37.

nearest relation on the opposite side of the table, and presently losing self-recollection again and muttering to himself, " Deil care, deil care, it's all true." Or there is the less pointed story told by Archdeacon Sinclair of another occasion when Smith was dining at Dalkeith, and two sons of Lord Dorchester were of the company. The conversation all turned on Lord Dorchester's estates and Lord Dorchester's affairs, and at last Smith interposed and said, " Pray, who is Lord Dorchester? I have never heard so much of him before." The former anecdote shows at once that Smith was in the habit of speaking his mind with considerable plainness, and that he shrank at the same time from everything like personal discourtesy; and the latter, like other stories of his absence of mind, is hardly worth repeating, except for showing that he continued to possess a redeeming infirmity.

From Dalkeith Smith returns to Kirkcaldy and his work. We find him in 1768 in correspondence with the Duke's law-agent, Mr. A. Campbell, W.S., and with Sir James Johnstone of Westerhall, about some investigation, apparently of no public importance, into the genealogy of the Scotts, in connection with which he first got Campbell to make a search in the charter-room of Dalkeith for ancient papers connected with the Scotts of Thirlestane, and then wanted to know the explanation Sir James Johnstone had given of Scott of Davington's claim as heir of Rennaldburn upon the Duke of Buccleugh.[1] It shows Smith, however, taking an interest, as if he were entitled to do so, in the business affairs of the Duke. We find him too in correspondence with Lord Hailes on historical points of some consequence to the economic inquiries he was now busy upon. Lord Hailes was one of the precursors of sound historical investigation in this country, and to Smith, with whom he was long intimate,

[1] Fraser's *Scotts of Buccleuch*, I. lxxxviii., II. 406.

he afterwards paid the curious compliment of translating his letter to Strahan on the death of Hume into Latin.

Of Smith's correspondence with Hailes only two letters have been preserved. The first is as follows :—

KIRKALDY, *5th March* 1769.

MY LORD—I should now be extremely obliged to your Lordship if you would send me the papers you mentioned upon the prices of provisions in former times. In order that the conveyance may be perfectly secure, if your Lordship will give me leave I shall send my own servant sometime this week to receive them at your Lordship's house at Edinburgh. I have not been able to get the papers in the cause of Lord Galloway and Lord Morton. If your Lordship is possessed of them it would likewise be a great obligation if you would send me them. I shall return both as soon as possible. If your Lordship will give me leave I shall transcribe the manuscript papers ; this, however, entirely depends upon your Lordship.

Since the last time I had the honour of writing to your Lordship I have read over with more care than before the Acts of James I., and compared them with your Lordship's remarks. From this last I have received both much pleasure and much instruction. Your Lordship's remarks will, I plainly see, be of much more use to me than, I am afraid, mine will be to you. I have read law entirely with a view to form some general notion of the great outlines of the plan according to which justice has been administered in different ages and nations ; and I have entered very little into the detail of particulars of which I see your Lordship is very much master. Your Lordship's particular facts will be of great use to correct my general views ; but the latter, I fear, will always be too vague and superficial to be of much use to your Lordship.

I have nothing to add to what your Lordship has observed upon the Acts of James I. They are framed in general in a much ruder and more inaccurate manner than either the English statutes or French ordinances of the same period ; and Scotland seems to have been, even during this vigorous reign, as our historians represent it, in greater disorder than either France or England had been from the time of the Danish and Norwegian incursions. The 5, 24, 56, and 85 statutes seem all to attempt a remedy to one and the same abuse. Travelling, from the disorders of the country, must have been extremely dangerous, and consequently very rare. Few people therefore would propose to live by entertaining travellers, and consequently there would be few or no inns. Travellers would be obliged to have recourse to the hospitality of private families in the same manner as in all other barbarous countries ; and being in this situation real objects of compassion, private families would think themselves obliged to receive them even though this hospitality was extremely oppressive. Strangers, says Homer, are sacred persons, and under the protection of Jupiter, but no wise man would ever choose to send for a stranger unless he was a bard or a soothsayer. The danger too of travelling either alone or with few attendants made all men of consequence carry along with them a numerous suite of retainers, which rendered this hospitality still more oppressive. Hence the orders to build hostellaries in 24 and 85 ; and as many people had chosen to follow the old fashion and to live rather at the expense of other people than at their own, hence the complaint of the keepers of the hostellaries and the order thereupon in Act 85.

I cannot conclude this letter, though already too long, without expressing to your Lordship my concern, and still more my indignation, at what has lately passed both at London and at Edinburgh. I have often thought that the Supreme Court of the United Kingdom very much resembled a jury. The law lords generally take upon them to sum up the evidence and to explain the law to the other peers, who generally follow their opinion implicitly. Of the two law lords who upon this occasion instructed them, the one has always run after the applause of the mob ; the other, by far the most intelligent, has always shown the greatest dread of popular odium, which, however, he has not been able to avoid. His inclinations also have always been suspected to favour one of the parties. He has upon this occasion, I suspect, followed rather his fears and his inclinations than his judgment. I could say a great deal more upon this subject to your Lordship, but I am afraid I have already said too much. I would rather, for my own part, have the solid reputation of your most respectable president, though exposed to the insults of a brutal mob, than all the vain and ·flimsy applause that has ever yet been bestowed upon either or both the other two.—I have the honour to be, with the highest esteem and regard, my Lord, your Lordship's most obliged and obedient servant,

ADAM SMITH.[1]

[1] Brougham's *Men of Letters*, ii. 219.

A week later Smith wrote Lord Hailes another letter, "giving," says Lord Brougham, "what is evidently the beginning of his speculations on the price of silver," but the letter seems to be now lost, and Lord Brougham quotes from it only the following sentences on the Douglas cause. "If the rejoicings which I read of in the public papers in different places on account of the Douglas cause, had no more foundation than those which were said to have been in this place, there has been very little joy upon the occasion. There was here no sort of rejoicing of any kind, unless four schoolboys having set up three candles upon the trone by way of an illumination, is to be considered as such."[1]

The first of these letters was written almost immediately after Smith heard of the decision of the House of Lords in the famous Douglas case. The news of the decision only reached Edinburgh on the 2nd of March, and was received with such popular enthusiasm that the whole city was illuminated. Smith walking by the shore at Kirkcaldy would have seen the bonfires blazing on Salisbury Crags, and he seems to have heard before writing that the house of the Lord President of the Court of Session, who was opposed to the Douglas claim, was attacked by the mob, and the President himself insulted next morning in the street on his way to Court. No civil lawsuit ever excited so much popular interest or feeling. The question, it will be remembered, was whether Mr. Douglas, who had been served heir to the estates of the late Duke of Douglas, was really the son of the Duke's sister, Lady Jane, by her husband, Sir John Stewart of Grandtully, whom she had secretly married abroad when she was already fifty years old, or whether he was an impostor, the son of a Frenchwoman, whom Lady Jane had brought up as her own son with a view to the inheritance of those estates. Everybody in Scotland was for the time either a Douglas or a Hamilton,

[1] Brougham's *Men of Letters*, ii. 219.

and the sentimental elements in the case had enlisted popular sympathy strongly on the Douglas side. Smith, as will be seen from those letters, was quite as strong and even impassioned a partisan on the unpopular and losing side, and Lord Hailes having been one of the judges who voted with the Lord President for the decision against Mr. Douglas which the House of Lords now reversed, he feels he can give free vent to his disappointment. Brougham, in publishing the letters, calls the opinion Smith gives not only "very strong" but "very rash," and his impeachment of the impartiality of the two great English judges — Lord Camden and Lord Mansfield — cannot seem defensible. But David Hume, though a Tory and an Under Secretary of State, is not a whit less sparing in his denunciation of those two law lords and in his contempt for the general body of the peers than Smith. "To one who understands the case as I do," he writes to Dr. Blair, "nothing could appear more scandalous than the pleading of the two law lords. Such curious misrepresentation, such impudent assertions, such groundless imputations, never came from that place ; but they were good enough for the audience, who, bating their quality, are most of them little better than their brothers the Wilkites of the streets."

Hume, having lost his place with a change of ministry, returned to Edinburgh for good in August 1769, and presently wrote Smith inviting him over :—

JAMES'S COURT, 20*th August* 1769.

DEAR SMITH—I am glad to have come within sight of you, and to have a view of Kirkaldy from my windows, but as I wish also to be within speaking terms of you, I wish we could concert measures for that purpose. I am miserably sick at sea, and regard with horror and a kind of hydrophobia the great gulf that lies between us. I am also tired of travelling as much as you ought naturally to be of staying at home. I therefore propose to you to come hither and pass some days with me in this solitude. I want to know what you have been doing, and purpose to exact a rigorous account of the method in which you have employed yourself during your retreat. I am positive you are in the wrong in many of your speculations, especially when you have the misfortune to differ from me. All these are reasons for our meeting, and I wish you would make me some reasonable proposal for that purpose. There is no habitation on the island of Inchkeith, otherwise I should challenge you to meet me on that spot, and neither of us ever to leave the place till we were fully agreed on all points of controversy. I expect General Conway here to-morrow, whom I shall attend to Roseneath, and I shall remain there a few days. On my return I expect to find a letter from you containing a bold acceptance of this defiance. I am, dear Smith, yours sincerely.[1]

Smith seems to have made such progress with his work in the two years of what Hume here calls his retreat at Kirkcaldy that in the beginning of 1770 there was some word of his going up with it to London for publication. For on the 6th of February Hume again writes him : "What is the meaning of this, dear Smith, which we hear, that you are not to be here above a day or two on your passage to London? How can you so much as entertain a thought of publishing a book full of reason, sense, and learning to those wicked abandoned madmen?"[2]

He had probably completed his first draft of the work from beginning to end, but he kept constantly amplifying and altering parts of it for six years more. He did not go to London in 1770, if he ever contemplated doing so, but he came to Edinburgh and received the freedom of the city in June. He seems to have received this honour for the merits of the Duke of Buccleugh rather than for his own. For the entry in the minutes of the Council of 6th June 1770 runs thus : "Appoint the Dean of Guild and his Council to admit and receive their Graces the Duke of Buccleugh and the Duke of Montagu in the most ample form, for good services done by them and their noble ancestors to the kingdome. And also Adam Smith, LL.D., and

---

[1] Burton's *Life of Hume*, ii. 429.   [2] *Ibid.*, ii. 433.

the Reverend Mr. John Hallam to be Burgesses and Gild Brethren of this city in the most ample form.

(Signed)   JAMES STUART, Provost."

The Duke of Montagu was the Duke of Buccleugh's father-in-law, and the Rev. Mr. John Hallam—afterwards Dean of Windsor, and father of Henry Hallam, the historian—was the Duke's tutor at Eton, as Adam Smith was his tutor abroad. The freedom was therefore given to the Duke of Buccleugh and party. Smith's burgess-ticket is one of the few relics of him still extant; it is possessed by Professor Cunningham of Belfast.

Smith promised Hume a visit about Christmas 1771, but the visit was postponed in consequence of the illness of Hume's sister, and on the 28th of January he received the following letter, in reply apparently to a request for the address of the Comtesse de Boufflers in Paris :—

EDINBURGH, 28*th January* 1772.

DEAR SMITH—I should certainly before this time have challenged the Performance of your Promise of being with me about Christmas had it not been for the misfortunes of my family. Last month my sister fell dangerously ill of a fever, and though the fever be now gone, she is still so weak and low, and recovers so slowly, that I was afraid it would be but a melancholy house to invite you to. However, I expect that time will reinstate her in her former health, in which case I shall look for your company. I shall not take any excuse from your own state of health, which I suppose only a subterfuge invented by indolence and love of solitude. Indeed, my dear Smith, if you continue to hearken to complaints of this nature, you will cut yourself out entirely from human society, to the great loss of both parties.

The Lady's Direction is Mᵉ la Comtesse de B., Douanière au Temple. She has a daughter-in-law, which makes it requisite to distinguish her.—Yours sincerely,   DAVID HUME.

P.S.—I have not yet read *Orlando Inamorato*. I am now in a course of reading the Italian historians, and am confirmed in my former opinion that that language has not produced one author who knew how to write elegant correct prose though it contains several excellent poets. You say nothing to me of your own work.[1]

Smith seems to have perhaps sent him _Orlando Inamorato_, or at any rate to have been previously in communication, either by letter or conversation, on the subject, for the Italian poets were favourite reading of his. But a more important point in the letter is the indication it affords that Smith's labours and solitude were beginning to tell on the state of his health. Indeed, poor health had now become one of the chief causes of his delay in finishing his work, and it continued to go from bad to worse. He writes his friend Pulteney in September that his book would have been ready for the press by the first of that winter if it were not for the interruptions caused by bad health, " arising," he says, " from want of amusement and from thinking too much upon one thing," together with other interruptions of an equally anxious nature, occasioned by his endeavours to extricate some of his personal friends from the difficulties in which they were involved by the commercial crisis of that time.

KIRKALDY, _5th September_ 1772.

MY DEAR PULTENEY—I have received your most friendly letter in due course, and I have delayed a great deal too long to answer it. Though I have had no concern myself in the Public calamities, some of the friends in whom I interest myself the most have been deeply concerned in them ; and my attention has been a good deal occupied about the most proper method of extricating them.

In the Book which I am now preparing for the press I have treated fully and distinctly of every part of the subject which you have recommended to me ; and I intended to send you some extracts from it ; but upon looking them over I find that they are too much interwoven with other parts of the work to be easily separated from it. I have the same opinion of Sir James Stewart's book that you have. Without once mentioning it, I flatter myself

---

[1] _Hume MSS._, R.S.E. Library. Partially published by Burton.

that any fallacious principle in it will meet with a clear and distinct confutation in mine.[1]

I think myself very much honoured and obliged to you for having mentioned me to the E. India Directors as a person who would be of use to them. You have acted in your old way of doing your friends a good office behind their backs, pretty much as other people do them a bad one. There is no labour of any kind which you can impose upon me which I will not readily undertake. By what Mr. Stewart and Mr. Ferguson hinted to me concerning your notice of the proper remedy for the disorders of the coin in Bengal, I believe our opinions upon that subject are perfectly the same.

My book would have been ready for the press by the beginning of this winter, but interruptions occasioned partly by bad health, arising from want of amusement and from thinking too much upon one thing, and partly by the avocations above mentioned, will oblige me to retard its publication for a few months longer.— I ever am, my dearest Pulteney, most faithfully and affectionately your obliged servant,   ADAM SMITH.

To WILLIAM PULTENEY, Esq., *Member of Parliament,*
          BATH HOUSE, LONDON.[2]

The public calamities to which Smith refers in the opening paragraph of his letter are the bankruptcies of the severe commercial crisis of that year, and the friends he was so much occupied in extricating from its results were, I think it most likely, the family of Buccleugh. The crash was especially disastrous in Scotland; only three private banks in Edinburgh out of thirty survived it, and a large joint-stock bank, Douglas Heron and Company, started only three years before, for the public-spirited purpose of promoting improvements, particularly improvements of land, now seemed to shake all commercial Scotland with its fall. In this company the Duke of Buccleugh was one of the largest shareholders, and,

---

[1] Sir James Steuart's *Inquiry into the Principles of Political Economy* was published in 1767.

[2] Published by Professor Thorold Rogers in the *Academy* of 28th February 1885.

liability being unlimited, it was impossible to foresee how much of its £800,000 of liabilities his Grace might be eventually called upon to pay. The suggestion that Smith was much consulted by the Duke and his advisers about this grave business is to some extent confirmed by the familiarity which he shows with the whole circumstances of this bank at the time of its failure in the second chapter of the second book of the *Wealth of Nations*.

The situation for which Pulteney had recommended him to the Court of Directors of the East India Company was, no doubt, a place as member of the Special Commission of Supervision which they then contemplated establishing. In 1772 the East India Company was in extremities; in July they were nearly a million and a half sterling behind for their next quarter's payments; and they proposed to send out to India a commission of three independent and competent men, with full authority to institute a complete examination into every detail of the administration, and to exercise a certain supervision and control of the whole. Burke had already been offered one of the seats on this commission, but had refused it on finding that Lord Rockingham was unwilling to part with him; and at the time this letter was written two of Smith's own Scotch friends, whose names he happens to mention in the letter—Adam Ferguson and Andrew Stuart, M.P.—were actually candidates for the places, and had apparently been recently seeing Pulteney in London on the subject. Pulteney, who had great influence at the India House, had probably mentioned the names of Smith, Ferguson, and Stuart to the Court of Directors at the same time, and if so, that must have been at least two months before Smith wrote this letter, for Ferguson was in the month of July getting influence brought to bear on the Edinburgh Town Council to secure their permission to retain his professorship in the event of his going to India.[1] Ferguson pushed his candidature vigorously, and

[1] *Caldwell Papers*, iii. 207.

went to London repeatedly about it between July and November, but Smith, although he would have accepted the post if he received the offer of it, does not seem to have taken any steps to procure it, and did not even answer Pulteney's letter till September. Stuart's candidature was defeated, Horace Walpole says, by Lord Mansfield, but eventually no appointment was made, because Parliament intervened, and forbade any such commission to be sent out at all.

In sending the letter to the *Academy* for publication Professor Rogers observes that it is plain the delay in the publication of the *Wealth of Nations* was due to the negotiations which Mr. Pulteney was evidently making for the purpose of getting Smith appointed to this place. "Had he succeeded," proceeds Mr. Rogers, "it is probable that the *Wealth of Nations* would never have seen the light ; for every one knows that in the first and second books of that work the East India Company is criticised with the greatest severity. . . . I have no doubt that owing to Pulteney's negotiations it lay unrevised and unaltered during four years in the author's desk."

With all respect, this is a strange remark to fall from an editor of the *Wealth of Nations*, for the evidences of continuous revision and alteration during those four years are very numerous in the text of the work itself. He made many changes or additions in 1773 ; for example, the remarks on the price of hides,[1] in the chapter on Rent, were written in February 1773 ; and those on the decline of sugar-refining in colonies taken from the French, in the chapter on the Colonies,[2] were written in October ; while the passage on American wages, in the chapter on Wages, was inserted some time in the same year. The extensive additions in the chapters on the Revenue, occasioned by reading the *Mémoires concernant les Droits*, must have been written after 1774, because Smith probably obtained that

[1] *Wealth of Nations*, Book I. chap. xi.
[2] *Ibid.*, Book IV. chap. vii.

book after Turgot became Minister in the middle of that
year; his remarks, in the chapter on Colonies, on the
effects of recent events on the trade with North America,[1]
and his remarks on the Irish revenue in the chapter on
Public Debts, were added in 1775.[2] The chapter on the
Regulated Companies, in which the East India Company
receives most systematic attention, and which did not
appear in the first edition of the book, was apparently not
written till 1782.[3]

The book therefore did not lie "unrevised and
unaltered" in the author's desk from 1772 to 1776; on
the contrary, the chief cause of the four years' delay was
the revision and alteration to which it was being incessantly
subjected during that whole term. The particular Indian
appointment for which Pulteney had recommended him
could have nothing to do with the delay, inasmuch as the
proposed office was suppressed altogether within two months
after this letter was written; and even if he entertained
expectations of any other sort from the East India Company, there is no reason why he should on that account
have withheld his work from publication. The more
elaborate criticism of that Company in the chapter on
Public Works did not appear in the original edition of the
book at all, but the only remarks on Indian administration
which did appear in that edition, although they are merely
incidental in character, are very strong and decided, and
might easily have been omitted, had the author been so
minded, to please the Company, without any injury to the
general argument with which they are connected.

On the other hand, there exists abundance of evidence
that Smith was busy for most of three years after this date,
and mainly in London, altering, improving, and adding
to the manuscript of the book. New lines of investigation
would suggest themselves, new theories to be thought out,
and the task would grow day by day by a very simple but

---

[1] *Wealth of Nations*, Book IV. chap. vii.
[2] *Ibid.*, Book V. chap. iii.   [3] *Ibid.*, Book V. chap. i.

unforeseen process of natural accretion. Hume thought it near completion in 1769 ; but towards the end of 1772, a couple of months after Smith's answer to Pulteney, he gives it most of another year yet for being finished. He writes from his new quarters in St. Andrew Square, asking Smith to break off his studies for a few weeks' relaxation with him in Edinburgh about Christmas, and then to return and finish his work before the following autumn.

ST. ANDREW'S SQUARE, 23rd *November* 1772.

DEAR SMITH—I should agree to your Reasoning if I could trust your Resolution. Come hither for some weeks about Christmas ; dissipate yourself a little ; return to Kirkaldy ; finish your work before autumn ; go to London, print it, return and settle in this town, which suits your studious, independent turn even better than London. Execute this plan faithfully, and I forgive you. . . .

Ferguson has returned fat and fair and in good humour, notwithstanding his disappointment,[1] which I am glad of. He comes over next week to a house in this neighbourhood. Pray come over this winter and join us.—I am, my dear Smith, ever yours,

DAVID HUME.[2]

While Pulteney was suggesting Smith's name for employment under the East India Company, Baron Mure was trying to secure his services as tutor to the Duke of Hamilton, and Lord Stanhope possibly offered him the position of tutor to his lordship's ward, the young Earl of Chesterfield. Baron Mure was one of the guardians of the young Duke of Hamilton (the son of the beautiful Miss Gunning), and had in that capacity had the chief responsibility in raising and carrying on the great Douglas cause. He was a man of great sagacity and weight, whom we have seen in communication with Hume and Oswald on economic subjects ; he had long been also on terms of personal intimacy with Smith, and he seems to have been anxious in 1772 to send Smith abroad with the Duke of Hamilton, as he

---

[1] From the suppression of the Indian supervisorship ; see p. 255.
[2] *Hume MSS.*, R.S.E. Library.

had already been sent abroad with the Duke of Buccleugh.
Smith would appear to have been sounded on the subject,
and even to have given what was considered a favourable
reply, for Andrew Stuart, a fellow-guardian of the Duke
along with Mure, writes the latter acknowledging receipt
of his letter " intimating "—these are the words—" the
practicability of having Mr. Smith," but the Duke's mother
(then Duchess of Argyle) and the Duke himself preferred
Dr. John Moore, the author of *Zelucco*, who was the
family medical attendant, and was indeed chosen because
he could act in that capacity to his very delicate young
charge, though he was strictly required to drop the
" doctor," and was severely censured by the Duchess for
assisting at a surgical operation in Geneva, inasmuch as if it
got known that he was a medical man it would be a bar to
their reception in the best society.[1]   Accordingly Mure
was told that it was " the united opinion of all concerned
that matters go no further with Mr. Smith."

   The circumstance that so wise and practical a head as
Baron Mure's should have thought of Smith for this post
is at least a proof that the Buccleugh tutorship had been a
success, and that Smith was not considered by other men
of the world who knew him well as being so unfit for the
situation of travelling tutor as some of his friends thought
him.

   During this period of severe study in Kirkcaldy his
fits of absence might be expected to recur occasionally, and
Dr. Charles Rogers relates an anecdote of one of them,
which may be repeated here, though Dr. Rogers omits
mentioning any authority for it ; and stories of that kind
must naturally be accepted with scruples, because they are
so apt to agglomerate round any person noted for the
failing they indicate.

   According to Dr. Rogers, however, Smith, during his
residence in Kirkcaldy, went out one Sunday morning in
his dressing-gown to walk in the garden, but once in the

[1] *Caldwell Papers*, i. 192.

garden he went on to the path leading to the turnpike road, and then to the road itself, along which he continued in a condition of reverie till he reached Dunfermline, fifteen miles distant, just as the bells were sounding and the people were proceeding to church. The strange sound of the bells was the first thing that roused the philosopher from the meditation in which he was immersed.[1] The story is very open to criticism, but if correct it points to sleepless nights and an incapacity to get a subject out of the head, due to over-application.

The persistency of his occupation with his book, according to Robert Chambers in his *Picture of Scotland*, left a mark on the wall of his study which remained there till the room was repainted shortly before that author, wrote of it in 1827. Chambers says that it was Smith's habit to compose *standing*, and to dictate to an amanuensis. He usually stood with his back to the fire, and unconsciously in the process of thought used to make his head vibrate, or rather, rub sidewise against the wall above the chimney-piece. His head being dressed, in the ordinary style of that period, with pomatum, could not fail to make a mark on the wall.

M'Culloch says Smith dictated the *Wealth of Nations* but did not dictate the *Theory of Moral Sentiments*. Whether he had any external ground for making this assertion I cannot tell, and, apart from such, the probability would seem to be that if he dictated his lectures in Edinburgh to an amanuensis, as seems probable, as well as his *Wealth of Nations*, he would have done the same with his *Theory*. But M'Culloch professes to see internal evidences of this difference of manual method in the different style of the respective works. Moore met M'Culloch one evening at Longman's, and they were discussing writers who were in the habit of dictating as they composed. One of the party said the habit of dictating always bred a diffuse style, and M'Culloch supported this view by the example

[1] Rogers' *Social Life of Scotland*, iii. 181.

of Adam Smith, whose *Wealth of Nations*, he said, was very diffuse because it had been dictated, while his *Theory*, which was not dictated, was admirable in style. But in reality there is probably more diffuse writing in the *Theory* than in the *Wealth of Nations*, which is for the most part packed tightly enough. Another Scotch critic, Archibald Alison the elder, the author of the *Essay on Taste*, even surpasses M'Culloch in his keenness in detecting the effects of this dictating habit. He says that Smith used to walk up and down the room while he dictated, and that the consequence is that his sentences are nearly all the same length, each containing as much as the amanuensis could write down while the author took a single turn.[1] This is excessive acuteness. Smith's sentences are not by any means all of one length, or all of the same construction. It need only be added that the habit of dictating would in his case arise naturally from his slow and laboured penmanship.

As I have mentioned the house in which the *Wealth of Nations* was composed, it may be added that it stood in the main street of the town, but its garden ran down to the beach, and that it was only pulled down in 1844, without anybody in the place realising at the moment, though it has been a cause of much regret since, that they were suffering their most interesting association to be destroyed. An engraving of it, however, exists.

[1] Sinclair's *Old Times and Distant Places*, p. 9.

CHAPTER XVII

LONDON

1773–1776.   *Aet.* 50–53

In the spring of 1773, Smith, having, as he thought, virtually completed the *Wealth of Nations*, set out with the manuscript for London, to give it perhaps some finishing touches and then place it in the hands of a publisher. But his labours had told so seriously on his health and spirits that he thought it not improbable he might die, and even die suddenly, before the work got through the press, and he wrote Hume a formal letter before he started on his journey, constituting him his literary executor, and giving him directions about the destination of the various unpublished manuscripts that lay in his depositories :—

My dear Friend—As I have left the care of all my literary papers to you, I must tell you that except those which I carry along with me, there are none worth the publishing but a fragment of a great work which contains a history of the astronomical systems that were successively in fashion down to the time of Descartes. Whether that might not be published as a fragment of an intended juvenile work I leave entirely to your judgment, tho’ I begin to suspect myself that there is more refinement than solidity in some parts of it. This little work you will find in a thin folio paper book in my writing-desk in my book-room. All the other loose paper which you will find either in that desk or within the glass folding-doors of a bureau which stands in my bedroom, together with about eighteen thin paper folio books, which you will likewise find within the same glass folding-doors, I desire may be destroyed without any examination. Unless I die very suddenly,

I shall take care that the Papers I carry with me shall be carefully sent to you.—I ever am, my dear friend, most faithfully yours,

ADAM SMITH.

EDINBURGH, 16*th April* 1773.

To DAVID HUME, Esq., 9 St. Andrew's Square, Edinburgh.[1]

Smith went to London shortly after writing this letter, and spent most of the next four years there. We find him there in May 1773, for he is admitted to the Royal Society on the 27th of that month ; he is there in September, for Ferguson then writes to him as if he were still there. He is there in February 1774, for Hume writes him in that month, " Pray what accounts are these we hear of Franklyn's conduct ? "—a question he would hardly have addressed except to one in a better position for hearing the truth about Franklin than he was himself. He is there in September 1774, for he writes Cullen from town in that month, and speaks of having been for some time in it. He is there in January 1775, for on the 11th Bishop Percy met him at dinner at Sir Joshua Reynolds', along with Johnson, Burke, Gibbon, and others.[2] He is there in February, for a young friend, Patrick Clason, addresses a letter to him during that month to the care of Cadell, the bookseller, in the Strand. He is there in December, for on the 27th Horace Walpole writes the Countess of Ossory that " Adam Smith told us t'other night at Beauclerk's that Major Preston—one of two, but he is not sure which—would have been an excellent commander some years hence if he had seen any service. I said it was a pity that the war had not been put off till the Major should be

---

[1] *Hume MSS.*, R.S.E. Library.

[2] Add. MSS., 32,336. It must have been during this period that Smith entertained Reynolds at dinner at Mrs. Hill's, Dartmouth Street, Westminster, on Sunday 11th March, and not, as Mr. Tom Taylor places it, in 1764, from finding the dinner engagement noted on " a tiny old-fashioned card bearing the name of ' Mr. Adam Smith ' " lying in one of Reynolds' pocket-books for 1764. In March 1764 Smith, as we know, was in France, and Mr. Taylor must have mistaken the year for 1774, unless, indeed, it may have been 1767.

some years older." [1]　He returned to Scotland in April
1776, about a month after his book was issued, but we
find him back again in London in January 1777, for his
letter to Governor Pownall in that month is dated from
Suffolk Street.　Whether the first three years of his stay
in London was continuous I cannot say, but it would
almost appear so from the circumstance that nothing
remains to indicate the contrary.

Those three years were spent upon the *Wealth of
Nations*.　Much of the book as we know it must have
been written in London.　When he went up to London
he had no idea that any fresh investigations he contemplated instituting there would detain him so long.　He
wrote Pulteney, as we have seen, even in the previous
September that the book would be finished in a few
months, and he led not only Hume but Adam Ferguson
also to look for its publication in 1773.　In a footnote to
the fourth edition of his *History of Civil Society*, published
in that year, Ferguson says, " The public will probably soon
be furnished (by Mr. Smith, author of the *Theory of Moral
Sentiments*) with a theory of national economy equal to
what has ever appeared on any subject of science whatever."　But the researches the author now made in
London must have been much more important than he
expected, and have occasioned extensive alterations and
additions, so that Hume, in congratulating him on the
eventual appearance of the work in 1776, writes, " It is
probably much improved by your last abode in London."
Whole chapters seem to have been put through the forge
afresh ; and on some of them the author has tool-marked
the date of his handiwork himself.

A very circumstantial account of Smith's London
labours at the book comes from America.　Mr. Watson,
author of the *Annals of Philadelphia*, says: " Dr. Franklin once told Dr. Logan that the celebrated Adam Smith
when writing his *Wealth of Nations* was in the habit of

[1] Walpole's *Letters*, vi. 302.

bringing chapter after chapter as he composed it to himself, Dr. Price, and others of the literati ; then patiently hear their observations and profit by their discussions and criticisms, sometimes submitting to write whole chapters anew, and even to reverse some of his propositions." [1]

Franklin's remark may have itself undergone enlargement before it appeared in print, but though it may have been exaggerated, there seems no ground for rejecting it altogether. Smith became acquainted with Franklin in Edinburgh in 1759, and could not fail to see much of him in London, because some of the most intimate of his own London friends, Sir John Pringle and Strahan, for example, were also among the most intimate friends of Franklin. Then a considerable proportion of the additions, which we know from the text of the *Wealth of Nations* itself to have been made to the work during this London period, bear on colonial or American experience.[2] And as Smith always obtained a great deal of his information from the conversation of competent men, no one would be more likely than Franklin to be laid under contribution or to be able to contribute something worth learning on such questions. The biographer of Franklin states that his papers which belong to this particular period " contain sets of problems and queries as though jotted down at some meeting of philosophers for particular consideration at home," and then he adds : " A glance at the index of the *Wealth of Nations* will suffice to show that its author possessed just that kind of knowledge of the American Colonies which Franklin was of all men the best fitted to impart. The allusions to the Colonies may be counted by hundreds ; illustrations from their condition and growth occur in nearly every chapter. We may go further and say that the American Colonies constitute the experimental evidence of the essential truth of the book, without which many of its leading positions had been little

---

[1] Watson's *Annals of Philadelphia*, i. 533.
[2] See above, pp. 256-7.

more than theory."[1] It ought of course to be borne in mind that Smith had been in the constant habit of hearing much about the American Colonies and their affairs during his thirteen years in Glasgow from the intelligent merchants and returned planters of that city.

After coming to London Smith seems to have renewed his acquaintance with Lord Stanhope, who sought Smith's counsel as to a tutor for his ward the Earl of Chesterfield, and appointed Adam Ferguson on Smith's recommendation. The negotiations with Ferguson were conducted through Smith, and some of Ferguson's letters to Smith on the matter still exist, but contain nothing of any interest for the biography of the latter. But in contemplation of Ferguson's going abroad with the Earl of Chesterfield, Hume, ever anxious to have his friend near him, sounds Smith on the possibility of his agreeing to act during Ferguson's absence as his substitute in the Moral Philosophy chair at Edinburgh. Smith, however, was apparently unwilling to undertake that duty. As we have already seen, he was strongly opposed to professorial absenteeism, and in the present case it was associated with unpleasant circumstances. The Town Council, the administrators of the College, refused to sanction Ferguson's absence, and called upon him either to stay at home or to resign his chair. Ferguson merely snapped his fingers, appointed young Dugald Stewart his substitute, and went off on his travels, quietly remarking that fools and knaves were necessary in the world to give other people something to do. Hume's letter is as follows :—

St. Andrew's Square, 13*th February* 1774.

Dear Smith—You are in the wrong for never informing me of your intentions and resolutions, if you have fix'd any. I am now obliged to write to you on a subject without knowing whether the proposal, or rather Hint, which I am to give you be an absurdity or not. The settlement to be made on Ferguson is

---

[1] Parton's *Life of Franklin*, i. 537.

a very narrow compensation for his class if he must lose it.   He
wishes to keep it and to serve by a Deputy in his absence.   But
besides that this scheme will appear invidious and is really scarce
admissible, those in the Town Council who aim at filling the
vacancy with a friend will strenuously object to it, and he himself
cannot think of one who will make a proper substitute.   I fancy
that the chief difficulty would be removed if you could offer to
supply his class either as his substitute or his successor, with a
purpose of resigning upon his return.   This notion is entirely my
own, and shall never be known to Ferguson if it appear to you
improper.   I shall only say that he deserves this friendly treatment
by his friendly conduct of a similar kind towards poor Russell's
family.

Pray what strange accounts are these we hear of Franklyn's
conduct ?   I am very slow in believing that he has been guilty in
the extreme degree that is pretended, tho' I always knew him to
be a very factious man, and Faction next to Fanaticism is of all
passions the most destructive of morality.   I hear that Wedderburn's treatment of him before the Council was most cruel without
being in the least blamable.   What a pity ! [1]

Smith's headquarters in London, to which Hume's
letters to him were addressed, was the British Coffee-House
in Cockspur Street, a great Scotch resort in last century, kept,
as I have said, by a sister of his old Balliol friend, Bishop
Douglas, " a woman," according to Henry Mackenzie, " of
uncommon talents and the most agreeable conversation."
Wedderburn founded a weekly dining club in this house,
which Robertson and Carlyle used to frequent when they
came to town, and no doubt Smith would do the same,
for many of his Scotch friends belonged to it—Dr. William
Hunter, John Home, Robert Adam the architect, and Sir
Gilbert Elliot.   Indeed, though men like Goldsmith, Sir
Joshua Reynolds, Garrick, and Richard Cumberland were
members, it was predominantly a Scotch club, and both
Carlyle and Richard Cumberland say an extremely agree-
able one.   But during his residence at this period in
London Smith was in 1775 admitted to the membership

[1] *Hume MSS.*, R.S.E. Library.

of a much more famous club, the Literary Club of John-son and Burke and Reynolds at the Turk's Head in Gerrard Street, and he no doubt attended their fortnightly dinners. The only members present on the night of his election were Beauclerk, Gibbon, Sir William Jones, and Sir Joshua Reynolds. Boswell, writing his friend Temple on 28th April 1776, immediately after the *Wealth of Nations* was published, says, " Smith too is now of our club. It has lost its select merit." But another member of the club, Dean Barnard—husband of the authoress of " Auld Robin Gray "—appreciates his worth better, though he wrote the lines in which his appreciation occurs before the *Wealth of Nations* appeared, and his words may therefore be taken perhaps to convey the impression made by Smith's conversation. One of the Dean's verses runs—

> If I have thoughts and can't express 'em,
> Gibbon shall teach me how to dress 'em
>   In form select and terse ;
> Jones teach me modesty and Greek,
> Smith how to think, Burke how to speak,
>   And Beauclerk to converse.

Smith's conversation seems, from all the accounts we have of it, to have been the conversation of a thinker, often lecturing rather than talk, but always instructive and solid. William Playfair, the brother of Professor John Playfair, the mathematician, says, " Those persons who have ever had the pleasure to be in his company may recollect that even in his common conversation the order and method he pursued without the smallest degree of formality or stiffness were beautiful, and gave a sort of pleasure to all who listened to him." [1]

Bennet Langton mentions the " decisive professorial manner " in which he was used to talk, and according to Boswell, Topham Beauclerk conceived a high opinion of

[1] Playfair's edition of *Wealth of Nations*, I. xiii.

Smith's conversation at first, but afterwards lost it, for reasons unreported, though if Beauclerk was himself, as Dean Barnard indicates, the model converser of the club, he would probably grow tired of expository lectures, however excellent and instructive. A criticism of Garrick's is more curious. After listening to Smith one evening, the great player turned to a friend and whispered, "What say you to this? eh, flabby, eh?" but whatever may have been the case that particular evening, flabbiness at least was not a characteristic of Smith's talk. It erred rather in excess of substance. He had Johnson's solidity and weight, without Johnson's force and vivacity. Henry Mackenzie, author of the *Man of Feeling*, talking of Smith soon after his death with Samuel Rogers, said of him, "With a most retentive memory, his conversation was solid beyond that of any man. I have often told him after half an hour's conversation, 'Sir, you have said enough to make a book.'"[1] His conversation, moreover, was particularly wide in its range. Dugald Stewart says that though Smith seldom started a topic of conversation, there were few topics raised on which he was not found contributing something worth hearing, and Boswell, no very partial witness, admits that his talk evinced "a mind crowded with all manner of subjects." Like Sir Walter Scott, Smith has been unjustly accused of habitually abstaining from conversing on the subjects he had made his own. Boswell tells us that Smith once said to Sir Joshua Reynolds that he made it a rule in company never to talk of what he understood, and he alleges the reason to have been that Smith had bookmaking ever in his mind, and the fear of the plagiarist ever before his eyes. But the fact thus reported by Boswell cannot be accepted exactly as he reports it, and his explanation cannot be accepted at all. Men able to converse on a variety of subjects will naturally prefer to converse on those unconnected with their own shop, because they go into company for diver-

[1] Clayden's *Early Life of Samuel Rogers*, p. 168.

sion from their own shop, but it is a question of company and circumstances. If Smith ever made any such rule as Boswell speaks of, he certainly seems to have honoured it as often by the breach as by the observance, for when his friends brought round the conversation to his special lines of research, he never seems to have failed to give his ideas quite freely, nay, as may be seen from the remark just quoted from Henry Mackenzie, not freely merely but abundantly—as many as would make a book. He does not appear to have been in this respect a grudging giver. I have already quoted his remark on hearing of Blair's borrowing some of his juridical ideas, "There's enough left." When Sir John Sinclair was writing his *History of the Revenue* Smith offered him the use of everything, either printed or manuscript, in his possession bearing upon the subject. And if it is true that he was discussing his own book chapter by chapter with Franklin, Price, and others, about the very period when this remark to Sir Joshua purports to have been made, it appears most unlikely that he could have thought of setting any churlish watch on his lips in ordinary conversation. But however it be with his disposition to talk about his own pursuits, we know from Dugald Stewart that he was very fond of talking of subjects remote from them, and as Stewart says, he was never more entertaining than when he gave a loose rein to his speculation on subjects off his own line. "Nor do I think," says Stewart, "I shall be accused of going too far when I say that he was scarcely ever known to start a new topic himself, or to appear unprepared upon those topics that were introduced by others. Indeed, his conversation was never more amusing than when he gave a loose rein to his genius upon the very few branches of knowledge of which he only possessed the outlines."[1] One of his defects, according to both Stewart and Carlyle, was his poor penetration into personal character ; but he was very fond of drawing the character of any person whose name came

[1] *Works*, v. 519.

up in conversation, and Stewart says his judgments of this kind, though always decided and lively, were generally too systematic to be just, leaning ever, however, to charity's side, and erring by partiality rather than prejudice ; while Carlyle completes the description by stating that when any one challenged or disputed his opinion of a character, he would retrace his steps with the greatest ease and nonchalance and contradict every word he had been saying. Carlyle's statement is confirmed by the remarks of certain of Smith's other friends who speak incidentally of the amusing inconsistencies in which he indulged in private conversation. He was fond of starting theories and supporting them, but it is not so easy to explain a man on a theory as to explain some abstract subject on a theory.

His voice seems to have been harsh, his utterance often stammering, and his manner, especially among strangers, often embarrassed, but many writers speak of the remarkable animation of his features as he warmed to his subject, and of the peculiar radiancy of his smile. " His smile of approbation," says Dr. Carlyle, " was captivating." " In the society of those he loved," says Stewart, " his features were often brightened with a smile of inexpressible benignity."

While living in London, Smith, along with Gibbon, attended Dr. William Hunter's lectures on anatomy,[1] as we are told by a writer who was one of Hunter's students at the time, and during that very period he had an opportunity of vindicating the value of the lectures of private teachers of medicine like Hunter against pretensions to monopoly set up at the moment on behalf of the universities. In a long letter written to Cullen in September 1774 Smith defends with great vigour and vivacity the most absolute and unlimited freedom of medical education, treating the University claims as mere expressions of the craft spirit, and recognising none of those exceptional features of medical education which have constrained even

---

[1] Taylor's *Records of my Life*, ii. 262.

the most extreme partisans of economic liberty now to approve of government interference in that matter.

The letter was occasioned by an agitation which had been long gathering strength in Scotch medical circles against the laxity with which certain of the Scotch universities —St. Andrews and Aberdeen in particular—were in the habit of conferring their medical degrees. The candidate was not required either to attend classes or to pass an examination, but got the degree by merely paying the fees and producing a certificate of proficiency from two medical practitioners, into whose qualifications no inquiry was instituted. In London a special class of agent—the broker in Scotch degrees—sprang up to transact the business, and England was being overrun with a horde of Scotch doctors of medicine who hardly knew a vein from an artery, and had created south of the Border a deep prejudice against all Scotch graduates, even those from the unoffending Universities of Edinburgh and Glasgow. A case seemed to be brought home even to Edinburgh in the year 1771. The offender—one Leeds—had not, indeed, got his degree from Edinburgh without examination, but he showed his competency to be so doubtful in his duties at the London Hospital that the governors made it a condition of the continuance of his services that he should obtain the diploma of the London College of Physicians, and he failed to pass this London examination and was deprived of his post. This case created much sensation both in London and Edinburgh, and when the Duke of Buccleugh was elected an honorary Fellow of the College of Physicians of Edinburgh in 1774, he made that body something like an offer to take up the question of examination for medical degrees in Parliament and try what could be done to remove this reproach from his country. The College of Physicians thereupon drew up a memorial to Government for the Duke of Buccleugh to present, praying for the prohibition of the universities from granting medical degrees, except honorary ones, to any person in

absence, or to any person without first undergoing a
personal examination into his proficiency, and bringing a
certificate of having attended for two years at a university
where physic was regularly taught, and of having applied
himself to all branches of medical study. They add that
they fix on two years not because they think two years
enough, but because that was the term adopted by the
London College of Physicians, and they suggest the appointment of a royal commission of inquiry if Government is
not prepared for immediate action.

The Duke of Buccleugh sent the memorial for the
consideration of Adam Smith, and asked him to write to
Cullen his views on the subject. Smith thought that it was
not very practicable in any event for the public to obtain a
satisfactory test of medical efficiency, that it was certainly
not practicable if the competition by the private teachers
were suppressed, that otherwise the medical examination
might become as great a quackery as the medical degree,
and that the whole question was a mere squabble between
the big quack and the little one. He unfolds his views
in the following letter :—

DEAR DOCTOR—I have been very much in the wrong both
to you and to the Duke of Buccleugh, to whom I certainly
promised to write you in a post or two, for having delayed so long
to fulfil my promise. The truth is that some occurrences which
interested me a good deal, and which happened here immediately
after the Duke's departure, made me forget altogether a business
which, I do acknowledge, interested me very little.

In the present state of the Scotch universities I do most
sincerely look upon them as, in spite of all their faults, without
exception the best seminaries of learning that are to be found
anywhere in Europe. They are perhaps, upon the whole, as
unexceptionable as any public institutions of that kind, which all
contain in their very nature the seeds and causes of negligency
and corruption, have ever been or are ever likely to be. That,
however, they are still capable of amendment, and even of considerable amendment, I know very well, and a Visitation (that is,
a Royal Commission) is, I believe, the only proper means of

procuring them this amendment.   Before any wise man, however, would apply for the appointment of so arbitrary a tribunal
in order to improve what is already, upon the whole, very well, he
ought certainly to know with some degree of certainty, first, who
are likely to be appointed visitors, and secondly, what plan of
reformation those visitors are likely to follow ; but in the present
multiplicity of pretenders to some share in the prudential management of Scotch affairs, these are two points which, I apprehend,
neither you nor I, nor the Solicitor-General nor the Duke of
Buccleugh, can possibly know anything about.   In the present
state of our affairs, therefore, to apply for a Visitation in order to
remedy an abuse which is not perhaps of great consequence to the
public, would appear to me to be extremely unwise.   Hereafter,
perhaps, an opportunity may present itself for making such an
application with more safety.

With regard to an admonition, or threatening, or any other
method of interfering in the affairs of a body corporate which is
not perfectly and strictly regular and legal, these are expedients
which I am convinced neither his Majesty nor any of his present
Ministers would choose to employ either now or at any time
hereafter in order to obtain an object even of much greater consequence than this reformation of Scottish degrees.

You propose, I observe, that no person should be admitted to
examination for his degrees unless he brought a certificate of his
having studied at least two years in some university.   Would not
such a regulation be oppressive upon all private teachers, such as
the Hunters, Hewson, Fordyce, etc. ?   The scholars of such
teachers surely merit whatever honour or advantage a degree
can confer much more than the greater part of those who have
spent many years in some universities, where the different branches
of medical knowledge are either not taught at all, or are taught
so superficially that they had as well not be taught at all.   When
a man has learnt his lesson very well, it surely can be of little
importance where or from whom he has learnt it.

The monopoly of medical education which this regulation
would establish in favour of universities would, I apprehend, be
hurtful to the lasting prosperity of such bodies corporate.   Monopolists very seldom make good work, and a lecture which a certain
number of students must attend, whether they profit by it or no,
is certainly not very likely to be a good one.   I have thought a
great deal upon this subject, and have inquired very carefully into
the constitution and history of several of the principal universities
of Europe ; I have satisfied myself that the present state of degra-

dation and contempt into which the greater part of these societies
have fallen in almost every part of Europe arises principally, first,
from the large salaries which in some universities are given to
professors, and which render them altogether independent of
their diligence and success in their professions ; and secondly,
from the great number of students who, in order to get degrees
or to be admitted to exercise certain professions, or who, for the
sake of bursaries, exhibitions, scholarships, fellowships, etc., are
obliged to resort to certain societies of this kind, whether the
instructions which they are likely to receive there are or are not
worth the receiving.   All these different cases of negligence and
corruption no doubt take place in some degree in all our Scotch
universities.   In the best of them, however, these cases take place
in a much less degree than in the greater part of other considerable
societies of the same kind ; and I look upon this circumstance as
the real cause of their present excellence.   In the Medical College
of Edinburgh in particular the salaries of the professors are insignificant.   There are few or no bursaries or exhibitions, and their
monopoly of degrees is broken in upon by all other universities,
foreign and domestic.   I require no other explication of its
present acknowledged superiority over every other society of the
same kind in Europe.

   To sign a certificate in favour of any man whom we know
little or nothing about is most certainly a practice which cannot
be strictly vindicated.   It is a practice, however, which from mere
good-nature and without interest of any kind the most scrupulous
men in the world are sometimes guilty of.   I certainly do not
mean to defend it.   Bating the unhandsomeness of the practice,
however, I would ask in what manner does the public suffer by
it ?   The title of Doctor, such as it is, you will say, gives some
credit and authority to the man upon whom it is bestowed ; it
extends his practice and consequently his field for doing mischief ;
it is not improbable too that it may increase his presumption and
consequently his disposition to do mischief.   That a degree
injudiciously conferred may sometimes have some little effect of
this kind it would surely be absurd to deny, but that this effect
should be very considerable I cannot bring myself to believe.
That Doctors are sometimes fools as well as other people is not in
the present time one of those profound secrets which is known
only to the learned.   The title is not so very imposing, and it
very seldom happens that a man trusts his health to another
merely because that other is a Doctor.   The person so trusted
has almost always some knowledge or some craft which would

procure him nearly the same trust, though he was not decorated with any such title. In fact the persons who apply for degrees in the irregular manner complained of are, the greater part of them, surgeons or apothecaries who are in the custom of advising and prescribing, that is, of practising as physicians ; but who, being only surgeons and apothecaries, are not fee-ed as physicians. It is not so much to extend their practice as to increase their fees that they are desirous of being made Doctors. Degrees conferred even undeservedly upon such persons can surely do very little harm to the public. When the University of St. Andrews very rashly and imprudently conferred a degree upon one Green who happened to be a stage-doctor, they no doubt brought much ridicule and discredit upon themselves, but in what respect did they hurt the public ? Green still continued to be what he was before, a stage-doctor, and probably never poisoned a single man more than he would have done though the honours of graduation had never been conferred upon him. Stage-doctors, I must observe, do not much excite the indignation of the faculty ; more reputable quacks do. The former are too contemptible to be considered as rivals ; they only poison the poor people ; and the copper pence which are thrown up to them in handkerchiefs could never find their way to the pocket of a regular physician. It is otherwise with the latter : they sometimes intercept a part of what perhaps would have been better bestowed in another place. Do not all the old women in the country practise physic without exciting murmur or complaint ? And if here and there a graduated Doctor should be as ignorant as an old woman, where can be the great harm ? The beardless old woman indeed takes no fees ; the bearded one does, and it is this circumstance, I strongly suspect, which exasperates his brethren so much against him.

There never was, and I will venture to say there never will be, a university from which a degree could give any tolerable security that the person upon whom it had been conferred was fit to practise physic. The strictest universities confer degrees only upon students of a certain standing. Their real motive for requiring this standing is that the student may spend more money among them and that they may make more profit by him. When he has attained this standing therefore, though he still undergoes what they call an examination, it scarce ever happens that he is refused his degree. Your examination at Edinburgh, I have all reason to believe, is as serious, and perhaps more so, than that of any other university in Europe ; but when a student has resided a few years among you, has behaved dutifully to all his professors, and has attended regularly all their lectures, when he comes to his examination I suspect you are disposed to be as good-natured as other people. Several of your graduates, upon applying for license from the College of Physicians here, have had it recommended to them to continue their studies. From a particular knowledge of some of the cases I am satisfied that the decision of the College in refusing them their license was perfectly just—that is, was perfectly agreeable to the principles which ought to regulate all such decisions ; and that the candidates were really very ignorant of their profession.

A degree can pretend to give security for nothing but the science of the graduate ; and even for that it can give but a very slender security. For his good sense and discretion, qualities not discoverable by an academical examination, it can give no security at all ; but without these the presumption which commonly attends science must render it in the practice of physic ten times more dangerous than the grossest ignorance when accompanied, as it sometimes is, with some degree of modesty and diffidence.

If a degree, in short, always has been, and, in spite of all the regulations which can be made, always must be, a mere piece of quackery, it is certainly for the advantage of the public that it should be understood to be so. It is in a particular manner for the advantage of the universities that for the resort of students they should be obliged to depend, not upon their privileges but upon their merit, upon their abilities to teach and their diligence in teaching ; and that they should not have it in their power to use any of those quackish arts which have disgraced and degraded the half of them.

A degree which can be conferred only upon students of a certain standing is a statute of apprenticeship which is likely to contribute to the advancement of science, just as other statutes of apprenticeship have contributed to that of arts and manufactures. Those statutes of apprenticeship, assisted by other corporation laws, have banished arts and manufactures from the greater part of towns corporate. Such degrees, assisted by some other regulations of a similar tendency, have banished almost all useful and solid education from the greater part of universities. Bad work and high price have been the effect of the monopoly introduced by the former ; quackery, imposture, and exorbitant fees have been the consequences of that established by the latter. The industry of manufacturing villages has remedied in part the inconveniences which the monopolies established by towns corporate had occasioned. The private interest of some poor Professors of Physic in some poor universities inconveniently situated for the resort of students has in part remedied the inconveniences which would certainly have resulted from that sort of monopoly which the great and rich universities had attempted to establish. The great and rich universities seldom graduated anybody but their own students, and not even these till after a long and tedious standing ; five and seven years for a Master of Arts ; eleven and sixteen for a Doctor of Law, Physic, or Divinity. The poor universities on account of the inconvenience of their situation, not being able to get many students, endeavoured to turn a penny in the only way in which they could turn it, and sold their degrees to whoever would buy them, generally without requiring any residence or standing, and frequently without subjecting the candidate even to a decent examination. The less trouble they gave, the more money they got, and I certainly do not pretend to vindicate so dirty a practice. All universities being ecclesiastical establishments under the immediate protection of the Pope, a degree from one of them gave all over Christendom very nearly the same privileges which a degree from any other could have given ; and the respect which is to this day paid to foreign degrees, even in Protestant countries, must be considered as a remnant of Popery. The facility of obtaining degrees, particularly in physic, from those poor universities had two effects, both extremely advantageous to the public, but extremely disagreeable to graduates of other universities whose degrees had cost them much time and expense. First, it multiplied very much the number of doctors, and thereby no doubt sunk their fees, or at least hindered them from rising so very high as they otherwise would have done. Had the universities of Oxford and Cambridge been able to maintain themselves in the exclusive privilege of graduating all the doctors who could practise in England, the price of feeling the pulse might by this time have risen from two and three guineas, the price which it has now happily arrived at, to double or triple that sum ; and English physicians might, and probably would, have been at the same time the most ignorant and quackish in the world. Secondly, it reduced a good deal the rank and dignity of a doctor, but if the physician was a man of sense and science it would not surely prevent his being respected and employed as a man of sense and science. If he was neither the one nor the other, indeed, his doctorship would no doubt avail him the less. But ought it in this case to avail him at all ? Had the hopeful project of the rich and great universities succeeded, there would have been no occasion

for sense or science. To have been a doctor would alone have
been sufficient to give any man rank, dignity, and fortune enough.
That in every profession the fortune of every individual should
depend as much as possible upon his merit and as little as possible
upon his privilege is certainly for the interest of the public. It is
even for the interest of every particular profession, which can
never so effectually support the general merit and real honour of
the greater part of those who exercise it, as by resting on such
liberal principles. Those principles are even most effectual for
procuring them all the employment which the country can afford.
The great success of quacks in England has been altogether owing
to the real quackery of the regular physicians. Our regular
physicians in Scotland have little quackery, and no quack accordingly has ever made his fortune among us.

After all, this trade in degrees I acknowledge to be a most
disgraceful trade to those who exercise it ; and I am extremely
sorry that it should be exercised by such respectable bodies as any
of our Scotch universities. But as it serves as a corrective of
what would otherwise soon grow up to be an intolerable nuisance,
the exclusive and corporation spirit of all thriving professions
and of all great universities, I deny that it is hurtful to the
public.

What the physicians of Edinburgh at present feel as a hardship
is perhaps the real cause of their acknowledged superiority over
the greater part of other physicians. The Royal College of
Physicians there, you say, are obliged by their charter to grant a
license without examination to all the graduates of Scotch universities. You are all obliged, I suppose, in consequence of this,
to consult sometimes with very unworthy brethren. You are all
made to feel that you must rest no part of your dignity upon your
degree, a distinction which you share with the men in the world
perhaps whom you despise the most, but that you must found the
whole of it upon your merit. Not being able to derive much
consequence from the character of Doctor, you are obliged perhaps
to attend more to your character as men, as gentlemen, and as
men of letters. The unworthiness of some of your brethren may
perhaps in this manner be in part the cause of the very eminent
and superior worth of many of the rest. The very abuse which
you complain of may in this manner perhaps be the real source of
your present excellence. You are at present well, wonderfully
well, and when you are so, be assured there is always some danger
in attempting to be better.

Adieu, my dear Doctor ; after having delayed to write to you

I am afraid I shall *get my lug* (ear) *in my lufe* (hand), as we say, for what I have written. But I ever am, most affectionately yours,

ADAM SMITH.

LONDON, 20*th September* 1774.[1]

Whether this decided expression of unfavourable opinion on the part of his old and venerated tutor altered the Duke of Buccleugh's mind on the subject, or in any way prevented him from persevering in his contemplated application to Government, we have no means of knowing, but at any rate no further action seems to have been taken in the matter, and it was left to the Scottish universities themselves to remedy abuses which were seriously telling on their own interest and good name.

The last year of Smith's residence in London was overcast by growing anxiety about the condition of his friend Hume, who had always enjoyed fairly good health till the beginning of the year 1775, and then seemed to fall rapidly away. As Smith said one evening at Lord Shelburne's to Dr. Price, who asked him about Hume's health, it seemed as if Hume was one of those persons who after a certain time of life go down not gradually but by jumps.[2] Under those circumstances Smith had determined as soon as his new book was out to go down to Edinburgh and if possible persuade Hume to come back with him to London, to try the effect of change of scene and a little wholesome diversion. But, bad correspondent that he was, he appears to have left Hume to gather his intentions from the reports of friends, and consequently received from Hume the following remonstrance a few weeks before the publication of his work :—

EDINBURGH, 8*th February* 1776.

DEAR SMITH—I am as lazy a correspondent as you, but my anxiety about you makes me write.

By all accounts your book has been printed long ago, yet it

---

[1] Thomson's *Life of Cullen*, i. 481.
[2] Notes of S. Rogers' Conversation. Add. MSS., 32,571.

has never yet been so much as advertised. What is the reason ?
If you wait till the fate of Bavaria be decided you may wait long.

By all accounts you intend to settle with us this spring, yet we
hear no more of it. What is the reason ?   Your chamber in my
house is always unengaged ; I am always at home ; I expect you
to land here.

I have been, am, and shall be probably in an indifferent state
of health. I weighed myself t'other day, and find I have fallen
five compleat stones. If you delay much longer I shall probably
disappear altogether.

The Duke of Buccleugh tells me that you are very zealous in
American affairs. My notion is that this matter is not so important as is commonly imagined. If I be mistaken I shall probably
correct my error when I see you or read you.   For navigation and
general commerce may suffer more than our manufactures.
Should London fall as much in its size as I have done it will be
the better.   It is nothing but a Hulk of bad and unclean Humours.[1]

The American question was of course the great
question of the hour, for the Colonies were already a year
in active rebellion, and they issued their declaration of
independence but a few months later.   Smith followed the
struggle, as we see from many evidences in the concluding portion of the *Wealth of Nations*, with the most
patriotic interest and anxiety, and having long made a
special study of the whole problem of colonial administration, had arrived at the most decided opinions not only on
the rights and wrongs of the particular quarrel then at
issue, but on the general policy it was requisite to adopt in
the government of dependencies.   Hume was in favour of
separation, because he believed separation to be inevitable
sooner or later in the ordinary course of nature, like the
separation of the fruit from the tree or the child from the
parent.   But Smith, shunning all such misleading meta-
phors, held that there need never be any occasion for
separation as long as mother country and dependency were
wise enough to keep together, and that the sound policy to
adopt was really the policy of closer union—of imperial

[1] Burton's *Life of Hume*, ii. 483.

federation, as we should now call it. He would not say,
"Perish dependencies," but "Incorporate them." He would
treat a colony as but a natural expansion of the territory
of the kingdom, and have its inhabitants enjoy the same
rights and bear the same burdens as other citizens.   He did
not think it wrong to tax the Colonies ; on the contrary,
he would make them pay every tax the inhabitants of
Great Britain had to pay ; but he thought it wrong to put
restrictions on their commerce from which the commerce
of Great Britain was free, and he thought it wrong to tax
them for imperial purposes without giving them representation in the Imperial Parliament—full and equal representation, " bearing the same proportion to the produce of their
taxes as the representation of Great Britain might bear to
the produce of the taxes levied upon Great Britain."   The
union he contemplated was to be more than federal ; it was
to preclude home rule by local assemblies ; it was to be like the
union which had been established with Scotland, and which
he strongly desired to see established with Ireland ; and the
Imperial Parliament in London was to make laws for the
local affairs of the provinces across the Atlantic exactly as
it made laws for the local affairs of the province across
the Tweed.   He shrank from none of the consequences of
his scheme, admitting even that when the Colonies grew in
population and wealth, as grow they must, till the real centre
of empire changed, the time would then arrive when the
American members of the Imperial Parliament would far
outnumber the British, and the seat of Parliament itself
would require to be transferred from London to some
Constantinople on the other side of the Atlantic.

He was quite sensible that this scheme of his would be
thought wild and called a " new Utopia," but he was
not one of those who counted the old Utopia of Sir
Thomas More to be either useless or chimerical, and he
says that this Utopia of his own is " no more useless or
chimerical than the old one."   The difficulties it would
encounter came, he says, " not from the nature of things,

but from the prejudices and opinions of the people both
on this and on the other side of the Atlantic." He held,
moreover, very strongly that a union of this kind was the
only means of making the Colonies a useful factor instead
of a showy and expensive appendage of the empire, and the
only alternative that could really prevent their total
separation from Great Britain. He pleaded for union, too,
not merely for the salvation of the Colonies to the mother
country, but even more for the salvation of the Colonies to
themselves. Separation merely meant mediocrity for Great
Britain, but for the Colonies it meant ruin. There would
no longer be any check on the spirit of rancorous and
virulent faction which was always inseparable from small
democracies. The coercive power of the mother country
had hitherto prevented the colonial factions from breaking
out into anything worse than brutality and insult, but if
that coercive power were entirely taken away they would
probably soon break out into open violence and bloodshed.[1]

The event has falsified the last anticipation, but this is
not the place to criticise Smith's scheme. It was only
requisite to recall for a moment the ideas which, according
to the Duke of Buccleugh's statement to Hume, Smith was
at this time so zealously working for in the important
circles in which he then moved in London.

[1] *Wealth of Nations*, Book V. chap. iii.

CHAPTER XVIII

"THE WEALTH OF NATIONS"

1776. *Aet.* 52

THE *Inquiry into the Nature and Causes of the Wealth of Nations* was at length published on the 9th of March 1776. Bishop Horne, one of Smith's antagonists, of whom we shall presently hear more, said the books which live longest are those which have been carried longest in the womb of the parent. The *Wealth of Nations* took twelve years to write, and was in contemplation for probably twelve years before that. It was explicitly and publicly promised in 1759, in the concluding paragraph of the *Theory of Moral Sentiments*, though it is only the partial fulfilment of that promise.

The promise is : "I shall in another discourse endeavour to give an account of the general principles of law and government, and of the different revolutions they have undergone in the different ages and periods of society, not only in what concerns justice, but in what concerns policy revenue and arms, and whatever else is the object of law." In speaking of this promise in the preface of the sixth edition of the *Theory* in 1790, Smith says, "In the *Inquiry concerning the Nature and Causes of the Wealth of Nations* I have partially executed this promise, at least so far as concerns policy revenue and arms." Now doubtless when Smith began writing his book in Toulouse he began it on the large plan originally in contemplation, and some part of the long delay that took place in its composition is probably to be explained by the fact that he would have possibly been a considerable time at work before he determined to break his book in two, and push on meanwhile with the section on policy revenue and arms, leaving to a separate publication in the future his discussion of the theory of jurisprudence.

The work was published in two vols. 4to, at the price of £1 : 16s. in boards, and the author uses this time all his honours on the title-page, describing himself as Adam Smith, LL.D. and F.R.S., formerly Professor of Moral Philosophy in the University of Glasgow. What was the extent of this edition, or the terms, as between author and publisher, on which it was put out, is not exactly known. The terms were not half-profits, for that arrangement is proposed by Smith for the second edition as if it were a new one, and is accepted in the same way by Strahan, who in a letter which I shall presently quote, pronounces it a " very fair " proposal, " and therefore very agreeable to Mr. Cadell and me " ; nor was it printed for the author, for the presentation copies he gave away were deducted from the copy money he received. On the whole, it seems most probable that the book was purchased from him for a definite sum, and as he mentions in his letter of the 13th November 1776 that he had received £300 of his money at that time, and had still a balance owing to him, one may reasonably conjecture that the full sum was £500— the same sum Cadell's firm had paid for the last economic work they had undertaken, Sir James Steuart's *Inquiry into the Principles of Political Economy*.

The book sold well. The first edition, of whose extent, however, we are ignorant, was exhausted in six months, and the sale was from the first better than the publishers expected, for on the 12th of April, when it had only been a month out, Strahan takes notice of a remark of David Hume that Smith's book required too much thought to be as popular as Gibbon's, and states, " What you say of Mr. Gibbon's and Dr. Smith's book is exactly just. The former is the most popular work ; but the sale of the latter, though not near so rapid, has been more than I could have expected from a work that requires much thought and reflection (qualities that do not abound among modern readers) to peruse to any purpose."[1] The sale is the more remarkable because it was scarce to any degree helped on by reviews, favourable or otherwise. The book was not noticed at all, for example, in the *Gentleman's Magazine*, and it was allowed only two pages in the *Annual Register*, while in the same number Watson's *History of Philip* got sixteen. This review of the book, however, was probably written by Burke.

Smith speaks in one of his letters to Strahan of having distributed numerous presentation copies. One of the first of these was of course sent to his old friend David Hume, and that copy, by the way, with its inscription, probably still exists, having been possessed for a time by the late Mr. Babbage. Hume acknowledged receipt of it in the following letter, which shows among other things that not even Hume had seen the manuscript of the book before publication :—

EDINBURGH, 1*st April* 1776.

EUGE ! BELLE ! DEAR MR. SMITH—I am much pleased with your performance, and the perusal of it has taken me from a state of great anxiety. It was a work of so much expectation, by yourself, by your friends, and by the public, that I trembled for its appearance, but am now much relieved. Not but that the reading of it necessarily requires so much attention, and the public is disposed to give so little that I shall still doubt for some time of its being at first very popular, but it has depth and solidity and acuteness, and is so much illustrated by curious facts that it must at last attract the public attention. It is probably much improved by your last abode in London. If you were here at my fireside, I should dispute some of your principles. I cannot think that the rent of farms makes any part of the price of the produce, but that the price is determined altogether by the quantity and the demand. It appears to me impossible that the King of France

---

[1] *Hume MSS.*, R.S.E.

can take a seignorage of 8 per cent upon the coinage. Nobody would bring bullion to the mint, it would be all sent to Holland or England, where it might be coined and sent back to France for less than 2 per cent. Accordingly Necker says that the French king takes only 2 per cent of seignorage. But these and a hundred other points are fit only to be discussed in conversation, which till you tell me the contrary I still flatter myself with soon. I hope it will be soon, for I am in a very bad state of health and cannot afford a long delay. I fancy you are acquainted with Mr. Gibbon. I like his performance extremely, and have ventured to tell him that had I not been personally acquainted with him I should never have expected such an excellent work from the pen of an Englishman. It is lamentable to consider how much that nation has declined in literature during our time. I hope he did not take amiss this national reflection.

All your friends here are in deep grief at present for the death of Baron Mure, which is an irreparable loss to our society. He was among the oldest and best friends I had in the world.[1]

On the same day as Hume wrote this letter from Edinburgh, Gibbon wrote from London to Adam Ferguson and said among other things, " What an excellent work is that with which our common friend Mr. Adam Smith has enriched the public! An extensive science in a single book, and the most profound ideas expressed in the most perspicuous language. He proposes visiting you very soon, and I find he means to exert his most strenuous endeavours to persuade Mr. Hume to return with him to town. I am sorry to hear that the health and spirits of that truly great man are in a less favourable state than his friends could wish, and I am sure you will join your efforts in convincing him of the benefits of exercise, dissipation, and change of air."

Some of Smith's personal friends seem to have entertained the common prejudice that a good work on commerce could not be reasonably expected from a man who had never been engaged in any branch of practical business, and seemed in outward air and appearance so ill fitted to succeed in such a line of business if he had

---

[1] Burton's *Life of Hume*, ii. 487.

engaged in it. One of these was Sir John Pringle, President of the Royal Society, and formerly, like Smith himself, Professor of Moral Philosophy at a Scotch university. When the *Wealth of Nations* appeared Sir John Pringle remarked to Boswell that Smith, having never been in trade, could not be expected to write well on that subject any more than a lawyer upon physic, and Boswell repeated the remark to Johnson, who at once, however, sent it to the winds. " He is mistaken, sir," said the Doctor ; " a man who has never been engaged in trade himself may undoubtedly write well upon trade, and there is nothing that requires more to be illustrated by philosophy than does trade. As to mere wealth—that is to say, money—it is clear that one nation or one individual cannot increase its store but by making another poorer ; but trade procures what is more valuable, the reciprocation of the peculiar advantages of different countries. A merchant seldom thinks but of his own particular trade. To write a good book upon it a man must have extensive views ; it is not necessary to have practised to write well upon a subject."

It is not within the scope of a work like the present to give an account of the doctrines of the *Wealth of Nations*, or any estimate of their originality or value, or of their influence on the progress of science, on the policy and prosperity of nations, or on the practical happiness of mankind. Buckle, as we know, declared it to be " in its ultimate results probably the most important book that has ever been written " ; a book, he said, which has " done more towards the happiness of man than has been effected by the united abilities of all the statesmen and legislators of whom history has preserved an authentic account " ;[1] and even those who take the most sober view of the place of this work in history readily admit that its public career, which is far from being ended yet, is a very remarkable story of successive conquest.

It has been seriously asserted that the fortune of the

[1] Buckle's *History of Civilisation*, ed. 1869, i. 214.

book in this country was made by Fox quoting it one
day in the House of Commons. But this happened in
November 1783, after the book had already gone through
two editions and was on the eve of appearing in a third.
It is curious, however, that that was the first time it was
quoted in the House, and it is curious, again, that the person
to quote it then was Fox, who was neither an admirer of the
book, nor a believer in its principles, nor a lover of its subject. He once told Charles Butler that he had never read
the book, and the remark must have been made many years
after its publication, for it was made at St. Anne's Hill,
to which Fox only went in 1785. " There is something
in all these subjects," the statesman added in explanation,
" which passes my comprehension ; something so wide that
I could never embrace them myself nor find any one who
did."[1] On another occasion, when he was dining one evening
in 1796 at Sergeant Heywood's, Fox showed his hearty
disdain for Smith and political economy together. The
Earl of Lauderdale, who was himself an economist of great
ability, and by no means a blind follower of Smith, made the
remark that we knew nothing of political economy before
Adam Smith wrote. " Pooh," said Fox, " your Adam
Smiths are nothing, but " (he added, turning to the company) " that is his love ; we must spare him there."
" I think," replied Lauderdale, " he is everything."
" That," rejoined Fox, " is a great proof of your affection."
Fox was no believer in free trade, and actively opposed
the Commercial Treaty with France in 1787 on the
express and most illiberal ground that it proceeded from a
novel system of doctrines, that it was a dangerous departure
from the established principles of our forefathers, and that
France and England were enemies by nature, and ought
to be kept enemies by legislation.

It is curious therefore that in a House where Smith had
many admirers and not a few disciples, his book was never
mentioned for near eight years after its appearance, and was

[1] Butler's *Reminiscences*, i. 176.

mentioned then by an enemy of its principles. Fox's quotation from it on that occasion was of the most unimportant character. It was in his speech on the Address of Thanks to the Throne, and he said : " There was a maxim laid down in an excellent book upon the Wealth of Nations which had been ridiculed for its simplicity, but which was indisputable as to its truth. In that book it was stated that the only way to become rich was to manage matters so as to make one's income exceed one's expenses. This maxim applied equally to an individual and to a nation. The proper line of conduct therefore was by a well-directed economy to retrench every current expense, and to make as large a saving during the peace as possible." [1] To think of this allusion having any influence on the fortunes of the work is of course out of reason. It was never even mentioned in the House again till the year 1787, when Mr. Robert Thornton invoked it in support of the Commercial Treaty with France, and Mr. George Dempster read an extract from it in the debate on the proposal to farm the post-horse duties. It was quoted once in 1788, by Mr. Hussy on the Wool Exportation Bill, and not referred to again until Pitt introduced his Budget on the 17th February 1792. In then explaining the progressive accumulation of capital that was always spontaneously going on in a country when it was not checked by calamity or by vicious legislation, that great minister, a deep student of Smith's book and the most convinced of all Smith's disciples, made the remark: " Simple and obvious as this principle is, and felt and observed as it must have been in a greater or less degree even from the earliest periods, I doubt whether it has ever been fully developed and sufficiently explained but in the writings of an author of our own time, now unfortunately no more (I mean the author of the celebrated treatise on the *Wealth of Nations*), whose extensive knowledge of detail and depth of philosophical research will, I believe, furnish

[1] *Parliamentary History*, xxiii. 1152.

the best solution of every question connected with the history of commerce and with the system of political economy." [1] In the same year it was quoted by Mr. Whitbread and by Fox (from the exposition of the division of labour in the first book) in the debate on the armament against Russia, and by Wilberforce in his speech introducing his Bill for the Abolition of the Slave Trade.

It was not mentioned in the House of Lords till 1793, when in the debate on the King's Message for an Augmentation of the Forces it was referred to by Smith's two old friends, the Earl of Shelburne (now Marquis of Lansdowne) and Alexander Wedderburn (now Lord Loughborough, and presiding over the House as Lord Chancellor of England). The Marquis of Lansdowne said : " With respect to French principles, as they had been denominated, those principles had been exported from us to France, and could not be said to have originated among the population of the latter country. The new principles of government founded on the abolition of the old feudal system were originally propagated among us by the Dean of Gloucester, Mr. Tucker, and had since been more generally inculcated by Dr. Adam Smith in his work on the *Wealth of Nations*, which had been recommended as a book necessary for the information of youth by Mr. Dugald Stewart in his *Elements of the Philosophy of the Human Mind.*" The Lord Chancellor in replying merely said that "in the works of Dean Tucker, Adam Smith, and Mr. Stewart, to which allusion had been made, no doctrines inimical to the principles of civil government, the morals or religion of mankind, were contained, and therefore to trace the errors of the French to these causes was manifestly fallacious." [2]

Lord Lansdowne's endeavour to shield Smith's political orthodoxy under the countenance lent to his book by so safe and trusted a teacher of the sons of the Whig nobility as Dugald Stewart, is hardly less curious than his unreserved

[1] *Parliamentary History*, xxix. 834.
[2] *Ibid.*, xxx. 330, 334.

identification of the new political economy with that moving cloud of ideas which, under the name of French principles, excited so much alarm in the public mind of that time. For Dugald Stewart was in that same year 1793 (on the evenings of 21st January and 18th March) reading his *Memoir of Adam Smith* to the Royal Society of Edinburgh, and he tells us himself (in 1810) how he was compelled to abandon the idea of giving a long account of Smith's opinions which he intended to have done, because at that period, he says, "it was not unusual, even among men of some talents and information, to confound studiously the speculative doctrines of political economy with those discussions concerning the first principles of government, which happened unfortunately at that time to agitate the public mind. The doctrine of a Free Trade was itself represented as of a revolutionary tendency, and some who had formerly prided themselves on their intimacy with Mr. Smith, and on their zeal for the propagation of his liberal system, began to call in question the expediency of subjecting to the disputation of philosophers the arcana of State policy, and the unfathomable wisdom of feudal ages."[1] People's teeth had been so set on edge by the events in France that, as Lord Cockburn tells us, when Stewart first began to give a course of lectures in the University on political economy in the winter 1801-2, the mere term "political economy" made them start. "They thought it included questions touching the constitution of governments, and not a few hoped to catch Stewart in dangerous propositions."[2]

The French Revolution seems to have checked for a time the growing vogue of Smith's book and the advance of his principles in this country, just as it checked the progress of parliamentary and social reform, because it filled men's mind with a fear of change, with a suspicion of all novelty, with an unreasoning dislike of anything in

[1] Stewart's *Works*, x. 87.
[2] Cockburn's *Memorials of My Own Time*, p. 174.

the nature of a general principle.   By French principles
the public understood, it is true, much more than the
abolition of all commercial and agrarian privilege which
was advocated by Smith, but in their recoil they made no
fine distinctions, and they naturally felt their prejudices
strongly confirmed when they found men like the Marquis
of Lansdowne, who were believers in the so-called French
principles and believers at the same time in the principles
of Adam Smith, declaring that the two things were substantially the same.   Whether and how far Smith or
Tucker had any influence on that development of
opinion which eventuated in the Revolution, it would be
difficult to gauge.   Before Lord Lansdowne made this
speech in 1793 two different translations of the *Wealth
of Nations* into French had already been published ; a
third (by the Abbé Morellet) had been written but not
published, and a fourth was possibly under way, for it
appeared in a few years.   The first and worst of these
translations, moreover (Blavet's), had already gone through
three separate editions, after having originally run
through a periodical in monthly sections for two years.
These are all tokens that the work was unquestionably
influencing French opinion.

But if the French Revolution stopped for a time, as is
most likely, the onward advance of Smith's free-trade
principles, it does not seem to have exercised the same
effect on the actual sale of the book.   I do not know
whether the successive editions were uniform in number of
copies, but as many editions of the *Wealth of Nations*—four
English and one Irish—appeared between the years 1791
and 1799 as between the years 1776 and 1786, and since
none was called for from 1786 till 1791, the edition of
1786 took longer to sell off than the subsequent editions
of 1791, 1793, and 1796.   It is quite possible—indeed
it is only natural—that the wave of active antagonism
which, according to Stewart's testimony, rose against the
principles of the book after the outbreak of the French

Revolution would have helped on the sale of the book itself by keeping it more constantly under public attention, discussion, and, if you will, vituperation. The fortune of a book, like that of a public man, is often made by its enemies.

But the very early influence of the *Wealth of Nations* in the English political world is established by much better proofs than quotations in Parliament. It had actually shaped parts of the policy of the country years before it was ever publicly alluded to in either House. The very first budget after its publication bore its marks. Lord North was then on the outlook for fresh and comparatively unburdensome means of increasing the revenue, and obtained valuable assistance from the *Wealth of Nations.* He imposed two new taxes in 1777, of which he got the idea there; one on man-servants, and the other on property sold by auction. And the budget of 1778 owed still more important features to Smith's suggestions, for it introduced the inhabited house duty so strongly recommended by him, and the malt tax.[1] Then in the following year 1779 we find Smith consulted by statesmen like Dundas and the Earl of Carlisle on the pressing and anxious question of giving Ireland free trade. His answers still exist, and will appear later on in this work.[2]

[1] See Dowell's *Taxation*, ii. 169.
[2] See below, pp. 350, 352.

CHAPTER XIX

THE DEATH OF HUME

1776

AFTER the publication of his book in the beginning of March, Smith still dallied in London, without taking any steps to carry out his plan of going to see Hume in Edinburgh and bring him up to London. But some hope seems to have been entertained of Hume coming up even without Smith's persuasion and escort. John Home, who was in London and was in correspondence with him, thought so, but he at length received a direct negative to the idea in a letter from Hume himself, written on the 12th of April; and then Smith and John Home set out together immediately for the northern capital, but when the coach stopped at Morpeth, whom should they see standing in the door of the inn but Colin, their friend's servant? Hume had determined to undertake the journey to London after all to consult Sir John Pringle, and was now so far on his way. John Home thereupon accompanied Hume back to London, but Smith, having heard of his mother being taken ill, and being anxious about her, as she was now over eighty years old, continued his journey on to Kirkcaldy. At Morpeth, however, he and Hume had time to discuss the question of the publication, in the event of Hume's death, of certain of his unpublished works. Hume had already on the 4th of January 1776 made Smith his literary executor by will, leaving him full power over all his papers except the *Dialogues on Natural*

Religion, which he explicitly desired him to publish. It was years since this work had been written, but its publication had been deferred in submission to the representations of Sir Gilbert Elliot and other friends as to the annoying clamour it was sure to excite. Its author, however, had never ceased to cherish a peculiar paternal pride in the work, and now that his serious illness forced him to face the possibility of its extinction, he resolved at last to save it from that fate, clamour or no clamour. If he lived, he would publish it himself; if he died, he charged his executor to do so.

But this was a duty for which Smith had no mind. He was opposed to the publication of these *Dialogues* on general grounds and under any editorship whatever, as will appear in the course of the correspondence which follows, but he had also personal scruples against editing them, of the same character as those which had already so long prevented their author himself from publishing them. He shrank from the public clamour in which it would involve him, and the injury it might do to his prospects of preferment from the Crown. When he met Hume at Morpeth accordingly he laid his mind fully before his friend, and the result was that Hume agreed to leave the whole question of publication or no publication absolutely to Smith's discretion, and on reaching London sent Smith a formal letter of authority empowering him to deal with the *Dialogues* as he judged best.

LONDON, *3rd May* 1776.

MY DEAR FRIEND—I send you enclosed a new ostensible letter, conformably to your desire. I think, however, your scruples groundless. Was Mallet anywise hurt by his publication of Lord Bolingbroke? He received an office afterwards from the present king and Lord Bute, the most prudent men in the world, and he always justified himself by his sacred regard to the will of a dead friend. At the same time I own that your scruples have a specious appearance, but my opinion is that if upon my death you determine never to publish these papers, you should leave them sealed up with my brother and family, with some inscription that you reserve to yourself the power of reclaiming them whenever you think proper. If I live a few years longer I shall publish them myself. I consider an observation of Rochefoucault that the wind, though it extinguishes a candle, blows up a fire.

You may be surprised to hear me talk of living years, considering the state you saw me in and the sentiments both I and all my friends at Edinburgh entertained on that subject. But though I cannot come up entirely to the sanguine notions of our friend John, I find myself very much recovered on the road, and I hope Bath waters and further journies may effect my cure.

By the little company I have seen I find the town very full of your book, which meets with general approbation. Many people think particular parts disputable, but this you certainly expected. I am glad that I am one of the number, as these parts will be the subject of future conversation between us. I set out for Bath, I believe, on Monday, by Sir John Pringle's directions. He says that he sees nothing to be apprehended in my case. If you write to me (hem ! hem !)—I say if you write to me, send your letter under cover to Mr. Strahan, who will have my direction.[1]

The ostensible letter which accompanied the other is—

LONDON, *3rd May* 1776.

MY DEAR SIR—After reflecting more maturely on that article of my will by which I leave you the disposal of all my papers, with a request that you should publish my *Dialogues concerning Natural Religion*, I have become sensible that both on account of the nature of the work and of your situation it may be improper to hurry on that publication. I therefore take the present opportunity of qualifying that friendly request. I am content to leave it entirely to your discretion at what time you will publish that piece, or whether you will publish it at all.

You will find among my papers a very inoffensive piece called " My Own Life," which I composed a few days before I left Edinburgh, when I thought, as did all my friends, that my life was despaired of. There can be no objection that the small piece should be sent to Messrs. Strahan and Cadell and the proprietors of my other works, to be prefixed to any future edition of them.[2]

---

[1] Burton's *Life of Hume*, ii. 492.   [2] *Ibid.* ii. 493.

The ink of those letters was scarcely dry before Hume's heart softened again towards his *Dialogues*, and in order to make more sure of their eventual publication than he could feel while they were entrusted to Smith's hands, he wrote Strahan from Bath on the 8th of June asking if he would agree to act as literary executor and undertake the editing and publishing of the work. In this letter he says: "I have hitherto forborne to publish it because I was of late desirous to live quietly and keep remote from all clamour, for though it be not more exceptionable than some things I had formerly published, yet you know some of them were thought exceptionable, and in prudence perhaps I ought to have suppressed them. I there intro- duce a sceptic who is indeed refuted and at last gives up the argument; nay, confesses that he was only amusing himself by all his cavils, yet before he is silenced he advances several topics which will give umbrage and will be deemed for bold and free as well as much out of the common road. As soon as I arrive at Edinburgh I intend to print a small edition of 500, of which I may give away about 100 in presents, and shall make you the property of the whole, provided you have no scruple, in your present situation, of being the editor. It is not necessary you should prefix any name to the Title-page. I seriously declare that after Mr. Miller and you and Mr. Cadell have publicly avowed your publication of the *Inquiry concerning Human Understanding*, I know no reason why you should have the least scruple with regard to these *Dialogues*. They will be much less obnoxious to the Law and not more exposed to popular clamour. Whatever your resolution be, I beg you would keep an entire silence on this subject. If I leave them to you by will, your executing the desire of a dead friend will render the publication still more excusable. Mallet never suffered anything by being the editor of Bolingbroke's works." [1]

Strahan agreed to undertake this duty, and Hume on

[1] Hill's *Letters of Hume to Strahan*, p. 330.

the 12th of June added a codicil to his will making
Strahan his literary executor and entire master of all his
manuscripts. Hume, however, got rapidly worse in
health, so that he never printed the small edition he
spoke of, and feeling his end to be near, he added a fresh
codicil to his will on the 7th of August, desiring Strahan
to publish the *Dialogues* within two years, and adding
that if they were not published in two years and a half
the property should return to his nephew (afterwards
Baron of Exchequer), " whose duty," he says, " in publishing them, as the last request of his uncle, must be
approved of by all the world." [1]

Hume had meanwhile on the 4th of July 1776 gathered
his group of more intimate friends about him to eat together a last farewell dinner before he made the great
departure. Smith was present at this touching and unusual reunion, and may possibly have remained some days
thereafter, for he speaks in a letter in the following month
of having had several conversations with Hume lately,
among them being that which he afterwards published in
his letter to Strahan. But he was in Kirkcaldy again in
the beginning of August, and received there on the 22nd
of August the following letter which Hume had written
on the 15th, and which, having gone, through some mistake, by the carrier instead of the post, had lain for a week
at the carrier's house without being delivered. The delay
occasioned by this accident was the more unfortunate on
account of the earnest appeal for an early answer with
which the letter closes, and which seems to contain a
recollection of many past transgressions, for Smith was
always a dilatory and backward correspondent, the act of
writing, as he repeatedly mentions, being a real pain to him.

> EDINBURGH, 15*th August* 1776.
>
> MY DEAR SMITH—I have ordered a new copy of my *Dia-*
> *logues* to be made besides that wh. will be sent to Mr. Strahan,

---

[1] Burton's *Life of Hume*, ii. 494.

and to be kept by my nephew. If you will permit me, I shall order a third copy to be made and consigned to you. It will bind you to nothing, but will serve as a security. On revising them (which I have not done these five years) I find that nothing can be more cautiously and more artfully written. You had certainly forgotten them. Will you permit me to leave you the property of the copy, in case they should not be published in five years after my decease? Be so good as write me an answer soon. My state of health does not permit me to wait months for it.—Yours affectionately,   DAVID HUME.[1]

To this letter Smith, immediately on receiving it, sent the following reply :—

KIRKALDY, *22nd August* 1776.

MY DEAREST FRIEND—I have this moment received yr. letter of the 15th inst. You had, in order to save me the sum of one penny sterling, sent it by the carrier instead of the Post, and (if you have not mistaken the date) it has lain at his quarters these eight days, and was, I presume, very likely to lie there for ever.

I shall be very happy to receive a copy of your *Dialogues*, and if I should happen to die before they are published, I shall take care that my copy shall be as carefully preserved as if I was to live a hundred years. With regard to leaving me the property in case they are not published within five years after yr. decease, you may do as you think proper. I think, however, you should not menace Strahan with the loss of anything, in case he does not publish yr. work within a certain time. There is no probability of his delaying it, and if anything could make him delay it, it wd. be a clause of this kind, wh. wd. give him an honourable pretence for doing so. It would then be said I had published, for the sake of an emolument, not from respect to the memory of my friend, what even a printer, for the sake of the same emolument, had not published. That Strahan is sufficiently jealous you will see by the enclosed letter, wh. I will beg the favour of you to return to me, but by the Post, and not by the carrier.

If you will give me leave I will add a few lines to yr. account of your own life, giving some account in my own name of your behaviour in this illness, if, contrary to my own hopes, it should prove your last. Some conversations we had lately together, particularly that concerning your want of an excuse to make to

---

[1] *Hume Correspondence*, R.S.E. Library.

Charon, the excuse you at last thought of, and the very bad reception wh. Charon was likely to give it, would, I imagine, make no disagreeable part of the history.   You have in a declining state of health, under an exhausting disease, for more than two years together now looked at the approach of death with a steady cheerfulness such as very few men have been able to maintain for a few hours, tho' otherwise in the most perfect Health.

I shall likewise, if you give me leave, correct the sheets of the new edition of your works, and shall take care that it shall be published exactly according to your last corrections.   As I shall be at London this winter, it will cost me very little trouble.

All this I have written upon the supposition that the event of yr. disease should prove different from what I still hope it may do.   For your spirits are so good, the spirit of life is still so very strong in you, and the progress of your disorder is so slow and gradual, that I still hope it may take a turn.   Even the cool and steady Dr. Black, by a letter I received from him last week, seems not to be averse to the same hopes.

I hope I need not repeat to you that I am ready to wait on you whenever you wish to see me.   Whenever you do so I hope you will not scruple to call on me.   I beg to be remembered in the kindest and most respectful manner to yr. Brother, your sister, your nephew, and all other friends.—I ever am, my dearest friend, most affectionately yours,   ADAM SMITH.[1]

Hume answered this letter next day.

EDINBURGH, 23*rd August* 1776.

MY DEAREST FRIEND—I am obliged to make use of my nephew's hand in writing to you, as I do not rise to-day.

There is no man in whom I have a greater confidence than Mr. Strahan, yet I have left the property of that manuscript to my nephew David, in case by any accident it should not be published within three years after my decease.   The only accident I could foresee was one to Mr. Strahan's life, and without this clause my nephew would have had no right to publish it.   Be so good as to inform Mr. Strahan of this circumstance.

You are too good in thinking any trifles that concern me are so much worth of your attention, but I give you entire liberty to make what additions you please to the account of my life.

I go very fast to decline, and last night had a small fever, wh.

_____

[1] *Hume Correspondence*, R.S.E. Library.

I hoped might put a quicker period to this tedious illness, but unluckily it has in a great measure gone off. I cannot submit to your coming over here on my account, as it is possible for me to see you so small a portion of the day, but Dr. Black can better inform you concerning the degree of strength which may from time to time remain with me.—Adieu, my dearest friend,

DAVID HUME.

P.S.—It was a strange blunder to send yr. letter by the carrier.[1]

These were the last words of this long and memorable friendship. Two days after they were written Hume passed peacefully away, and his bones were laid in the new cemetery on the Calton Crags, and covered a little later, according to his own express provision, with that great round tower, designed by Robert Adam, which Smith once pointed out to the Earl of Dunmore as they were walking together down the North Bridge, and said, "I don't like that monument; it is the greatest piece of vanity I ever saw in my friend Hume."

Smith was no doubt at the funeral, and seems to have been present when the will was read, and to have had some conversation about it with Hume's elder brother, John Home of Ninewells,[2] for on the 31st of August he writes from Dalkeith House, where he had gone on a visit to his old pupil, discharging Ninewells of any obligation to pay the legacy of £200 which he had been left by Hume in consideration of acting as his literary executor, and which had not been revoked in the codicil superseding him by Strahan. This legacy Smith felt that he could not in the circumstances honourably accept, and he consequently lost no time in forwarding to Ninewells the following letter :—

DALKEITH HOUSE, 31*st August* 1776.

DEAR SIR—As the Duke proposes to stay here till Thursday next I may not have an opportunity of seeing you before yr. return

---

[1] *Hume Correspondence*, R.S.E. Library.
[2] Hume's brother always spelt his name with an *o*.

to Ninewells. I therefore take the opportunity of discharging you and all others concerned of the Legacy which you was so good as to think might upon a certain event become due to me by your Brother's will, but which I think could upon no event become so, viz. the legacy of two hundred pounds sterling. I hereby therefore discharge it for ever, and least this discharge should be lost I shall be careful to mention it in a note at the bottom of my will. I shall be glad to hear that you have received this letter, and hope you will believe me to be, both on yr. Brother's account and your own, with great truth, most affectionately yours,   ADAM SMITH.

P.S.—I do not hereby mean to discharge the other Legacy, viz. that of a copy of his works.[1]

Mr. Home answered him on the 2nd of September as follows :—

DEAR SIR—I was favoured with yours of Saturday, and I assure you that on perusing the destination I was more of oppinion than when I saw you that the pecuniary part of it was not altered by the codicil, and that it was intended for you at all events, that my brother, knowing your liberal way of thinking, laid on you something as an equivalent, not imagining you would refuse a small gratuity from the hands it was to come from as a testimony of his friendship, and tho' I most highly esteem the motives and manner, I cannot agree to accept of your renunciation, but leave you full master to dispose of it which way is most agreeable to you.

The copys of the *Dialogues* are finished, and of the life, and will be sent to Mr. Strahan to-morrow, and I will mention to him your intention of adding to the last something to finish so valuable a life, and will leave you at liberty to look into the correction of the first as it either answers your leisure or ideas with regard to his composition or what effects you think it may have with regard to yourself. The two copys intended for you will be left with my sister when you please to require them, and the copy of the new edition of his works you shall be sure to receive, tho' you have no better title to that part than the other, tho' much you have to the friendship and esteem, dr. sir, of him who is most sincerely yours,   JOHN HOME.

EDINBURGH, *2nd September* 1776.[2]

---

[1] *Hume Correspondence*, R.S.E. Library.   [2] *Ibid.*

Smith's reply was that though the legacy might be due to him in strict law, he was fully satisfied it was not due to him in justice, because it was expressly given in the will as a reward for a task which he had declined to undertake. This reply was given in a letter of the 7th October, in which he enclosed a copy of the account of Hume's death which he proposed to add to his friend's own account of his life.

DEAR SIR—I send you under the same cover with this letter what I propose should be added to the account which your never-to-be-forgotten brother has left of his own life. When you have read it I beg you will return it to me, and at the same time let me know if you wd. wish to have anything either added to it or taken from it. I think there is a propriety in addressing it as a letter to Mr. Strahan, to whom he has left the care of his works. If you approve of it I shall send it to him as soon as I receive it from you.

I have added at the bottom of my will the note discharging the legacy of two hundred pounds which your brother was so kind as to leave me. Upon the most mature deliberation I am fully satisfied that in justice it is not due to me. Tho' it should be due to me therefore in strict law, I cannot with honour accept of it. You will easily believe that my refusal does not proceed from any want of the highest respect for the memory of your deceased brother.—I have the honour to be, with the highest respect and esteem, dear sir, most sincerely and affectionately yours,   ADAM SMITH.

KIRKALDY, FIFESHIRE, 7*th October* 1776.[1]

Mr. Home returned Smith's manuscript to him on the 14th of October, and expressed his entire approbation of it except " that as it is to be added to what is wrote in so short and simple a manner, he would have wished that the detail had been less minutely entered into, particularly of the journey which, being of a private concern and having drawn to no consequences, does not interest the publick," but still he expressed that opinion, he

---

[1] *Hume Correspondence*, R.S.E. Library.

said, with diffidence, and thought the piece would perhaps
best stand as it was.   He says, too, that instead of the
words, " as my worst enemies could wish " in the remark
to Dr. Dundas, he was told that the words his brother
actually used were, " as my enemies, if I have any, could
wish "—a correction which was adopted by Smith.   And
he repeats that by his interpretation of his brother's will
he considers the legacy to belong to Smith both in law
and in equity.

Meanwhile Smith had also written Strahan from
Dalkeith :—

MY DEAR STRAHAN—By a codicil to the will of our late
most valuable friend Mr. Hume, the care of his manuscripts is left
to you.   Both from his will and from his conversation I understand that there are only two which he meant should be published—
an account of his life and *Dialogues concerning Natural Religion*.
The latter, tho' finely written, I could have wished had remained in manuscript to be communicated only to a few people.
When you read the work you will see my reasons without my
giving you the trouble of reading them in a letter.   But he has
ordered it otherwise.   In case of their not being published within
three years after his decease, he has left the property of them to
his nephew.   Upon my objecting to this clause as unnecessary
and improper, he wrote to me by his nephew's hand in the following terms : " There is no man in whom I have a greater confidence
than Mr. Strahan, yet have I left the property of that manuscript
to my nephew David, in case by any accident they should not be
published within three years after my decease.   The only accident
I could foresee was one to Mr. Strahan's life, and without this
clause my nephew would have had no right to publish it.   Be so
good as inform Mr. Strahan of this circumstance."   Thus far
this letter, which was dated on the 23rd of August.   He dyed on
the 25th at 4 o'clock afternoon.   I once had persuaded him to
leave it entirely to my discretion either to publish them at what
time I thought proper, or not to publish them at all.   Had he
continued of this mind the manuscript should have been most
carefully preserved, and upon my decease restored to his family ;
but it never should have been published in my lifetime.   When
you have read it you will perhaps think it not unreasonable to
consult some prudent friend about what you ought to do.

I propose to add to his Life a very well authenticated account of his behaviour during his last illness. I must, however, beg that his life and those *Dialogues* may not be published together, as I am resolved for many reasons to have no concern in the publication of the *Dialogues*. His life, I think, ought to be prefixed to the next edition of his former works, upon which he has made many very proper corrections, chiefly in what concerns the language. If this edition is published while I am at London, I shall revise the sheets and authenticate its being according to his last corrections. I promised him that I would do so.

If my mother's health will permit me to leave her, I shall be in London by the beginning of November. I shall write to Mr. Home to take my lodgings as soon as I return to Fife, which will be on Monday or Tuesday next. The Duke of Buccleugh leaves this on Sunday. Direct for me at Kirkaldy, Fifeshire, where I shall remain all the rest of the season.—I remain, my dear Strahan, most faithfully yours, ADAM SMITH.

DALKEITH HOUSE, *5th September* 1776.

Let me hear from you soon.[1]

To this Strahan replied on the 16th of September, and then towards the end of October Smith wrote the following answer, of which the first draft, in Smith's own handwriting, unsigned and undated and containing considerable erasures, exists in the R.S.E. Library. It shows that Smith submitted his account of Hume's illness to the whole circle of Hume's intimate friends, and that at the moment of writing he was waiting for the arrival of John Home, the poet, in Edinburgh, to obtain his remarks upon it.

DEAR SIR—When I received your last letter I had not begun the small addition I proposed to make to the life of our late friend. It is now more than three weeks since I finished it, and sent one

---

[1] *New York Evening Post*, 30th April 1887. Original in possession of Mr. Worthington C. Ford of Washington, U.S.A. The first draft of this letter, in Smith's handwriting but without the last paragraph and the signature, seems to have been preserved by him as a copy for reference, and having been sent by him with his other Hume letters to the historian's nephew, is now in the Royal Society Library, Edinburgh.

copy to his brother and another to Dr. Black. That which I sent to his brother is returned with remarks, all of which I approve of and shall adopt. Dr. Black waits for John Home, the Poet, who is expected every day in Edinburgh, whose remarks he proposes to send along with those of all our common friends. The work consists only of two sheets, in the form of a letter to you, but without one word of flattery or compliment. It will not cost my servant a forenoon to transcribe it, so that you will receive it by the first post after it is returned to me.

I am much obliged to you for so readily agreeing to print the life together with my additions separate from the *Dialogues*. I even flatter myself that this arrangement will contribute not only to my quiet but to your interest. The clamour against the *Dialogues*, if published first, might hurt for some time the sale of the new edition of his works, and when the clamour has a little subsided the *Dialogues* may hereafter occasion a quicker sale of another edition.

I do not propose being with you till the Christmas holidays; in the meantime I should be glad to know how things stand between us, what copies of my last book are either sold or unsold, and when the balance of our bargain is likely to be due to me. I beg my most respectful and affectionate compliments to Mr. Cadell; I should have written him, but you know the pain it gives me to write with my own hand, and I look upon writing to him and you as the same thing. I have been since I came to Scotland most exceedingly idle. It is partly in order to bring up in some measure my leeway that I propose to stay here two months longer than I once intended. If my presence, however, was at all necessary in London, I could easily set out immediately.

I beg the favour of you to send the enclosed to Mr. Home. The purpose of it is to bespeak my lodgings.[1]

The second and third paragraphs of this letter as they stood at first are erased entirely, but their original substance is in no way altered in their corrected form. One of the original sentences about the clamour he dreaded may perhaps be transcribed. " I am still," he says, " uneasy about the clamour which I foresee they will excite." It may also be noticed that he does not

[1] *Hume Correspondence*, R.S.E. Library.

seem to have dictated his account of Hume's illness to his amanuensis, but to have written it with his own hand and then got his amanuensis to transcribe it. The Mr. Home whom he wishes to bespeak lodgings for him must be John Home the poet, in spite of the circumstance that he speaks of John Home the poet as being expected in Edinburgh every day at the time of writing; and in the event Home does not seem to have come to Edinburgh, for in a subsequent letter to Strahan on 13th of November Smith again mentions having written Mr. Home to engage lodgings for him from Christmas. This letter is as follows :—

DEAR SIR—The enclosed is the small addition which I propose to make to the account which our late invaluable friend left of his own life.

I have received £300 of the copy money of the first edition of my book. But as I got a good number of copies to make presents of from Mr. Cadell, I do not exactly know what balance may be due to me. I should therefore be glad he would send me the account. I shall write to him upon this subject.

With regard to the next edition, my present opinion is that it should be printed in four vol. octavo ; and I would propose that it should be printed at your expense, and that we should divide the profits. Let me know if this is agreeable to you.

My mother begs to be remembered to Mrs. Strahan and Miss Strahan, and thinks herself much obliged both to you and them for being so good as to remember her.—I ever am, dear sir, most affectionately yours, ADAM SMITH.

KIRKALDY, FIFESHIRE, 13*th November* 1776.

I shall certainly be in town before the end of the Christmas holidays. I do not apprehend it can be necessary for me to come sooner. I have therefore written ·to Mr. Home to bespeak my lodgings from Christmas.[1]

Strahan acknowledges this letter on the 26th of November, and asks Smith's opinion on an idea that has

---

[1] *New York Evening Post*, 30th March 1887. Original in possession of Mr. Worthington C. Ford of Washington, U.S.A.

occurred to him of publishing the interesting series of letters from Hume to himself which he possessed, and which, after a curious and remarkable history, have been now preserved for the world through the liberality of Lord Rosebery and the learned devotion of Mr. Birkbeck Hill. To these letters Strahan, if he obtained Smith's concurrence, would like to add those of Hume to Smith himself, to John Home, to Robertson, and other friends, which have now for the most part been lost. But Smith put his foot on this proposal decisively, on the ground apparently that it was most improper for a man's friends to publish anything he had written which he had himself given no express direction or leave to publish either by his will or otherwise. Strahan's letter runs thus :—

DEAR SIR — I received yours of the 13th enclosing the addition to Mr. Hume's Life, which I like exceedingly. But as the whole put together is very short and will not make a volume even of the *smallest size*, I have been advised by some very good judges to annex some of his letters to me on political subjects. What think you of this ? I will do nothing without your advice and approbation, nor would I for the world publish any letter of his but such as in yr. opinion would do him honour. Mr. Gibbon thinks such as I have shown him would have that tendency. Now if you approve of this in any manner, you may perhaps add partly to the collection from your own cabinet and those of Mr. John Home, Dr. Robertson, and others of your mutual friends which you may pick up before you return hither. But if you wholly disapprove of this scheme say nothing of it, here let it drop, for without your concurrence I will not publish a single word of his. I should be glad, however, of your sentiments as soon as you can, and let me know at the same time as nearly as may be what day you purpose to be in London, for I must again repeat to you that without your approbation I will do nothing.

Your proposal to print the next edition of your work in 4 vols. octavo at *our* expense and to divide the Profits is a very fair one, and therefore very agreeable to Mr. Cadell and me. Enclosed is the List of Books delivered to you of the 1st edit.

My wife and daughter join kindest compliments to your amiable Parent, who, I hope, is still able to enjoy your company, which must be her greatest comfort.—Dear sir, your faithful and affectionate humble servant, WILL. STRAHAN.

LONDON, 26*th November* 1776.[1]

The following is Smith's reply :—

DEAR SIR—It always gives me great uneasiness whenever I am obliged to give an opinion contrary to the inclination of my friend. I am sensible that many of Mr. Hume's letters would do him great honour, and that you would publish none but such as would. But what in this case ought principally to be considered is the will of the Dead. Mr. Hume's constant injunction was to burn all his Papers except the *Dialogues* and the account of his own life. This injunction was even inserted in the body of his will. I know he always disliked the thought of his letters ever being published. He had been in long and intimate correspondence with a relation of his own who dyed a few years ago. When that gentleman's health began to decline he was extremely anxious to get back his letters, least the heir should think of publishing them. They were accordingly returned, and burnt as soon as returned. If a collection of Mr. Hume's letters besides was to receive the public approbation, as yours certainly would, the Curls of the times would immediately set about rummaging the cabinets of all those who had ever received a scrap of paper from him. Many things would be published not fit to see the light, to the great mortification of all those who wish well to his memory. Nothing has contributed so much to sink the value of Swift's works as the undistinguished publication of his letters ; and be assured that your publication, however select, would soon be followed by an undistinguished one. I should therefore be sorry to see any beginning given to the publication of his letters. His life will not make a volume, but it will make a small pamphlet. I shall certainly be in London by the tenth of January at furthest. I have a little business at Edinburgh which may detain me a few days about Christmas, otherwise I should be with you by the new year. I have a great deal more to say to you ; but the post is just going. I shall write to Mr. Cadell by next post.—I ever am, dear sir, most affectionately yours,

ADAM SMITH.

KIRKALDY, 2*nd December* 1776.[2]

---

[1] *Hume Correspondence*, R.S.E. Library.
[2] Hill's *Letters of Hume*, p. 351.

When we consider Smith's concern about the clamour he expected to arise from the *Dialogues*, and his entire unconcern about the clamour he did not expect to arise from the letter to Strahan on Hume's last illness, the actual event seems one of those teasing perversities which drew from Lord Bolingbroke the exclamation, "What a world is this, and how does fortune banter us!" The *Dialogues* fell flat; the world had apparently had its surfeit of theological controversy. A contemporary German observer of things in England states that while the book made something of a sensation in his own country, it excited nothing of that sort here, and was already at the moment he wrote (1785) entirely forgotten.[1]

The letter to Strahan, on the other hand, excited a long reverberation of angry criticism. Smith had certainly in writing it no thought of undermining the faith, or of anything more than speaking a good word for the friend he loved, and putting on record some things which he considered very remarkable when he observed them, but in the ear of that age his simple words rang like a challenge to religion itself. Men had always heard that without religion they could neither live a virtuous life nor die an untroubled death, and yet here was the foremost foe of Christianity represented as leading more than the life of the just, and meeting death not only without perturbation, but with a positive gaiety of spirits. His cheerfulness without frivolity, his firmness, his magnanimity, his charity, his generosity, his entire freedom from malice, his intellectual elevation and strenuous labour, are all described with the affection and confidence of a friend who had known them well ; and they are finally summed up in the conclusion: "Upon the whole I have always considered him, both in his lifetime and since his death, as approaching as nearly to the idea of a perfectly wise and virtuous man as perhaps the nature of human frailty will permit."

Hume's character was certainly one of great beauty

---

[1] Wendeborn, *Zustand des Staats, etc., in Gross-britannien*, ii. 365.

and nobleness, and churchmen who knew him well speak of him in quite as strong admiration as Smith. Robertson used to call him " the virtuous heathen" ; Blair said every word Smith wrote about him was true ; and Lord Hailes, a grave religious man and a public apologist of Christianity, showed sufficient approbation of this letter to translate it into Latin verse. But in the world generally it raised a great outcry. It was false, it was incredible, it was a wicked defiance of the surest verities of religion. Even Boswell calls it a piece of "daring effrontery," and as he thinks of it being done by his old professor, says, "Surely now have I more understanding than my teachers." Though nothing was further from the intention of the author, it was generally regarded as an attack upon religion, which imperatively called for repulsion ; and a champion soon appeared in the person of Dr. George Horne, President of Magdalen College, Oxford, author of a well-known commentary on the Psalms, and afterwards Bishop of Norwich. In an anonymous pamphlet, entitled " A Letter to Adam Smith, LL.D., on the Life, Death, and Philosophy of David Hume, Esq., by one of the People called Christians," which ran rapidly through a number of editions, Horne, begging the whole question he raises, contends that a man of Hume's known opinions could not by any possibility be the good and virtuous man Smith represented him to be, for had he been really generous, or compassionate, or good-natured, or charitable, or gentle-minded, he could never have thought of erasing from the hearts of mankind the knowledge of God and the comfortable faith in His fatherly care, or been guilty of " the atrocious wickedness of diffusing atheism through the land." Horne goes on to charge this "atrocious wickedness" against Smith too. " You would persuade us," he says, " by the example of David Hume, Esq., that atheism is the only cordial for low spirits and the proper antidote against the fear of death, but surely he who can reflect with complacency on friend thus employing his talents in this life, and thus

amusing himself with Lucian, whist, and Charon at his
death, can smile over Babylon in ruins, esteem the earth-
quakes which destroyed Lisbon as agreeable occurrences,
and congratulate the hardened Pharaoh on his overthrow
in the Red Sea."

Smith never wrote any reply to this attack, nor took
any public notice of it whatever, though he had too much
real human nature in him to agree with Bishop Horne's
own ethereal maxim that "a man reproached with a crime
of which he knows himself to be innocent should feel no
more uneasiness than if he was said to be ill when he felt
himself in perfect health." It was of course quite unjust
to accuse Smith of atheism, or of desiring to propagate
atheism. His published writings, which the Bishop
ought in fairness to have consulted, show him to have
been a Theist, and there is some ground for thinking that
he believed Hume, as many others of Hume's personal
friends did, to have been a Theist likewise. Though
Hume was philosophically a doubter about matter, about
his own existence, about God, he did not practically think
so differently from the rest of the world about any of the
three as was often supposed. Dr. Carlyle always thought
him a believer. Miss Mure of Caldwell, the sister of his
great friend the Baron of Exchequer, says he was the most
superstitious man she ever knew.[1] He told Holbach that
an atheist never existed, and once, while walking with
Adam Ferguson on a beautiful clear night, he stopped
suddenly and exclaimed, pointing to the sky, "Can any
one contemplate the wonders of that firmament and not
believe that there is a God?"[2] That Smith would not
have been surprised to hear his friend make such a confession is apparent from the well-known anecdote told of
his absence of mind in connection with Henry Mackenzie's
story of "La Roche." That story was written soon after
Hume's death; it was published in the *Mirror* in 1779,
while Horne's agitation was raging; and the author intro-

[1] *Caldwell Papers*, i. 41.   [2] Burton's *Hume*, ii. 451.

duced Hume as one of the characters of the piece for the very purpose of presenting this more favourable view of the great sceptic's religious position with which Mackenzie had been impressed in his own intercourse with him. Hume appears in the story as a visitor in Switzerland, an inmate of the simple household of the pastor La Roche, and after describing him as being deeply taken with the sweet and unaffected piety of this family's life and with the faith that sustained them in their troubles, the author goes on to observe, " I have heard him long after confess that there were moments when, amidst the pride of philosophical discovery and the pride of literary fame, he recalled to his mind the venerable figure of the good La Roche and wished he had never doubted." Before publishing his story Mackenzie read it to Adam Smith, in order to be told whether anything should be omitted or altered as being out of keeping with Hume's character, and so completely was Smith carried away by the verisimilitude that he not only said he found not a syllable to object to, but added that he was surprised he had never heard the anecdote before. In his absence of mind he had forgotten for the moment that he had been asked to listen to the story as a work of fiction, and his answer was the best compliment Mackenzie could receive to his fidelity to the probabilities of character.[1]

[1] See Mackenzie's "La Roche," and Mackenzie's *Works of J. Home*, i. 21.

CHAPTER XX

LONDON AGAIN—APPOINTED COMMISSIONER OF CUSTOMS

Smith remained at Kirkcaldy from May to December 1776, except for occasional visits to Edinburgh or Dalkeith, but his thoughts, as we have noticed from time to time, were again bent on London, as soon as his mother's health should permit of his leaving home. He seems to have enjoyed London thoroughly during his recent prolonged sojourn, and inspired some hopes in friends like Strahan that he might even settle there as a permanent place of residence. After his departure for Scotland in April Strahan used to write him from time to time a long letter of political news keeping him abreast of all that was going on, and in a letter of the 16th of September he says : " I hope your mother's health will not prevent you from returning hither at the time you propose. You know I once mentioned to you how happy I thought it would make you both if you could bring her along with you to spend the remainder of her days in this Place, but perhaps it will not be easy to remove her so far at this time of her life. I pray you offer her the respectful compliments of my family, who do not forget her genteel and hospitable reception at Kircaldy some years ago." [1] The time Smith proposed to return, as he had written Strahan early in September, was November, but he afterwards put the journey off for two months on account of

[1] *Hume MSS.*, R.S.E. Library.

his own health, which had suffered from his long spell of literary labour, and was in need of more rest ; and he might have postponed it still further but for the visit being necessary in order to carry the second edition of his work through the press. Early in January 1777 he is already in London, having found lodgings in Suffolk Street, near the British Coffee-House, and on the 14th of March we find him attending a dinner of the Literary Club, with Fox in the chair, and Gibbon, Garrick, Reynolds, Johnson, Burke, and Fordyce for the rest of the company.[1]

His great work had not yet attracted much public notice. Its merits were being fully recognised by the learned, and it was already leaving its mark on the budget of the year ; but it was probable Smith was more talked about in general company at the time for his letter to Strahan than for his *Wealth of Nations*. In one little literary circle he was being zealously but most unjustly decried for taking a shabby revenge on a worthy young Scotch poet who had ventured to differ from him in opinion about the merits of the East India Company. Mickle, the author of the popular song " There's nae luck aboot the hoose," published his translation of the *Lusiad* of Camoens in 1775, and dedicated the book by permission to the Duke of Buccleugh, whose family had been his father's patrons, and from whose interest he hoped to obtain some advancement himself. When the work appeared the author sent a nicely-bound presentation copy to the Duke, but received no acknowledgment, and at length a common friend waited on his Grace, and, says one of Mickle's biographers, " heard with the indignation and contempt it deserved, a declaration that the work was at that time unread, and had been represented not to have the merit it had been first said to possess, and therefore nothing could be done on the subject of his mission." A dedication in those days was often only a more dignified begging letter, and

[1] Leslie and Taylor, *Life of Reynolds*, ii. 199.

Mickle's friends declared that he had been cruelly wronged, because the Duke had not only done nothing for him himself, but by accepting the dedication had prevented the author from going to some other patron who might have done something. Whatever could have been the reason for this sudden coolness of the Duke? Mickle and his little group of admirers declared it was all due to an ill word from the Duke's great mentor, Adam Smith, whom they alleged to have borne Mickle a grudge for having in the preface to the _Lusiad_ successfully exposed the futility of some of the views about the East India Company propounded in the _Wealth of Nations_.[1]

But since the _Wealth of Nations_ was only published in 1776, its opinions obviously could not, even with the vision and faculty divine of the poet, be commented on either favourably or unfavourably in the _Lusiad_, which was published in 1775. The comments on Smith's views appeared first in subsequent editions of Mickle's work, and were probably effects of the injury the author fancied himself to have suffered. Anyhow they could not have been its causes, and the whole story, so thoroughly opposed to the unusual tolerancy and benevolence of Smith's character, merits no attention. It sprang manifestly from some imaginary suspicion of a sensitive minor poet, but Mickle used to denounce Smith without stint, and, thinking he had an opportunity for retaliation when the letter to Strahan appeared, he wrote a satire entitled, " An Heroic Epistle from Hume in the Shades to Dr. Adam Smith," which he never published indeed, though he showed it about among his friends, but in which, says Sim, who had seen it, Smith and his noble pupil were rather roughly handled.[2] Mickle afterwards burnt this _jeu d'esprit_, and very probably came to entertain better views of Smith, for he seems to have been not only quick to suspect injuries, but ready after a space to perceive his error. He once inserted an angry

---

[1] Sim's _Works of Mickle_, Preface, xl.
[2] _Ibid_, Preface, xliii.

note in one of his poems against Garrick, who had, as he imagined, used him ill ; but going afterwards to see the great actor in *King Lear*, he listened to the first three acts without saying a word, and after a fine passage in the fourth, heaved a deep sigh, and turning to his companion said, " I wish that note was out of my book." Had he foreseen the noise his several friends continued to make, even after his death, about this purely imaginary offence on the part of Adam Smith, the poet would not improbably wish the polemical prefaces out of his book. Smith did not think much of Mickle's translation of the *Lusiad*, holding the French version to be much superior,[1] but if he happened to express this unfavourable opinion to the Duke of Buccleugh, it could not have been with any thought of injuring a struggling and meritorious young author. He has never shown any such intolerance of public contradiction as Mickle's friends chose to attribute to him. Dr. James Anderson, the first and true author of what is known as Ricardo's theory of rent, won Smith's friendship by a controversial pamphlet challenging some of his doctrines ; Bentham won — what is rarer — his conversion from the doctrines impugned, and a very kindly letter still exists which Smith wrote to another hostile critic, Governor Pownall, and which I shall give here, as it was one of the first things he did after now arriving in London. Pownall had been Governor of Massachusetts, a man of much activity of mind and experience of affairs, and author of respectable works on the *Principles of Polity*, the *Administration of the Colonies*, and the *Middle States of America*. He was one of the forty-two persons to whom the authorship of the letters of Junius has been attributed. He differed strongly from many of Smith's views, especially from his condemnation of the monopoly of the colonial trade, and wrote a pamphlet setting forth his criticisms in the form of a letter to Adam Smith. This pamphlet Smith received in Edinburgh, just before his departure for

[1] The *Bee*, 1st May 1791.

London, and when he arrived he wrote the Governor as follows :—

Sir—I received the day before I left Edinburgh the very great honour of your letter. Though I arrived here on Sunday last, I have been almost from the day of my arrival confined by a cold, which I caught upon the road ; otherwise I should before this time have done myself the honour of waiting on you in person, and of thanking you for the very great politeness with which you have everywhere treated me. There is not, I give you my word, in your whole letter a single syllable relating to myself which I could wish to have altered, and the publication of your remarks does me much more honour than the communication of them by a private letter could have done.

I hope in a few days to have the honour of waiting on you, and of discussing in person with you both the points on which we agree and those on which we differ. Whether you will think me, what I mean to be, a fair disputant, I know not ; I can venture to promise you will not find me an irascible one. In the meantime I have the honour to be, with the highest respect and esteem, etc. etc.   ADAM SMITH.

Suffolk Street, 12*th January* 1777.[1]

The gentleman who forwarded this letter to the editor of the *Gentleman's Magazine* in 1795, but whose name is not published, states, in further evidence, as he says, of Smith's liberality of mind, that " he altered in his second edition some of the parts objected to, and instead of a reply, sent to Governor Pownall a printed copy of this second edition so altered, and there all contest closed." Smith, however, does not appear to have made any such alterations. In fact, in the second edition he hardly made more than three or four alterations, and these were confined to the introduction of an additional fact or two in confirmation of his argument ; and besides, when we refer to Pownall's pamphlet we find that their differences were all about points on which Smith's views were mature and the Governor's raw.

[1] *Gentleman's Magazine*, lxv. 635.

Smith probably remained most of the year 1777 in London, for, as we have seen, one of his reasons for being there was to see the second edition of his work through the press, and the second edition of his work did not appear till 1778. But he was back in Kirkcaldy again before December, and while there he received from Lord North the appointment of Commissioner of Customs in Scotland, vacant through the death of Mr. Archibald Menzies. The offence he unexpectedly gave to the world's religious sensibilities by his account of Hume's last days had not interfered, as he feared such an offence would, with his prospects of employment in the public service, nor, what is quite as remarkable, had his political opinions. For he was always a strong Whig, and the preferment was bestowed by a Tory ministry. It is usually attributed to the influence of the Duke of Buccleugh and Henry Dundas, then a member of the ministry as Lord Advocate for Scotland, and their word may no doubt have helped; but there is reason to believe that the appointment was really a direct reward to the author of the *Wealth of Nations* for the benefit Lord North, who was Chancellor of the Exchequer as well as Prime Minister, derived from that book in preparing the budgets for the years 1777 and 1778. Smith himself, in a letter to Strahan which will presently appear (p. 323) attributes the appointment largely to the favour of Sir Grey Cooper, who had been Secretary to the Treasury since 1765, and was naturally Lord North's right-hand man in the preparation of his budgets. At the time the *Wealth of Nations* appeared the English Chancellor of the Exchequer was at his wits' end for fresh and convenient and easy means of increasing the revenue to carry on the American war, and the book was a mine of suggestions to him. He imposed two new taxes in 1777, of which he got the idea there,—one on man-servants, estimated by him to bring in £105,000, though in the event it yielded only £18,000, and the other on property sold by auction, which was to bring in £37,000 ; but in the budget of 1778, which he would have under consideration at the very moment of Smith's appointment, he introduced two new taxes recommended by Smith,—the inhabited house duty, estimated to yield £264,000, and the malt tax, estimated to yield £310,000. Under those circumstances Smith's appointment to the Commissionership of Customs is to be regarded not as a private favour to the Duke of Buccleugh, but as an express recognition on the part of the Premier of the public value of Smith's work, and the more honourable because rendered to a political opponent who had condemned important parts of the ministerial policy—their American policy, for example—in his recent work.

The appointment was worth £600 a year,—£500 for the Commissionership of Customs and £100 for the Commissionership of the Salt Duties ; and Smith still retained his pension of £300 from the House of Buccleugh. When he obtained this place he thought himself bound in honour to give up his Buccleugh pension, possibly because of the assistance he may have believed the Duke to have given in securing it ; but he was informed that the pension was meant to be permanent and unconditional, and that if he were consulting his own honour in offering to give it up, he was not thinking of the honour of the Duke of Buccleugh. Smith now settled in Edinburgh accordingly with an assured income of £900 a year, and £900 a year was a comparatively princely revenue in the Scottish capital at a time when a Lord of Session had only £700 a year, and a professor in the best chair in the University seldom made as much as £300.

Though the appointment was made probably in November 1777, Smith did not receive the Commission till January 1778, and there were still fees to pay and other business to transact about the matter, which he got Strahan to do for him. That occasioned the following letters :—

DEAR SIR—The last letter I had the pleasure of receiving from you congratulated me upon my being appointed one of the Commissioners of Customs in Scotland. You told me at

the same time that you had dined that day with Sir Grey
Cooper, and that you had both been so good as to speak very
favourably of me. I have received from London several other
congratulations of the same kind. But I have not yet received,
nor has the office here received, any official information that any
such appointment had been made. It is possible that the Commission is not made out on account of the fees. If this is the
case, you may either draw upon me for the amount, which I
understand to be about £160, or you may write to me, and I
shall by return of post remit you the money to London. Whatever be the cause of the delay, I beg you will endeavour to find it
out and let me know as soon as possible, that I may at least be at
the end of my hope. Remember me most affectionately to all
your family, and believe me to be, most faithfully yours,

ADAM SMITH.

EDINBURGH, 20*th December* 1777.

Neither you nor Mr. Cadell have wrote me anything concerning the new Edition of my Book. Is it published? does it
sell well? does it sell ill? does it sell at all? I left directions
with Mr. Cadell to send copies of it to several of my friends. If
John Hunter was not among the number, put him in *ex dono
authoris*, and desire Cadell to send me the account of the whole,
that I may pay it. I should write to him, but it would only be
plaguing him. If you draw upon me make your bill payable at
five days' sight. I return to Kirkaldy on Christmas Day.[1]

On returning to Kirkcaldy Smith again wrote
Strahan :—

DEAR SIR—I should have sent you the enclosed bill the day
after I received your letter accompanyed with a note from Mr.
Spottiswood, had not Mr. Charteris, the Solicitor of the Customs
here, told me that the fees were not paid in London, but at
Edinburgh, where Mr. Shadrach Moyes acted as receiver and
agent for the officers of the treasury at London. I have drawn
the bill for £120, in order to pay, first, what you have advanced
for me; secondly, the exchange between Edinburgh and London;
and lastly, the account which I shall owe to Mr. Cadell, after he
has delivered the presents I desired him to make of the second
edition of my book. To this I beg he will add two copies, hand-

---

[1] Original with Mr. F. Barker.

somely bound and guilt (*sic*), one to Lord North, the other to Sir Gray Cooper. I received Sir Gray's letter, and shall write to him as soon as the new Commission arrives, in order not to trouble him with answering two Letters. I believe that I have been very highly obliged to him in this business. I shall not say anything to you of the obligations I owe you for the concern you have shewn and the diligence you have exerted on my account. Remember me to Mr. Spottiswood. I shall write to him as soon as the affair is over. Would it be proper to send him any present or fee? I am much obliged to him, and should be glad to express my sense of it in every way in my power.

I would not make any alteration in my title-page on account of my new office.

Remember me to Mrs. and Miss Strahan, likewise to the Homes and the Hunters. How does the Painter go on? I hope he thrives.—I ever am, my dear sir, most faithfully and affectionately yours,   ADAM SMITH.

KIRKALDY, 14*th January* 1777.[1]

The Mr. Spottiswood mentioned in this letter was a nephew of Strahan, and no doubt an ancestor of Strahan's present successor in his printing business. The Hunters are John and William Hunter, the Homes are John Home and his wife, and the painter is Allan Ramsay.

In the course of a fortnight the Commission arrived, and Smith then wrote Strahan again:—

EDINBURGH, 5*th February* 1778.

MY DEAR STRAHAN—I received the Commission in due course, and have now to thank you for your great attention to my interest in every respect, but above all, for your generosity in so readily forgiving the sally of bad humour which, in consequence of General Skeenes, who meant too very well, most unreasonably broke out upon you. I can only say in my own vindication that I am not very subject to such sallies, and that upon the very few occasions on which I have happened to fall into them, I have soon recovered from them. I am told that no commission ever came so soon to Edinburgh, many having been delayed 3 weeks or a month after appearing in the Gazette. This extraordinary

---

[1] Original in possession of Mr. Alfred Morrison.

despatch I can impute to nothing but your friendly diligence and that of Mr. Spottiswood, to whom I beg to be remembered in the most respectful manner.

You have made a small mistake in stating our account. You credit me with £150 only, instead of £170; the first bill for £120, the second for £50. Cadell, however, still remains unpaid. As soon as I understand he has delivered the books, or before it, if he will send me the account of them, I shall send him the money.—I ever am, dear sir, most faithfully yours,

ADAM SMITH.[1]

What was the cause of Smith's outbreak of very unhabitual irritation with Strahan on the occasion alluded to in this letter, I cannot say, nor probably does it in the least matter. His temper, indeed, was one of unusual serenity and constancy, and but for his own confession in this letter, we should never have known that it was liable, like others, to occasional perturbations, from which it appears, however, he speedily recovered, and of which he is evidently heartily ashamed. General Skeenes was probably one of his relations, the Skenes of Pitlour.

The money transactions mentioned in the concluding paragraph refer doubtless to his Commission fees, which from some calculations made, probably by Strahan, on the back of the letter, seem to have come to £147 : 18s. But the reference to Mr. Cadell's account shows that the second edition of his book had now appeared. It was not published in four volumes octavo, as he originally proposed to Strahan, but, like the former edition, in two volumes quarto, and the price was now raised from £1 : 16s. to two guineas, so that under the half-profit arrangement which was agreed upon, he must have obtained a very reasonable sum out of this edition, and we can understand how, from the four authorised editions published during his lifetime, he made, according to his friend Professor Dalzel, a " genteel fortune," as genteel fortunes went in those days.

[1] Original in possession of Mr. Alfred Morrison.

CHAPTER XXI

IN EDINBURGH

1778–1790. *Aet.* 55–67

ON settling in Edinburgh Smith took a house in the Canongate—Panmure House, at the foot of Panmure Close, one of the steep and narrow wynds that descend from the north side of the Canongate towards the base of the Calton Hill ; and this house was his home for the rest of his days, and in it he died. The Canongate—the old Court end of the Scottish capital—was still at the close of last century the fashionable residential quarter of the city, although Holyrood had then long lain deserted— as Hamilton of Bangour called it,

> A virtuous palace where no monarch dwells.

The Scottish nobility had their town-houses in its gloomy courts, and great dowagers and famous generals still toiled up its cheerless stairs. Panmure House itself had been the residence of the Panmure family before Smith occupied it, and became the residence of the Countess of Aberdeen after his death. Most of his own more particular friends too—the better aristocracy of letters and science—lived about him here. If it was to Edinburgh, as Gibbon remarks, that " taste and philosophy seemed to have retired from the smoke and hurry of the immense capital of London," it was in the ancient smoke and leisure of the Canongate they found their sanctuary. Robertson flitted out, indeed, to the Grange House ; Black—Smith's special

crony in this Edinburgh period—to the present Blind
Asylum in Nicolson Street, then a country villa; and Adam
Ferguson to a place at the Sciennes which, though scarce two
miles from the Cross, was thought so outrageously remote
by the people of the compact little Edinburgh of those
days, that his friends always called it Kamtschatka, as if it
lay in the ends of the earth. But Kames and Hailes still
lived in New Street, Sir John Dalrymple and Monboddo
and many other notabilities in St. John Street, Cullen in the
Mint, and Dugald Stewart in the Lothian Hut (the town-
house of the Marquis of Lothian) in the Horse Wynd.

Panmure House is still standing. It is a much more
modern structure than the houses near it, having been
built towards the middle of last century; and although its
rooms are now mostly tenantless, and its garden a cooper's
yard, it wears to this day an air of spacious and substantial
comfort which is entirely wanting in the rest of the
neighbourhood. William Windham, the statesman, who
dined in it repeatedly when he was in Edinburgh with
Burke in 1785, thought it a very stately house indeed for
a philosopher. "House magnificent," he enters in his
diary, "and place fine," and one can still imagine how it
would appear so when the plastered walls were yet white,
and the eye looked over the long strip of terraced garden
on to the soft green slopes of the Calton. There was
then no building of any kind on or about the Calton Hill,
except the Observatory, and Dugald Stewart, who was very
fond of rural scenery, always said that the great charm of
his own house a few closes up was its view of the Calton
crags and braes.

Smith brought over his mother and his cousin, Miss
Douglas, from Kirkcaldy, and a few months later the
youngest son of his cousin, Colonel Douglas of Strathendry,
who was to attend school and college with a view to the bar,
and whom he made his heir. Windham, after visiting them,
makes the same note twice in his diary, "Felt strongly the
impression of a family completely Scotch." Smith's house

was noted for its simple and unpretending hospitality. He liked to have his friends about him without the formality of an invitation, and few strangers of distinction visited Edinburgh without being entertained in Panmure House. His Sunday suppers were still remembered and spoken of in Edinburgh when M'Culloch lived there as a young man. Scotch Sabbatarianism had not at that time reached the rigour that came in with the evangelical revival in the beginning of this century, and the Sunday supper was a regular Edinburgh institution. Even the Evangelical leaders patronised it. Lord Cockburn and Mrs. Somerville both speak with very agreeable recollections of the Sunday supper parties of the Rev. Sir Harry Moncreiff, and Boswell mentions being invited to one by another Evangelical leader, Dr. Alexander Webster.

His mother, his friends, his books — these were Smith's three great joys. He had a library of about 3000 volumes, as varied a collection in point of subject-matter as it would be possible to find. Professor Shield Nicholson, who saw a large portion of it, says : " I was most struck by the large number of books of travel and of poetry, of some of which there were more than one edition, and occasionally *éditions de luxe*. I had hoped to find marginal notes or references which might have thrown light on the authorities of some passages in the *Wealth of Nations* (for Smith gives no references), but even the ingenious oft-quoted author of the *Tracts on the Corn Laws* has escaped without a mark. At the same time pamphlets have been carefully bound together and indexes prefixed in Smith's own writing." [1]

Mr. James Bonar has been able to collect a list of probably two-thirds of Smith's books—about 1000 books, or 2200 volumes.[2] Nearly a third of the whole are in French, another third in Latin, Greek, and Italian, and

[1] Nicholson's edition of *Wealth of Nations*, p. 8.
[2] Bonar's *Catalogue of the Library of Adam Smith*, p. viii.

a little more than a third in English.   According to Mr.
Bonar's analysis, a fifth of them were on Literature and Art ;
a fifth were Latin and Greek classics; a fifth on Law, Politics,
and Biography ; a fifth on Political Economy and History ;
and the remaining fifth on Science and Philosophy.   One
cannot help remarking, as an indication of the economist's
tastes, the almost complete absence of works in theology
and prose fiction.   Hume's *Dialogues on Natural Religion*
and Pascal's *Pensées* belong as much to philosophy as theology ; Jeremy Taylor's *Antiquitates Christianae*, Father
Paul Sarpi's *History of the Council of Trent*, and Ruchat's
Histoire de la Reformation de la Suisse belong as much
to history ; and except these the only representatives of
theology on Smith's shelves were the English Bible,
Watson's edition, 1722—probably his parents' family Bible
—a French translation of the Koran, and Van Maestricht's
Theologia.   The only sermons, except those of Massillon
in French, are the *Sermons of Mr. Yorick*.   Those
sermons, however, were the only representative of Sterne.
Goldsmith was represented by his poems, but not by his
fiction ; and Defoe, Fielding, Richardson, and Smollett were
not represented at all.   One or two French novels were
there, but except Gulliver, which came in with the complete
edition of Swift's works in 1784, the only English novel
Smith seems to have possessed was the *Man of the World*,
by his friend Henry Mackenzie.   It is perhaps stranger
that he ignored the novel than that he ignored theology,
for the novel was then a very rising and popular literary
form, and Smith began life as a professed literary critic.   His
mind seems to have been too positive to care much for
tales.   On the other hand, of the Greek and Latin classics
he not unfrequently had several different editions.   He
had eight, for example, of *Horace*, who seems to have been
an especial favourite.

Like most men who are fond of books, he seems to
have bound them well, and often elegantly.   Smellie, the
printer, says that the first time he happened to be in

Smith's library he was "looking at the books with some degree of curiosity, and perhaps surprise, for most of the volumes were elegantly, and some of them superbly bound," when Smith, observing him, said, "You must have remarked that I am a beau in nothing but my books."[1] M'Culloch, however, who had seen the books, doubts whether their condition warranted the account given of them by Smellie, and says that while they were neatly, and in some cases even elegantly bound, he saw few or none of which the binding could with propriety be called superb.

The Custom House was on the upper floors of the Royal Exchange, in Exchange Square, off the High Street; and Kay, standing in his shop over at the corner of the Parliament Close, must often have seen Smith walk past from his house to his office in the morning exactly as he has depicted him in one of his portraits,—in a light-coloured coat, probably linen; knee-breeches, white silk stockings, buckle shoes, and flat broad-brimmed beaver hat; walking erect with a bunch of flowers in his left hand, and his cane, held by the middle, borne on his right shoulder, as Smellie tells us was Smith's usual habit, "as a soldier carries his musket." When he walked his head always moved gently from side to side, and his body swayed, Smellie says, "vermicularly," as if at each alternate step "he meant to alter his direction, or even to turn back." Often, moreover, his lips would be moving all the while, and smiling in rapt conversation with invisible companions. A very noticeable figure he was as he went up and down the High Street, and he used to tell himself the observations of two market women about him as he marched past them one day. "Hegh sirs!" said one, shaking her head significantly. "And he's weel put on too!" rejoined the other, surprised that one who appeared from his dress to be likely to have friends should be left by them to walk abroad alone.

There were five Commissioners in the Scotch Board of

[1] Smellie's *Life of Smith*, p. 297.

Customs, but Smith's colleagues were none of them men of any public reputation at the time, and they are now mere names ; but the name of the Secretary of the Board, R. E. Phillips, may be mentioned for the circumstance that, after living to the great age of 104, he was buried— for what reason I know not—in the same grave with Adam Smith in Canongate Churchyard. The business of the office was mostly of a routine and simple character : considering appeals from merchants against the local collector's assessments ; the appointment of a new officer here, the suppression of one there ; a report on a projected colliery ; a plan for a lighthouse, a petition from a wine importer, or the owner of a bounty sloop ; a representation about the increase of illicit trade in Orkney, or the appearance of smuggling vessels in the Minch ; the despatch of troops to repress illegal practices at some distillery, or to watch a suspected part of the coast ; the preparation of the annual returns of income and expenditure, the payment of salaries, and transmission of the balance to the Treasury.

Smith attended to those duties with uncommon diligence ; he says himself, in his letter to the Principal of Glasgow College in 1787 on his appointment to the Rectorship, that he was so regular an attendant at the Custom House that he could " take the play for a week at any time " without giving offence or provoking comment. He was evidently a very conscientious and on the whole, no doubt, a satisfactory administrator, though he may have been in some things slower than a clerk bred to business would have been, and caused occasionally a ludicrous mistake through his incidental absence of mind. Sir Walter Scott relates two anecdotes illustrative of that weakness, on the authority of one of Smith's colleagues on the Board of Customs. Having one day to sign an official document as Commissioner, Smith, instead of signing his own name, wrote an imitation of the signature of the Commissioner who had written before him. The other story, though, possibly enough, embellished unconsciously by the teller in some details, is yet of too distinct and peculiar a character to be easily rejected, and for the same reason will best be given in Scott's own words:—

"That Board (the Board of Customs) had in their service as porter a stately person, who, dressed in a huge scarlet gown or cloak covered with frogs of worsted lace, and holding in his hand a staff about seven feet high as an emblem of his office, used to mount guard before the Custom House when a Board was to be held. It was the etiquette that as each Commissioner entered the porter should go through a sort of salute with his staff of office, resembling that which officers used formerly to perform through their spontoon, and then marshal the dignitary to the hall of meeting. This ceremony had been performed before the great economist perhaps five hundred times. Nevertheless one day, as he was about to enter the Custom House, the motions of this janitor seem to have attracted his eye without their character or purpose reaching his apprehension, and on a sudden he began to imitate his gestures as a recruit does those of his drill serjeant. The porter having drawn up in front of the door, presented his staff as a soldier does his musket. The Commissioner, raising his cane and holding it with both hands by the middle, returned the salute with the utmost gravity. The inferior officer, much annoyed, levelled his weapon, wheeled to the right, stepping a pace back to give the Commissioner room to pass, lowering his staff at the same time in token of obeisance. Dr. Smith, instead of passing on, drew up on the opposite side and lowered his cane to the same angle. The functionary, much out of consequence, next moved upstairs with his staff upraised, while the author of the *Wealth of Nations* followed with his bamboo in precisely the same posture, and his whole soul apparently wrapped in the purpose of placing his foot exactly on the same spot of each step which had been occupied by the officer who preceded him. At the door of the hall the porter again drew off, saluted with his staff, and bowed reverentially. The philosopher again imitated his motions, and returned his bow with the most profound gravity. When the Doctor entered the apartment the spell under which he seemed to act was entirely broken, and our informant, who, very much amused, had followed him the whole way, had some difficulty to convince him that he had been doing anything extraordinary."[1]

This inability to recollect in a completely waking state what had taken place during the morbid one separates this story from all the rest that are told of Smith's absence of mind. For his friends used always to observe of his fits of abstraction what a remarkable faculty he possessed of recovering, when he came to himself, long portions of the conversation that had been going on around him while his mind was absent. But here there is an entire break between the one state and the other ; the case seems more allied to trance, though it doubtless had the same origin as the more ordinary fits of absence, and, like them, was only one of the penalties of that power of profound and prolonged concentration to which the world owes so much ; it was thinker's cramp, if I may use the expression.

In one way Smith took more interest in his official work than ordinary Commissioners would do, because he found it useful to his economic studies. In 1778 he wrote Sir John Sinclair, who had desired a loan of the French inquiry entitled *Mémoires concernant les Impositions*, that "he had frequent occasion to consult the book himself both in the course of his private studies and in the business of his present employment," and Sir John states that Smith used to admit "that he derived great advantage from the practical information he derived by means of his official situation, and that he would not have otherwise known or believed how essential practical knowledge was to the thorough understanding of political subjects."[2] This is

---

[1] *Quarterly Review*, xxxvi. 200.
[2] *Sir J. Sinclair's Correspondence*, i. 389.

confirmed by the fact that most of the additions and corrections introduced into the third edition of the *Wealth of Nations*—the first published after his settlement in the Customs—are connected with that branch of the public service.

Still his friends were perhaps right in lamenting that the duties of this office, light though they really were, used up his time and energy too completely to permit his application to the great work on government which he had projected. "Though they required little exertion of thought, they were yet," says Dugald Stewart, "sufficient to waste his spirits and dissipate his attention ; and now that his career is closed, it is impossible to reflect on the time they consumed without lamenting that it had not been employed in labours more profitable to the world and more equal to his mind. During the first years of his residence in this city his studies seemed to be entirely suspended, and his passion for letters served only to amuse his leisure and to animate his conversation. The infirmities of age, of which he very early began to feel the approach, reminded him at last, when it was too late, of what he yet owed to the public and to his own fame. The principal materials of the works which he had announced had been long ago collected, and little probably was wanting but a few years of health and retirement to bestow on them that systematical arrangement in which he delighted." [1]

His leisure seems to have been passed during these later years of his life very largely in the study of the Greek poets, and he frequently remarked to Dugald Stewart, when found in his library with Sophocles or Euripides open before him on the table, that of all the amusements of old age, the most grateful and soothing was the renewal of acquaintance with the favourite studies and the favourite authors of our youth.[2] Besides, the work of

[1] Stewart's *Works*, x. 73.
[2] Stewart's *Life of Reid*, sec. iii.

composition seems to have grown really more arduous to him. He was always a slow composer, and had never acquired increased facility from increased practice.

Much of his time too was now given to the enjoyments of friendship. I have already mentioned his Sunday suppers, but besides these he founded, soon after settling in Edinburgh, in co-operation with the two friends who were his closest associates during the whole of this last period of his career—Black the chemist, and Hutton the geologist—a weekly dining club, which met every Friday at two o'clock in a tavern in the Grassmarket. Dr. Swediaur, the Paris physician, who spent some time in Edinburgh in 1784 making researches along with Cullen, and was made a member of this club during his stay, writes Jeremy Bentham : "We have a club here which consists of nothing but philosophers. Dr. Adam Smith, Cullen, Black, Mr. M'Gowan, etc., belong to it, and I am also a member of it. Thus I spend once a week in a most enlightened and agreeable, cheerful and social company." And of Smith, with whom he says he is intimately acquainted, he tells Bentham he "is quite our man"—in opinion and tendencies, I presume. Ferguson was a member of the club, though after being struck with paralysis in 1780 he never dined out ; but among the constant attenders were Henry Mackenzie, Dugald Stewart, Professor John Playfair, Sir James Hall the geologist ; Robert Adam, architect ; Adam's brother-in-law, John Clerk of Eldin, inventor of the new system of naval tactics ; and Lord Daer—the "noble youthful Daer"—who was the first lord Burns ever met, and taught the poet that in a lord he after all but "met a brither," with nothing uncommon about him,

> Except good sense and social glee,
> An' (what surprised me) modesty.

Lord Daer was the eldest son of the fourth Earl of Selkirk, and, on the outbreak of the French Revolution, a few years

after Burns met him, became one of the most ardent of the
" Friends of the People " ; and was intimate with Mirabeau, to whom he ventured to speak a word for the king's
safety, and was told that the French would not commit
the English blunder of cutting off their king's head,
because that was the usual way to establish a despotism.[1]
Great expectations were cherished of Lord Daer's future,
but they were defeated by his premature death in 1794.
The Mr. M'Gowan mentioned by Swediaur is little known
now, but he was an antiquary and naturalist, a friend and
correspondent of Shenstone, Pennant, and Bishop Percy.
M'Gowan kept house with a friend of his youth, who had
returned to him after long political exile, Andrew Lumisden,
Prince Charlie's Secretary, who was also a warm friend of
Smith, and whose portrait by Tassie is one of the few
relics of Smith's household effects which still exist.
Lumisden had been Hamilton of Bangour's companion in
exile at Rouen, and was no doubt also a member of this
club.

According to Playfair, the chief delight of the club
was to listen to the conversation of its three founders.
" As all the three possessed great talents, enlarged views,
and extensive information, without any of the stateliness and
formality which men of letters think it sometimes necessary
to affect, as they were all three easily amused, and as the
sincerity of their friendship had never been darkened by
the least shade of envy, it would be hard to find an
example where everything favourable to good society was
more perfectly united, and everything adverse more entirely excluded." [2] This friendship of Smith, Black, and
Hutton, if not so famous as the friendship between Smith
and Hume, was not less really memorable. Each of them
had founded—or done more than any other single person
to found—a science ; they may be called the fathers of
modern chemistry, of modern geology, and of modern

[1] Sinclair's *Old Times and Distant Places*, p. 7.
[2] *Transactions*, R.S.E., v. 98.

political economy ; and for all their great achievements, they were yet men of the most unaffected simplicity of character. In other respects they were very different from one another, but their differences only knit them closer together, and made them more interesting to their friends.

Black was a man of fine presence and courtly bearing, grave, calm, polished, well dressed, speaking, what was then rare, correct English without a trace of Scotch accent, and always with sense and insight even in fields beyond his own. Smith used to say that he never knew a man with less nonsense in him than Dr. Black, and that he was often indebted to his better discrimination in the judgment of character, a point in which Smith, not only by the general testimony of his acquaintance, but by his own confession, was by no means strong, inasmuch as he was, as he acknowledges, too apt to form his opinion from a single feature. Now the judgment of character was, according to Robison, Black's very strongest point. " Indeed," says Robison, " were I to say what natural talent Dr. Black possessed in the most uncommon degree, I should say it was his judgment of human character, and a talent which he had of expressing his opinion in a single short phrase, which fixed it in the mind never to be forgotten." [1] He was a very brilliant lecturer, for Brougham, who had been one of his students, said that he had heard Pitt and Fox and Plunket, but for mere intellectual gratification he should prefer sitting again on the old benches of the chemistry class-room, "while the first philosopher of his age was the historian of his own discoveries " ; and, adored as he was by his students, he was the object of scarce less veneration and pride to the whole body of his fellow-citizens. Lord Cockburn tells us how even the wildest boys used to respect Black. " No lad," says he, " could ever be irreverent towards a man so pale, so gentle, so elegant, and so illustrious."

Hutton was in many respects the reverse of Black.

[1] Black's *Works*, I. xxxii.

He was a dweller out of doors, a man of strong vitality and high spirits, careless of dress and appearance, setting little store by the world's prejudices or fashions, and speaking the broadest Scotch, but overflowing with views and speculations and fun, and with a certain originality of expression, often very piquant. Every face brightened, says Playfair, when Hutton entered a room. He had been bred a doctor, though he never practised, but, devoting himself to agriculture, had been for years one of the leading improvers of the Border counties, and is said, indeed, to have been the first man in Scotland to plough with a pair of horses and no driver, the old eight-ox plough being then in universal use. Between his early chemical studies and his later agricultural pursuits, his curiosity was deeply aroused as he walked about the fields and dales, not merely concerning the composition but the origin of the soils and rocks and minerals that lay in the crust of the globe, and he never ceased examining and speculating till he completed his theory of the earth which became a new starting-point for all subsequent geological research. He was a bold investigator, and Playfair distinguishes him finely in this respect from Black by remarking that "Dr. Black hated nothing so much as error, and Dr. Hutton nothing so much as ignorance. The one was always afraid of going beyond the truth, and the other of not reaching it." He went little into general society, but Playfair says that in the more private circles which he preferred he was the most delightful of companions.

The conversation of the club was often, as was to be expected from its composition, scientific, but Professor Playfair says it was always free, and never didactic or disputatious, and that "as the club was much the resort of the strangers who visited Edinburgh from any objects connected with art or with science, it derived from them an extraordinary degree of vivacity and interest." [1]

Its name was the Oyster Club, and it may be thought

[1] *Transactions*, R.S.E., v. 98.

from that circumstance that those great philosophers did not spurn the delights of more ordinary mortals. But probably no three men could be found who cared less for the pleasures of the table. Hutton was an abstainer ; Black a vegetarian, his usual fare being " some bread, a few prunes, and a measured quantity of milk diluted with water " ; and as for Smith, his only weakness seems to have been for lump sugar, according to an anecdote preserved by Scott, which, trivial though it be, may be repeated here, under the shelter of the great novelist's example and of Smith's own biographical principle that nothing about a great man is too minute not to be worth knowing.

Scott, speaking apparently as an eye-witness, says : " We shall never forget one particular evening when he (Smith) put an elderly maiden lady who presided at the tea-table to sore confusion by neglecting utterly her invitation to be seated, and walking round and round the circle, stopping ever and anon to steal a lump from the sugar basin, which the venerable spinster was at length constrained to place on her own knee, as the only method of securing it from his uneconomical depredations. His appearance mumping the eternal sugar was something indescribable." It is probably the same story Robert Chambers gives in his *Traditions of Edinburgh*, and he makes the scene Smith's own parlour, and the elderly spinster his cousin, Miss Jean Douglas. It may have been so, for Scott, as a school companion of young David Douglas, would very likely have been occasionally at Panmure House.

CHAPTER XXII

Soon after Smith settled in Edinburgh he received from his old French friends, the Duchesse d'Enville and her son the Duc de la Rochefoucauld, a presentation copy of a new edition of their ancestor's *Maximes*, accompanied by the following letter from the Duke himself, in which he informs Smith of the interesting circumstance that, in spite of the way his famous ancestor is mentioned in the *Theory of Moral Sentiments*, he had himself at one time undertaken a translation of that work, and only abandoned the task when he found himself anticipated by the publication of the translation by Abbé Blavet in 1774. It is a little curious that a disciple of Quesnay, a regular frequenter of Mirabeau's economic dinners, should take no notice in his letter of Smith's greater work, so lately published.

PARIS, 3 *mars* 1778.

Le désir de se rappeller à votre souvenir, monsieur, quand on a eu l'honneur de vous connoître doit vous paroître fort naturel ; permettez que nous saisissons pour cela, ma mère et moi, l'occasion d'une édition nouvelle des *Maximes de la Rochefoucauld*, dont nous prenons la liberté de vous offrir un exemplaire. Vous voyez que vous n'avons point de rancune, puisque le mal que vous avez dit de lui dans la *Théorie des Sentimens Moraux* ne nous empêche point de vous envoyer ce même ouvrage. Il s'en est même fallu de peu que je ne fisse encore plus, car j'avois eu peutêtre la témérité d'entreprendre une traduction de votre *Théorie ;* mais comme je venois de terminer la première partie, j'ai vu paroître la traduction de M. l'Abbé Blavet, et j'ai été forcé de renoncer au plaisir que j'aurois eu de faire passer dans ma langue un des meilleurs ouvrages de la vôtre.

Il auroit bien fallu pour lors entreprendre une justification de mon grandpère. Peutêtre n'auroit-il pas été difficile première-ment de l'excuser, en disant, qu'il avoit toujours vu les hommes à la Cour, et dans la guerre civile, *deux théâtres sur lesquels ils sont certainement plus mauvais qu'ailleurs ;* et ensuite de justifier, par la conduite personnelle de l'auteur, les principes qui sont certainement trop généralisés dans son ouvrage. Il a pris la partie pour le tout ; et parceque les gens qu'il avoit eu le plus sous les yeux étoient animés par *l'amour-propre,* il en a fait le mobile général de tous les hommes. Au reste quoique son ouvrage mérite à certains égards d'être combattu, il est cependant estimable même pour le fond, et beaucoup pour la forme.

Permettez-moi de vous demander, si nous aurons bientôt une édition complète des œuvres de votre illustre ami M. Hume ? Nous l'avons sincèrement regretté.

Recevez, je vous supplie, l'expression sincère de tous les senti-mens d'estime et d'attachement avec lesquels j'ai l'honneur d'être, monsieur, votre très humble et très obéissant serviteur,

LE DUC DE LA ROCHEFOUCAULD.[1]

What immediate answer Smith gave to this letter is unknown, and he certainly suffered the offending allusion to his correspondent's ancestor to remain unmodified in the new edition of the *Theory* which appeared in 1781, but eventually at any rate he came to think that he had done the author of the *Maximes* an injustice by associating him in the same condemnation with Mandeville, and when Dugald Stewart visited Paris in 1789 he was commissioned by Smith to express to the Duc de la Rochefoucauld his sincere regret for having done so, and to inform him that the error would be repaired in the forthcoming edition of the work, which was at that time in preparation.[2] This was done. In that final edition the allusion to Rochefou-cauld was entirely suppressed, and the censure confined to Mandeville alone.

While Smith's French friends were remonstrating with

[1] Stewart's *Works*, x. 46.   [2] *Ibid.*, v. 256.

him about an incidental allusion in the *Theory of Moral Sentiments*, his old friend, Lord Kames—still at eighty-three as keen for metaphysical controversy as he had been with Bishop Butler sixty years before—was preparing an elaborate attack upon the theory of the book itself, which he proposed to incorporate in a new edition of his own *Principles of Morality and Religion*. Before publishing this examination of the theory, however, he sent the manuscript to Smith for perusal, and received the following reply :—

16th November 1778.

My DEAR LORD—I am much obliged to you for the kind communication of the objections you propose to make in yr. new edition to my system. Nothing can be more perfectly friendly and polite than the terms in which you express yourself with regard to me, and I should be extremely peevish and ill-tempered if I could make the slightest opposition to their publication. I am no doubt extremely sorry to find myself of a different opinion both from so able a judge of the subject and from so old and good a friend ; but differences of this kind are inevitable, and besides, *Partium contentionibus respublica crescit.* I should have been waiting on your Lordship before this time, but the remains of a cold have for these four or five days past made it inconvenient for me to go out in the evening. Remember me to Mrs. Drummond,[1] and believe me to be, my dear Lord, your most obliged and most humble servant,   ADAM SMITH.

Smith had most probably discussed the merits of Lord Kames's objections with his lordship already, so that he saw no occasion to reply to them in his letter. What Kames principally combated was the idea that sympathy with the sufferings of another originated in any way in our imagining what would be our own feelings if we were in the sufferer's place. He contends, on the contrary, that

[1] Mrs. Drummond is Lord Kames's wife. She had succeeded to the estate of her father, Mr. Drummond of Blair Drummond, and having along with her husband assumed her father's surname in addition to her own, was now Mrs. Home Drummond. It may perhaps be necessary to add that the title of a Scotch judge is not extended, even by courtesy, to his wife.

it is excited directly by the perception of the screams, contortions, tears, or other outward signs of the pain that is endured ; and that trying to put ourselves in the sufferer's place produces really a self-satisfaction, on account of our own immunity from his troubles, which has the effect not of awakening the feeling of pity but of moderating and diminishing it.

A second objection he raises is that if Smith's theory were true, those in whom the power of imagination was strongest would feel the force of the moral duties most sensibly, and *vice versâ*, which, he says, is contradicted by experience. His last objection is that while the theory proposes to explain the origin of the moral sentiments so far as they respect other persons, it fails entirely to account for those sentiments in regard to ourselves. Our distress on losing an only son and our gratitude for a kindly office neither need to be explained nor can they be explained by imagining ourselves to be other persons.

One of the first acquaintances Smith made in Edinburgh was a young Caithness laird who was presently to make a considerable figure in public life—the patriotic and laborious Sir John Sinclair, founder of the Board of Agriculture, promoter of the Statistical Account of Scotland, and author of the *History of the Public Revenue, the Code of Agriculture, the Code of Health*, and innumerable pamphlets on innumerable subjects. Sinclair was not yet in Parliament when Smith came to Edinburgh in the end of 1777, but his hands were already full of serious work. He was busy with his *History of the Public Revenue*, in which Smith gave him every assistance in his power, and he had actually finished a treatise on the Christian Sabbath, which, in deference to Smith's advice, he never gave to the press. The object of this treatise was to show that the puritanical Sabbath observance of Scotland had no countenance in Holy Scripture, and that, while part of the day ought certainly to be devoted to divine service, the rest might be usefully employed in occupations of a character

not strictly religious without infringing any divine law.
When the work was completed, Sinclair showed the manuscript to Smith, who dissuaded him strongly from printing
it. "Your work, Mr. Sinclair," said he, "is very ably
written, but I advise you not to publish it, for rest assured
that the Sabbath as a political institution is of inestimable
value independently of its claim to divine authority." [1]

One day Sinclair brought Smith the news of the surrender of Burgoyne at Saratoga in October 1777, and exclaimed in the deepest concern that the nation was ruined.
' There is a great deal of ruin in a nation," was Smith's
calm reply. In November 1778 Sinclair wanted Smith to
send him to Thurso Castle the loan of the important
French book on contemporary systems of taxation,
which is so often quoted in the *Wealth of Nations*—the
Mémoires concernant les Impositions—and of which only 100
copies were originally printed, and only four apparently
found their way to this country. Smith naturally hesitated to send so rare a book so far, but promised his young
correspondent to give him, when he returned to Edinburgh,
not only that book but everything else, printed or written,
which he possessed on the subject. Smith's letter is as
follows :—

Mr. Smith presents his most respectful compliments to Mr.
Sinclair of Ulbster.

The *Mémoires sur les Finances* [2] are engaged for four months to
come to Mr. John Davidson ; [3] when he is done with them Mr.
Smith would be very happy to accommodate Mr. Sinclair, but
acknowledges he is a little uneasy about the safety of the conveyance and the greatness of the distance. He has frequent occasion to
consult the book himself, both in the course of his private studies

---

[1] Sinclair's *Memoirs of Sir John Sinclair*, i. 36.

[2] Smith, writing from memory and without the book at hand, makes
a verbal mistake in the title.

[3] Doubtless John Davidson, W.S., a well-known antiquary of the
period, who is mentioned favourably in the preface to Robertson's
History of Scotland as a special authority on certain facts of the life of
Mary Stuart.

and in the business of his present employment, and is therefore not very willing to let it go out of Edinburgh. The book was never properly published, but there were a few more copies printed than was necessary for the Commission, for whose use it was compiled.

One of these I obtained by the particular favour of Mr. Turgot, the late Controller-General of the Finances. I have heard but of three copies in Great Britain : one belongs to a noble lord, who obtained it by connivance, as he told me ;[1] one is in the Secretary of State's office, and the third belongs to a private gentleman. How these two were obtained I know not, but suspect it was in the same manner. If any accident should happen to my book, the loss is perfectly irreparable. When Mr. Sinclair comes to Edinburgh I shall be very happy to communicate to him not only that book, but everything else I have upon the subject, both printed and manuscript, and am, with the highest respect for his character his most obedient humble servant,   ADAM SMITH.

EDINBURGH, 24*th November* 1778.[2]

The *Mémoires* was printed in 1768, but it may be reasonably inferred, from Smith's account of the extreme difficulty of getting a copy, that he only obtained his in 1774, on the advent of Turgot to power. If that be so, much in the chapters on taxation in the *Wealth of Nations* must have been written in London after that date.

Sir John's biographer quotes a passage from another letter of Smith in connection with his correspondent's financial studies. This letter—which Archdeacon Sinclair describes as a " holograph letter in six folio pages "—is no longer extant, but it concluded with the following remarks on the taxation of the necessaries and luxuries of the poor :—

I dislike all taxes that may affect the necessary expenses of the poor. They, according to circumstances, either oppress the

---

[1] Probably Lord Rosslyn, for Bentham, in writing to advise Lord Shelburne to procure a copy of this book, mentions that he knew Lord Rosslyn had a copy, which he had obtained from Mr. Anstruther, M.P., who happened to be in Paris when it was printed, and contrived to get a copy somehow there.

[2] *Sir J. Sinclair's Correspondence*, i. 388.

people immediately subject to them, or are repaid with great interest by the rich, *i.e.* by their employers in the advanced wages of their labour.   Taxes on the *luxuries* of the poor, upon their beer and other spirituous liquors, for example, as long as they are so moderate as not to give much temptation to smuggling, I am so far from disapproving, that I look upon them as the best of sumptuary laws.

I could write a volume upon the folly and the bad effects of all the legal encouragements that have been given either to the linen manufacture or to the fisheries.—I have the honour to be, with most sincere regard, my dear friend, most affectionately yours,   ADAM SMITH.[1]

[1] Sinclair's *Life of Sir J. Sinclair*, i. 39.

CHAPTER XXIII

In 1779 Smith was consulted by various members of the Government with respect to the probable effects of the contemplated concession of free trade to Ireland, and two letters of Smith still remain—one to the Earl of Carlisle, First Lord of Trade and Plantations, and the other to Henry Dundas—which state his views on this subject. A few preliminary words will explain the situation. The policy of commercial restriction has probably never been used with more cruelty or more disaster than it was used against the people of Ireland between the Restoration and the Union. They were not allowed to trade as they would with Great Britain or her colonies, because they were aliens, and they were not allowed to trade as they would with foreign countries, because they were British subjects. There were various industries they had special advantages for establishing, but the moment they began to export the products the English Parliament, or their own Irish Parliament under English influence, closed the markets against them. Living in an excellent grazing country, their first great product was cattle, and the export of cattle was prohibited. When stopped from sending live meat, they tried to send dead, but the embargo was promptly extended to salt provisions. Driven from cattle, they betook themselves to sheep, and sent over wool; that was stopped, allowed, and stopped again. When their raw wool was denied a market, they next tried cloth, but England then bargained for the suppression of the chief branches of Irish woollen manufacture by promising Ireland a monopoly of the manufacture of linen. Other infant industries which gave signs of growing to prosperity were by the same means crushed in the cradle, and Ireland was in consequence never able to acquire that nest-egg of industrial capital and training which England won in the eighteenth century.

All this systematic oppression of national industry had produced its natural fruit in a distressing scarcity of employment, and in 1778, though it was a year of plenty, and meal was at its cheapest, many thousands of the population were starving because they had not the means to buy it ; the farmers were unable to pay their rents because they got such poor prices ; processions of unemployed paraded the streets of Dublin carrying a black fleece in token of their want ; and the Viceroy from the Castle warned the English ministry that an enlargement of the trade of Ireland had become a matter of the merest necessity, without which she could never pay her national obligations to the English Exchequer.

But it was neither the voice of justice nor the cry of distress that moved the Government ; it was the alarm of external danger. The strength of England was then strained as it has never been before or since in an unequal war with the combined forces of France, Spain, and America, and it was no time either to feed or to neglect discontent at home. Ireland had already sent many recruits to the revolutionary army in America, and at this very moment the Irish Protestants, incensed at the indifference of Government to the protection of their ports, had, under the lead of Lord Charlemont, raised an illegal army of 42,000 volunteers, and placed them under arms without the consent of the Crown.

The demand of free trade for Ireland came therefore with sanctions that could not be ignored, and Lord North's first idea was to give Ireland the same rights of trading with the colonies and foreign countries as England enjoyed, except in the two particulars of the export of wool and glass and the import of tobacco. This proposal was not satisfactory to the Irish, because it failed to remove their chief grievance, the restriction on their trade in woollen goods, but it provoked a storm of indignation in Liverpool, Manchester, Glasgow, and all the great manufacturing and trading centres of Great Britain. They petitioned the Government declaring that the proposed measure would ruin them, for a reason with which we are still very familiar, because it would be impossible for any English or Scotch manufacturer to compete against the pauper labour of Ireland. Lord North, frightened, as Burke said, into some concessions by the menaces of Ireland, was now frightened out of them again by the menaces of England, and he cut down his original proposals till the Irish thought he was merely trifling with their troubles, and their whole island was aflame. Associations were formed, commotions broke out; a great meeting in Dublin in April 1779 pledged itself to buy nothing of English or Scotch manufacture; many of the county meetings instructed their representatives in Parliament to vote no money bill for more than six months till Irish grievances were redressed; and the Lord-Lieutenant wrote the Government that popular discontent was seriously increasing, that French and American emissaries were actively abroad, that the outlook was black indeed if next session of Parliament passed without giving the Irish a satisfactory measure of free trade, and that " nothing short of permission to export coarse woollen goods would in any degree give general satisfaction."

As soon as the Irish Parliament met in October a new member of the House, who was presently to become a new power in the country, Henry Grattan, rose and moved an amendment to the address, urging the necessity for a free export trade; and the amendment was, on the suggestion of Flood, extended to a general demand for free trade,

including imports as well as exports, and in this form was
carried without a division. The reply to the address,
however, seemed studiously ambiguous, and inflamed the
prevailing discontent. On King William's birthday the
statue of that monarch in Dublin was hung over with
expressive placards, and the city volunteers turned out and
paraded round it ; a few days later a mob from the
Liberties attacked the house of the Attorney-General, and
proceeding to Parliament, swore all the members they
found to vote only short money bills till free trade were
conceded ; and then Grattan, in his place in the House,
carried by three to one a resolution to grant no new taxes
and to give only six months' bills for the appropriated
duties.

The Government was now thoroughly alarmed ; they
must at last face the question of free trade for Ireland in
dead earnest, and applied themselves without delay to
learn from all who understood the subject what would be
the real effect on England of removing the Irish restrictions.
They requested many of the leading public men whom
they trusted in Ireland—Lord Lifford, Hely Hutchinson,
Henry Burgh, and others—to prepare detailed statements
of their views on the commercial grievances of their
country and the operation of the proposed remedies. Mr.
Lecky, who has seen those statements at the Record Office,
says they are conspicuous for their clear grasp of the principles of free trade, and I think that they may with great
probability be considered a fruit of Smith's then recently
published work, because Hely Hutchinson's statement, or
its substance, has been published—it was, indeed, the last
book publicly burned in this country—and it makes
frequent quotations from the *Wealth of Nations*. It was
in these circumstances that the Board of Trade made a
double application to Adam Smith for his opinion on the
subject. Lord Carlisle, the head of the Board, applied to
him through Adam Ferguson, who had been Secretary of
the Commission, of which Lord Carlisle had been President,

sent out to America the year before to negotiate terms of peace ; and Mr. William Eden, Secretary of the Board, applied to him through Henry Dundas. With Eden (afterwards the first Lord Auckland) Smith became later on well acquainted ; he was married in 1776 to a daughter of Smith's old friend, Sir Gilbert Elliot, but at the date of this correspondence their personal acquaintance does not seem to have been intimate.

Smith's letter to Lord Carlisle is as follows :—

MY LORD—My friend Mr. Ferguson showed me a few days ago a letter.in which your Lordship was so good as to say that you wished to know my opinion concerning the consequence of granting to the Irish that *free trade* which they at present demand so importunately. I shall not attempt to express how much I feel myself flattered by your Lordship's very honourable remembrance of me, but shall without further preface endeavour to explain that opinion, such as it may be, as distinctly as I can.

Till we see the heads of the bill which the Irish propose to send over, it is impossible to know precisely what they mean by a free trade.

It is possible they may mean by it no more than the freedom of exporting all goods, whether of their own produce or imported from abroad, to all countries (Great Britain and the British settlements excepted) subject to no other duties or restraints than such as their own Parliament may impose. At present they can export glass, tho' of their own manufacture, to no country whatever. Raw silk, a foreign commodity, is under the same restraint. Wool they can export only to Great Britain. Woollen manufactures they can export only from certain ports in Ireland to certain ports in Great Britain. A very slender interest of our own manufacturers is the foundation of all these unjust and oppressive restraints. The watchful jealousy of those gentlemen is alarmed least the Irish, who have never been able to supply compleatly even their own market with glass or woollen manufactures, should be able to rival them in foreign markets.

The Irish may mean by a *free trade* to demand, besides, the freedom of importing from wherever they can buy them cheapest all such foreign goods as they have occasion for. At present they can import glass, sugars of foreign plantations, except those of Spain or Portugal, and certain sorts of East India goods, from no country but Great Britain. Tho' Ireland was relieved from these and from all restraints of the same kind, the interest of Great Britain could surely suffer very little. The Irish probably mean to demand no more than this most just and reasonable freedom of exportation and importation ; in restraining which we seem to me rather to have gratified the impertinence than to have promoted any solid interest of our merchants and manufacturers.

The Irish may, however, mean to demand, besides, the same freedom of exportation and importation to and from the British settlements in Africa and America which is enjoyed by the inhabitants of Great Britain. As Ireland has contributed little either to the establishment or defence of these settlements, this demand would be less reasonable than the other two. But as I never believed that the monopoly of our Plantation trade was really advantageous to Great Britain, so I cannot believe that the admission of Ireland to a share in that monopoly, or the extension of this monopoly to all the British islands, would be really dis-advantageous.

Over and above all this, the Irish may mean to demand the freedom of importing their own produce and manufactures into Great Britain, subject to no other duties than such as are equiva-lent to the duties imposed upon the like goods of British produce or manufacture. Tho' even this demand, the most unreason-able of all, should be granted, I cannot believe that the interest of Britain would be hurt by it. On the contrary, the competition of Irish goods in the British market might contribute to break down in part that monopoly which we have most absurdly granted to the greater part of our own workmen against ourselves. It would, however, be a long time before this competition could be very considerable. In the present state of Ireland centuries must pass away before the greater part of its manufactures could vie with those of England. Ireland has little coal, the coallieries about Lough Neagh being of little consequence to the greater part of the country ; it is ill provided with wood : two articles essentially necessary to the progress of great manufactures. It wants order, police, and a regular administration of justice, both to protect and to restrain the inferior ranks of people : articles more essential to the progress of industry than both coal and wood put together, and which Ireland must continue to want as long as it continues to be divided between two hostile nations, the oppressors and the oppressed, the Protestants and the Papists.

Should the industry of Ireland, in consequence of freedom and good government, ever equal that of England, so much the better would it be not only for the whole British Empire, but for the particular province of England. As the wealth and industry of Lancashire does not obstruct but promote that of Yorkshire, so the wealth and industry of Ireland would not obstruct but promote that of England.

It makes me very happy to find that in the midst of the public misfortunes a person of your Lordship's rank and elevation of mind doth not despair of the commonwealth, but is willing to accept of an active share in administration. That your Lordship may be the happy means of restoring vigour and decision to our counsels, and in consequence of them, success to our arms, is the sincere wish of, my Lord, your Lordship's most obliged and most obedient servant, ADAM SMITH.[1]

EDINBURGH, 8*th November* 1779.

The letter to Dundas was published in the *English Historical Review* for April 1886 (p. 308), by Mr. Oscar Browning, from a copy in the Auckland papers then in his possession. Mr. Browning gives at the same time the previous letters of Dundas to Eden and Smith respectively. To Eden he writes :—

MELVILLE, 30*th October* 1779.

MY DEAR SIR—I received yours last night and have sent it this morning to Smith. When I see or hear from him you shall hear again from me upon the different parts of your letter. The enclosed is a copy of my letter to Smith, which will show you what are my present crude ideas upon the subject of Ireland.— Yours faithfully, HENRY DUNDAS.

His letter to Smith is as follows :—

MELVILLE, 30*th October* 1779.

DEAR SIR—I received the enclosed last night from Mr. Eden. The questions he puts would require a Volume to answer them in place of a Letter. Think of it, however, and let me have your ideas upon it. For my own part I confess myself little alarmed about what others seem so much alarmed. I doubt much if a free trade to Ireland is so very much to be dreaded. There is trade enough

---

[1] Morrison MSS.

in the World for the Industry both of Britain and Ireland, and if two or three places either in South or North Britain should suffer some damage, which, by the bye, will be very gradual, from the loss of their monopoly, that is a very small consideration in the general scale and policy of the country. The only thing to be guarded against is the people in Ireland being able to undersell us in foreign mercates from the want of taxes and the cheapness of Labour. But a wise statesman will be able to regulate that by proper distribution of taxes upon the materials and commodities of the respective Countrys. I believe a Union would be best if it can be accomplished ; if not the Irish Parliament might be managed by the proper distribution of the Loaves and Fishes, so that the Legislatures of the two countrys may act in union together. In short, it has long appeared to me that the bearing down of Ireland was in truth bearing down a substantial part of the Naval and Military strength of our own Country. Indeed, it has often shocked me in the House of Commons for these two years past, when anything was hinted in favour of Ireland by friends of giving them only the benefit of making the most of what their soil and climate afforded them, to hear it received as a sufficient answer that a town in England or Scotland would be hurt by such an Indulgence. This kind of reasoning will no longer do. But I find, in place of asking yours, I am giving you my opinion. So adieu.—Yours sincerely,   HENRY DUNDAS.

To this manly, but somewhat inconsistent letter, acknowledging the full right of a people to make the most of what their soil and climate afforded, but yet afraid to give them the whole advantage of their cheapness of labour, Smith sent the following reply, probably on the 1st of November :—

MY DEAR LORD [1]—I am very happy to find that Your Lordship's opinion concerning the circumstance of granting a free trade to Ireland coincides so perfectly with my own.

I cannot believe that the manufacturers of Great Britain can for a century to come suffer much from the Rivalship of those of Ireland, even though the Irish should be indulged in a free trade. Ireland has neither the skill nor the stock which would enable Her to rival England, and tho' both may be acquired in time,

---

[1] The Lord Advocate is usually addressed as My Lord.

to acquire them completely will require the opperation of little less than a Century. Ireland has neither coal nor wood ; the former seems to have been denied to her by nature ; and though her Soil and Climate are perfectly suited for raising the Latter, yet to raise it to the same degree as in England will require more than a Century. I perfectly agree with your Lordship too that to Crush the Industry of so great and so fine a Province of the Empire in order to favour the monopoly of some particular Towns in Scotland or England is equally injurious and impolitic. The general opulence and improvement of Ireland must certainly, under proper management, afford much greater Resources to Government than can ever be drawn from a few mercantile or manufacturing Towns.

Till the Irish Parliament sends over the Heads of their proposed Bill, it may perhaps be uncertain what they understand by a Free Trade.

They may perhaps understand by it no more than the power of exporting their own produce to the foreign country where they can find the best mercate. Nothing can be more just and reasonable than this demand, nor can anything be more unjust and unreasonable than some of the restraints which their Industry in this respect at present labours under. They are prohibited under the heaviest penalties to export Glass to any Country. Wool they can export only to Great Britain. Woolen goods they can export only from certain Ports in their own Country and to certain Ports in Great Britain.

They may mean to demand the Power of importing such goods as they have occasion for from any Country where they can find them cheapest, subject to no other duties and restraints than such as may be imposed by their own Parliament. This freedom, tho' in my opinion perfectly reasonable, will interfere a little with some of our paltry monopolies. Glass, Hops, Foreign Sugars, several sorts of East Indian goods can at present be imported only from Great Britain.

They may mean to demand a free trade to our American and African Plantations, free from the restraints which the 18th of the present King imposed upon it, or at least from some of those restraints, such as the prohibition of exporting thither their own Woolen and Cotton manufactures, Glass, Hatts, Hops, Gunpowder, etc. This freedom, tho' it would interfere with some of our monopolies, I am convinced, would do no harm to Great Britain. It would be reasonable, indeed, that whatever goods were exported from Ireland to these Plantations should be subject to the like duties as those of the same kind exported from England in the terms of the 18th of the present King.

They may mean to demand a free trade to Great Britain, their manufactures and produce when Imported into this country being subjected to no other duties than the like manufactures and produce of our own. Nothing, in my opinion, would be more highly advantageous to both countries than this mutual freedom of trade. It would help to break down that absurd monopoly which we have most absurdly established against ourselves in favour of almost all the different Classes of our own manufacturers.

Whatever the Irish mean to demand in this way, in the present situation of our affairs I should think it madness not to grant it. Whatever they may demand, our manufacturers, unless the leading and principal men among them are properly dealt with beforehand, will probably oppose it. That they may be so dealt with I know from experience, and that it may be done at little expense and with no great trouble. I could even point to some persons who, I think, are fit and likely to deal with them successfully for this purpose. I shall not say more upon this till I see you, which I shall do the first moment I can get out of this Town.

I am much honoured by Mr. Eden's remembrance of me. I beg you will present my most respectful compliments to him, and that you will believe me to be, my dear Lord, most faithfully yours,   ADAM SMITH.

1st November 1779.

I cannot explain the allusion in the closing parts of the letter to the writer's personal experience of the ease with which the opposition of manufacturers to proposed measures of public policy could be averted by sagacious management and a little expenditure of money. Nor can I say what persons he had in view to recommend as likely to do this work successfully; but his advice seems to imply that he agreed with the political maxim that the opposition of the pocket is best met through the pocket.

He takes no notice of Dundas's suggestion of a union with Great Britain, but we know from the *Wealth of Nations* that he was a strong advocate of a union—not, of course, on Dundas's ground that a union would better enable the English Parliament to counteract the effects of the competition of Irish pauper labour, but for a reason which will sound curiously perhaps in the middle of our present agitations, that a union would deliver the Irish people from the tyranny of an oppressive aristocracy, which was the great cause of that kingdom being then divided into "two hostile nations," to use his words to Lord Carlisle, "the oppressors and the oppressed." He avers in the *Wealth of Nations* that "without a union with Great Britain the inhabitants of Ireland are not likely for many ages to consider themselves one people." [1]

[1] Book V. chap. iii.

CHAPTER XXIV

WHILE these communications with leading statesmen were showing the impression the *Wealth of Nations* had made in this country, Smith was receiving equally satisfactory proofs of its recognition abroad. The book had been translated into Danish by F. Dräbye, and the translation published in two volumes in 1779-80. Apparently the translator was contemplating the publication of a second edition, for he communicated with Smith through a Danish friend, desiring to know what alterations Smith proposed to make in his second edition, of whose appearance the translator had manifestly not heard. Smith thereupon wrote Strahan the following letter, asking him to send a copy of the second edition to Dräbye :—

DEAR SIR—I think it is predestined that I shall never write to you except to ask some favour of you or to put you to some trouble. This letter is not to depart from the style of all the rest. I am a subscriber for Watt's Copying Machine. The price is six guineas for the machine and five shillings for the packing-box ; I should be glad too he would send me a ream of the copying paper, together with all the other specimens of ink, etc., which commonly accompany the machine. For payment of this to Mr. Woodmason, the seller, whose printed letter I have enclosed, you will herewith receive a bill of eight Guineas payable at sight. If, after paying for all these, there should be any remnant, there is a tailour in Craven Street, one Heddington, an acquaintance of James M'Pherson, to whom I owe some shillings, I believe under ten, certainly under twenty ; pay him what I owe. He is a very honest man, and will ask no more than is due. Before I left London I had sent several times for his account, but he always put it off.

I had almost forgot I was the author of the inquiry concerning the Wealth of Nations, but some time ago I received a letter from a friend in Denmark telling me that it had been translated into Danish by one Mr. Dreby, secretary to a new erected board of trade and Economy in that Kingdom. My correspondent, Mr. Holt, who is an assessor of that Board, desires me, in the name of Mr. Dreby, to know what alterations I propose to make in a second Edition. The shortest answer to this is to send them the second edition. I propose, therefore, by this Post to desire Mr. Cadell to send three copies of the second Edition, handsomely bound and gilt, to Mr. Anker, Consul-General of Denmark, who is an old acquaintance—one for himself and the other two to be by him transmitted to Mr. Holt and Mr. Dreby. At our final settlement I shall debit myself with these three Books. I suspect I am now almost your only customer for my own book. Let me know, however, how matters go on in this respect.

After begging your pardon a thousand times for having so long neglected to write you, I shall conclude with assuring you that notwithstanding this neglect I have the highest respect and esteem for you and for your whole family, and that I am, most sincerely and affectionately, ever yours,   ADAM SMITH.

EDINBURGH, CANONGATE, 26 *Oct.* 1780.[1]

As this Danish translation has come up, it may be mentioned here that the *Wealth of Nations* had already been translated into several other languages. The Abbé Blavet's French version ran through the pages of the *Journal de l'Agriculture, des Commerce, des Finances, et des Arts* month by month in the course of the years 1779 and 1780, and was then published in book form in 1781. This was not a satisfactory translation, though through mere priority of occupation it held the field for a number of years and went through a number of editions. In

[1] *New York Evening Post*, 30th April 1887. Original in possession of Mr. Worthington C. Ford, Washington, U.S.A.

1790 a second translation appeared by Roucher and the Marquise de Condorcet, and in 1802 a third, the best, by Germain Garnier. Smith's own friend Morellet, receiving a presentation copy from the author through Lord Shelburne on its publication, carried it with him to Brienne, the seat of his old Sorbonne comrade the Archbishop of Toulouse, and set at work to translate it there. But he tells us himself that the ex-Benedictine Abbé (Blavet), who had formerly murdered the *Theory of Moral Sentiments* by a bad translation, anticipated him by his equally bad translation of the *Wealth of Nations*; and so, adds Morellet, " poor Smith was again betrayed instead of being translated, according to the Italian proverb, *Tradottore traditore.*"[1] Morellet still thought, however, of publishing his own version, offering it to the booksellers first for 100 louis-d'or and then for nothing, and many years afterwards he asked his friend the Archbishop of Toulouse, when he had become Minister of France, for a grant of 100 louis to pay for its production, but was as unsuccessful with the Minister as he was with the booksellers. All the good Abbé says is that he is sure the money would have been well spent, because the translation was carefully done, and he knew the subject better than any of the other translators. Everything that was abstract in the theory of Smith was, he says, quite unintelligible in Blavet's translation, and even in Roucher's subsequent one, and could be read to more advantage in his own ; but after a good translation was published by Garnier in 1802, the Abbé gave up all thought of giving his to the press.

A German translation by J. F. Schuler appeared, the first volume in 1776 and the second in 1778, but Roscher says it is worse done than Blavet's translation ; and little attention was paid to Smith or his work in Germany until about the close of the century, when a new translation was published by Professor Garve, the

[1] Morellet, *Mémoires*, i. 244.

metaphysician. Roscher observes that neither Frederick the Great nor the Emperor Joseph, nor any of the princes who patronised the Physiocrats so much, paid the least heed to the *Wealth of Nations*; that in the German press it was neither quoted nor confuted, but merely ignored ; and that he himself had taken the trouble to look through the economic literature published between 1776 and 1794, to discover any marks of the reception of the book, and found that Smith's name was very seldom mentioned, and then without any idea of his importance. One spot ought to be excepted—the little kingdom of Hanover, which, from its connection with the English Crown, participated in the contemporary French complaint of Anglomania. Göttingen had its influential school of admirers of English institutions and literature ; the *Wealth of Nations* was reviewed in the *Gelehrte Anzeigen* of Göttingen early in 1777, and one of the professors of the University there announced a course of lectures upon it in the winter session of 1777-78.[1] But before Smith died his work was beginning to be clearly understood among German thinkers. Gentz, the well-known politician, writes a friend in December 1790 that he had been reading the book for the third time, and thought it "far the most important work which is written in any language on this subject" ;[2] and Professor C. J. Kraus writes Voigt in 1796 that the world had never seen a more important work, and that no book since the New Testament has produced more beneficial effects than this book would produce when it got better known. A few years later it was avowedly shaping the policy of Stein.

It was translated into Italian in 1780, and in Spain it had the curious fortune of being suppressed by the Inquisition on account of "the lowness of its style and the looseness of its morals." Sir John Macpherson—Warren

---

[1] Roscher, *Geschichte*, p. 599.
[2] Gentz, *Briefe an Christian Garve*, p. 63.

Hastings' successor as Governor-General of India—writes Gibbon as if he saw the sentence of the Inquisition posted on the church doors in a Spanish tour he made in 1792 ;[1] but a change must have speedily come over the censorial mind, for a Spanish translation by J. A. Ortez was published in four volumes in 1794, with additions relating to Spain.

Smith continued, as he says, to be a good customer for his own book. There is another letter which, though undated and unaddressed, was evidently written about this time to Cadell, directing presentation copies of both his books to be sent to Mrs. Ross of Crighton, the wife of his own " very near relation," Colonel Patrick Ross.

DEAR SIR—Mrs. Ross of Crighton, now living in Welbeck Street, is my particular friend, and the wife of Lieutenant-Collonel (*sic*) Patrick Ross, in the service of the East India Company, my very near relation. When she left this she seemed to intimate that she wished to have a copy of my last book from the author. May I therefore beg the favour of you to send her a copy of both my books, viz. of the Theory of Moral Sentiments and of the Enquiry concerning the " Wealth of Nations," handsomely bound and gilt, placing the same to my account, and writing upon the blank-leaf of each, *From the Authour.* Be so good as to remember me to Mrs. Cadell, Mr. Strahan and family, and all other friends, and believe me, ever yours,

ADAM SMITH.[2]

Smith's new duties did not pre-engage his pen from higher work altogether, for before the close of 1782 he had written some considerable additions to the *Wealth of Nations*, which he proposed to insert in the third edition, among them a history of the trading companies of Great Britain, including, no doubt, his history of the East India Company, which Mr. Thorold Rogers supposed him to

---

[1] Gibbon's *Miscellaneous Works*, ii. 479.
[2] *New York Evening Post*, 30th April 1887. Original in possession of Mr. Worthington C. Ford, Washington, U.S.A.

have written ten years before and kept in his desk.　He writes Cadell on the 7th December 1782 :—

I have many apologies to make to you for my idleness since I came to Scotland.　The truth is, I bought at London a good many partly new books or editions that were new to me, and the amusement I found in reading and diverting myself with them debauched me from my proper business, the preparing a new edition of the *Wealth of Nations*.　I am now, however, heartily engaged at my proper work, and I hope in two or three months to send you up the second edition corrected in many places, with three or four very considerable additions, chiefly to the second volume.　Among the rest is a short but, I flatter myself, a complete history of all the trading companies in Great Britain. These additions I mean not only to be inserted at their proper places into the new edition, but to be printed separately and to be sold for a shilling or half-a-crown to the purchasers of the old edition.　The price must depend on the bulk of the additions when they are all written out.　It would give me great satisfaction if you would let me know by the return of the Post if this delay will not be inconvenient.　Remember me to Strahan.　He will be so good as excuse my not writing to him, as I have nothing to say but what I have now said to you, and he knows my aversion to writing. [1]

The additions of which he speaks in this letter were published separately in 1783 in quarto, so as to suit the two previous editions of the work, and the new edition containing them was published in the end of 1784 in three volumes octavo, at the price of a guinea.　The delay was due to booksellers' reasons.　Dr. Swediaur, the eminent Paris physician, who was resident in Edinburgh at the time studying with Cullen, wrote Bentham in November 1784 that Smith, whom he used to see at least once a week, had shown him the new edition printed and finished, but had told him that Cadell would not publish it till all the people of fashion had arrived in London, and would then at once push a large sale.　Swediaur adds that

---

[1] Printed in a catalogue of a sale of autographs at Messrs. Sotheby, Wilkinson, and Hodge's on 26th and 27th November 1891.

he found this was a bookseller's trick very generally practised, and of Smith himself he says he found him " a very unprejudiced and good man." [1]

The principal additions are the result of investigations to which he seems to have been prompted by current agitations of the stream of political opinion. He gives now, for example, a fuller account of the working of the bounty system in the Scotch fisheries, which was then the subject of a special parliamentary inquiry, and on which his experience as a Commissioner of Customs furnished him with many opportunities of gaining accurate information; and he enters on a careful examination of the chartered and regulated corporations, and especially of the East India Company, whose government of the great oriental dependency was at the moment a question of such urgency that Fox introduced his India Bill which killed the Coalition Ministry in 1783, and Pitt established the Board of Control in 1784.

The new matter contains two recommendations which have attracted comment as ostensible contraventions of free trade doctrine. One of them is the recommendation of a tax on the export of wool ; but then the tax was to take the place of the absolute prohibition of the export which then existed, and it was not to be imposed for protectionist reasons, but for the simple financial purpose of raising a revenue. Smith thought few taxes would yield so considerable a revenue with so little inconvenience to anybody. The other supposed contravention of free trade doctrine is the sanction he lends to temporary commercial monopolies ; but then this is avowedly a device for an exceptional situation in which a project promises great eventual benefit to the public, but the projectors might without the monopoly be debarred from undertaking it by the magnitude of the risk it involved. He places this temporary monopoly in the same category with authors' copyrights and inventors' patents ; it was the easiest and

[1] Add. MSS., 33,540.

most natural way of recompensing a projector for hazarding a dangerous and expensive experiment of which the public was afterwards to reap the benefit.[1]   It was only to be granted for a fixed term, and upon proof of the ultimate advantage of the enterprise to the public.

[1] *Wealth of Nations*, Book V. chap. i.

CHAPTER XXV

In his letter to Cadell Smith reproaches himself with his idleness during his first few years in Edinburgh. He had bought a good many new books in London, or new editions of old ones, and, says he, " The amusement I found in reading and diverting myself with them debauched me from my proper business, the preparing a new edition of the *Wealth of Nations*." While he was engaged in this dissipation of miscellaneous reading a young interviewer from Glasgow, who happened to be much in his company in connection with business in the year 1780, elicited his opinions on most of the famous authors of the world, noted them down, and gave them to the public after Smith's death in the pages of the *Bee* for 1791. In introducing these recollections the editor of the *Bee*, Dr. James Anderson—author of Ricardo's rent theory—says that even if they had not been sent to him with the strongest assurances of authenticity, he could entertain no doubt on that point after their perusal from the coincidence of the opinions reported in them with those he himself had heard Smith express. The writer, who takes the name Amicus, describes himself as " young, inquisitive, and full of respect " for Smith, and says their conversation, after they finished their business, always took a literary turn, and Smith was " extremely communicative, and delivered himself with a freedom and even boldness quite opposite to the apparent reserve of his appearance."

The first author Amicus mentions is Dr. Johnson, of whom he thought Smith had a " very contemptuous opinion." " I have seen that creature," said Smith, " bolt up in the midst of a mixed company, and without any previous notice fall upon his knees behind a chair, repeat the Lord's Prayer, and then resume his seat at table. He has played this trick over and over, perhaps five or six times in the course of an evening. It is not hypocrisy but madness. Though an honest sort of man himself, he is always patronising scoundrels. Savage, for example, whom he so loudly praises, was but a worthless fellow ; his pension of £50 never lasted him longer than a few days. As a sample of his economy you may take a circumstance that Johnson himself once told me. It was at that period fashionable to wear scarlet cloaks trimmed with gold lace, and the Doctor met him one day just after he had got his pension with one of those cloaks on his back, while at the same time his naked toes were sticking through his shoes." He spoke highly, however, of Johnson's political pamphlets on the American question, in spite of his disapproval of their opinions, and he was especially charmed with the pamphlet about the Falkland Islands, because it presented in such forcible language the madness of modern wars.

" Contemptuous opinion " is too strong an expression for Smith's view of Johnson, but it is certain he never rated him so high as the world did then or does now. He told Samuel Rogers that he was astonished at Johnson's immense reputation, but, on the other hand, he frequently praised some of the Doctor's individual writings very highly, as he did to this young gentleman of Glasgow. He once said to Seward that Johnson's preface to Shakespeare was " the most manly piece of criticism that was ever published in any country." [1]

Amicus then inquired of Smith his opinion of his countryman Dr. Campbell, author of the *Political Survey*,

[1] Seward's *Anecdotes*, ii. 464.

and Smith replied that he had never met him but once, but that he was one of those authors who wrote on from one end of the week to the other, and had therefore with his own hand produced almost a library of books. A gentleman who met Campbell out at dinner said he would be glad to have a complete set of his works, and next morning a cart-load came to his door, and the driver's bill was £70. He used to get a few copies of each of his works from the printers, and keep them for such chances as that. A visitor one day, casting his eye on these books, asked Campbell, " Have you read all these books ? " " Nay," said the other, " I have written them."

Smith often praised Swift, and praised him highly, saying he wanted nothing but inclination to have become one of the greatest of all poets. " But in place of that he is only a gossiper, writing merely for the entertainment of a private circle." He regarded Swift, however, as a pattern of correctness both in style and sentiment, and he read to his young friend some of the short poetical addresses to *Stella*. Amicus says Smith expressed particular pleasure with one couplet—

> Say, Stella, feel you no content,
> Reflecting on a life well spent ?

But it was more probably not so much of these two lines as of the whole passage of which they are the opening that Smith was thinking. He thought Swift a great master of the poetic art, because he produced an impression of ease and simplicity, though the work of composition was to him a work of much difficulty, a verse coming from him, as Swift himself said, like a guinea. The Dean's masterpiece was, in Smith's opinion, the lines on his own death, and his poetry was on the whole more correct after he settled in Ireland, and was surrounded, as he himself said, " only by humble friends."

Among historians Smith rated Livy first either in the ancient or the modern world. He knew of no other who had even a pretence to rival him, unless David Hume perhaps could claim that honour.

When asked about Shakespeare Smith quoted with apparent approval Voltaire's remarks that *Hamlet* was the dream of a drunken savage, and that Shakespeare had good scenes but not a good play ; but Amicus gathered that he would not permit anybody else to pass such a verdict with impunity, for when he himself once ventured to say something derogatory of *Hamlet*, Smith replied, "Yes, but still *Hamlet* is full of fine passages." This opinion of Shakespeare was of course common to most of the great men of last century. They were not so much insensible to the poet's genius as perplexed by it. His plays were full of imagination, dramatic power, natural gifts of every kind—that was admitted ; but then they seemed wild, unregulated, savage—even "drunken savage," to use Voltaire's expression ; they were magnificent, but they were not poetry, for they broke every rule of the art, and poetry after all was an art. And so we find Addison at the beginning of last century writing on the greatest English poets and leaving the name of Shakespeare out ; and we find Charles James Fox, a true lover of letters, telling Reynolds at the close of the century that Shakespeare's reputation would have stood higher if he had never written *Hamlet*. Smith thought Shakespeare had more than ten times the dramatic genius of Dryden, but Dryden had more of the poetic art.

He praised Dryden for rhyming his plays, and said— as Pope and Voltaire used also to say—that it was nothing but laziness that prevented our tragic poets from writing in rhyme like those of France. "Dryden," said he, "had he possessed but a tenth part of Shakespeare's dramatic genius, would have brought rhyming tragedies into fashion here as they were in France, and then the mob would have admired them just as much as they then pretended to despise them." Beattie's *Minstrel* he would not allow to be called a poem at all, because it had no plan,

no beginning, middle, or end. It was only a series of
verses, some of them, however, he admitted, very happy.
As for Pope's translation of the *Iliad*, he said, "They do
well to call it Pope's *Iliad*, for it is not Homer's *Iliad*.
It has no resemblance to the majesty and simplicity of the
Greek."

He read over to Amicus Milton's *L'Allegro* and *Il
Penseroso*, and explained the respective beauties of each ;
but he added that all the rest of Milton's short poems
were trash. He could not imagine what made Johnson
praise the poem on the death of Mrs. Killigrew, and compare it with *Alexander's Feast*. Johnson's praise of it
had induced him to read the poem over and with attention
twice, but he could not discover even a spark of merit in it.
On the other hand, Smith considered Gray's *Odes*, which
Johnson had damned, to be the standard of lyric excellence.

The Gentle Shepherd he did not admire much. He
preferred the *Pastor Fido*, of which, says Amicus, he
"spoke with rapture," and the *Eclogues* of Virgil.
Amicus put in a word in favour of the poet of his own
country, but Smith would not yield a point. "It is the
duty of a poet," he said, "to write like a gentleman. I
dislike that homely style which some think fit to call the
language of nature and simplicity and so forth. In Percy's
Reliques too a few tolerable pieces are buried under a heap
of rubbish. You have read perhaps *Adam Bell*, *Clym
of the Cleugh, and William of Cloudesley*." "Yes," said
Amicus. "Well then," continued Smith, "do you think
that was worth printing ? "

Of Goldsmith Smith spoke somewhat severely — of
Goldsmith as a man apparently, not as a writer—relating
some anecdotes of his easy morals, which Amicus does not
repeat. But when Amicus mentioned some story about
Burke seducing a young lady, Smith at once declared it
an invention. "I imagine," said he, "that you have got
that fine story out of some of the Magazines. If anything
can be lower than the Reviews, they are so. They once

had the impudence to publish a story of a gentleman having debauched his own sister, and on inquiry it came out that the gentleman never had a sister. As to Mr. Burke, he is a worthy, honest man, who married an accomplished girl without a shilling of fortune." Of the Reviews Smith never spoke but with ridicule and detestation. Amicus tried to get the *Gentleman's Magazine* exempted from the general condemnation, but Smith would not hear of that, and said that for his part he never looked at a Review, nor even at the names of the publishers.

Pope was a great favourite with him as a poet, and he knew by heart many passages from his poems, though he disliked Pope's personal character as a man, saying he was all affectation, and speaking of his letter to Arbuthnot when the latter was dying as a consummate piece of canting. Dryden was another of his favourite poets, and when he was speaking one day in high praise of Dryden's fables, Amicus mentioned Hume's objections, and was told, " You will learn more as to poetry by reading one good poem than by a thousand volumes of criticism." Smith regarded the French theatre as the standard of dramatic excellence.

Amicus concludes his reminiscences by quoting one of Smith's observations on a political subject. He said that at the beginning of the reign of George the Third the dissenting ministers used to receive £2000 a year from Government, but that the Earl of Bute had most improperly deprived them of this allowance, and that he supposed this to be the real motive of their virulent opposition to Government.

These recollections of Amicus provoked a letter in a succeeding number of the *Bee* from Ascanius (the Earl of Buchan) complaining of their publication, not as in any way misrepresenting any of Smith's views, but as obtruding the trifles of the ordinary social hour upon the learned world in a way Smith himself would have extremely disliked. Smith, he says, would rather have had his body injected by Hunter and Monro, and exhibited in Fleet Street or in Weir's Museum. That may very possibly be so ; but though Smith, if he were to give his views on literary topics to the public, might prefer putting them in more elaborate dress, yet the opinions he expressed were, it must be remembered, mature opinions on subjects on which he had long thought and even lectured, and if neither Dr. Anderson nor the Earl of Buchan has any fault to find with the correctness of Amicus's report of them, Smith cannot be considered to be any way wronged. The Earl complains too of the matter of the letter being "such frivolous matter" ; but it is not so frivolous, and, if it were, is it not Smith himself who used to say to his class at Glasgow, as we are informed by Boswell, that there was nothing too frivolous to be learnt about a great man, and that, for his own part, he was always glad to know that Milton wore latchets to his shoes and not buckles?

In 1781 Gibbon seems to have been in doubt as to continuing his *History*, and desired Robertson, who happened to be up in London at the time, to talk the matter over with Smith after his return to Edinburgh. The result of this consultation is communicated in a letter from Robertson to Gibbon on 6th November 1781. " Soon after my return," says Robertson, " I had a long conversation with our friend Mr. Smith, in which I stated to him every particular you mentioned to me with respect to the propriety of going on with your work. I was happy to find that his opinion coincided perfectly with that which I had ventured to give you. His decisions, you know, are both prompt and vigorous, and he could not allow that you ought to hesitate a moment in your choice. He promised to write his sentiments to you very fully, but as he may have neglected to do this, for it is not willingly he puts pen to paper, I thought it might be agreeable to you to know his opinion, though I imagine you could hardly entertain any doubt concerning it." [1]

---

[1] Gibbon's *Miscellaneous Works*, ii. 255.

Professor B. Faujas Saint Fond, Professor of Geology in the Museum of Natural History at Paris and member of the National Institute of France, paid a visit to Edinburgh in October or November 1782 in the course of a tour he made through Scotland, and received many civilities from Adam Smith, as he mentions in the account of his travels which he published in 1783. Saint Fond says there was nobody in Edinburgh he visited more frequently than Smith, and nobody received him more kindly or studied more to procure for him every information and amusement Edinburgh could afford. He was struck with Smith's numerous and, as he says, excellently chosen library. " The best French authors occupied a distinguished place in his library, for he was fond of our language." " Though advanced in years, he still possessed a fine figure ; the animation of his countenance was striking when he spoke of Voltaire." I have already quoted the remark he made (p. 190).

One evening when the geologist was at tea with him, Smith spoke about Rousseau also, and spoke of him " with a kind of religious respect." " Voltaire," he said, " set himself to correct the vices and follies of mankind by laughing at them, and sometimes by treating them with severity, but Rousseau conducts the reader to reason and truth by the attractions of sentiment and the force of conviction. His ' Social Compact ' will one day avenge all the persecutions he suffered."

Smith asked the Professor if he loved music, and on being told that it was one of his chief delights whenever it was well executed, rejoined, " I am very glad of it ; I shall put you to a proof which will be very interesting for me, for I shall take you to hear a kind of music of which it is impossible you can have formed any idea, and it will afford me great pleasure to know the impression it makes upon you." The annual bagpipe competition was to take place next day, and accordingly in the morning Smith came to the Professor's lodgings at nine o'clock, and they proceeded at ten to a spacious concert-room, plainly but neatly decorated, which they found already filled with a numerous assembly of ladies and gentlemen. A large space was reserved in the middle of the room and occupied by gentlemen only, who, Smith said, were the judges of the performances that were to take place, and who were all inhabitants of the Highlands or Islands. The prize was for the best execution of some favourite piece of Highland music, and the same air was to be played successively by all the competitors. In about half an hour a folding door opened at the bottom of the hall, and the Professor was surprised to see a Highlander advance playing on a bagpipe, and dressed in the ancient kilt and plaid of his country. " He walked up and down the vacant space in the middle of the hall with rapid steps and a martial air playing his noisy instrument, the discordant sounds of which were sufficient to rend the ear. The tune was a kind of sonata divided into three periods. Smith requested me to pay my whole attention to the music, and to explain to him afterwards the impression it made upon me. But I confess that at first I could not distinguish either air or design in the music. I was only struck with a piper marching backward and forward with great rapidity, and still presenting the same warlike countenance, he made incredible efforts with his body and his fingers to bring into play the different reeds of his instrument, which emitted sounds that were to me almost insupportable. He received, however, great praise." Then came a second piper, who seemed to excel the first, judging from the clapping of hands and cries of bravo that greeted him from every side ; and then a third and a fourth, till eight were heard successively ; and the Professor began at length to realise that the first part of the music was meant to represent the clash and din and fury of war, and the last part the wailing for the slain,—and this last part, he observed, always drew tears from the eyes of a number of " the beautiful Scotch ladies " in the audience. After the music came a "lively and animated dance," in which some of the pipers engaged, and the rest all played together "suitable airs possessing expression and character, though the union of so many bagpipes produced a most hideous noise." He does not say whether his verdict was satisfactory to Smith, but the verdict was that it seemed to him like a bear's dancing, and that "the impression the wild instrument made on the greater part of the audience was so different from the impression it made on himself, that he could not help thinking that the lively emotion of the persons around him was not occasioned by the musical effect of the air itself, but by some association of ideas which connected the discordant sounds of the pipe with historical events brought forcibly to their recollection." [1]

Nor were these annual competitions the only local institutions in which Smith took a more or less active interest. One of the duties of a citizen which he undertook will perhaps occasion surprise—he became a Captain of the City Guard. He was made Honorary Captain of the Trained Bands of Edinburgh—the City Guard—on the 4th of June 1781, "with the usual solemnity," the minutes state, "and after spending the evening with grate joy, the whole corps retired, but in distinct divisions and good order, to quarters." [2]

The business of this body, according to its minutes, seems practically to have been mostly of a convivial character, and we can sympathise with the honest pride of the clerk in recording in what a condition of good order they were able to retire after celebrating that auspicious occasion with the joy it deserved. Smith no doubt attended their periodical festivities, or paid his fine of eight magnums of claret for absence. But their business was not all claret and punch. On the 8th September 1784, for example, the captains, lieutenants, and ensigns of the Trained Bands were called out, in consequence of an order from the

---

[1] Saint Fond, *Travels in England, Scotland, and the Hebrides,* ii. 241.
[2] Skinner's *Society of Trained Bands of Edinburgh,* p. 99.

Lord Provost, "to attend the wheeping of Paull and Anderson, actors in the late riots at Cannonmills." A rescue riot was apprehended, and the Trained Bands met in the old Justiciary Court-room, and were armed there with "stowt oaken sticks." Marching forth in regular order, they acted as guard to the magistrates during the day, and "by their formidable and respectable appearance had the good effect of detering the multitude so that they became only peaceable spectators." Whether an honorary captain could be called upon for active service in an emergency I cannot say, but Smith's name is not mentioned in the list of absentee captains upon this occasion.

In 1783 Smith joined Robertson and others in founding the Royal Society of Edinburgh. Robertson had long entertained the idea of establishing a society on the model of the foreign academies for the cultivation of every branch of science, learning, and taste, and he was at length moved into action by the steps taken in 1782 by the Earl of Buchan and others to obtain a royal charter for the Society of Antiquaries of Scotland, founded two years before. Robertson was very anxious to have only one learned society in Edinburgh, of which antiquities might be made a branch subject, and he even induced the University authorities to petition Parliament against granting a charter of incorporation to the Antiquarian Society. In this strong step the University was seconded by the Faculty of Advocates and the old Philosophical Society, founded by Colin Maclaurin in 1739, but their efforts failed. Out of the agitation, however, the Royal Society came into being. Whether Smith actively supported Robertson, or supported him at all, in his exertions against the Antiquarian Society, I do not know. He was not, as Robertson was, a member of the Society of Antiquaries. But he was one of the original members of the Royal Society. The society was divided into two branches,—a physical branch or class devoted to science ; and a literary branch or class devoted to history and polite letters,—and Smith was one of the four presidents of the literary class. The Duke of Buccleugh was President of the whole society ; and Smith's colleagues in the presidency of the literary class were Robertson, Blair, and Baron Gordon (Cosmo Gordon of Cluny, a Baron of Exchequer and most accomplished man).

Smith never read a paper to this society, nor does he ever seem to have spoken in it except once or twice on a matter of business which had been entrusted to him. The only mention of his name in the printed *Transactions* is in connection with two prizes of 1000 ducats and 500 ducats respectively, which were offered to all the world in 1785 by Count J. N. de Windischgraetz for the two most successful inventions of such legal terminology for every sort of deed as, without imposing any new restraints on natural liberty, would yet leave no possible room for doubt or litigation, and would thereby diminish the number of lawsuits. The Count wished the prizes to be decided by three of the most distinguished literary academies in Europe, and had chosen for that purpose the Royal Academy of Science in Paris, which had already consented to undertake the duty ; the Royal Society of Edinburgh, whose consent the Count now sought ; and one of the academies of Germany or Switzerland which he was after- wards to name. He addressed his communication to the society through Adam Smith, who must therefore be assumed to have had some private acquaintance or connec- tion with him ; and on the 9th of July Smith laid the proposal before the Council of the society, and, as is reported in the *Transactions*, " signified to the meeting that although he entertained great doubt whether the problem of the Count de Windischgraetz admitted of any complete and rational solution, yet the views of the proposer being so highly laudable, and the object itself being of that nature that even an approximation to its attainment would be of importance to mankind, he was therefore of opinion that the society ought to agree to the request that was made to them. He added that it was his intention to communicate his sentiments on the subject to the Count by a letter which he would lay before the Council at a subsequent meeting." [1] This letter was read to the Council on the 13th of December, and after being approved, a copy of it was requested for preservation among their papers, as the author " did not incline that it should be published in the *Transactions* of the society."

Nothing further is heard of this business till the 6th of August 1787, when " Mr. Commissioner Smith acquainted the society that the Count de Windischgraetz had transmitted to him three dissertations offered as solutions of his problem, and had desired the judgment of the society upon their merits. The society referred the consideration of these papers to Mr. Smith, Mr. Henry Mackenzie of the Exchequer, and Mr. William Craig, advocate, as a committee to appraise and consider them, and to report their opinion to the society at a subsequent meeting." At length, on the 21st January 1788, Mr. Commissioner Smith reported that this committee thought none of the three dissertations amounted either to a solution or an approximation to a solution of the Count's problem, but that one of them was a work of great merit, and the society asked Mr. A. Fraser Tytler, one of their secretaries, to send on this opinion to the Count as their verdict.[2]

---

[1] *Transactions*, R.S.E., i. 39.   [2] *Ibid.*, R.S.E., ii. 24.

CHAPTER XXVI

THE AMERICAN QUESTION AND OTHER POLITICS

NOTWITHSTANDING the patronage he received from Lord
North and his relations of friendship and obligation with
the Duke of Buccleugh and Henry Dundas, Smith continued to be a warm political supporter of the Rockingham
Whigs and a warm opponent of the North ministry.   The
first Earl of Minto (then Sir Gilbert Elliot) visited Edinburgh in 1782, and wrote in his journal · "I have found one
just man in Gomorrah, Adam Smith, author of the *Wealth
of Nations*.   He was the Duke of Buccleugh's tutor, is a
wise and deep philosopher, and although made Commissioner of the Customs here by the Duke and Lord Advocate,
is what I call an *honest fellow*.   He wrote a most kind as
well as elegant letter to Burke on his resignation, as I
believe I told you before, and on my mentioning it to him
he told me he was the only man here who spoke out for
the Rockinghams." [1]   This letter is now lost, but Burke's
answer to it remains, and was sold at Sotheby's a few years
ago.   Smith must have expressed the warmest approval of
the step Fox and Burke had taken, on the death of the
Marquis of Rockingham in July 1782, in resigning their
offices in the Ministry rather than serve under their
colleague Lord Shelburne, and he must have felt strongly
on the subject to overcome his aversion to letter-
writing on the occasion.   Fox and Burke have been
much censured for their refusal to serve under Shelburne,

[1] Lady Minto's *Life of the Earl of Minto*, i. 84.

inasmuch as that refusal meant a practical disruption of the Whig party ; and Burke could not help feeling strengthened, as he says he was in his letter, by the approval of a man like Smith, who was not only a profound political philosopher, but a thorough and loyal Whig. Notwithstanding his personal friendship with Lord Shelburne, Smith never seems to have trusted him as a political leader. We have already seen him condemning Shelburne at the time of that statesman's first collision with Fox—the " pious fraud " occasion—and now nineteen years later he shows the same distrust of Shelburne, and doubtless for the same reason, that he believed Shelburne was willing to be subservient to the king's designs, and to increase the power of the Crown, which it had ever been the aim of the Whigs to limit. Shelburne's acceptance of office, after the king's positive refusal to listen to the views of the Rockinghams themselves regarding the leadership of their own party, was probably regarded by Smith as a piece of open treason to the popular cause, and open espousal of the cause of the Court.

In those critical times the thoughts of even private citizens brooded on the arts of war. An Edinburgh lawyer who had never been at sea invented the system of naval tactics which gave Rodney his victories, and here is a Highland laird, who had spent his days among his herds in Skye, writing Smith about a treatise he has composed on fortification, which he believes to contain original discoveries of great importance, and which he sends up to Smith and Henry Mackenzie, with a five-pound note to pay the expenses of its publication. The author was Charles Mackinnon of Mackinnon, the chief of his clan, who fell into adverse circumstances shortly after the date of this correspondence, and parted with all the old clan property, and the treatise on fortification itself still exists among the manuscripts of the British Museum. It is certainly a poor affair, from which the author could have reaped nothing but disappointment, and Smith, who seems to have held Mr. Mackinnon in high esteem personally, strongly dissuades him from giving it to the press. This opinion is communicated in the following candid but kind letter :—

DEAR SIR—I received your favour of the 13th of this month, and am under some concern to be obliged to tell you that I have not only not got out of the press, but that I have not yet gone into it, and would most earnestly once more recommend it to your consideration whether upon this occasion we should go into it at all. It was but within these few days that I could obtain a meeting with Mr. Mackinzie, who was occupied with the Exchequer Business. I find he had seen your papers before, and was of the same opinion with me that in their present condition they would not do you the honour we wish you to derive from whatever work you publish. We read them over together with great care and attention, and we both continued of our first opinion. I hope you will pardon me if I take the liberty to tell you that I cannot discover in them those original ideas which you seem to suppose that they contain. I am not very certain whether I understand what you hint obscurely in your former letter, but it seems to me as if you had some fear that some person might anticipate you, and claim the merit of your discoveries by publishing them as his own. From the character of the gentleman to whom your property has been communicated, I should hope there is no danger of this. But to prevent the Possibility of the Public being imposed upon in this manner, your Papers now lie sealed up in my writing Desk, superscribed with directions to my executors to return them unopened to you or your heirs as their proper owners. In case of my death and that of Mr. M'Kinzie, the production of these papers under my seal and superscribed by my hand will be sufficient to refute any plagiarism of this kind. While we live our evidence will secure to you the reputation of whatever discoveries may be contained in them. I return you the five Pound note, in hopes that you will not insist upon this publication, at least for some time ; at any rate, I shall always be happy to advance a larger sum upon your account, though I own I could wish it was for some other purpose. I have not shown your Papers to Smellie. It will give me great pleasure to hear from you, and to be informed that you forgive the freedom I have used in offering you, I am afraid, a disagreeable advice. I can assure you that nothing but the respect which I think I owe to the character of a person whom I know to be a man of worth, delicacy, and honour, could have extorted it from me.—I ever am, dear sir, most faithfully yours,   ADAM SMITH.

CUSTOM HOUSE, EDINBURGH,
  21*st August* 1782.

If you should not chuse that your Papers should remain in my custody, I shall either send them to you or deliver to whom you please.[1]

While one Highland laird was planning to save his country by an improved system of fortification, another was conceiving a grander project of saving her by continental alliances. The moment was among the darkest England has ever passed through. We were engaged in a death-struggle against France, Spain, and the American colonies combined. Cornwallis had just repeated at Yorktown the humiliating surrender of Burgoyne at Saratoga. Elliot lay locked in Gibraltar. Ireland was growing restive and menacing on one side, and the Northern powers of Europe on the other—the Armed Neutrality, as they were called—sat and watched, with their hands on their sword-hilts and a grudge against England in their hearts. Now Sir John Sinclair believed that these neutral powers held the key of the situation, and wrote a pamphlet in 1782, which he proposed to translate into their respective tongues for the purpose of persuading them to join this country in a crusade against the House of Bourbon, and " to emancipate the colonies both in the West Indies and on the continent of America for the general interest of all nations." The price he was prepared to offer these powers for their adhesion was to be a share in the colonial commerce of England, and the acquisition of some of the French and Spanish colonial dependencies for themselves. Sinclair sent his pamphlet to Smith, apparently with a request for his opinion on the advisability of translating it for the conversion of the powers, and he received the following

[1] Add. MSS., 5035.

reply. I may add that I have not been able to see this pamphlet, but that it is evidently not the pamphlet entitled " Impartial Considerations on the Propriety of retaining Gibraltar," as Sinclair's biographer supposes ; for in the former pamphlet Sinclair is advocating not only a continuance, but an extension of the war, whereas in the latter he has come round to the advocacy of peace, and instead of contemplating the deprivation of France and Spain of their colonies, he recommends the cession of Gibraltar as a useless and expensive possession, using very much the same line of argument which Smith suggests in this letter. Smith's letter very probably had some influence in changing his views, though it is true the idea of ceding Gibraltar was in 1782 much favoured by a party in Lord Shelburne's government, and even by the king himself.

Smith's letter ran thus :—

My DEAR SIR—I have read your pamphlet several times with great pleasure, and am very much pleased with the style and composition. As to what effect it might produce if translated upon the Powers concerned in the Armed Neutrality, I am a little doubtful. It is too plainly partial to England. It proposes that the force of the Armed Neutrality should be employed in recovering to England the islands she has lost, and the compensation which it is proposed that England should give for this service is the islands which they may conquer for themselves, with the assistance of England indeed, from France and Spain. There seems to me besides to be some inconsistency in the argument. If it be just to emancipate the continent of America from the dominion of every European power, how can it be just to subject the islands to such dominion ? and if the monopoly of the trade of the continent be contrary to the rights of mankind, how can that of the islands be agreeable to these rights ? The real futility of all distant dominions, of which the defence is necessarily most expensive, and which contribute nothing, either by revenue or military forces, to the general defence of the empire, and very little even to their own particular defence, is, I think, the subject on which the public prejudices of Europe require most to be set right. In order to defend the barren rock of Gibraltar (to the possession of which

we owe the union of France and Spain, contrary to the natural
interests and inveterate prejudices of both countries, the important
enmity of Spain and the futile and expensive friendship of Portugal)
we have now left our own coasts defenceless, and sent out a great
fleet, to which any considerable disaster may prove fatal to our
domestic security ; and which, in order to effectuate its purpose,
must probably engage a fleet of superior force. Sore eyes have
made me delay writing to you so long.—I ever am, my dear sir,
your most faithful and affectionate humble servant,

ADAM SMITH.

CUSTOM HOUSE, EDINBURGH,
14*th October* 1782.[1]

The strong opinion expressed in this letter of the
uselessness of colonial dependencies, which contributed
nothing to the maintenance of the mother country, had of
course been already expressed in the *Wealth of Nations*.
" Perish uncontributing colonies " is the very pith of the
last sentence of that work. " If any of the provinces of
the British Empire cannot be made to contribute towards
the support of the whole empire, it is surely time that Great
Britain should free herself from the expense of defending
those provinces in time of war and of supporting any part
of their civil or military establishments in time of peace ;
and endeavour to accommodate her future views and designs to the real mediocrity of her circumstances."

The principles of free trade presently got an impetus
from the conclusion of peace with America and France in
1783. Lord Shelburne wrote Abbé Morellet in 1783
that the treaties of that year were inspired from beginning
to end by " the great principle of free trade," and that " a
peace was good in the exact proportion that it recognised
that principle." A fitting opportunity was thought to
have arisen for making somewhat extended applications of
the principle, and many questions were asked about how
far such applications should go in this direction or that.
When the American Intercourse Bill was before the House
in 1783, one of Lord Shelburne's colleagues in the

[1] *Correspondence of Sir John Sinclair*, i. 389.

Ministry, William Eden, approached Smith in considerable perplexity as to the wisdom of conceding to the new republic free commercial intercourse with this country and our colonies. Eden had already done something for free trade in Ireland, and he was presently to earn a name as a great champion of that principle, after successfully negotiating with Dupont de Nemours the Commercial Treaty with France in 1786 ; but in 1787 he had not accepted the principle so completely as his chief, Lord Shelburne. Perhaps, indeed, he never took a firm hold of the principle at any time, for Smith always said of him, " He is but a man of detail." [1] Anyhow, when he wrote Smith in 1783 he was under serious alarm at the proposal to give the United States the same freedom to trade with Canada and Nova Scotia as we enjoyed ourselves. Being so near those colonies, the States would be sure to oust Great Britain and Ireland entirely out of the trade of provisioning them. The Irish fisheries would be ruined, the English carrying trade would be lost. The Americans, with fur at their doors, could easily beat us in hats, and if we allowed them to import our tools free, they would beat us in everything else for which they had the raw materials in plenty. Eden and Smith seem to have exchanged several letters on this subject, but none of them remain except the following one from Smith, in which he declares that it would be an injustice to our own colonies to restrict their trade with the United States merely to benefit Irish fish-curers or English hatters, and to be bad policy to impose special discouragements on the trade of one foreign nation which are not imposed on the trade of others. His argument is not, it will be observed, for free trade, which he perhaps thought then impracticable, but merely for equality of treatment,—equality of treatment between the British subject in Canada and the British subject in England, and equality of treatment between the American nation and the Russian, or French, or Spanish.

---

[1] Mackintosh, *Miscellaneous Works*, iii. 17.

DEAR SIR—If the Americans really mean to subject the goods of all different nations to the same duties and to grant them the same indulgence, they set an example of good sense which all other nations ought to imitate. At any rate it is certainly just that their goods, their naval stores for example, should be subjected to the same duties to which we subject those of Russia, Sweden, and Denmark, and that we should treat them as they mean to treat us and all other nations.

What degree of commercial connection we should allow between the remaining colonies, whether in North America or the West Indies, and the United States may to some people appear a more difficult question. My own opinion is that it should be allowed to go on as before, and whatever inconveniences result from this freedom may be remedied as they occur. The lumber and provisions of the United States are more necessary to our West India Islands than the rum and sugar of the latter are to the former. Any interruption or restraint of commerce would hurt our loyal much more than our revolted subjects. Canada and Nova Scotia cannot justly be refused at least the same freedom of commerce which we grant to the United States.

I suspect the Americans do not mean what they say. I have seen a Revenue Act of South Carolina by which two shillings are laid upon every hundredweight of brown sugar imported from the British plantations, and only eighteenpence upon that imported from any foreign colony. Upon every pound of refined sugar from the former one penny, from the latter one halfpenny. Upon every gallon of French wine twopence ; of Spanish wine threepence ; of Portuguese wine fourpence.

I have little anxiety about what becomes of the American commerce. By an equality of treatment of all nations we must soon open a commerce with the neighbouring nations of Europe infinitely more advantageous than that of so distant a country as America. This is an immense subject upon which when I wrote to you last I intended to have sent you a letter of many sheets, but as I expect to see you in a few weeks I shall not trouble you with so tedious a dissertation. I shall only say at present that every extraordinary, either encouragement or discouragement that is given to the trade of any country more than to that of another may, I think, be demonstrated to be in every case a complete piece of dupery, by which the interest of the state and the nation is constantly sacrificed to that of some particular class of traders. I heartily congratulate you upon the triumphant manner in which the East India Bill has been carried through the Lower House.

I have no doubt of its passing through the Upper House in the same manner. The decisive judgment and resolution with which Mr. Fox has introduced and supported that Bill does him the highest honour.—I ever am, with the greatest respect and esteem, dear sir, your most affectionate and most humble servant,

ADAM SMITH.

EDINBURGH, 15*th December* 1783.[1]

Fox's East India Bill, of which Smith expresses such unqualified commendation, proposed to transfer the government of British India from the Court of Directors of the East India Company to a new board of Crown nominees. This measure was entirely to Smith's mind. He had already in the former editions of his book condemned the company which, as he says, "oppresses and domineers in India," and in the additional matter which he wrote about the company immediately before this bill was introduced he declared of them that "no other sovereigns ever were, or, from the nature of things, ever could be, so perfectly indifferent about the happiness or misery of their subjects, the improvement or waste of their dominions, the glory or disgrace of their administration, as, from irresistible moral causes, the greater part of the proprietors of such a mercantile company are and necessarily must be."

---

[1] *Journals and Correspondence of Lord Auckland,* i. 64.

CHAPTER XXVII

BURKE IN SCOTLAND

1784–1785

BURKE had been elected Lord Rector of the University of Glasgow in November 1783 in succession to Dundas, and he came down to Scotland to be installed in the following April. He spent altogether eight or ten days in the country, and he spent them all in the company of Smith, who attended him wherever he went. Burke and Smith, always profound admirers of one another's writings, had grown warm friends during the recent lengthened residence of the latter in London. Even in the brilliant circle round the brown table in Gerrard Street there was none Burke loved or esteemed more highly than Smith. One of the statesman's biographers informs us, on the authority of an eminent literary friend, who paid him a visit at Beaconsfield after his retirement from public life, that he then spoke with the warmest admiration of Smith's vast learning, his profound understanding, and the great importance of his writings, and added that his heart was as good and rare as his head, and that his manners were " peculiarly pleasing." [1] Smith on his part was drawn to Burke by no less powerful an attraction. He once paid him a compliment with which the latter appears to have been particularly gratified, for he repeated it to his literary friend on this same occasion. "Burke," said the economist, "is the only man I ever knew who thinks on economic subjects exactly as I do,

[1] Bisset's *Life of Burke*, ii. 429.

without any previous communications having passed between us." [1]

The installation of Lord Rector was to take place on Saturday the 10th of April, and Burke arrived in Edinburgh on Tuesday or Wednesday previous. Whether he was Smith's guest while there I am unable to say, but at any rate it was Smith who did the honours of the town to him, and accompanied him wherever he went. Dalzel, the Greek professor, gives an account of the statesman's visit, to his old friend and class-fellow, Sir Robert Liston, and states that " Lord Maitland attended him constantly and Mr. Adam Smith. They brought him," he adds, " to my house the day after he arrived." Lord Maitland was the eldest son of the Earl of Lauderdale, and became a well-known figure both in politics and in scientific economics after he succeeded to the peerage himself. I have already mentioned him for his admiration of Smith, and his defence of him from the disparaging remarks of Fox, though he was himself no blind follower of the *Wealth of Nations*, but one of the earliest and not the least acute of the critics of that work. He was at this time one of the rising hopes of the Whigs in the House of Commons, which he had entered as representative of a Cornish borough in 1780. Dalzel had been his tutor, and had accompanied him in that capacity to Oxford ; and being also a great favourite with Smith, whom he respected above all things for his knowledge of Greek, he was naturally among the first of the eminent citizens to whom they introduced their distinguished guest.

On Thursday morning Burke and Smith went out with Lord Maitland to Hatton, the Lauderdale seat in Midlothian, to dine and stay the night there on their way to Glasgow, and Dugald Stewart and Dalzel joined them later in the day after they had finished their college classes. The conversation happened very naturally to touch on party prospects, for they were at the moment in the thick

[1] Bisset's *Life of Burke*, ii. 429.

of a general election—the famous election of 1784, so
fatal to the Whigs, when near 160 supporters of the
Coalition Ministry—"Fox's martyrs"—lost their seats, and
Pitt was sent back with an enormous majority behind him.
Parliament had been dissolved a fortnight before, and many
of the elections were already past; Burke himself had been
returned for Malton on his way north, but the battle was
still raging; in Westminster, where the Whig chief was
himself fighting, it lasted a month longer, and in many
other constituencies the event was as yet undecided. As
far as returns had been made, however, things had gone hard
with the Whigs, and Burke was despondent. He had
been some twenty years in public life without his party
being in power as many months, and since the party seemed
now doomed, as indeed it was, to twenty years of opposition again, he turned to Lord Maitland and said, "Lord
Maitland, if you want to be in office, if you have any
ambition or wish to be successful in life, shake us off, give
us up." But Smith intervened, and with singular hopeful-
ness ventured to prophesy that in two years things would
certainly come round again. "Why," replied Burke, "I
have already been in a minority nineteen years, and your
two years, Mr. Smith, will just make me twenty-one,
and it will surely be high time for me to be then in my
majority." [1]

Smith's hearty remark implies his continued loyalty to
the Rockinghams, and shows that just as he two years
before approved of their separation from Lord Shelburne,
which many Whig critics have censured, so he now
equally approved of their coalition with their old adversary, Lord North, which Whig critics have censured more
severely still. But his sanguine forecast was far astray.
Burke never again returned to office, and the whole conversation reads strangely in the light of subsequent events.
Only a few years more and Burke had himself shaken off

[1] Innes's Memoir of Dalzel in Dalzel's *History of University of
Edinburgh*, i. 42.

his friends—from no view to power, it is true—and the young nobleman to whom he gave the advice in jest was to take the lead in avenging the desertion, and to denounce the pension it was proposed to give him as the wages of apostasy. The French Revolution, which drove Burke back to a more conservative position, carried Lord Maitland, who had drunk in Radicalism from Professor John Millar, forward into the republican camp. He went over to Paris with Dugald Stewart and harangued the mob on the streets *pour la liberté*,[1] and he said one day to the Duchess of Gordon, "I hope, madame, ere long to have the pleasure of introducing Mrs. Maitland to Mrs. Gordon."[2]

On the present occasion at Hatton, however, they were all one in their lamentations over the temporary eclipse the cause of liberty had suffered. On the following morning they all set out together for Glasgow, Stewart and Dalzel being able to accompany them because it was Good Friday, and Good Friday was then a holiday at Edinburgh University. They supped that evening with Professor John Millar, Smith's pupil and Lord Maitland's master, and next day they assisted at the ceremony of installation. The chief business was of course the Rector's address, described in the *Annual Register* of the year as "a very polite and elegant speech suited to the occasion." Tradition says Burke broke down in this speech, and after speaking five minutes concluded abruptly by saying he was unable to proceed, as he had never addressed so learned an audience before; but though the tradition is mentioned by Jeffrey, who was a student at Glasgow only three years afterwards, and is more definitely stated by Professor Young of the same University in his *Lectures on Intellectual Philosophy* (p. 334), there appears to be no solid foundation for it whatever. It is not mentioned by Dalzel, who would be unlikely to omit so interesting a

---

[1] Add. MSS., 32,567.
[2] Best's *Anecdotes*, p. 25.

circumstance in the gossiping account of the affair which
he gives in his letter to Sir R. Liston.

After the installation they adjourned to the College
chapel for divine service, where they heard a sermon from
Professor Arthur, and then they dined in the College
Hall. On Sunday Stewart and Dalzel returned to Edin-
burgh for their classes next day, but Smith and Lord
Maitland accompanied Burke on an excursion to Loch
Lomond, of which we know Smith was a great admirer.
He said to Samuel Rogers it was the finest lake in Great
Britain, and the feature that pleased him particularly was
the contrast between the islands and the shore.[1] They did
not return to Edinburgh till Wednesday, and they returned
then by way of Carron, probably to see the ironworks.
On Thursday evening they dined at Smith's, Dalzel being
again of the party. Burke seems to have been at his best
—" the most agreeable and entertaining man in conversation I ever knew," says Dalzel. " We got a vast deal of
political anecdotes from him, and fine pictures of political
characters both dead and living. Whether they were
impartially drawn or not, that is questionable, but they
were admirably drawn."[2]

The elections were still proceeding, and the 29th of
April was fixed for the election in Lanarkshire, which had
been represented for the previous ten years by a strong
personal friend of Smith, Andrew Stuart of Torrance.
I have already mentioned Stuart's name in connection with
his candidature for the Indian Commissionership, for which
Sir William Pulteney thought of proposing Smith. Though
now forgotten, he was a notable person in his day. He
came first strongly into public notice during the proceedings in the Douglas cause. Having, as law-agent for the
Duke of Hamilton, borne the chief part in preparing the
Hamilton side of the case, he was attacked in the House
of Lords—and attacked with quite unusual virulence—

[1] Clayden's *Early Life of Samuel Rogers*, p. 92.
[2] Dalzel's *History of the University of Edinburgh*, i. 42.

both by Thurlow, the counsel for the other side, and by
Lord Mansfield, one of the judges; and he met those
attacks by fighting a duel with Thurlow, and writing a
series of letters to Lord Mansfield, which obtained much
attention and won him a high name for ability. Shortly
thereafter—in 1774—he entered Parliament as member for
Lanarkshire, and made such rapid mark that he was
appointed a Commissioner of Trade and Plantations in
1779, and seemed destined to higher office. But now in
1784, on the very eve of the election, Stuart suddenly
retired from the field, in consequence apparently of some
personal considerations arising between himself and the
Duke of Hamilton. He was extremely anxious to have
his reasons for this unexpected step immediately and fully
explained to his personal friends in Edinburgh, and on
the 22nd of April—the day before he wrote his resignation—he sent his whole correspondence with the Duke of
Hamilton about the matter through to John Davidson,
W.S., for their perusal, and especially, it would appear, for
the perusal of Smith, the only one he names. "There is
particularly," he says, "one friend, Mr. Adam Smith,
whom I wish to be fully informed of everything." Being
the only friend specifically named in the letter, Smith
seems to have been consulted by Davidson as to any other
"particular friends" to whom the correspondence should
be submitted, and he wrote Davidson on the 7th of May
1784 advising him to show it to Campbell of Stonefield,
one of the Lords of Session, and a brother-in-law of Lord
Bute. He says—

My Lord Stonefield is an old attached and faithful friend of
A. Stuart. The papers relative to the County of Lanark may
safely be communicated to him. He is perfectly convinced of the
propriety of what you and I agreed upon, that the subject ought
to be talked of as little as possible, and never but among his most
intimate and cordial friends. A. SMITH.

Friday, 7th May.[1]

---

[1] Edinburgh University Library.

After being brightened by the agreeable visit of Burke, Smith was presently cast into the deepest sadness by what seems to have been the first trouble of his singularly serene and smooth life—the death of his mother. She died on the 23rd of May, in her ninetieth year. The three avenues to Smith, says the Earl of Buchan, were always his mother, his books, and his political opinions —his mother apparently first of all. They had lived together, off and on, for sixty years, and being most tenderly attached to her, he is said, after her death, never to have seemed the same again. According to Ramsay of Ochtertyre, he was so disconsolate that people in general could find no explanation except in his supposed unbelief in the resurrection. He sorrowed, they said, as those who have no hope. People in general would seem to have little belief in the natural affections; but while they extracted from Smith's filial love a proof of his infidelity, Archdeacon John Sinclair seeks to extract from it a demonstration of his religious faith. It appears that when Mrs. Smith was visited on her deathbed by her minister, her famous son always remained in the room and joined in the prayers, though they were made in the name and for the sake of Christ ; and the worthy Archdeacon thinks no infidel would have done that.

The depression Smith showed after his mother's death, however, was unfortunately due in part to the fact that his own health was beginning to fail. He was now sixty-one ; as Stewart tells us, he aged very rapidly, and in two years more he was in the toils of the malady that carried him off. The shock of his mother's death could not help therefore telling severely upon him in his declining bodily condition.

Burke was—no doubt at Smith's instance—elected Fellow of the Royal Society of Edinburgh in June 1784, in spite of several black balls ; for, as Dalzel observes, "it would seem that there are some violent politicians among us" ; and in August 1785 he was again in Scotland attending to the duties of his Rectorship. He was accompanied this time by Windham, who was the most attached and the most beloved of his political disciples, and who had been a student at Glasgow himself in 1766. If Dalzel was delighted with Burke, he was enchanted with Windham, for, says he to Liston, " besides his being a polite man and a man of the world, he is perhaps the very best Greek scholar I ever met with. He did me the honour of breakfasting with me one morning, and sat for three hours talking about Greek. When we were at Hatton he and I stole away as often as we could from the rest of the company to read and talk about Greek. . . . You may judge how I would delight in him." Smith was not at Hatton with them this time, but he saw much of them in Edinburgh.

Smith had probably known Windham already, but at any rate, as soon as Burke and he arrived in Edinburgh on the 24th of August and took their quarters in Dun's Hotel, they paid a visit to Smith, and next day they dined with him at his house. Among the guests mentioned by Windham as being present were Robertson ; Henry Erskine, who had recently been Burke's colleague in the Coalition Ministry as Lord Advocate ; and Mr. Cullen, probably the doctor, though it may have been his son (afterwards a judge), who lives in fame chiefly for his feats as a mimic. Windham gives us no scrap of their conversation except a few remarks of Robertson about Holyrood ; and though he says he recollected no one else of the company except those he has mentioned, there was at least one other guest whose presence there that evening he was shortly afterwards to have somewhat romantic occasion to recall. This was Sir John Sinclair, who had just re-entered Parliament for a constituency at the Land's End, after having been defeated in the Wick burghs by Fox. Burke and Windham proposed making a tour in the Highlands, and Sir John advised them strongly, when they came to the beautiful district between Blair-Athole and Dunkeld, to leave their post-chaise for that stage and

walk through the woods and glens on foot. They took
the advice, and about ten miles from Dunkeld came upon
a young lady, the daughter of a neighbouring proprietor,
reading a novel under a tree. They entered into conversation with her, and Windham was so much struck with
her smartness and talent that though he was obliged at
the time, as he said, most reluctantly to leave her, he, three
years afterwards, came to Sinclair in the House of Commons and said to him, "I have never been able to get
this beautiful mountain nymph out of my mind, and I
wish you to ascertain whether she is married or single."
Windham was too late. She was already married to Dr. Dick
—afterwards a much-trusted medical adviser of Sir Walter
Scott—and had gone with her husband to the East Indies.

They returned to Edinburgh on the 13th of September,
and, says Windham, "after dinner walked to Adam
Smith's. Felt strongly the impression of a family completely Scotch. House magnificent and place fine. . . .
Found there Colonels Balfour and Ross, the former late
aide-de-camp to General Howe, the latter to Lord Cornwallis. Felt strongly the impression of a company completely Scotch."

Colonel Nesbit Balfour, who won great distinction in
the American war, was the son of one of Smith's old Fifeshire neighbours, a proprietor in that county, and became
afterwards well known in Parliament, where he sat from
1790 to 1812. Colonel (afterwards General) Alexander
Ross had also taken a distinguished part in the American
war, and was Cornwallis's most intimate friend and
correspondent. He was at this time Deputy-Adjutant-
General of the Forces in Scotland. Whether he was a
relation of the Colonel Patrick Ross of whom Smith speaks
in one of his letters as a kinsman of his own,[1] I cannot say.

Next day, the 14th, Burke and Windham dined with
Smith. There was no other guest except a Mr. Skene, no
doubt one of Smith's cousins from Pitlour, probably the

[1] See above, p. 361.

Inspector-General of Scotch Roads already mentioned.[1] On the following morning the two statesmen proceeded on their way southward.

One of the visits Burke paid in Edinburgh was to a charming poet, to whom fortune has been singularly unkind, not only treating him cruelly when alive, but instead of granting the usual posthumous reparation, treating him even more cruelly after his death. I mean John Logan, the author of the *Ode to the Cuckoo*, which Burke thought the most beautiful lyric in the language. Logan was at the moment in the thick of his troubles. He had written a tragedy called *Runnymede*, which, though accepted by the management of Covent Garden, was prohibited by the Lord Chamberlain, who scented current politics in the bold speeches of the Barons of King John, but it was eventually produced in the Edinburgh theatre in 1783. Its production immediately involved the author, as one of the ministers of Leith, in difficulties with his parishioners and the ecclesiastical courts similar to those which John Home had encountered twenty years before, and the trouble ended in Logan resigning his charge in December 1786 on a pension of £40 a year. Smith, who was an admirer and, as Dr. Carlyle mentions to Bishop Douglas, a "great patron" of Logan, stood by him through these troubles. When they first broke out in 1783 he wished, as Logan himself tells his old pupil Sir John Sinclair, to get the poet transferred if possible from his parish in Leith to the more liberal and enlightened parish of the Canongate, and when Logan eventually made up his mind to take refuge in literature, Smith gave him the following letter of introduction to Andrew Strahan, who had, since his father's death, become the head of the firm :—

Dear Sir—Mr. Logan, a clergyman of uncommon learning, taste, and ingenuity, but who cannot easily submit to the puri-

---

[1] See above, p. 243.

tanical spirit of this country, quits his charge and proposes to settle in London, where he will probably exercise what may be called the trade of a man of letters. He has published a few poems, of which several have great merit, and which are probably not unknown to you. He has likewise published a tragedy, which I cannot say I admire in the least. He has another in manuscript, founded and almost translated from a French drama, which is much better. But the best of all his works which I have seen are some lectures upon universal history, which were read here some years ago, but which, notwithstanding they were approved and even admired by some of the best and most impartial judges, were run down by the prevalence of a hostile literary faction, to the leaders of which he had imprudently given some personal offence. Give me leave to recommend him most earnestly to your countenance and protection. If he was employed on a review he would be an excellent hand for giving an account of all books of taste, of history, and of moral and abstract philosophy.—I ever am, my dear sir, most faithfully and affectionately yours,

ADAM SMITH.[1]

EDINBURGH, 29*th September* 1785.

The lectures which Smith praises so highly were published in 1779, and are interesting as one of the first adventures in what was afterwards known as the philosophy of history. But his memory rests now on his poems, which Smith thought less of, and especially on his *Ode to the Cuckoo*, which he has been accused so often of stealing from his deceased friend Michael Bruce, but to which his title has at last been put beyond all doubt by Mr. Small's publication of a letter, written to Principal Baird in 1791, by Dr. Robertson of Dalmeny, who acted as joint editor with him of their common friend Bruce's poems.[2]

[1] Morrison MSS.
[2] Small, *Michael Bruce and the Ode to the Cuckoo*, p. 7.

CHAPTER XXVIII

THE POPULATION QUESTION

Dr. Richard Price had recently stirred a sensation by his attempt to prove that the population of England was declining, and had actually declined by nearly 30 per cent since the Revolution, and the first to enter the lists against him was William Eden, who in his *Fifth Letter to the Earl of Carlisle*, published in 1780, exposes the weakness of Price's statistics, and argues that both the population and the trade of the country had increased. Price replied to these criticisms in the same year, and now in 1785 Eden appears to have been contemplating a return to the subject and the publication of another work upon it, in connection with which he entered upon a correspondence with Smith, for the two following letters bearing on this population question of last century, though neither of them bears any name or address, seem most likely to have been written to that politician.

Price had drawn his alarmist conclusions from rough estimates founded on the revenue returns. From a comparison of the hearth-money returns before the Revolution with the window and house tax returns of his own time he guessed at the number of dwelling-houses in the country, and from the number of dwelling-houses he guessed at the number of inhabitants by simply supposing each house to contain five persons. He further tried to support his conclusion by figures drawn from bills of mortality and by references to colonial emigration, consolidation of farms, the growth of London, and the progress of luxury.

Smith thought very poorly of those ill-founded speculations, and even of their author generally, and he appears
to have called Eden's attention to a population return
relative to Scotland which furnished a sounder basis for a
just estimate of the numbers of the people than the statistics
on which Price relied.   This was a return of the number
of examinable persons in every parish of Scotland which
had been obtained in 1755 by Dr. Alexander Webster, at
the desire of Lord President Dundas, for the information
of the Government.   Public catechisings were then, and
in many parishes are still, part of the ordinary duties of
the minister, who visited each hamlet and district of his
parish successively for the purpose every year, and consequently every minister kept a list of the examinable
persons in his parish—the persons who were old enough to
answer his questions on the Bible or Shorter Catechism.
None were too old to be exempt.   Webster procured copies
of these lists for every parish in Scotland, and when he
added to each a certain proportion to represent the number
of persons under examinable age, he had a fairly accurate
statement of the population of the country.   He appears to
have procured the lists for 1779 as well as those for 1755,
and to have ascertained from a comparison of the two that
the population of Scotland had remained virtually stationary
during that quarter of a century, the increase in the commercial and manufacturing districts being counterbalanced by a
diminution in the purely agricultural districts, due to the
consolidation of farms.   That, at least, was the impression
of the officials of the Ministers' Widows' Fund, through
whom the correspondence on the subject with the ministers
had been conducted ; and they threw doubt on an observation of a contrary import—apparently to the effect that the
population of Scotland was increasing—which Smith heard
Webster make in one of those hours of merriment for
which that popular and useful divine seems destined to be
remembered when his public services are forgotten.

Smith's first letter runs thus :—

SIR—I have been so long in answering your very obliging letter of the 8th inst. that I am afraid you will imagine I have been forgetting or neglecting it. I hoped to send one of the accounts by the post after I received your letter, but some difficulties have occurred which I was not aware of, and you may yet be obliged to wait a few days for it. In the meantime I send you a note extracted from Mr. Webster's book by his clerk, who was of great use to him in composing it, and who has made several corrections upon it since.

My letters as a Commissioner of the Customs are paid at the Custom House, and my correspondents receive them duty free. I should otherwise have taken the liberty to enclose them, as you direct, under Mr. Rose's cover. It may perhaps give that gentleman pleasure to be informed that the net revenue arising from the customs in Scotland is at least four times greater than it was seven or eight years ago. It has been increasing rapidly these four or five years past, and the revenue of this year has overleaped by at least one-half the revenue of the greatest former year. I flatter myself it is likely to increase still further. The development of the causes of this augmentation would require a longer discussion than this letter will admit.

Price's speculations cannot fail to sink into the neglect that they have always deserved. I have always considered him as a factious citizen, a most superficial philosopher, and by no means an able calculator.—I have the honour to be, with great respect and esteem, sir, your most faithful humble servant,

ADAM SMITH.

CUSTOM HOUSE, EDINBURGH, 22*nd December* 1785.

I shall certainly think myself very much honoured by any notice you may think proper to take of my book.[1]

The second letter followed in a few days :—

EDINBURGH, 3*rd January* 1786.

SIR—The accounts of the imports and exports of Scotland which you wanted are sent by this day's post to Mr. Rose.

Since I wrote to you last I have conversed with Sir Henry Moncreiff, Dr. Webster's successor as collector of the fund for

---

[1] Original in possession of Mr. Alfred Morrison.

the maintenance of clergymen's widows, and with his clerk, who was likewise clerk to Dr. Webster, and who was of great use to the Doctor in the composition of the very book which I mentioned to you in a former letter. They are both of opinion that the conversation I had with Dr. Webster a few months before his death must have been the effect of a momentary and sudden thought, and not of any serious or deliberate consideration or inquiry. It was, indeed, at a very jolly table and in the midst of much mirth and jollity, of which the worthy Doctor, among many other useful and amiable qualities, was a very great lover and promoter. They told me that in the year 1779 a copy of the Doctor's book was made out by his clerk for the use of my Lord North. That at the end of that book the Doctor had subjoined a note to the following purpose, that though between 1755 and 1779 the numbers in the great trading and manufacturing towns and villages were considerably increased, yet the Highlands and Islands were much depopulated, and even the low country, by the enlargement of farms, in some degree ; so that the whole numbers, he imagined, must be nearly the same at both periods. Both these gentlemen believe that this was the last deliberate judgment which Dr. Webster ever formed upon this subject. The lists mentioned in the note are the lists of what are called examinable persons—that is, of persons upwards of seven or eight years of age, who are supposed fit to be publicly examined upon religious and moral subjects. Most of our country clergy keep examination rolls of this kind.

My Lord North will, I dare to say, be happy to accommodate you with the use of this book. It is a great curiosity, though the conversation I mentioned to you had a little shaken my faith in it —I am glad now to suppose, without much reason.—I have the honour to be, with the highest regard, sir, your most obedient humble servant,   ADAM SMITH.[1]

A new edition of the *Wealth of Nations*—the fourth—appeared in 1786, without any alteration in the text from the previous one, but the author prefixed to it an advertisement acknowledging the very great obligations he had been under to Mr. Henry Hope, the banker at Amsterdam, for (to quote the words of the advertisement) " the most distinct as well as the most liberal information concerning a

[1] Original in Edinburgh University Library.

very interesting and important subject, the Bank of Amsterdam, of which no printed account has ever appeared to me satisfactory or even intelligible. The name of that gentleman is so well known in Europe, the information which comes from him must do so much honour to whoever has been favoured with it, and my vanity is so much interested in making this acknowledgment, that I can no longer refuse myself the pleasure of prefixing this advertisement to this new edition of my book."

Smith had now, as he says in the following letter, reached his grand climacteric—his sixty-third year, according to the old belief, the last and most dangerous of the periodical crises to which man's bodily life was supposed to be subject—and the winter of 1786-87 laid him so low with a chronic obstruction of the bowels that Robertson wrote Gibbon they were in great danger of losing him. That was the winter Burns was in Edinburgh, and it was doubtless owing to this illness and Smith's consequent inability to go into society, that he and the poet never met. Burns obtained a letter of introduction to Smith from their common friend Mrs. Dunlop, but writes her on the 19th of April that when he called he found Smith had gone to London the day before, having recovered, as we know he did, sufficiently in spring to go up there for the purpose of consulting John Hunter. He was still in Edinburgh in March, however, and wrote Bishop Douglas a letter introducing one of his Fifeshire neighbours, Robert Beatson, the author of the well-known and very useful *Political Index*. Beatson had been an officer of the Engineers, but had retired on half-pay in 1766 and become an agriculturist in his native county. While there he compiled his unique and valuable work, which he published in 1786 and dedicated to his old friend Adam Smith. A new edition was called for within a year, and the author proposed to add some new matter, on which he desired the advice of Bishop Douglas. Hence this letter :—

DEAR SIR—This letter will be delivered to you by Mr. Robert Beatson of Vicars Grange, in Fifeshire, a very worthy friend of mine, and my neighbour in the country for more than ten years together. He has lately published a very useful book called a Political Index, which has been very successful, and which he now proposes to republish with some additions. He wishes much to have your good advice with regard to these additions, and indeed with regard to every other part of his book. And indeed, without flattering you, I know no man so fit to give him good advice upon this subject. May I therefore beg leave to introduce him to your acquaintance, and to recommend him most earnestly to your best advice and assistance. You will find him a very good-natured, well-informed, inoffensive, and obliging companion.

I was exceedingly vexed and not a little offended when I heard that you had passed through this town some time ago without calling upon me, or letting me know that you was in our neighbourhood. My anger, however, which was very fierce, is now a good deal abated, and if you promise to behave better for the future, it is not impossible that I may forgive the past.

This year I am in my grand climacteric, and the state of my health has been a good deal worse than usual. I am getting better and better, however, every day, and I begin to flatter myself that with good pilotage I shall be able to weather this dangerous promontory of human life, after which I hope to sail in smooth water for the remainder of my days.—I am ever, my dear sir, most faithfully and affectionately yours,   ADAM SMITH.

EDINBURGH, *6th March* 1787.[1]

---

[1] Egerton MSS., British Museum, 2181.

CHAPTER XXIX

IN April he had improved enough to undertake the journey to London to consult Hunter, but he was wasted to a skeleton. William Playfair—brother of his friend the Professor of Mathematics, and afterwards one of the early editors of the *Wealth of Nations*—met him soon after his arrival in London, and says he was looking very ill, and was evidently going to decay. While in his usual health he was, though not corpulent, yet rather stout than spare, but he was now reduced to skin and bone. He was able, however, to move about in society and see old friends and make new. Windham in his *Diary* mentions meeting him at several different places, and he was now introduced for the first time to the young statesman who was only a student in the Temple when he was last in London in 1777, but who was already one of the most powerful ministers England had ever seen, and was at the moment reforming the national finances with the *Wealth of Nations* in his hand. Pitt always confessed himself one of Smith's most convinced disciples. The first few years of his long ministry saw the daybreak of free trade. He brought in a measure of commercial emancipation for Ireland ; he carried a commercial treaty with France ; he passed, in accordance with Smith's recommendations, laws simplifying the collection and administration of the revenue. In this very year 1787 he introduced his great

Consolidation Bill, which created order out of the previous chaos of customs and excise, and was so extensive a work that it took 2537 separate resolutions to state its provisions, and these resolutions had only just been read on the 7th of March, a few weeks before Smith arrived in London.

No one in London therefore was more interested to meet Smith than the young minister who was carrying the economist's principles out so extensively in practical legislation. They met repeatedly, but they met on one occasion, of which recollection has been preserved, at Dundas's house on Wimbledon Green,—Addington, Wilberforce, and Grenville being also of the company; and it is said that when Smith, who was one of the last guests to arrive, entered the room, the whole company rose from their seats to receive him and remained standing. " Be seated, gentlemen," said Smith. " No," replied Pitt ; " we will stand till you are first seated, for we are all your scholars." This story seems to rest on Edinburgh tradition, and was first published, so far as I know, in the 1838 edition of Kay's *Portraits*, more than half a century after the date of the incident it relates. Most of the biographies contained in that work were written by James Paterson, but a few of the earliest, including this of Smith, were not. They were all written, however, from materials which had been long collected by Kay himself, who only died in 1832, or which were obtained before the time of publication from local residents who had known the men themselves, or had mingled with those who did. The whole were edited by the well-known and learned anti-quary, James Maidment, whose acceptance of the story is some security that it came from an authoritative though unnamed source.

Smith was highly taken with Pitt, and one evening when dining with him, he remarked to Addington after dinner, " What an extraordinary man Pitt is ; he understands my ideas better than I do myself." [1]   Other

[1] Pellew's *Life of Sidmouth*, i. 151.

statesmen have been converts to free trade. Pitt never had any other creed ; it was his first faith. He was forming his opinions as a young man when the *Wealth of Nations* appeared, and he formed them upon that work. Smith saw much of this group of statesmen during his visit to the capital in that year.[1] We find Wilberforce sounding him about some of his philanthropic schemes, Addington writing an ode to him after meeting him at Pitt's, and Pitt himself seeking his counsels concerning some contemplated legislation, and perhaps setting him to some task of investigation for his assistance. Bentham had in the early part of 1787 sent from Russia the manuscript of his *Defence of Usury*, written in antagonism to Smith's doctrine on the subject, to his friend George Wilson, barrister, and Wilson a month or two later—14th of July —writes of " Dr. Smith," who can, I think, be no other than the economist : " Dr. Smith has been very ill here of an inflammation in the neck of the bladder, which was increased by very bad piles. He has been cut for the piles, and the other complaint is since much mended. The physicians say he may do some time longer. He is much with the Ministry, and the clerks of the public offices have orders to furnish him with all papers, and to employ additional hands, if necessary, to copy for him. I am vexed that Pitt should have done so right a thing as to consult Smith, but if any of his schemes are effectuated I shall be comforted."[2] It may be, of course, that Smith was examining papers in the public offices in connection with his own work on Government, but Wilson's statement rather leaves the impression that the researches were instituted in pursuance of some idea of Pitt's, probably related to the reform of the finances. If the Dr. Smith of Wilson's letter is the economist, he would appear to have stayed in London a considerable time on this occasion, and to have suffered a serious relapse of ill-health during his stay there.

[1] Wilberforce's *Correspondence*, i. 40.
[2] Bowring's Memoir of Bentham, Bentham's *Works*, x. 173.

Wilberforce did not think quite so highly of Smith as Pitt did, being disappointed to find him too hard-headed to share his own enthusiasm about a great philanthropic adventure of the day, which, to the very practical mind of the economist, seemed entirely wanting in the ordinary conditions of success. With some of the other philanthropic movements in which Wilberforce was interested—with his anti-slavery agitation, for example, begun in that very year 1787—he would have found no more cordial sympathiser than Smith, who had condemned slavery so strongly in his book. The Sunday school movement, too, started by Thomas Raikes two or three years before, won Smith's strongest commendation ; for Raikes writes William Fox on 27th July of this same year, and writes as if the remark had been made in conversation with himself, " Dr. Adam Smith, who has very ably written on the Wealth of Nations, says : ' No plan has promised to effect a change of manners with equal ease and simplicity since the days of the Apostles.' " These schools were instituted for the purpose of giving gratuitous instruction to all comers for four or five hours every Sunday in the ordinary branches of primary education, and they were opposed by some leading ecclesiastics—among others by a liberal divine like Bishop Horsley—on the ground that they might become subservient to purposes of political propagandism. The ecclesiastical mind is too often suspicious of the consequences of mental improvement and independence, but to Smith these were merely the first broad conditions of all popular progress.

No man could be less chargeable with indifference to honest and practicable schemes of philanthropy, but the particular scheme towards which Wilberforce found him " characteristically cool " was one which, in his opinion, held out extravagant expectations that could not possibly be realised. It was a project—first suggested, I believe, by Sir James Steuart, the economist, and taken up warmly after him by Dr. James Anderson, and especially by that earliest and

most persistent of crofters' friends, John Knox, bookseller
in the Strand—for checking the depopulation and distress
of the Scotch Highlands by planting a series of fishing
villages all round the Highland coast. Knox's idea was
to plant forty fishing villages at spots twenty-five miles
apart between the Mull of Cantyre and the Dornoch Firth
at a cost of £2000 apiece, or at least as many of them as
money could be obtained to start; and the scheme rose
high in public favour when the parliamentary committee
on Scotch Fisheries gave it a general recommendation in
1785, and suggested the incorporation of a limited liability
company by Act of Parliament in order to carry it out.

The Scotch nobility adopted the suggestion with great
spirit, and in 1786 the British Society for extending the
Fisheries was incorporated for that purpose by Royal
Charter with a capital of £150,000, with the Duke of
Argyle for Governor, and many leading personages, one
of them being Wilberforce, for directors. It was indeed
the grand philanthropic scheme of the day. The shares
were rapidly subscribed for sufficiently to justify a start,
and when Smith was in London in 1787 the society had
just begun operations on a paid-up capital of £35,000.
One of the directors, Isaac Hawkins Browne, M.P.,
was actually down in Scotland choosing the sites for the
villages; and Wilberforce was already almost hearing the
"busy hum" of the little hives of fishermen, coopers,
boat-builders, and ropemakers, whom they were settling
along the desolate coasts.

He naturally spoke to Smith about this large and
generous project for the benefit of his countrymen, but
was disappointed to find him very sceptical indeed as to
its practical results. "Dr. Smith," writes Wilberforce to
Hawkins Browne, "with a certain characteristic coolness,
observed to me that he looked for no other consequence
from the scheme than the entire loss of every shilling
that should be expended on it, granting, however, with
uncommon candour, that the public would be no great

sufferer, because he believed the individuals meant to put
their hands only in their own pockets." [1]

The event, however, has justified the sagacity of Smith's
prognostication.   The society began by purchasing the
ground for three fishing settlements on the west coast,—one
at Ullapool, in Ross-shire; a second at Lochbeg, in Inverness-shire; and a third at Tobermory, in Argyle.   They
prepared their feuing plans, built a few houses at their
own cost, tried to attract settlers by offering building feus
at low rents and fishing-boats on credit at low rates, but,
except to a slight extent at Ullapool, their offers were not
taken ; not a single boat ever sailed from Tobermory
under their auspices, and before many years elapsed the
society deserted these three original west coast stations
and sold its interest in them at a loss of some £2000.   But
meanwhile the directors had in 1803 bought land at a
small port on the east coast, Wick, where a flourishing
fishery with 400 boats had already been established by local
enterprise without their aid, and they founded there the
settlement of Pulteneytown (named by them after Smith's
friend, Sir William Pulteney), which has grown with the
industry of the port.   The society never again tried to
resume its original purpose of creating new fishing centres,
and here in Pulteneytown it has obviously only acted the
part of the shrewd building speculator, investing in the
ground-rents of a rising community and prudently helping
in its development.   Through this change of purpose it has
contrived to save some of its capital, and having recently
resolved to be wound up, it sold its whole estate in 1893
for £20,000, and after all claims are met may probably
have £15,000 of its original capital of £35,000 left to
divide.   The net result of the scheme therefore on the
development of Highland fisheries has been as near *nil* as
Smith anticipated ; and if the shareholders have not, as he
predicted, lost every shilling of their money, they have lost
half of it, and only saved the other half by abandoning

[1] Wilberforce's *Correspondence*, i. 40.

the scheme for which it was subscribed. In the whole course of its one hundred and eight years' existence the society never paid more than eleven annual dividends, because for many years it saved up its income for building an extension to its harbour, and eventually lost all these savings and £100,000 of Government money besides in a great breakwater, which proved an irremediable engineering failure, and lies now in the bottom of the sea.

Smith returned to Edinburgh deeply pleased with the reception he met with from the ministers and the progress he saw his principles making. He came back, says the Earl of Buchan, " a Tory and a Pittite instead of a Whig and a Foxite, as he was when he set out. By and by the impression wore off and his former sentiments returned, but unconnected either with Pitt, Fox, or anybody else." [1] Had the impression remained till his death, it would be no matter for wonder. A Liberal has little satisfaction in contemplating the conflict of parties during the first years of Pitt's long administration, and seeing the young Tory minister introducing one great measure of commercial reform after another, while his own Whig chief, Charles Fox, offers to every one of them a most factious and unscrupulous opposition.

Soon after his return Smith received another, and to him a very touching, recognition of his merit in being chosen in November Lord Rector of his old *alma mater*, the University of Glasgow. The appointment lay with the whole University, professors and students together, but as the students had the advantage of numbers, the decision was virtually in their hands, and their unanimous choice came to Smith (as Carlyle said a similar choice came to him) at the end of his labours like a voice of " Well done " from the University which had sent him forth to do them, and from the coming generation which was to enter upon the fruits of them. There was at first some word of opposition to his candidature, on the good old

[1] The *Bee*, vol. iii. p. 165.

electioneering plea that he was the professors' nominee, and that it was essential for the students to resent dictation and assert their independence. One of Smith's keenest opponents among the students was Francis Jeffrey, who was then a Tory. Principal Haldane, who was also a student at Glasgow at the time, used to tell of seeing Jeffrey—a little, black, quick-motioned creature with a rapid utterance and a prematurely-developed moustache, on which his audience teased him mercilessly—haranguing a mob of boys on the green and trying to rouse them to their manifest duty of organising opposition to the professors' nominee. His exertions failed, however, and Smith was chosen without a contest.

On receiving intimation of his appointment Smith wrote to Principal Davidson the following reply :—

REVEREND AND DEAR SIR—I have this moment received the honour of your letter of the 15th instant. I accept with gratitude and pleasure the very great honour which the University of Glasgow have done me in electing me for the ensuing year to be the Rector of that illustrious Body. No preferment could have given me so much real satisfaction. No man can own greater obligations to a Society than I do to the University of Glasgow. They educated me, they sent me to Oxford, soon after my return to Scotland they elected me one of their own members, and afterwards preferred me to another office to which the abilities and virtues of the never-to-be-forgotten Dr. Hutcheson had given a superior degree of illustration. The period of thirteen years which I spent as a member of that Society, I remember as by far the most useful and therefore as by far the happiest and most honourable period of my life ; and now, after three-and-twenty years' absence, to be remembered in so very agreeable a manner by my old friends and protectors gives me a heartfelt joy which I cannot easily express to you.

I shall be happy to receive the commands of my colleagues concerning the time when it may be convenient for them to do me the honour of admitting me to the office. Mr. Millar mentions Christmass. We have commonly at the Board of Customs a vacation of five or six days at that time. But I am so regular an attendant that I think myself entitled to take the play for a

week at any time.   It will be no inconveniency to me therefore
to wait upon you at whatever time you please.   I beg to be
remembered to my colleagues in the most respectful and the most
affectionate manner ; and that you would believe me to be, with
great truth, reverend and dear sir, your and their most obliged,
most obedient, and most humble servant,   ADAM SMITH.

EDINBURGH, 16*th November* 1787.

The Rev. Dr. ARCHIBALD DAVIDSON,
Principal of the College, Glasgow.[1]

He was installed as Rector on the 12th December 1787
with the usual ceremonies.   He gave no inaugural address,
nor apparently so much as a formal word of thanks.   At least
Jeffrey, who might have been present, though he does
not seem to speak from personal recollection, says he
remained altogether silent.   His predecessor, Graham of
Gartmore, held the Rector's chair for only one year, but
Smith, like Burke and Dundas, was re-elected for a second
term, and was Rector therefore from November 1787 till
November 1789.

One of the new friends Smith made during his last
visit to London was Sir Joseph Banks, President of the
Royal Society, who seems to have shown him particular
attentions, and shortly after his return he gave a young Scotch
scientific man a letter of very warm recommendation to Sir
Joseph.   The young man of science was John Leslie, afterwards Sir John, the celebrated Professor of Natural Philosophy in Edinburgh University.   Leslie, who belonged to
the neighbourhood of Smith's own town of Kirkcaldy, had
been employed by him for the previous two years as tutor
to his cousin and heir, David Douglas, and being thus a
daily visitor at Smith's house, had won a high place in his
affections and regard.   Accordingly when Leslie in 1787
gave up his original idea of entering the Church, and
resolved to migrate to London with a view to literary or
scientific employment, Smith furnished him with a number

[1] Glasgow College Minutes.

of letters of introduction, and, as Leslie informed the
writer of his biography in Chambers's *Biographical Dictionary*, advised him, when the letter was addressed to an
author, to be always sure to read that author's book before
presenting it, so as to be able to speak of the book should
a fit opportunity occur.   The letter to Sir Joseph Banks
runs as follows :—

Sir—The very great politeness and attention with which you
was so good as to honour me when I was last in London has
emboldened me to use a freedom which I am afraid I am not
entitled to, and to introduce to your acquaintance a young gentleman of very great merit, and who is very ambitious of being
known to you.   Mr. Leslie, the bearer of this letter, has been
known to me for several years past.   He has a very particular
happy turn for the mathematical sciences.   It is no more than
two years and a half ago that he undertook the instruction of a
young gentleman, my nearest relation, in some of the higher parts
of these sciences, and acquitted himself most perfectly both to
my satisfaction and to that of the young gentleman.   He proposes
to pursue the same lines in London, and would be glad to accept
of employment in some of the mathematical academies.   Besides
his knowledge in mathematics he is, I am assured, a tolerable
Botanist and Chymist.   Your countenance and good opinion,
provided you shall find he deserves them, may be of the highest
importance to him.   Give me leave, upon that condition, to
recommend him in the most anxious and earnest manner to your
protection.   I have the honour to be, with the highest respect
and regard, sir, your most obliged and most obedient humble
servant,   ADAM SMITH.[1]

EDINBURGH, 18*th December* 178 (*sic*).

Sir JOSEPH BANKS.

Why does so large a proportion of Smith's extant
letters consist of letters of introduction ?   Have they a
better principle of vitality than others, that they should be
more frequently preserved?   There certainly seems less
reason to preserve them, but then there is also less reason
to destroy them.

[1] Morrison MSS.

Smith's health appears to have improved so much during the spring of 1788 that his friends, who, as we know from Robertson's letter to Gibbon, had been seriously alarmed about his condition, were now again free from anxiety. He seemed to them to be " perfectly re-established." But in the autumn he suffered another great personal loss in the death of his cousin, Miss Jean Douglas, who had lived under his roof for so many years. His home was now desolate. His mother and his cousin—the two lifelong companions of his hearth—were both gone ; his young heir was only with him during the vacations from Glasgow College, where he was now living with Professor John Millar, and being a man for whom the domestic affections went for so much, there seemed, amid all the honour, love, obedience, troops of friends that enrich the close of an important career, to remain a void in his life that could not be filled.

Gibbon had sent him a present of the three concluding volumes of the *Decline and Fall*, and Smith writes him in November a brief letter of thanks, in which he sets the English historian where he used to set Voltaire, at the head of all living men of letters.

EDINBURGH, 18*th December* 1788.

MY DEAR FRIEND—I have ten thousand apologies to make for not having long ago returned you my best thanks for the very agreeable present you made me of the three last volumes of your History. I cannot express to you the pleasure it gives me to find that by the universal consent of every man of taste and learning whom I either know or correspond with, it sets you at the very head of the whole literary tribe at present existing in Europe.— I ever am, my dear friend, most affectionately yours,

ADAM SMITH.[1]

In this letter Smith makes no complaint of his condition of health, but he seems to have got worse again in the course of the winter, for we find Gibbon writing Cadell,

[1] Gibbon's *Miscellaneous Works*, ii. 429.

the bookseller, with some apparent anxiety on the 11th of
February 1789 : "If you can send me a good account of
Adam Smith, there is no man more sincerely interested in
his welfare than myself."   If, however, he were ill then,
he recovered in the summer, and was in excellent spirits in
July, when Samuel Rogers saw him often during a week he
spent in Edinburgh.

CHAPTER XXX

1789

THE author of the *Pleasures of Memory*, going to Scotland to make the home tour, as it was called, then much in vogue, brought with him letters of introduction to Smith from Dr. Price and Dr. Kippis, the editor of the *Biographia Britannica*. The poet was then a young man of twenty-three, who had published nothing but his *Ode to Superstition*, and these old Unitarian friends of his father were as yet his chief acquaintances in the world of letters. Their names, notwithstanding the disparaging allusion Smith makes to Price in a letter previously given, won for Rogers the kindest possible reception, and even a continuous succession of civilities, of which he has left a grateful record in the journal he kept during his tour. This journal has been published in Mr. Clayden's *Early Years of Samuel Rogers*, and a few additional particulars omitted in it are found in Dyce's published and Mitford's unpublished recollections of Rogers's table-talk.

Rogers arrived in Edinburgh apparently on the 14th of July—that momentous 14th of July 1789 which set the world aflame, though not a spark of information of it had reached Edinburgh before he left the city on the 21st; and on the morning of the 15th he walked down Panmure Close and paid his first visit to the economist. He found Smith sitting at breakfast quite alone, with a dish of strawberries before him, and he has preserved some scraps of the conversation, none of them in any way remarkable. Starting from the business then on hand, Smith said that fruit was his favourite diet at that season of the year, and that Scotland produced excellent strawberries, for the strawberry was a northern fruit, and was at its best in Orkney or Sweden. Passing to the subject of Rogers's tour, he said that Edinburgh deserved little notice, that the old town had given Scotland a bad name (for its filth, presumably), and that he himself was anxious to remove to the newer quarters of the town, and had set his heart on George Square (the place where Walter Scott was brought up and Henry Dundas died). He explained that Edinburgh was entirely supported by the three Courts of Session, Exchequer, and Justiciary (possibly to account for the filth of the place, in accordance with his theory that there was always more squalor and misery in a residential than in an industrial town). While thus apparently slighting or ignoring the beauties of Edinburgh, which were all there then as they are now, he praised Loch Lomond highly. It was the finest lake in Great Britain, the islands being very beautiful and forming a very striking contrast to the shores. The conversation passed from the scenery of Scotland to the soil, and Smith said Scotland had an excellent soil, but a climate so severe that its harvests were too often overtaken by winter before they were housed. The consequence was that the Scotch on the Borders were still in extreme poverty, just as he had noticed half a century before when he rode across the Borders as a student to Oxford, and was greatly struck with the different condition of things he saw as he approached Carlisle. From agriculture they passed on to discuss the corn trade, and Smith denounced the Government's late refusal of corn to France, saying it ought to excite indignation and contempt, inasmuch as the quantity required was so trifling that it would not support the population of Edinburgh for a single day. The population of Edinburgh suggested their houses, and Smith said that the houses were piled high on one another in Paris as well as in Edinburgh. They then touched on Sir John Sinclair, of whom Smith spoke disparagingly in certain aspects, but said that he never knew a man who was in earnest and did not do something at last. Before leaving to return to his hotel Rogers seems to have asked Smith if he knew Mrs. Piozzi, who was then living there, and had called upon Rogers after learning from the landlord that Smith and Robertson had left cards for him, and Smith said he did not know her, but believed she was spoiled by keeping company with odd people. Smith then invited his visitor to dine with him next day at the usual Friday dinner of the Oyster Club, and Rogers came away delighted with the interview, and with the illustrious philosopher's genuine kindness of heart.

On Friday, as appointed, Rogers dined with the Oyster Club as Smith's guest, but he has made no specific entry of the event in his journal, and no record of the conversation. Black and Playfair seem to have been there, and possibly other men of eminence; but the whole talk was usurped by a commonplace member, and Smith felt—and possibly Rogers too—that the day was lost. For next time they met Smith asked Rogers how he liked the club, and said, "*That* Bogle, I was sorry he talked so much; he spoiled our evening." That Bogle was the Laird of Daldowie, on the Clyde. His father had been Rector of Glasgow University in Smith's professorial days, and one of his brothers, George Bogle, attained some eminence through the embassy on which he was sent by Warren Hastings to the Llama of Thibet, and his account of which has been published quite recently; and the offender himself was a man of ability and knowledge, who had been a West India merchant for many years, was well versed in economic and commercial subjects, and very fond of writing to the Government of the day long communications on those subjects, which seem to have been generally read, and sometimes even acted upon. In society, as we are told by one of his relations, Mr. Morehead, he was generally con-

sidered very "tedious, from the long lectures on mercantile
and political subjects (for he did not converse when he
entered on these, but rather declaimed) which he was in
the habit of delivering in the most humdrum and mono-
tonous manner."[1] His tedious lectures must, however,
have had more in them than ordinary hearers appreciated,
for Smith thought so highly of Bogle's conversation that
when he invited Rogers to the club on this particular
occasion he mentioned that Bogle, a very clever person,
was to be there, and said "I must go and hear Bogle
talk."[2]

Rogers was with Smith again on Sunday the 19th, and
used ever afterwards to speak of that particular Sunday as
the most memorable in his life, for he breakfasted with
Robertson, heard him preach in the Old Greyfriars in the
forenoon, heard Blair preach in the High Church in the
afternoon, drank coffee thereafter with Mrs. Piozzi, and
finished the day by supping with Adam Smith. He had
called on Smith "between sermons," as they say in Scotland, and apparently close on the hour for service, since
"all the bells of the kirks" were ringing. But Smith
was going for an airing, and his chair was at the door.
The sedan was much in vogue in Edinburgh at that
period, because it threaded the narrow wynds and alleys
better than any other sort of carriage was able to do.
Smith met Rogers at the door, and after exchanging the
few observations about Bogle and the club to which I
have already alluded, he invited his young friend to come
back to supper in the evening, and also to dinner on
Monday, because he had asked Henry Mackenzie, the
author of the *Man of Feeling*, to meet him. "Who could
refuse?" writes Rogers. Smith then set out in his sedan,
and Rogers walked up to the High Church to hear Blair.
Returning to Panmure House at nine, he found there, he
says, all the company who were at the club on Friday

[1] Morehead's *Life of the Rev. R. Morehead*, p. 43.
[2] Add. MSS., 32,566.

except Bogle and Macaulay, and with the addition of a Mr. Muir from Göttingen. (I do not know who Macaulay and Muir were.) They spoke of Junius, and Smith suspected Single-speech Hamilton of the author-ship, on the ground of the well-known story, which seems to have been then new to Rogers, and which Smith had been told by Gibbon, that on one occasion when Hamilton was on a visit at Goodwood, he informed the Duke of Richmond that there was a devilish keen letter from Junius in the *Public Advertiser* of that day, and men-tioned even some of the points it made; but when the Duke got hold of the paper he found the letter itself was not there, but only an apology for its absence. From this circumstance Hamilton's name came to be mentioned in connection with the authorship of the letters, and they ceased to appear. Smith's argument was that so long as the letters were attributed to men who were not their writers, such as Lord Lansdowne or Burke, they continued to go on, but immediately the true author was named they stopped. The conversation passed on to Turgot and Voltaire and the Duke of Richelieu, and its particulars have been stated already in previous parts of this work.[1]

On Monday Rogers dined at Smith's house to meet Henry Mackenzie, as had been arranged, and the other guests seem to have been the Mr. Muir of the evening before and Mr. M'Gowan—John M'Gowan, Clerk of the Signet, already referred to. Dr. Hutton came in after-wards and joined them at tea. The chief share in the conversation seems to have been taken by Mackenzie, who, as we know from Scott, was always "the life of company with anecdotes and fun," and related on this occasion many stories of second sight in the Highlands, and especially of the eccentric Caithness laird, who used the pretension as a very effectual instrument for maintain-ing authority and discipline among his tenantry. They spoke much too about the poetesses,—Hannah More, and

[1] See above, pp. 189, 190, 205.

Mrs. Charlotte Smith, and Mrs. John Hunter, the great surgeon's wife; but it appears to have still been Mackenzie who bore the burden of the talk. The only thing Rogers reports Smith as saying is a very ordinary remark about Dr. Blair. They had been speaking, as was natural, about the sermon which Rogers—and Mackenzie also—had heard the previous afternoon on "Curiosity concerning the Affairs of Others," and one passage in which, though it reads now commonplace enough in the printed page, Rogers seems to have admired greatly. Smith observed that Blair was too puffed up, and the worthy divine would have been more or less than human if he had escaped the necessary effects of the excessive popularity he so long enjoyed at once as a preacher and as a critic. It will be remembered how Burns detested Blair's absurd condescension and pomposity.

From Smith's the company seems to have proceeded in a body to a meeting of the Royal Society, of which all were members except Muir and Rogers himself. Before going Mackenzie repeated an epigram which had been written on Smith sleeping at the meetings of this society, but the epigram has not been preserved. Only seven persons were present—Smith and his guests and the reader of the paper for the day, who happened to be the economist, Dr. James Anderson, already mentioned repeatedly in this book as the original propounder of Ricardo's theory of rent. His paper was on "Debtors and the Revision of the Laws that respect them," and Rogers says it was "very long and dull," and, as a natural consequence, "Mr. Commissioner Smith fell asleep, and Mackenzie touched my elbow and smiled,"[1]—a curious tableau. When the meeting was over Rogers took leave of his host, went to the play with Mrs. Piozzi, and, though he no doubt saw Smith again before finally quitting Edinburgh, mentions him no more.

Having been so much with Smith during those few

[1] Clayden's *Early Life of Samuel Rogers*, p. 96.

days, Rogers's impressions are in some respects of considerable value. He was deeply impressed with the warmth of Smith's kindness. "He is a very friendly, agreeable man, and I should have dined and supped with him every day, if I had accepted all his invitations." [1] He was very communicative,[2] and to Rogers's surprise, considering the disparity of their years and the greatness of his reputation, Smith was "quite familiar." "Who shall we have to dinner?" he would ask. Rogers observed in him no sign of absence of mind,[3] and felt that as compared with Robertson, Smith was far more of a man who had seen much of the world. His communicativeness impressed itself also upon other casual visitors, because his first appearance sometimes gave them the opposite suggestion of reserve. "He was extremely communicative," says the anonymous writer who sent the first letter of reminiscences to the editor of the *Bee*, "and delivered himself on every subject with a freedom and boldness quite opposite to the apparent reserve of his appearance."

Another visitor to Scotland that year who enjoyed a talk with Smith, and has something interesting to communicate about the conversation, is William Adam, barrister and M.P., afterwards Chief Commissioner of the Jury Court in Scotland, who was a nephew of Smith's schoolfellow and lifelong friend, Robert Adam, the architect. William Adam was an intimate personal friend of Bentham since the days when they ate their way to the bar together and spent their nights in endless discussions about Hume's philosophy and other thorny subjects, and when in Scotland in the summer of 1789 he met Smith, and drew the conversation to his friend Bentham's recently published *Defence of Usury*. This book, it will be remembered, was written expressly to

---

[1] Clayden's *Early Life of Samuel Rogers*, p. 90.
[2] Dyce's *Recollections of the Table-talk of Samuel Rogers*, p. 45.
[3] Add. MSS., 32,566.

controvert Smith's recommendation of a legal limitation of the rate of interest, and from this conversation with Adam there seems to be some ground for thinking that the book had the very unusual controversial effect of converting the antagonist against whom it was written. Smith's reason for wanting to fix the legal rate of interest at a maximum just a little above the ordinary market rate was to prevent undue facilities being given to prodigals and projectors ; but Bentham replied very justly that, whatever might be said of prodigals, projectors at any rate were one of the most useful classes a community could possess, that a wise government ought to do all it could to encourage their enterprise instead of thwarting it, and that the best policy therefore was to leave the rate of interest alone. In conducting his polemic Bentham wrote as an admiring pupil towards a venerated master, to whom he said he owed everything, and over whom he could gain no advantage except, to use his own words, " with weapons which you have taught me to wield and with which you have furnished me ; for as all the great standards of truth which can be appealed to in this line owe, as far as I can understand, their establishment to you, I can see scarce any other way of convicting you of an error or oversight than by judging you out of your own mouth." [1]

Smith was touched with the handsome spirit in which his adversary wrote, and candidly admitted to Adam the force of his assaults. The conversation is preserved in a letter written to Bentham on the 4th December 1789 by another friend and fellow-barrister, George Wilson, as he apparently had the story from Adam's own lips.

"Did we ever tell you," writes Wilson, "what Dr. Adam Smith said to Mr. William Adam, the Council M.P., last summer in Scotland ? The Doctor's expressions were that 'the *Defence of Usury* was the work of a very superior man, and that tho' he had given

[1] Bentham's *Works*, iii. 21.

him some hard knocks, it was done in so handsome a way that he could not complain,' and seemed to admit that you were right." [1] This admission, though apparently not made in so many words by Smith, but rather inferred by Adam from the general purport of the conversation, is still not far removed from the confession so definitely reported that his position suffered some hard knocks from the assaults of Bentham. After that confession it is reasonable to think that if Smith had lived to publish another edition of his work, he would have modified his position on the rate of interest.

[1] Bentham MSS., British Museum.

CHAPTER XXXI

A REVISION of the *Theory of Moral Sentiments* was a task Smith had long had in contemplation. The book had been thirty years before the world and had passed through five editions, but it had never undergone any revision or alteration whatever. This was the task of the last year of the author's life. He made considerable changes, especially by way of addition, and though he wrote the additions, as Stewart informs us, while he was suffering under severe illness, he has never written anything better in point of literary style. Before the new edition appeared there was a preliminary difference between author and publisher regarding the propriety of issuing the additions as the additions to the *Wealth of Nations* had been issued, in a separate form, for the use of those who already possessed copies of the previous editions of the book. Cadell favoured that course, notwithstanding that it would obviously interfere with the sale of the new book, because he was unwilling to incur the charge of being illiberal in his dealings with the public. But Smith refused to assent to it, for reasons quite apart from the sale, but connected, whatever they were, with "the nature of the work." He communicated his decision through Dugald Stewart, who was in London in May 1789 on his way to Paris, and Stewart reports the result of his interview with Cadell in the following letter, bearing the post stamp of 6th May 1789 :—

DEAR SIR—I was so extremely hurried during the very short stay I made in London that I had not a moment's time to write you till now. The day after my arrival I called on Cadell, and luckily found Strachan (*sic*) with him. They both assured me in the most positive terms that they had published no Edition of the *Theory* since the *Fifth*, which was printed in 1781, and that if a 6*th* has been mentioned in any of the newspapers, it must have been owing to a typographical mistake. For your farther satisfaction Cadell stated the fact in his own handwriting on a little bit of paper which I send you enclosed.

I mentioned also to Cadell the resolution you had formed not to allow the Additions to the *Theory* to be printed separately, which he said embarrassed him much, as he had already in similar circumstances more than once incurred the charge of illiberality with the public. On my telling him, however, that you had made up your mind on the subject, and that it was perfectly unnecessary to write to you, as the nature of the work made it impossible for you to comply with his proposal, he requested of me to submit to your consideration whether it might not (be) proper for you to mention this circumstance, for his justification, in an advertisement prefixed to the Book. This was all, I think, that passed in the course of our conversation.

I write this from Dover, which I am just leaving with a fair wind, so that I hope to be in Paris on Thursday. It will give me great pleasure to receive your commands, if I can be of any use to you in executing any of your commissions.—I ever am, dear sir, your much obliged and most obedient servant,

DUGALD STEWART.[1]

In the preface to the 1790 edition the author refers to the promise he had made in that of 1759 of treating in a future work of the general principles of law and government, and of the different revolutions they had undergone in the different ages and periods of society, not only in what concerns justice, but in what concerns policy, revenue, and arms, and whatever else is the object of law ; and he says that in the *Wealth of Nations* he had executed this promise so far as policy, revenue, and arms were concerned, but that the remaining part of the task, the theory of jurisprudence, he had been prevented from executing by the

---

[1] Original in possession of Professor Cunningham, Belfast.

same occupations which had till then prevented him from revising the *Theory*. He adds: "Though my very advanced age leaves me, I acknowledge, very little expectation of ever being able to execute this great work to my own satisfaction, yet, as I have not altogether abandoned the design, and as I wish still to continue under the obligation of doing what I can, I have allowed the paragraph to remain as it was published more than thirty years ago, when I entertained no doubt of being able to execute everything which it announced."

The most important of the new contributions to this last edition of the *Theory* is the chapter "on the corruption of our moral sentiments, which is occasioned by our disposition to admire the rich and the great, and to despise or neglect persons of poor and mean condition." In spite of his alleged republicanism he was still a sort of believer in the principle of birth. It was not, in his view, a rational principle, but it was a natural and beneficial delusion. In the light of reason the vulgar esteem for rank and fortune above wisdom and virtue was utterly indefensible, but it had a certain advantage as a practical aid to good government. The maintenance of social order required the establishment of popular deference to some species of superiority, and the superiorities of birth and fortune were at least plain and palpable to the mob of mankind who have to be governed, whereas the superiorities of wisdom and virtue were often invisible and uncertain, even to the discerning. But however useful this admiration for the wrong things might be for the establishment of settled authority, he held it to be "at the same time the great and most universal cause of the corruption of our moral sentiments."[1]

But the additions attracted little notice compared with the deletions—the deletion of the allusion to Rochefoucauld associating that writer in the same condemnation with Mandeville, and the deletion of the passage in which the revealed doctrine of the atonement was stated to coincide

[1] *Theory*, ed. 1790, i. 146.

with the repentant sinner's natural feeling of the necessity of some other intercession and sacrifice than his own. The omission of the reference to Rochefoucauld has been blamed as a concession to feelings of private friendship in the teeth of the claims of truth; but Stewart, who knew the whole circumstances, says that Smith came to believe that truth as well as friendship required the emendation, and there is certainly difference enough between Rochefoucauld and Mandeville to support such a view.

The suppression of the passage about the atonement escaped notice for twenty years, till a notable divine, Archbishop Magee, in entire ignorance of the suppression, quoted the passage from one of the earlier editions as a strong testimony to the reasonableness of the Scriptural doctrine of the atonement from a man whose intellectual capacity and independence were above all dispute. "Such," he says, "are the reflections of a man whose powers of thinking and reasoning will surely not be pronounced inferior to those of any, even of the most distinguished champions of the Unitarian school, and whose theological opinions cannot be charged with any supposed taint from professional habits or interests. A layman (and he too a familiar friend of David Hume), whose life was employed in scientific, political, and philosophical researches, has given to the world those sentiments as the natural suggestions of reason. Yet these are the sentiments which are the scoff of sciolists and witlings."[1]

The sciolists and witlings were not slow in returning the scoff, and pointing out that while Smith was, no doubt, as an intellectual authority all that the Archbishop claimed for him, his authority really ran against the Archbishop's view and not in favour of it, inasmuch as he had withdrawn the passage relied on from the last edition of his work. Dr. Magee instantly changed his tune, and without thinking whether he had any ground for the statement, attributed the omission to the unhappy influence over

[1] Magee's *Works*, p. 138.

Smith's mind of the aggressive infidelity of Hume. " It adds one proof more," says his Grace, who, having failed to make Smith an evidence for Christianity, will now have him turned into a warning against unbelief,—"it adds one proof more to the many that already existed of the danger, even to the most enlightened, from a familiar contact with infidelity." His intercourse with Hume was at its closest when he first published the passage in 1759, whereas Hume was fourteen years in his grave when the passage was omitted ; besides there is probably as much left in the context which Hume would object to as is deleted, and in any case, there is no reason to believe that Smith's opinion about the atonement was anywise different in 1790 from what it was in 1759, or for doubting his own explanation of the omission, which he is said to have given to certain Edinburgh friends, that he thought the passage unnecessary and misplaced.[1] As if taking an odd revenge for its suppression, the original manuscript of this particular passage seems to have reappeared from between the leaves of a volume of Aristotle in the year 1831, when all the rest of the MS. of the book and of Smith's other works had long gone to destruction.[2] It may be added, as so much attention has been paid to Smith's religious opinions, that he gives a fresh expression to his belief in a future state and an all-seeing Judge in one of the new passages he wrote for this same edition of his *Theory*. It is in connection with his remarks on the Calas case. He says that to persons in the circumstances of Calas, condemned to an unjust death, " Religion can alone afford them every effectual comfort. She also can tell them that it is of little importance what men may think of their conduct while the all-seeing Judge of the world approves of it. She alone can present to them a view of another world,—a world of more candour, humanity, and justice than the present, where their innocence is in due time to be declared and

---

[1] Sinclair's *Life of Sir John Sinclair*, i. 40.
[2] Add. MSS., 32,574.

their virtue to be finally rewarded, and the same great principle which can alone strike terror into triumphant vice affords the only effectual consolation of disgraced and insulted innocence." [1] Whatever may have been his attitude towards historical Christianity, these words, written on the eve of his own death, show that he died as he lived, in the full faith of those doctrines of natural religion which he had publicly taught.

[1] *Theory*, ed. 1790, i. 303, 304.

CHAPTER XXXII

LAST DAYS

THE new edition of the *Theory* was the last work Smith published. A French newspaper, the *Moniteur Universelle* of Paris, announced on 11th March 1790 that a critical examination of Montesquieu's *Esprit des Lois* was about to appear from the pen of the celebrated author of the *Wealth of Nations*, and ventured to predict that the work would make an epoch in the history of politics and of philosophy. That at least, it added, is the judgment of well-informed people who have seen parts of it, of which they speak with an enthusiasm of the happiest augury. But notwithstanding this last statement the announcement was not made on any good authority. Smith may probably enough have dealt with Montesquieu as he dealt with many other topics in the papers he had prepared towards his projected work on government, but there is no evidence that he ever intended to publish a separate work on that remarkable writer, and before March 1790 his strength seems to have been much wasted. The Earl of Buchan, who had some time before gone to live in the country, was in town in February, and paid a visit to his old professor and friend. On taking leave of him the Earl said, " My dear Doctor, I hope to see you oftener when I come to town next February," but Smith squeezed his lordship's hand and replied, " My dear Lord Buchan,[1] I may be alive then

---

[1] " My dear Ascanius " are the words of the text, because Ascanius was the pseudonym under which the Earl happened to be writing.

and perhaps half a dozen Februaries, but you never will see your old friend any more. I find that the machine is breaking down, so that I shall be little better than a mummy "—with a by-thought possibly to the mummies of Toulouse. "I found a great inclination," adds the Earl, "to visit the Doctor in his last illness, but the mummy stared me in the face and I was intimidated." [1]

During the spring months Smith got worse and weaker, and though he seemed to rally somewhat at the first approach of the warm weather, he at length sank again in June, and his condition seemed to his friends to be already hopeless. Long and painful as his illness was, he bore it throughout not with patience merely but with a serene and even cheerful resignation. On the 21st of June Henry Mackenzie wrote his brother-in-law, Sir J. Grant, that Edinburgh had just lost its finest woman, and in a few weeks it would in all probability lose its greatest man. The finest woman was the beautiful Miss Burnet of Monboddo, whom Burns called "the most heavenly of all God's works," and the greatest man was Adam Smith. "He is now," says Mackenzie, "past all hopes of recovery, with which about three weeks ago we had flattered ourselves."

A week later Smellie, the printer, wrote Smith's young friend, Patrick Clason, in London : "Poor Smith! we must soon lose him, and the moment in which he departs will give a heart-pang to thousands. Mr. Smith's spirits are flat, and I am afraid the exertions he sometimes makes to please his friends do him no good. His intellect as well as his senses are clear and distinct. He wishes to be cheerful, but nature is omnipotent. His body is extremely emaciated, and his stomach cannot admit of sufficient nourishment ; but, like a man, he is perfectly patient and resigned." [2]

In all his own weakness he was still thoughtful of the care of his friends, and one of his last acts was to commend

---

[1] The *Bee*, 1791, iii. 166.
[2] Kerr's *Memoirs of W. Smellie*, i. 295.

to the good offices of the Duke of Buccleugh the children of
his old friend and physician, Cullen, who died only a few
months before himself. "In many respects," says Lord
Buchan, "Adam Smith was a chaste disciple of Epicurus
as that philosopher is properly understood, and Smith's
last act resembled that of Epicurus leaving as a legacy to
his friend and patron the children of his Metrodorus, the
excellent Cullen."[1]

When it became evident that the sickness was to prove
mortal, Smith's old friend Adam Ferguson, who had been
apparently estranged from him for some time, immediately
forgot their coolness, whatever it was about, and came and
waited on him with the old affection. "Your friend
Smith," writes Ferguson on 31st July 1790, announcing
the death to Sir John Macpherson, Warren Hastings' successor as Governor-General of India—"your old friend
Smith is no more. We knew he was dying for some
months, and though matters, as you know, were a little
awkward when he was in health, upon that appearance I
turned my face that way and went to him without further
consideration, and continued my attentions to the last."[2]

Dr. Carlyle mentions that the harmony of the famous
Edinburgh literary circle of last century was often ruffled
by little tifts, which he and John Home were generally
called in to compose, and that the usual source of the
trouble was Ferguson's "great jealousy of rivals," and
especially of his three more distinguished friends, Hume,
Smith, and Robertson. But it would not be right to
ascribe the fault to Ferguson merely on that account, for
Carlyle hints that Smith too had "a little jealousy in his
nature," although he admits him to have been a man of
"unbounded benevolence." But whatever it was that
had come between them, it is pleasant to find Ferguson
dismissing it so unreservedly, and forgetting his own
infirmities too—for he had been long since hopelessly

[1] The *Bee*, 1791, iii. 167.
[2] Original letter in Edinburgh University Library.

paralysed, and went about, Cockburn tells us, buried in furs "like a philosopher from Lapland"—in order to cheer the last days of the friend of his youth.

When Smith felt his end to be approaching he evinced great anxiety to have all his papers destroyed except the few which he judged to be in a sufficiently finished state to deserve publication, and being apparently too feeble to undertake the task himself, he repeatedly begged his friends Black and Hutton to destroy them for him. A third friend, Mr. Riddell, was present on one of the occasions when this request was made, and mentions that Smith expressed regret that " he had done so little." " But I meant," he said, " to have done more, and there are materials in my papers of which I could have made a great deal, but that is now out of the question." [1] Black and Hutton always put off complying with Smith's entreaties in the hope of his recovering his health or perhaps changing his mind ; but at length, a week before his death, he expressly sent for them, and asked them then and there to burn sixteen volumes of manuscript to which he directed them. This they did without knowing or asking what they contained. It will be remembered that seventeen years before, when he went up to London with the manuscript of the *Wealth of Nations*, he made Hume his literary executor, and left instructions with him to destroy all his loose papers and eighteen thin paper folio books " without any examination," and to spare nothing but his fragment on the history of astronomy. When the sixteen volumes of manuscript were burnt Smith's mind seemed to be greatly relieved. It appears to have been on a Sunday, and when his friends came, as they were accustomed to do, on the Sunday evening to supper— and they seem to have mustered strongly on this particular evening—he was able to receive them with something of his usual cheerfulness. He would even have stayed up and sat with them had they allowed him, but they pressed

[1] Stewart's *Works*, x. 74.

him not to do so, and he retired to bed about half-past
nine.   As he left the room he turned and said, " I love
your company, gentlemen, but I believe I must leave you
to go to another world."   These are the words as reported
by Henry Mackenzie, who was present, in giving Samuel
Rogers an account of Smith's death during a visit he paid
to London in the course of the following year.[1]   But
Hutton, in the account he gave Stewart of the incident,
employs the slightly different form of expression,   " I
believe we must adjourn this meeting to some other
place."   Possibly both sentences were used by Smith, for
both are needed for the complete expression of the parting
consolation he obviously meant to convey—that death is
not a final separation, but only an adjournment of the
meeting.

That was his last meeting with them in the earthly
meeting-place.   He had gone to the other world before
the next Sunday came round, having died on Saturday the
17th of July 1790.   He was buried in the Canongate
churchyard, near by the simple stone which Burns placed
on the grave of Fergusson, and not far from the statelier
tomb which later on received the remains of his friend
Dugald Stewart.   The grave is marked by an unpretending monument, stating that Adam Smith, the author of the
Wealth of Nations, lies buried there.

His death made less stir or rumour in the world than
many of his admirers expected.   Sir Samuel Romilly, for
example, writing on the 20th of August to a French lady
who had wanted a copy of the new edition of the *Theory of
Moral Sentiments*, says : " I have been surprised and, I own,
a little indignant to observe how little impression his death
has made here.   Scarce any notice has been taken of it,
while for above a year together after the death of Dr.
Johnson nothing was to be heard of but panegyrics of him,—
lives, letters, and anecdotes,—and even at this moment there
are two more lives of him to start into existence.   Indeed,

---

[1] Clayden's *Early Life of Samuel Rogers*, p. 168.

one ought not perhaps to be very much surprised that the public does not do justice to the works of A. Smith since he did not do justice to them himself, but always considered his *Theory of Moral Sentiments* a much superior work to his *Wealth of Nations*."[1]   Even in Edinburgh it seemed to make less impression than the death of a bustling divine would have made—certainly considerably less than the death of the excellent but far less illustrious Dugald Stewart a generation later.   The newspapers had an obituary notice of two small paragraphs, and the only facts in his life the writers appear to have been able to find were his early abduction by the gipsies, of which both the *Mercury* and the *Advertiser* give a circumstantial account, and the characteristics which the *Advertiser* mentions, that " in private life Dr. Smith was distinguished for philanthropy, benevolence, humanity, and charity."   Lord Cockburn, who was then beginning to read and think, was struck with the general ignorance of Smith's merits which his fellow-citizens exhibited shortly after his death. " The middle-aged seemed to me to know little about the founder of the science (political economy) except that he had recently been a Commissioner of Customs and had written a sensible book.   The young—by which I mean the Liberal young of Edinburgh—lived upon him."[2] Stewart was no sooner dead than a monument was raised to him on one of the best sites in the city.   The greater name of Smith has to this day no public monument in the city he so long adorned.

Black and Hutton were his literary executors, and published in 1795 the literary fragments which had been spared from the flames.   By his will, dated 6th February 1790, he left his whole property to his cousin, David Douglas, afterwards Lord Reston, subject to the condition that the legatee should follow the instructions of Black and Hutton in disposing of the MSS. and writings, and

[1] *Memoirs of Sir Samuel Romilly*, i. 403.
[2] Cockburn's *Memorials of My Own Time*, p. 45.

pay an annuity of £20 a year to Mrs. Janet Douglas, and after her death, a sum of £400 to Professor Hugh Cleghorn of St. Andrews and his wife.[1] The property Smith left, however, was very moderate, and his friends could not at first help expressing some surprise that it should have been so little, because, though known to be very hospitable, he had never maintained anything more than a moderate establishment. But they had not then known, though many of them had long suspected, that he gave away large sums in secret charity. William Playfair mentions that Smith's friends, suspecting him of doing this, had sometimes in his lifetime formed special juries for the purpose of discovering evidences of it, but that the economist was "so ingenious in concealing his charity" that they never could discover it from witnesses, though they often found the strongest circumstantial evidence of it.[2] Dugald Stewart was more fortunate. He says : "Some very affecting instances of Mr. Smith's beneficence in cases where he found it impossible to conceal entirely his good offices have been mentioned to me by a near relation of his and one of his most confidential friends, Miss Ross, daughter of the late Patrick Ross, Esq., of Innernethy. They were all on a scale much beyond what would have been expected from his fortune, and were combined with circumstances equally honourable to the delicacy of his feelings and the liberality of his heart." One recalls the saying of Sir James Mackintosh, who was a student of Cullen and Black's in Smith's closing years, and used occasionally to meet the economist in private society. " I have known," said Mackintosh to Empson many years after this—" I have known Adam Smith slightly, Ricardo well, and Malthus intimately. Is it not something to say for a science that its three greatest masters were about the three best men I ever knew ?"[3]

[1] Bonar's *Library of Adam Smith*, p. xiv.
[2] Playfair's edition of *Wealth of Nations*, p. xxxiv.
[3] *Edinburgh Review*, January 1837, p. 473.

Smith never sat for his picture, but nevertheless we possess excellent portraits of him by two very talented artists who had many opportunities of seeing and sketching him. Tassie was a student at Foulis's Academy of Design in Glasgow College when Smith was there, and he may possibly even then have occasionally modelled the distinguished Professor, for we hear of models of Smith being in all the booksellers' windows in Glasgow at that time, and these models would, for a certainty, have been made in the Academy of Design. However that may be, Tassie executed in later days two different medallions of Smith. Raspe, in his catalogue of Tassie's enamels, describes one of these in a list of portraits of the largest size that that kind of work admitted of, as being modelled and cast by Tassie in his hard white enamel paste so as to resemble a cameo. From this model J. Jackson, R.A., made a drawing, which was engraved in stipple by C. Picart, and published in 1811 by Cadell and Davies. Line engravings of the same model were subsequently made by John Horsburgh and R. C. Bell for successive editions of the *Wealth of Nations*, and it is accordingly the best known, as well as probably the best, portrait of the author of that work. It is a profile bust showing rather handsome features, full forehead, prominent eyeballs, well curved eyebrows, slightly aquiline nose, and firm mouth and chin, and it is inscribed, "Adam Smith in his 64th year, 1787. Tassie F." In this medallion Smith wears a wig, but Tassie executed another, Mr. J. M. Gray tells us, in what he called "the antique manner," without the wig, and with neck and breast bare. "This work," says Mr. Gray, "has the advantage of showing the rounded form of the head, covered with rather curling hair and curving upwards from the brow to a point above the large ear, which is hidden in the other version." [1] It bears the same date as the former, and it appears never to have been engraved. Raspe mentions a third medallion of Smith in his catalogue

[1] Bonar's *Library of Adam Smith*, p. xxii.

of Tassie's enamels—"a bust in enamel, being in colour an imitation of chalcedony, engraved by F. Warner, after a model by J. Tassie,"—but this appears from Mr. Gray's account to be a reduced version of the first of the two just mentioned. Kay made two portraits of Smith : the first, done in 1787, representing him as he walked in the street, and the second, issued in 1790, and occasioned, no doubt, by his death, representing him as he has entered an office, probably the Custom House. There is a painting by T. Collopy in the National Museum of Antiquities at Edinburgh, which is thought to be a portrait of Adam Smith from the circumstance that the title *Wealth of Nations* appears on the back of a book on the table in the picture ; but in the teeth of Stewart's very explicit statement that Smith never sat for his portrait, the inference drawn from that circumstance cannot but remain very doubtful. All other likenesses of Smith are founded on those of Tassie and Kay. Smith was of middle height, full but not corpulent, with erect figure, well-set head, and large gray or light blue eyes, which are said to have beamed with "inexpressible benignity." He dressed well—so well that nobody seems to have remarked it ; for while we hear, on the one hand, of Hume's black-spotted yellow coat and Gibbon's flowered velvet, and on the other, of Hutton's battered attire and Henry Erskine's gray hat with the torn rim, we meet with no allusion to Smith's dress either for fault or merit.

Smith's books, which went on his death to his heir, Lord Reston, were divided, on the death of the latter, between his two daughters ; the economic books going to Mrs. Bannerman, the wife of the late Professor Bannerman of Edinburgh, and the works on other subjects to Mrs. Cunningham, wife of the Rev. Mr. Cunningham of Prestonpans. Both portions still exist, the former in the Library of the New College, Edinburgh, to which they have been presented by Dr. D. Douglas Bannerman of Perth ; and the latter in the possession of Professor Cunningham of

Queen's College, Belfast, except a small number which were sold in Edinburgh in 1878, and a section, consisting almost exclusively of Greek and Latin classics, which Professor Cunningham has presented to the library of the college of which he is a member. Among other relics of Smith that are still extant are four medallions by Tassie, which very probably hung in his library. They are medallions of his personal friends : Black, the chemist ; Hutton, the geologist ; Dr. Thomas Reid, the metaphysician ; and Andrew Lumisden, the Pretender's old secretary, and author of the work on the antiquities of Rome.

INDEX

THE END